AUTOMATIC TRANSMISSIONS AND TRANSAXLES

FOURTH EDITION

Tom Birch
Chuck Rockwood

Prentice Hall
Upper Saddle River, New Jersey
Columbus, Ohio

Library of Congress Cataloging-in-Publication Data

Birch, Thomas W. (Thomas Wesley)
  Automatic transmissions and transaxles/Tom Birch, Chuck Rockwood.—4th ed.
    p. cm.
  Includes bibliographical references and index.
  ISBN 0-13-505135-5
1. Automobiles—Transmission devices, Automatic.   2. Automobiles—Transmission
devices, Automatic—Maintenance and repair.   I. Rockwood, Chuck.   II. Title.

TL263.B57 2010
629.2′4460288—dc22

2008049452

Editor in Chief: Vernon Anthony
Acquisitions Editor: Wyatt Morris
Editorial Assistant: Christopher Reed
Production Coordination: Erin Melloy, S4Carlisle
Project Manager: Holly Shufeldt
Operations Specialist: Laura Weaver
Art Director: Candace Rowley
Cover Designer: John Cave
Cover and chapter opener photo: iStockphoto
Director of Marketing: David Gesell
Marketing Assistant: Les Roberts

This book was set in Weidmann by S4Carlisle and was printed and bound by Edwards Brothers. The cover was printed by Lehigh-Phoenix Color Corp.

Pearson Education Ltd., London
Pearson Education Singapore Pte. Ltd.
Pearson Education Canada, Inc.
Pearson Education—Japan

Pearson Education Australia Pty. Limited
Pearson Education North Asia Ltd., Hong Kong
Pearson Educación de Mexico, S.A. de C.V.
Pearson Education Malaysia Pte. Ltd.

Prentice Hall
is an imprint of

www.pearsonhighered.com

10 9 8 7 6 5 4 3 2 1
ISBN-13: 978-0-13-505135-1
ISBN-10:   0-13-505135-5

PREFACE

PROFESSIONAL TECHNICIAN SERIES

Part of Prentice Hall Automotive's Professional Technician Series, the fourth edition of *Automatic Transmissions and Transaxles* presents students and instructors with a practical, real-world approach to automotive technology and service. The series includes textbooks that cover all eight ASE certification test areas of automotive service: Engine Repair (A1), Automatic Transmissions and Transaxles (A2), Manual Drivetrains and Axles (A3), Steering and Suspension (A4), Brakes (A5), Electrical/Electronic Systems (A6), Heating and Air Conditioning (A7), and Engine Performance (A8).

Current revisions are written by experienced authors and peer reviewed by automotive instructors and experts in the field to ensure technical accuracy.

UPDATES TO THE FOURTH EDITION

- An index of the "How To" service operations contained in the service chapters of the text.
- Expanded content describing some of the newer transmissions.
- Expanded automatic transmission and transaxle testing, diagnosis, and service procedures to reflect new tools, equipment, and service procedures.
- Expanded electrical/electronic content for testing, diagnosis, and repair.
- A worktext (available separately) for use while doing actual service and repair procedures.

ASE AND NATEF CORRELATED

NATEF-certified programs need to demonstrate that they use course materials that cover NATEF and ASE tasks. This textbook has been correlated to the ASE and NATEF task lists and offers comprehensive coverage of all tasks. A **NATEF TASK CORRELATION CHART** and an **ASE TEST CORRELATION CHART** are located in the appendices to the book.

A COMPLETE INSTRUCTOR AND STUDENT SUPPLEMENTS PACKAGE

This textbook is accompanied by a full package of instructor and student supplements. See page vi for a detailed list of all supplements available with this book.

A FOCUS ON DIAGNOSIS AND PROBLEM SOLVING

The Professional Technician series has been developed to satisfy the need for a greater emphasis on problem diagnosis. Automotive instructors and service managers agree that students and beginning technicians need more training in diagnostic procedures and skill development. To meet this need and demonstrate how real-world problems are solved, the "Real World Fix" features are included throughout and highlight how real-life problems are diagnosed and repaired.

The following pages highlight the unique core features that set the Professional Technician Series apart from other automotive textbooks.

IN-TEXT FEATURES

OBJECTIVES and **KEY TERMS** appear at the beginning of each chapter to help students and instructors focus on the most important material in each chapter. The chapter objectives are based on specific ASE and NATEF tasks.

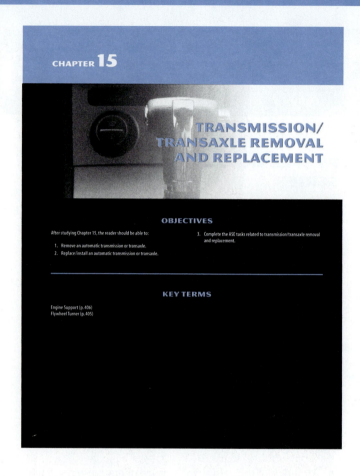

CHAPTER **15**

TRANSMISSION/ TRANSAXLE REMOVAL AND REPLACEMENT

OBJECTIVES

After studying Chapter 15, the reader should be able to:

1. Remove an automatic transmission or transaxle.
2. Replace/install an automatic transmission or transaxle.
3. Complete the ASE tasks related to transmission/transaxle removal and replacement.

KEY TERMS

Engine Support (p. 406)
Flywheel Turner (p. 405)

TECH TIP

Synthetic wintergreen oil, available at drugstores, is an excellent penetrating oil. The next time you

SAFETY TIP

Always dispose of oily shop cloths in an enclosed container to prevent a fire (Figure 1-37). Whenever oily cloths are thrown together on the floor or workbench, a chemical reaction can occur, which can ignite the cloth even

REAL WORLD FIX

The 1997 Dodge Caravan (123,000 miles) transmission was bucking and slipping under a load. A scan tool check revealed no DTCs. A remanufactured transmission was installed, but this did not help. A new transmission controller was installed, but this did not help.

Fix. Following advice, the technician removed the flexplate so it could be thoroughly inspected. The flexplate was checked visually when the transmission was replaced, but this vehicle has a large washer that hides the inner portion. The flexplate appeared fine,

FREQUENTLY ASKED QUESTION

The word *gauge* means "measurement or dimension to a standard of reference." The word *gauge* can also be spelled *gage*. Therefore, in most cases, the words mean the same.

NOTE: One vehicle manufacturing representative mentioned that *gage* was used rather than *gauge* because even though it is the second acceptable spelling of the word, it is correct and it saved the company a lot of money in printing costs because the word *gage* has one less letter! One letter multiplied by the millions of times that *gage* is used in service manuals adds up to a big savings for the manufacturer.

TECH TIPS feature real-world advice and "tricks of the trade" from ASE-certified master technicians.

SAFETY TIPS alert students to possible hazards on the job and how to avoid them.

REAL WORLD FIXES AND PROBLEMS present students with actual automotive service scenarios and show how these common (and sometimes uncommon) problems were diagnosed and repaired.

FREQUENTLY ASKED QUESTIONS are based on the author's own experience and provide answers to many of the most common questions asked by students and beginning service technicians.

NOTES provide students with additional technical information to give them a greater understanding of a specific task or procedure.

CAUTIONS alert students about potential damage to the vehicle that can occur during a specific task or service procedure.

WARNINGS alert students to potential dangers to themselves during a specific task or service procedure.

NOTE: Removing the ignition key will shut off the HV system. It is recommended to place the key in your pocket or tool box to prevent someone from putting it back in the ignition switch. *Smart keys* must be disabled before working on the vehicle.

CAUTION: Eyes and skin should always be protected when you are performing operations during which refrigerant might escape.

WARNING: Some vehicles with electronic fuel injection have a fuel pressure test port that uses a 1/4-inch flare fitting, the same as an R-12 service port. Make sure that the refrigerant recovery unit is connected into the A/C system and not the fuel system.

STEP-BY-STEP photo sequences show in detail the steps involved in performing a specific task or service procedure.

HOISTING A VEHICLE Step-by-Step

(Photos courtesy of James Halderman)

STEP 1 The first step in hoisting a vehicle is to center the vehicle on the hoist.

STEP 2 Most vehicles will be correctly positioned when the left front tire is centered on the tire pad.

STEP 3 Many pads at the end of the hoist arms can be rotated to allow for many different types of vehicles.

STEP 4 The arms of the lifts can be retracted or extended to accommodate vehicles of different lengths and widths.

The **SUMMARY, REVIEW QUESTIONS,** and **CHAPTER QUIZ** at the end of Chapters 1 to 19 help students review the material presented in the chapter and test themselves to see how much they've learned.

Transmission/Transaxle Removal and Replacement   419

SUMMARY

1. Transmissions are removed to make repairs, overhaul, or replacement.
2. The removal and replacement procedures are similar for most transmissions and transaxles.
3. Always check the service information before removing an automatic transmission.
4. Never force the transmission onto the back of the engine during installation.
5. It may be necessary the check the wheel alignment after installing a transaxle.

REVIEW QUESTIONS

The following questions are provided to help you study as you read the chapter.

1. A special _____ support is used when removing a front wheel drive transaxle.
2. A _____ manual should be consulted for the suggested removal and installation procedures for a particular transmission.
3. The first thing removed when removing an RWD transmission from a vehicle is the _____ ground _____.
4. Before unbolting the torque converter, put match marks on the converter and the _____ to aid installation.
5. As the transmission is removed from the vehicle, install a bracket to the _____ _____ to prevent it from sliding out of the transmission.
6. The first thing removed when removing an FWD transmission from a vehicle is the _____ ground _____.
7. To prevent leakage once the drive shaft has been removed from an RWD vehicle, the _____ needs to be plugged.
8. When removing a drive shaft, always put _____ marks on the drive shaft and the differential flange to aid in reassembly.
9. When removing the drive shafts from a FWD vehicle, it is not advisable to let the brake _____ or the _____ hang free.
10. Since the front suspension is removed during removal of an FWD transaxle, it may be necessary to check the _____ of the front end at completion of the job.
11. After the transmission or transaxle is installed in the vehicle, check that the torque converter will rotate freely to ensure that the converter is not _____ into the pump or pump drive and the flexplate.
12. During installation, the transmission should fit easily up against the engine. Never use _____ to connect the transmission to the engine.
13. A _____ converter housing or other serious problem could result if anything is caught between the converter housing and the engine.
14. After the installation of the transmission or transaxle is complete, check the _____ level after shifting the transmission through its gear ranges.
15. After the installation of the transmission or transaxle is complete, the last step is to _____ _____ the vehicle.

CHAPTER QUIZ

The following questions will help you check the facts you have learned. Select the answer that completes each statement correctly.

1. Student A says that the torque converter is usually left on the engine when removing a transmission. Student B says that it is more difficult to remove a transaxle than a transmission. Who is correct?
   a. Student A
   b. Student B
   c. Both A and B
   d. Neither A nor B

2. Student A says that you should be able to rotate the converter to align the bolt holes with the flexplate after the transmission has been bolted to the engine. Student B says that a transmission overhaul is not complete until it passes a road test. Who is correct?
   a. Student A
   b. Student B
   c. Both A and B
   d. Neither A nor B

SUPPLEMENTS

The comprehensive **INSTRUCTOR'S MANUAL** includes chapter outlines, answers to all questions from the book, teaching tips, and additional exercises.

Included with every copy of the book is access to the following website: **www.pearsonhighered.com/autostudent.** This resource contains:

- A complete text-specific **TEST BANK WITH TEST CREATION SOFTWARE**
- A comprehensive, text-specific **POWERPOINT PRESENTATION** featuring much of the art from the text as well as video clips and animations
- An **IMAGE LIBRARY** featuring additional images to use for class presentations
- Additional student activities including **CROSSWORD PUZZLES, WORD SEARCHES,** and other worksheets
- A **SAMPLE ASE TEST** as well as the complete **ASE TASK LIST**

To access supplementary materials online, instructors need to request an instructor access code. Go to www.pearsonhighered.com/irc, where you can register for an instructor access code. Within 48 hours after registering, you will receive a confirming e-mail, including an instructor access code. Once you have received your code, go to the site and log on for full instructions on downloading the materials you wish to use.

Available to be packaged with the book, the **STUDENT WORKTEXT (NATEF CORRELATED TASK SHEETS)**, includes 100% of the job sheets tied to the Automatic Transmissions and Transaxles (A2) NATEF tasks. Contact your local Prentice Hall representative for information on ordering the textbook packaged with the student worktext.

STUDENT SUPPLEMENTS

Pearson has a large array of supplemental material available for students. In the past these materials were included on a CD. They are now hosted at the following URL for easy access and convenience:

www.pearsoned.com/autostudent

Resources there include:

- Power Point Slides
- Chapter Objectives
- Chapter Summaries
- Image Bank
- Flash Cards
- English/Spanish Glossary
- NATEF/ASE Correlations

ACKNOWLEDGMENTS

The authors wish to thank the following reviewers for their helpful comments and suggestions. Elizabeth Dorries, Vermont Technical College; Sumner Huckaby, Greenville Technical College; and Stewart Sikora, Triton College.

This book has the support of much of the automatic transmission repair industry. The authors are grateful to the following companies and individuals for their contributions:

A-1 Automatic Transmissions
AceomaticRecon
AFM, Raytech Automotive Components Comp.
Alto Products Corp.
American Honda Motor Company
ATEC Trans-Tool and Cleaning Systems
Autotrans
AxiLine, Hicklin Engineering
Borg Warner, Morse TEC
Tom Broxholm, Skyline College
Chassis Ear, Steelman
DaimlerChrysler Corporation
Ethyl Corporation
Mark Ferner, Pennzoil-Quaker State
Fluke Corporation
Ford Motor Company
G-Tec
General Motors Corporation
Goodall Manufacturing Co.
Roger Griffen, Nissan North America, Inc.
James Halderman
Tony Jewel, Reedley College
J.S. Products/Steelman

KD Tools
Kent-Moore, SPX Corporation
Life Automotive Products
Dennis Madden, ATRA
The Mighty Mover
Mooq Automotive Division, Federal-Moqul Corp.
NEAPCO Inc.
Nissan North America, Inc.
OTC, SPX Corporation
Pennzoil-Quaker State Comp.
Raybestos Aftermarket Products Co.
Ken Redick
Rostra Precision Controls
Slauson Transmission Parts, Christopher Wilson
Snap-on Tools
Sonnax Industries
SPX Filtran
Superior Transmission Parts
T.C.R.S. Inc., Hicklin Engineering
Tribco, Inc.
Toyota Motor Sales, U.S.A., Inc.
Waekon Corporation
Williams Technology Inc., Division of Delco Remy Int.
Yank Converters
ZF Group North American Operations
Zoom Technology
"Portions of materials contained herein have been reprinted with permission of General Motors Corporation, Service Operations."

BRIEF CONTENTS

CONTENTS

xiv   Contents

"HOW TO" SERVICE OPERATIONS

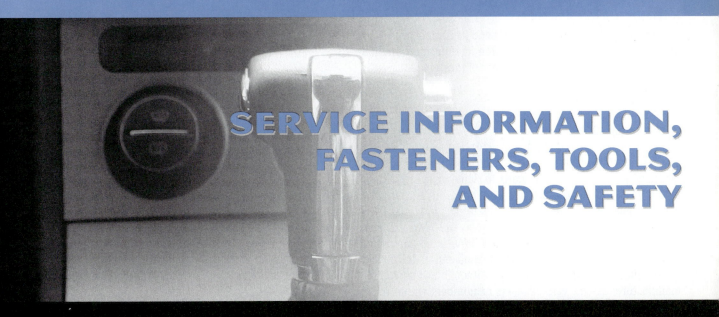

SERVICE INFORMATION, FASTENERS, TOOLS, AND SAFETY

OBJECTIVES

After studying Chapter 1, the reader should be able to:

1. Retrieve vehicle service information.
2. Identify the strength ratings of threaded fasteners.
3. Explain how to safely use hand tools.
4. Describe how to safely hoist a vehicle.
5. Identify the personal safety equipment that all service technicians should wear.
6. Understand the ASE requirements for vehicle identification and the proper use of tools and shop equipment.

KEY TERMS

Aftermarket (p. 3)
Barrel (p. 13)
Bolt (p. 5)
Bump Cap (p. 14)
Cap Screw (p. 5)
Grade (p. 6)
Lock Washer (p. 7)
Loctite (p. 7)

Micrometer (p. 13)
Nut (p. 7)
OEM (p. 3)
Pitch (p. 5)
Spontaneous Combustion (p. 16)
Stud (p. 5)
Vernier Dial Caliper (p. 14)
Washer (p. 7)

1.1 VEHICLE IDENTIFICATION

All service work requires the vehicle and its components to be properly identified. The most common identification method is verifying the make, model, and year of the vehicle:

Make: e.g., Chevrolet
Model: e.g., Trailblazer
Year: e.g., 2003

The year of the vehicle is often difficult to determine exactly. Typically, a new model year starts in September or October of the year prior to the actual model year, but not always. A model may be introduced as the next year's model as soon as January of the previous year. This is why the *vehicle identification number,* usually abbreviated *VIN,* is so important (Figure 1-1). Since 1981 all vehicle manufacturers have used a VIN that is 17 characters long. Although every vehicle manufacturer assigns various letters or numbers within these 17 characters, there are some constants, including:

- The first number or letter designates the country of origin.

1 = United States	K = Korea
2 = Canada	L = Taiwan
3 = Mexico	S = England
4 = United States	V = France
6 = Australia	W = Germany
9 = Brazil	Y = Sweden
J = Japan	Z = Italy

- The model of the vehicle is commonly the fourth or fifth character.

- The eighth character is often the engine code. (Some engines cannot be determined by the VIN.)
- The tenth character represents the year on all vehicles.

A = 1980	L = 1990	Y = 2000
B = 1981	M = 1991	1 = 2001
C = 1982	N = 1992	2 = 2002
D = 1983	P = 1993	3 = 2003
E = 1984	R = 1994	4 = 2004
F = 1985	S = 1995	5 = 2005
G = 1986	T = 1996	6 = 2006
H = 1987	V = 1997	7 = 2007
J = 1988	W = 1998	8 = 2008
K = 1989	X = 1999	9 = 2009

1.1.1 VECI Label

The *vehicle emissions control information (VECI)* label located under the hood of the vehicle shows informative settings and emission hose routing information (Figure 1-2). The VECI label (sticker) can be located on the underside of the hood, the radiator fan shroud, radiator core support, or on the strut towers. The VECI label usually includes the following information:

Engine identification
Emissions control information
Vacuum hose routing diagram
Base ignition timing (if adjustable)
Spark plug type and gap
Valve lash
Emission calibration code

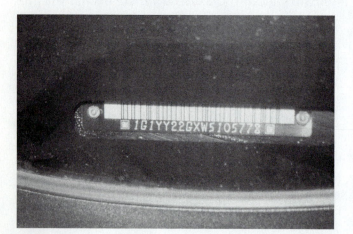

FIGURE 1-1 The vehicle identification number (VIN) is at the top front of the instrument panel and is visible through the windshield.

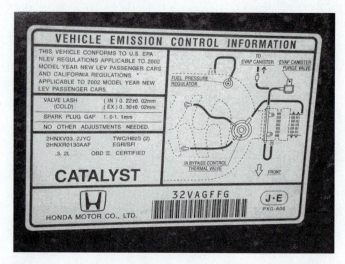

FIGURE 1-2 The VECI, vehicle emission control information, label is attached to an underhood portion of the vehicle.

FIGURE 1-3   The sticker attached to this control module indicates the calibration code.

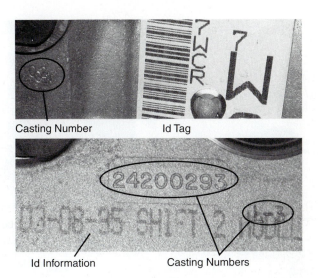

FIGURE 1-4   The two transmission cases show casting numbers that are cast as part of the case. They also have an ID tag or painted-on ID information.

1.1.2 Calibration Codes

Calibration codes are usually located on powertrain control modules (PCMs) or other controllers. Whenever diagnosing an engine concern, it may be necessary to use the calibration code to determine if the vehicle is the subject of a technical service bulletin (TSB) or other service procedure (Figure 1-3).

1.1.3 Casting Numbers

Whenever an engine part, such as a block, is cast, a number is put into the mold to identify the casting (Figure 1-4). The casting number can be used to identify the part, check dimensions such as the cubic inch displacement, and identify other information such as year of manufacture. Sometimes changes are made to the mold, yet the casting number is not changed. The casting number is often the best piece of identifying information that is available.

1.2 SERVICE INFORMATION

Service information is used by the service technician to determine specifications, service procedures, and any required special tools.

1.2.1 Service Manuals

The original equipment manufacturer, or **OEM,** and **aftermarket** service manuals contain specifications and service

FIGURE 1-5   The factory service manual is the most complete source of service and repair information for a vehicle.

procedures. While OEM service manuals cover just one year and one or more models of the same vehicle, most aftermarket service manufacturers cover multiple years and/or models in one manual (Figure 1-5). Included in most service manuals are the following:

- Capacities and recommended specifications for all fluids
- Specifications including engine and routine maintenance items
- Testing procedures
- Service procedures including the use of special tools

FIGURE 1-6   Electronic service information, available from several independent sources, is read using a computer and monitor.

1.2.2 Electronic Service Information

Electronic service information is available on CD, DVD, or the Internet. A subscription is usually required for access to an Internet site where current service and repair information is available (Figure 1-6). Most vehicle manufacturers also offer electronic service information to their dealers and to schools that offer corporate training programs.

1.2.3 Technical Service Bulletins

Technical service bulletins, often called *TSBs,* are issued by the vehicle manufacturer to notify service technicians of a problem, and include the necessary corrective action. Technical service bulletins are designed for OEM dealership technicians but are republished by aftermarket companies and made available to shops and vehicle repair facilities (Figure 1-7).

1.2.4 Internet

The Internet has opened the field for information exchange and access to technical advice. A very useful site is the *international Automotive Technicians' Network (iATN)* at *www.iatn.net.* This is a free site, but service technicians must register to join. If a small monthly sponsor fee is paid, the shop or service technician can gain access to the archives, which include thousands of successful repairs in a searchable database.

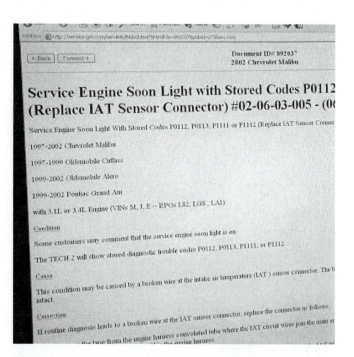

FIGURE 1-7   This TSB, technical service bulletin, describes a condition that causes the "Service Engine Soon Light" to come on for certain vehicles, and it describes the correction procedure for this concern. Note that it is in an electronic form.

1.3 STEEL CLASSIFICATION

Steel is the base material for automotive parts that require high strength. Steel is iron that has been refined to the point where little carbon remains. Even a very small percentage of carbon in steel has a great deal of significance in the physical characteristics. The classifications of steel were established by the Society of Automotive Engineers (SAE) and are referred to as the SAE numbers.

The classification number usually contains four numbers, such as SAE 1040 steel. The first number (on the left) identifies the basic type (alloy) of the steel.

1	carbon steel (no other alloy)
2	nickel alloy
3	nickel-chromium (includes stainless steels)
4	molybdenum alloy (includes chromium-molybdenum alloys)
5	chromium
6	chromium-vanadium
9	silicon-manganese

(Other numbers are used to represent triple-alloy steels.)

The second number represents the percent of alloy in the steel or is used to identify percentage ranges of alloy if more than one alloy is used in the steel.

The last two numbers represent the points of carbon, and a small change in carbon content means a big difference in the characteristics of the steel (1% contains 100 points; therefore, 35 points of carbon means the steel contains 0.35% carbon). Generally, the higher the carbon content of the steel, the harder the steel.

Low-carbon steels	0.08% to 0.20% (8 to 20 points) carbon
Medium-carbon steels	0.20% to 0.45% (20 to 45 points) carbon
High-carbon steels	0.45% to 0.65% (45 to 65 points) carbon
Tool steel	above 0.65% (65 points) carbon

1.3.1 Steel Classification Examples

SAE 4130 is commonly used for high-strength tubing for race car roll cages:

4	chromium molybdenum
1	1% alloy
30	0.30% carbon

SAE 5140 is commonly used as the billet (block) of steel for some stabilizer bars:

5	chromium
1	1% alloy
40	0.40% carbon

Besides carbon content, the hardness of the steel is determined by heat treatment procedures, cooling times, temperatures, and even by what material is used to cool the steel. For example, *water-hardened* steel is quenched (cooled) by submerging the hot steel in water.

Rockwell Hardness Test. The harder the steel, the more it resists the penetration of another object. A Rockwell hardness tester uses the principle of measuring the distance a hard 1/16″ diameter ball dents the metal sample under a given load. Different scales are used to test various types of materials. The Rockwell *C* scale is the most common hardness scale used for hardened and alloy steels. A typical camshaft lobe in an automotive engine should have a hardness of 45 on the Rockwell *C* scale. This is often abbreviated as 45 HRC.

1.4 THREADED FASTENERS

Most of the threaded fasteners used on vehicles are **cap screws,** which are fasteners that are threaded into a casting or part. Automotive service technicians usually refer to these fasteners as

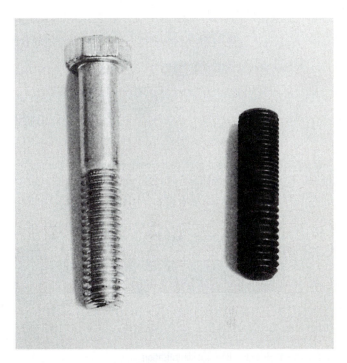

FIGURE 1-8   Typical bolt on the left and stud on the right. Note the different thread pitch on the top and bottom portions of the stud.

bolts, regardless of how they are used. In this book, they are called bolts, although bolts are normally used with nuts. Sometimes, **studs,** short rods with threads on both ends, are used for threaded fasteners. A stud will often have coarse threads on one end and fine threads on the other end. The end of the stud with coarse threads is screwed into the casting, and a nut is used on the opposite end to hold the parts together (Figure 1-8).

The fastener threads *must* match the threads in the casting or nut. The threads may be measured either in fractions of an inch (called *fractional*) or in metric units.

1.4.1 Fractional Bolts

Fractional bolts have either fine or coarse threads. The coarse threads are called *Unified National Coarse (UNC),* and the fine threads are called *Unified National Fine (UNF).* Standard combinations of sizes and number of threads per inch (called **pitch**) are used. Pitch can be measured with a thread pitch gauge, as shown in Figure 1-9.

Bolts are identified by their diameter and length as measured from below the head, as shown in Figure 1-10. Fractional thread sizes are specified by the diameter in fractions of an inch and the number of threads per inch. For example, a 5/16–18 bolt has threads that are 5/16 of an inch in diameter and 18 threads per inch of length. Typical UNC thread sizes would be 5/16–18 and 1/2–13. Similar UNF thread sizes would be 5/16–24 and 1/2–20.

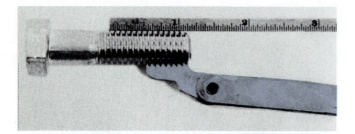

FIGURE 1-9 Thread pitch gauge used to measure the pitch of the thread. This is a 1/2-in. diameter bolt with 13 threads to the inch (1/2–13).

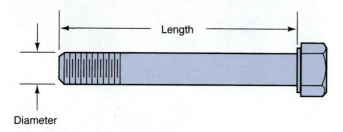

FIGURE 1-10 Bolt size identification.

1.4.2 Metric Bolts

The size of a metric bolt is specified by the letter *M* followed by the diameter in millimeters (mm) across the outside (crest) of the threads. Typical metric sizes would be M8 and M12. Fine metric threads (pitch) are specified by the thread diameter followed by X and the distance between the threads measured in millimeters (M8 X 1.5). Typical metric sizes would be M8 X 1.5 (coarse thread), M8 X 1.25 (medium thread), and M8 X 1.0 (fine thread).

1.4.3 Bolt Grade

Bolts are made from many different types of steel, and for this reason some are stronger than others. The strength or classification of a bolt is called the **grade** and is marked on the bolt

TECH TIP

Synthetic wintergreen oil, available at drugstores, is an excellent penetrating oil. The next time you can't get that rusted bolt loose, head for the drugstore (Figure 1-11).

FIGURE 1-11 Synthetic wintergreen oil can be used as a penetrating oil to loosen rusted bolts or nuts.

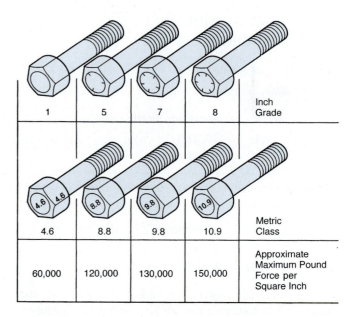

1	5	7	8	Inch Grade
4.6	8.8	9.8	10.9	Metric Class
60,000	120,000	130,000	150,000	Approximate Maximum Pound Force per Square Inch

FIGURE 1-12 Typical bolt (cap screw) grade markings and approximate strength.

head. Fractional bolts have lines on the head to indicate the grade, as shown in Figure 1-12, the actual grade being two more than the number of lines on the bolt head. More lines or a higher grade number indicate a stronger bolt. Grade 5 and better bolts usually have threads that are rolled rather than cut, which also makes them stronger. In some cases, nuts and machine screws have similar grade markings. Metric bolts are marked with a decimal number to indicate the grade.

CAUTION: *Never* use hardware store (nongraded) bolts, studs, or nuts on any vehicle steering, suspension, brake, or clutch component (Figure 1-13). Always use the exact size and grade of hardware that is specified and used by the vehicle manufacturer.

TECH TIP

A common mistake is to think that the size of a bolt or nut is the size of the wrench used to turn the fastener. The size of the bolt or nut (outside diameter of the threads) is usually smaller than the size of the wrench or socket that fits the head of the bolt or nut. Examples are given in the following table:

Wrench Size	Thread Size
7/16 in.	1/4 in.
1/2 in.	5/16 in.
9/16 in.	3/8 in.
5/8 in.	7/16 in.
3/4 in.	1/2 in.
10 mm	6 mm
12 mm or 13 mm*	8 mm
14 mm or 17 mm*	10 mm*

* European (Système International d'Unités—SI) metric.

1.4.4 Nuts

Most **nuts** used on bolts have the same hex size as the bolt head. Some inexpensive nuts use a hex size larger than the cap screw head. Metric nuts are often marked with dimples to show their strength—more dimples indicate stronger nuts. Some nuts, commonly called *self-locking nuts*, use interference fit threads to keep them from accidentally loosening. They are made so that the shape of the nut is slightly distorted or a section of the threads is deformed. Nuts can also be kept from loosening with a nylon washer fastened in the nut or with a nylon patch or strip on the threads (Figure 1-14).

NOTE: An open-end wrench can be used to gauge bolt sizes by placing the wrench opening across the threads. For example, a 3/8-in. wrench will closely fit the threads of a 3/8-in. bolt.

Most "locking nuts" are grouped together and are commonly referred to as *prevailing torque* nuts. This means that the nut will hold its tightness or torque and not loosen with movement or vibration. Most prevailing torque nuts should be replaced whenever removed to ensure that the nut will not loosen during service. Always follow the manufacturer's recommendations. Anaerobic sealers, such as **Loctite,** are used

FIGURE 1-13   Every shop should have an assortment of high-quality bolts and nuts.

FIGURE 1-14   Types of lock nuts. On the left, a nylon ring; in the center, a distorted shape; and on the right, a castle used with a cotter key.

on the threads where the nut or cap screw must be both locked and sealed.

1.4.5 Washers

Washers are often used under cap screw heads and under nuts. Plain, flat washers are used to provide an even clamping load around the fastener and to protect the part being assembled. **Lock washers** are added to prevent accidental loosening. Some manufacturers lock the washer onto a cap screw by placing it into position before rolling the threads.

1.5 BASIC TOOLS

Every automotive technician should possess the hand tools to turn fasteners (bolts, nuts, and screws). The following list does not include specialty tools, and items marked with an asterisk (*) are only needed if working on older vehicles.

Tool Chest

1/4-in. drive socket set (Figure 1-15):
  1/4- to 9/16-in. standard and deep sockets (Figure 1-16)*
  6- to 15-mm standard and deep sockets
  1/4-in. drive ratchet
  1/4-in. drive 2-in. and 6-in. extension
  1/4-in. drive handle

3/8-in. drive socket set:
  *3/8- to 7/8-in. standard and deep sockets (Figure 1-17)
  10- to 19-mm standard and deep sockets
  3/8-in. drive Torx set, T40, T45, T50, and T55
  3/8-in. drive 5/8-in. and 13/16-in. spark plug socket
  3/8-in. drive ratchet
  3/8-in. drive 1 1/2-in., 3-in., 6-in., and 12-in. extension (Figure 1-18)
  3/8-in. drive universal
  Crowfoot set (fractional inch* and metric)
  Hex/Allen socket

1/2-in. drive socket set:
  1/2- to 1-in. standard and deep sockets*
  1/2-in. drive ratchet
  1/2-in. drive breaker bar
  1/2-in. drive 5-in. and 10-in. extension
  3/8- to 1/4-in. adapter (Figure 1-19)
  1/2- to 3/8-in. adapter
  3/8- to 1/2-in. adapter
3/8- through 1-in. combination wrench set (Figure 1-20)
10- to 19-mm combination wrench set
1/16- to 1/4-in. hex wrench set
2- to 12-mm hex wrench set
5/16- to 9/16-in. flare-nut wrench set (Figure 1-21)*
10- and 12-, 14- and 17-mm flare-nut wrench set
Diagonal, needle nose, adjustable-jaw, locking, snap-ring, and electrical stripping or crimping pliers (Figure 1-22)

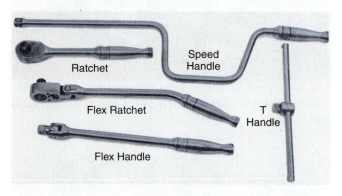

FIGURE 1-15   Typical drive handles for sockets.

FIGURE 1-16   Standard 12-point short socket (left), universal joint socket (center), and deep-well socket (right). Both the universal and deep-well are 6-point sockets.

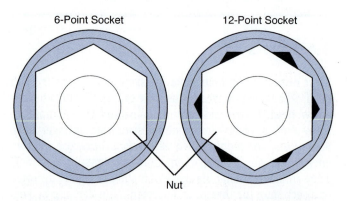

FIGURE 1-17   A 6-point socket fits the head of the bolt or nut on all sides. A 12-point socket can round off the head of a bolt or nut if a lot of force is applied.

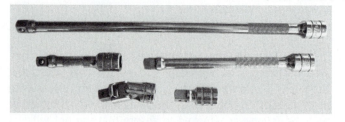

FIGURE 1-18   Various socket extensions. The universal joint (U-joint) (upper left) is useful for gaining access in tight areas.

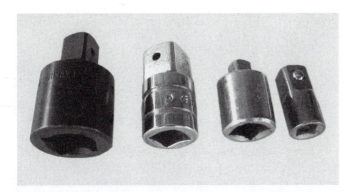

FIGURE 1-19   Socket drive adapters. These adapters permit the use of a 3/8-in. drive ratchet with 1/2-in. drive sockets, or other combinations as the various adapters permit. Adapters should be used carefully where a larger tool could break or damage a smaller-sized socket.

FIGURE 1-20   Combination wrench. The openings are the same size at both ends. Notice the angle of the open end to permit use in close spaces.

FIGURE 1-21   Flare-nut wrench. Also known as a *line wrench, fitting wrench,* or *tube-nut wrench.* This style of wrench is designed to grasp most of the flats of a six-sided (hex) tubing fitting to provide the most grip without damage to the fitting.

Ball-peen, rubber, and dead-blow hammers (Figure 1-23)
Five-piece standard screwdriver set (Figure 1-24)
Four-piece Phillips screwdriver set
#15 and #20 Torx screwdriver
Awl
Mill file
Center and pin punches (Figure 1-25)
Chisel
Utility knife
Valve core tool
Filter wrench (large and small filters)

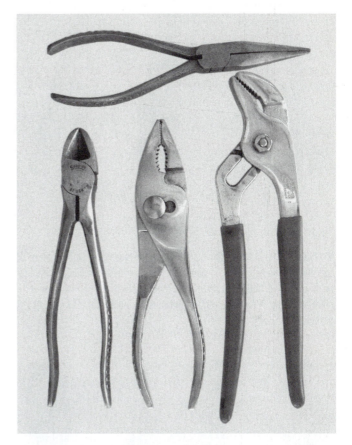

FIGURE 1-22   Assortment of pliers. Slip-joint pliers (center) are often confused with water-pump pliers (lower right).

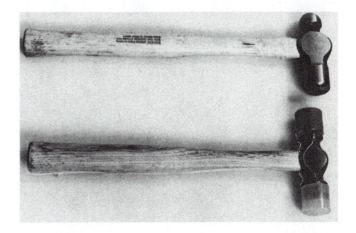

FIGURE 1-23   A ball-peen hammer (top) is purchased according to weight (usually in ounces) of the head of the hammer. At bottom is a soft-faced (plastic) hammer. Always use a hammer that is softer than the material being driven. Use a block of wood or similar material between a steel hammer and steel or iron parts to prevent damage to the part.

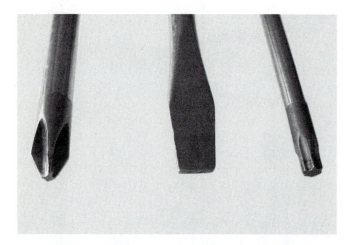

FIGURE 1-24 A flat-blade (or straight-blade) screwdriver (center) is specified by the length of the screwdriver and width of the blade. A Phillips-head screwdriver (left) is specified by the length of the handle and the size of the point at the tip. A Torx screwdriver (right) uses a numerical (#15 or #20) size designation.

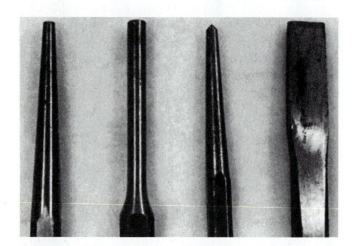

FIGURE 1-25 From the left, a starting punch, pin punch, center punch, and chisel.

Safety glasses
Circuit tester
Feeler gauge set
Gasket scraper
Pinch bar
Magnet

1.5.1 Tool Sets and Accessories

A beginning service technician may wish to start with a small set of tools before purchasing an expensive, extensive tool set (Figure 1-26).

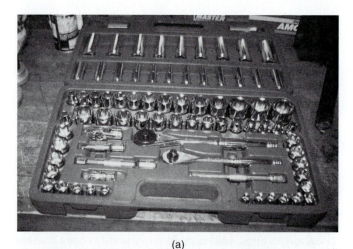

(a)

(b)

FIGURE 1-26 (a) A beginning technician can start with some simple basic hand tools. (b) An experienced, professional technician will spend several thousand dollars a year for tools like these stored in a large and expensive tool box.

NOTE: Most service technicians agree that it is okay for a beginning technician to borrow a tool occasionally. However, if a tool has to be borrowed more than twice, it should be purchased as soon as possible. Also, whenever a tool is borrowed, be sure you return the tool clean and show the technician you borrowed the tool from that you are returning the tool.

An apprentice technician started working for a dealership and put his top tool box on a workbench. Another technician observed that along with a complete set of good-quality tools, the box contained several adjustable wrenches. The more experienced technician said, "Hide those from the boss." If any adjustable wrench is used on a bolt or nut, the movable jaw often moves or loosens and starts to round the head of the fastener. If the head of the bolt or nut becomes rounded, it becomes that much more difficult to remove.

Apply a small amount of valve grinding compound to a Phillips or Torx screw or bolt head. The gritty valve grinding compound "grips" the screwdriver or tool bit and prevents the tool from slipping up and out of the screw head. Valve grinding compound is available in a tube from most automotive parts stores.

1.5.2 Brand Name Versus Proper Term

Technicians often use slang or brand names of tools rather than the proper term. This results in some confusion for new technicians. Some examples are given in the following table.

Brand Name	Proper Term	Slang Name
Crescent wrench	Adjustable wrench	Monkey wrench
Vise Grips	Locking pliers	
Channel Locks	Water pump pliers or multigroove adjustable pliers	Pump pliers
	Diagonal cutting pliers	Dikes or side cutters

NOTE: Whenever removing any automotive component, it is wise to note the length, diameter, thread pitch, and condition of each bolt. This will help you identify damaged fasteners and to remember where to reinstall them.

NOTE: Normally, a bolt should be long enough to thread into the part a distance that is equal to or about half again the bolt diameter.

1.5.3 Safety Tips for Using Hand Tools

The following safety tips should be kept in mind whenever you are working with hand tools:

- Always use the proper tool for the job.
- Always *pull* a wrench toward you for best control and safety. Avoid pushing a wrench. If you do and a bolt or nut loosens, your entire weight will propel your hand(s) forward. This usually results in cuts, bruises, or other painful injury.
- Keep all hand tools clean. This prevents rust and provides a better, firmer grip.
- Always use a 6-point socket or a box-end wrench to break loose a tight bolt or nut.
- Use a box-end wrench for torque and the open-end wrench for speed.
- Never use a pipe extension or other type of "cheater bar" on a wrench or ratchet handle. If more force is required, use a larger tool or use penetrating oil and/or heat on the frozen fastener. (If heat is used on a bolt or nut to remove it, always replace it with a new part.)
- Never expose any tool to excessive heat. High temperatures can reduce the strength ("draw the temper") of metal tools.
- Never use a hammer on any wrench or socket handle unless you are using a special wrench designed to be used with a hammer.
- Replace any tools that are damaged or worn.

NOTE: Punches, made from soft materials like brass or aluminum, are available for striking a shaft, gear, or other object.

1.5.4 Automatic Transmission Special Service Tools

Specialized service tools are required to properly disassemble and assemble an automatic transmission. Manufacturers have developed *special service tools (SSTs)* to meet this need (Figure 1-27). They are available from the vehicle or drivetrain manufacturer and/or their tool supplier. Many technicians do not have access to the SSTs, so they use generic versions that are available from aftermarket sources.

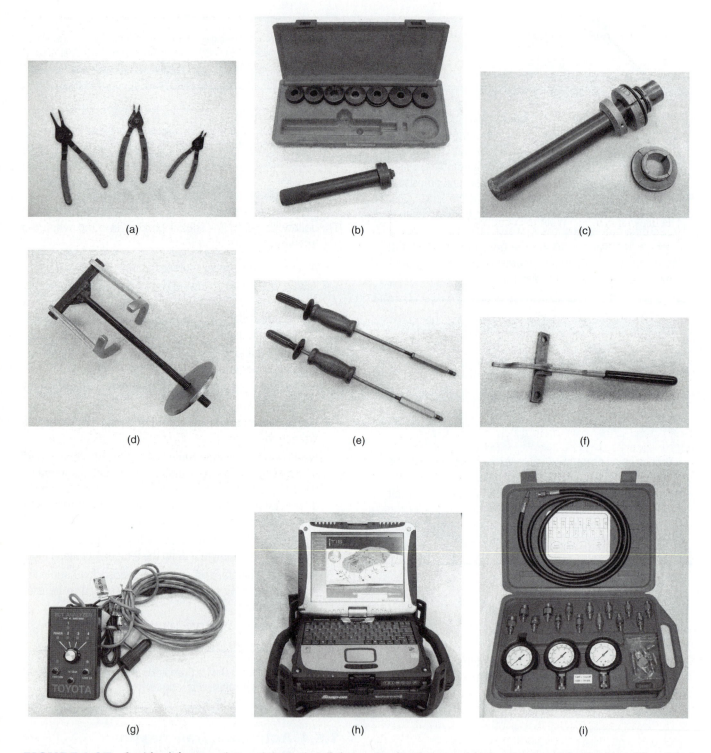

FIGURE 1-27 Special tools for automatic transmission service include snap-ring pliers that are available in various sizes (a), bushing drivers (b), specialized pullers (c), clutch spring compressor (d), slide hammers (e), servo cover compressor (f), electronic transmission tester (g), scan tool (h), and a set of pressure gauges (i).

TECH TIP

If you must strike or pound on something, be sure to use a tool that is softer than what you are about to strike to avoid damage. Examples are given in the following table.

The Material Being Pounded	What to Pound With
Steel or cast iron	Brass or aluminum hammer or punch
Aluminum	Plastic or rawhide mallet or plastic-covered dead-blow hammer
Plastic	Rawhide mallet or plastic dead-blow hammer

1.6 MEASURING TOOLS

The purpose of any repair is to restore the vehicle to factory-specified tolerance. Many repair procedures involve measuring. The service technician must measure twice:

- First, the original components must be measured to see if correction is necessary to restore the component or part to factory specifications.
- Second, the replacement parts and finished machined areas must be measured to ensure proper dimension before the component is assembled.

1.6.1 Micrometer

A **micrometer** is a commonly used measuring instrument (Figure 1-28). The *thimble* rotates over the **barrel** on a screw that has 40 threads per inch. Every revolution of the thimble moves the *spindle* 0.025 in. The thimble is graduated into 25 equally spaced lines; therefore, each line represents 0.001 in. An outside micrometer has a measuring range of one inch. Micrometers should be checked for calibration on a regular basis (Figure 1-29).

1.6.2 Telescopic Gauge

A *telescopic gauge* is used with a micrometer to measure the inside diameter of a hole or bore.

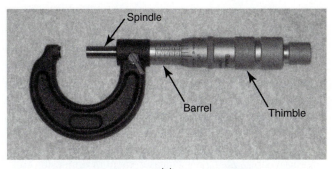

(a)

(b)

FIGURE 1-28 Typical micrometers used for dimensional measurements (a). A vernier scale (inset) allows measuring to the ten-thousandths of an inch. This set of micrometers can measure sizes between 0 and 4 inches (b).

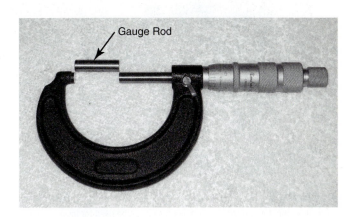

FIGURE 1-29 All micrometers should be checked and calibrated as needed using a gauge rod.

FREQUENTLY ASKED QUESTION

The word *gauge* means "measurement or dimension to a standard of reference." The word *gauge* can also be spelled *gage*. Therefore, in most cases, the words mean the same.

NOTE: One vehicle manufacturing representative mentioned that *gage* was used rather than *gauge* because even though it is the second acceptable spelling of the word, it is correct and it saved the company a lot of money in printing costs because the word *gage* has one less letter! One letter multiplied by the millions of times that *gage* is used in service manuals adds up to a big savings for the manufacturer.

1.6.3 Vernier/Dial Caliper

A **vernier dial caliper** can be used to measure outside diameter (OD), inside diameter (ID), as well as depth of a hole. Although not as accurate as a micrometer, a vernier caliper is faster and covers a wider measuring range (Figure 1-30). Dial calipers have become very popular because they are easy to read and more versatile than a micrometer.

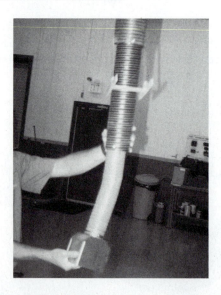

FIGURE 1-30   (a) A typical vernier dial caliper. This is a very useful measuring tool for automotive work because it can be used for inside, outside, and depth measurements. (b) To read a vernier dial caliper, simply add the reading on the blade to the reading on the dial.

1.6.4 Dial Indicator

A **dial indicator** is used to measure movement like shaft runout, gear lash/clearance, and end play (see Figures 16-16 and 16-17).

1.7 SAFETY TIPS FOR TECHNICIANS

Safety is not just a buzzword on a poster in the work area. Safe work habits can reduce accidents and injuries, ease the workload, and keep employees pain-free. Suggested safety tips include the following:

- *Wear safety glasses at all times while servicing any vehicle* (Figure 1-31).
- Watch your toes—always keep your toes protected with steel-toed safety shoes (Figure 1-32). If safety shoes are not available, then leather-topped shoes offer more protection than canvas or cloth.
- Wear gloves to protect your hands from rough or sharp surfaces. Thin rubber gloves are recommended when working around automotive liquids such as engine oil, antifreeze, transmission fluid, or any other liquids that may be hazardous.
- Service technicians working under a vehicle should wear a **bump cap** to protect the head against under-vehicle objects and the pads of the lift (Figure 1-33).
- Remove all jewelry that may get caught on something or act as a conductor to an exposed electrical circuit (Figure 1-34).
- Take care of your hands. Keep your hands clean by washing frequently with soap and hot water of at least 110°F (43°C).
- Avoid loose or dangling clothing.
- Ear protection should be worn if the sound around you requires that you raise your voice (sound level higher than 90 dB). (A typical lawn mower produces noise at a level of about 110 dB. This means that everyone who uses a lawn mower or other lawn or garden equipment should wear ear protection.)
- When lifting any object, get a secure grip with solid footing. Keep the load close to your body to minimize the strain. Lift with your legs and arms, not your back.
- Do not twist your body when carrying a load. Instead, pivot your feet to help prevent back strain.
- Ask for help when moving or lifting heavy objects.
- Push a heavy object rather than pull it. This is opposite to the way you should work with tools.
- Always connect an exhaust hose to the tailpipe of any vehicle running in a closed garage to prevent the buildup of carbon monoxide (Figure 1-35).
- When standing, keep objects, parts, and tools with which you are working between chest height and waist height. If seated, work at tasks that are at elbow height.
- Always be sure the hood is securely held open (Figure 1-36).

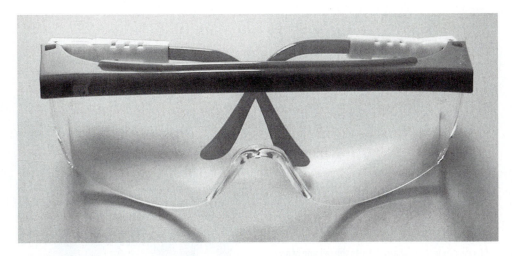

FIGURE 1-31   Safety glasses should be worn at all times when working on or around any vehicle or servicing any component.

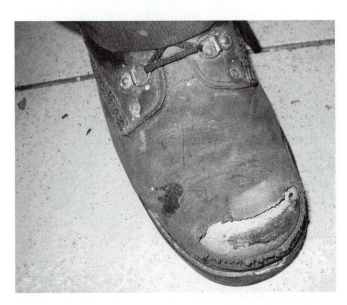

FIGURE 1-32   Steel-toed shoes are a worthwhile investment to help prevent foot injury due to falling objects. Even this well-worn shoe can protect the foot of this technician.

FIGURE 1-33   A bump cap provides a shield and padding to protect the head while working under a vehicle.

1.7.1 Vehicle Lifting (Hoisting) Safety

Many chassis and underbody service procedures require that the vehicle be hoisted or lifted off the ground. The simplest methods involve the use of drive-on ramps or a floor jack and safety (jack) stands. Hydraulic or electric in-ground or surface-mounted lifts provide greater access. **Setting the pads is a critical part of the lifting procedure.**

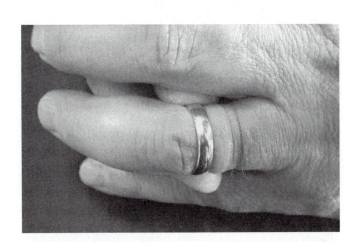

FIGURE 1-34   All jewelry such as rings and watches should be re-moved when working on vehicles.

FIGURE 1-35 Always connect an exhaust hose to the tailpipe of a vehicle running inside a building.

(a)

(b)

FIGURE 1-36 A crude but effective method to secure a hood is to use locking pliers on the hood strut shaft (a). Locking pliers should only be used on defective struts because the jaws of the pliers can damage the strut shaft. A commercially available hood clamp (b); remember to remove the clamp before attempting to close the hood.

SAFETY TIP

Always dispose of oily shop cloths in an enclosed container to prevent a fire. Whenever oily cloths are thrown together on the floor or workbench, a chemical reaction can occur, which can ignite the cloth even without an open flame. This process of ignition without an open flame is called **spontaneous combustion.**

TECH TIP

SHOCK CONTROL

To avoid impact damage from your impact wrench on your hand, take the rubber covering from an old electric fuel pump and fit it on the handle of the gun to soften the blow.

All automobile and light-truck service manuals include recommended locations to be used when hoisting (lifting) (Figure 1-37) a vehicle. Newer vehicles have a triangle decal on the driver's door indicating the recommended lift points (Figure 1-38). The recommended standards for the lift points and lifting procedures are found in SAE standard JRP-2184. These recommendations typically include the following points:

1. The vehicle, with the doors, hood, and trunk closed, should be centered on the lift or hoist so as not to overload one side or put too much load toward the front or rear of the hoist.
2. The pads of the lift should be spread as far apart as possible to provide a stable platform.
3. Each pad should be placed under a part of the vehicle that is strong and capable of supporting the weight of the vehicle.

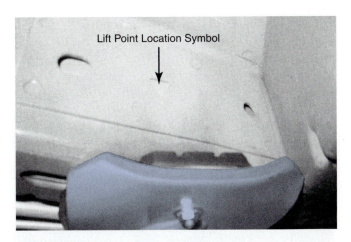

FIGURE 1-37 Most newer vehicles have a triangle symbol indicating the recommended hoisting life points.

FIGURE 1-38 Many vehicles have a triangle symbol indicating the recommended hoisting lift points.

(a)

(b)

FIGURE 1-39 This vehicle fell from the hoist because the pads were not set correctly. No one was hurt, but the vehicle was a total loss.

a. Pinch welds at the bottom edge of the body are generally considered to be strong enough lift points.

CAUTION: Even though pinch weld seams are the recommended location for hoisting many vehicles with unitized bodies (unit-body), care should be taken when placing the pad(s). Incorrect placement of the vehicle on the lift could cause the vehicle to be imbalanced, and the vehicle could fall. This is exactly what happened to the vehicle in Figure 1-39. Be aware that a tall vehicle might hit the ceiling or suspended lights.

b. Boxed areas of the body are the best places to position the pads on a vehicle without a frame. Be careful to note whether the arms of the lift might come into contact with other parts of the vehicle before the pad touches the intended location. Commonly damaged areas include the following:
   1. rocker panel moldings,
   2. exhaust system (including catalytic converter), and
   3. tires or body panels

4. The vehicle should be raised about a foot (30 centimeters [cm]) off the floor, then stopped and shaken to check for stability. If the vehicle appears stable, continue raising the vehicle and watch the vehicle until it has reached the desired height.

CAUTION: Do not look away from the vehicle while it is being raised (or lowered) on a hoist. One side or one end of the hoist can stop or fail, resulting in the vehicle being slanted enough to slip or fall, creating physical damage not only to the vehicle and/or hoist but also to the technician or others who may be nearby.

NOTE: Most hoists can be safely placed at any desired height. When removing and replacing components such as an axle, it is not necessary to work on them down near the floor or over your head. Raise the hoist so that the components are at a comfortable work height (chest level).

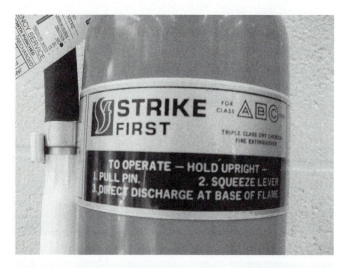

FIGURE 1-40 A typical fire extinguisher design to be used on Class A, B, or C fires.

FIGURE 1-41 A CO_2 fire extinguisher being used on a fire set in an open steel drum during a demonstration at a fire department training center.

5. Before lowering the hoist, the safety latch(es) must be released and the direction of the controls reversed. The speed downward is often adjusted to be as slow as possible for additional safety.

1.8 HYBRID VEHICLE CAUTIONS

Hybrid vehicles combine a gasoline engine, electric motor/generator, and a high-voltage battery pack. Technicians and first-responders (emergency workers such as firefighters, ambulance crews, and vehicle recovery personnel) must be aware of the potential hazards of these vehicles. The biggest hazard is electric shock. The use of nickel-cadmium batteries has minimized hazardous electrolyte spills. Battery pack voltage varies between different makes, but it is about 150 to 275 volts of direct current (dc), ample to kill or seriously injure.

A hybrid vehicle can be identified by a hybrid label on the trunk lid or rear lift gate, on the hood, or front doors. There is often a label on the engine. Bright orange warning decals are also placed under the hood and in the vicinity of the major high-voltage components. Wires used to connect the high-voltage components are bright orange. DO NOT TOUCH ANY BRIGHT ORANGE WIRING OR COMPONENT WITHOUT FOLLOWING THE VEHICLE MANUFACTURER'S PROCEDURE AND WEARING THE PROPER PROTECTIVE GEAR.

If necessary, turn off the high-voltage current by turning the ignition key to "off" and removing the key to prevent it from being turned back "on." Next, disconnect the 12-volt dc battery to prevent vehicle operation; this will shut off the high-voltage battery pack on some vehicles. Many hybrid

vehicles also have a high-voltage shutoff switch/plug that completely shuts off the high-voltage circuit (Figure 1-42).

CAUTION: Always remember these things concerning hybrid vehicles:

- Orange insulation = high voltage (HV).
- If the ignition is off, then the high-voltage circuits are open.
- Shut off the HV system if any work is to be done on HV components.
- A HV circuit can retain voltage for up to 5 minutes after being shut off.
- HV batteries retain a HV charge.
- Wear HV insulated gloves whenever working on HV components.
- Never lean on HV components; you might create a path to ground.
- Don't wear metal near HV components.
- Any one wearing a pacemaker should stay away from HV devices.
- Test for voltage with a meter that is labeled CAT III before touching an HV component.
- Always place the ignition key in your pocket, except for with auto-start vehicles, you should place the key at least 15 feet away from the vehicle.

1.9 ELECTRICAL CORD SAFETY

Use correctly grounded three-prong sockets and extension cords to operate power tools. Use only double-insulated power tools. Some modern tools use polarized two-prong plugs that have one wide and one narrow prong. When not in use, keep

SAFETY TIP

Improper use of an air nozzle can cause blindness or deafness. If an air nozzle is used to dry and clean parts, make sure the airstream is directed away from anyone else in the immediate area. Clean, coil, and store air hoses when they are not in use.

electrical cords off the floor to prevent tripping over them. Tape the cords to the floor if they are placed in high-foot-traffic areas.

1.10 FIRE EXTINGUISHERS

There are four classes of fire extinguishers. Each class should be used on specific fires only:

- **Class A** is designed for use on general combustibles, such as cloth, paper, and wood.
- **Class B** is designed for use on flammable liquids and greases, including gasoline, oil, thinners, and solvents.
- **Class C** is used only on electrical fires.
- **Class D** is effective only on combustible metals such as powdered aluminum, sodium, or magnesium.

The class rating is clearly marked on the side of every fire extinguisher. Many extinguishers are good for multiple types of fires (Figure 1-40).

When using a fire extinguisher, remember the word *PASS*:

P = Pull the safety pin.
A = Aim the nozzle of the extinguisher at the base of the fire.
S = Squeeze the lever to actuate the extinguisher.
S = Sweep the nozzle from side to side at the base of the flame.

See Figure 1-41.

1.10.1 Types of Fire Extinguishers

The various types of fire extinguishers include:

- Water—A water fire extinguisher is usually in a pressurized container and is good to use on Class A fires because it reduces the temperature to the point where a fire cannot be sustained.
- Carbon Dioxide (CO_2)—A carbon dioxide fire extinguisher is good for almost any type of fire, especially Class B or Class C materials. A CO_2 fire extinguisher works by removing the oxygen from the fire. The cold CO_2 also helps reduce the temperature of the fire.
- Dry Chemical (yellow)—A dry chemical fire extinguisher is good for Class A, B, or C fires and works by coating the flammable materials to eliminate the oxygen from the fire. A dry chemical fire extinguisher tends to be very corrosive and will cause damage to electronic devices.

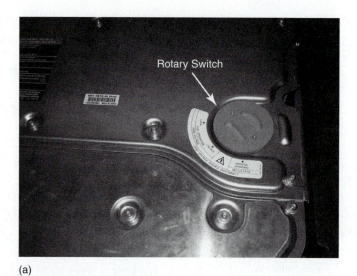

(a)

Locations of HV Batteries and Service Switch /Plugs

Model (year)	HV Battery Pack Location	HV Safety Switch / Plug Location
Honda Insight 2000-2006	144v unit under hatch floor.	Under hatch carpet, remove small plate in center
Civic / Accord Hybrid 2003 - 2006 +	144v unit (158v 06 Civic) behind back seat upright cushion	Behind back seat upright cushion, remove small oval plate in center
Toyota Prius 2001 - 2003	275v unit in trunk, under carpet, lower front area	In lower front left area corner of HV battery.
Toyota Prius 2004 - 2006 +	201v unit in front of spare tire	In front of spare tire, lower front left area of HV battery pack around the corner. Plug removes toward left side of car.
Toyota / Lexus SUV RX400h / Highlander 2006+	288v unit under rear seat in 3 compartments	In lower rear seat left side under trim small rectangular panel. Plug removes toward left side of SUV
Ford Escape 2005+	330v unit under carpet, rear floor	Under rear carpet, round orange switch on right side in plain view
Mercury Mariner 2006 +	330v unit under carpet, rear floor	Under rear carpet, round orange switch on right side in plain view

Note: The GM hybrid truck is not listed because it is only 42 volts and not considered a shock hazard.

(b)

FIGURE 1-42   This hybrid vehicle has a rotary switch in the rear compartment; turning the switch disconnects the high-voltage electricity (a). Locations of the HV batteries and safety switches or plugs (b).

HOISTING A VEHICLE Step-by-Step

(Photos courtesy of James Halderman)

STEP 1 The first step in hoisting a vehicle is to center the vehicle to the hoist.

STEP 2 Most vehicles will be correctly positioned when the left front tire is centered on the tire pad.

STEP 3 Many pads at the end of the hoist arms can be rotated to allow for many different types of vehicles.

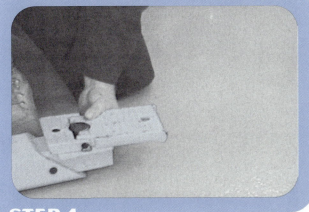

STEP 4 The arms of the lifts can be retracted or extended to accommodate vehicles of different lengths and widths.

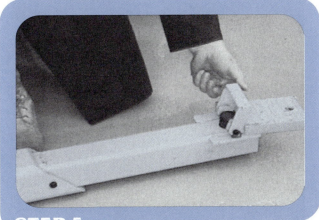

STEP 5 Most lifts are equipped with short pad extensions to contact the frame of a vehicle without causing the arm of the lift to damage parts of the body.

STEP 6 Tall pad extensions can also be used to gain access to the frame of a vehicle. This position is needed to safely hoist many pickups, vans, and sport-utility vehicles (SUVs).

(continued)

HOISTING A VEHICLE continued

STEP 7 An additional extension may be necessary to hoist a truck or van equipped with running boards to provide the necessary clearance.

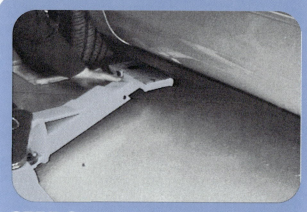

STEP 8 Position the front hoist pads under the recommended locations.

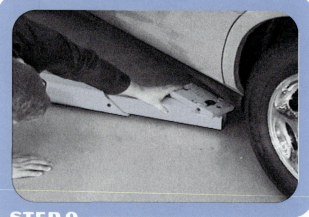

STEP 9 Position the rear pads under the vehicle in the recommended locations.

STEP 10 An asymmetrical lift has front arms that are shorter than the rear arms. This design allows the driver to easily exit the vehicle because the door can be opened wide.

STEP 11 After being sure all pads are correctly positioned, use the electromechanical controls to raise the vehicle.

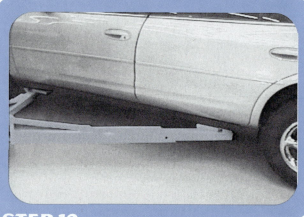

STEP 12 Raise the vehicle about 1 foot (30 cm) and stop to double-check that all pads contact the body or frame in the correct positions.

HOISTING A VEHICLE continued

STEP 13 With the vehicle raised about 1 foot, push down on the vehicle to check to see if it is stable on the pads. If the vehicle rocks, lower the vehicle and reset the pads.

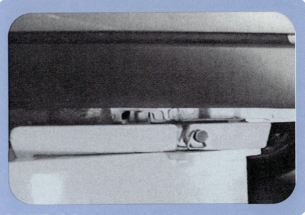

STEP 14 This photo shows the pads set flat and contacting the pinch welds of the body. This method spreads the load over the entire length of the pad and is less likely to dent or damage the pinch weld area.

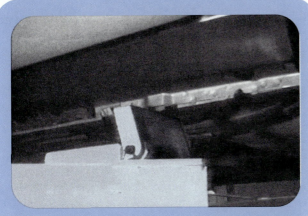

STEP 15 Where additional clearance is necessary, the pads can be raised and placed under the pinch weld area as shown.

STEP 16 When the service work is completed, raise the hoist slightly and release the safety lock before using the hydraulic lever to lower the vehicle.

STEP 17 After lowering the vehicle and before moving the vehicle, be sure all arms of the lift are moved out of the way.

STEP 18 Carefully back the vehicle out of the stall. Notice that all of the lift arms have been neatly moved out of the way to provide clearance so that the tires will not contact the lift arms.

SUMMARY

1. Vehicles carry several different identification numbers:

    VIN: identifies the vehicle as well as where and when it was assembled.

    VECI: Necessary vehicle emission control information

    Calibration codes

    Casting number on major components

2. Vehicle service information is available in printed and electronic format as service manuals and TSBs.

3. Bolts, nuts, studs, and threaded fasteners use fractional inch or metric sizes; they also come in a series of grades.

4. Technicians have a tool set of hand tools in a variety of sizes. A technician must be able to use tools properly to prevent injury.

5. A technician must be aware of potential safety hazards when working on and around motor vehicles.

REVIEW QUESTIONS

The following questions are provided to help you study as you read the chapter.

1. The two common types of fractional bolt sizes are _____ and _____.

2. A 5/16–18 bolt has _____ threads per inch and a _____ diameter of 5/16″.

3. A M8 X 1.5 bolt has a thread diameter of _____ _____ and a _____ of 1.5 mm.

4. A grade 8 bolt is _____ than a grade 5 bolt.

5. Loctite is an _____ compound used to _____ the nut on the bolt.

6. A Crescent wrench should properly be called an _____ _____.

7. When you loosen a tight nut or bolt, you should _____ on the wrench.

8. The best tool to loosen a really tight nut is either a _____ _____ socket or a _____ _____ wrench.

9. A _____ is a good tool to measure a shaft to see if it is worn.

10. A _____ _____ can be used to measure shaft end play or flywheel runout.

11. An oily shop cloth can ignite and burn without an open flame because of _____ _____.

12. A critical step in lifting a vehicle on a hoist is to _____ the _____.

13. The third prong of a three-prong electrical plug is for _____.

14. Class B fire extinguishers are designed to extinguish _____ _____ fires.

15. A _____ _____ fire extinguisher is good for most types of fire.

CHAPTER QUIZ

The following questions will help you check the facts you have learned. Select the answer that completes each statement correctly.

1. Student A says that if a micrometer thimble is rotated two complete revolutions, the spindle will move 0.050″. Student B says the micrometer barrel has 40 threads per inch. Who is correct?

    a. Student A

    b. Student B

    c. Both A and B

    d. Neither A nor B

2. Two students are discussing bolts. Student A says the wrench used with a bolt is the same size as the bolt. Student B says the thread diameter is the bolt size. Who is correct?

    a. Student A

    b. Student B

    c. Both A and B

    d. Neither A nor B

3. Student A says a micrometer can be used to measure parts to 0.001″. Student B says vernier calipers can be used to measure

depth as well as the inside and outside diameter of a part. Who is correct?

   a. Student A
   b. Student B
   c. Both A and B
   d. Neither A nor B

4. Student A says it is a good idea to get help when you need to lift a heavy object. Student B says you should lift heavy objects using your legs, not your back. Who is correct?

   a. Student A
   b. Student B
   c. Both A and B
   d. Neither A nor B

5. A vehicle is being hoisted on a lift. Student A says to put the pads of a lift under a notch at the pinch weld of a unit-body vehicle. Student B says to place the pads on the four corners of the frame of a full-frame vehicle. Who is correct?

   a. Student A
   b. Student B
   c. Both A and B
   d. Neither A nor B

6. The correct location for the pads when hoisting or jacking the vehicle can often be found in the _____.

   a. service manual
   b. shop manual
   c. owner's manual
   d. all of the above

7. For the best working position, the work should be _____.

   a. at neck or head level
   b. at knee or ankle level
   c. overhead by about 1 foot
   d. at chest or elbow level

8. When working with hand tools, always _____.

   a. push a wrench—don't pull toward you
   b. pull a wrench—don't push a wrench

9. Student A says that the fire extinguisher should be aimed at the base of a fire. Student B says that fire extinguishers remove either heat or oxygen from the burning material. Who is correct?

   a. Student A
   b. Student B
   c. Both A and B
   d. Neither A nor B

10. The strength of a fractional bolt is identified by _____.

   a. a UNC symbol
   b. lines on the head
   c. strength letter codes
   d. the coarse threads

11. A fastener that uses threads on both ends is called a _____.

   a. cap screw
   b. stud
   c. machine screw
   d. crest fastener

12. The proper term for Channel Locks is _____.

   a. Vise Grips
   b. Crescent wrench
   c. locking pliers
   d. multigroove adjustable pliers

13. The proper term for Vise Grips is _____.

   a. locking pliers
   b. slip-joint pliers
   c. side cuts
   d. multigroove adjustable pliers

14. What is *not* considered to be personal safety equipment?

   a. air impact wrench
   b. safety glasses
   c. rubber gloves
   d. hearing protection

15. Student A says that a typical fire extinguisher is designed to be used on class A, B, or C fires. Student B says that a different fire extinguisher is needed for each class of fire. Who is correct?

   a. Student A
   b. Student B
   c. Both A and B
   d. Neither A nor B

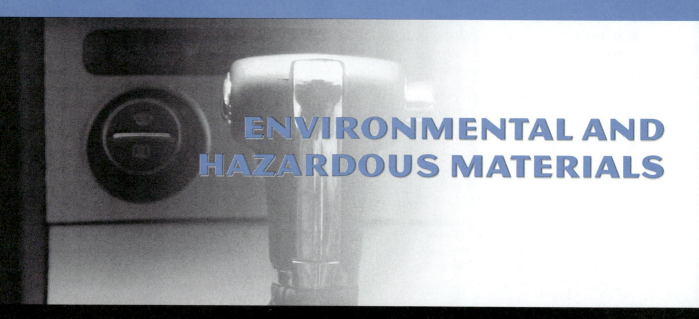

ENVIRONMENTAL AND HAZARDOUS MATERIALS

OBJECTIVES

After studying Chapter 2, the reader should be able to:

1. Define the Occupational Safety and Health Act.
2. Explain the term *material safety data sheet (MSDS).*
3. Identify hazardous waste materials in accordance with state and federal regulations.

4. Describe the steps required to safely handle and store automotive chemicals and waste.
5. Follow proper safety precautions while handling hazardous waste materials.
6. Understand the ASE requirements for all service technicians in order to adhere to environmentally appropriate actions and behavior.

KEY TERMS

Blood-borne Pathogens (p. 35)
High-efficiency Particulate Air (HEPA) Filter (p. 29)
Occupational Safety and Health Act (p. 27)
Solvent (p. 31)

Used Brake Fluid (p. 30)
Used Coolant (p. 33)
Used Oil (p. 30)
Workplace Hazardous Materials Information Systems (WHIMS) (p. 28)

2.1 INTRODUCTION

The safe handling of hazardous waste materials is extremely important in the automotive shop. The improper handling of hazardous material affects everyone, not just those in the shop. Shop personnel are required by right-to-know laws to be informed of their rights and responsibilities regarding hazardous waste disposal. Shop personnel must also be familiar with any hazardous materials being used and the proper disposal methods for these materials according to state and federal regulations.

2.2 OCCUPATIONAL SAFETY AND HEALTH ACT (OSHA)

The U.S. Congress passed the **Occupational Safety and Health Act** in 1970. The purpose of this legislation is to assist and encourage the citizens of the United States in their efforts to assure safe and healthful working conditions. The Occupational Safety and Health Administration (OSHA) provides research, information, education, and training in the field of occupational safety and health. It also assures safe and healthful working conditions by authorizing enforcement of OSHA standards. Since approximately 25% of workers are exposed to health and safety hazards on the job, the OSHA standards are necessary to monitor, control, and educate workers regarding health and safety in the workplace.

2.2.1 Health Care Rights

The OSHA regulations concerning on-the-job safety place certain responsibilities on the employer and give employees specific rights. Any person who feels there might be unsafe conditions in the workplace, whether asbestos exposure, chemical poisoning, or any other problem, should discuss the issue with fellow workers, the union representative (where applicable), and the supervisor or employer. If no action is taken and there is reason to believe the employer is not complying with OSHA standards, a complaint can be filed with OSHA, which will be investigated. The law forbids employers from taking action against employees who file a complaint concerning a health or safety hazard. However, if workers fear reprisal as the result of a complaint, they may request that OSHA withhold their names from the employer.

2.3 HAZARDOUS WASTE

Hazardous waste materials are chemicals, or components, that the shop no longer needs and pose a danger to the environment and people if they are disposed of in ordinary garbage cans or sewers. However, one should note that no material is considered hazardous waste until the shop has finished using it and is ready to dispose of it. The *Environmental Protection Agency (EPA)* publishes a list of hazardous materials that is included in the Code of Federal Regulations. The EPA considers waste hazardous if it is included on the EPA list of hazardous materials or if it can be described in one or more of the following ways:

Reactive. Any material that reacts violently with water or any other chemical is considered hazardous.

Corrosive. If a material burns the skin or dissolves metals and other materials, a technician should consider it hazardous. A pH scale of 0 to 14 is used, with the number 7 indicating neutral. Pure water has a pH of 7. Lower numbers indicate an acidic solution and higher numbers indicate a caustic solution. If, when exposed to low-pH acid solutions, a material releases cyanide gas, hydrogen sulfide gas, or similar gases, it is considered hazardous.

Toxic. Materials are hazardous if they leak one or more of eight different heavy metals in concentrations greater than 100 times the primary drinking water standard.

Ignitable. A liquid is hazardous if it has a flash point below 140°F (60°C), and a solid is hazardous if it ignites spontaneously.

Radioactive. Any substance that emits measurable levels of radiation is hazardous. When individuals bring containers of highly radioactive substances into the shop environment, qualified personnel with the appropriate equipment must test them.

CAUTION: When handling hazardous waste material, one must always wear proper protective clothing and use equipment detailed in the right-to-know laws, including respirator equipment when needed. All recommended procedures must be followed accurately. Personal injury may result from improper clothing, equipment, and/or procedures when handling hazardous materials.

WARNING: Hazardous waste disposal laws include serious penalties for anyone responsible for breaking these laws.

2.4 RESOURCE CONSERVATION AND RECOVERY ACT (RCRA)

Federal and state laws control the disposal of hazardous waste materials. Every shop employee must be familiar with these laws. Hazardous waste disposal laws include the Resource Conservation and Recovery Act (RCRA), which states that hazardous material users are responsible for hazardous materials from the time they become a waste until the proper waste disposal is completed. Many shops hire an independent hazardous waste hauler to dispose of hazardous waste material. The shop owner, or manager, should have a written contract with the waste hauler. In this case, the user must store hazardous waste material properly and safely and be responsible for its transportation until it arrives at an approved hazardous waste disposal site and is processed according to the law. A shop may also choose to recycle the hazardous waste material in the shop rather than have it hauled to an approved hazardous waste disposal site. The RCRA identifies these types of automotive waste:

- paint and body repair products waste,
- solvents for parts and equipment cleaning,
- batteries and battery acid,
- mild acids used for metal cleaning and preparation,
- waste oil and engine coolants or antifreeze,
- air conditioning refrigerants and oils, and
- engine oil filters.

The *right-to-know laws* state that employees have a right to know when the materials they use at work are hazardous. The right-to-know laws started with the *Hazard Communication Standard* published by the Occupational Safety and Health Administration in 1983. Originally, this document was intended for chemical companies and manufacturers that required employees to handle hazardous materials in their work situation. Meanwhile, the federal courts have decided to apply these laws to all companies, including automotive service shops. Under the right-to-know laws, the employer has responsibilities regarding the handling of hazardous materials by employees. All employees must be trained about the types of hazardous materials they will encounter in the workplace, and the employees must be informed about their rights under legislation regarding the handling of hazardous materials.

2.5 CLEAN AIR ACT

Air-conditioning (A/C) systems and refrigerant are regulated by the Clean Air Act, Title VI, Section 609. Technician certification and service equipment is also regulated. Any technician working on automotive A/C systems must be certified. A/C refrigerants must not be released or vented into the atmosphere, and used refrigerants must be recovered.

2.6 MATERIAL SAFETY DATA SHEETS (MSDSs)

All hazardous materials must be properly labeled, and information about each hazardous material must be posted on *material safety data sheets (MSDSs),* available from the manufacturer (Figure 2-1). In Canada, MSDSs are called **workplace hazardous materials information systems (WHIMS).**

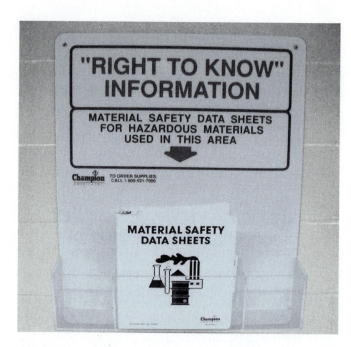

FIGURE 2-1   Material safety data sheets (MSDSs) should be readily available for use by anyone in the area who may come into contact with hazardous materials.

The employer has a responsibility to place MSDSs where they are easily accessible by all employees. The MSDSs provide the following information about the hazardous material: chemical name, physical characteristics, protective handling equipment, explosion/fire hazards, incompatible materials, health hazards, medical conditions aggravated by exposure, emergency and first-aid procedures, safe handling, and spill/leak procedures.

The employer also has a responsibility to make sure that all hazardous materials are properly labeled. The label information must include health, fire, and reactivity hazards posed by the material and the protective equipment necessary to handle the material. The manufacturer must supply all warning and precautionary information about hazardous materials, and this information must be read and understood by the employee before handling the material.

2.7 ASBESTOS EXPOSURE HAZARD

Friction materials such as brake and clutch linings may contain asbestos. Although asbestos has been eliminated from most original equipment friction materials, the automotive service technician cannot know whether the vehicle being serviced is or is not equipped with friction materials containing asbestos. It is important that all friction materials be handled as if they contain asbestos.

Asbestos exposure can cause scar tissue to form in the lungs. This condition, called *asbestosis*, causes gradually increasing shortness of breath and permanent scarring of the lungs. Even low exposures to asbestos can cause *mesothelioma*, a type of fatal cancer of the lining of the chest or abdominal cavity. Asbestos exposure can also increase the risk of lung cancer as well as cancer of the voice box, stomach, and large intestine. It usually takes 15 to 30 years or more for cancer or asbestos lung scarring to show up after exposure. (Scientists call this the *latency period*.)

Government agencies recommend that asbestos exposure be eliminated or controlled to the lowest level possible, and they have developed recommendations and standards that the automotive service technician and equipment manufacturers should follow. These agencies include the National Institute for Occupational Safety and Health (NIOSH), the Occupational Safety and Health Administration (OSHA), and the Environmental Protection Agency (EPA).

2.7.1 OSHA Asbestos Standards

The Occupational Safety and Health Administration (OSHA) has established three levels of asbestos exposure. Any vehicle service establishment that does either brake or clutch work must limit employee exposure to asbestos to less than 0.2 fibers per cubic centimeter (cc) as determined by an air sample. If the level of employee exposure is greater than specified, corrective measures must be taken and a large fine may be imposed.

NOTE: Research has found that worn asbestos fibers, such as from automotive brakes or clutches, may not be as hazardous as first believed. Worn asbestos fibers do not have sharp, flared ends that can latch onto tissue, but rather are worn down to a dust form that resembles talc. Grinding or sawing operations on unworn brake shoes or clutch discs *will* contain *harmful* asbestos fibers. To limit health damage, always use proper handling procedures while working around any component that may contain asbestos.

2.7.2 EPA Asbestos Regulations

The federal Environmental Protection Agency (EPA) has established procedures for the removal and disposal of asbestos. The EPA procedures require that products containing asbestos be "wetted" to prevent the asbestos fibers from becoming airborne. According to the EPA, asbestos-containing materials can be disposed of as regular waste—asbestos is only considered hazardous when it is airborne.

2.7.3 Asbestos-Handling Guidelines

The air in the shop area can be tested by a testing laboratory, but this can be expensive. Tests have determined that asbestos levels can easily be kept below the recommended levels by using a solvent or a special vacuum.

FIGURE 2-2   Brakes should be washed with liquid to help keep brake dust from becoming airborne.

NOTE: Even though manufacturers are removing asbestos from brake and clutch lining materials, the service technician cannot tell whether the old brake pads or shoes or clutch discs contain asbestos. Therefore, to be safe, the technician should assume that all brake pads or shoes or clutch discs contain asbestos.

HEPA Vacuum. A special **high-efficiency particulate air (HEPA) filter** vacuum system has been proven to be effective in keeping asbestos exposure levels below 0.1 fibers per cubic centimeter.

Liquid/Solvent Brake Cleaners. Many technicians use an aerosol can of brake cleaning solvent to wet the brake dust and prevent it from becoming airborne. Some of the brake cleaning solvents may be hazardous; be sure to read the product label. Commercial brake cleaners are available that use a concentrated cleaner that is mixed with water (Figure 2-2). The waste liquid is filtered, and when dry, the filter can be disposed of as solid waste.

CAUTION: Never use compressed air to blow brake dust. The fine, talc-like brake dust can create a health hazard even if asbestos is not present or is present in dust rather than fiber form.

Disposal of Brake Dust and Brake Shoes. As mentioned, the hazard of asbestos occurs when asbestos fibers are airborne.

Once the asbestos has been wetted down, it is then considered to be solid waste, not hazardous waste. Old brake shoes and pads should be enclosed, preferably in a plastic bag, to help prevent any of the brake material from becoming airborne.

2.8 PROPER DISPOSAL

Always follow current federal and local laws considering disposal of all waste.

2.8.1 Used Brake Fluid

Most brake fluid is made from polyglycol; it is water soluble and can be considered hazardous if it has absorbed metals from the brake system.

- Collect **used brake fluid** in containers clearly marked to indicate that they are dedicated for that purpose.
- If your used brake fluid is hazardous, manage it appropriately and use only an authorized waste receiver for its disposal.
- If your used brake fluid is nonhazardous, your local solid waste collection provider will tell you how to dispose of it properly.
- Do not mix used brake fluid with used engine oil.
- Do not pour used brake fluid down drains or onto the ground.
- Recycle used brake fluid through a registered recycler.

2.8.2 Used Oil

Used oil is identified as any petroleum-based or synthetic oil that has been used. During normal use, impurities such as dirt, metal scrapings, water, or chemicals can get mixed with the oil. Eventually, this used oil must be replaced with virgin or re-refined oil. The EPA's used oil management standards include a three-pronged approach to determine if a substance meets the definition of used oil. To meet this definition, a substance must satisfy each of the following three criteria:

1. **Origin.** The first criterion for identifying used oil is based on the origin of the oil. Used oil must have been refined from crude oil or made from synthetic materials. Animal and vegetable oils are excluded from the EPA's definition of used oil.
2. **Use.** The second criterion is based on whether and how the oil is used. Oils used as lubricants, hydraulic fluids, heat transfer fluids, and for other similar purposes are considered used oil. Unused oil, such as bottom clean-out waste from virgin fuel oil storage tanks or virgin fuel oil recovered from a spill, do not meet the EPA's definition of used oil because these oils have never been

"used." The EPA's definition also excludes products used as cleaning agents or solely for their solvent properties, as well as certain petroleum-derived products such as antifreeze and kerosene.
3. **Contaminants.** The third criterion is based on whether the oil is contaminated with either physical or chemical impurities. Oil that is physically or chemically contaminated is considered used oil by the EPA's definition and includes residues and contaminants generated from handling, storing, and processing used oil.

NOTE: The release of only 1 gallon of used oil (a typical oil change) can make a million gallons of fresh water undrinkable.

If used oil is dumped down the drain and enters a sewage treatment plant, concentrations as small as 50 to 100 ppm (parts per million) in the wastewater can foul the sewage treatment processes. Never mix a listed hazardous waste, gasoline, wastewater, hologenated solvents, antifreeze, or an unknown waste material with used oil. Adding any of these substances will cause the used oil to become contaminated, which classifies it as hazardous waste.

Disposal of Used Oil. Once oil has been used, it can be collected, recycled, and reused. An estimated 380 million gallons of used oil are recycled each year. Recycled used oil can sometimes be used again for the same job or for a completely different task. For example, used motor oil can be re-refined and sold as motor oil or processed for heating fuel. After collecting used oil in an appropriate container (for example, a 55-gallon steel drum), the material must be disposed of in one of two ways:

- Shipped off-site for recycling
- Burned in an on-site or off-site EPA-approved heater for energy recovery

Used Oil Storage. Used oil must be stored in compliance with existing *underground storage tank (UST)* or an *aboveground storage tank (AGST)* standards or kept in separate containers. Containers are portable receptacles, such as a 55-gallon steel drum.

Keep used-oil storage drums in good condition. This means that they should be covered, secured from vandals, properly labeled, and maintained in compliance with local fire codes. Frequent inspections for leaks, corrosion, spillage, and so on are an essential part of container maintenance.

Never store used oil in anything other than the proper tanks and storage containers. Used oil may also be stored in containers that are permitted to store regulated hazardous waste.

Follow used oil filters disposal regulations. Used oil filters contain used engine oil that may be hazardous. Before an oil filter is placed in the trash or sent for recycling, it must be drained using one of the following hot-draining methods approved by the EPA:

- Puncture the filter anti-drain-back valve or filter dome end and hot-drain for at least 12 hours.
- Hot-drain and crush.
- Dismantle and hot-drain.
- Use any other hot-draining method that will remove all the used oil from the filter.

After the oil has been drained from the oil filter, the filter housing can be disposed of in any of the following ways:

- Recycling
- Pickup by a service contract company
- Disposed of in regular trash

2.8.3 Solvents

The major sources of chemical danger are liquid and aerosol brake cleaning fluids that contain chlorinated hydrocarbon **solvents.** The most common of these solvents are 1,1,1-trichloroethane, trichloroethylene, and tetrachloroethylene, which is also known as perchloroethylene, or "perk" for short. These solvents are all members of the same chemical family and share the same basic characteristics. They are colorless liquids with an odor of chloroform or ether. In large enough quantities these solvents can dull the senses, induce sleep, or cause a stupor. Very high levels of exposure over even a short period of time can be fatal. Repeated exposure to these solvents, in high concentrations and over long periods of time, can result in liver, kidney, and lung damage and may potentially cause cancer. Additionally, if these solvents are exposed to high heat or an open flame, they decompose into deadly gases such as hydrogen chloride, phosgene, and carbon monoxide.

Because 1,1,1-trichloroethane and trichloroethylene are known to be ozone depleters, the EPA prohibited their manufacture after January 1, 1996. "Perks" do not deplete the ozone and their use continues. Several other chemicals that do not deplete the ozone, such as heptane, hexane, and xylene, are now being used in nonchlorinated brake cleaning solvents. Some manufacturers are also producing solvents they describe as environmentally responsible that are biodegradable and noncarcinogenic.

Another solvent that can affect health is *n*-Hexane, a major component in several brands of automotive and industrial cleaners.

Some local areas, such as the South Coast Air Quality Management District in Southern California, have regulations and standards for air quality and various chemicals that can affect air quality, including chemicals such as solvents that evaporate.

Sources of Chemical Poisoning. The health hazards presented by automotive cleaning solvents occur from three different forms of exposure: ingestion, inhalation, or physical contact. It should be obvious that swallowing automotive cleaning solvent is harmful, and such occurrences are not common. Automotive cleaning solvents should always be handled and stored properly and kept out of reach of children. The dangers of inhalation are perhaps the most serious problem—even very low levels of solvent vapors are hazardous. For example, the current OSHA standard (1910.1000) for airborne trichloroethylene is 100 ppm (parts per million) in the ambient air averaged over an 8-hour period. The ceiling level for exposure is 200 ppm, and there is a maximum acceptable peak level of 300 ppm for 5 minutes in any 2-hour period. The limits for other chlorinated hydrocarbon solvents, and for other chemicals replacing the chlorinated ones, are similar. These alternative chemicals are being used because they do not deplete the ozone layer, not because they are necessarily any safer to breathe, ingest, or touch.

Ingestion and inhalation are common forms of poisoning from many hazardous substances, but allowing automotive cleaning solvents to come in contact with the skin presents a danger unknown to many people. Not only do these solvents strip natural oils from the skin and cause irritation of the tissues, they also have the ability to be absorbed through the skin directly into the bloodstream. The transfer begins immediately upon contact and continues until the liquid is wiped or washed away.

There is no specific standard for physical contact with chlorinated hydrocarbon solvents or the chemicals replacing them. All contact should be avoided whenever possible. The law requires an employer to provide appropriate protective equipment and ensure proper work practices by an employee handling these chemicals.

Effects of Chemical Poisoning. The effects of exposure to chlorinated hydrocarbon and other types of solvents can take many forms. Short-term exposure at low levels can cause headache, nausea, drowsiness, dizziness, lack of coordination, or unconsciousness. It may also cause irritation of the eyes, nose, and throat and flushing of the face and neck. Short-term exposure to higher concentrations can cause liver damage with symptoms such as yellow jaundice or dark urine. Liver damage may not become evident until several weeks after the exposure. Long-term or repeated exposure to perk (1,1,1-tetrachloroethylene) may cause irritation or burning of the skin. It also increases the risk of damage to the liver or kidneys. If you experience any of these symptoms, seek medical treatment immediately, and tell the doctor about your exposure to brake cleaning solvents.

Chemical Precautions. Unlike many industrial applications of chlorinated hydrocarbon solvents, automotive parts/brake cleaning sprays and liquids present relatively limited opportunity for exposure to dangerous levels of contamination. The possibility still exists, however, and just as with asbestos, there are safety precautions that should be followed to minimize the risk.

SAFETY TIP

HAND SAFETY

Service technicians should wear protective rubber or rubberlike gloves or wash their hands with soap and water after handling engine oil, differential or transmission fluids, or other shop chemicals (Figure 2-3).

The service technician should not wear watches, rings, or other jewelry that could come in contact with electrical or moving parts of a vehicle.

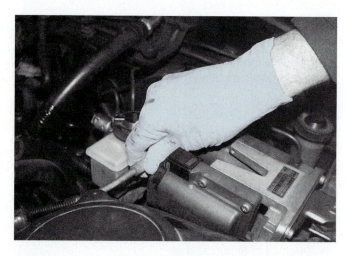

FIGURE 2-3   Protective gloves should be worn whenever working around grease or oil to help prevent possible skin problems. They help keep your hands clean, too!

Always use automotive cleaning solvents in an open, well-ventilated area and avoid breathing the vapors. Take precautions to prevent physical contact with the liquid solvent and clean any spills from the skin promptly, using soap and water. Wear protective clothing and immediately remove any piece of clothing that becomes dampened with solvent. Do not wear the item again until it has been cleaned. Wear safety goggles or other eye protection when spraying brake cleaning solvents. The safest procedure is to avoid using these chemicals completely.

Status of Solvents as Hazardous and Regulatory Status.   Most used solvents are classified as hazardous wastes. Other characteristics include:

- Solvents with flash points below 140°F are considered flammable and, like gasoline, are federally regulated by the *Department of Transportation (DOT)*.
- Solvents and oils with flash points above 140°F are considered combustible and are regulated by DOT.

It is the responsibility of the repair shop to determine if its spent solvent is hazardous waste. Waste solvents that are considered hazardous waste have a flash point below 140°F (60°C). Hot water or aqueous parts cleaners may be used to avoid disposing of spent solvent as hazardous waste. Solvent-type parts cleaners with filters are available to greatly extend solvent life and reduce spent solvent disposal costs. Solvent reclaimers are available that clean and restore the solvent so that it lasts indefinitely.

Used Solvents.   Used or spent solvents are liquid materials that have been generated as waste and may contain xylene, methanol, ethyl ether, and methyl isobutyl ketone (MIBK). These materials must be stored in OSHA-approved safety containers with tightly closed lids or caps (Figure 2-4). These storage receptacles must show no signs of leaks or significant damage due to dents or rust. In addition, the containers must

FIGURE 2-4   Typical fireproof flammable storage cabinet.

be stored in a protected area equipped with secondary containment or spill protectors, such as a spill pallet. Additional requirements include:

- Containers should be clearly labeled "Hazardous Waste" and include the date the material was first placed into the storage receptacle.
- Labeling is not required for solvents being used in a parts washer.
- Used solvents will not be counted toward a facility's monthly output of hazardous waste if the vendor under contract removes the material.

FIGURE 2-5   All solvents and other hazardous waste should be disposed of properly.

FIGURE 2-6   Used antifreeze coolant should be kept separate and stored in a leak-proof container until it can be recycled or disposed of according to federal, state, and local laws. Note that the storage barrel is placed inside another container to catch any coolant that may spill out of the inside barrel.

- Used solvents may be disposed of by recycling with a local vendor, such as SafetyKleen, who removes the used solvent according to specific terms in the vendor agreement. See Figure 2-5.

2.8.4 Coolant Disposal

Coolant is a mixture of antifreeze and water. Proper disposal of **used coolant** applies to all types of antifreeze coolant, including the following:

- **Ethylene glycol.** This coolant type has been used almost exclusively since the 1950s. It is sweet-tasting and can harm or kill humans, wild animals, or pets if swallowed (usually yellow-green).

  NOTE: There is no universal color standard for antifreeze.

- **Propylene glycol.** Similar to ethylene glycol, this type of coolant is less harmful to pets and animals because it is not sweet-tasting, although it is still harmful if swallowed.
- **Organic acid technology (OAT).** antifreeze coolant (orange).
- **Hybrid organic acid technology (HOAT).** (orange, yellow, or green).
- **VW/Audi pink.** Most of these coolants are HOAT (ethylene glycol-based with some silicate and containing an organic acid) and are phosphate-free.

- **Asian red.** This coolant is ethylene glycol-based and is silicate-free, yet contains phosphate.
- **Mercedes yellow.** This conventional ethylene glycol coolant has low amounts of silicate and no phosphates.
- **Korean or European blue.** This conventional ethylene glycol coolant has low amounts of silicate and no phosphates.

New antifreeze is not considered to be hazardous even though it can cause death if ingested. Used antifreeze may be hazardous due to dissolved metals from engine and other components of the cooling system. These metals include iron, steel, aluminum, copper, brass, and lead (from older radiators and heater cores).

1. Coolant should be recycled either on-site or off-site.
2. Used coolant should be stored in a sealed and labeled container (Figure 2-6).
3. With a permit, used coolant can be disposed of by pouring into municipal sewers. Check with local authorities and obtain a permit before discharging used coolant into sanitary sewers.

2.8.5 Lead–Acid Battery Waste

About 70 million spent lead–acid batteries are disposed of each year in the United States alone. Lead is classified as a toxic metal and the acid used in lead–acid batteries is highly corrosive. The vast majority (95–98%) of these batteries are recycled through lead reclamation operations and secondary lead smelters for use in the manufacture of new batteries.

Status of Batteries as Hazardous and Regulatory Status.
Used lead–acid batteries must be reclaimed or recycled. Leaking batteries must be stored and transported as hazardous waste. Some states have stricter regulations that require special handling procedures and transportation. According to the Battery Council International (BCI), battery laws usually

- prohibit lead–acid battery disposal in landfills or incinerators,
- require batteries to be delivered to a battery retailer, wholesaler, recycling center, or lead smelter, and
- require all retailers of automotive batteries to post a sign that displays the universal recycling symbol and indicates the retailer's specific requirements for accepting used batteries.

CAUTION: Battery electrolyte contains sulfuric acid, which is a very corrosive substance capable of causing serious personal injury, such as skin burns and eye damage. In addition, the battery plates contain lead, which is highly poisonous. For this reason, disposing of batteries improperly can cause environmental contamination and lead to severe health problems.

Battery Handling and Storage. Batteries, whether new or used, should be kept indoors. The storage location should be an area specifically designated for battery storage and must be well ventilated. If outdoor storage is the only alternative, a sheltered and secured area with acid-resistant secondary containment is strongly recommended. It is also advisable that acid-resistant secondary containment be used for indoor storage. In addition, batteries should be placed on acid-resistant pallets and never stacked!

2.8.6 Fuel Safety and Storage

Gasoline is very explosive. The expanding vapors are extremely dangerous and are present even in cold temperatures. The vapors that form in many vehicle gasoline tanks are controlled, but vapors from stored gasoline may escape from the can, resulting in a hazardous situation. Therefore, place gasoline storage containers in a well-ventilated space. Although diesel fuel is not as volatile as gasoline, the same basic rules apply.

- Approved gasoline storage cans have a flash-arresting screen at the outlet. These screens prevent external ignition sources from igniting the gasoline in the can when pouring the gasoline or diesel fuel.
- Technicians must always use approved *red* gasoline containers to allow for proper hazardous substance identification (Figure 2-7).
- Do not fill gasoline containers completely full. Always leave at least 1 inch from the top of the container. This will allow room for the gasoline to expand at higher temperatures. If the containers are completely full, the expanding gasoline will be forced from the can, creating a dangerous spill.

FIGURE 2-7 This portable gasoline supply is a sealed steel container that is painted red.

- If gasoline or diesel fuel containers must be stored, place them in a designated storage locker or facility.
- Never leave gasoline containers open except while filling or pouring gasoline from the container.
- Never use gasoline as a cleaning agent.
- Always connect a ground strap to containers when filling or transferring fuel or other flammable products from one container to another, in order to prevent static electricity that could result in explosion and fire. These ground wires prevent the buildup of a static electric charge, which could result in a spark and a disastrous explosion.

2.8.7 Air-Bag Handling

Air-bag modules are pyrometer devices that can be ignited if exposed to an electrical charge or if the front or sides of the vehicle are subjected to a sudden shock. Air-bag safety should include the following precautions:

1. Disarm the air bag(s) if you will be working in the area where a discharged bag could make contact with any part of your body. Consult service information for the exact procedure to follow for the vehicle being serviced.
2. Do not expose an air bag to extreme heat or fire.
3. Always carry an air bag pointing away from your body.

4. Place an air-bag module facing upward.
5. Always follow the manufacturer's recommended procedure for air-bag disposal or recycling, including the proper packaging to use during shipment.
6. Always wash your hands or body well if exposed to a deployed air bag. The chemicals involved can cause skin irritation and a possible rash to develop.
7. Wear protective gloves if handling a deployed air bag.

2.8.8 Used Tire Disposal

Used tires are an environmental concern for several reasons, including:

1. In a landfill, they tend to "float" up through the other trash and rise to the surface.
2. Tires trap and hold rainwater, which is a breeding ground for mosquitoes. Mosquito-borne diseases include encephalitis and dengue fever.
3. Used tires present a fire hazard, and when they burn they create a large amount of black smoke that contaminates the air.

Used tires can be reused until the end of their useful life and then should be disposed of in one of the following ways:

1. Tires can be retreaded.
2. Tires can be recycled by shredding for use in asphalt.
3. Tires, removed from the wheel, can be sent to a landfill (most landfill operators will shred the tires because it is illegal in many states to landfill whole tires).
4. Tires can be burned in cement kilns or other power plants where the smoke can be controlled.

Use only a registered scrap tire handler to transport tires for disposal or recycling.

2.8.9 Air-Conditioning Refrigerant Oil Disposal

Air-conditioning refrigerant oil contains dissolved refrigerant and is therefore considered hazardous waste. This oil must be

FIGURE 2-8 Used refrigerant oil should be stored in a clearly labeled, secure container.

SAFETY TIP

INFECTION CONTROL PRECAUTIONS

Working on a vehicle can result in personal injury, including the possibility of being cut severely enough to cause serious bleeding. Some infections such as hepatitis B, HIV (which can cause acquired immunodeficiency syndrome [AIDS]), hepatitis C virus, plus others are transmitted in the blood. These infections are commonly called **blood-borne pathogens.** Report any injury that involves blood to your supervisor and take the necessary precautions to avoid coming in contact with blood from another person.

kept separate from other waste oil or the entire amount of oil must be treated as hazardous. Used refrigerant oil must be sent to a licensed hazardous waste disposal company for recycling or disposal (Figure 2-8).

SUMMARY

1. OSHA enforces workplace health and safety.
2. Hazardous waste includes reactive, corrosive, ignitable, and radioactive substances that are identified for disposal.
3. MSDSs provide information about potentially hazardous materials.
4. Asbestos is a hazardous material that must be handled and disposed of properly as required by federal and local laws and regulations.
5. Some chemicals and components used in motor vehicle service also must be disposed of properly.

REVIEW QUESTIONS

The following questions are provided to help you study as you read the chapter.

1. OSHA is short for _____ _____ and _____ _____.

2. Hazardous waste materials are _____ or _____ that the shop no longer needs and that pose a danger.

3. EPA is short for _____ _____ _____.

4. A _____ material can burn skin or dissolve metal.

5. MSDS is short for _____ _____ _____ _____.

6. An MSDS contains information about a _____ _____.

7. _____ _____ or _____ _____ might contain asbestos.

8. Asbestos exposure can cause _____.

9. Used engine oil should be _____ so it can be used over and over.

10. Automotive solvents that contain _____ _____ solvents can cause health and environmental problems.

11. Cleaning solvents can strip _____ _____ from skin.

12. Some cleaning solvents have the ability to enter your _____ _____.

13. Technicians should wear protective _____ and _____ protection.

14. Antifreeze can cause death if _____.

15. _____ is a very explosive liquid.

CHAPTER QUIZ

The following questions will help you check the facts you have learned. Select the answer that completes each statement correctly.

1. Student A says the Occupational Safety and Health Act was passed in 1970 to protect workers. Student B says that the Environmental Protection Agency publishes a list of hazardous materials. Who is correct?
   a. Student A
   b. Student B
   c. Both A and B
   d. Neither A nor B

2. Hazardous materials include all of the following except _____.
   a. engine oil
   b. asbestos
   c. water
   d. brake cleaner

3. Student A says that employees have a right to know if materials that they are working with are hazardous. Student B says that all employees must be trained about hazardous materials. Who is correct?
   a. Student A
   b. Student B
   c. Both A and B
   d. Neither A nor B

4. Student A says that any technician working on an automotive A/C system must be certified. Student B says that all hazardous materials must be labeled. Who is correct?
   a. Student A
   b. Student B
   c. Both A and B
   d. Neither A nor B

5. To determine if a product or substance being used is hazardous, consult _____.
   a. a dictionary
   b. an MSDS
   c. EPA guidelines
   d. SAE standards

6. Student A says that right-to-know laws state that employees have the right to know when they are working with hazardous materials. Student B says the right-to-know laws state that the employer has the responsibility to train employees about the hazardous wastes they will encounter in their workplace. Who is correct?
   a. Student A
   b. Student B
   c. Both A and B
   d. Neither A nor B

7. Student A says that hazardous waste is material that the shop no longer needs that can pose a danger to people and the environment. Student B says that material safety data sheets (MSDSs) must be provided to all employees. Who is correct?

   a. Student A
   b. Student B
   c. Both A and B
   d. Neither A nor B

8. Student A says that exposure to asbestos can cause serious health problems. Student B says that all brake and clutch lining materials should be treated as if they contain asbestos. Who is correct?

   a. Student A
   b. Student B
   c. Both A and B
   d. Neither A nor B

9. Student A says that used motor oil should be recycled. Student B says that 1 gallon of used motor oil will make 1 million gallons of freshwater undrinkable. Who is correct?

   a. Student A
   b. Student B
   c. Both A and B
   d. Neither A nor B

10. Solvents are often used in automotive repair. Student A says that physical contact with solvents should be avoided. Student B says that all solvents should be used in open, well-ventilated areas. Who is correct?

    a. Student A
    b. Student B
    c. Both A and B
    d. Neither A nor B

11. Student A says that used coolant can be recycled or, with a permit, disposed of by pouring it down a drain. Student B says that new or used antifreeze can cause death if it is swallowed. Who is correct?

    a. Student A
    b. Student B
    c. Both A and B
    d. Neither A nor B

12. Student A says that the lead in batteries is toxic and battery acid is corrosive. Student B says that used batteries must be recycled. Who is correct?

    a. Student A
    b. Student B
    c. Both A and B
    d. Neither A nor B

13. Student A says gasoline vapors are very dangerous. Student B says that gasoline should never be used to clean parts. Who is correct?

    a. Student A
    b. Student B
    c. Both A and B
    d. Neither A nor B

14. Air bags should be handled with caution. Student A says that air-bag systems should always be disarmed when working near them. Student B says that air bags should never be exposed to extreme heat or fire. Who is correct?

    a. Student A
    b. Student B
    c. Both A and B
    d. Neither A nor B

15. Two students are discussing used tire disposal. Student A says that recycled tires can be added to asphalt for roads. Student B says that used tires are a fire hazard. Who is correct?

    a. Student A
    b. Student B
    c. Both A and B
    d. Neither A nor B

CHAPTER 3

INTRODUCTION TO TRANSMISSIONS

OBJECTIVES

After studying Chapter 3, the reader should be able to:

1. Explain the requirements for an automotive drivetrain.
2. Identify the major components of an automatic transmission and transaxle.

3. Explain how different gear ratios can be obtained in a planetary gearset.
4. Describe the systems within an automatic transmission and how they relate to each other.

KEY TERMS

3.1 TRANSMISSIONS: THEIR PURPOSE

A vehicle would be difficult to operate without a **transmission.** Every driver is familiar with the gear shift lever that is moved to control a vehicle's motion. This lever determines gear selection in the transmission, which determines the driving mode of the vehicle. The transmission provides the various gear ratios for forward and reverse operation as well as two methods for the engine to run without moving the vehicle. These selections are:

P: Park, allows the engine to run without moving the vehicle and mechanically locks the drivetrain to hold the vehicle stationary.

R: Reverse, allows the vehicle to be driven backward.

N: Neutral, allows the engine to run without moving the vehicle or locking the drivetrain.

O or **OD:** Overdrive, allows the engine to run slower while cruising for improved fuel mileage and lower emissions, shifts automatically from 1st through OD.

D: Allows automatic shifts from 1st through D, drives high gear with a 1:1 ratio.

I: Intermediate, prevents high-gear operation and provides compression braking.

L: Low gear, multiplies the engine's torque so there will be enough power to move the vehicle in difficult conditions, prevents upshifts, and provides compression braking.

At one time, most vehicles had the transmission mounted behind the engine and used a *drive shaft,* also called a *propeller shaft* or drive line, to transfer power to the rear axle and driving wheels. This *drivetrain* is called *rear wheel drive (RWD)* (Figure 3-1). Many vehicles use a transaxle to drive the front wheels *(FWD).*

Most FWD vehicles have the engine mounted in a *transverse* position, crosswise in the vehicle. Some are **longitudinal** mounted, in a lengthwise position as in RWD vehicles. A **transaxle** is a combination of the transmission and final *drive axle* (Figure 3-2). Two short drive shafts are used to connect the transaxle to the front wheels. Driving only two wheels is adequate for most driving conditions.

Vehicles that can drive all four wheels are called *four wheel drive (4WD)* vehicles. The driver has the option of selecting two or four wheel drive. 2WD is used for normal driving conditions, and 4WD is normally used only for off-road driving or slippery conditions. Vehicles that drive all four wheels all of the time on all road surfaces are called **all wheel drive (AWD)** vehicles. 4WD and AWD are more complex, more expensive, and heavier than 2WD. 4WD or AWD are available on most pickups, sport-utility vehicles (SUVs), vans, and light trucks. AWD is available on some passenger cars, station wagons, vans, and SUVs. Because of the added traction, AWD can benefit winter and performance-oriented driving. A transfer case or transfer gear is required to deliver power to the

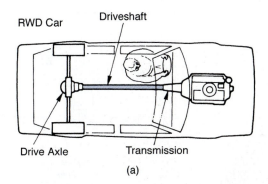

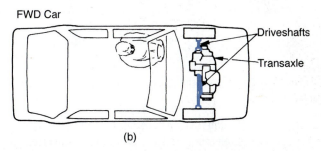

FIGURE 3-1 A RWD drivetrain uses a transmission to provide the necessary gear ratio and a single driveshaft to transfer power to the rear axle (a). A FWD drivetrain uses a transaxle that combines the transmission, final drive, and differential (b). A driveshaft is used for each of the two front drive wheels.

FREQUENTLY ASKED QUESTION

WHEN WERE AUTOMATIC TRANSMISSIONS DEVELOPED?

Before the 1940s, most vehicles used a clutch and *standard,* also called a *manual,* transmission. A well-known exception was the Model T Ford, which used a planetary gear transmission; this transmission used foot pedals to change gears. The first automatic transmission was the Hydra-Matic Drive introduced on the 1940 Oldsmobile; this option cost an additional $57. Since the 1960s, most of the domestic (U.S.-produced) and import (foreign-produced) vehicles are equipped with automatic transmissions. Currently, over 90% of the vehicles sold in the United States are equipped with an automatic transmission.

second drive axle, and it is usually mounted in or on the transmission or transaxle.

Automatic and manual transmissions serve the same purpose—the difference is how they are shifted. The driver with a manual transmission selects the gear and performs each

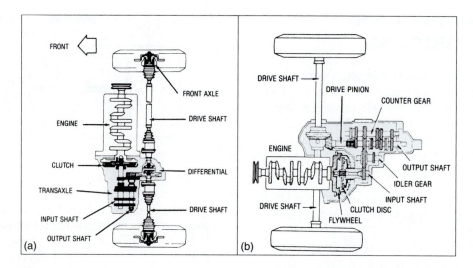

FIGURE 3-2   Transverse (a) and longitudinal (b) mounted FWD drivetrains. Note that B can easily be redesigned to drive a shaft to the rear wheels of a 4WD or AWD vehicle.

shift while depressing the clutch pedal. An automatic transmission has a self-releasing clutch, the torque converter, and upshifts and downshifts automatically. Some *Manumatic* transmissions are designed so the driver has more control of the shift points. In the past, several manufacturers offered semiautomatic transmissions; Chrysler Corporation's Fluid Drive and Volkswagen's Automatic Stick Shift are examples of semiautomatic transmissions. The driver had to perform each of the upshifts and downshifts, but did not need to operate a clutch.

Some manufacturers offer an optional **dual-clutch transmission.** This transmission uses a gear train similar to a manual transmission, but it has automatic shifts. Servos move the synchronizers, two automatic clutches are alternately applied to transfer torque, and electronic controls operate the servos and clutches. There is a more complete description in a following section.

3.2 TORQUE AND HORSEPOWER

Torque is a twisting force (Figure 3-3). We exert torque on a nut or bolt when it is tightened or loosened. Torque must be exerted at the drive axle in order to turn the wheels and move the vehicle.

Torque is commonly measured in *foot-pounds (ft-lb)*, *inch-pounds (in-lb),* or *Newton-meters (N-m)*. A foot-pound of torque is created when we exert a pound of force on a wrench that is one foot long. Force (in pounds) times the wrench length (in feet) equals the torque in foot-pounds. One foot-pound of torque is equal to 12 inch-pounds, or 1.356 N-m.

Torque is a form of mechanical energy and, like all other forms of energy, it cannot be created or destroyed. It can and is transformed from one form of energy to another. A vehicle's engine converts the potential heat energy of gasoline into

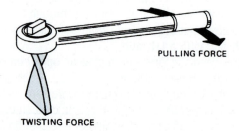

FIGURE 3-3   Torque is a twisting force like that produced when you pull on a wrench.

torque that rotates the flywheel. The transmission receives the torque and increases or decreases it according to the gear selected. The torque at the drive wheels is transformed into the kinetic energy of the moving vehicle.

Most of us are more familiar with the term *horsepower* than torque. Horsepower is a measurement of the energy developed in the engine. It is a product of torque and engine speed. To determine horsepower, an engineer uses a dynamometer to measure the amount of torque that the engine can produce at various points through its operating range. Then the formula torque times revolutions per minute (rpm) divided by 5,252 is used to convert torque at a certain rpm into a horsepower reading. The various readings are then plotted into a curve, as shown in Figure 3-4. A typical horsepower and torque curve shows us that an engine does not produce very much torque at low rpm. The most usable torque is produced in the mid-rpm range. Torque decreases with an increase of horsepower at a higher rpm.

The torque from an engine can be increased or decreased through the use of gears, belts, and chains (Figure 3-5). These are called *simple machines*. Gears are commonly used in transmissions. Transmissions of the future will probably make greater use of a belt with variable-size pulleys; this will be described later in this chapter. Gears, belts, or chains cannot increase horsepower;

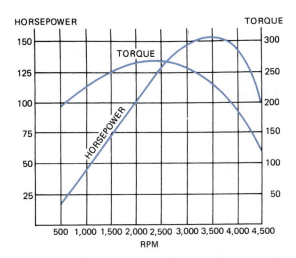

FIGURE 3-4   A typical automotive engine horsepower and torque chart. Note that the maximum horsepower (155) occurs at about 3,400 rpm and that maximum torque occurs between 2,000 and 2,500 rpm. The rpm range and maximum power output will vary depending on engine size and design.

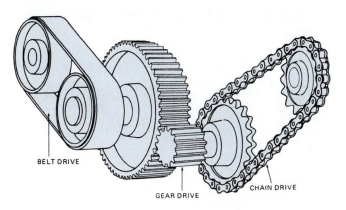

FIGURE 3-5   The common methods of transferring torque are belt, gear, and chain.

they can only modify its effect. A gearset can increase torque, but it will decrease speed the same amount. A driver feels the torque increase when he or she steps on the throttle. The different ratios are felt when the transmission shifts.

The maximum torque that a transmission can handle is referred to as *torque capacity.* Larger engines and heavier vehicles require larger transmissions with greater torque capacity than lighter vehicles with smaller engines. A transmission's torque capacity is determined by the size and strength of its internal components. Some manufacturers identify their transmissions by torque capacity (Figure 3-6).

3.3 GEAR RATIOS

The term *gear ratio* refers to the relative size of two gears (a *gearset*). The ratio can be determined using either the diameter or the number of teeth on the two gears. A pair of gears of

different size will have different numbers of teeth, and the number of teeth is directly related to the diameter of the gears (Figure 3-7). A pair of gears has one gear that is turning the other, called the drive gear. The other gear is being turned and is called the driven gear. When the drive gear is smaller than the driven gear, the ratio between the two gears produces more torque but less speed at the output shaft, this is called **gear reduction.** When the drive gear is larger than the driven gear, this produces an **overdrive.** Overdrive increases the output speed but reduces the torque at the output shaft. The gear ratio is determined by dividing the driven gear by the driving gear.

The motoring public is attached to the term overdrive. It has helped to sell automobiles since the 1930s when a car with a three-speed transmission with overdrive was first introduced.

Gear ratios can be easily calculated. If, for example, a gear has 15 teeth and is meshed with a gear that has 30 teeth, the 30-tooth gear is exactly twice the diameter of the 15-tooth gear. If the 15-tooth gear is the input drive gear, it has to rotate two revolutions for each revolution of the 30-tooth-driven gear. This gear ratio is 2:1, and the output shaft has twice the torque and half the speed as the input shaft (Figure 3-8). The first/left number of a ratio tells how far the driving gear turns for one revolution of the driven gear.

When calculating gear ratios, divide the number of teeth on the driven gear by the number of teeth on the drive gear: gear ratio = driven gear ÷ drive gear. If the drive gear has 12 teeth and the driven gear 36 teeth, the ratio will be 36 ÷ 12, or 3:1, a *reduction,* and the input shaft will turn three revolutions for each revolution of the output shaft. If we turn that gearset around, the ratio would be 12 ÷ 36, or 0.3:1, an *overdrive.* In this case, the input shaft would turn 0.3 turn for each revolution of the output shaft.

When power travels through more than one gearset, the overall ratio is determined by multiplying one gear ratio by the next. An example of this is the RWD, five-speed transmission (shown in Figure 3-9). A transmission with a first-gear ratio of 3.97:1 and a rear axle ratio of 3.55:1 produces an overall ratio of 3.97 × 3.55, or 14.09:1, in first gear. The engine will revolve 14.09 turns for each revolution of the drive axle. The overdrive ratio in fifth gear in this transmission is 2.84:1 (0.8:1 times the 3.55 rear-axle ratio). In fifth gear, the engine will revolve 2.84 turns for each drive axle revolution. This vehicle will have about one-fifth the torque it had in first gear but will be able to go about five times faster in fifth gear for each engine revolution.

Most gears have *external teeth,* where the teeth are cut around the outside of the gear. Some gears have the teeth cut on the inside of the gear's rim and are called **internal, ring,** or **annulus gears.** Most transmission gears are **helical gears** as compared with **spur gears** (Figure 3-10). The teeth of a spur gear are cut in a straight line, parallel to the axis of the gear and the shaft on which the gear is mounted. The teeth of a helical gear are cut on a spiral helix shape; a helix spirals continuously if it is extended sideways. A spur gear is less expensive to make,

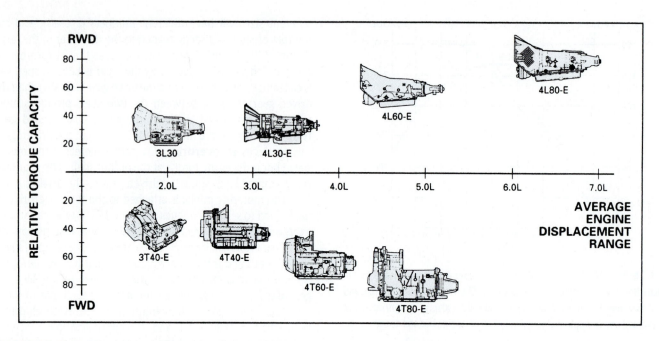

FIGURE 3-6 Transmissions and transaxles are designed with a torque capacity to match the engine with which it is used. *(Reprinted with permission of General Motors)*

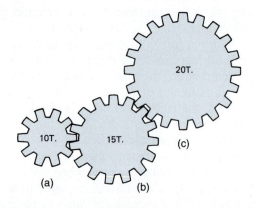

FIGURE 3-7 In a matched set of gears, the number of teeth on each gear is related to the diameter. Gear A is half the size of C and has half the number of teeth. Gear B is one and a half times the diameter of A and has one and a half times as many teeth.

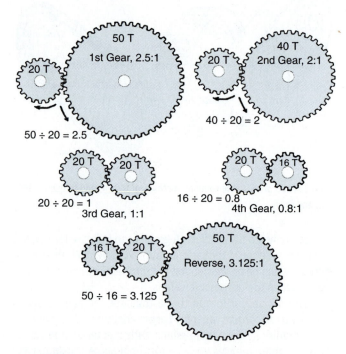

FIGURE 3-8 The gear ratio is determined by dividing the number of teeth on the driven (output) gear by the number of teeth on the driving (input) gear.

but it is noisier and not as strong as a helical gear. A helical gear tends to be quieter and stronger, but it has a tendency to slide sideways, out of mesh. This is called *side thrust*. The other major gear type, a **bevel gear,** is used to transfer power between shafts that are not parallel. Bevel gears are made in both a *spur bevel* and *spiral bevel* form (Figure 3-11). A **hypoid gear** is a variation of the spiral bevel gear and is commonly used in drive axles.

External gears reverse the direction of rotation when the drive gear transfers power to the driven gear. When it is necessary to change the ratio without changing the direction of power flow, an **idler gear** is added. An idler gear changes the rotational direction and does not affect the ratio (Figure 3-12).

Some important rules to learn about gearsets are:

- Two mated external gears will always rotate in opposite directions.
- Mated internal and external gears will rotate in the same direction.

Gear	Ratio	Final Drive Ratio	Overall Ratio	mph per 1000 rpm
I	3.97:1	3.55:1	14.09:1	4.5
II	2.34:1	3.55:1	8.31:1	9.2
III	1.46:1	3.55:1	5.18:1	14.7
IV	1:1	3.55:1	3.55:1	21.5
V	0.80:1	3.55:1	2.84:1	26.9

FIGURE 3-9   The forward gear ratios of a five-speed transmission are shown along with mph speed of the vehicle per 1,000 rpms of engine speed. The overall gear ratio is determined by multiplying the transmission gear ratio by the final drive ratio. A final drive ratio of 3.55:1 and a first-gear ratio of 3.97:1 will produce an overall ratio of 14.09:1.

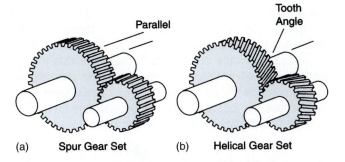

FIGURE 3-10   The teeth of a spur gear (a) are cut parallel to the shaft, which produces a straight pressure between the driving and driven gears. The teeth of a helical gear (b) are cut on a slant, which causes an axial or side thrust.

- An idler gear allows the drive and driven gears to rotate in the same direction.
- To find the ratio, divide the driven gear by the drive gear.
- When power transfers through an even number (two or four) of gears, the input and output gears will rotate in opposite directions.
- When power transfers through an uneven number (one, three, or five) of gears, the input and output gears will rotate in the same direction.
- To find the overall ratio of multiple gearsets, multiply the ratios of the gearsets.

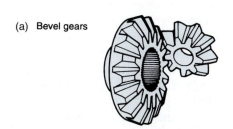

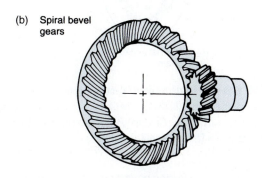

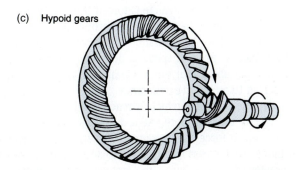

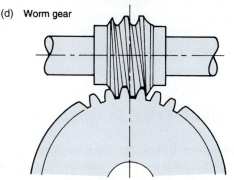

FIGURE 3-11   The three major styles of bevel gears are spur or plain bevel gears (a), spiral bevel gears (b), and hypoid gears (c). Note the differences in the shape of their teeth. A worm gearset (d) also transmits power between angled shafts. *(Reprinted with permission of General Motors)*

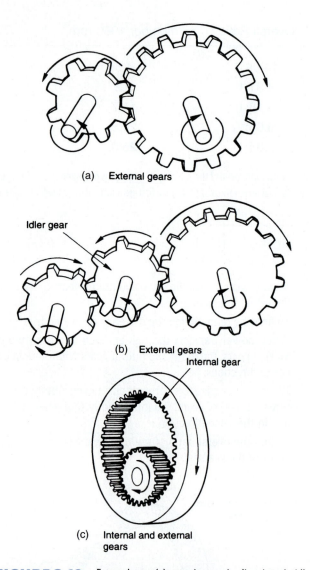

FIGURE 3-12   External gears (a) rotate in opposite directions. An idler gear in an external gearset (b) changes the direction of rotation so the input and output gears turn in the same direction without changing the ratio. An internal and external gearset (c) rotate in the same direction.

- Two gears transferring power push away from each other in an action called gear separation. The gear separation force is proportional to the torque being transferred.
- All gearsets have *backlash* to prevent binding (Figure 3-13).
- The smaller gear(s) in a gearset is often called a **pinion.**

3.4 TRACTIVE FORCE

An engineer uses the term *tractive force* to describe the power in a vehicle's drivetrain. It is a product of the engine's torque multiplied by the gear ratio and can be plotted in a graph (Figure 3-14). Note that a curve is shown for each of the transmission's gears. The second graph (B) shows drive shaft torque

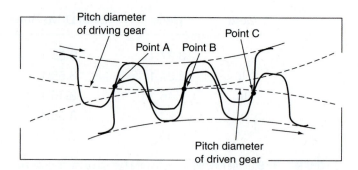

FIGURE 3-13   The pitch diameter is the effective diameter of a gear. Note how the contact points slide across the gear tooth. Backlash is the clearance on the nonloaded side of the gear tooth.

and engine speed relative to vehicle speed. It does not show engine rpm, but for each curve, the left end is plotted for 500 rpm and the right end for 4,500 rpm. As shown, first gear produces the most torque and fourth gear the most speed.

When discussing vehicle speed, remember that the tire diameter will affect vehicle speed. The larger the tire, the faster the vehicle will go at a particular axle rpm (Figure 3-15). You can use the following formula to determine the vehicle speed at a particular engine rpm or vice versa:

$$\text{Engine rpm} = \frac{\text{mph} \times \text{gear ratio} \times 336}{\text{tire diameter}}$$

$$\text{Vehicle rpm} = \frac{\text{rpm} \times \text{tire diameter}}{\text{gear ratio} \times 336}$$

The amount of horsepower required to reach a certain speed is influenced by the weight and shape of the vehicle and how level the road is. Vehicle movement is resisted by two types of friction: rolling and aerodynamic. Rolling friction is produced by the tires, axles, and other rotating parts of the power train. A heavier vehicle increases the rolling resistance because of the load on the tires and axles. Rolling resistance increases at a constant rate as the vehicle speed increases, and if speed is doubled, it requires twice as much power to overcome rolling resistance. Aerodynamic friction or drag is created as the body of the vehicle is forced through air. A large, boxy vehicle is much harder to push through air than a small, streamlined vehicle. Aerodynamic drag increases at the square of the vehicle's speed; if speed is doubled, the aerodynamic drag increases about four times. Combined, these two factors are referred to as *tractive resistance.*

The top speed of a vehicle is reached when tractive resistance equals tractive force. At low speeds, the lower gears produce more force than needed to overcome the tractive resistance. This excess force is used to accelerate the vehicle; the greater the excess force, the greater the rate of acceleration. Excess force is also convenient when going up hills, because the slope of the road increases the tractive resistance.

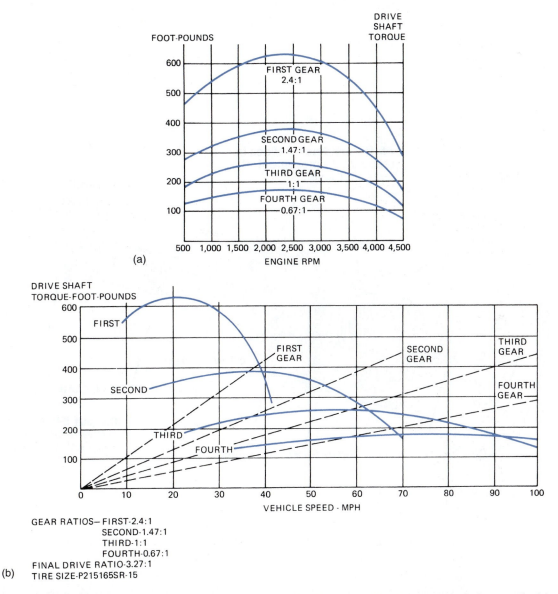

FIGURE 3-14 Tractive force (a) is determined by multiplying engine torque times the gear ratio. Note how it is greatest in first gear. The chart in (b) shows the same curves related to engine and vehicle speed. This curve is based on a typical 5-liter V8 engine.

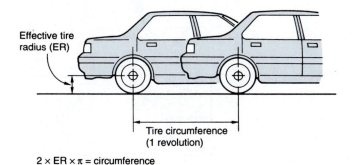

$2 \times ER \times \pi = $ circumference

FIGURE 3-15 The speed of a vehicle is determined by the diameter of the drive tires and how fast the tires are turned.

3.5 MANUAL TRANSMISSION AND CLUTCH

A manual transmission, also called a *standard transmission*, has several sets of gears to produce the necessary gear ratios (Figure 3-16). When a driver selects a gear, the power must flow through a specific path as it goes from the input shaft to the output shaft. A gear reduction or overdrive is produced when the power flows from the main drive gear on the input shaft to the cluster gear and from the cluster gear to a driven gear on the output shaft (Figure 3-17). The cluster gear is also called a *counter gear*. The actual shift is

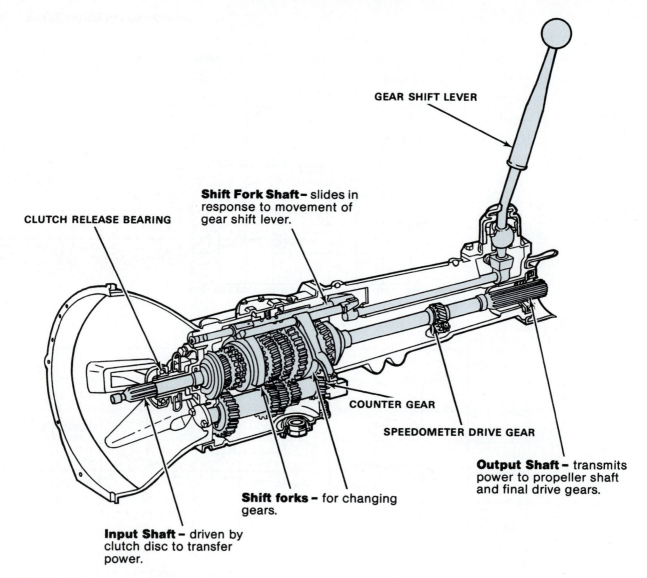

GEAR SHIFT LEVER

CLUTCH RELEASE BEARING

Shift Fork Shaft – slides in response to movement of gear shift lever.

COUNTER GEAR

SPEEDOMETER DRIVE GEAR

Output Shaft – transmits power to propeller shaft and final drive gears.

Shift forks – for changing gears.

Input Shaft – driven by clutch disc to transfer power.

FIGURE 3-16 A standard transmission provides several gear ratios and a method to shift them.

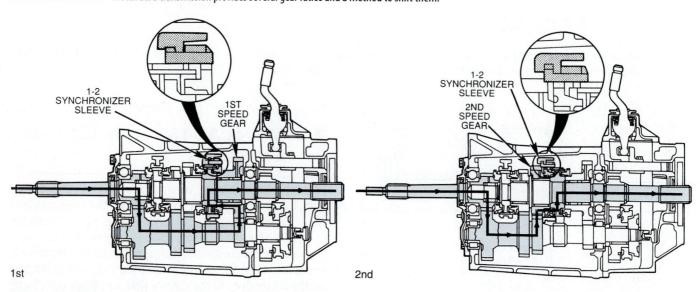

1-2 SYNCHRONIZER SLEEVE

1ST SPEED GEAR

1-2 SYNCHRONIZER SLEEVE

2ND SPEED GEAR

1st

2nd

FIGURE 3-17 Power flows through each of the gear ranges of a five-speed, RWD, standard transmission. Note that the synchronizer sleeves are used to shift the power flow. *(Courtesy of Chrysler Corporation)*

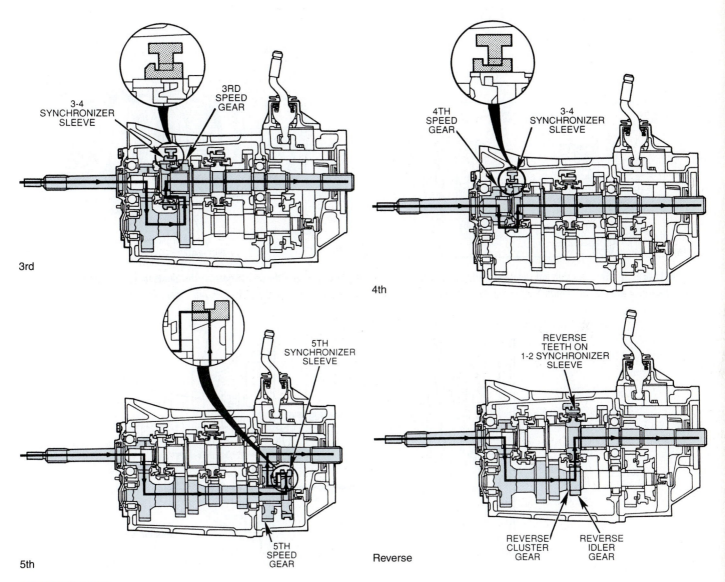

FIGURE 3-17   Continued

made by moving a **synchronizer sleeve** to couple the desired driven gear to the **synchronizer hub** and the output shaft (Figure 3-18).

A shift cannot be made while the power is flowing in a manual transmission. The power flow must be interrupted or disengaged by depressing the clutch pedal. Pushing the clutch pedal releases the pressure on the clutch disc and disengages the power flow (Figure 3-19). This allows the transmission gear being engaged to match the speed of the synchronizer sleeve during the shift. This is sometimes called a *nonpower* shift. The clutch is also needed so the transmission can be shifted from neutral to low or reverse.

A FWD transaxle is slightly different from a RWD unit in that power is always transferred through three or more shafts that are parallel to each other (Figure 3-20). The input comes from the clutch to the first/input shaft. The second (main) shaft transfers power through the pinion gear of the *final drive.* The third shaft is the ring gear of the final drive and the differential. The various transmission ratios are the different power paths between the first and second shafts. Like a RWD transmission, a synchronizer assembly is used to produce smooth shifts.

Unless it is important to be specific, most technicians will use the term *transmission* when referring to the transmission portion of a transaxle. Also, the front of a transmission or transaxle is the end closest to the engine, even though the engine might be mounted in a transverse or sideways position.

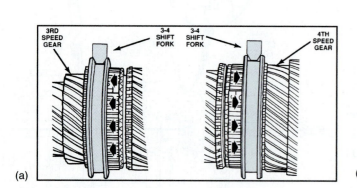

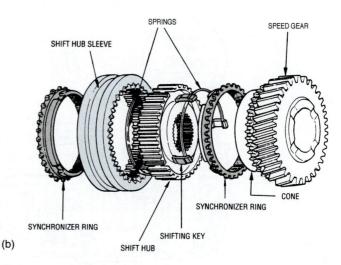

FIGURE 3-18 The shift fork slides the synchronizer sleeve into mesh with the dog teeth of the desired gear (a). This allows torque to be transferred between the speed gear and the synchronizer hub. An exploded view of a synchronizer assembly (b) shows all of the parts. *(a is courtesy of Chrysler Corporation)*

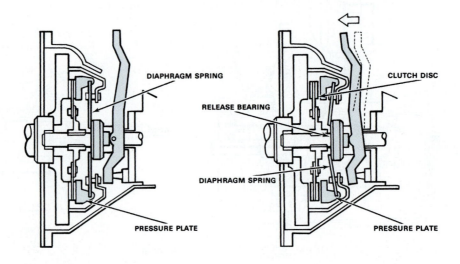

(a) **Clutch Engaged–** The flattened diaphragm spring pushes against the pressure plate.

(b) **Clutch Disengaged –** Release bearing flexes the diaphragm spring and frees the clutch disc.

FIGURE 3-19 A clutch cover (pressure plate assembly) is bolted onto the flywheel with the clutch disc between them (a). The release bearing and fork provide a method to release the clutch. When the clutch is engaged, the disc is squeezed against the flywheel by the pressure plate (b). Releasing the clutch separates the disc from the flywheel and pressure plate.

3.6 SIMPLE PLANETARY GEARSETS

A **planetary gearset** is a combination of a **sun gear,** two or more *planet gears,* a *planet carrier,* and a *ring gear.* The ring gear, also called an *annulus gear,* is an internal gear. All the other gears are external gears. The carrier holds the planet gears (also called *pinions*) in position and allows each of these gears to rotate in the carrier (Figure 3-21). When the gearset is assembled, the sun gear is in the center and meshed with the planet gears, which are located around it, somewhat like the planets in our solar system.

The ring gear is meshed around the outside of the planet gears.

The three main members of the planetary gearset, the sun gear, ring gear, and planet carrier, have two possible actions: They can rotate or stand still. The planet gears/pinions have three possible actions (Figure 3-22):

1. They can rotate on their shafts in a stationary carrier and act like idler gears.
2. They can rotate on their shafts in a rotating carrier; the planet gears are *walking.*
3. They can stand still on their shafts and rotate with the carrier.

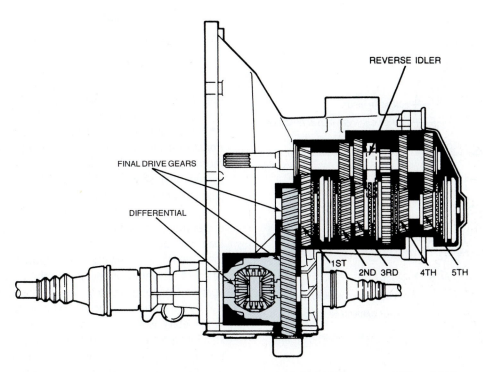

FIGURE 3-20   A FWD transaxle. Note that it combines a five-speed transmission with the final drive gears and differential. *(Courtesy of Chrysler Corporation)*

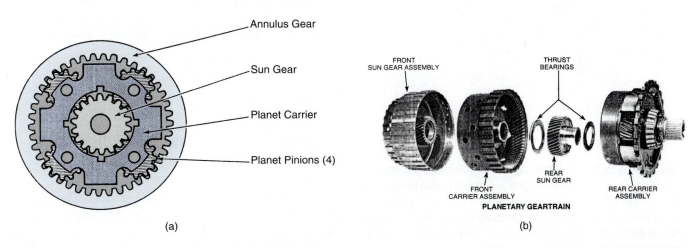

FIGURE 3-21   A simple planetary gearset is a combination of a sun gear, a planet carrier with a group of planet pinion gears, and an annulus/ring gear (a). A transmission planetary gear train contains a combination of complex gearsets (b). *(Courtesy of Chrysler Corporation)*

The planet gears can walk around the outside of a stationary sun or the inside of a stationary ring gear. The rotating carrier forces the planet gears to walk around the stationary sun or ring gear, which forces the planet gears to rotate on their shafts. This, in turn, will force the third member of the gearset to rotate.

Planetary gearsets are arranged so power enters one of the members and leaves through one of the other members while the third member is held stationary in reaction. One of the basic physical laws states that for every action, there is an equal and opposite reaction. In a gearset, the action is usually an increase in torque; the reaction is an equal amount of torque that tries to turn the gear box in a reverse direction. For example, watch a short-wheelbase truck-tractor pull a heavy trailer from a dead stop. The action needed is to turn the drive wheels and move the truck, the reaction is a lifting of the frame at the left front wheel. The front of the truck lifts in reaction to the drive axle torque, and the left side lifts in reaction to the drive shaft torque. Getting back to the planetary gearset, one of the three members has to be held stationary in reaction to obtain either the torque or speed increase

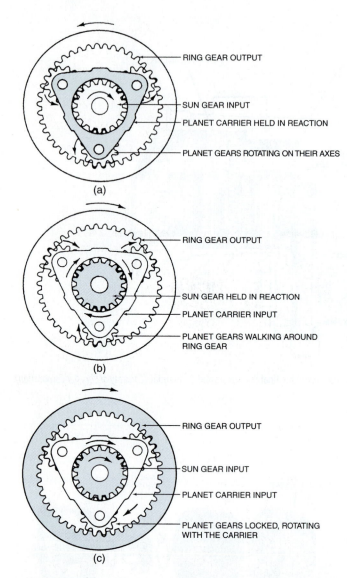

FIGURE 3-22   If the planet carrier is held with the sun gear rotating, the planet gears simply rotate in the carrier and act as idler gears between the sun and ring gears (a). If the sun or ring is held, the planet gears will walk around that stationary gear; they rotate on their shafts as the carrier rotates (b). If two parts are driven and no parts are held, the planet gears are stationary on their shafts, and the whole assembly rotates as a unit (c).

in the gear box. There cannot be a ratio change without a reaction member.

Power flow through a planetary gearset is controlled by clutches, bands, and one-way clutches. One or more clutches will control the power coming to a planetary member and one or more reaction members can hold a gearset member stationary. The third planetary member will be the output. One simple planetary gearset can produce:

- a neutral if either the input clutch or reaction member is not applied,
- a 1:1, direct-drive ratio if two gearset members are driven,

- two reduction ratios,
- two overdrive ratios, or
- two reverse ratios, one a reduction and one an overdrive.

The reduction, overdrive, and reverse ratios will require one driving member, one output member, and one reaction member in the gearset (Figure 3-23).

Planetary gearsets offer several advantages over conventional gearsets. Because of the multiple planet gears, there is more than one gear transferring power, so the torque load is spread over several gear teeth. Because of this, planetary gearsets are quieter and stronger. Also, any gear separation forces (as gears transfer power, they tend to push away from each other) are contained within the ring gear, preventing this load from being transmitted to the transmission case. This allows the transmission case to be thinner and therefore lighter. Another advantage is the small relative size of the planetary gearset. Conventional gears are normally side by side, and for a 2:1 gear ratio, one gear has to be twice the size of the other. A planetary gearset can easily produce this same ratio in a smaller package. Also, planetary gearsets are in constant mesh; no coupling or uncoupling of the gears is required.

As illustrated in Figure 3-23, there can be seven possible power flow conditions and a neutral in a planetary gearset. A 1:1 ratio occurs if you drive any two members without a reaction member. Neutral occurs if there is no driving member or no reaction member. This effectively stops the power flow for the neutral condition. In the other six power flows, there is:

- one driving or input member,
- one driven or output member, and
- one stationary or *reaction* member.

3.7 COMPOUND PLANETARY GEARSETS

Most automatic transmissions use a more complicated *compound planetary gearset* that combines a simple planetary gearset with portions of one or more planetary gearsets in such a way that three or more gear ratios are possible. In many four-speed transmissions, a simple planetary gearset is used along with a compound set to provide an additional overdrive or reduction ratio.

The most common compound planetary gearset used in three-speed transmissions is known as the *Simpson gear train*, named after its designer, Howard Simpson. This gearset uses one common sun gear with two ring gears and two planet carriers (Figure 3-24). The rear ring gear and the front carrier are attached to the output shaft, so they are the driven or output members. Three inputs are possible: either (1) the front ring gear, (2) the sun gear, or (3) both. Also, two reaction members are possible: either (1) the sun gear or (2) the rear carrier. In some transmissions, a stepped sun gear of two sizes is used.

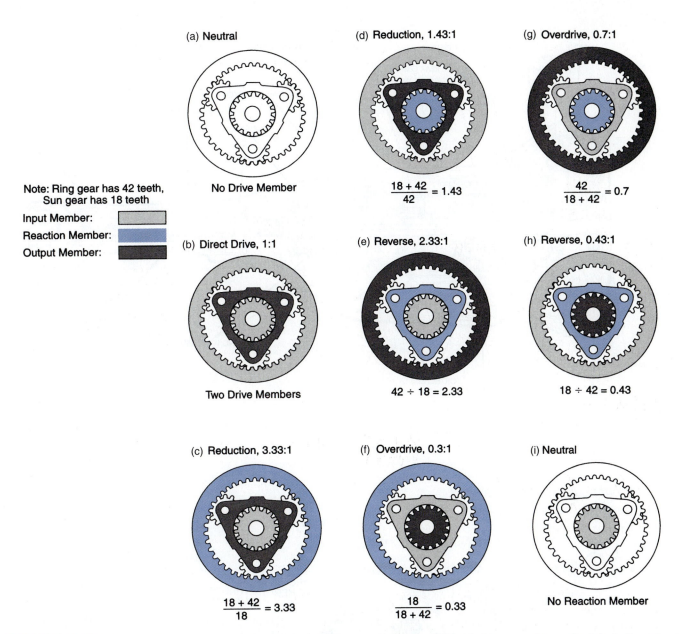

(a) Neutral

No Drive Member

Note: Ring gear has 42 teeth,
Sun gear has 18 teeth

Input Member:
Reaction Member:
Output Member:

(d) Reduction, 1.43:1

$$\frac{18 + 42}{42} = 1.43$$

(g) Overdrive, 0.7:1

$$\frac{42}{18 + 42} = 0.7$$

(b) Direct Drive, 1:1

Two Drive Members

(e) Reverse, 2.33:1

$$42 \div 18 = 2.33$$

(h) Reverse, 0.43:1

$$18 \div 42 = 0.43$$

(c) Reduction, 3.33:1

$$\frac{18 + 42}{18} = 3.33$$

(f) Overdrive, 0.3:1

$$\frac{18}{18 + 42} = 0.33$$

(i) Neutral

No Reaction Member

FIGURE 3-23   Nine possible modes of operation for a simple planetary gearset. In all cases, solid black indicates a reaction member, light shading an input member, and medium shading the output member.

This allows lower first- and second-gear ratios. We will describe the power flow through this gearset as well as other common gearset arrangements in more detail in Chapter 5.

3.8 CONTROL DEVICES

Power flow through a gearset is accomplished by the *control devices:* the **clutches, bands,** and **one-way clutches.** They are also called *apply devices* or friction members. A gearset has several paths for power flow, and each path provides a different gear ratio (Figure 3-25). The control devices determine the power flow path through the gearset.

A control device is either a driving or a reaction member. A driving member completes a path so power can transfer from one unit to another. A reaction member holds one of the gearset members from rotating so the power flow can occur. Because friction-type clutches and bands are used, the power flow does not have to be interrupted during a shift. This allows powered shifts to be made, and the drive wheels will have a constant flow of power during a shift.

Multiple-disc clutches are the driving devices that connect the transmission's input shaft to the gearset input member. These clutches are applied by **hydraulic** force. This type of clutch is made up of plates that are lined with friction material and unlined steel plates. The plates are stacked in an alternating

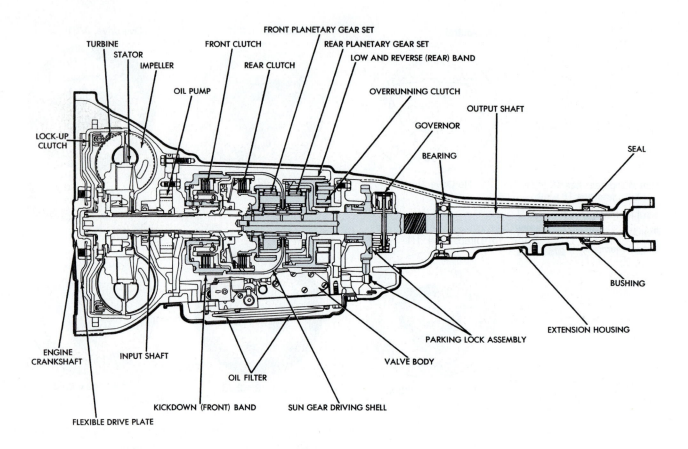

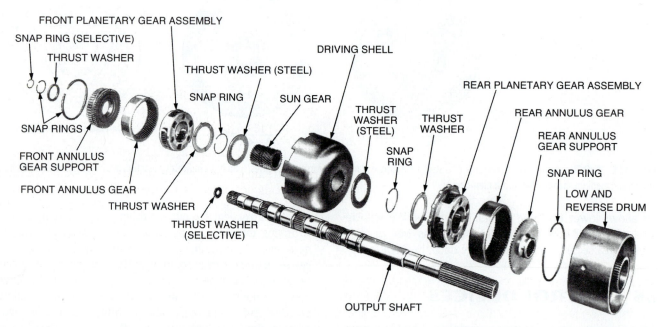

FIGURE 3-24 A cutaway and an exploded view of a Simpson gear train. Note that the gearset uses a double sun gear with two carriers and ring gears. The two clutches allow either the forward ring gear or the sun gear to be driven. The two bands allow either the sun gear or the rear carrier to be held in reaction. The one-way clutch will keep the rear carrier from turning counterclockwise. *(Courtesy of Chrysler Corporation)*

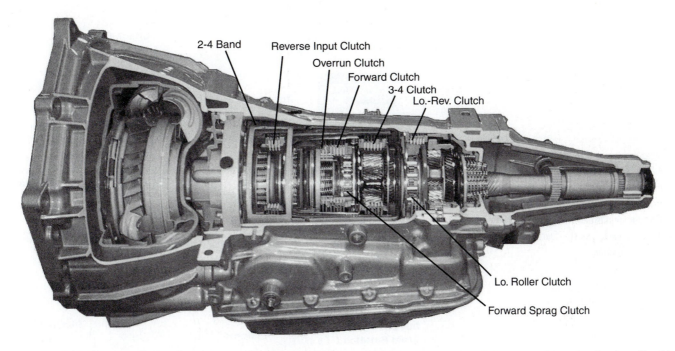

FIGURE 3-25 A sectioned view of a modern, four-speed, RWD transmission. You should be able to identify all of these parts, know what they do, and be able to service them at the completion of this book.

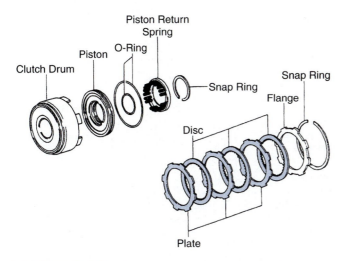

FIGURE 3-26 A multiple-disc clutch combines lined friction discs and unlined steel plates. *(Courtesy of Toyota Motor Sales USA, Inc.)*

fashion, with half of the plates splined to the input and the other half splined to the planetary member (Figure 3-26). When oil pressure is applied to the hydraulic piston, the clutch pack is squeezed together, applying the clutch (Figure 3-27). When the oil pressure is released, a return spring pushes the piston away from the clutch pack, releasing the clutch. A reaction device can be a band, a one-way clutch, or a multiple-disc clutch. Some transmission manufacturers call their reaction members *brakes* because they stop a gearset member from turning. A band is also

applied by hydraulic pressure and released by a spring or hydraulic pressure.

A band is a metal strap that is lined with friction material and wraps around a drum (Figure 3-28). When a band is applied, it is tightened around the drum, bringing it to a stop, and when released it allows the drum to rotate. The hydraulic device that applies a band is commonly called a **servo;** the servo is a hydraulic piston assembly.

A reaction clutch resembles a driving clutch except the unlined set of plates is connected to the transmission case. When it applies, the gearset member that it connects to will come to a stop.

A one-way clutch is a device that allows rotation in only one direction. One-way clutches are either *roller clutches, sprag clutches,* or *mechanical diodes* (Figure 3-29). Hydraulic and electronically operated valves control the control devices. By the time we combine the gearset, control devices, and hydraulic and electronic controls, the transmission appears rather complex. After studying each of these transmission systems, much of the complexity and mystery will disappear.

3.9 TRANSMISSION HYDRAULICS

As soon as the engine starts, a *pump* driven by the torque converter sends fluid into the transmission's *hydraulic* passages. Fluid is pumped from the sump in the transmission pan into

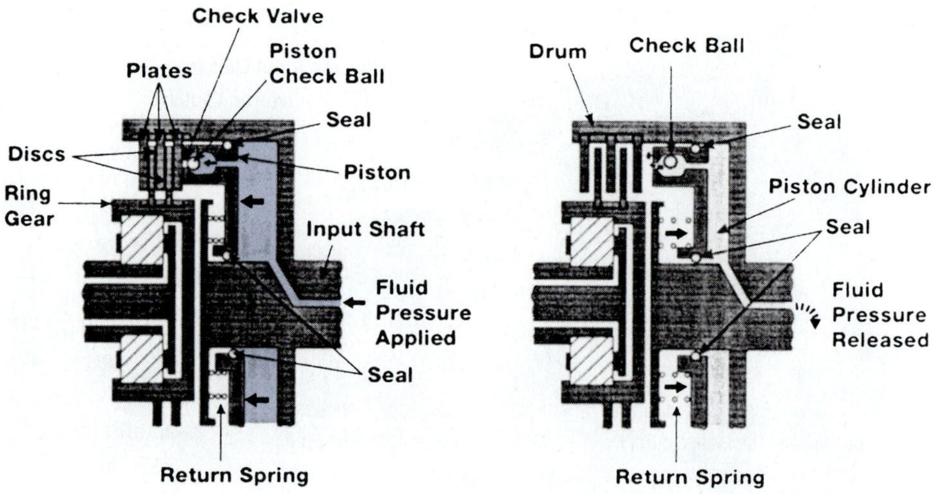

FIGURE 3-27 Fluid pressure forces the piston against the clutch pack to apply a clutch (left). When the fluid pressure is released, the return springs push the piston away from the clutch pack (right). *(Courtesy of Toyota Motor Sales USA, Inc.)*

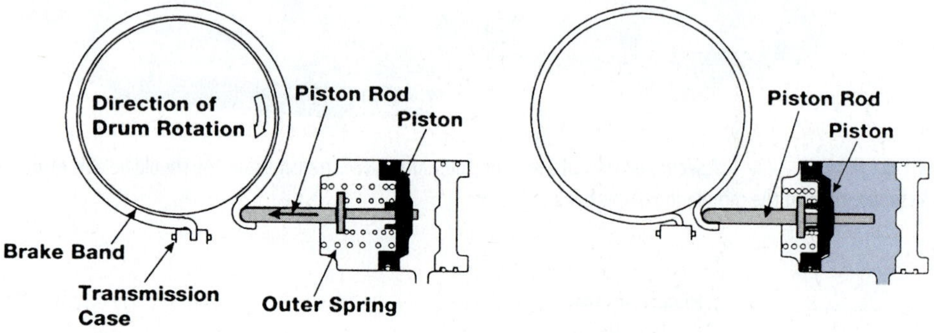

FIGURE 3-28 A band is applied when fluid pressure forces the piston and rod inward (right). When the pressure is released, a spring pushes the piston back (left). *(Courtesy of Toyota Motor Sales USA, Inc.)*

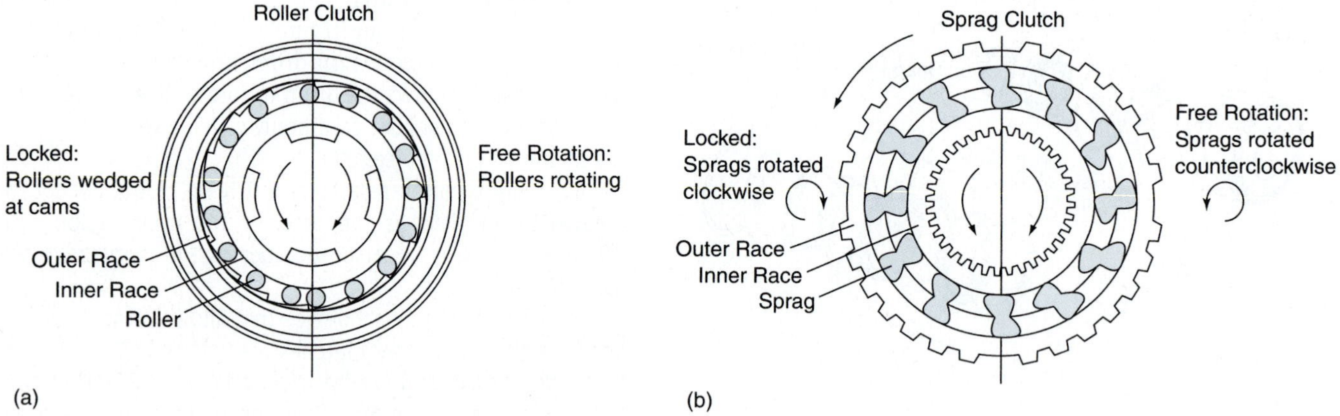

FIGURE 3-29 Two types of one-way clutches. The roller clutch (a) will release if the inner race turns clockwise and lock up if it turns counterclockwise. The sprag clutch (b) will operate in the same manner.

the hydraulic circuit where the pressure and flow is controlled by the valve body (Figure 3-30). This fluid pressure is used to:

- apply the clutches and bands,
- maintain a full torque converter so it can transmit power, and
- lubricate and cool the internal parts of the transmission.

A transmission has numerous passages that allow fluid to flow to the many different locations (Figure 3-31).

The valve body contains most of the transmission's control valves. Sometimes, there are one or more valves elsewhere. The major valves used in nonelectronic transmissions are as follows:

- **Manual valve** Operated by the shift linkage and used to select automatic forward gear ranges, nonautomatic forward gear ranges (manual first, second, etc.), reverse, as well as park and neutral.
- **Pressure regulator** Controls fluid pressure.

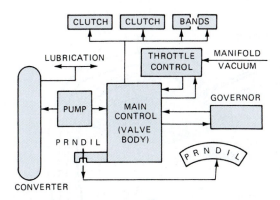

FIGURE 3-30 A simplified hydraulic control circuit for a nonelectronic transmission. The main control unit (valve body) sends oil pressure to the clutches and bands to control the shifts. It uses signals from the manual shift lever, governor, and throttle valve.

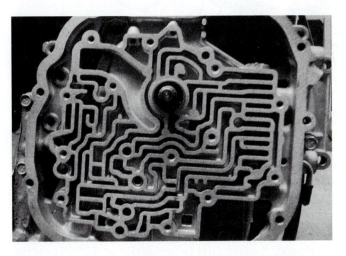

FIGURE 3-31 The end of this transmission case shows most of the fluid passages. These connect the valve body to passages in the case.

- **Throttle or modulator valve** Tailors the pressure regulator to the operation of the transmission and delays upshifts as the throttle is opened.
- **Governor** Operated by the output shaft speed; causes upshifts.
- **Shift valves** One for each shift; controls upshifts and downshifts.
- **Shift modifier valves** Valves that change the quality and timing of an upshift or downshift to ensure proper operation.
- **Torque converter clutch valve** Controls the apply and release of the torque converter clutch.

Modern transmissions use electronic controls to improve shift timing and quality and to integrate transmission operation more closely with engine operation. Some vehicles electronically reduce engine torque during shifts to smooth out the shifts and increase transmission life. Electronic controls include *electronic sensors* that provide input to an *electronic control module (ECM),* which operates *solenoids* inside the transmission that control hydraulic fluid flow (Figure 3-32). Transmission electronics is described more completely in Chapter 8.

In reality, the hydraulic system is rather complex. It will be discussed more thoroughly in Chapters 6 and 7. A competent service technician has a good understanding of what the various valves do and what the fluid pressures should be at a specific location in a given gear range. The technician will often refer to a hydraulic diagram when trying to solve a problem. Many automatic transmission problems are caused by a loss of fluid pressure, sticky control valves, or faulty electronic controls.

3.10 TORQUE CONVERTERS

Every automatic transmission uses a **torque converter** to transfer power from the engine to the transmission (Figure 3-33). It serves as an automatic fluid clutch as well as converting torque (as its name implies). It can multiply torque much like a gearset.

A torque converter is normally made up of three members: an *impeller,* a *turbine,* and a *stator.* To operate properly, it must be completely filled with transmission fluid. The impeller, also called a *pump,* is built into the housing that connects to the engine crankshaft. When the engine runs, the impeller produces fluid flow inside the converter.

The turbine is splined to the transmission input shaft. Oil flowing from the impeller causes the turbine to rotate and drive the transmission.

The stator is splined to the *stator support,* a stationary shaft extending from the transmission case. A one-way clutch connects the stator to the stator support so the stator can rotate in only one direction. The stator changes the direction of the fluid flow from the turbine back to the impeller.

At slow engine speeds, fluid flow inside the converter is not strong enough to rotate the turbine and the transmission input shaft. As the throttle is opened and engine speed increases, fluid flow becomes strong enough to rotate the turbine and move the vehicle. During slow turbine speeds, the stator redirects and increases the force of the fluid flow. This has the effect of increasing the torque, producing a ratio of about 2:1.

In a torque converter all of the power is transferred by fluid. Because of this, it always has some slippage; this slippage reduces the efficiency and fuel mileage. Modern torque converters have an internal clutch, called the **torque converter clutch (TCC);** it will produce torque converter lockup to eliminate slipping during cruising conditions. A TCC improves fuel mileage about 1 to 3 miles per gallon. Torque converter operation will be described in more detail in Chapter 9.

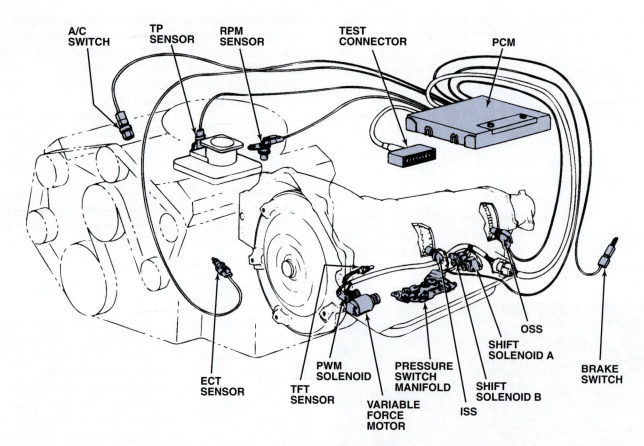

FIGURE 3-32 The electronic controls for an electronic transmission include input sensor signals from the engine and the transmission to the PCM and output devices in the transmission. The test connector is the diagnostic link used to diagnose transmission problems.

3.11 TRANSAXLE FINAL DRIVE AND DIFFERENTIAL

The difference between a transmission and a transaxle is the **final drive** unit and the output shafts. An RWD transmission has a single output shaft that connects to the drive shaft and rear-axle assembly. A transaxle has two output shafts, one for each front wheel. Also, the final drive gear reduction and the differential must fit into the area between the transmission's output and the two drive shafts.

The final drive is the gear reduction that determines the overall tractive force of the vehicle. It also determines the engine operating rpm at cruising speed. In an RWD vehicle, the final drive gears are the *ring and pinion* located in the rear axle. In an FWD vehicle, the ring and pinion are located inside the transaxle. The drive pinion gear is mounted on either the transmission mainshaft or a transfer shaft. The ring gear is mounted on the *differential case,* sometimes called a *carrier.* Helical gears are normally used in transverse-mounted transaxles because the transmission shaft is parallel to the differential (Figure 3-34). Some transaxles use a planetary gearset

to produce the final drive reduction (Figure 3-35). The planetary members are arranged so:

- the output shaft of the transmission drives a sun gear that is the input to the final drive;
- the ring gear is secured into the transmission case so it is the reaction member; and
- the planet carrier is the output member and doubles as the differential case.

Longitudinal-mounted transaxles use either spiral bevel or hypoid final drive gears. The smaller final drive pinion gear driving the larger ring gear provides the desired gear reduction.

A **differential** is a device that allows the axle shafts to rotate at different speeds. When a vehicle turns a corner, the outer tires must travel farther and therefore must go faster than the inner tires. Most differentials use a set of bevel gears, as shown in Figure 3-36. The differential case is made with a differential pinion shaft running across it; this shaft also passes through a pair of differential pinion gears with the gears free to turn on the shaft. A pair of differential side gears is meshed with both differential pinions. One of these side gears is attached to each drive wheel through a drive shaft or axle.

When the vehicle is going straight ahead, the equal load of each side gear prevents rotation of the pinion gears on their shaft. The entire differential assembly rotates as a unit, and both wheels revolve at the same speed. When the vehicle turns a corner, one side gear rotates slower than the differential case. When this occurs, the pinion gears rotate on their

shaft while walking around the slower axle side gear, causing the other side gear to rotate faster than the case. Both drive wheels receive the same torque, but they will rotate at different speeds.

3.12 FOUR WHEEL DRIVE

Four wheel drive (4WD) drivetrains can be based on any of the FWD or RWD engine-transmission variations (Figure 3-37). 4WD vehicles are usually *part-time 4WD,* where the driver performs the shift between 2WD and 4WD. 2WD is used on a street with good traction, and 4WD is used in poor-traction conditions such as mud, sand, snow, or ice. These conditions usually cause enough tire slippage so that the speed difference between the front and rear tires is not a problem.

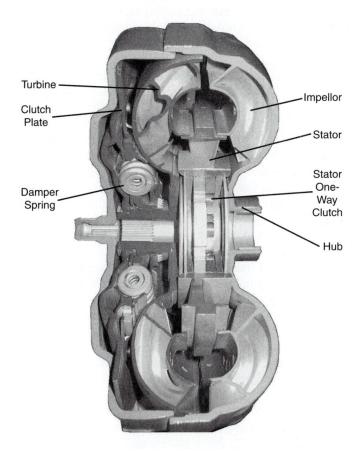

FIGURE 3-33   The torque converter transfers power from the engine to the transmission input shaft. It serves as an automatic clutch and multiplies torque during periods of engine load. This converter also has a clutch plate for the torque converter clutch.

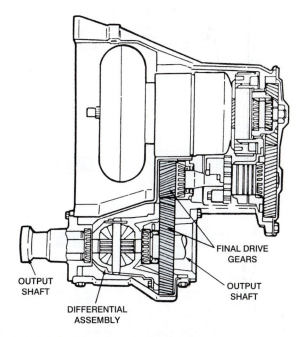

FIGURE 3-34   A pair of helical gears provides the final drive reduction. The final drive ring gear is attached to the differential assembly. *(Courtesy of Chrysler Corporation)*

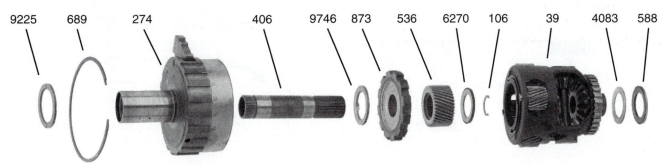

FIGURE 3-35   Some transaxles use a planetary gearset for the final drive reduction. Part 274 is the internal gear (stationary), 536 is the sun gear (input), and 39 is the planet carrier (output). The carrier also contains the differential gears. *(Courtesy of Slauson Transmission Parts, www.slauson.com)*

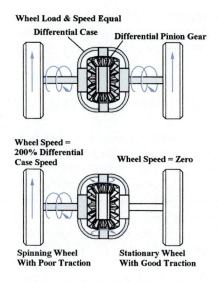

Wheel Load & Speed Equal

Differential Case | Differential Pinion Gear

Wheel Speed =
200% Differential
Case Speed

Wheel Speed = Zero

Spinning Wheel
With Poor Traction

Stationary Wheel
With Good Traction

FIGURE 3-36 Normally, an equal load from each wheel keeps the differential pinion gears stationary on their shaft (top). An equal load will cause the differential pinion gears to rotate and drive the axle shafts at unequal speeds (bottom).

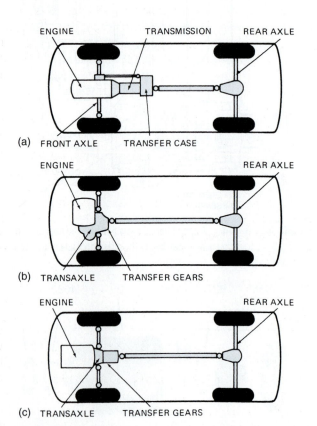

(a) FRONT AXLE   TRANSFER CASE

ENGINE   TRANSMISSION   REAR AXLE

(b) TRANSAXLE   TRANSFER GEARS

ENGINE   REAR AXLE

(c) TRANSAXLE   TRANSFER GEARS

ENGINE   REAR AXLE

FIGURE 3-37 Three major 4WD configurations. The traditional form (a) uses a transfer case to split the torque for the front and rear drive axles. (b) and (c) are typical AWD configurations.

Full-time 4WD is also called all wheel drive (AWD). Driving all of the wheels of a vehicle creates a few problems if driving on hard surfaces. One of the greatest is that all of the wheels rotate at different speeds when a vehicle turns corners (Figure 3-38), because each of the wheels travels around a circle that has a different radius and circumference. Vehicles normally drive only two wheels, and the differential in the drive axle provides for the speed difference between the inner and outer drive wheels. Vehicles with AWD need three differentials: one between the drive wheels of each axle and another between the two axles. The center, or *interaxle,* differential allows the front wheels to travel faster than the rear wheels on corners.

AWD becomes more complex because the power that leaves the transmission must first go to the center differential and then split to the front and rear axles. Some center differentials are torque biasing: They have the ability to split the torque unequally and send more torque to the rear axle. Most center differentials include a lockout feature so both front and rear axles can be driven equally. This ensures that at least one front tire and one rear tire will be driven, and it is only used in poor-traction conditions.

The 4WD version of an RWD automatic transmission is basically the same as the transmission used in two wheel drive (2WD) vehicles. A transfer case is attached to the rear of the transmission case by omitting the extension housing and using a shortened transmission output shaft (Figure 3-39). The transfer case contains the mechanism to allow engagement and disengagement of 4WD and also the universal joint connection for the drive shaft to the front and rear drive axles. Gears or a chain and sprockets transfer the power flow to the front drive shaft.

There are two 4WD/AWD versions for FWD vehicles, and these depend on the direction that the transmission shafts run. A few FWD vehicles use an engine and transmission that are positioned lengthwise in the vehicle. This makes it relatively easy to install a transfer clutch in the rear of the transmission

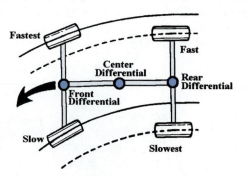

FIGURE 3-38 When a vehicle turns a corner, the front wheels must go faster than the rear, and the outside wheels must turn faster than the inside wheels.

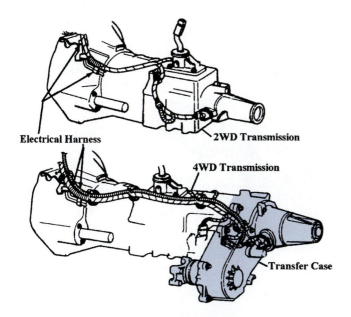

Electrical Harness   **2WD Transmission**

4WD Transmission

Transfer Case

FIGURE 3-39   The 4WD version of an RWD transmission often replaces the extension housing with an adapter and the transfer case.

FIGURE 3-40   This AWD transaxle has an output shaft to drive the rear wheels (at left). The interaxle differential is between the transfer gears for the rear and those that send power to the front final drive gears and differential. *(Courtesy of ZF Group North American Operations)*

(Figure 3-40). The clutch can operate an output shaft that runs out the back of the transmission to connect with the drive shaft for the rear axle.

When the engine and transmission are mounted in a transverse position, 4WD becomes more complicated. The power flow must be turned 90° to travel down the vehicle before turning another 90° at the rear axle. The *power transfer unit* for a transverse transaxle must include a pair of bevel gears in order to change the direction of power flow (Figure 3-41). The transfer case also includes a dog clutch to engage and disengage the power flow to the rear axle.

3.13 NONPLANETARY GEAR AUTOMATIC TRANSMISSIONS

3.13.1 Automatic Layshaft Transmissions

Honda and early Saturn automatic transmissions do not use planetary gearsets. The gear train used is much like that of a standard transmission with the gears in constant mesh (Figure 3-42). The major difference is that the synchronizer assemblies are replaced with multidisc clutches. The fully automatic shifts are made when the multiple-disc clutch for each gear is engaged (Figure 3-43). The shifts are accomplished by hydraulic pressure using a hydraulic system like that of other automatic transmissions. Also like other automatic transmissions, a torque converter is used between the transmission and engine.

3.13.2 Dual-Clutch Transmissions

A dual-clutch transmission is essentially an automatically controlled manual transmission that uses two clutches and two countershafts. Gear section is determined by which clutch is applied. The clutches are applied, one at a time, to transfer power to the appropriate gearset. The shifts can occur very rapidly, being controlled by how fast the two clutches can be applied and released. This transmission is presently available in some models of the Audi TT and Volkswagen Golf and is called a *direct-shift gearbox* (DSG).

The gear arrangement shown in Figure 3-44 illustrates how the odd-numbered gears, 1–3 and 5, are driven by clutch #1. The even-numbered gears, 2–4 and 6-reverse are driven by clutch #2. The two clutches are built into one DualTronic™ clutch assembly. Vehicle movement begins when the 1–3 synchronizer is shifted to first gear and the clutch #1 is applied. The 2–4 synchronizer is then shifted into second gear by a hydraulic servo. The 1–2 upshift will occur when clutch #1 is released and clutch #2 is applied. The remaining upshifts occur in the same manner, with the synchronizer shifted early and the actual shift occurring when the clutches are cycled.

The driver can control the automatic operation by using a floor-mounted shifter or one of a pair of paddles mounted in front of the steering wheel. Clutch #1 and #2 are applied by hydraulic pressure, similar to automatic transmission clutches. As mentioned, the synchronizer sleeves are shifted by hydraulic servos. An electronic control module controls the hydraulic flow to the clutches and servos. The control module contains the hydraulic valve body, solenoids, a microprocessor, and the external electrical connectors. Sensors monitor shift lever position, upshift and downshift paddles, engine RPM, and fluid temperatures. The control module uses the information from these sensors to determine the proper clutch and servo operation.

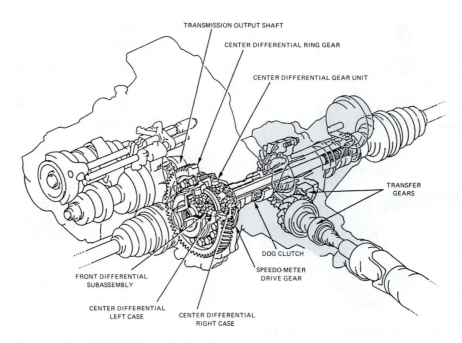

TRANSMISSION OUTPUT SHAFT

CENTER DIFFERENTIAL RING GEAR

CENTER DIFFERENTIAL GEAR UNIT

TRANSFER GEARS

DOG CLUTCH

SPEEDO-METER DRIVE GEAR

FRONT DIFFERENTIAL SUBASSEMBLY

CENTER DIFFERENTIAL LEFT CASE

CENTER DIFFERENTIAL RIGHT CASE

FIGURE 3-41 This transaxle has an output shaft for each of the front wheels plus a dog clutch and transfer gears to drive a rear axle (lower right).

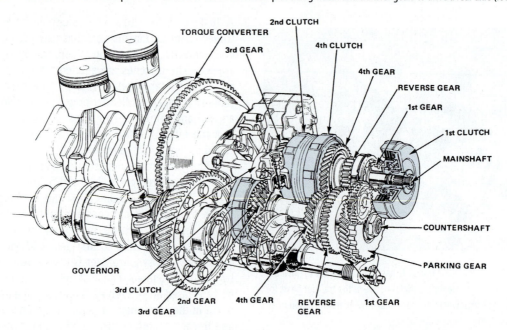

TORQUE CONVERTER

2nd CLUTCH

3rd GEAR

4th CLUTCH

4th GEAR

REVERSE GEAR

1st GEAR

1st CLUTCH

MAINSHAFT

COUNTERSHAFT

PARKING GEAR

GOVERNOR

3rd CLUTCH

3rd GEAR

2nd GEAR

4th GEAR

REVERSE GEAR

1st GEAR

FIGURE 3-42 This four-speed, automatic transaxle combines helical gears, as in a standard transmission, with four multiple-disc clutches and a torque converter. *(Courtesy of American Honda Motor Company)*

3.13.3 Continuously Variable Transmission (CVT)

In some vehicles, the planetary gear transmission is replaced by a simpler **continuously variable transmission (CVT).**

At this time, the CVT is used in smaller vehicles. It uses a metal V-belt and two variable-size pulleys to produce continuous gear ratios (Figure 3-45). This transmission does not shift

gears; the ratio gradually changes from the lowest ratio at a stop to the highest ratio for cruising speeds. While accelerating, the engine runs at almost a constant speed as the transmission varies the ratio. For low gear, a small input pulley drives a large output pulley (Figure 3-46). As the vehicle speed increases, the diameter of the input pulley becomes larger while the output pulley diameter becomes smaller. This is accomplished by moving the sides of each pulley together or

CLUTCH APPLICATION CHART

	1st CLUTCH	2nd CLUTCH	3rd CLUTCH	4th CLUTCH	SPRAG CLUTCH
DRIVE 1	APPLIED	RELEASED	RELEASED	RELEASED	ON
DRIVE 2	APPLIED	APPLIED	RELEASED	RELEASED	OFF
DRIVE 3	APPLIED	RELEASED	APPLIED	RELEASED	OFF
DRIVE 4	APPLIED	RELEASED	RELEASED	APPLIED	OFF
MANUAL 2	RELEASED	APPLIED	RELEASED	RELEASED	OFF
REVERSE	RELEASED	RELEASED	RELEASED	APPLIED	OFF

Power Flow

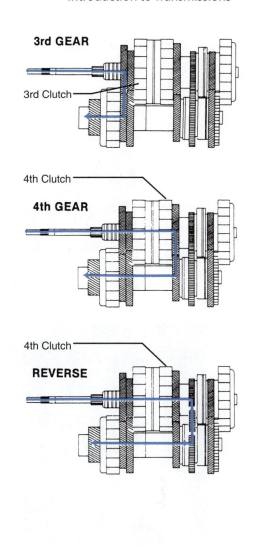

FIGURE 3-43 The power flows through this four-speed HondaMatic are controlled by applying the different clutches. *(Courtesy of American Honda Motor Company)*

apart. At cruising speeds (high gear), a large input pulley drives a small output pulley. Hydraulic controls are used to change the pulley diameter in response to throttle position (vehicle load) and output shaft speed (vehicle speed). A CVT uses an electronic magnetic clutch or a torque converter so the vehicle can be stopped and a planetary gearset for reverse.

3.14 HYBRID DRIVE SYSTEM

Hybrid drive systems were developed to help meet the demands for lower exhaust emissions and improved fuel economy. Hybrid drive combines an internal combustion engine, either gasoline or diesel, with an electric motor. An internal combustion engine is most efficient if it can be designed to run at a constant operating speed. Electrical-powered vehicles have a very limited operating range because they rely on batteries that need recharging. Combining the high torque at low rpm of an electric motor with the

optimized, constant-speed, internal combustion engine to generate electricity produces a vehicle that has smooth, quiet acceleration with very low emissions.

Optimizing an internal combustion engine to constant rpm operation allows improvement of these characteristics:

- reduced strength and weight of the internal moving components,
- optimized air–fuel mixture,
- accurate ignition spark advance,
- variable intake and exhaust valve timing, and
- reduced engine idling.

Electric vehicles offer advantages in efficiency, but they have severely limited operating ranges, about 40 miles. Some electric vehicles can extend the operating range by using *regenerative* braking. This system slows the vehicle by converting the kinetic energy of the moving vehicle into electricity to

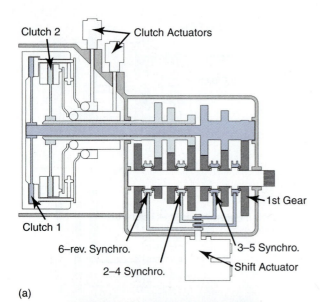

(a)

(b)

(c)

FIGURE 3-44 A dual-clutch transmission, also called an *automated manual transmission (AMT)*, uses two clutches (a). One of them drives the odd-numbered gears, and other drives the even-numbered ones (b). The acuators that apply the clutches and shift the synchronizers are operated by a control module (c).

FIGURE 3-45 A continuously variable transmission (CVT) uses a steel belt to transfer power from the drive pulley to the driven pulley. The two pulleys change diameter to obtain the various gear ratios. *(Courtesy of ZF Group North American Operations)*

recharge the batteries. A conventional brake system wastes this energy by converting it to heat and then dissipating the heat to air moving past the brakes.

General Motors recently introduced an electric vehicle that utilizes an engine to recharge the batteries as they run low. While parked, the vehicle is plugged into a household electrical outlet to recharge the batteries. With the batteries charged, it will run on the electric motor for the first 40 miles, then, as needed, the engine will start to recharge the batteries. This is an electric vehicle since the engine cannot mechanically drive the vehicle. This system should have a substantial impact on emissions and fuel economy since 78% of commuters drive less than 40 miles.

Another fuel-saving feature is called *idle-stop*. This feature saves the fuel the engine would normally use while waiting at a stoplight. When the vehicle comes to a stop with the driver's foot on the brake, the engine will shut off. When the driver depresses the accelerator, the electric motor will start the vehicle moving and restart the engine to accelerate.

Hybrid vehicles can be grouped into two categories; mild and true hybrid. Mild hybrids provide minimal electrical power to assist the internal combustion engine and recharge the batteries with regenerative braking and use idle-stop technology. True hybrids provide regenerative braking, idle-stop technology, engine generator for battery charging, and use electric power to propel the vehicle.

3.14.1 Honda Hybrid

Honda hybrid vehicles use a gasoline engine that has advanced variable valve timing coupled to a CVT or five-speed automatic transmission. This system, called Integrated Motor

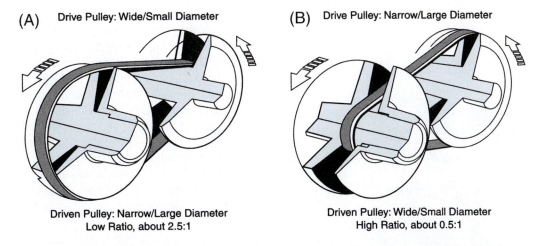

(A) Drive Pulley: Wide/Small Diameter

(B) Drive Pulley: Narrow/Large Diameter

Driven Pulley: Narrow/Large Diameter
Low Ratio, about 2.5:1

Driven Pulley: Wide/Small Diameter
High Ratio, about 0.5:1

FIGURE 3-46 CVTs in low (a) and high (b) ratios. The ratio changes to high ratio because the drive pulley squeezes together, moving it to maximum diameter; the driven pulley will spread apart for minimum diameter. When the vehicle is at rest, the drive pulley will be spread apart and the driven pulley will be squeezed together.

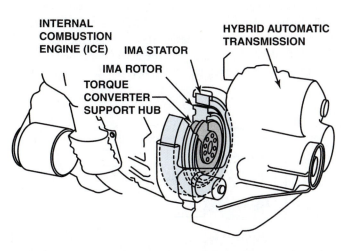

INTERNAL COMBUSTION ENGINE (ICE)

IMA STATOR

HYBRID AUTOMATIC TRANSMISSION

IMA ROTOR

TORQUE CONVERTER SUPPORT HUB

FIGURE 3-47 The assist motor is sandwiched between the engine and the transmission.

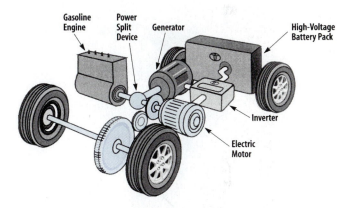

Gasoline Engine

Power Split Device

Generator

High-Voltage Battery Pack

Inverter

Electric Motor

FIGURE 3-48 This hybrid drive system (HDS) combines a gasoline engine, an electric motor, and a generator with some rather complex electronic controls. The vehicle can be powered by the electric motor along with the engine as needed. The generator will help stop the vehicle using regenerative braking.

Assist (IMA), uses an electric assist motor that is sandwiched between the engine and transmission (Figure 3-47). As the name implies, the electric motor is used to assist the engine. When the vehicle is stationary the engine is off. During startup and acceleration the engine starts and powers the vehicle with the assist of the electric motor. Rapid acceleration will cause the engine to change valve timing to increase the engine's power, and the electric motor to provide additional assist. Under very light loads the engine will shut off and the electric motor will provide the power. While decelerating, the batteries are recharged by braking regeneration.

3.14.2 Toyota Hybrid

The Toyota hybrid drive system combines an internal combustion engine and an electric motor to improve economy and reduce emissions. This drive system uses the electric motor as the primary driving force. The gasoline engine powers a generator that produces electricity for the electric motor and to charge the batteries, and it is also a supplementary driving force during acceleration (Figure 3-48). The electric motor can be coupled directly to the drive wheels through a set of reduction gears. Electric motors develop enough low-speed torque that a normal transmission is not required. Changing the polarity to the motor causes it to run backward for reverse. During deceleration, this motor is converted electrically to become a generator for regenerative braking to charge the batteries.

A large battery pack is required to store the electrical energy. Thirty-eight individual battery modules are wired in series for an operating voltage of 274 volts. Caution should be exercised with these systems as the voltage is high enough to cause a fatal shock.

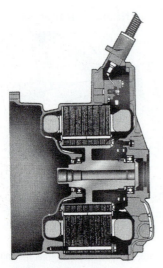

(a) Electric Motor

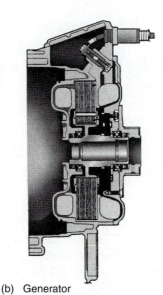

(b) Generator

(c) Power Split Device

FIGURE 3-49 This HDS motor uses 274 volts to produce 44 horsepower (a). The generator (b) can be driven by the engine when electricity is needed or the drive wheels during braking. The power split device (c) allows the engine to drive either the rear wheels or the generator.

A power divider, also called a power split device, is used to couple the engine to both the generator and the drivetrain to the wheels (Figure 3-49). The power split device is a simple planetary gearset. The engine is connected to the planet carrier, the sun gear is connected to the generator, and the ring gear is connected to the drivetrain. The power split device acts like a type of differential so the engine can run at its designed speed and add power to the drivetrain that might be turning at various speeds. The generator can operate at any speed, and its load can be adjusted electronically so the engine power can be split as needed for vehicle operation.

A complex set of electronic controls uses the shift lever position, accelerator position, and brake pedal position to control the motor and engine operation (Figure 3-50). This includes an inverter to convert dc electricity of the batteries to ac current at the motor and generator.

The hybrid engine does not run when the ignition is turned to start, but a ready light will come on to inform the driver that the operating sequence has begun. When the shift selector is moved to drive and the accelerator is depressed, the vehicle can begin moving using the electric motor. The engine might start and run at its design speed as determined by the ECU. The determining inputs to the ECU for engine operation are the rate of acceleration being requested, state of battery

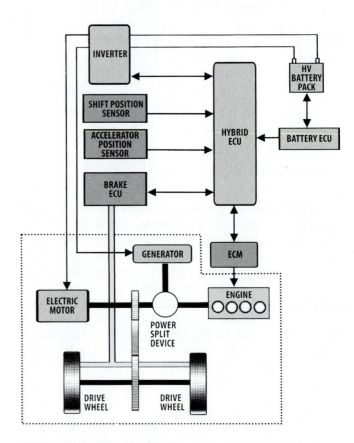

FIGURE 3-50 The HDS vehicle drive system and electrical system.

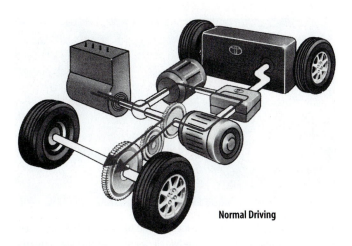

Normal Driving

FIGURE 3-51 When a vehicle is accelerating, the wheels are driven by the electric motor with an assist from the engine. The engine is also driving the generator through the power split device.

charge, outside temperature, use of air conditioning, and if the vehicle is traveling over a level road or going up- or downhill. If engine operation is required, the generator works as a starter; then after the engine starts, it becomes a load device providing electricity (Figure 3-51). As soon as the engine is no longer needed, it is shut off, and the vehicle operates using the motor and batteries.

3.14.3 Ford Hybrid

The Ford hybrid operation is similar to that of the Toyota system.

3.14.4 General Motors Hybrid

General Motors has mild and true hybrid systems in production.

The parallel hybrid system uses a compact 14-kW electric motor/starter generator between the engine and transmission. The electric motor's stator is positioned on dowels and clamped between the engine and transmission (Figure 3-52). The rotor is bolted to the engine's crankshaft and extends over the torque converter. When slowing or stopping, the fuel to the engine is shut off. The electric motor is used to restart the engine. A 42-volt battery is used to store the electricity generated by the motor and provide electricity used to restart the engine. It is classified as a mild hybrid.

The belt alternator starter (BAS) system is another mild hybrid system that provides idle-stop, electrically controlled creep, and regenerative braking. The system uses a belt-driven alternator/starter that looks similar to an alternator. The reinforced belt that drives the alternator/starter utilizes a dual tensioner system that will control the bi-directional

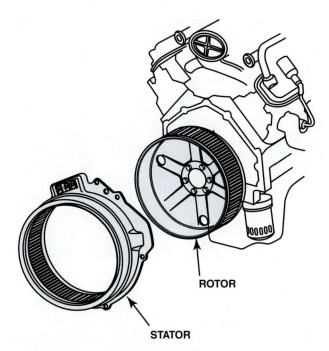

ROTOR

STATOR

FIGURE 3-52 The motor/generator uses a rotor that is bolted to and turns with the crankshaft, and a stator that is sandwiched between the engine and transmission around the rotor.

loads (Figure 3-53). The alternator/starter is used to start the engine and provide some torque. During deceleration, power is passed back through the belt to turn the alternator/starter to recharge the batteries. The system provides idle-stop to conserve fuel and reduce exhaust emissions about 10% to 12%.

The General Motors two-mode system was developed jointly by General Motors, Chrysler, and BMW (Figure 3-54). The system optimizes power train output and fuel economy at various driving conditions. The transmission can operate as a CVT with four fixed ratios, with power input from the engine and/or the two electric motors. There are two modes of operation. Mode one provides fuel saving in low speed, stop-and-go operation, and mode two provides fuel savings at highway speeds while also providing power for trailer towing or steep grades.

The two-mode hybrid transmission contains two internal 60-kW motors that operate from a three-phase, 288-volt power source, three planetary gearsets, and four clutches (Figure 3-55). There are four fixed ratios: 3.7:1, 1.7:1, 1:1, and .07:1. The fixed ratios save battery power that would otherwise be used to keep the engine in its optimal operating range. Other advantages of the fixed ratios are overdrive and faster overall vehicle speed. The system provides a fuel improvement of up to 25%.

As the vehicle accelerates the engine can be off and the electric motors will propel the vehicle and start the engine. Once the engine is running the computer will control

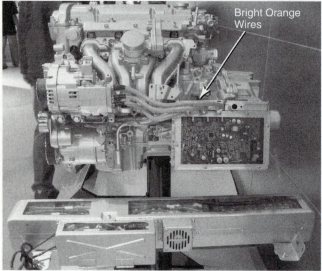

FIGURE 3-54 The two-mode hybrid transmission has two, three-wire sets of HV wires connected to the two electric motors/generators inside the transmission.

FIGURE 3-55 The two-mode hybrid uses two motors/generators, three planetary gearsets, and four hydraulic clutches. This simplified, schematic view illustrates the internal parts.

FIGURE 3-53 The dual tensioner system allows the drive belt to turn the alternator/starter during charging mode and allows the alternator/starter to turn the crankshaft during starting (a). Note the three idlers (arrows) to keep the belt very tight. The controller and orange HV wires are shown in (b).

the engine and electric power to operate in the most efficient range.

One electric motor controls the speed ratio of the sun gear of the planetary set and the second motor generates electricity to power the first motor and can supply torque, if needed to the output shaft. This allows the transmission to work like two transmissions connected together: the first transmission is continuously variable and the other is a conventional transmission. The fixed ratios are used when the electric motors are ineffective in high-load conditions. When this happens, the motors act as generators to recharge the batteries.

3.14.5 Nissan Hybrid

The Nissan hybrid operation is similar to that of the Toyota system.

SUMMARY

1. Transmissions provide the needed gear ratios to operate a vehicle.

2. Gear ratios multiply torque and reduce the speed or increase the speed as torque decreases.

3. Planetary gearsets are the most common automatic transmission gear trains.

4. A simple planetary gearset can provide seven driving modes and neutral.

5. Combinations of planetary gearsets provide two, three, four, or more forward gear ranges.

6. Clutches, band clutches, and one-way clutches are used to control planetary members.

7. Automatic transmissions are controlled hydraulically and/or electronically.

8. Torque converters provide the engine-to-transmission coupling and provide an automatic clutch.

9. In an effort to better control emissions and fuel economy, new automatic transmission drivetrains are being developed.

REVIEW QUESTIONS

The following questions are provided to help you study as you read the chapter.

1. The abbreviation used to describe front wheel drive is _____, and the engine is usually mounted in a _____ position.

2. Torque is a twisting force that is commonly measured in _____, _____, and _____.

3. Five foot-pounds of torque equals _____ inch-pounds.

4. When the transmission increases torque, _____ is decreased.

5. Many transmission manufacturers include the _____ as part of the identifying code for the transmission.

6. A gearset with a 12-tooth drive gear and a 24-tooth driven gear has a gear ratio of _____.

7. A gearset with a 10-tooth drive gear and a 24-tooth driven gear has a gear ratio of _____.

8. If a transmission has a gear ratio of 3:1 in first gear and the final drive ratio is 4:1, the overall ratio would be _____.

9. Three names used to describe an internal cut transmission gear are _____, _____, and _____.

10. Two meshed external gears will rotate in the _____ direction. An external gear meshed with an internal gear will rotate in the _____ direction.

11. A vehicle with a tire diameter of 48 inches and a gear ratio of 12:1 is traveling at 30 mph. How fast is the engine turning?

12. How fast would a vehicle be traveling if the engine was turning at 3,500 rpm, if the overall drive ratio was 10:1, and the tires were 45 inches in diameter?

13. A standard transmission will shift smoothly if the synchronizer sleeve and driven gear are turning at the same _____.

14. The front of the transmission is the part that is closest to the _____.

15. The three members of a simple planetary set are the _____, _____, and _____.

16. When the planet gears move around a stationary gear, the action is known as _____.

17. The most common compound planetary gearset is known as the _____ gear train.

18. The three types of control (apply) devices used in automatic transmissions are _____, _____, and _____.

19. List seven major valves used in a valve body of an automatic transmission.

20. The four major components of a typical, modern torque converter are _____, _____, _____, and _____.

21. Modern torque converters have a _____ that is applied during cruise conditions to eliminate torque converter slippage.

22. The _____ allows the drive wheels to rotate at different speeds when rounding a corner.

23. The two types of drivetrains that power all four wheels of a vehicle are _____ and _____.

24. _____ and _____ are vehicle manufacturers that do not use planetary gearsets in their automatic transmissions.

25. An alternative to the conventional automatic transmission for small vehicles is known as a _____, _____, _____.

26. The use of an internal combustion engine and an electric motor is known as a _____ drive system.

CHAPTER QUIZ

The following questions will help you check the facts you have learned. Select the response that completes each statement correctly.

1. The transmission provides _____.
   a. several gear ratios.
   b. a means of backing up.
   c. a neutral power path.
   d. All of these

2. Student A says that the turning force produced in an engine is called horsepower. Student B says that the turning force produced by an engine is called torque. Who is correct?
   a. Student A
   b. Student B
   c. Both A and B
   d. Neither A nor B

3. Student A says that a 2:1 gear ratio will double the amount of torque. Student B says that a 2:1 gear ratio will reduce the speed by half. Who is correct?
   a. Student A
   b. Student B
   c. Both A and B
   d. Neither A nor B

4. A gear ratio of 0.75:1 _____.
   a. is an overdrive ratio
   b. will offer only a small amount of torque increase
   c. is a very low gear ratio
   d. All of these

5. If the gear on the input shaft has 9 teeth and the gear on the output shaft has 27 teeth, the gear ratio will be _____.
   a. 2.5:1
   b. 0.33:1
   c. 3:1
   d. None of these

6. A vehicle has a transmission with a low gear ratio of 2.5:1 and a final drive ratio of 3.5:1. The overall gear ratio while operating in first gear will be _____.
   a. 2.5:1
   b. 3.5:1
   c. 6:1
   d. 8.75:1

7. When one external gear drives another external gear of the same size, the rotation of the driven gear will be _____.
   a. at a slower speed
   b. at a faster speed
   c. in the opposite direction
   d. All of these

8. The clearance between two meshed gears is called _____.
   a. backlash
   b. side clearance
   c. side thrust
   d. end play

9. The speed of a vehicle is determined by the _____.
   a. speed of the engine
   b. gear ratio
   c. tire diameter
   d. All of these

10. The amount of torque developed in a vehicle's drivetrain is called _____.
    a. power
    b. tractive force
    c. power train torque
    d. All of these

11. A planetary gearset is made up of a _____.
    a. sun gear
    b. ring gear
    c. carrier and planet gears
    d. All of these

12. When the carrier is held and the sun or ring gear is driven, the action of the planet gears will be to _____.
    a. walk
    b. be motionless in the carrier
    c. idle
    d. None of these

13. When the carrier is driven while the sun gear is held, the action of the planet gears will be to _____.
    a. walk
    b. be motionless in the carrier
    c. idle
    d. None of these

14. A Simpson gear train uses _____.
    a. two ring gears, two carriers, and two sun gears
    b. two ring gears, one carrier, and two sun gears
    c. one ring gear, one carrier, and one sun gear
    d. two ring gears, two carriers, and one sun gear

15. Student A says that a clutch in an automatic transmission is applied by spring pressure and released by fluid pressure. Student B says that a band in an automatic transmission is applied by fluid pressure and released by fluid or spring pressure. Who is correct?
    a. Student A
    b. Student B
    c. Both A and B
    d. Neither A nor B

16. Student A says that a reaction member keeps a part of the gearset from rotating. Student B says that a reaction member is always applied by hydraulic pressure. Who is correct?
    a. Student A
    b. Student B
    c. Both A and B
    d. Neither A nor B

17. The transmission's hydraulic circuit _____.
    a. controls clutch and band operation
    b. produces upshifts and downshifts
    c. controls shift quality and timing
    d. All of these

18. A lockup torque converter is used in transmissions to _____.
    a. increase first-gear torque
    b. improve fuel mileage
    c. reduce engine operating speed
    d. All of these

19. Student A says that when a vehicle is going around a corner, the differential pinion gears are rotating on their shafts. Student B says that when a car is going around a corner, the differential pinion gears are in mesh with the axle side gears. Who is correct?
    a. Student A
    b. Student B
    c. Both A and B
    d. Neither A nor B

20. The job of the center differential of an AWD vehicle is to _____.
    a. allow the front axle to go faster than the rear axle
    b. force all four wheels to rotate at the same speed
    c. work the same as in 2WD vehicles
    d. None of these

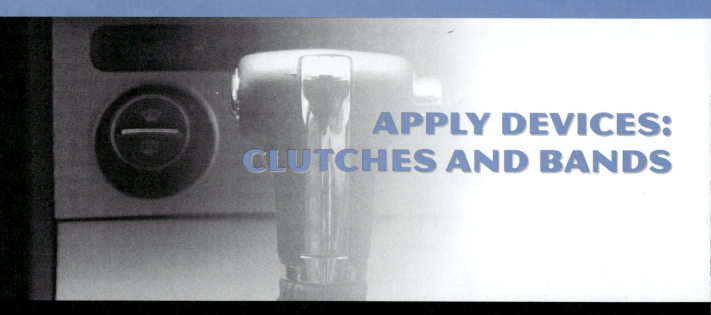

APPLY DEVICES: CLUTCHES AND BANDS

OBJECTIVES

After studying Chapter 4, the reader should be able to:

1. Describe the power flow through a planetary gearset.
2. Identify the components of a multiple-disc clutch and describe how it operates.
3. Identify a one-way clutch and describe how it operates.
4. Identify a band and servo and describe how they operate.

KEY TERMS

Belleville Spring (p. 72)
Driving Devices (p. 71)
Dynamic Friction (p. 76)
Front Clutch (p. 71)
Garage Shifts (p. 77)
High-Reverse Clutch (p. 71)
Hub (p. 72)
Lined Plates (p. 72)

Mechanical Diode (p. 79)
Pressure Plate (p. 72)
Shift Feel (p. 83)
Static Friction (p. 76)
Steels (p. 73)
Strut (p. 81)
Synchronous (p. 71)

4.1 INTRODUCTION

There are several paths for power to flow through an automatic transmission, and each path provides a different gear ratio. These power paths are controlled by the driving and reaction devices, also called driving and reaction members. The **driving devices** connect the turbine shaft from the torque converter to a member of the planetary gear train. The **reaction devices** connect a member of the gear train to the transmission case. There are usually two or more driving devices and two or more reaction devices in a three- or four-speed automatic transmission (Figure 4-1).

4.2 DRIVING DEVICES

The driving devices provide the input to the gearset. The turbine shaft is normally built as part of or splined to one or more of the driving devices. Driving devices are usually multiple-plate disc clutches. In most cases, they will be at the front of the transmission, just behind the pump.

A few transmissions have a one-way (roller or sprag) clutch positioned between the multiple-disc clutch and the input member of the planetary gearset. One-way clutches transfer power in only one direction. A one-way clutch in a driving position will become effective and transfer power when the multiple-disc clutch is applied. It will release or overrun, becoming ineffective when the driving member for a higher gear applies, and this allows the part held by the roller clutch to increase speed.

A common problem that students and technicians have concerning automatic transmissions is the lack of common terms. Although the parts perform the same job, the driving clutches are often given different names by different manufacturers. An example of this involves the two clutches in front of a Simpson gear train transmission.

- Chrysler Corporation calls the first clutch the **front clutch;**
- Ford Motor Company calls it a **high-reverse clutch;**
- General Motors Corporation and Toyota call it a *direct clutch;*
- Toyota uses the term direct clutch but more commonly calls it C2.

4.2.1 Synchronizing Shifts

Automatic shifts must be timed to happen quickly without the possibility of being in two gears at the same time. There are two strategies used by transmission manufacturers. One strategy is call **synchronous,** *overlap,* or *clutch-to-clutch* shifting. This requires that one apply device be timed or synchronized with the application of the apply device for the next gear range. The other strategy is called *nonsychronous, asynchronous,* or *freewheel shifts.* These shifts use one or more one-way clutches as driving or reaction devices. A one-way clutch will self-release during a shift as soon as the next clutch applies, eliminating the need to time the shifts.

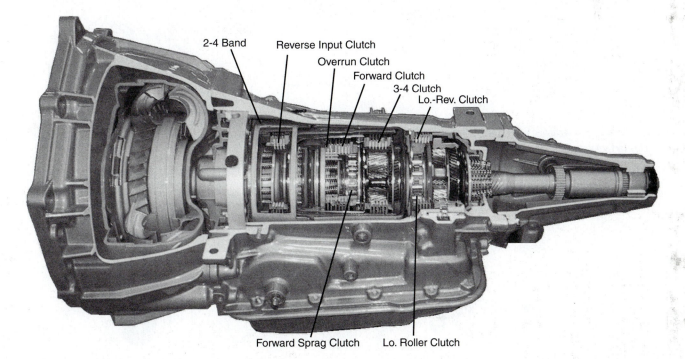

FIGURE 4-1 The 4L60 (THM 700) has one band, five multiple-disc clutches, and two one-way clutches to control the power flow. The reverse input, overrun, forward, and 3–4 clutches along with the forward sprag clutch are driving members. The 2–4 band, low roller clutch, and low-reverse clutch are reaction members.

4.3 MULTIPLE-DISC DRIVING CLUTCHES

The parts of a clutch assembly are: the *drum,* **hub,** *lined plates, unlined plates,* **pressure plate,** apply piston, and piston return springs. The drum, also called a *housing,* has splines inside its outer edge for the externally lugged plates, usually the unlined plates. The inner diameter of the drum is machined for the apply piston and its inner and outer seals (Figure 4-2). The drum of the rear, or forward, clutch is usually built as part of or splined to the input or turbine shaft. A clutch can be built as a single unit or combined with another drum or hub of a second clutch assembly. For example, the input drum of a General Motors 4L60 (THM 700-R4) transmission contains three different clutches as well as the hub for a fourth clutch (Figure 4-3).

NOTE: The model designation for some transmissions has changed. In this text, the new designation for common transmissions will be given first and the older one will follow inside parentheses.

A clutch hub is splined or lugged on its outer diameter to accept the internal lugs of the lined clutch plates. The clutch pack is made up by alternately stacked unlined and lined plates, and this stack is contained in the drum. The clutch pack is held in place by a thick pressure plate retained by a large retaining ring in the drum. The clutch hub is often built as part of the unit being driven, such as a ring gear or a carrier.

The doughnut-shaped apply piston is sealed at both its inner and outer diameter to trap the fluid entering the cylinder. During clutch application, fluid pressure forces the piston to squeeze the clutch pack against the pressure plate (Figure 4-4). When the fluid pressure is released, one or more piston return springs push the piston back to its released position. Clutch assemblies use a group of small coil springs; a single, large coil spring; a single, large Belleville spring; or a wave spring (Figure 4-5). When the clutch is released, the plates separate, creating a clearance between each plate.

A **Belleville spring,** also called a *diaphragm spring,* resembles a metal washer that is slightly cone shaped. Spring action occurs when this spring is flattened. A *wave spring* also resembles a large washer. It is not flat; it is bent back and forth. The action of a Belleville or wave spring cushions clutch

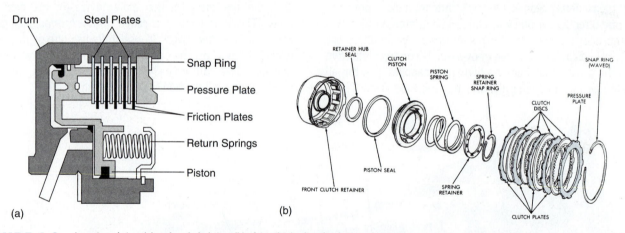

FIGURE 4-2   A sectioned view (a) and exploded view (b) of a multiple-disc clutch. Note the piston to apply the clutch and the spring(s) to release it. *(b is courtesy of Chrysler Corporation)*

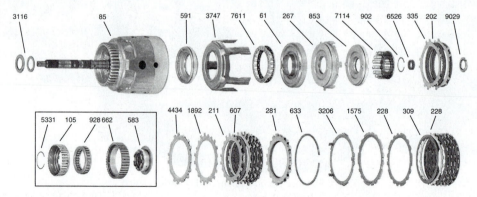

FIGURE 4-3   A 4L60 input clutch assembly has three separate clutch packs: 202 is the overrun clutch; 607 is the forward clutch; and 228 is the 3–4 clutch. The input sprag assembly is at the bottom left. *(Courtesy of Slauson Transmission Parts, www.slauson.com)*

TECH TIP

If the fluid does not exhaust from the clutch apply chamber of a spinning clutch, centrifugal force will force the fluid to the outer edge of the chamber (Figure 4-6). This trapped fluid can cause partial clutch apply and unwanted clutch drag.

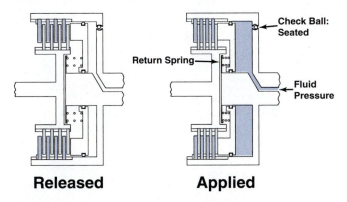

Released   **Applied**

FIGURE 4-4   The apply piston is released (left) by the coil springs. Fluid pressure moves the piston to apply the clutch (right).

application. Some clutches position a Belleville spring between the piston and the clutch pack so it serves as an apply lever as well as a return spring. The force increase from this leverage increases the strength of the clutch.

4.3.1 Clutch Plates

The unlined plates are called **steels,** or *separator plates.* They are flat pieces of steel stamped into the desired shape. A steel plate is usually about 0.070 to 0.100 in. (1.78 to 2.54 mm) thick. After being stamped, the plate is carefully flattened. An out-of-flat plate will use up clutch clearance and cause drag while released. A steel plate has a surface roughness of 12 to 15 micro-in (Figure 4-7). An unlined steel plate usually has lugs on its outer diameter to engage with the clutch drum/housing or transmission case. The steel plates used in current automatic transmissions are very smooth; some have a polished appearance. Steel plates have a secondary purpose of serving as heat sinks to help remove heat from the lined friction plates.

Lined plates are called *friction plates* or simply *frictions.* These plates are also made from stamped steel with lining material bonded to each side. The engagement lugs are usually

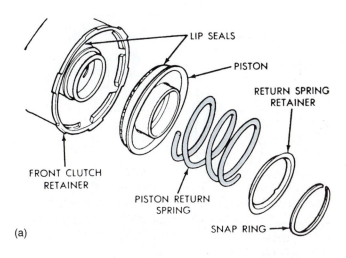

(a)

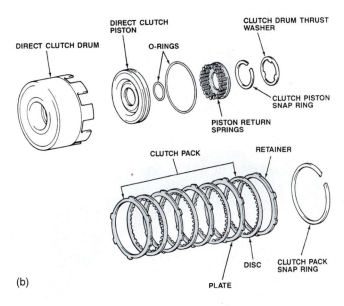

(b)

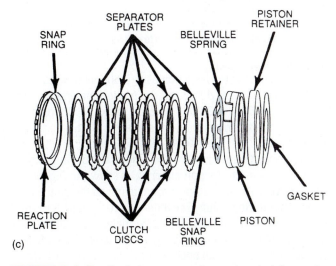

(c)

FIGURE 4-5   Clutch piston return springs can be a single large spring (a), a group of small springs (b), or a single Belleville spring (c). *(Courtesy of Chrysler Corporation)*

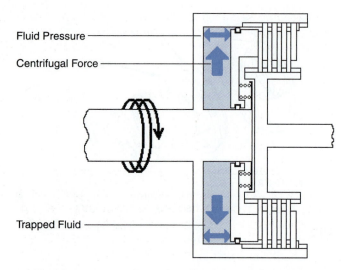

Fluid Pressure

Centrifugal Force

Trapped Fluid

FIGURE 4-6   Any fluid left in the apply chamber of a spinning clutch will be pushed outward by centrifugal force. This force can cause the fluid to push on the piston and partially apply a clutch.

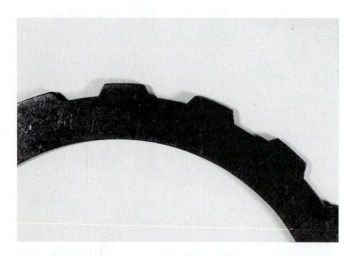

FIGURE 4-7   A close-up view of the surface finish on a steel plate. Note the small nicks and grooves that tend to hold fluid.

on the inner diameter. A friction plate is about 0.063 to 0.086 in. (1.6 to 2.18 mm) thick, and the friction material is about 0.015 to 0.030 in. (0.38 to 0.76 mm) thick. The lining material can have a plain, smooth, flat surface or a grooved friction surface.

A grooved plate can have one of several grooving patterns cut or stamped into friction material, as shown in Figure 4-8. The grooves help fluid leave or enter between the unlined and lined plates during a shift. The different grooving patterns help control how fast the fluid leaves the friction area to produce different shift-quality characteristics. The faster the oil leaves, the faster the clutch can apply, but the longer the oil stays between the plates, the more heat can be absorbed by the oil. Different clutch packs for the same transmission will often use lined plates with different grooving patterns. Clutches that

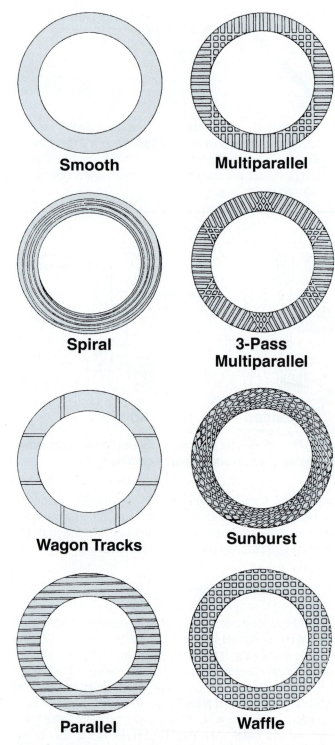

Smooth

Multiparallel

Spiral

3-Pass Multiparallel

Wagon Tracks

Sunburst

Parallel

Waffle

FIGURE 4-8   Friction plates often have a groove pattern to help wipe fluid away, dissipate heat, eliminate clutch noise, and change friction qualities during apply and release. A smooth plate is the coolest and slowest to apply; the waffle plate will apply the fastest, but it will have less heat removed by the oil. *(Courtesy of Raybestos)*

apply with the vehicle at rest can be smooth because apply rate is not important. Clutches that are used for upshifts will often have a groove pattern. Some new clutch designs use friction plates with *directional grooving* (Figure 4-9). These are a slanted groove that must face the proper direction. Some have an inner spline shape that allows the plate to be installed only in the proper direction.

Clutch lining material is a mix of natural and man-made fibers, fillers, and binders. The exact mixture is selected to provide the desired clutch apply, duration, and heat resistance characteristics. The natural fibers come from cotton or wood (Figure 4-10).

The man-made fibers are aramid/Kevlar, glass, and carbon. Fillers help determine the density, porosity, and flexibility; common fillers are diatomaceous earth, graphite/carbon, and friction particles. Binders hold the mix together; the most common binders are thermosetting phenolic resins.

The clutches are flooded with transmission fluid while released, and during application this fluid prevents any heat generated by friction from overheating the lining. Theoretically, there will always be a film of fluid between the friction and steel plates.

Manufacturers often provide some means of adjusting the released clearance in a clutch pack. There must be sufficient clearance between the plates to ensure that there is no drag when released. This clearance should be about 0.010 to 0.015 in. (0.25 to 0.38 mm) between each friction surface-lined and unlined plate. Clutch pack clearance is also called *piston travel.* The most common methods of adjusting clutch pack clearance are selective size retaining rings or pressure plates (Figure 4-11). A selective part is available in several thicknesses, and when a clutch is assembled, the correct width or thickness is selected.

Double- and Single-Sided Friction Plates. The clutch just described uses double-sided friction plates. *Single-sided plates* have friction material on one side only, and half of the plates have lugs on the inner diameter while the other half have lugs on the outer diameter (Figure 4-12). Single-sided plates run cooler than two-sided plates, and this feature allows for more power transfer. The plates can be made thinner so that more plates can be put into a clutch pack. Single-sided plates have encountered problems of uneven heating because one side gets hotter, and the plate tends to deform into a conical shape. This problem has been cured by mechanically distorting the plates slightly or by specially designed grooves cut in the end plates.

FIGURE 4-9 This friction plate has directional grooves. The lugs (center inset) are assymmetrical, so the plate cannot be installed incorrectly. *(Courtesy of Raybestos)*

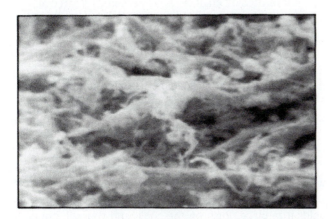

FIGURE 4-10 A microscopic view of the surface of paper friction plate lining. Friction material is formed on the lined plate to establish a cross-linked matrix. Note the large cavities between the paper fibers that can store relatively large amounts of fluid. *(Courtesy of Raybestos)*

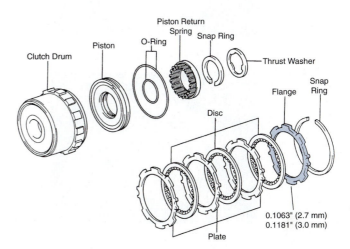

FIGURE 4-11 In this clutch assembly, clutch stack clearance is adjusted using either the large or small flange (backing plate). Other clutches may use a selective snap ring. *(Courtesy of Toyota Motor Sales USA, Inc.)*

4.3.2 Clutch Operation

When a clutch is applied, the plates are squeezed together and torque is transferred from the friction plates to the steel plates. The amount of torque that can be transferred is determined by the following factors: diameter and width of the friction

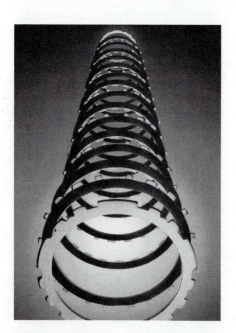

(a)

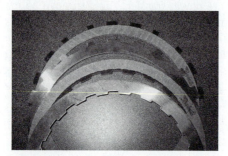

(b)

(c)

FIGURE 4-12 The ZPAK is a single-sided clutch design (a). Both sides of the two different plates show a lined and unlined side (b). The clutch pack requires proper placement of the end plates (c). *(Courtesy of Raybestos)*

surfaces, number of friction surfaces (two per lined plate), and the amount of force being applied (hydraulic pressure times the piston area). The greater the plate area, number of plates, piston size, or hydraulic pressure, the greater the torque capacity. The formula used to determine clutch capacity is:

$$T = \frac{N[[D + d]\ F\mu]}{4}$$

where:

T = torque capacity (in inch-pounds)
N = number of active friction surfaces
D = outside diameter of clutch facings (in inches)
d = inside diameter of clutch facings (in inches)
F = total force on clutch pack (in pounds)
μ = coefficient of friction

A clutch with sufficient capacity will transfer torque without slipping. Many transmissions are made with varying torque capacities depending on the engine with which they will be used. Transmissions used with high-torque engines have more plates in the clutch packs.

When a clutch is released, there must be clearance between the plates. There is often a considerable speed differential between the friction and steel plates. For example, during first gear in a Simpson gear train, the sun gear revolves at a 2.5:1 ratio in reverse (counterclockwise). Imagine the speed difference in a released high-gear clutch with the input shaft, clutch hub, and lined plates revolving at an engine speed of 3,000 rpm in a clockwise direction and the drum and the unlined plates turning 7,500 rpm in a counterclockwise direction (Figure 4-13). Without sufficient clearance and lubrication, these plates would surely drag, create friction, and burn up. The oil flow through the grooves and between the plates helps cool the friction surfaces.

A transmission engineer is concerned with three different friction conditions in a clutch:

- While the clutch is released, there should be no friction or drag.
- While applied, there should be sufficient **static friction** to transfer torque without slippage.
- While applying, there should be the proper **dynamic friction** to get a good, smooth shift.

An example of static and dynamic friction can be seen if we place a book on a table. With the book sitting still, the static (stationary) friction between the book and the table holds it in place. Push on the book, and you will notice the amount of force it takes to overcome this static friction (Figure 4-14). Also notice how much force it takes to keep the book sliding; this is the dynamic or sliding friction. Static friction is always greater than dynamic friction.

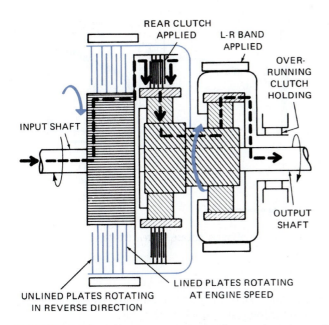

FIGURE 4-13   When this transmission is in first gear, the sun gear and unlined plates of the front clutch rotate counterclockwise while the hub and lined plates of this clutch rotate clockwise. Any drag will produce heat that can cause clutch burnout.

FIGURE 4-14   If you push against a stationary book, you will notice the static friction that resists motion. Pushing against the same book while it is sliding is easier because the dynamic friction is somewhat less.

Several terms are used to describe a shift. *Shift quality* describes how smooth or rough a shift feels. *Shift pattern* is used by General Motors to describe when the shift occurs, the vehicle speed and load to produce the upshift or downshift. The transmission industry uses the term *shift timing* for this same purpose. General Motors uses *shift timing* to describe the

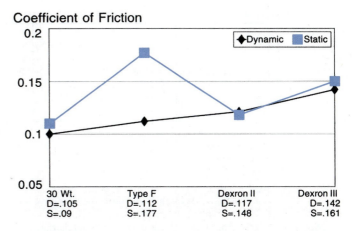

Coefficient of Friction

| | 30 Wt.
D=.105
S=.09 | Type F
D=.112
S=.177 | Dexron II
D=.117
S=.148 | Dexron III
D=.142
S=.161 |

FIGURE 4-15   A comparison of the dynamic and static coefficients of friction with motor oil and three types of ATF. *(Courtesy of Raybestos)*

length of time required to completely apply or release the components involved in the shift. The transmission industry calls this *shift duration.*

The friction characteristics of a clutch are designed to work with the friction characteristics of the transmission fluid. The various types of automatic transmission fluid (ATF) use different friction modifiers (Figure 4-15). A vehicle manufacturer specifies the fluid type to be used in its transmissions.

Some clutches in an automatic transmission are applied while the vehicle is at rest; the neutral-to-drive and neutral-to-reverse shifts are called **garage shifts.** The clutches for first or reverse gear need a high amount of static friction because of the amount of torque required to start the vehicle moving. The garage shifts can occur slowly so they are usually less severe than the 1–2, 2–3, or 3–4 shifts; they may take 3 or 4 seconds to apply. Clutches that are applied while the vehicle is in motion and are called *power shift* elements. They are applied under power and have to transfer substantial torque as they are applied (Figure 4-16). These clutches must have a high dynamic coefficient of friction.

4.3.3 Wet Friction

Wet friction occurs because ATF fills the space between the clutch plates. This ATF film transmits torque between the clutch plates as the clutch is being applied. The action of the film of fluid is called *fluid shear.*

As the clutch is applied, the clutch plate clearance reduces as the fluid is squeezed from between the plates, leaving a film of fluid. This hydrodynamic film begins transferring torque. Fluid shear, the resistance to motion, is the primary torque transmitting force at the start of a shift. As the plate clearance is reduced, fluid viscosity increases and its resistance to shear increases. The clutch plates make physical contact at the end of application. Since there is no movement between the plates at this time, friction lining wear is minimized.

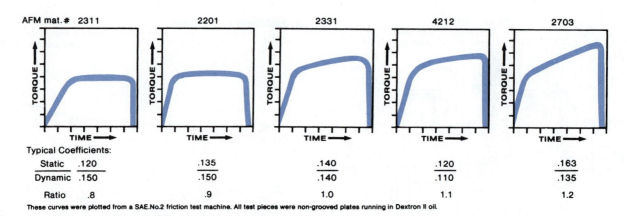

AFM mat. # 2311	2201	2331	4212	2703

Typical Coefficients:

Static	.120	.135	.140	.120	.163
Dynamic	.150	.150	.140	.110	.135
Ratio	.8	.9	1.0	1.1	1.2

These curves were plotted from a SAE.No.2 friction test machine. All test pieces were non-grooved plates running in Dextron II oil.

FIGURE 4-16   The clutch apply curves of five different clutches. The dynamic friction is the rate of torque increase, whereas the static friction is the amount of torque at the left. *(Courtesy of AFM)*

FIGURE 4-17   The four slots in this steel plate, called a turbulator plate, promote a fluid layer on each side of the stationary plate. *(Courtesy of Raybestos)*

Open Pack Drag.   Open pack drag refers to the torque that is required to spin a clutch that is released. Remember that during cruise operation, one or two of the clutch packs will be released, and any drag within the released clutches reduces transmission efficiency and fuel mileage. Fluid shear between the rotating plates increases parasitic drag. *Turbulator steels* have small holes drilled through them. The holes create a turbulence that tends to center the plate and separate the pack (Figure 4-17). The turbulator holes also provide additional escape paths for fluid during clutch apply. Another design to reduce drag is a precision wave friction plate. The wave is very

small, about 0.010 in. (0.0004 mm), just enough to help center the friction plate between the steels.

PROBLEM SOLVING 4-1 Imagine that you are working in a shop that specializes in transmission repair, and these problems are brought to you.

Case 1 A 1982 Chevrolet pickup starts okay in first gear, but the 1–2 shift is long and drawn out. A full-throttle shift has an engine speed flare with indications of slippage. What part of the transmission is faulty? What do you think is causing this problem?

Case 2 A 1995 Nissan Sentra shifts good going into the forward ranges, but there is no reverse; it acts just like neutral. How can you determine the faulty part?

4.4 ONE-WAY DRIVING CLUTCHES

Two styles of one-way clutches are used in automatic transmissions: *roller clutches* and *sprag clutches*. One-way clutches are also called *overrunning clutches*. A one-way clutch is sometimes called a mechanical diode; like an electronic diode, it allows travel in one direction only.

4.4.1 Roller Clutch

A roller clutch is made up of a smooth inner race, a ramped outer race, a series of rollers and energizing springs, and a cage or guide to locate the springs (Figure 4-18). Some roller clutches are made with a ramped inner race and a smooth outer race. Each roller fits in the ramp or cam section of the race (Figure 4-19). An energizing spring pushes the roller so there is a light contact between the roller, the ramp, and the smooth race. Counterclockwise rotation of the hub will

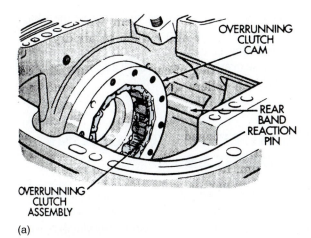

(a)

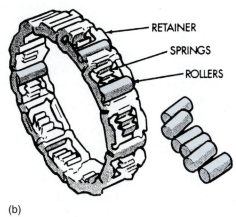

(b)

FIGURE 4-18   This overrunning clutch assembly is a roller clutch with the clutch cam secured to the transmission case (a). It uses a set of spring-loaded rollers in the retainer (b). *(Courtesy of Chrysler Corporation)*

wedge the rollers so they become locked between the inner and outer races. When locked, they will block any further rotation in that direction. Clockwise rotation will unwedge the rollers, and each roller will simply rotate, much like a roller bearing. The inner hub will rotate freely or overrun in a clockwise direction.

4.4.2 Sprag Clutch

A sprag clutch uses smooth, hardened inner and outer races and a series of sprags that are mounted in a special cage. A sprag is an odd-shaped part that somewhat resembles an hourglass or fat letter *S* when viewed from the end. A sprag has two effective diameters. The major diameter is greater than the space between the inner and outer races, and the minor diameter is smaller than this space. The sprags are mounted in a cage that spring loads each sprag in a direction to "stand up" or wedge the major diameter between the two races. A clockwise rotation of the inner race causes the sprags to rotate in the stand-up direction. This causes them to wedge

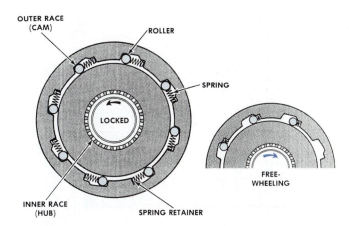

FIGURE 4-19   If this inner race tries to turn counterclockwise, the rollers will wedge at the narrow part of the cams and lock the clutch. Movement of the inner race in a clockwise direction will move the rollers to the wide part of the cams, where they will roll freely. *(Courtesy of Chrysler Corporation)*

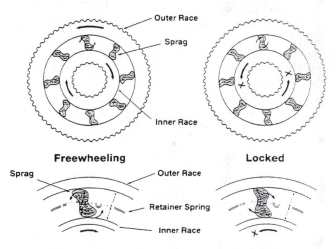

FIGURE 4-20   Each sprag has a major and minor diameter. The major diameter is greater than the distance between the two races (right); the minor diameter is smaller (left). *(Courtesy of Toyota Motor Sales USA, Inc.)*

firmly between the two races and lock the races together. A counterclockwise rotation of the inner race rotates the sprags in the opposite (laydown) direction (Figure 4-20). Each sprag tends to lay down so its minor diameter is between the races, and the inner race rotates freely.

4.4.3 Mechanical Diode

A **mechanical diode** is a relatively new type of one-way clutch. It uses spring-loaded, rectangular struts in the face of one clutch ring, the pocket plate that can engage notches in the face of another ring, and the notch plate (Figure 4-21). The struts are pushed into their pockets when the clutch is overrunning, and they can move outward, about 15 degrees, to

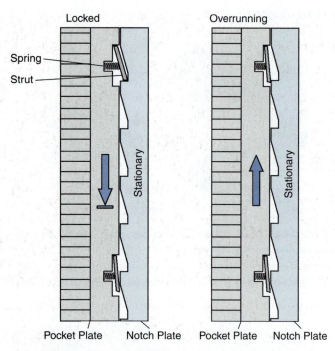

FIGURE 4-21 A mechanical diode. The struts can move out of the pocket plate to engage the notch plate, and this will lock the pocket plate. The pocket plate can overrun in the opposite direction.

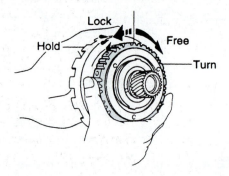

FIGURE 4-22 This clutch hub and sprag clutch should rotate freely in a clockwise direction but should lock up in the opposite direction. *(Courtesy of Toyota Motor Sales USA, Inc.)*

engage the notch plate to lock up. Because the compressive forces though the strut are in the load direction, only one or two of the struts need to engage. A mechanical diode is much stronger than a roller or sprag clutch.

4.4.4 Clutch Operation

A one-way clutch can be placed as an input to a gearset. In transmissions like the Ford 5R55E, a one-way clutch is always driving the forward planetary gearset at input shaft speed. In other transmissions, such as the General Motors 4T60-E, one-way clutches are driven through multiple-disc clutches to become effective in first and third gears (Figure 4-22). One-way clutches will overrun as the transmission shifts into the next higher gear.

One-way clutches require continuous lubrication. In most automatic transmissions, one or more one-way clutches are overrunning in high gear. The constant motion would quickly cause overheating and wear if a good flow of fluid was not available at all times.

4.5 HOLDING/REACTION DEVICES

A holding member acts as a brake to hold a planetary gearset member in reaction. Three types of holding devices are used: multiple-disc clutches, bands, and one-way clutches. Multiple-disc clutches and bands are applied by hydraulic pressure and are controlled by the valve body. A one-way clutch is mechanically controlled; it allows rotation in one direction only. In most transmissions, a one-way clutch allows rotation in a clockwise direction but blocks counterclockwise rotation. Applying and holding in a one-way clutch is often referred to as holding or being *effective,* and releasing it is called ineffective or *noneffective.*

Although reaction devices do not rotate, there can be a substantial load on these devices. Remember that for every action, there is an equal and opposite reaction. A General Motors 4L60 (THM 700-R4) transmission uses a 2:1 torque converter ratio and a 3.06:1 first gear. If the engine develops 100 ft-lb (135.6 N-m) of torque, there is 2×100, or 200, ft-lb (271 N-m) of torque coming from the torque converter and 200×3.06, or 612, ft-lb (829.8 N-m) of torque at the drive shaft. There will also be the same 612 ft-lb load on the reaction member, trying to turn it inside the transmission case.

4.6 MULTIPLE-DISC HOLDING CLUTCHES

A multiple-disc holding clutch is quite similar to a driving clutch. The difference is the transmission case is the drum, and the clutch plates splined to it do not rotate. Some manufacturers call these clutches a *brake.* The lugs on the outside of the unlined plates fit into slots built into the case (Figure 4-23). Like a driving clutch, the lugs on the inner diameter of the lined plates fit over the hub, which is often a part of the gear train or the outer race of a one-way clutch.

The hydraulic piston can be built into the case, the back of the front pump assembly, or in a center support (Figure 4-24). The stationary position of the piston and cylinder make it relatively easy to provide fluid to it. Like a driving clutch, the piston is normally returned to a released position by springs.

4.7 ONE-WAY HOLDING CLUTCHES

One-way clutches are commonly used as reaction devices. The outer race is often secured directly to the transmission case so it cannot rotate. The one-way clutch (F2) in the transmission illustrated in Figure 4-24 has the ability to hold the

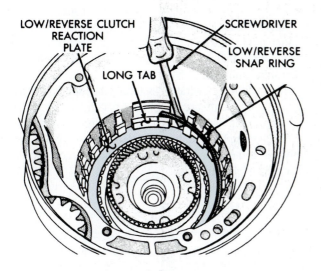

FIGURE 4-23   The 41TE transaxle low/reverse clutch is a holding clutch. Note the splines in the case for the clutch plates. *(Courtesy of Chrysler Corporation)*

rear carrier stationary in drive-1. The carrier can rotate clockwise in any of the other gears. This carrier can also be held stationary by the first and reverse clutch in manual-1 and reverse to provide compression (engine) braking.

4.8 BANDS

A band is a circular strip of metal that has lining bonded to the inner surface. It wraps around the smooth surface of a drum. There are three types: a single thick, heavy band; a single thin, light band; and a split, *double-wrap*, heavy *band*. The heavy, single-wrap band is also called a *rigid band*. The thin, single-wrap band is called a *flexible* or *flex band* (Figure 4-25). A rigid band is strong and provides a good heat sink to absorb some of the friction heat during application. The disadvantage with a rigid band is that it is relatively expensive and does not always conform to the shape of the drum. A flex band is less expensive and, because of its flexibility, can easily conform to the shape of the drum. Double-wrap bands give more holding power, and are often used for reverse or manual first gears. Each band type has end lugs so it can be attached to the anchor and the servo. A small link, commonly called a **strut,** is often used to connect the lugs of the band to the anchor or the servo piston rod (Figure 4-26).

The friction material used on a band is similar to that used on clutch plates. Paper- and cloth-based materials are normally used. Metallic and semimetallic materials tend to cause severe wear of the drum. The drum must be a smooth cylinder with

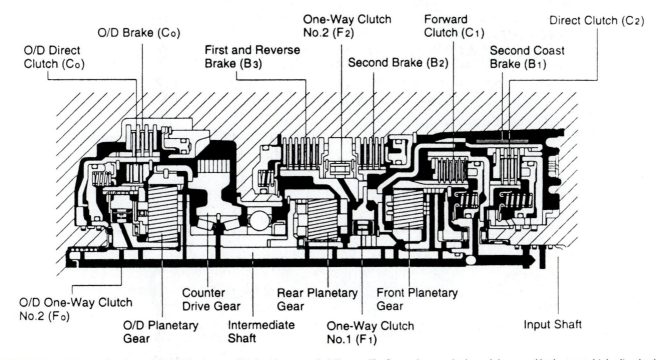

FIGURE 4-24   The plates of the O/D brake are splined to the transaxle O/D case. The first and reverse brake and the second brake are multiple-disc clutches that are splined to the transaxle case. *(Courtesy of Toyota Motor Sales USA, Inc.)*

straight sides in order to have complete contact with the band lining. The lining surface of the band is often grooved to help control fluid flow during apply and release operations. Similar to a clutch, band friction material and grooving are designed to operate with a specified fluid to ensure good shift quality and long life.

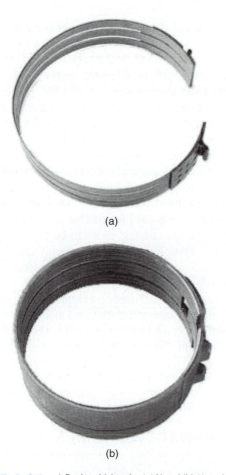

(a)

(b)

FIGURE 4-25   A flex band (a) and a rigid band (b). Note the flex band has circumferential grooves for improved conformity, fluid flow, and performance. Note that this is a double-wrap rigid band. Single-wrap rigid bands are also used. *(Courtesy of Raybestos)*

The band is anchored at the trailing end so drum rotation will tend to pull the band tightly into engagement (Figure 4-27). A double-wrap band design takes advantage of this wrapping tendency and applies smoother and stronger than a single-wrap band. The band tries to rotate with its drum, and the band, anchor, and servo must be designed to absorb this load.

The anchor for the band can be a fixed or adjustable point in the transmission case. An adjustable anchor provides a method of adjusting the clearance between the band and the drum. There must be enough clearance to ensure there is no band-to-drum contact with the band released, but too much clearance might cause slippage if the band does not apply completely. A band that is too loose or too tight has an adverse effect on shift timing.

The servo is the hydraulic assembly that applies the band; its main components are a cylinder, piston, piston rod/pin, and return spring (Figure 4-28). The piston rod pushes directly on the end of the band on most servos. Some servo pistons are connected to the band through a lever or linkage attached to the band strut (Figure 4-29).

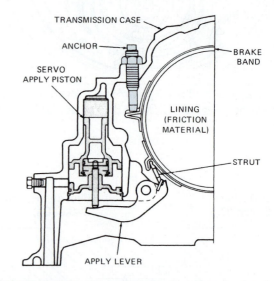

FIGURE 4-26   This band uses an adjustable anchor that allows the clearance to be easily adjusted. *(Courtesy of Chrysler Corporation)*

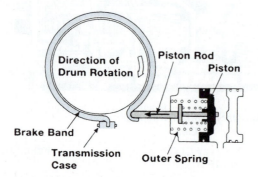

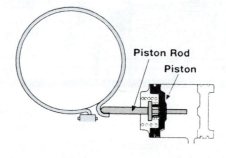

FIGURE 4-27   A band is normally anchored at the trailing end so its rotation will pull the band tighter. Note that this servo is applied by fluid pressure and released by a spring. *(Courtesy of Toyota Motor Sales USA, Inc.)*

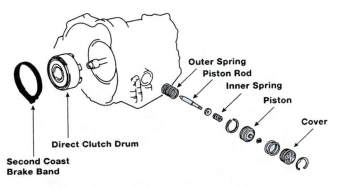

FIGURE 4-28 Fluid pressure acting on the piston forces the piston and piston rod inward to apply the band. The band is released by the outer spring pushing outward on the piston. *(Courtesy of Toyota Motor Sales USA, Inc.)*

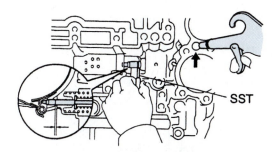

FIGURE 4-30 Air pressure can be used to apply the band while the length of the piston stroke is measured. Piston stroke is used to determine the correct piston rod and adjust band clearance. *(Courtesy of Toyota Motor Sales USA, Inc.)*

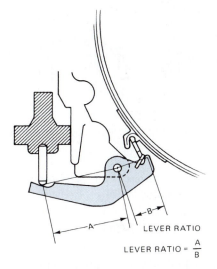

FIGURE 4-29 This band apply lever increases servo force by about two and a half times. The apply speed will be decreased the same amount because the servo must travel a greater distance. *(Courtesy of Chrysler Corporation)*

A band lever provides a force increase because of the lever ratio. The ratio will require more piston travel to apply the band but increases the application force acting on the end of the band. Some manufacturers incorporate a band adjustment screw in the apply lever. Other manufacturers use selective-sized servo piston rods for band adjustment (Figure 4-30).

4.8.1 Band Operation

When fluid pressure enters the servo, the servo piston strokes to tighten the band around the drum. The amount of torque that a band can absorb before slipping is determined by the band-to-drum contact area, type of band, drum diameter, fluid type, and the force squeezing the band onto the drum.

When a band releases, the servo piston backs off, and the springy, elastic nature of the band causes it to move away from the drum. A servo piston can be released by either spring pressure and/or hydraulic pressure.

- When the shift is to neutral, the release speed is not important. Normally, servos use only a release spring.
- During an upshift, the band release must be fast and carefully timed. The release of many bands is done by using fluid pressure from the clutch being applied (Figure 4-31). For example, in a Simpson gear train transmission during a 2–3 shift, the fluid pressure to apply the third-gear clutch is also used to release the second-gear band.
- During a downshift, band apply must be quick and firm.

PROBLEM SOLVING 4-2 Imagine that you are working in a shop that specializes in transmission repair, and these problems are brought to you.

Case 1 A 1996 Dodge Ram pickup drives okay in all gears, but there is a bump, like a small bind-up, during the 2–3 shift. This transmission has a band-to-clutch operation during this shift. Would a worn band cause this problem? Could a sticking band servo cause it? How about a worn third-gear clutch? Could the band be out of adjustment?

Case 2 A 1989 Chevrolet Caprice with a 200-4R transmission does not move forward with the shift selector in OD. It does work normally when shifted to manual-1, and then if shifted to OD, it works well. What do you think might be wrong with this transmission?

4.9 SHIFT QUALITY

As a power shift occurs, there must be a smooth transition from one apply device to the next. The smoothness of the shift is referred to as shift quality or **shift feel.** For example, when a Simpson gear train transmission starts a 2–3 (second [1.5:1 ratio] to third [1:1 ratio] gear) shift, the third-gear clutch drum

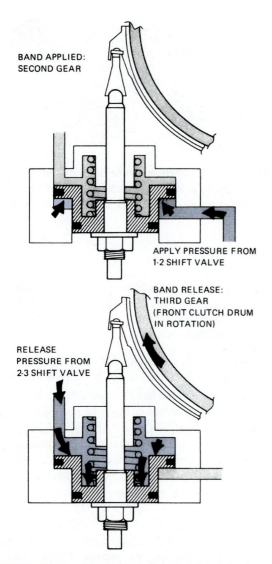

BAND APPLIED:
SECOND GEAR

APPLY PRESSURE FROM
1-2 SHIFT VALVE

BAND RELEASE:
THIRD GEAR
(FRONT CLUTCH DRUM
IN ROTATION)

RELEASE
PRESSURE FROM
2-3 SHIFT VALVE

FIGURE 4-31 This band is applied when 1–2 shift valve pressure pushes upward on the servo piston. It will release when 2–3 shift valve pressure pushes the piston downward. Note the larger area above the piston.

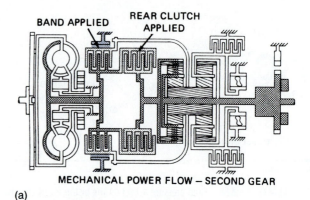

BAND APPLIED

REAR CLUTCH
APPLIED

MECHANICAL POWER FLOW – SECOND GEAR

(a)

FRONT CLUTCH
APPLIED

REAR CLUTCH
APPLIED

MECHANICAL POWER FLOW – THIRD GEAR

(b)

FIGURE 4-32 In second gear, the sun gear and front clutch drum are held stationary by the band (a). In third gear, the clutch is applied so drum and sun gear are rotating at engine speed (b). The driver feels this change as shift quality. *(Courtesy of Nissan North America, Inc.)*

is held stationary by a band, and the hub and lined plates are rotating at engine speed. During this shift, the band is released, and the clutch is applied to turn the clutch at engine speed. Imagine that as the shift begins, the engine is at 3,000 rpm and the vehicle is going about 45 mph (72 km/h). In second gear, with a transmission ratio of 1.5:1, the drive shaft will be turning at 2,000 rpm. The time duration of the shift must be gradual enough so the engine's rpm will be smoothly lowered (in this case, from 3,000 to 2,000 rpm). The resulting 1:1 third-gear ratio will have the input turning the same speed as the drive shaft (Figure 4-32).

A shift should be smooth without any unusual noises. In order for this to occur, the clutches and bands must apply smoothly and quietly. The timing of the band releasing from

second gear and the clutch applying for third gear must be precise. Any improper noises such as squeaks, squawks, or shrieks or operation such as engine rpm flare, jerks, bumps, or harsh application are considered faults that need to be corrected.

When one apply device is released as another one is applied it is called a synchronous shift. The release and application of the two elements, the intermediate band and the high clutch, must be synchronized.

Clutch shift quality is controlled by the type of lining material and grooving, the use of wave or Belleville plates, the type of fluid used, and the speed at which fluid moves the piston.

A *wave plate* is an unlined plate that is wavy, not flat. A *Belleville plate,* like a Belleville spring, is also not flat (Figure 4-33). These are often called *cushion plates.* If either plate is used in a clutch pack, it will be placed between the piston and the first unlined plate or between the last unlined plate and the pressure plate. Both plates are designed to compress slightly under pressure during clutch application. The result is to slightly prolong the clutch apply time.

Again consider the time just before the 2–3 shift. The high clutch drum and unlined plates are stationary, and the hub and lined plates are revolving at about 3,000 rpm. Transmission

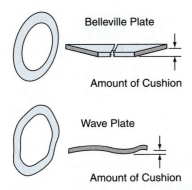

FIGURE 4-33 Two cushion plates: the Belleville plate has a coned shape. The wave plate has a wavy shape. Both of them will flatten slightly as the clutch is applied.

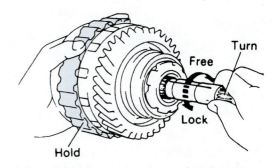

FIGURE 4-34 This one-way clutch allows the shaft to overrun in a clockwise direction. *(Courtesy of Toyota Motor Sales USA, Inc.)*

fluid enters the cylinder behind the clutch piston and starts the piston moving, reducing the clutch pack clearance. When the clearance has diminished, pressure will start squeezing the plates together. Suddenly, there is dynamic friction between the plates, and a power transfer takes place. If a cushion plate is used, clutch apply is slightly longer and a slight slippage occurs. This gives a smoother, less severe clutch application.

Many transmissions do not use Belleville or wave plates. Hydraulic controls (accumulators and orifices) are used to control piston movement and the desired shift quality. Electronically controlled transmissions have even greater ability to alter shift quality. The shift solenoids and hydraulic pressure control solenoids can be turned off and on, or cycled to produce the desired shifts. Electronic shift control will be described more completely in Chapter 8.

4.9.1 Shifts Involving One-Way Clutches

A one-way clutch is an ideal driving or reaction member for automatic shifts. It applies or holds when it is needed and self-releases or overruns when it is not needed. Its operation is controlled by the load direction on the inner or outer race so

shift timing is automatic. When the transmission upshifts, the reaction or driving member for the next gear is applied, and the one-way clutch simply overruns.

This is called a *nonsynchronous* or *asynchronous shift;* the shift elements do not need to be synchronized. It is also called a *freewheeling shift.*

4.9.2 Deceleration with One-Way Clutches

When the throttle is released while in a gear that uses a one-way clutch, the transmission will go into neutral as the one-way clutch overruns. This action is good if the vehicle is coasting to a stop, but can be a problem if going down a steep hill.

One-way clutches are normally used in the automatically selected drive gears, such as drive-1 or drive-2. The manually selected gears such as manual-1 or manual-2 will apply a reaction member like the low-reverse band or second-gear coast brake (a clutch) (Figure 4-34). The second reaction member locks the gearset into the desired gear during deceleration and coasting. This helps control vehicle speed while descending hills by using the engine's compression, commonly called compression braking. The added clutch or band also provides a stronger reaction member while pulling heavy loads such as a trailer.

SUMMARY

1. The power flow through a gearset is controlled by driving and reaction devices.

2. The driving and reaction devices are multiple-disc clutches, one-way clutches, and bands.

3. Multiple-disc clutches are the primary driving devices and are also used to hold planetary members in reaction.

4. One-way clutches primarily are used to hold planetary members in reaction, but can be used with a multiple-disc clutch to be a driving device.

5. Bands are used to hold a planetary member in reaction.

6. The timing of the apply and release of the apply devices has a direct effect on shift quality.

REVIEW QUESTIONS

The following questions are provided to help you study as you read the chapter.

1. The power flow through an automatic transmission is controlled by the _____ and _____ devices.

2. The most common driving member is the _____ _____ _____; a(n) _____ _____ is also used as a driving member.

3. List the seven major parts of a clutch assembly.

4. Usually the lined plates of a driving multiple-disc clutch are splined to the clutch _____, and the unlined plates are splined to the clutch _____.

5. List the four types of return springs used in a multiple-disc clutch are.

6. Piston travel or clutch plate clearance can be adjusted by replacing the _____ or _____.

7. The multiple-disc clutch torque capacity can be increased by increasing the _____ area, number of _____, _____ size, or by increasing the _____ pressure.

8. *Shift quality* is a term used to describe the _____ of a shift.

9. The two types of one-way clutches used in an automatic transmission are the _____ and _____.

10. One-way clutches _____ when turned in one direction and _____ when rotated in the other direction.

11. One-way clutches can be used as a _____ or a _____ apply device.

12. List the three types of apply devices that can be used to hold a planetary member.

13. A one-way clutch that is holding is referred to as being _____.

14. A multiple-disc clutch that is used in reaction has the steel plates splined to the _____.

15. Bands are applied by _____ pressure and released by _____ or _____ pressure.

16. A _____ shift sequence is a shift where the apply and release of the apply devices must be carefully timed.

17. A shift sequence that does not need to be timed is known as a _____ or _____ shift.

18. One-way clutches are only used in the _____ gear ranges.

19. The disadvantage of one-way clutches is that they do not provide _____ on deceleration.

20. Manual gear ranges use an additional _____ or _____ to provide more holding power when pulling a heavy load.

CHAPTER QUIZ

The following questions will help you check the facts you have learned. Select the answer that completes each statement correctly.

1. Student A says that in order for a planetary gearset to change the ratio and transmit torque, there must be an input and a reaction member. Student B says that the turbine shaft is the primary input to the transmission. Who is correct?

   a. Student A

   b. Student B

   c. Both A and B

   d. Neither A nor B

2. Student A says that neutral in a planetary gearset can be obtained by releasing all of the driving clutches. Student B says that neutral in a planetary gearset can be obtained by not applying any reaction members. Who is correct?

   a. Student A

   b. Student B

   c. Both A and B

   d. Neither A nor B

3. The apply device that is most commonly used as a driving member is a

   a. cone clutch.

   b. multiple-disc clutch.

   c. one-way clutch.

   d. band.

4. Student A says that some of the plates used in a multiple-disc clutch are lined with paper friction material. Student B says that some of the plates used in a multiple-disc clutch are unlined steel plates. Who is correct?

   a. Student A

   b. Student B

   c. Both A and B

   d. Neither A nor B

5. The ideal unlined steel plates _____.

   a. are perfectly flat

   b. have many very small nicks in their surface

   c. are not extremely smooth

   d. All of these

6. The most common material that the friction plate lining is made from is _____.

   a. paper

   b. asbestos

   c. inorganic fibers

   d. Any of these

7. A multiple-disc clutch is applied by _____.

   a. one or more coil springs

   b. a piston and air pressure

   c. hydraulic pressure pushing against a piston

   d. None of these

8. The grooves in the surface of a lined clutch plate _____.

   a. help cool the friction material

   b. allow oil to flow between the plates more easily

   c. are cut using different patterns depending on the clutch

   d. All of these

9. The torque-carrying capacity of a clutch is determined by the _____.

   a. number of plates

   b. amount of lining area on the plates

   c. amount of pressure squeezing the plates together

   d. All of these

10. Commonly used holding or reaction members are _____.

   a. bands

   b. one-way clutches

   c. multiple-disc clutches

   d. All of these

11. Student A says that a band is applied by a hydraulic servo and released by a spring or hydraulic pressure. Student B says that a clutch is applied by hydraulic pressure and released by a spring or hydraulic pressure. Who is correct?

   a. Student A

   b. Student B

   c. Both A and B

   d. Neither A nor B

12. When a multiple-disc clutch is used as a holding member, the lugs of the unlined plates are splined into _____.

   a. a very large drum

   b. the reaction carrier

   c. the transmission case

   d. the output shaft

13. The strongest of the band designs is the _____.

   a. single wrap

   b. heavy band

   c. double wrap

   d. flexible

14. Band clearance can be adjusted using a _____.

   a. threaded adjuster at the band anchor

   b. threaded adjuster at the servo lever

   c. selective sized servo piston rod

   d. Any of these, depending on the transmission

15. Student A says that the inner and outer races of a sprag clutch are perfectly round and smooth. Student B says that one of the races of a roller clutch is perfectly round and smooth while the other one has a series of ramps in it. Who is correct?

   a. Student A

   b. Student B

   c. Both A and B

   d. Neither A nor B

16. When a sprag clutch locks, the sprags _____.

   a. try to rotate but wedge between the two races

   b. roll down the ramps and wedge into place

   c. rotate into a position that unlocks them

   d. rotate with the free or rotating race

17. When a roller clutch unlocks, the rollers _____.

   a. are wedged between the two races

   b. rotate between the two races like a series of bearing rollers

   c. rotate to a position where they allow both inner and outer races to rotate

   d. None of these

18. A one-way clutch in a reverse direction _____.

   a. is applied by hydraulic pressure

   b. is released by a group of springs

   c. self-applies whenever one of the races tries to rotate in a reverse direction

   d. Any of these

19. The term used to describe when the apply devices do not need to be timed when shifting gears is _____.

   a. shift feel

   b. asynchronous

   c. shift quality

   d. All of these

20. The term used to describe the condition when the engine is used to slow the vehicle is _____.

   a. compression braking

   b. compression gear

   c. low gear

   d. forced braking

CHAPTER 5

POWER FLOW THROUGH TRANSMISSION GEARSETS

OBJECTIVES

After studying Chapter 5, the reader should be able to:

1. Explain how power can be transferred through a planetary gearset to produce the various ratios.

2. Identify the major components of simple, compound, and complex planetary gearsets.

3. Explain the role of the driving and reaction members in producing the different power flows.

4. Identify the basic gear train arrangements used in automatic transmissions.

5. Trace the power flow through various planetary gear trains.

KEY TERMS

5.1 RULES OF POWER TRANSFER

The gearset in an automatic transmission must provide a **neutral,** one or more **gear reductions,** a 1:1 or **direct-drive ratio,** a *reverse,* and an **overdrive.** Some manufacturers are currently using five-, six-, seven, and even eight-speed transmissions.

To provide the various gear ratios, planetary gearsets are combined in different arrangements. The same gearset design can be found in more than one make or model of transmission. A simple planetary gearset has a sun gear, ring gear, and planet carrier with two or more planet gears (Figure 5-1). Two or more simple gearsets can also be combined using different arrangements to provide more gear ratios. A complex planetary gearset combines one or more of the planetary members. Two examples of compound gearsets are:

- *Simpson gear train,* which combines one sun gear with two carriers with planet gears and two ring gears (Figure 5-2); and
- *Ravigneaux gearset,* which combines one carrier that has two sets of planet gears with two sun gears, and one ring gear (Figure 5-3).

Gearsets can be used in combination, which will result in additional ratios.

- A simple planetary gearset and a Simpson gearset can be combined to get four- and five-speed transmissions.
- A Ravigneaux gearset and a simple planetary gearset can be combined to get six, seven, and eight speeds. This arrangement is known as the **LePelletier gear train.**

FREQUENTLY ASKED QUESTION

HOW MANY SPEEDS WERE AVAILABLE IN EARLY AUTOMATIC TRANSMISSIONS?

At one time, Chevrolet used a transmission (the Turboglide) that had only a single forward speed. There were several two-speed transmissions: the Chrysler Powerflite, Ford Fordomatic and Merc-O-matic two-speed, General Motors Powerglide, Toyota Toyoglide, and Honda Hondamatic. These transmissions had a reduction and a direct drive. During the 1960s and 1970s, most automatic transmissions were three speeds, with high gear being a direct drive. The demand in the 1970s and 1980s for improved fuel economy and reduced emissions resulted in four-speed transmissions, with fourth gear being an overdrive.

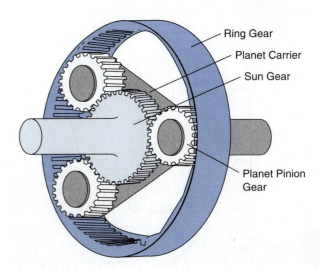

FIGURE 5-1   A simple planetary gearset consists of a sun gear, ring gear, planet carrier, plus a group of planet pinion gears. To produce a power flow, one part is the input, one part is held in reaction, and one part becomes the output.

Knowledge of the arrangement or type of gearset will help to understand similar transmissions without memorizing the power flow for each transmission.

The power flow through the gearset (the gear ratio) is changed by applying or releasing the appropriate driving device(s) and reaction device(s). The following rules of power flow explain the power flow through a gearset.

- One planetary member must provide input (usually by applying a clutch). This *driving member* or input member will be turned by the engine through the torque converter.
- One planetary member must drive the output shaft; this will be the output member.
- To produce a ratio change, one planetary member must be a **reaction member** (usually by applying a band, holding clutch, or self-applying **one-way clutch**).
- To get a 1:1 ratio, two planetary members must be driven, and there can be no reaction device.
- Neutral occurs when none of planetary members are driving or held in reaction

To understand the power flow through a particular automatic transmission, consider each part of the gearset as a simple planetary gearset. Identify which planetary member is driven for the input, which one is held in reaction, and which one is the output for each of the gear ratios (Table 5-1).

5.1.1 Planetary Gear Ratios

A simple planetary gearset can produce seven different gear ratios, plus neutral. Changing the gear ratios is done by changing the input (driving) and the reaction (held) member. These

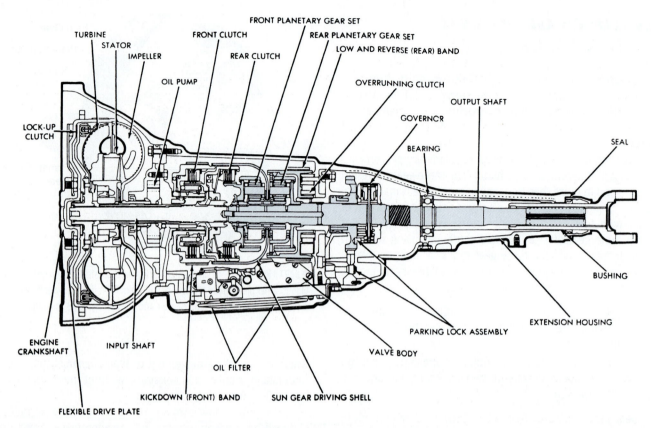

FIGURE 5-2 A Simpson gear train transmission. Note that the two gearsets (front and rear) use the same sun gear. Also note that one carrier and the sun gear can be the reaction members. The sun gear and one ring gear can be input members, and the other carrier and ring gear can be output members. *(Courtesy of Chrysler Corporation)*

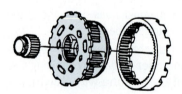

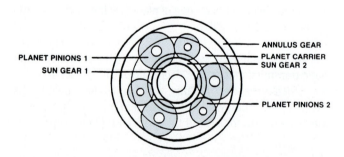

FIGURE 5-3 A Ravigneaux gearset has two sun gears (one small [sun gear 1] and one large [sun gear 2]), one carrier with a set of short pinions (planet pinions 1) and a set of long pinions (planet pinions 2), and a single ring gear. *(Courtesy of Chrysler Corporation)*

various conditions are illustrated in Figure 5-4 and described as follows:

A: If the ring gear is held and the sun gear is driven, the planet gears are forced to rotate as they walk around inside the ring gear. The result is a torque increase and a speed reduction. The formula for calculating the gear ratio is (sun + ring) ÷ sun.

B: If the ring gear is held and the carrier is driven, the planet gears are forced to rotate as they walk around inside the ring gear. This is the reciprocal, or inverse (opposite), of A. The opposite of a reduction ratio is an overdrive ratio. The formula for calculating the gear ratio is sun ÷ (sun + ring).

C: If the sun gear is held in reaction and the ring gear is driven, the planet gears are forced to rotate as they walk around the sun gear. The result is a torque increase and a speed reduction. The formula for calculating the gear ratio is (sun + ring) ÷ ring.

D: If the sun gear is held and the carrier is driven, the planet gears are forced to rotate as they walk around the sun gear. The result is a speed increase and a torque reduction. The

TABLE 5-1   Planetary rules

Neutral, Forward, or Reverse	Reduction, Overdrive, or Direct Drive	Planetary Gear Action
Neutral		When there is no driving member or reaction member, neutral results.
Forward	Direct Drive, 1:1	When there are two driving members, direct drive occurs.
Forward	Reduction	When the carrier is the output, a forward reduction occurs.
Forward	Overdrive	When the carrier is the input, an overdrive occurs.
Reverse	Reduction or OD	When the carrier is the reaction member, a reverse occurs.
F or R	OD	When the sun gear is the output, an overdrive occurs.
F or R	Reduction	When the sun gear is the input, a reduction occurs.
Reverse	Reduction or OD	When one external gear drives another, reverse rotation occurs.
Forward	Any	When an external gear drives an internal gear or vice versa, same-direction rotation occurs.

formula for calculating the gear ratio is ring ÷ (sun + ring). This ratio is the reciprocal of C.

E: If the carrier is held and the sun gear is driven, the planet gears will rotate and act as idlers; the planet gears drive the ring gear in a direction opposite to the sun gear. The result is a reverse with a torque increase and a speed reduction. The formula for calculating the gear ratio is ring ÷ sun.

F: If the carrier is held and the ring gear is driven, the planet gears will rotate and act as idlers, driving the sun gear in a direction opposite to the ring. The result is a reverse with a speed increase and a torque reduction. The formula for calculating the gear ratio is sun ÷ ring. This ratio is the reciprocal of E.

A technician rarely needs to calculate planetary gearset ratios. The gear ratio formulas are shown here for those who are interested or for reference.

When discussing transmission power flow, the input shaft usually turns in a clockwise direction. The direction of rotation for a rear wheel drive (RWD) transmission is normally viewed from the front of the transmission looking rearward. With a transaxle, this can become confusing because the front of the transmission is usually facing toward the right side of the vehicle. The right and left sides of a vehicle are determined by the driver's view of the vehicle from the driver's seat. When viewing a transaxle from the right side, the input shaft will turn in a clockwise direction. Some transmissions and transaxles use a drive chain to couple the torque converter and pump to the main gear section. On these units, the first input will be clockwise (viewed from the right), and the second input into the main case is considered to be counterclockwise, because it is normally viewed from the left (Figure 5-5).

(Imagine watching a clock's hands rotate from the back side.) An exception is that the engine and transaxle in some Hondas rotate in a counterclockwise direction.

5.2 TRANSAXLES

The following descriptions of transmission power flows also apply to transaxles. Most features of a transaxle are the same as those of a transmission; in the following discussions, we will treat them as the same and only refer specifically to a transmission or a transaxle when necessary. With the exception of CVTs that use an electromagnetic clutch, all automatic transmissions have the torque converter mounted on the input shaft at the front of the transmission. RWD transmissions have a single output shaft that connects to either the drive shaft of 2WD vehicles or transfer case for 4WD vehicles.

Most FWD vehicles have transverse-mounted engines, and the engine-transmission package must fit between the front suspension. A transaxle includes the transmission, final drive reduction gears, and the differential with its two output shafts. Ideally, these two shafts will exit the transaxle at the center of the vehicle to provide equal-length drive shafts.

Many transaxles have the differential mounted off-center; the result is unequal-length drive shafts (Figure 5-6). Unequal-length drive shafts can cause the vehicle to pull to one side during acceleration; this is called *torque steer*. Torque steer is caused by the unequal CV joint angles, by the length of the shafts, and by the tendency for the longer drive shaft to twist. The vehicle turns toward the side that has the longer drive shaft. Some vehicles use a short intermediate drive shaft to shorten the length of the long axle and equalize the CV joint angles.

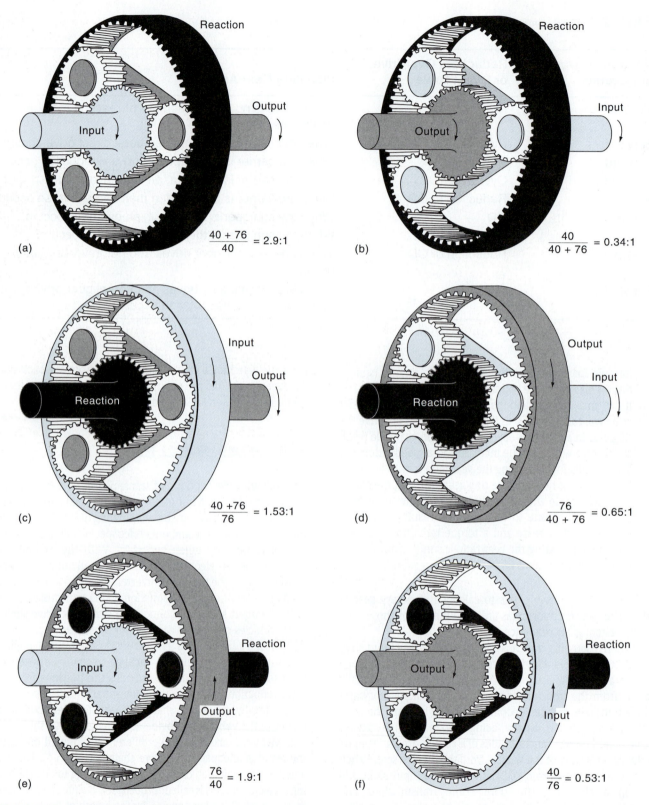

Reaction

Output

Input

$$\frac{40 + 76}{40} = 2.9:1$$

(a)

Reaction

Output

Input

$$\frac{40}{40 + 76} = 0.34:1$$

(b)

Input

Output

Reaction

$$\frac{40 + 76}{76} = 1.53:1$$

(c)

Output

Input

Reaction

$$\frac{76}{40 + 76} = 0.65:1$$

(d)

Input

Reaction

Output

$$\frac{76}{40} = 1.9:1$$

(e)

Output

Reaction

Input

$$\frac{40}{76} = 0.53:1$$

(f)

FIGURE 5-4 The gear ratio through a planetary gearset depends on which part is driven, which part is held, and which part is the output. The formula used to calculate the ratio is included with each illustration. Each gear set uses a 40-tooth sun gear and a 76-tooth ring gear.

Various designs are used to shorten transaxle length and equalize drive shaft length. One design mounts the torque converter, pump, and valve body above the main case, and a drive chain and sprockets connect the torque converter with the transmission input shaft. The General Motors transaxles and the Ford AX4N and AX4S are examples of this arrangement (Figure 5-7). The Chrysler 31TH uses a gear train at the output of the gearset and a short intermediate shaft to position the final drive closer to the center of the vehicle (Figure 5-8). The

Ford CD4E uses a drive chain and sprockets to connect the gearset output with the final drive and differential (Figure 5-9).

Some FWD vehicles mount the engine lengthwise, longitudinal, to allow a longer transaxle. Longitudinal transaxles

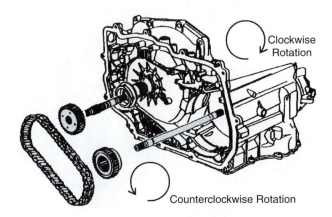

FIGURE 5-5   When a transmission or transaxle is viewed from the engine end, the rotation of the torque converter and input shaft is in a clockwise direction. If the gearset is driven by a chain and sprockets, the rotation is counterclockwise.

FIGURE 5-7   This transaxle uses a drive chain and two sprockets to transfer torque from the torque converter at the left to the gear train. *(Courtesy of BorgWarner, Morse TEC)*

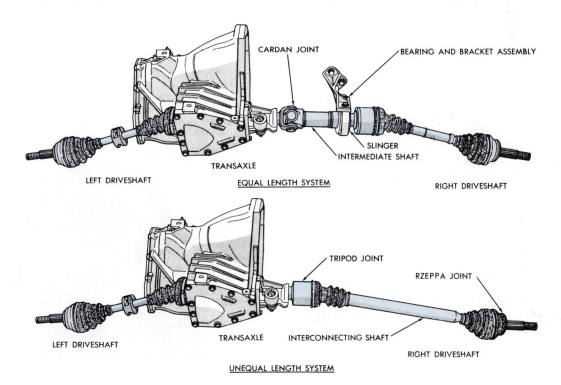

FIGURE 5-6   This transaxle has a drive shaft for each front wheel. To reduce torque steer, the top unit has equal-length shafts; note the two-part right drive shaft. The lower unit uses a larger tubular shaft on the right side. *(Courtesy of Chrysler Corporation)*

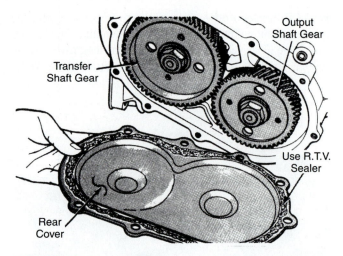

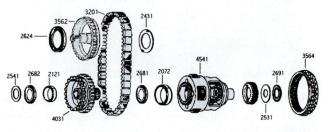

FIGURE 5-8 This transaxle uses a pair of transfer gears to transfer torque to the transfer shaft and final drive gears. *(Courtesy of Chrysler Corporation)*

FIGURE 5-9 A CD4E transaxle uses a chain (3201) to transfer torque from the planetary gearset (3562) to the final drive (4031) and differential (4541). *(Courtesy of Aceomatic Recon)*

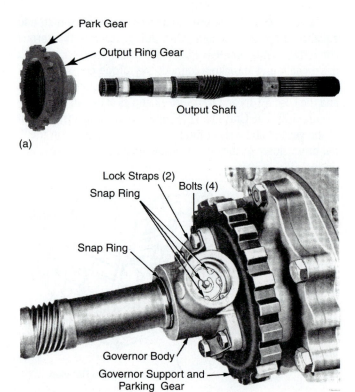

FIGURE 5-10 The park gear can be built into one of the planetary output members like this output ring gear (a) or as a separate member attached to the transmission output shaft (b). Note that B also supports the governor. *(a is courtesy of Slauson Transmission Parts, www.slauson.com; b is courtesy of Chrysler Corporation)*

are used exclusively by Subaru (the Justy is an exception) and in some Chrysler, Honda, Toyota, and Volkswagen vehicles.

Other important design features of new transaxles are lighter weight and reduced friction. Current engine designs tend to have smaller displacement with reduced torque output. All of these features improve vehicle efficiency. Improved fuel mileage and reduced emissions become more important every year.

5.3 PARK

Every automatic transmission and transaxle includes a *park* range. A shift into park prevents the transmission's output shaft from turning, holding the vehicle stationary. The parking gear has gearlike teeth and is mounted on the output member of the transmission (Figure 5-10). The park pawl (sometimes called a lever) moves on a pivot pin in the case.

In all gear positions except park, the park pawl is held away from the park gear teeth by a spring. When the gear selector is moved to PARK, a circular cam on the end of the park actuating rod pushes the pawl into mesh with the gear teeth. This holds the gear and output shaft stationary (Figure 5-11).

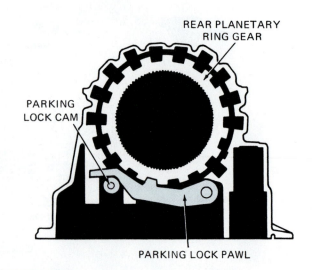

FIGURE 5-11 When the control rod is moved, the locking cam pushes the pawl into engagement with the parking gear. *(Courtesy of Chrysler Corporation)*

The actuating cam is spring loaded. If the gear teeth and pawl are not aligned, the gear selector lever can still be shifted into park. When the output shaft rotates slightly, the spring moves the cam, which in turn moves the pawl into engagement.

The shift into park is a mechanical connection that should be made with the drive shaft stopped. It is recommended that the shift to park should be made after the parking brake is applied. If the vehicle is rolling as park is engaged, damage to the park pawl or gear could result.

5.4 TRANSMISSION SCHEMATICS

Transmission parts and operation are often illustrated using pictures and cutaway drawings. They show the bare essentials of the transmission gear train in the simplest way possible. When you look at the typical cutaway view of a gear train, the transmission is usually split lengthwise through the middle. This shows the relationship of the parts, but in many cases, it is difficult to tell where one part stops and another begins, making it difficult to trace the path of the power flow. Many exploded views of the internal parts show the front or back of a clutch, carrier, or gear, but it is difficult to tell what the backside connects to unless a separate view is given. Exploded views are typically used by parts personnel to identify parts.

An easier way to view transmission operation is by using schematics. Transmission schematics resemble stick drawings (Figure 5-12). Schematics use symbols for the parts and a line shows the link between the parts. Similar to electrical schematics, the major objective is to simplify the transmission as much as possible (Figure 5-13). A schematic is most useful when tracing the power flow. At this time, there is no industry-wide standard for automatic transmission symbols.

The Type 1 gear train schematic (Figure 5-14) shows that the transmission input from the torque converter splits and goes to two clutches. One clutch can drive the front (left side) ring gear, and the other clutch can drive the sun gear that is common to both gearsets. The sun gear can also be held in reaction by the **intermediate band.** The other reaction member is the rear carrier, and it can be held by either the low-reverse

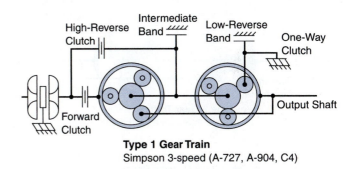

Type 1 Gear Train
Simpson 3-speed (A-727, A-904, C4)

FIGURE 5-12 The Type 1 gearset is a three-speed Simpson gear train that uses bands to hold the sun gear and reaction carrier. Note that the reaction carrier can also be held by a one-way clutch.

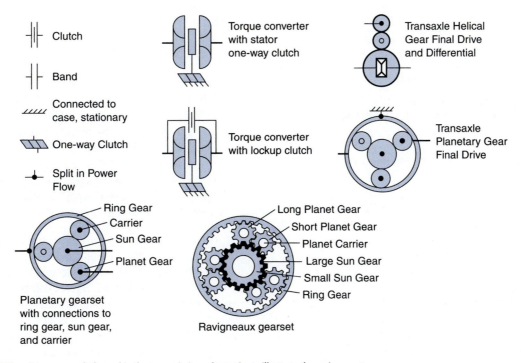

FIGURE 5-13 Common symbols used in the transmission schematics to illustrate the various parts.

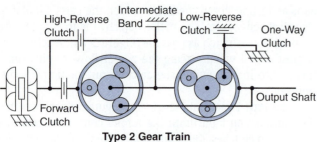

Type 2 Gear Train
Simpson 3-speed (C6)

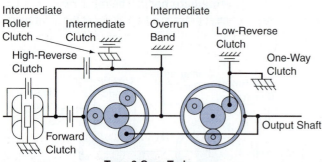

Type 3 Gear Train
Simpson 3-speed (THM 350)

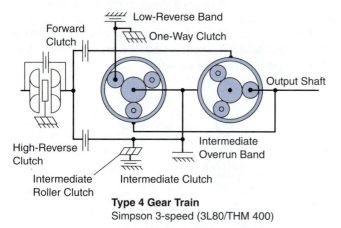

Type 4 Gear Train
Simpson 3-speed (3L80/THM 400)

FIGURE 5-14 These gear train types are all Simpson three-speed units that use different apply devices or, in the Type 4, a different gearset arrangement.

band or the one-way clutch. The output of the gearset is either the front carrier or the rear ring gear because they both connect to the output shaft.

5.5 SIMPSON GEAR TRAIN TRANSMISSIONS

The Simpson gear train is a compound gearset commonly used in many three-speed transmission/transaxles. Most of the automatic transmissions used in domestic vehicles during the

1960s and 1970s used this gear train. The better known Simpson gear train transmissions are:

Aisin-Warner: Three-speed models
Chrysler Corporation: 36 and 37 RH (Torqueflite A-727 and A-904) transmissions and the 31TH (A-404, A-413, A-415, and A470) transaxles
Ford Motor Company: Cruisomatic C3, C4, C5, and C6 and JATCO transmissions
General Motors: The 3L80 (THM 400), THM 200, 250, 350, 375, and 425 transmissions and 3T40 (THM 125) and THM 325 transaxles
JATCO: Three-speed models
Toyota: A40, A41, A130, A131, and A132

NOTE: Aisin-Warner AW and JATCO (Japanese Automatic Transmission Company) are independent transmission manufacturers; they manufacture transmissions that are used by various vehicle manufacturers.

NOTE: Manufacturers occasionally change transmission model designations. In this book, the older designations are placed in parentheses, for example, current designation: 3T40; old designation: (THM 125). These are also listed in Appendix B.

Although transmissions using a Simpson gear train are similar, they are not identical. The power flow through the gearset is essentially the same. They all have two input or driving clutches and a one-way reaction clutch, but the reaction members vary (Figure 5-14). To help understand these different arrangements, we will group them into similar types:

- Type 1 transmissions use a band for both reaction members.
- Type 2 transmissions use a multiple-disc clutch for the reaction carrier and a band to hold the sun gear.
- Type 3 transmissions use a multiple-disc clutch, a one-way clutch, and an overrun band for the sun gear reaction member and a multiple-disc clutch to hold the reaction carrier.
- Type 4 transmissions use a multiple-disc clutch, a one-way clutch, and an overrun band for the sun gear reaction member and a band to hold the reaction carrier.

The major difference between these transmissions is the type of reaction member. A multiple-disc clutch can handle more torque than a band. It has a much larger friction area and multiple case connections. A clutch is more complex than a band and requires more space. Type 3 and 4 units are **nonsynchronous** (asynchronous) designs. The 2–3 upshift timing is less critical because the disc clutch is used with a one-way clutch; the clutch stays applied while the one-way clutch simply overruns as the upshift occurs (Figure 5-15). The band used in **synchronous**

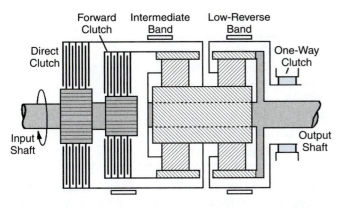

FIGURE 5-15   The one-way clutch of this Type 1 gearset serves as the reaction member in Drive 1. The low-reverse band is applied in manual 1 to allow compression braking.

designs must be released at an exact time for the upshift, and it must reapply at the exact time during a downshift.

The nonsynchronous arrangement is great for upshifts, but is ineffective during deceleration. Similar to the one-way clutch in first gear, the one-way clutch overruns during deceleration. An overrun band is used in manual-2 range for compression braking.

Type 4 transmissions, the 3L80 (THM 400), have the gearset turned end for end. In this arrangement, the input ring gear is at the back of the transmission, and the output ring gear is at the front. This transmission uses a center support to hold the inner race of the low-roller clutch and house the intermediate clutch piston. Type 4 units are nonsynchronous because of the two one-way clutches.

As mentioned, the Simpson gearset consists of a double sun gear that is meshed with the planet gears of the two carriers (Figure 5-16). This sun gear is also called a compound or common sun gear. One of the carriers (usually the front) is attached to the output shaft, and the other carrier serves as a reaction member. It is called the reaction carrier in some transmissions. One ring gear (usually the front) is the input and is splined to a driving clutch. The other ring gear is the output ring gear, and it is attached to the output shaft. The sun gear is attached to a driving clutch through an input shell, making it an input member, but it can also be a reaction member, held stationary by a band or a multiple-disc holding clutch (Table 5-2). In most transmissions, the sun gear is the same size at both ends, but in some transmissions, the rear section has a smaller sun gear so first and reverse gears have lower ratios.

Manufacturers usually provide clutch and band application charts for their transmissions, and these charts show which apply devices are used for each gear range. Each apply device drives a particular gearset member or holds it in reaction. Clutch and band charts are very helpful in understanding the power flow through a transmission. They are also very helpful when diagnosing transmission failures (Table 5-3).

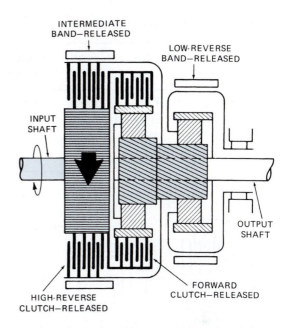

FIGURE 5-16   If both the high-reverse and forward clutches are released, then the transmission is in neutral. Note that the sun gear can be of two different sizes.

TABLE 5-2   Planetary gear actions

Ring Gear	Sun Gear	Planet Carrier	Ratio
Held	Input	Output	Reduction
Held	Output	Input	Overdrive
Input	Held	Output	Reduction
Input	Output	Held	Reverse Overdrive
Output	Held	Input	Overdrive
Output	Input	Held	Reverse Reduction
Input	Input	Output	Direct Drive

5.5.1 Neutral

Neutral is achieved by not applying the input clutches. Power enters the transmission from the torque converter but only travels as far as the released clutches (Figure 5-17). When shifted into neutral, some transmissions apply one of the clutches needed for first or reverse to prevent a harsh engagement when the vehicle is shifted into gear.

5.5.2 First Gear

The Simpson gearset has two slightly different first gears—drive-1 and manual-1—and the difference is how the reaction carrier is held. In both gear ranges, power flows through the gearset when the front ring gear is driven and the reaction

TABLE 5-3   Simpson gear train summary

Gear	Front Ring	Front Carrier	Sun	Rear Carrier	Rear Ring
First	Input	Reaction	Output/input	Reaction	Output
Second	Input	Output	Reaction	—	—
Third	Input	Output	Input	—	—
Reverse	—	—	Input	Reaction	Output

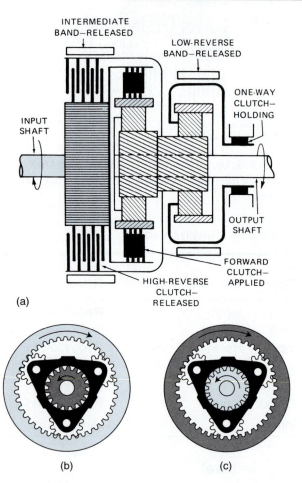

FIGURE 5-17   In drive-1, the front ring gear is driven while the rear carrier is held by the one-way clutch (a). A reverse reduction occurs in both the front unit (b) and the rear unit (c).

carrier is held. All Simpson gearsets use a clutch to drive the front (input) ring gear. Transmission Types 1 and 4 use a one-way clutch and a band and Types 2 and 3 use a one-way clutch and a holding clutch to hold the reaction carrier. In drive-1, the one-way clutch is used; it provides self-application and release. In manual-1, a band or holding clutch is applied to provide engine compression braking during deceleration.

When manual-1 (low) is selected, the one-way clutch is assisted by either a band (Types 1 and 4) or multiple-disc clutch (Types 2 and 3). The band is called the *low and reverse* or *low-reverse band*. The multiple-disc clutch is called a **low-reverse clutch**. The power flow is exactly the same as drive-1 except that power can be transmitted from the drive shaft to the engine during deceleration. This provides engine (compression) braking as the vehicle slows. Engine braking is easily noticed by comparing the deceleration of a vehicle in drive-1 and manual-1. For simplicity, we will call this holding member either a low-reverse band or a low-reverse clutch in this text.

Power Flow: Simpson Drive-1.   In drive-1 (low):

- The **forward clutch** is applied to drive the input ring gear in a clockwise direction.
- The output/front carrier will not rotate because it is connected to the drive shaft.

NOTE: The front carrier becomes a rotating reaction member when the vehicle starts moving.

- The front planet gears are driven clockwise.
- The sun gear is driven in a reverse direction (counterclockwise) at a reduction speed.
- The reaction carrier is held from turning counterclockwise by the one-way clutch (or the low-reverse band or clutch in manual-1).
- The rear planet gears are driven clockwise.
- The rear ring gear is driven clockwise at a reduced speed.
- The output shaft and drive shaft are driven clockwise at a reduced speed.

The gearset is producing two reverse reduction ratios, and the result is a forward (clockwise) rotation of the drive shaft. The overall ratio will be about 2.45:1 to 2.74:1 depending on the size of the gears.

5.5.3 Second Gear

The sun gear must be held stationary in second gear. This is done by a band in Type 1 and 2 transmissions or a multiple-disc clutch plus a one-way clutch in Type 3 and 4 transmissions. Type 3 and 4 transmissions use an **intermediate clutch** and an *intermediate one-way clutch* (Figure 5-18). When the intermediate clutch is applied, it holds the outer race of the intermediate roller clutch stationary. The one-way clutch locks,

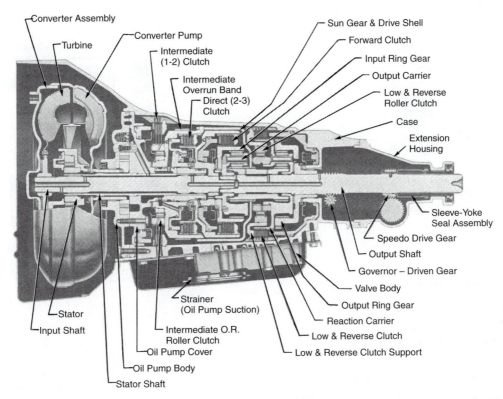

FIGURE 5-18   The intermediate clutch and intermediate roller clutch hold the sun gear from rotating in second gear in the THM 350, Type 3 gearset. The intermediate overrun band is used in manual-2 for compression braking. *(Reprinted with permission of General Motors)*

holding the sun gear from rotating counterclockwise. Because the one-way clutch will only hold in one direction, these units have two slightly different power flows in second gear: *drive-2* and **manual-2.** Manual-2 applies an intermediate overrun band to provide engine compression braking during deceleration. For simplicity, we will call this reaction member either an intermediate band or intermediate clutch in this text.

Power Flow: Simpson Drive-2.

In drive-2 (intermediate):

- The forward clutch stays applied to drive the input ring gear clockwise (Figure 5-19).
- The intermediate band or clutch applies to hold the sun gear stationary.
- The front planet gears are driven clockwise and walk around the sun gear.
- The front carrier is driven clockwise.
- The front carrier drives the output shaft clockwise at about a 1.5:1 ratio.

5.5.4 Third Gear

Third gear in this gearset is direct drive with a 1:1 ratio. It is produced by applying both driving clutches (forward and high-reverse) and either releasing the intermediate

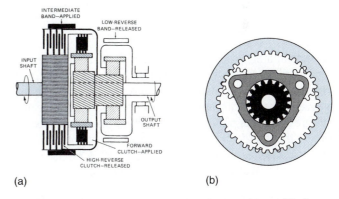

(a)   (b)

FIGURE 5-19   In second gear, the ring gear is driven while the sun gear is held, the planet gears walk around the sun gear and force the carrier to revolve at a reduced speed.

band in synchronous transmissions (Types 1 and 2) or allowing the intermediate roller clutch to overrun in nonsynchronous transmissions (Types 3 and 4). The gearset locks up because the ring gear is trying to turn the planet pinions clockwise while the sun gear is trying to turn them counter clockwise.

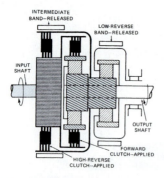

FIGURE 5-20 In third gear, both driving clutches are applied so two members (the ring and sun gears) of the same gearset are driven. This locks the gears and produces a 1:1 gear ratio.

Power Flow: Simpson Drive-3.

In drive-3 (high):

- The forward clutch stays applied to drive the input ring gear clockwise.
- The **high-reverse clutch** applies to drive the sun gear clockwise.
- The front planet gears become locked in the carrier.
- The front carrier is driven clockwise at the same speed as the ring and sun gears (Figure 5-20).
- The front carrier drives the output shaft clockwise at a 1:1 ratio.

5.5.5 Reverse

Reverse in a Simpson gear train occurs when the high-reverse clutch and the low-reverse band or clutch are applied. The high-reverse clutch drives the sun gear while the carrier in the rear gearset is held stationary by the low-reverse band or clutch (Figure 5-21). The planet gears act as idlers, reversing the power flow as they transfer power from the smaller sun gear to the larger ring gear. Gear action is shown in Figure 5-4E. A reverse reduction is produced at the output ring gear of about 2.07:1 to 2.22:1.

Power Flow: Simpson Reverse.

In reverse:

- The high-reverse clutch is applied to drive the sun gear clockwise.
- The low-reverse band or clutch is applied to hold the rear carrier.
- The rear planet gears are driven counterclockwise.
- The rear ring gear is driven counterclockwise at a speed reduction.
- The rear ring gear drives the output shaft counterclockwise at a 2.07:1 to 2.22:1 ratio.

A summary of the Simpson gear train members used to produce the two reduction ratios, one direct and one reverse,

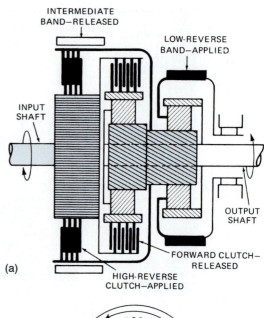

(a)

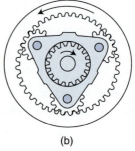

(b)

FIGURE 5-21 In reverse, the sun gear is driven while the carrier is held. The planet gears act as idlers and cause the ring gear to revolve in a reverse direction at a reduced speed.

is provided in Table 5-3. Clutch and band application charts for Type 1 and 3 gear trains are provided in Tables 5-4 and 5-5.

PROBLEM SOLVING 5-1 Imagine that you are working in a shop that specializes in transmission repair, and these problems are given to you:

Case 1 A 1970 Dodge pickup with an A727 transmission (Type 1) drives normally in all ranges, except there is an engine flare, indicating slippage, during a full-throttle 1–2 shift. Do you think a driving or reaction member could be faulty? If so, which one?

Case 2 A 1986 Chevrolet with a THM 350C transmission (Type 3) has no second gear. It has a delayed shift from first into third. There is a second gear if you shift manually from manual-1 to manual-2. What would be the cause of this problem? Which driving or reaction member is at fault?

5.6 SHIFT TIMING

As a vehicle accelerates from a stop to cruising speed, the driving and reaction members have to apply and release in an exact operating sequence. When they apply, they must come

TABLE 5-4   Simpson gear train band and clutch application, type 1

Gear	Forward Clutch	High-Rev. Clutch	Intermediate Band	Low-Rev. Band	One-Way Clutch
D1	Applied				Effective
D2	Applied		Applied		
D3	Applied	Applied			
M1	Applied			Applied	Effective
M2	Applied		Applied		
R		Applied		Applied	
Planetary Member	Drives Input Ring	Drives Sun	Holds Sun	Holds Reaction Carrier	Holds Reaction Carrier

TABLE 5-5   Simpson gear train band and clutch application, type 3

Gear	Forward Clutch	Hi-Rev. Clutch	Inter. Clutch	Inter. One-Way Clutch	Inter. Band	Low-Rev. Clutch	One-Way Clutch
D1	Applied						Effective
D2	Applied		Applied	Effective			
D3	Applied	Applied	Applied	Over running			
M1	Applied					Applied	Effective
M2	Applied		Applied	Effective	Applied		
R		Applied				Applied	
Planetary Member	Drives Input Ring	Drives Sun	Holds Sun	Holds Sun	Holds Sun	Holds Reaction Carrier	Holds Reaction Carrier

on at a precise rate. To illustrate this, we will follow an upshift sequence during a hard acceleration with shift points occurring at 4,800 rpm (Figure 5-22).

In first gear, the ratio will be 2.5:1, so the vehicle drive shaft will be revolving at 1,920 rpm (4,800 ÷ 2.5) when the 1–2 upshift occurs. Second gear has a ratio of 1.5:1, so the engine speed will drop from 4,800 to 2,800 rpm (1,920 × 1.5) during the shift.

The forward clutch is used in all the forward gear ranges. It is applied when the driver makes the neutral-to-drive shift, and it will stay applied through all forward gears, driving the front ring gear at input shaft speed. In first gear, the sun gear is revolving in a reverse direction. During the 1–2 shift, the intermediate reaction member must apply gradually, smoothly, and firmly so the sun gear will come to a stop during the time duration required for the shift. If it stops too fast, the shift will be harsh. The shift will be long and drawn out if it stops too slowly. This shift is relatively easy to accomplish because the one-way clutch will overrun and release the reaction carrier as the intermediate reaction member is applied (nonsynchronous shift). The duration or timing of this shift will be controlled by how fast the intermediate reaction member is applied. Some of the variables that affect application time are servo diameter,

fluid feed orifice diameter, and use of an accumulator. These are described in Chapter 7. Shift timing can also be controlled electronically as described in Chapter 8.

When the 2–3 shift occurs, the vehicle drive shaft will be turning at 3,200 rpm (4,800 ÷ 1.5), and during the shift the engine speed will drop from 4,800 to 3,200 rpm. Remember that this is a 1:1 gear ratio, and the sun gear speed must increase from a stop to input shaft speed as the direct clutch is applied.

The synchronous Type 1 and 2 transmissions that use a band for the intermediate reaction member have a potential timing problem during the 2–3 shift. The band must release as the direct clutch is applied. If the band releases too quickly, the transmission will fall back into first gear, and an engine overspeed or flare will occur (3,200 × 2.5 = 8,000 rpm). If the band releases too slowly or the direct clutch applies too rapidly, the combination will try to bring the engine and the vehicle to a stop. This produces a very harsh shift.

The intermediate overrunning clutch in the Type 3 or 4 transmission eliminates any timing problem. As the direct clutch applies, the sun gear picks up speed because the overrunning clutch simply overruns.

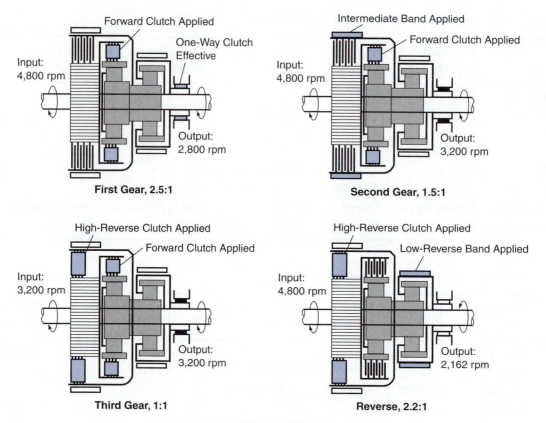

Triple 1 Shift Sequence

FIGURE 5-22 The full-throttle shift sequence for a Type 1 transmission showing the apply devices and the output shaft speed at the 1–2 and 2–3 upshifts. Reverse is also shown.

5.7 SIMPSON GEAR TRAIN PLUS AN ADDITIONAL GEARSET

The Simpson gear train with an additional simple planetary gearset is used to produce a four-speed overdrive transmission or transaxle.

The overdrive planetary gearset provides two speeds: direct 1:1 and overdrive. When the overdrive planetary gearset is in direct drive it turns the Simpson planetary gearset input at engine speed. When the overdrive gear train is in direct drive 1:1 the Simpson gear train will shift from first to second and then to third. If the overdrive planetary gearset is in overdrive it will turn the Simpson planetary gearset input faster than engine speed. The three-speed Simpson gear train will operate as described earlier. To get overdrive, the overdrive planetary gearset will be in overdrive and the Simpson gear set will be in direct 1:1. To get reverse, the overdrive gearset will be in direct and the Simpson will be in reverse.

The more common transmissions using this gearset are:

Chrysler 42RH (A-500), 46RH (A-518)
Ford 4R44E (A4LD), 5R55E, and E4OD

GM 4T80-E, THM-2004R, and 325–4L
Jeep AW-4
Nissan E4N7IB
Toyota A40 and A340 series

5.7.1 Overdrive

In most of these transmissions, the overdrive gearset is built into the area at the front of the case between the torque converter and the main gearset (Figure 5-23). The input shaft from the torque converter is connected to the carrier of the overdrive gearset, and the ring gear of the overdrive gearset is arranged so it becomes the input of the main gearset. The Chrysler 42RH and 46RH have the overdrive gearset built into the transmission extension housing to cause a speed increase between the main gearset and the output shaft (Figure 5-24). Each of these transmissions uses a different arrangement of bands and clutches so they fall into a different transmission category or type.

The input member for the overdrive gearset (a simple planetary gearset) is the planet carrier, and the output is the ring gear (Figure 5-25). The sun gear is a reaction member and can be held stationary by either a band or a multiple-disc

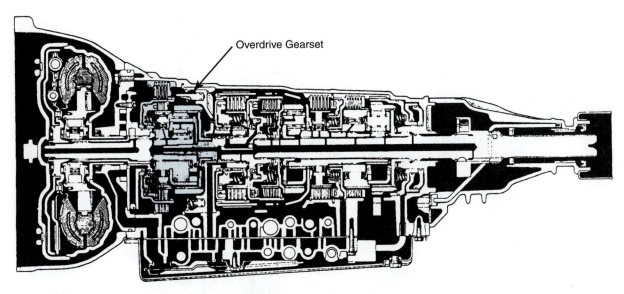

FIGURE 5-23   This A340E transmission sectional view shows the overdrive section between the pump and three-speed planetary gear section. *(Courtesy of Toyota Motor Sales USA, Inc.)*

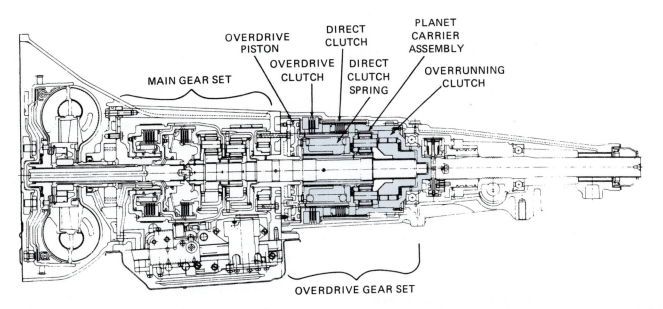

FIGURE 5-24   This Chrysler 42RH transmission cutaway view shows a three-speed, Simpson Type 1 gearset with an overdrive unit at the output end of the transmission. *(Courtesy of Chrysler Corporation)*

clutch. There is also a multiple-disc clutch that can lock the carrier to the sun gear and a one-way clutch. In the 4R44E/5R55E, the one-way clutch is placed so the carrier can drive the ring gear. In the others, the one-way clutch is placed so the sun gear cannot turn faster than the carrier. The overdrive friction members have different names depending on the transmission manufacturer.

Power is transmitted through the overdrive gearset at a 1:1 ratio by the one-way clutch in drive-1, 2, and 3 (Figure 5-26).

The 42RH and 46RH are a little unusual in that one hydraulic piston and return spring is used for both the direct clutch and the overdrive clutch (Type 5 gear train). The very strong return spring is used to release the overdrive clutch and apply the direct clutch. Hydraulic pressure at the piston releases the direct clutch and then almost immediately applies the overdrive clutch. With this arrangement, the gearset is locked in either direct drive or overdrive with the overrunning clutch transferring power while the upshift or downshift is made.

In the 4R44E/5R55E (Type 6), the power is transferred directly from the carrier to the ring gear. In the 2004R (Type 7), the gearset is locked because the one-way clutch does not

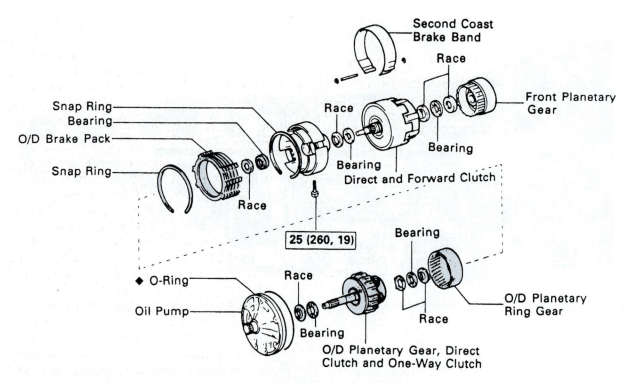

FIGURE 5-25   An exploded view of the A340E overdrive unit. The O/D one-way clutch provides a 1:1 ratio in D1, D2, and D3. The O/D direct clutch is used in manual gear ranges. The O/D brake pack is applied in D4. *(Courtesy of Toyota Motor Sales USA, Inc.)*

allow the sun gear to overrun the carrier. The Type 8 gear train illustrates the power flow through a Jeep AW-4 transmission.

Like other power flows using a one-way clutch, these gearsets overrun during deceleration and do not produce engine (compression) braking. To prevent this in manual-1, M2, or M3, the overdrive clutch in the 4R44E/5R55E, overrun clutch in the 200–4R, or the O/D direct clutch in the AW-4 are applied. This locks the overdrive gear assembly so it operates in direct drive in both acceleration and deceleration.

A shift sequence for a Type 6 transmission is illustrated in Figure 5-27, and a band and clutch chart is shown in Table 5-6. A summary of the input, reaction, and output members of the overdrive gearsets to produce the various ratios is given in Tables 5-7 and 5-8.

Power Flow: Overdrive Gearset.   In the overdrive gearset:

- The overdrive carrier is driven by the input shaft.
- The band or clutch is applied to hold the overdrive sun gear.
- The overdrive planet gears are driven clockwise and walk around the sun gear.
- The overdrive ring gear is driven clockwise at an overdrive speed.
- The overdrive ring gear drives the main gearset at a 0.69:1 to 0.75:1 ratio.

PROBLEM SOLVING 5-2   Imagine that you are working in a shop that specializes in transmission repair, and these problems are given to you:

Case 1   A 1998 Ford Ranger pickup with a 4R44E transmission (Type 6) drives normally in all ranges, except there is an engine flare, indicating slippage, during a full-throttle 1–2 shift. Do you think one driving or reaction member could be faulty? If so, which one?

Case 2   A 1990 Chevrolet Caprice with a TH 200-4R transmission (Type 7) does not move when in drive. It has manual-1, and there is a second gear if you shift manually from manual-1 to manual-2. What would be the cause of this problem? Which driving or reaction member is at fault?

5.8 RAVIGNEAUX GEARSETS

The Ravigneaux gearset uses a single carrier that has two sets of intermeshed planet gears, two sun gears, and a single ring gear. The planet gears are different lengths. The two sun gears have different diameters and are independent of each other. The long pinion gears mesh with the large sun gear, short pinions, and ring gear. The short pinions mesh with the small sun gear and the long pinion gears (see Figure 5-3). In some transmissions, the ring gear is in

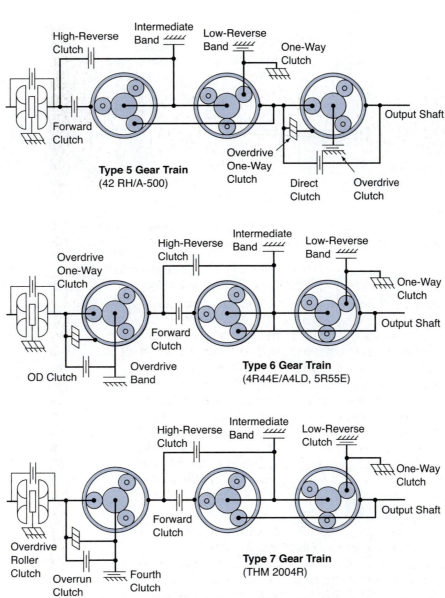

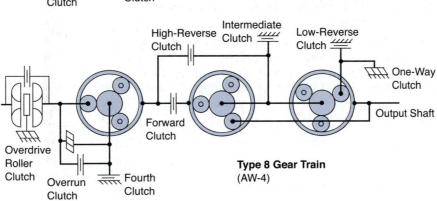

FIGURE 5-26   The Type 5, 6, 7, and 8 gearsets illustrate the different four-speed gear train arrangements that combine a Simpson three-speed gearset with an overdrive unit.

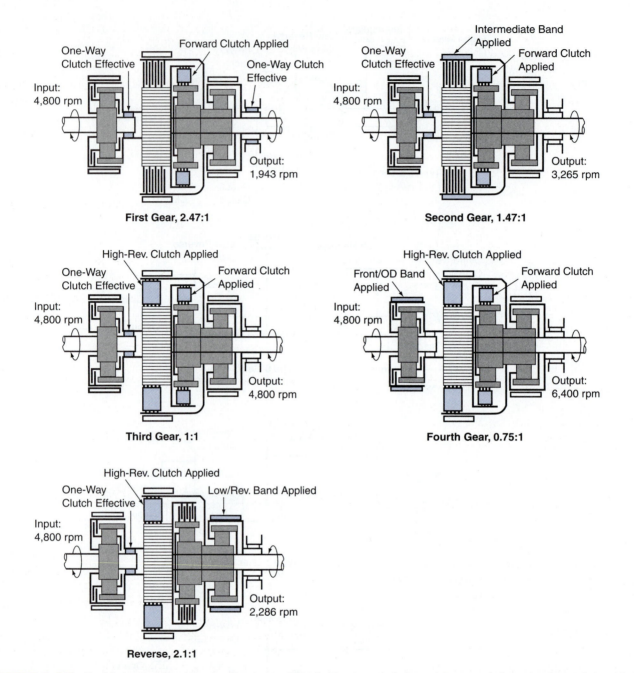

FIGURE 5-27 The full-throttle shift sequence for a Type 6 transmission showing the apply devices and the output shaft speed at the 1–2, 2–3, and 3–4 upshifts. Reverse is also shown.

mesh with the short pinions. The Ravigneaux gearset is used in:

Two-speed transmissions: the Chrysler Powerflite, the Ford two-speed, and the General Motors Powerglide, Dynaflow, and THM 300

Three-speed transmissions: the Ford FMX and General Motors 3L30 (THM 180)

Three-speed transaxles: the Ford ATX, KM 171 to 175 versions

Four-speed transmission: the Ford 4R70W (AOD)

Four-speed transaxles: the Ford 4EAT, KM 175 to 177, and ZF-4

NOTE: KM (Kyoto Transmission) and ZF (Zahnradfabrik Freidrichshafen) are independent transmission manufacturers; they manufacture transmissions that are used by various vehicle manufacturers.

TABLE 5-6 Simpson gear train plus overdrive band and clutch application, type 6

Gear	Forward Clutch	High-Reverse Clutch	Over-drive Clutch	O/D One-Way Clutch	Over-drive Band	Intermediate Band	Low/Rev. Band	Rear One-Way Clutch
D1	Applied			Effective				Effective
D2	Applied			Effective		Applied		
D3	Applied	Applied		Effective				
D4	Applied	Applied		Overrunning	Applied			
M1	Applied		Applied	Effective			Applied	Effective
M2	Applied		Applied	Effective		Applied		
M3			Applied	Effective				
R		Applied					Applied	
Planet Member	Drives Input Ring	Drives Forward Sun	Locks Front Sun & Ring	Drives Center Shaft	Holds Front Sun	Holds Forward Sun	Holds Reaction Carrier	Holds Reaction Carrier

TABLE 5-7 Shift strategy: four speed

Gear	Main Gearset	O/D Gearset	Ratio
1	1st gear	Direct	2.47:1
2	2nd gear	Direct	1.47:1
3	3rd gear	Direct	1:1
4	3rd gear	Overdrive	0.75:1

TABLE 5-8 Shift strategy: five speed

Gear	Main Gearset	O/D Gearset	Ratio
1	1st gear	Direct	2.47:1
2	1st gear	Overdrive	1.87:1
3	2nd gear	Direct	1.47:1
4	3rd gear	Direct	1:1
5	3rd gear	Overdrive	0.75:1

The exact arrangement of the gearset varies depending on the usage (Figure 5-28).

5.8.1 Two-Speed Ravigneaux Arrangement and Operation

Power Flows: Powerglide. In drive low:

- The primary sun gear is driven by the input shaft.
- The low band is applied to hold the secondary sun gear.

FREQUENTLY ASKED QUESTION

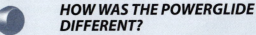

HOW WAS THE POWERGLIDE DIFFERENT?

Two-speed transmissions were used in the 1950s and 1960s. They are no longer in production, but so many were produced that they are still encountered. The most common was the Chevrolet Powerglide (Type 9 gearset).

In two-speed Ravigneaux transmissions, the small, **primary sun gear** is attached to the input shaft so it is always an input. The large sun gear, called the **secondary sun gear,** is either a reaction member or an input member. The carrier is the output member, and the ring gear can be a reaction member. A driving clutch is placed on the input shaft so the secondary sun gear can be driven, and a band, called a low band, is placed around the clutch drum so the secondary sun gear can be held in reaction. The clutch is often called the *high clutch,* and the band is called a *low band.* The ring gear is held by either a band (first version) or a multiple-disc clutch (second version), and this is called either a *reverse clutch* or a *reverse band* (Figure 5-29).

Neutral occurs in this gearset when none of the driving or reaction members are applied. The primary sun gear turns with the torque converter.

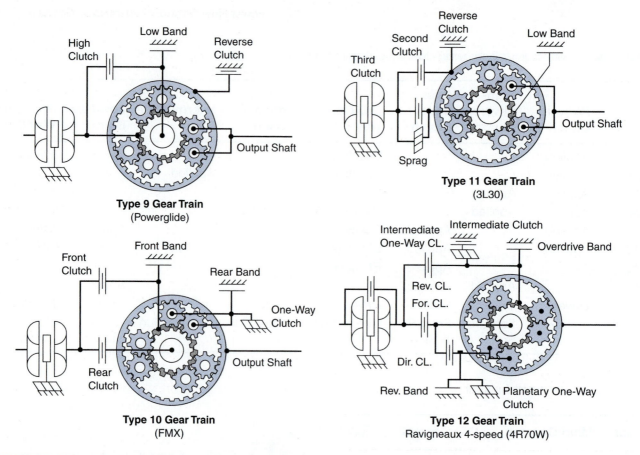

Type 9 Gear Train
(Powerglide)

Type 11 Gear Train
(3L30)

Type 10 Gear Train
(FMX)

Type 12 Gear Train
Ravigneaux 4-speed (4R70W)

FIGURE 5-28   The Type 9, 10, 11, and 12 gearsets illustrate the different three- and four-speed gear train arrangements that use a single Ravigneaux gearset.

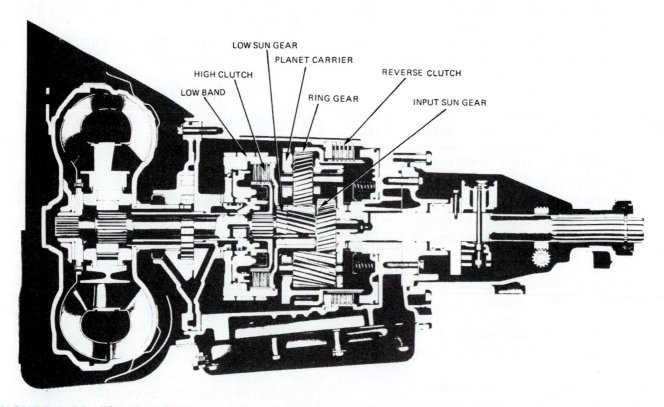

FIGURE 5-29   When a Powerglide is in low gear, the low band is applied to hold the low sun gear stationary; at this time, the long pinions will be driven by the input sun gear and walk around the low sun gear to drive the carrier. *(Reprinted with permission of General Motors)*

- The primary sun gear drives the long planet pinion gears counterclockwise.
- The long planet pinions drive the short planet pinions clockwise.
- The short planet pinions walk around the secondary sun gear.
- The planet carrier is driven clockwise at a reduction speed.
- The output shaft is driven clockwise at a 1.76:1 or 1.82:1 ratio.

In drive high:

- The primary sun gear is driven by the input shaft.
- The low band releases.
- The primary sun gear is driven by the input shaft.
- The long and short planet pinion gears become locked.
- The carrier is driven at input shaft speed.
- The output shaft is driven clockwise at a 1:1 ratio.

In reverse:

- The primary sun gear is driven by the input shaft.
- The reverse clutch is applied to hold the ring gear.
- The primary sun gear drives the long planet pinion gears counterclockwise.
- The long planet pinions drive the short planet pinions clockwise.
- The short planet pinions walk around inside the ring gear.
- The planet carrier is driven counterclockwise at a reduction speed.
- The output shaft is driven counterclockwise at a 1:76 to 1.82:1 ratio.

5.8.2 Three-Speed Ravigneaux Arrangement and Operation: First Version

There are two three-speed versions of the Ravigneaux gearset. The Ford FMX (Type 10 gearset) is the first version. It uses two driving clutches, two bands, and a one-way clutch. The ring gear is the output member, and the carrier with its two sets of planet pinion gears can be a reaction member held by either a band or the one-way clutch. The inner one-way clutch race is secured by a stationary transmission part called a *center support*. One sun gear (the smaller, rear, primary one) is driven by the front, *forward clutch*. The larger secondary sun gear is driven by the high-reverse clutch or held stationary by the intermediate band.

In neutral, both driving clutches are released, and the power flow from the torque converter goes no farther than the clutches.

Power Flows: FMX. In drive-1 (low):

- The forward clutch applies to drive the primary sun gear.
- The primary sun gear drives the short planet pinion gears counterclockwise.

- The carrier is held from turning counterclockwise by the one-way clutch (rear band in manual-1).
- The short planet pinions drive the long planet pinions clockwise.
- The long planet pinions drive the ring gear clockwise at a reduction speed.
- The output shaft is driven clockwise at a 2.4:1 ratio.

In drive-2 (intermediate):

- The forward clutch stays applied to drive the primary sun gear.
- The intermediate band applies to hold the secondary sun gear.
- The primary sun gear drives the short planet pinion gears counterclockwise.
- The short planet pinions drive the long planet pinions clockwise.
- The long planet pinions walk around the secondary sun gear.
- The long planet pinions drive the ring gear clockwise at a reduction speed.
- The output shaft is driven clockwise at a 1.47:1 ratio.

In drive-3 (high):

- The forward clutch stays applied to drive the primary sun gear.
- The intermediate band is released.
- The high-reverse clutch is applied to drive the secondary sun gear.
- The long and short planet pinion gears become locked.
- The ring gear is driven at input shaft speed.
- The output shaft is driven clockwise at a 1:1 ratio.

In reverse:

- The high-reverse clutch is applied to drive the secondary sun gear.
- The low-reverse band is applied to hold the carrier.
- The secondary sun gear drives the long planet pinion gears counterclockwise.
- The long planet pinions drive the ring gear counterclockwise at a reduction speed.
- The output shaft is driven in a reverse direction at a 2:1 ratio.

5.8.3 Three-Speed Ravigneaux Arrangement and Operation: Second Version

The General Motors 3L30 (THM 180) transmission (Type 11 gearset) and the Ford ATX transaxle use a slightly different arrangement of the Ravigneaux three-speed gearset. Both use two driving clutches, one holding clutch, a one-way clutch, and a band. The carrier with its two sets of planet pinion gears is the output member. The ring gear is meshed with the long planet pinion gearset and is arranged so it can be an input or a reaction member. We will use the 3L30 as an example while describing power flow through this gearset. Remember that power flow through an ATX is very similar.

The ring gear can be held stationary by the *reverse clutch*, or it can be driven by the *second clutch* (Figure 5-30). The smaller sun gear, called the input sun gear, can be driven by a clutch called the *third clutch*. There is also a one-way clutch in this sun gear drive arrangement that allows the sun gear to over-run the speed of the input shaft. The larger sun gear can be a re-action member. It is called the reaction sun gear and can be held by the *low band*.

Power Flow: 3L30. In drive-1 (low):

- The third clutch is applied to drive the input sun gear.
- The input sun gear drives the short planet pinion gears counterclockwise.
- The short planet pinions drive the long planet pinions clockwise.
- The low band is applied to hold the reaction sun gear.
- The long planet pinions walk around the reaction sun gear.

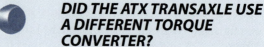

FREQUENTLY ASKED QUESTION

DID THE ATX TRANSAXLE USE A DIFFERENT TORQUE CONVERTER?

In some versions of the Ford ATX, a split-torque converter is used that has an internal planetary gearset. The ring gear of this set is connected to the front of the torque converter through a damper assembly so it will be driven at engine speed; the input sun gear is connected to the turbine shaft; and the carrier is connected to the intermediate shaft. The intermediate shaft (in the transaxles using this torque converter) drives the intermediate clutch in the main gear assembly. This arrangement produces a partial mechanical input of 38% in second gear and 94% in third gear, which reduces torque converter slippage and improves operating efficiency and fuel mileage.

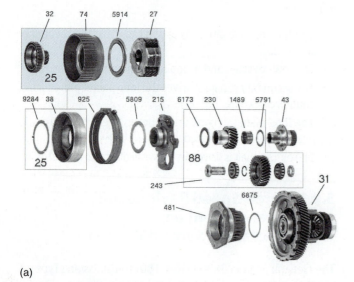

(a)

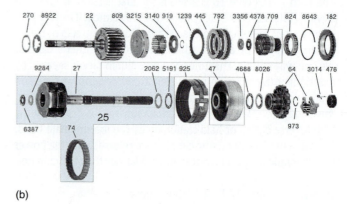

(b)

FIGURE 5-30 Exploded views of a Ford ATX (a) transaxle and a GM 3L30 (b) transmission gearset. Note the difference in the carriers (27). *(Courtesy of Slauson Transmission Parts, www.slauson.com)*

- The long planet pinions drive the carrier clockwise at a reduction speed.
- The output shaft is driven clockwise at a 2.4:1 to 2.8:1 ratio.

In drive-2 (intermediate):

- The second clutch is applied to drive the ring gear.
- The low band stays applied to hold the reaction sun gear.
- The ring gear drives the long planet pinions clockwise.
- The long plant pinions walk around the reaction sun gear.
- The long planet pinions drive the carrier clockwise at a reduction speed.
- The output shaft is driven clockwise at a 1.48:1 to 1.6:1 ratio.
- The long planet pinions drive the carrier clockwise at a reduction speed.
- The output shaft is driven clockwise at a 2.4:1 to 2.8:1 ratio.

In drive-3 (high):

- The second clutch stays applied to drive the ring gear.
- The third clutch is applied to drive the input sun gear.
- The long and short planet pinion gears become locked.
- The carrier is driven at input shaft speed.
- The output shaft is driven clockwise at a 1:1 ratio.

In reverse:

- The third clutch is applied to drive the input sun gear.
- The reverse clutch is applied to hold the ring gear.
- The input sun gear drives the short planet pinion gears counterclockwise.
- The short planet pinions drive the long planet pinions clockwise.
- The long planet pinions walk around inside the ring gear.
- The long planet pinions drive the carrier counterclockwise at a reduction speed.
- The output shaft is driven counterclockwise at a 1.9:1 to 2.1:1 ratio.

5.8.4 Four-Speed Ravigneaux Arrangement and Operation

The Ford 4R70W (AOD) (Type 12 gearset) uses a four-speed version of the Ravigneaux gear train. The gears in the 4R70W are arranged in a manner similar to the Type 10 Ford FMX. The first version of this transmission, the AOD, has an additional input shaft (the direct drive shaft) and an additional clutch (the direct clutch). These are arranged so the carrier can be an input member in third and fourth gears as well as a reaction member in first and reverse. The direct-drive shaft is driven by a damper assembly at the front of the

torque converter so it is a purely mechanical input into the gearset (Figure 5-31). Newer versions, such as the 4R70W, use a more conventional torque converter with a converter clutch and connect the direct clutch to the forward clutch by a short stub shaft.

The first-, second-, and reverse-gear power flows in the 4R70W are the same as those in the FMX, with the exception that the intermediate clutch is used to hold the carrier for a reaction member in second gear. In third gear, the direct-drive clutch is applied to drive the carrier while the forward clutch remains applied to drive the small, forward sun gear. This locks the planet gears and drives the ring gear in direct drive. The intermediate clutch remains applied, but it becomes ineffective because the intermediate one-way clutch overruns.

In summary, the input, reaction, and output members for the various power flows are shown in Figure 5-32. A clutch and band chart is shown in Table 5-9.

Power Flow: 4R70W. The 4R70W power flows for drive-1, D2, D3, and reverse are very similar to those of the FMX described in Section 5.8.2.1. The exception is that the drive-3 applies the forward and direct clutches.

In drive-4 (overdrive):

- The direct clutch stays applied to drive the carrier.
- The carrier drives the long planet pinion gears counterclockwise.
- The overdrive band is applied to hold the front sun gear.
- The long planet pinions walk around the front sun gear.
- The long planet pinions drive the ring gear clockwise at an overdrive speed.
- The output shaft is driven clockwise at a 0.67:1 ratio.

5.8.5 Four-Speed Ravigneaux Arrangement and Operation: Second Version

The General Motors 4L30-E transmission is a dual-unit transmission that is a combination of the Type 11 gear train with an overdrive unit at the front. This combination is similar to the Type 6, 7, and 8 gear trains. Like these other gearsets, the overdrive unit is kept in its lower ratio in first, second, and third and shifted into overdrive for fourth gear (Figure 5-33).

5.8.6 LePelletier Gear Train

The LePelletier gear train (Type 13 Gearset) is a recent development and combines a simple planetary gearset with a Ravigneaux gearset providing six forward speeds (Figure 5-34). The combination is fairly simple, using only five multiplate

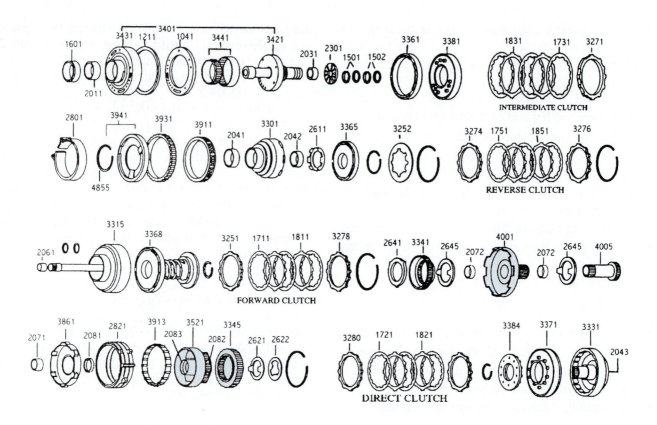

FIGURE 5-31   A stub shaft (not shown) is used to connect the turbine shaft and forward drum (3315) of the Ford 4R70W transmission to the direct clutch housing (3331). The direct clutch is used in third and fourth gears. *(Courtesy of Aceomatic Recon)*

clutches and, in some transmissions, a one-way clutch. Three of the clutches are driving members and the other two are used in reaction. This gearset is used in the Ford 6R60 and 6R80 and General Motors 6L80E transmissions, and transmissions produced by Aisin and ZF.

Because the ring gear is always an input and the sun gear is always a reaction member (it is splined to the back of the pump), the simple gearset is always in reduction. The C1 and C3 clutches can provide a reduced speed input to the Ravigneaux gearset. The Ravigneaux gearset is arranged like a Type 12 gearset, with three possible inputs and two reaction members.

This gearset has four reduction ratios and two overdrive ratios, with a gear ratio spread of over 6:1 (Figure 5-35). Compared to current five-speed transmissions, these six-speed transmissions have fewer control devices and weigh about 13% less. Because of the close gear ratios and lighter weight, they also promise fuel mileage increases of 5% to 7%, and provide faster acceleration.

PROBLEM SOLVING 5-3   Imagine that you are working in a shop that specializes in transmission repair, and these problems are given to you:

Case 1   A 1995 Ford Thunderbird with a 4R70W transmission (Type 12) drives normally in all ranges, except there is an engine flare, indicating slippage, during a full-throttle 1–2 shift. Do you think a driving or reaction member could be faulty? If so, which one?

Case 2   A 1978 Chevrolet Chevette with a TH 180C transmission (Type 11) has noisy first and second gears. It is okay in third gear. What would be the cause of this problem? Which driving or reaction member is at fault?

5.9 FOUR-SPEED OVERDRIVE GEARSET

A four-speed gearset was developed by General Motors and introduced in the 4L60 (THM 7004R) (Figure 5-36). It has two simple planetary gearsets that have the ring gears interconnected

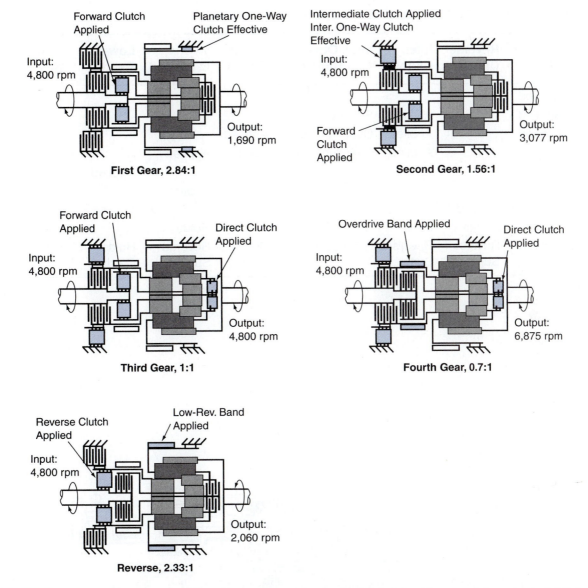

FIGURE 5-32   The full-throttle shift sequence for a Type 12 transmission showing the apply devices and the output shaft speed at the 1–2, 2–3, and 3–4 upshifts and reverse.

with the carriers of the other set. A second version of this gearset is used in the Chrysler 41TE (A-604) and 42LE and Ford AX4N, AX4S (AXOD), and CD4E units. General Motors uses this type of gearset in the 4T60E (THM 440), 4T65-E, and 4T80-E transaxles. The operation of the second version will be described later in this chapter.

The 4L60E (THM 7004R) is a Type 14 gear train and uses four multiple-disc clutches plus a one-way clutch as driving members and one multiple-disc clutch, a one-way clutch, and a band for holding members. The driving clutches are arranged so they can drive the sun gear and ring gear in the front gearset, called the *input gearset,* and the sun gear and carrier in the rear

gearset, called the **reaction gearset.** The input housing contains three of the driving clutches and the hub for the fourth. There are two ways that the front sun gear can be driven. One way is through the *forward clutch* and forward one-way clutch, called a **forward sprag,** and the other way is through the *overrun clutch.* The overrun clutch is used in manual-1, M2, and M3 to provide engine braking during deceleration.

The rear carrier (and front ring gear) can be held by the one-way clutch, *low-roller clutch,* or the multiple-disc *low and reverse clutch.* The rear sun gear can be held by the *2–4 band* to serve as a reaction member as well as a driving member.

TABLE 5-9   Four-speed Ravigneaux gear train band and clutch application, type 12

Gear	Forward Clutch	Reverse Clutch	Inter. Clutch	Inter. One-Way Clutch	Direct Clutch	O/D Band	Low-Rev. Band	Planetary One-Way Clutch
D1	Applied							Effective
D2	Applied		Applied	Effective				
D3	Applied		Applied	Over running	Applied			
D4			Applied	Over running	Applied	Applied		
M1	Applied						Applied	Effective
M2	Applied			Effective	Applied			
R		Applied					Applied	
Planet	Drives	Drives	Holds	Holds		Holds		
Member	Forward Sun	Reverse Sun	Reverse Sun	Reverse Sun	Drives Carrier	Reverse Sun	Holds Carrier	Holds Carrier

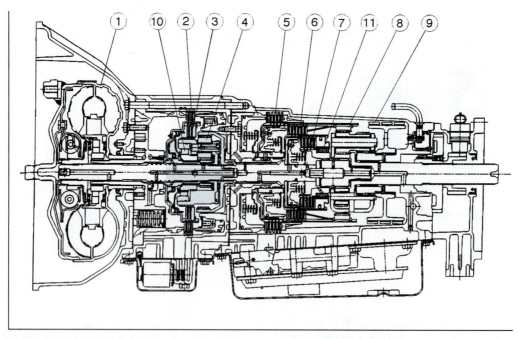

Legend

(1) Torque Converter Clutch (TCC)
(2) Fourth Clutch (C4)
(3) Overrun Clutch (OC)
(4) Overdrive Unit
(5) Reverse Clutch (RC)
(6) Second Clutch (C2)
(7) Third Clutch (C3)
(8) Ravigneaux Planetary Gear Set
(9) Brake Band (B)
(10) Overdrive Free Wheel (One Way Clutch) (OFW)
(11) Principle Sprag Assembly (One Way Clutch) (PFW)

FIGURE 5-33   This cutaway view of a GM 4L30 transmission shows an overdrive unit as the input of a Type 11, three-speed Ravigneaux gearset. *(Reprinted with permission of General Motors)*

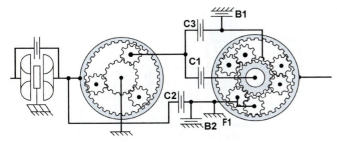

**Type 13 Gear Train
Lepelletier Principle**

(a)

Lepelletier Gear Ranges						
Range	C1	C2	C3	B1	B2	F1	Ratio
1	X					X	4.15:1
Manual 1	X				X		4.15:1
2	X			X			2.37:1
3	X		X				1.56:1
4	X	X					1.15:1
5		X	X				0.86:1
6		X		X			0.69:1
Reverse			X		X		3.39:1

(b)

FIGURE 5-34   A schematic view of a Type 13, LePelletier six-speed gearset (a) and a clutch application chart (b).

In neutral, all clutches are released so the power flows no farther than the input housing.

Figure 5-37 shows the shift sequence for the various power flows.

5.9.1 Power Flow: 4L60E

In drive-1 (low):

- The forward clutch is applied to drive the front sun gear.
- The front sun gear drives the front planet pinion gears counterclockwise.
- The front ring gear/rear carrier is held from turning counterclockwise by the low-roller clutch (low and reverse clutch in manual-1).
- The front planet pinions walk around inside the ring gear.
- The front carrier/rear ring gear is driven clockwise at a reduction speed.
- The output shaft is driven clockwise at a 3.06:1 ratio.

In drive-2:

- The forward clutch stays applied to drive the front sun gear.
- The 2–4 band applies to hold the rear sun gear.
- The front sun gear drives the front planet pinion gears counterclockwise.
- The front planet pinions drive the front ring gear/rear carrier clockwise.

- The rear planet pinions walk around the sun gear.
- The rear ring gear is driven clockwise at a reduction speed.
- The output shaft is driven clockwise at a 1.63:1 ratio.

In drive-3:

- The forward clutch stays applied to drive the front sun gear.
- The 2–4 band is released.
- The 3–4 clutch applies to drive the front ring/rear carrier.
- The front planet pinion gears become locked.
- The front carrier is driven at input shaft speed.
- The output shaft is driven clockwise at a 1:1 ratio.

In drive-4 (overdrive):

- The 3–4 clutch stays applied to drive the front ring/rear carrier.
- The 2–4 band applies to hold the rear sun gear.
- The rear planet pinion gears walk around the sun gear.
- The rear planet pinion gears drive the carrier clockwise at an overdrive.
- The output shaft is driven clockwise at a 0.7:1 ratio.
- The forward clutch stays applied, but the front sprag allows the sun gear to overrun.

In reverse:

- The reverse clutch applies to drive the rear sun gear.
- The low and reverse clutch applies to hold the rear carrier.
- The rear planet pinion gears are driven counterclockwise.
- The rear ring gear is driven counterclockwise at a reduction speed.
- The output shaft is driven counterclockwise at a 2.3:1 ratio.

5.9.2 Four-Speed Overdrive Gearset: Second Version

The 41TE (A-604) and 42LE (Type 15) use a similar gearset to the 4L60 (THM 700R4), with different input and output members and a reversal of the gearset so the front ring gear and the rear carrier are the output members (Figure 5-38). This produces slightly different power flows. The 41TE transmission is also unique in that no bands or one-way clutches are used.

Three of the multiple-disc clutches used in the 41TE are driving members and the other two clutches are holding members (Figure 5-39). The driving clutches are arranged so they can drive the front sun gear (closest to the engine), the front carrier, or the rear sun gear. Remember that driving the carrier in the front gearset also drives the ring gear in the rear gearset. The holding clutches are arranged so one clutch can hold the sun gear in the front gearset. The other clutch can hold the ring gear in the rear gearset as well as the carrier in the front set.

Clutch application is controlled by the manual valve and four solenoid valves. The solenoid valves are controlled by the

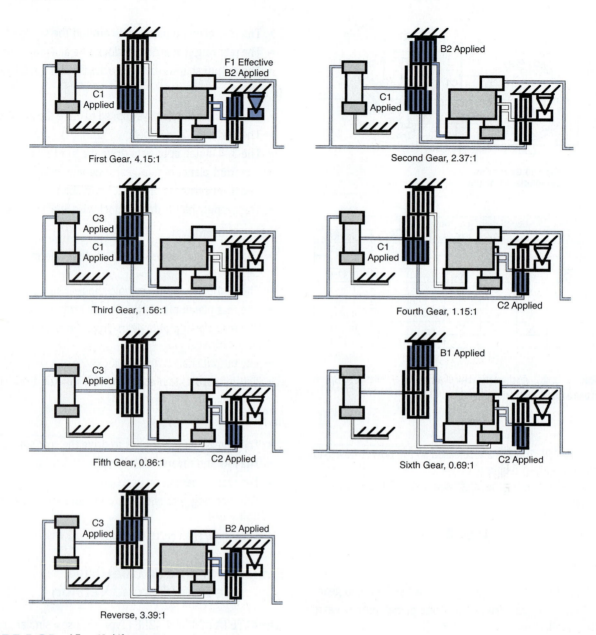

First Gear, 4.15:1

F1 Effective B2 Applied

C1 Applied

Second Gear, 2.37:1

B2 Applied

C1 Applied

Third Gear, 1.56:1

C3 Applied

C1 Applied

Fourth Gear, 1.15:1

C1 Applied

C2 Applied

Fifth Gear, 0.86:1

C3 Applied

C2 Applied

Sixth Gear, 0.69:1

B1 Applied

C2 Applied

Reverse, 3.39:1

C3 Applied

B2 Applied

FIGURE 5-35 A Type 13 shift sequence.

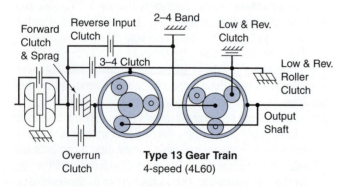

Forward Clutch & Sprag

Reverse Input Clutch

2–4 Band

Low & Rev. Clutch

3–4 Clutch

Low & Rev. Roller Clutch

Output Shaft

Overrun Clutch

Type 13 Gear Train 4-speed (4L60)

FIGURE 5-36 A schematic view of a Type 14, GM 4L60 four-speed gearset.

transaxle electronic control module, and they are opened and closed to produce the automatic upshifts and downshifts. They are also operated at the exact rate to produce the proper clutch application and release for good shift quality. These valves will be explained in more detail in Chapter 8.

In neutral, the three driving clutches are released. The low-reverse clutch is applied to hold the reaction member as soon as the transmission is shifted into first or reverse gear.

Power Flow: 42LE. In drive-1 (first):

- The underdrive clutch is applied to drive the rear sun gear.
- The low-reverse clutch is applied to hold the rear ring gear/front carrier.

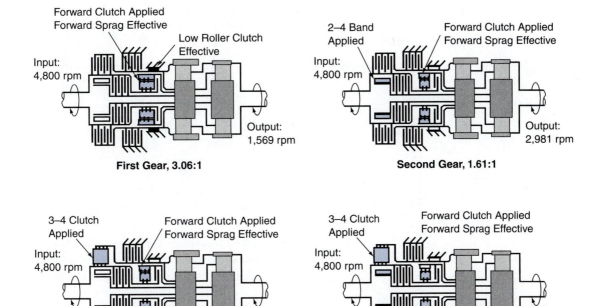

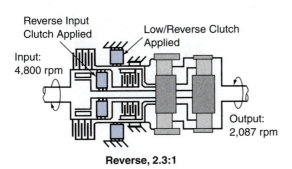

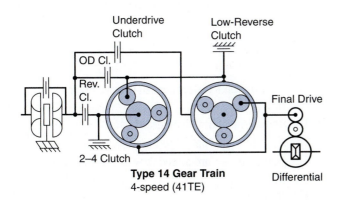

FIGURE 5-37 The full-throttle shift sequence for a Type 14, 4L60 transmission showing the apply devices and the output shaft speed at the 1–2, 2–3, and 3–4 upshifts and reverse.

FIGURE 5-38 A schematic view of a Type 15, Chrysler 41TE four-speed gearset.

- The rear planet pinion gears are driven counterclockwise.
- The rear planet pinions drive the rear carrier/front ring gear clockwise at a reduction speed.
- The output shaft is driven clockwise at a 2.84:1 ratio (Figure 5-40).

In drive-2 (second):

- The underdrive clutch stays applied to drive the rear sun gear.
- The low-reverse clutch is released.
- The 2–4 clutch is applied to hold the front sun gear.
- The rear planet pinion gears are driven counterclockwise.
- The rear planet pinions drive the rear carrier/front ring gear clockwise.

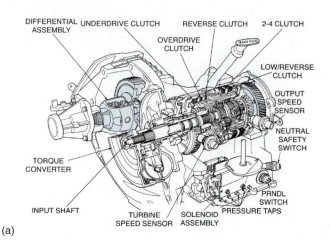

(a)

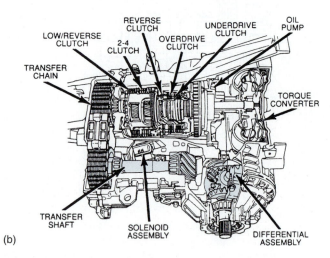

(b)

FIGURE 5-39   A 41TE (a) and a 42LE (b) transaxle use essentially the same transmission gear train with different final drives. The 41TE is mounted transversely, and the 42LE is mounted longitudinally. *(Courtesy of Chrysler Corporation)*

- The front planet pinions are forced to walk around the front sun gear.
- The front ring gear is driven clockwise at a reduction speed.
- The output shaft is driven clockwise at a 1.57:1 ratio (Figure 5-41).

In drive-3 (third):

- The underdrive clutch stays applied to drive the rear sun gear.
- The 2–4 clutch is released.
- The overdrive clutch is applied to drive the front carrier/rear ring gear.
- The front planet pinion gears become locked.
- The front carrier is driven at input shaft speed.
- The output shaft is driven clockwise at a 1:1 ratio (Figure 5-42).

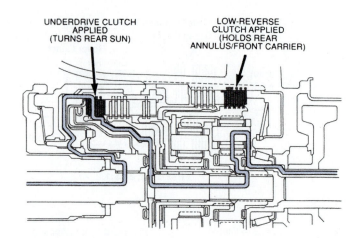

FIGURE 5-40   In first gear, the 41TE rear sun gear is driven by the underdrive clutch while the rear ring and front carrier are held by the low-reverse clutch. This forces the rear planet gears to walk around the inside of the ring gear and the rear carrier to rotate at a reduced speed. *(Courtesy of Chrysler Corporation)*

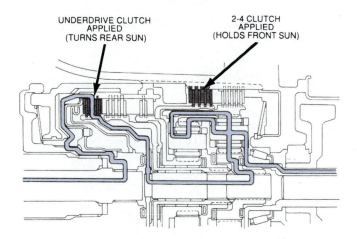

FIGURE 5-41   In second gear, the 41TE rear sun gear is driven by the underdrive clutch and the front sun gear is held by the 2–4 clutch. This forces the front planet gear to walk around the stationary sun gear and drive the front carrier and rear ring gear at a reduced speed. *(Courtesy of Chrysler Corporation)*

In drive-4 (overdrive):

- The overdrive clutch stays applied to drive the front carrier/rear ring gear.
- The underdrive clutch is released.
- The 2–4 clutch is applied to hold the front sun gear.
- The planet pinions are forced to walk around the sun gear.
- The front planet pinions drive the ring gear clockwise at an overdrive.
- The output shaft is driven clockwise at a 0.69:1 ratio (Figure 5-43).

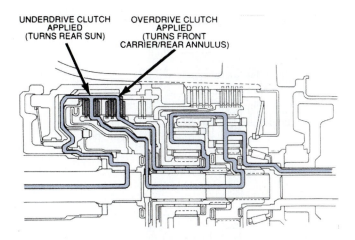

FIGURE 5-42 In third gear, the 41TE rear sun gear is driven by the underdrive clutch and the front carrier/rear ring gear is driven by the overdrive clutch. This locks the front gearset and produces a 1:1 ratio. *(Courtesy of Chrysler Corporation)*

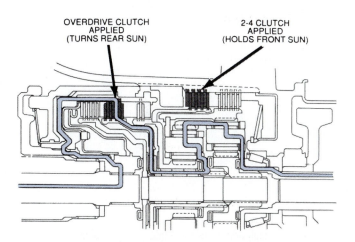

FIGURE 5-43 In fourth gear, the 41TE rear sun gear is driven by the overdrive clutch and the front sun gear is held by the 2–4 clutch. This forces the front planet gears to walk around the stationary sun gear and drives the front carrier at an overdrive ratio. *(Courtesy of Chrysler Corporation)*

In reverse:

- The reverse clutch is applied to drive the front sun gear.
- The low-reverse clutch is applied to hold the rear ring gear/front carrier.
- The front planet pinion gears are driven counterclockwise.
- The front ring gear is driven counterclockwise at a reduced speed.
- The output shaft is driven counterclockwise at a 2.21:1 ratio (Figure 5-44).

The shift sequence for the 42LE transaxle is shown in Figure 5-45. A clutch and band chart is shown in Table 5-10.

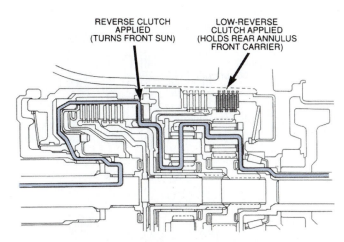

FIGURE 5-44 In reverse, the 41TE front sun gear is driven by the reverse clutch while the front carrier/rear ring gear is held by the low-reverse clutch. The front planet gears act as idlers, driving the front ring gear at a reverse, reduction ratio. *(Courtesy of Chrysler Corporation)*

5.9.3 Four-Speed Overdrive Gearset: Variation of Second Version

The General Motors 4T60-E (THM 440), 4T65-E, and 4T80-E and the Ford AX4N (AXOD), AX4S, and CD4E transaxles use gearsets that are very similar to the arrangement in the 41TE (Figure 5-46). These transaxles have the front carrier and the rear ring gears combined and are the output members. The rear carrier and the front ring gear can be a driving member, a reaction, or neither. The rear sun gear can only be a reaction member. The 4T60 is illustrated as a Type 16 gear train (Figure 5-47).

Power Flow: 4T60E. In drive-1 (low):

- The input clutch is applied to drive the input sun gear.
- The input sun gear drives the front planet pinion gears counterclockwise.
- The reaction sun gear is held by the 1–2 band (low and reverse clutch in manual-1).
- The reaction planet pinions walk around the reaction sun gear.
- The input carrier assembly is driven clockwise at a reduction speed.
- The output shaft is driven clockwise at a 2.92:1 ratio (Figure 5-48).

In drive-2:

- The 2nd clutch is applied to drive the rear ring gear (input carrier assembly).
- The 1–2 band stays applied to hold the reaction sun gear.
- The rear ring gear drives the rear planet pinion gears clockwise.

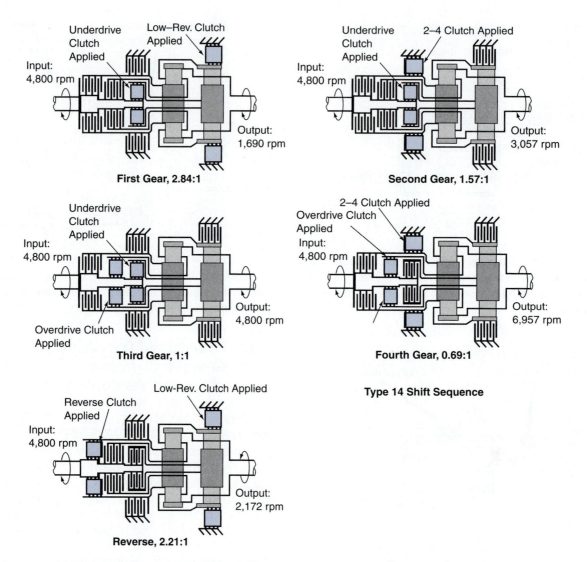

First Gear, 2.84:1

Second Gear, 1.57:1

Third Gear, 1:1

Fourth Gear, 0.69:1

Type 14 Shift Sequence

Reverse, 2.21:1

FIGURE 5-45 The full-throttle shift sequence for a Type 15, 41TE transmission showing the apply devices and the output shaft speed at the 1–2, 2–3, and 3–4 upshifts and reverse.

TABLE 5-10 Four-speed gear train band and clutch application, type 15

Gear	Underdrive Clutch	Low-Rev. Clutch	2–4 Clutch	Overdrive Clutch	Reverse Clutch
D1	Applied	Applied			
D2	Applied		Applied		
D3	Applied			Applied	
D4			Applied	Applied	
R		Applied			Applied
Planetary	Drives Rear	Holds Front	Holds	Drives Front	Drives
Member	Sun	Carrier & Rear Ring	Front Sun	Carrier & Rear Ring	Front Sun

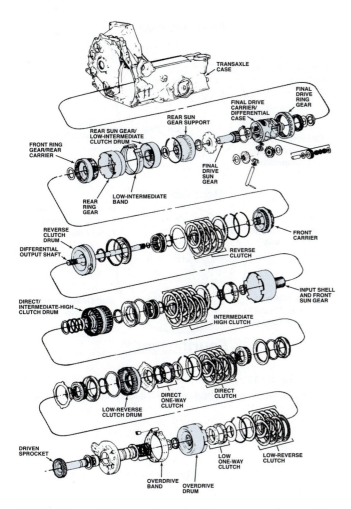

FIGURE 5-46   An exploded view of the Type 16 gear train used in an AXOD/AX4N transaxle.

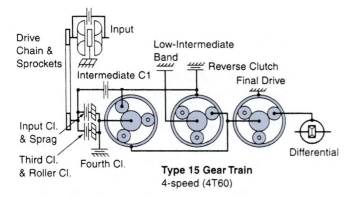

FIGURE 5-47   A schematic view of a Type 16, GM 4T60 four-speed gearset. The Ford AX4N gearset is similar.

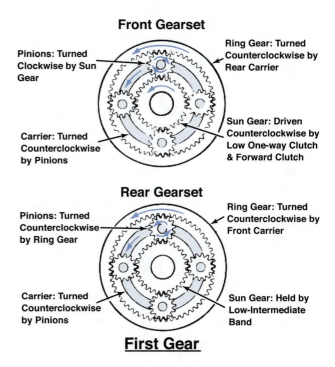

FIGURE 5-48   In first gear, the AXOD front sun gear is driven by the forward clutch and low one-way clutch while the rear sun gear is held by the low-intermediate band.

- The rear planet pinions walk around the sun gear.
- The rear planet pinions drive the front ring gear/rear carrier clockwise at a reduction speed.
- The output shaft is driven clockwise at a 1.57:1 ratio (Figure 5-49).

In drive-3:

- The 2nd clutch stays applied to drive the rear ring gear (input carrier assembly).
- The 1–2 band is released.
- The 3rd clutch applies to drive the front sun gear.
- The front planet pinions become locked.
- The front carrier is driven at input shaft speed.
- The output shaft is driven clockwise at a 1:1 ratio (Figure 5-50).

In drive-4 (overdrive):

- The 2nd clutch stays applied to drive the rear ring gear (input carrier assembly).
- The 4th clutch applies to hold the front sun gear.
- The front planet pinion gears walk around the sun gear.
- The front planet pinion gears drive the carrier clockwise at an overdrive.

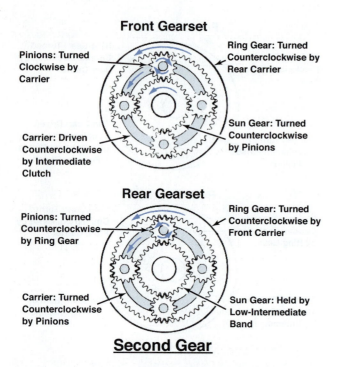

FIGURE 5-49 In second gear, the AXOD front carrier is driven by the intermediate clutch while the rear sun gear is held by the low-intermediate band.

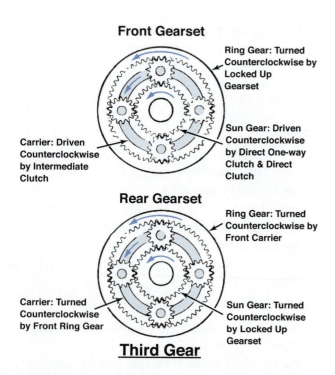

FIGURE 5-50 In third gear, the AXOD front gear is driven by the intermediate clutch while the front sun gear is driven by the forward clutch and low one-way clutch, and this locks up both gearsets to produce a 1:1 ratio.

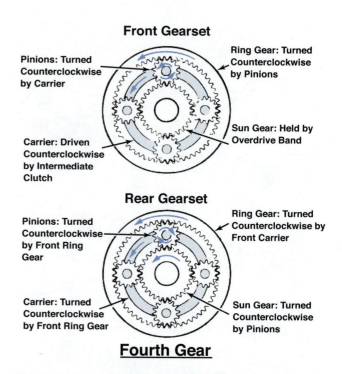

FIGURE 5-51 In fourth gear, the AXOD front carrier is driven by the intermediate clutch while the front sun gear is held by the overdrive band.

- The output shaft is driven clockwise at a 0.7:1 ratio (Figure 5-51).
- The 3rd clutch stays applied, but the 3rd sprag allows the sun gear to overrun.

In reverse:

- The input clutch applies to drive the front sun gear.
- The reverse band applies to hold the front carrier.
- The front planet pinion gears are driven counterclockwise.
- The front ring gear is driven counterclockwise at a reduction speed.
- The output shaft is driven counterclockwise at a 2.38:1 ratio (Figure 5-52).

5.9.4 Four-Speed Overdrive Gearset: Variation Two

The Ford CD4E is another version of the four-speed gearset; it is illustrated as a Type 17 gear train (Figure 5-53). It is a compact transaxle with a chain drive between the transmission gearset and the planetary reduction gears and differential of the final drive. The power flows through this gearset are quite similar to that of the other four-speed gearsets.

Front Gearset

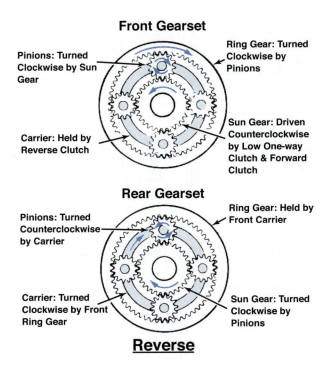

Ring Gear: Turned Clockwise by Pinions

Pinions: Turned Clockwise by Sun Gear

Carrier: Held by Reverse Clutch

Sun Gear: Driven Counterclockwise by Low One-way Clutch & Forward Clutch

Rear Gearset

Ring Gear: Held by Front Carrier

Pinions: Turned Counterclockwise by Carrier

Carrier: Turned Clockwise by Front Ring Gear

Sun Gear: Turned Clockwise by Pinions

Reverse

FIGURE 5-52   In reverse, the AXOD front sun gear is driven by the forward clutch and low one-way clutch while the carrier is held by the reverse clutch.

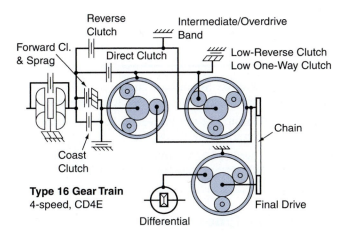

Type 16 Gear Train
4-speed, CD4E

Reverse Clutch
Forward Cl. & Sprag
Direct Clutch
Intermediate/Overdrive Band
Low-Reverse Clutch
Low One-Way Clutch
Chain
Coast Clutch
Differential
Final Drive

FIGURE 5-53   A schematic view of a Type 17, Ford CD4E four-speed gearset.

5.10 JOINT VENTURE, SIX-SPEED GEARSET

This gearset, Type 18, was developed jointly by Ford (6F50) and General Motors (6T70 and 6T75). It uses three simple planetary gearsets and has each carrier connected to the ring gear of another set (Figure 5-54). The sun gear of the center gearset is connected to the input shaft, so it is always driven.

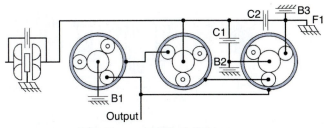

Joint Venture 6-Speed Gearset

Output

(a)

Joint Venture Gearset							
Range	C1	C2	B1	B2	B3	F1	Ratio
1			X			X	4.48:1
Manual 1			X		X		4.48:1
2			X	X			2.87:1
3	X		X				1.84:1
4		X	X				1.41:1
5	X	X					1:1
6		X			X		0.74:1
Reverse	X				X		2.88:1

(b)

FIGURE 5-54   A schematic view of a Type 18, Joint Venture six-speed gearset (a) and a clutch application chart (b).

It uses two driving clutches, four reaction clutches (brakes), and one mechanical diode (one-way clutch). The front carrier and rear ring gear are the output.

Except for first gear with the one-way clutch, it uses clutch-to-clutch shifts. It has a low 4.48:1 first gear, and an overdrive 0.74:1:1 sixth gear (Figure 5-55).

PROBLEM SOLVING 5-4   Imagine that you are working in a shop that specializes in transmission repair, and these problems are given to you:

Case 1   A 1992 Camaro with a TH 700-R4 transmission (Type 14) drives normally in all ranges, except there is an engine flare, indicating slippage, during a full-throttle 1–2 shift. Do you think a driving or reaction member could be faulty? If so, which one?

Case 2   A 1996 Dodge Intrepid with a 42LE transaxle (Type 15) has no second or fourth gear. With enough throttle, it will skip second and make a 1–3 shift. What would be the cause of this problem? Which driving or reaction member is at fault?

5.11 NONPLANETARY GEARSETS

Several automatic transmission designs do not use planetary gearsets. These designs are attempts to produce a smaller, simpler, lighter, and less expensive transmission that will

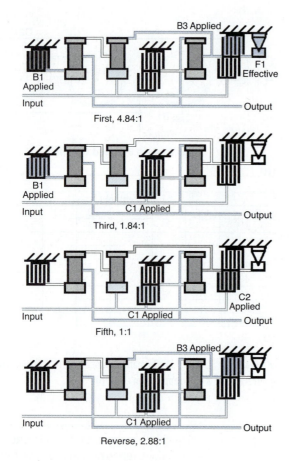

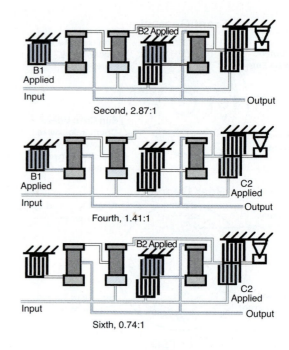

FIGURE 5-55   A Type 18 shift sequence.

produce better fuel mileage with lower exhaust emissions. Many consider the dual clutch transmissions to be automatic transmissions.

5.11.1 Helical Gear Types

The Hondamatic and the Saturn TAAT use constant-mesh helical gears, much like those in a manual transmission. The major difference is that manual transmissions use a mechanical clutch and synchronizer assemblies that are shifted through manual linkage, and the automatic transmissions use a torque converter and hydraulically applied clutch packs (Figure 5-56). The power flow for each gear range goes through a pair of gears and each gear range uses a different gearset (Figure 5-57).

A garage shift into first or reverse is made by applying that particular clutch pack. Upshifts and downshift timing and ratio changes are made by applying the next clutch pack while releasing the previous one (Figure 5-58). All shifts, with one exception, occur with the application of a single clutch pack. The exception is reverse, which requires the movement of the reverse selector and the engagement of the fourth clutch.

PROBLEM SOLVING 5-5 Imagine that you are working in a shop that specializes in transmission repair, and these problems are given to you:

Case 1 A 1998 Saturn slips during the 2–3 shift. Do you think a driving or reaction member could be faulty? If so, which one?

Case 2 A 1996 Honda has noisy second gear. What would be the cause of this problem? Which parts will probably need replacement?

5.11.2 CVT Types

A CVT (continuously variable transmission) has an infinite number of gear ratios between its lowest ratio, about 3.7:1, and its highest ratio, which is an overdrive. Ideally, it can keep the engine at the most efficient rpm. As the vehicle accelerates from a stop, the engine speed rises quickly from idle to the desired rpm. From that point on, the engine stays at the same speed, while the transmission ratio continuously changes to provide acceleration. CVT transmissions are commonly used in snowmobiles. The clutch used in top-fuel dragsters and "funny" cars could be considered a type of CVT transmission. CVT transmissions have been used in the Subaru Justy and are now used by Audi, Dodge, Honda, and Nissan.

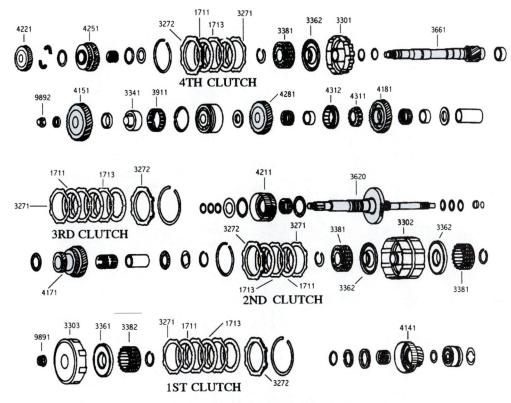

FIGURE 5-56 This parts catalog page shows an exploded view of a Saturn TAAT automatic transaxle. Note the helical gearset and the clutches for shift control. *(Courtesy of Aceomatic Recon)*

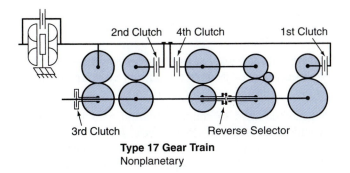

FIGURE 5-57 A schematic view of a Type 19, Honda four-speed gearset.

Automotive CVTs are used with multiplate clutches, magnetic particle clutches, and torque converters. A pair of hydraulically controlled, variable-size pulleys is used with a steel-link drive belt (Figure 5-59). This belt is often called a push belt because torque is transferred by the driving pulley pushing on the belt, which in turn pushes the driven pulley. At start, the pulley halves/discs on the primary input shaft are spread apart, and the pair of pulley halves on the secondary output shaft are pushed together. This produces a small pulley driving a large pulley, which produces the lowest drive ratio. When a ratio change is required, the primary pulley halves are

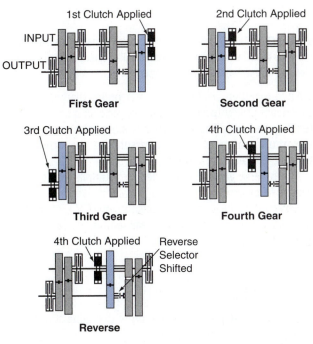

FIGURE 5-58 The shift sequence for a Type 19, four-speed transmission showing the apply devices.

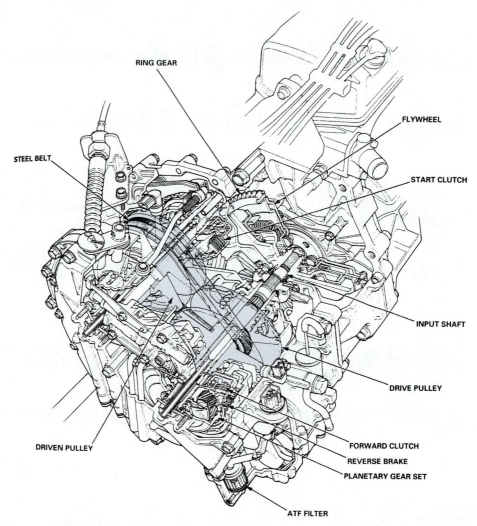

RING GEAR

FLYWHEEL

STEEL BELT

START CLUTCH

INPUT SHAFT

DRIVE PULLEY

DRIVEN PULLEY

FORWARD CLUTCH
REVERSE BRAKE
PLANETARY GEAR SET

ATF FILTER

FIGURE 5-59 Forward ratios in this CVT transmission are changed as the two halves of the drive pulley are forced together, increasing the diameter. At the same time, the two halves of the driven pulley spread apart to reduce its diameter. The planetary gearset at the rear of the input shaft is used to produce reverse. *(Courtesy of American Honda Motor Company)*

pushed together, producing a bigger pulley diameter, and the secondary pulley halves separate, producing a smaller diameter (Figure 5-60). This produces a higher gear ratio. Both pulleys must maintain enough pressure on the drive belt to transfer the required torque.

A reverse gearset, controlled by multiplate clutch packs, is used to produce reverse.

A continuously variable transmission, CVT, offers several advantages over a planetary-gear automatic transmission. These include:

- Compact, very short
- Lighter weight
- Constant, step-less acceleration with engine staying at the rpm for maximum power
- Efficient fuel use and emissions, cruise with engine staying at the rpm for maximum efficiency
- Lower internal power loss

One method used to compare transmissions is the engine revolutions for a specific driving cycle. A test vehicle using a 3.0-L engine and a CVT showed 3% fewer revolutions than the same vehicle with a five-speed transmission and 11% less than with a four-speed transmission. This should equal a gain of about 12% in fuel economy.

CVT Components, Pulleys. A CVT improves efficiency by changing ratios from underdrive/reduction to overdrive in a gradual, continuous manner. Two pulleys, also called *variators,* and a steel drive belt are used

The primary/drive pulley is attached to the input shaft. The secondary/driven pulley is on the output shaft and drives the final drive gears. Each pulley, also called a sheave, has two sides: one is fixed so it cannot move, and the other can float sideways to change pulley width. When the vehicle is at rest, the primary pulley is wide so the belt sits low on the pulley, and the secondary pulley is narrow so the belt sits high (Figure 5-61). This produces the lowest, underdrive ratio.

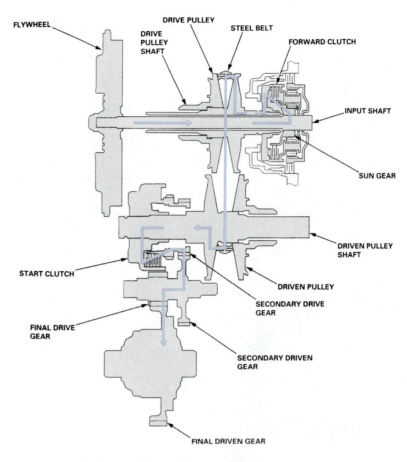

FIGURE 5-60   The shift sequence for a CVT transmission is a very smooth, stepless transition from a low ratio to a high ratio as the pulleys change diameter. The engine speed can stay constant as the vehicle speeds up. *(Courtesy of American Honda Motor Company)*

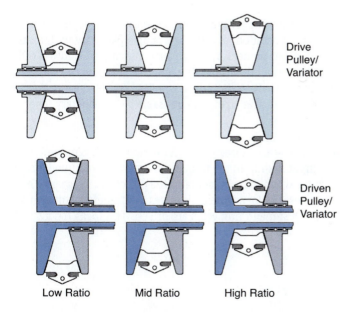

| Low Ratio | Mid Ratio | High Ratio |

FIGURE 5-61   The drive pulley is wide while the driven pulley is narrow for low ratio, vehicle start (left). The ratio changes by making the drive pulley narrow and the driven pulley wider.

As the vehicle moves, the floating side of the primary pulley moves inward, making the pulley narrower and forcing the belt to move out to a wider diameter. The belt is steel so it cannot stretch, so it will be forced deeper into the secondary pulley, forcing the pulley to become wider.

The floating side of each pulley can be thought of as a hydraulic piston. Fluid pressure is used to force the piston/pulley to a narrower position. The secondary pulley is spring loaded to force it to a narrow position and the drive piston to a wide (underdrive) position. The primary pulley is adjusted to control the gear ratio, and the secondary pulley is adjusted to maintain tension on the belt. The belt must never be loose between the pulleys.

CVT Components, Drive Belt.   Two different styles of fixed-length steel belts are used (Figure 5-62).

- One type is a push-belt made up of about 400 wedge-shaped segments that are held together by two steel bands. Each band is made from multiple layers to allow flexibility. The segment sides contact the pulley sides. A push-belt is often called the *Van Doorne design*. This style

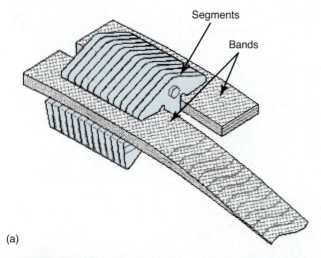

(a)

(b)

FIGURE 5-62   A push-belt is made from a few hundred steel segments held together by two bands that have multiple layers of thin steel (a). A pull-belt resembles a silent chain with exposed end links that grip the pulley sides (b).

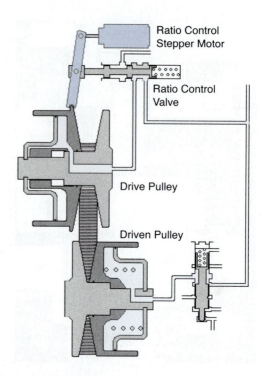

FIGURE 5-63   The ratio control valve and motor control the drive pulley fluid pressure, which in turn controls the pulley widths and ratio.

of belt is directional, and it usually is marked with an arrow to show belt direction.

- The other type is a pull-belt that is made up of links and link pins, much like a silent chain. The ends of the link pins contact the pulley sides. This style is also called a *Luk chain drive.*

CVT Operation.   With no fluid pressure, the secondary pulley spring forces the floating side to a narrow, high-belt position, which in turn moves the primary pulley to a wide, low-belt position. This produces an underdrive that is always used as the vehicle starts moving (Figure 5-63).

As the vehicle begins moving, the ratio control valve moves to send fluid pressure to the primary piston, and this forces the floating side to a more narrow position. The belt is forced outward, which in turn forces the secondary pulley to a lower-belt position. Continued fluid flow to the primary piston will change the ratio from an underdrive/reduction through 1:1 to an overdrive.

CVT Reverse.   A planetary gearset is needed for reverse-direction operation, and this is a simple planetary with a carrier that can be held by the reverse clutch (see Figure 5-60). The input shaft drives the ring/internal gear, and the sun gear drives the shaft to the primary pulley. Reverse gear ratio depends on the gear sizes; one transaxle has a planetary reverse ratio of 0.74:1.

CVT Forward Operation.   A forward clutch is mounted on the input shaft from the torque converter; it is mounted inside a clutch drum that also contains the planetary ring gear. When it applies, the forward clutch drives the planetary sun gear so both the sun and ring gears are driven. This locks the gearset to produce a 1:1 ratio.

SUMMARY

1. An understanding of the rules of power transfer through a planetary gearset is needed to trace the power through any planetary gearset.

2. A simple planetary gearset can produce seven different gear ratios.

3. Transmissions schematics are a helpful tool for understanding gear train power flow.

4. There are two basic types of planetary gearsets used: Simpson and Ravigneaux.

5. Combinations of Simpson or Ravigneaux gearsets with a simple planetary gearset will produce four, five, six, eight, or more gear ratios.

6. CVTs offer unique advantages, better fuel economy, lower emissions, and smoother operation.

REVIEW QUESTIONS

The following questions are provided to help you study as you read the chapter.

1. A simple planetary gearset has a _____ _____, a _____ _____, and a _____ that has two or more planet gears.

2. A Simpson gear train combines one _____ _____ with _____ planet gearsets and two _____ gears.

3. The right and left sides of a vehicle are determined by viewing from the _____ _____.

4. The transmission/transaxle can be mounted in either a _____ (lengthwise) or _____ (crosswise) position.

5. The lever or arm used to hold the vehicle stationary in park is called a parking _____.

6. _____ transmission designs require that during an upshift, the application of a clutch must be carefully timed with the release of a reaction member.

7. A _____ and _____ application chart shows the relationship between the apply devices used in each of the gear ranges.

8. Complete the following for a Simpson, Type 1 transmission.
   a. The forward clutch _____ the input ring gear.
   b. The one-way clutch holds the _____ _____.
   c. The high-reverse clutch _____ the _____ _____.

d. The intermediate band holds the _____ _____.

e. The low-reverse band _____ the _____ _____.

9. Which apply devices are working when a three-speed Simpson gear train is in third gear?

10. Variables that affect the speed of a band engagement include:
    a. _____ diameter.
    b. Fluid feed _____ diameter.
    c. Use of a(n) _____.

11. When an overdrive Simpson gear train is in third gear, what is the gear ratio in the overdrive planetary gearset? The main gearset?

12. A Ravigneaux gearset uses a _____ carrier that has _____ and _____ planet pinions, a _____ and a _____ sun gear, and a single _____ gear.

13. A single _____ gearset can be used in a two-, three-, or four-speed transmission or transaxle.

14. The gear train in the GM 4L60 has two _____ gearsets and has _____ apply devices.

15. The automatic transmissions used in most Honda and Saturn vehicles use _____ mesh _____ gears similar to conventional standard transmissions. In place of synchronizers, they use _____ disc _____.

16. A _____ _____ _____ has an infinite number of _____ ratios that should keep the engine at its most efficient _____.

CHAPTER QUIZ

The following questions will help you check the facts you have learned. Select the answer that completes each statement correctly.

1. Student A says that if the carrier is the input and the sun gear is the reaction member, the ring gear will rotate in a gear reduction. Student B says that if the carrier is the input and the sun gear is the reaction member, the ring gear rotates in reverse. Who is correct?
    a. Student A
    b. Student B
    c. Both A and B
    d. Neither A nor B

2. Student A says that a simple planetary gearset operates in neutral if there is no input member. Student B says that it will operate in neutral if there is no reaction member. Who is correct?
    a. Student A
    b. Student B
    c. Both A and B
    d. Neither A nor B

3. Student A says that driving the ring gear while the sun gear is held will make the planet gears walk around the sun gear. Student B says that driving the ring gear while holding the sun gear will force the carrier to rotate at a reduction speed. Who is correct?
    a. Student A
    b. Student B
    c. Both A and B
    d. Neither A nor B

4. Student A says that if the sun gear is driven while the ring gear is held, the planet gears will walk around the inside of the ring gear. Student B says that if the sun gear is driven while the carrier is held, the ring gear is forced to rotate at a slower speed than the sun gear. Who is correct?
    a. Student A
    b. Student B
    c. Both A and B
    d. Neither A nor B

5. If the ring gear is driven while the sun gear is held, the planet gears will
    a. merely rotate in the carrier.
    b. rotate as they walk around the sun gear.
    c. rotate with the carrier but not on their axis.
    d. be stationary in the carrier.

6. The term referring to the pull of a FWD vehicle under a hard acceleration is
    a. torque pull.
    b. steer pull.
    c. torque steer.
    d. acceleration steer.

7. In a three-speed Simpson gear train, if the sun gear is stationary, the transmission is in
    a. first gear.
    b. third gear.
    c. second gear.
    d. reverse.

8. When a three-speed Simpson gear train is in first gear, the sun gear is
    a. rotating clockwise
    b. stationary.
    c. rotating counterclockwise.
    d. freewheeling.

9. In a three-speed Simpson gear train, third gear occurs when the forward clutch is applied along with the
    a. rear band.
    b. one-way clutch.
    c. front band.
    d. None of these

10. In a three-speed Simpson gear train, the reaction carrier is held stationary by a
    a. one-way clutch.
    b. multiple-disc clutch.
    c. band.
    d. Any of these

11. Student A says that when a one-way clutch is used for a reaction member, the clutch will release if the vehicle decelerates in that gear. Student B says that when a one-way clutch is used for a reaction member, the clutch self-applies when the throttle is opened. Who is correct?
    a. Student A
    b. Student B
    c. Both A and B
    d. Neither A nor B

12. Driving two members of a planetary gearset while there is no reaction member will result in a(n) _____ ratio.

   a. overdrive

   b. reduction

   c. 1:1

   d. reverse, reduction

13. Student A says that in a four-speed Simpson gear train, the sun gear is the input member for the overdrive gearset. Student B says the ring gear is the output member. Who is correct?

   a. Student A

   b. Student B

   c. Both A and B

   d. Neither A nor B

14. Student A says that in Type 5, 6, 7, and 8 transmissions, both driving clutches in the main gearset are applied in third gear. Student B says that the overdrive gearset reaction member is applied in third gear. Who is correct?

   a. Student A

   b. Student B

   c. Both A and B

   d. Neither A nor B

15. A Ravigneaux gearset uses

   a. two sun gears.

   b. one ring gear.

   c. two sets of planet pinion gears.

   d. All of these

16. Student A says that in a two-speed Ravigneaux gear train, one sun gear is driven whenever the turbine shaft turns. Student B says that it will always be in neutral if there is no reaction member. Who is correct?

   a. Student A

   b. Student B

   c. Both A and B

   d. Neither A nor B

17. The Ravigneaux gear train can be arranged so it produces _____ forward speeds.

   a. 2

   b. 2 or 3

   c. 2, 3, or 4

   d. 2, 3, 4, or 5

18. Student A says that in a Ravigneaux gear train, the long pinion gears are meshed with the large sun gear. Student B says that the long pinion gears are meshed with the short pinion gears. Who is correct?

   a. Student A

   b. Student B

   c. Both A and B

   d. Neither A nor B

19. Student A says that in fourth gear, the sun gear is driven. Student B says the carrier is held stationary in fourth gear. Who is correct?

   a. Student A

   b. Student B

   c. Both A and B

   d. Neither A nor B

20. Student A says that when a simple planetary gearset is in reverse, the carrier is held stationary. Student B says the ring gear is the output member in reverse. Who is correct?

   a. Student A

   b. Student B

   c. Both A and B

   d. Neither A nor B

CHAPTER 6

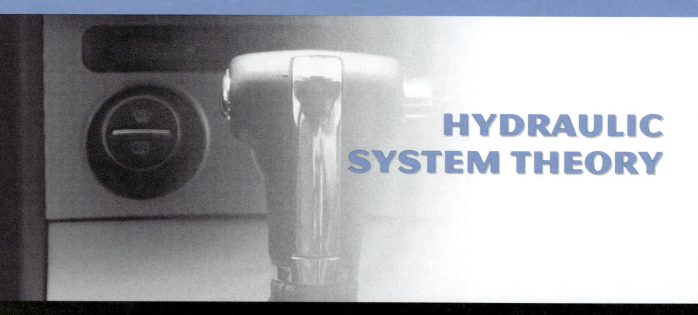

HYDRAULIC SYSTEM THEORY

OBJECTIVES

After studying Chapter 6, the reader should be able to:

1. Discuss hydraulic principles.
2. Describe how a hydraulic system operates.
3. Identify the parts of a transmission hydraulic system and explain their purpose.
4. Explain the requirements for a transmission hydraulic system.
5. Identify the requirements for automatic transmission fluid and the differences between fluids.

KEY TERMS

Accumulator (p. 153)
Area (p. 134)
Automatic Transmission Fluid (ATF) (p. 154)
Detent Valve (p. 144)
Fluid Power (p. 133)
Force (p. 133)
Governor Valve (p. 142)
Hydraulics (p. 133)
Internal-External Pump (p. 137)
Land (p. 141)
Manual Valve (p. 137)
Metal-Clad Lip Seal (p. 149)
Micron (p. 139)
Modulator Valve (p. 144)
Orifice (p. 153)
O-Ring (p. 148)
Pressure (p. 134)
Pressure Regulator Valve (p.136)
Pressure Relief Valve (p. 137)
Pump (p. 136)
Reaction Surface (p. 141)
Static Seal (p. 148)
Throttle Position Sensors (TPS) (p. 144)
Vehicle Speed Sensors (VSS) (p. 144)

6.1 INTRODUCTION

The automatic transmission's hydraulic system has several important functions (Figure 6-1). It must be able to:

- apply the clutches and bands and therefore control the transmission power flow,
- transmit sufficient force and motion to completely apply the control units to prevent slippage,
- maintain fluid flow through the torque converter for its proper operation,
- maintain fluid flow to lubricate and cool the moving parts of the gear train.

6.2 HYDRAULIC PRINCIPLES

Hydraulics, often called **fluid power,** is a method of transmitting motion and/or **force.** Hydraulics is based on the fact that liquids can flow easily through complicated paths, but they cannot be compressed. All the components in a hydraulic system are connected so that fluid pressure can be transmitted and allowed to work. Another important feature is that when fluids transmit pressure, that pressure is transferred equally in all directions and acts on all parts of a circuit at the same time with the same pressure (Figure 6-2). This is a simplified version of Pascal's law, which was developed by Blaise Pascal. It

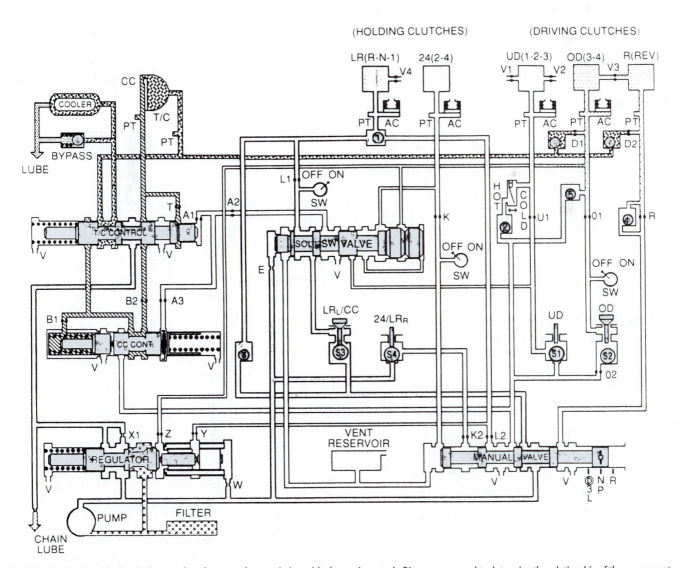

FIGURE 6-1   A hydraulic diagram for a four-speed transmission with electronic controls. Diagrams are used to determine the relationship of the components. They are often color-coded to help locate the circuits. *(Courtesy of Chrysler Corporation)*

states that pressure applied to a confined fluid at any point is transmitted undiminished throughout the fluid in all directions and acts upon every part of the confining vessel at right angles to its interior surfaces and equally upon equal areas.

If we were to fill a strong container with a liquid, it would be impossible to add more liquid, even by force (Figure 6-3). Once the container is full, any added force becomes fluid pressure. **Pressure** is defined as the amount of force applied to a given area. In the United States, pressure is commonly measured using *pounds per square inch (psi).* Ten pounds per square inch is equal to a force of 10 pounds pushing on an area of one square inch. In other parts of the world, the metric system is used. The metric system measures pressure using kilograms per square centimeter (kg/cm²), or bars (a bar is equal to 14.5 psi). Today, pressure is also measured in kilopascals (kPa); one psi is equal to 6.895 kPa, 0.07 kg/cm², or 0.0689 bar. The *kilopascal* is an international unit for measuring pressure.

Pressure can be created in a hydraulic system in several ways. It is easier to describe and understand if we use a piston as the pressure input and one or more pistons for the output. System pressure is a product of three things: the ability of the system to contain the pressure, the surface area of the input piston, and the amount of force applied to the piston (Figure 6-4).

The strength of the system is important because if the pressure gets too high for the system, the system will rupture and release the pressure.

When force is exerted on the piston of a closed system, that force becomes fluid pressure. Pressure is equal to the force divided by the **area** of the piston. A 100-lb (90.9-kg) force on a piston that is 10 in² (64.5 cm²) in area will generate a pressure of 10 psi (1.4 kg/cm²). The pressure can be converted to kilopascals by multiplying 6.895 by 10 psi (6.895 × 10). The pressure would be 68.95 kPa. The amount of pressure is determined by dividing the force by the area of the piston (Figure 6-5). This same 100-lb force acting on a 0.5-in² (3.2 cm²) piston generates a pressure of 100 ÷ 0.5, or 200, psi (28 kg/cm²) (1,399 kPa).

Fluid pressure is never greater than what is needed to overcome resistance to fluid flow. Using a vehicle's brake system as an example, it takes only a few pounds of force to push the brake pedal downward, and then after the pedal has moved an inch or so, it will not move any farther. During the first part of the pedal travel, the brake shoes or pads were moving to

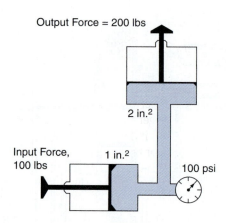

FIGURE 6-4 A 100-lb force applied on an input piston that has an area of 1 in. will produce a fluid pressure of 100 psi.

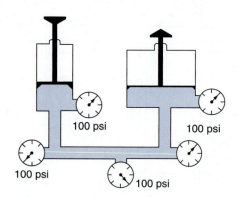

FIGURE 6-2 Fluid pressure is transmitted undiminished in all directions. Note that the pressure is equal throughout the system.

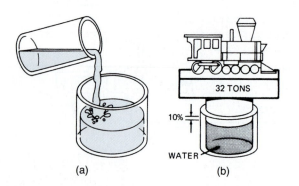

FIGURE 6-3 Fluids flow freely and will assume the shape of their container (a), yet they are virtually noncompressible (b).

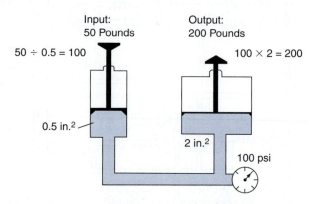

FIGURE 6-5 System pressure can be determined by dividing the input force (50 lb) by the area of the input piston (0.5 in²). Output force can be determined by multiplying the area of the output piston (2 in²) by the fluid pressure (100 psi).

make contact with the rotors and drums. The only resistance was the seals and brake shoe return springs. Only a relatively low pressure is needed to overcome the resistance and produce this movement, about 10 to 150 psi. After the shoes touch their friction surfaces, the pistons can move no farther; now the hydraulic system pressure will increase to whatever the driver demands through the amount of force applied to the pedal.

When discussing hydraulic pistons and computing fluid pressures and forces, it is important to use the area of the piston and not the diameter. The area of a piston or any circle can be determined using this formula:

$$\pi r^2 \text{ or } \pi\,(0.785d^2)$$

where:

$\pi = 3.1416$
$r = \text{one-half the diameter}$
$d = \text{diameter}$

The pressure in a hydraulic system becomes a force to produce work, and the amount of force can be determined by multiplying the area of the output piston by the system pressure. A pressure of 200 psi pushing on a piston with an area of 1 in² produces a force of 200 lb (200×1). This same pressure on a 4-in² (26.17-cm²) piston produces a force of 200×4, or 800 lb (363.6 kg). Application force is multiplied whenever the output piston is larger than the input. Force will decrease if the input piston is larger than the output piston. The simple memory triangle shown in Figure 6-6 can be used as an aid to determine area, force, or pressure.

A hydraulic system can only transmit the energy, force, and motion that is put into it; it cannot create energy. What goes in one end is all that can come out of the other. However, it is possible to change force to motion or vice versa. Most automotive brake systems multiply force with a loss in travel; other hydraulic systems are used to increase travel.

As the input piston moves, it displaces or pushes fluid through the passages or tubing of the system. The volume of fluid displaced is equal to the piston area times the length of piston stroke. A 1-in. (2.54-cm) diameter piston has an area of 0.785 in²(5.067 cm²); if this piston strokes 2 in. (5.08 cm), 1.57 in³ (25.7 cm³) of fluid is displaced (0.785 in² $\times$ 2 in.) (5.067 cm² $\times$ 5.08 cm). This much fluid can move a 1-in.

diameter output piston 2 in. If the output piston is larger, its larger area requires a larger volume of fluid, so its travel will be shorter.

6.3 SIMPLE HYDRAULIC SYSTEMS

Many hydraulic systems use an engine- or motor-driven pump to produce fluid movement. These systems normally consist of the pump, a fluid intake system usually equipped with a filter, a *fluid supply* (sump), control valves, and the actuators that provide the system output (Figure 6-7). In these systems, the pressure is determined by the amount of power turning the pump and the resistance to the fluid flow. Some factors that affect pressure are the speed and condition of the pump, the size of the fluid passage, and the strength of the system. Most systems use either a pressure relief valve or a pressure regulator valve to control the pressure below the point where damage occurs. The flow from the pump is a product of how much power is put into the pump, the size of the pump, and the quantity of fluid available. Pump output is normally rated as the number of gallons, quarts, or liters that a pump can deliver in a minute at a certain pressure.

The fluid pressure and flow are also related to the energy that is being put into the fluid at the pump. As described in Chapter 3, the mechanical horsepower of an engine is closely related to the torque and rpm of the engine. In a similar fashion, fluid horsepower is related to the pressure and the fluid flow. The formula for computing hydraulic, or fluid, horsepower is:

$$\text{hp} = \frac{\text{psi} \times \text{gpm}}{1{,}714}$$

where:

$\text{hp} = \text{horsepower}$
$\text{psi} = \text{fluid pressure in pounds per square inch}$
$\text{gpm} = \text{fluid flow in gallons per minute}$

FIGURE 6-6   A simple memory triangle will help you remember the commonly used hydraulic formulas.

FORCE = PRESSURE × AREA
PRESSURE = FORCE ÷ AREA
AREA = FORCE ÷ PRESSURE

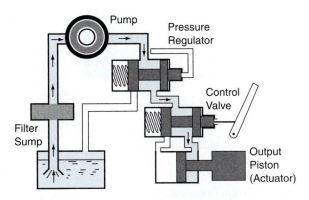

FIGURE 6-7   The basic components of a simple hydraulic system.

From this formula, we can see that the power needed for the transmission's hydraulic system is determined by how much fluid is being pumped and the system pressure.

Another concern related to fluid horsepower comes from another physical law: Energy can neither be created nor destroyed, but it can be converted from one form to another. Pumping fluid through a restriction like that of a relief valve heats the fluid; the lost fluid energy is converted to heat. A transmission is most efficient if it has only enough fluid pressure to do the required operation.

6.4 BASIC AUTOMATIC TRANSMISSION HYDRAULICS

In most automatic transmissions, the **pump** is built into the front or engine end of the transmission and is driven by the back of the torque converter (Figure 6-8). In some units, the pump is mounted deeper into the case and is driven by a shaft running from the torque converter (Figure 6-9). In either case, the pump begins moving fluid as soon as the engine starts. The pump is sized to produce enough fluid flow to fill the actuators and stroke the pistons during each shift in addition to keeping the torque converter filled and the transmission lubricated at all engine speeds.

The pump intake begins at the *filter,* which is positioned in the transmission's pan; in many cases, the filter is attached to the bottom of the valve body . The pan is the *fluid reservoir* or *sump,* and it contains more than enough fluid for normal operation.

All automatic transmissions use a variable **pressure regulator valve** that limits the operating pressure as well as providing the appropriate hydraulic pressure for the various

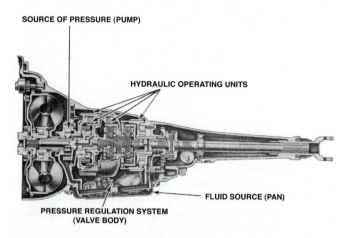

FIGURE 6-8 In many transmissions, the oil pump is at the front of the transmission and is driven by the torque converter hub. *(Courtesy of Chrysler Corporation)*

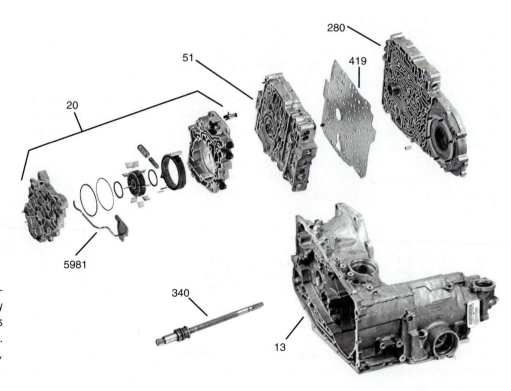

FIGURE 6-9 This pump assembly (20) is attached to the valve body (51) and channel plate (280). The pump is driven by the oil pump drive shaft (340). *(Courtesy of Slauson Transmission Parts, www.slauson.com)*

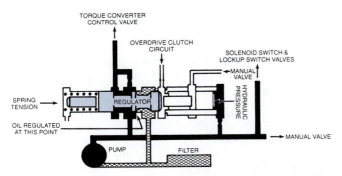

FIGURE 6-10   A pressure regulator valve. When fluid pressure acting on the right end of the valve exceeds spring tension, the valve will move to the left and open the passage back to the pump inlet. *(Courtesy of Chrysler Corporation)*.

operating conditions (Figure 6-10). The pressure regulator is normally found in the valve body. It is located in the pump body in some transmissions. In addition to the pressure regulator, some transmissions use a **pressure relief valve** to release excess pressure that might occur under certain operating conditions. Some transmissions use a *variable displacement* vane pump or a two-stage pump. These pumps can reduce their displacement and therefore the amount of fluid that is pumped when fluid demands are low.

Fluid flow through a transmission's hydraulic system is controlled by various valves, most of these are in the *valve body* (Figure 6-11). All transmissions have a **manual valve.** This valve is connected to the shift lever in the driver's compartment (Figure 6-12). Nearly all transmissions also have one *shift valve* for each automatic upshift (Figure 6-13). A two-speed transmission has one shift valve; a four-speed has three shift valves. Additional valves are used to tailor the timing, speed, and quality of the upshifts and downshifts.

The greatest fluid flow is to the **actuator,** which is usually a hydraulic piston. The hydraulic actuators of an automatic transmission are the servos that apply and release the bands and the pistons that apply the clutches.

In automatic transmissions, the valves are positioned so that fluid pressure is exerted on the actuator piston all the time that the actuator is applied. When the actuator is released, fluid pressure is exhausted (Figure 6-14). Many valves shuttle back and forth between the apply and exhaust ports.

6.5 PRODUCING FLUID FLOW AND PRESSURE

Three common types of rotary pumps are used to produce the fluid flow and resulting pressure in an automatic transmission. They are the **internal-external** gear with *crescent (crescent or gear) pump,* the *gerotor (rotor) pump,* and the *vane pump* (Figure 6-15). The pumping action in each of these is

essentially the same. The inner pumping member (external gear or inner rotor) is driven by the torque converter hub or a drive shaft, and the outer pumping member (the internal gear, outer rotor, or vane housing) is offset or eccentric relative to the inner gear or rotor.

As the inner member rotates, a series of chambers (between the gear teeth, the rotor lobes, or vanes) increases in volume in one area and decreases in another. A low-pressure area is created in the void area where the chamber volume increases. This area is connected to a passage leading to the filter that is submerged in fluid near the bottom of the sump. Atmospheric pressure inside the transmission pushes fluid into the filter, through the intake passage, and into the pump inlet (Figure 6-16). As the pump rotates, fluid fills the chambers just as fast as they enlarge.

On the other side of the pump the chambers get smaller, and the outlet port of the pump is positioned in this area. Here, the fluid is forced out of the pump and into the passage leading to the pressure control valve and the rest of the hydraulic system. The pressure regulated fluid is often called *supply* or *mainline pressure.*

Most automatic transmissions use a fixed-size, *positive displacement* pump. Every revolution of the pump will move the same volume of fluid. The faster the pump is turned, the more fluid will be pumped during a given time period. Both the gear pump and the rotor pump are positive displacement pumps. Variable vane pumps are also positive displacement in that they will pump a certain volume on each revolution, but the displacement, and therefore the fluid volume, can be changed. This is done by moving the vane housing to reduce the size of the pumping chambers (Figure 6-17). Variable displacement pumps allow a large output to produce the fluid volume needed for shifts and lubrication and a reduced output when it is not needed.

Some transmissions use a dual-stage gear pump, a combination of two positive displacement pumps. Both pumps supply fluid when demands are high. The output of the second-stage pump is released or vented when the primary stage can supply the needed flow and pressure. This system provides the volume of a large displacement pump at low speeds plus the economy of a small displacement pump at higher, cruising speeds (Figure 6-18).

The parts in a pump must fit together with a very little clearance to prevent the fluid from leaking across the pump from the high-pressure area to the areas of lower pressure. The fit provides just enough clearance for the parts to move without excess drag.

6.6 PROVIDING CLEAN FLUID

A filter is located at the pump inlet to trap dirt, metal, and any other foreign particles that might cause wear in the pump, bearings, bushings, and gear train or cause sticking of the

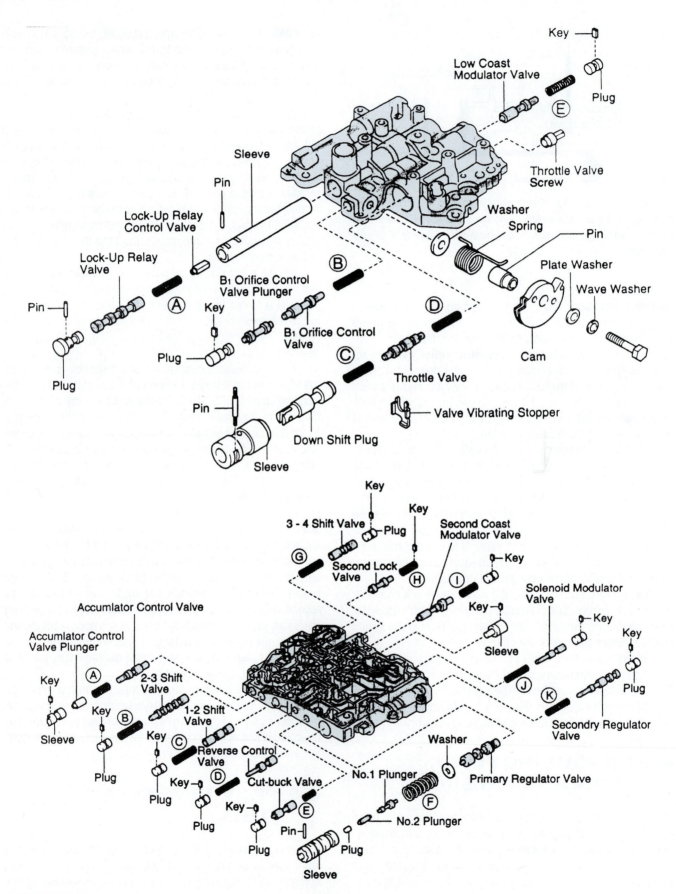

FIGURE 6-11   This valve body has two sections that contain 11 sets of valves.

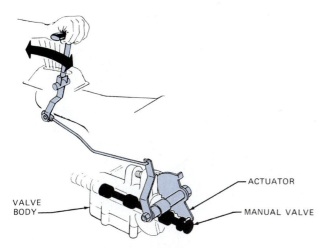

FIGURE 6-12   The manual valve is connected to the gear shift lever so movement of the lever will slide the valve along its bore. *(Courtesy of Nissan North America, Inc.)*

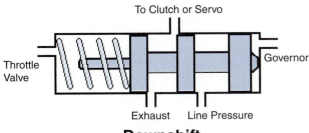

Downshift

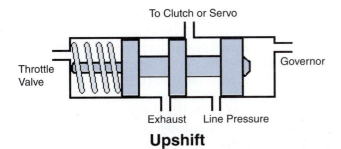

Upshift

FIGURE 6-13   A typical shift valve has a spring to move the valve to a downshift position; throttle pressure works with this spring. When governor pressure gets high enough, the valve will move to an upshift position.

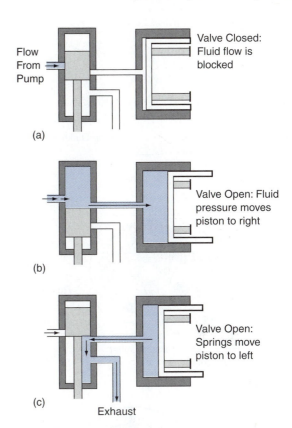

FIGURE 6-14   Operation of the valve controls fluid flow to the actuator. It can block operation (a), cause apply (b), or cause release (c).

various valves. Three types of filters are used: surface, depth, and paper (Figure 6-19). Filters offer a potential problem in that as they do their job, they will eventually plug up. This might cause an excessive pressure drop across the filter and fluid starvation to the pump.

A *surface filter* traps the foreign particles at the outer surface (Figure 6-20). This filter can be a woven screen of metal or synthetic material such as dacron or polyester. Some sources consider a *paper filter* to be a surface filter. With a metal or synthetic screen, the size of the openings vary from rather large to very fine, in the range of 50 to 100 μm (micrometer, micron). A **micron** is one millionth of a meter or 39 millionths of an inch. The symbol for micron is μm. The disadvantage of a surface filter is that it has limited surface area that limits it's capacity. The mesh openings are the usable area. A large portion of a filter's surface is the fibers or wires that make up the filter, with the remainder being the openings (Figure 6-21). The filter can quickly become plugged. The filter material must be strong enough to prevent collapse or tearing of the filter.

A *depth filter* traps particles as they try to pass through the filter material. Depth filters use felt or a synthetic material of various thickness (Figure 6-22). The depth of the material allows room to trap particles as well as room for fluid flow. It also offers the ability to trap smaller particles, more capacity to trap particles, and the ability to flow better for a longer period of time (Figure 6-23). Some depth filters trap particles as small as 10 μm.

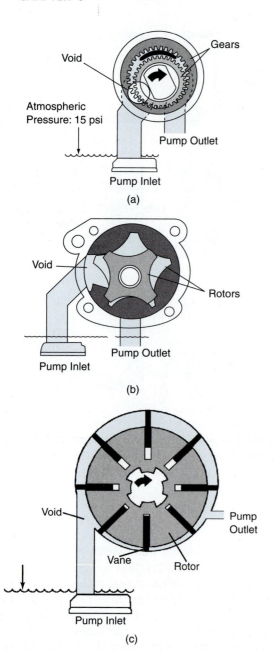

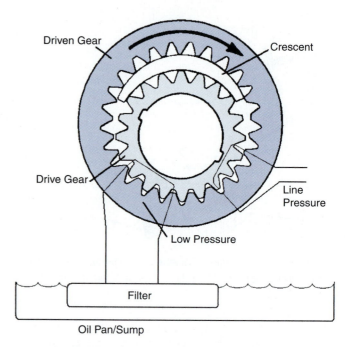

FIGURE 6-16   As a pump rotates, a low pressure/vacuum is created as the pumping members move apart in one area, and atmospheric pressure will force fluid into this area. Pressure is created where the pumping members move together.

eight different transmissions used less than 3,000 miles found:

- 1 to 20 particles in the 50-μm size
- 800 to 8,000 particles in the 15-μm size
- More than 50,000 particles in the 5-μm size

Normally, the pan is the sump or reservoir for the fluid, and the filter is positioned close to the bottom of the pan. General Motors transaxles use two reservoirs; one is the bottom pan and the other is the valve body cover or side pan (Figure 6-24). When the unit is cold, all the fluid is kept in the bottom pan. As the transaxle warms up, the thermostatic element closes to retain fluid in the side pan.

FIGURE 6-15   An internal-external gear pump (a), gerotor pump (b), and vane pump (c).

Particle size is important when we consider the space between a bushing and the shaft. This clearance is about 0.001 to 0.003 in. (0.025 to 0.076 mm), but if the shaft is loaded to one side by gear pressure, this clearance might be only the width of two or three oil molecules. A hard, abrasive particle in this area will produce wear that, in turn, will produce small metal particles that cause more wear. Dirt or other particles that enter the valve body may cause a valve to stick in its bore. This can cause a no-shift problem or a partial shift with low pressure. A recent study of the fluid from

PROBLEM SOLVING 6-1   Imagine that you are working in a shop that specializes in transmission repair, and these problems are brought to you:

Case 1   A 1996 Toyota Camry drives okay in all gears, but it seems to go into neutral when it makes sharp turns. What could cause this problem? What should you first check?

Case 2   A 1989 Chevrolet Caprice with a 200–4R transmission does not move, forward or backward, with the shift selector in any position. What do you think might be wrong with this transmission? Where would you begin your checks?

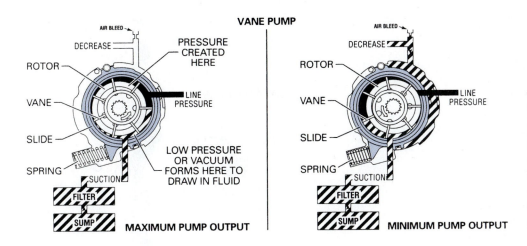

FIGURE 6-17 A variable displacement vane pump in maximum and minimum output positions. The slide is moved to the high-output position by the spring moving the slide. Decreased pressure comes from the pressure regulator valve. *(Reprinted with permission of General Motors)*

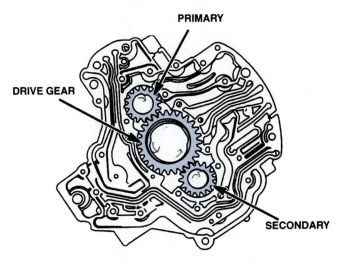

FIGURE 6-18 This transmission uses a dual-stage, external gear pump. Both stages are used at low engine speeds to produce enough fluid for the transmission's needs. At higher engine speeds, the secondary stage is vented. *(Courtesy of Chrysler Corporation)*

6.7 CONTROLLING FLUID FLOW

The fluid flow from the pressure regulator valve to the manual valve and into the control circuit is called *mainline, line,* or *control pressure.* Flow to and from a transmission hydraulic actuator is controlled by one or more valves. Spool valves sliding in a round bore are used for this purpose. A *spool valve* gets its name from its resemblance to a spool used for thread (Figure 6-25). A spool valve can have two or more **lands** that fit the valve bore tightly enough so that fluid cannot escape past the valve land but loosely enough so that the valve can slide

freely in the bore (Figure 6-26). The annular grooves (valleys) between the lands is where the fluid flows through the valve. Typically the valve-to-bore clearance is about 0.003 to 0.004 in. (80 to 100 microns). The close fit requires the valve to expand and contract at the same rate as the valve body. This prevents the valve from sticking or having excessive leakage. The outer edges of the lands have sharp corners to help prevent debris from wedging between the land and the valve bore. The valleys or grooves between the lands serve as fluid passages. The faces serve as pressure surfaces, called **reaction surfaces,** to produce valve movement. Some valves are relatively long with a series of lands and grooves so fluid flow through two or more passages are controlled at the same time. The lands of a spool valve often have different diameters in order to provide different-size reaction areas. Some valves are used with bushings, also called sleeves, that allow the manufacturer to easily change valve diameter and fluid passages (Figure 6-27).

A spool valve bore has fluid passages entering from the sides, which connect to the grooves (valleys) that extend clear around the valve. This is done to produce the same pressure entirely around the valve. If pressure were exerted on only one side of the valve, the valve would be *side loaded.* This can force the valve sideways and lock the valve in the bore. Only a very few manual valves are designed with side loading. These valves have one or more grooves running along part of the valve's length. As a spool valve is slid along the bore, the lands open up or close off the side passages and block or allow fluid flow from one place to another or to the sump to allow pressure to be exhausted.

The position of a valve can be controlled by the following:

- mechanical linkage
- hydraulic pressure
- spring
- centrifugal force
- engine vacuum
- electric solenoids

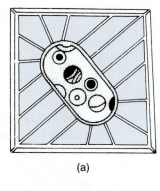

(a)

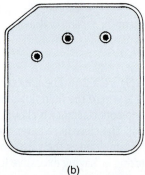

(b)

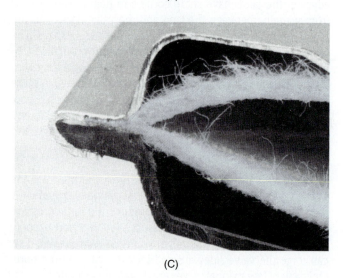

(C)

FIGURE 6-19   Two filters: a surface/screen filter (a) and a depth/felt filter (b and c).

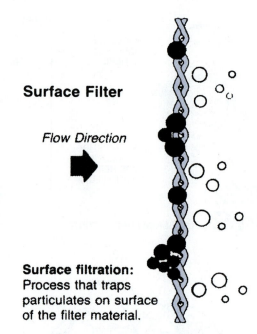

Surface Filter

Flow Direction

Surface filtration:
Process that traps
particulates on surface
of the filter material.

FIGURE 6-20   A surface filter traps particles that are too big to pass through the openings in the screen. *(Courtesy of SPX Filtran)*

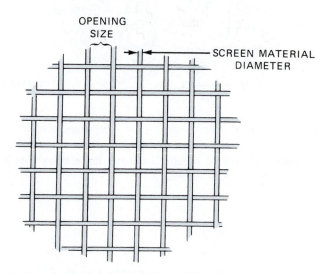

OPENING
SIZE

SCREEN MATERIAL
DIAMETER

FIGURE 6-21   The surface area of a surface filter is reduced somewhat by the material that makes up the screen. The size of the screen openings determines how small of a particle can be filtered.

The manual valve (a spool valve) is moved mechanically by the shift lever. Movement of the shift lever slides the manual valve along its bore, opening or closing the desired passages. Fluid will be sent to the appropriate apply devices and valves for the selected gear range.

Most of the spool valves in a valve body are positioned by a spring at one end and fluid pressure at the other (Figure 6-28). The spring tries to hold the valve in one position, and when

fluid pressure gets stronger than the spring, it will move the valve (Figure 6-29). Some valves act as a servo to produce motion (usually of another valve), redirect fluid flow, or regulate fluid pressure. They will be described more completely in Chapter 7.

Nonelectronic transmissions use a mechanical **governor valve** and either a mechanical or vacuum-operated throttle valve. *Shift timing,* also called *shift points,* is controlled by the governor and throttle valves. Newer transmissions use electronic controls with *vehicle speed sensors (VSS)* and *throttle position sensors (TPS)* for this purpose. An *electronic control module (ECM)* uses signals from these two sensors as well as other sensors to determine shift points, and the ECM activates electronic *solenoid valves* to produce the shifts. Electronic shift control is described more completely in Chapter 8.

Governor valves are spun by the transmission output shaft so the valve is thrown outward by centrifugal force. Hydraulic pressure from the governor and a light spring is used to

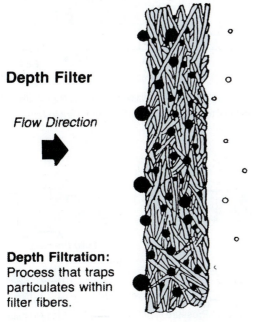

FIGURE 6-22 A depth filter is a group of woven fibers of a certain thickness. Foreign particles are trapped at different levels as they try to flow through. *(Courtesy of SPX Filtran)*

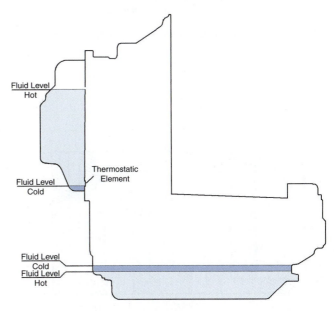

FIGURE 6-24 General Motors transaxles have two fluid reservoirs. One is the lower pan, and one is the valve body cover. The thermostatic element closes when the fluid heats up to raise the fluid level in the upper pan. *(Reprinted with permission of General Motors)*

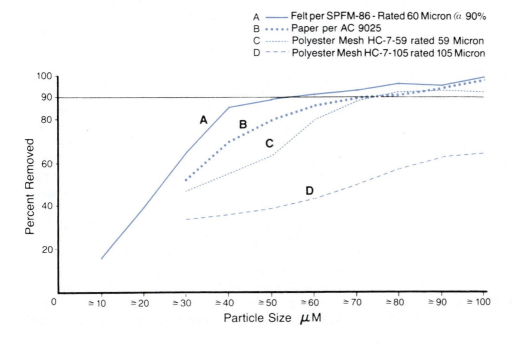

FIGURE 6-23 Comparison of the filtering ability of four types of filters. *(Courtesy of SPX Filtran)*

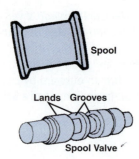

FIGURE 6-25   A spool valve resembles a spool for thread (top).

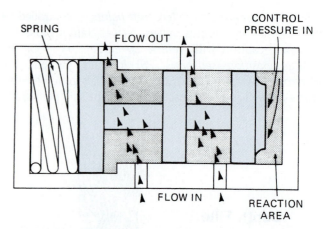

FIGURE 6-28   When a valve moves in its bore, the side passages are opened or closed to control fluid flow. *(Courtesy of Chrysler Corporation)*

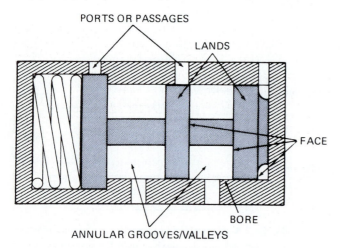

FIGURE 6-26   A spool valve and its bore. Note the names of the various parts. *(Courtesy of Chrysler Corporation)*

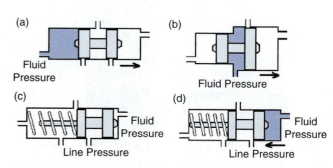

FIGURE 6-29   Fluid pressure acting on the surface area of the valve face can move the valve along the bore.

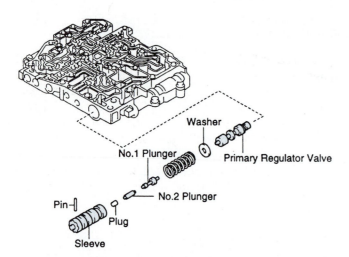

FIGURE 6-27   The sleeve allows the larger primary regulator valve to enter its part of the bore and also provides the bore for the smaller No. 1 and No. 2 plungers. *(Courtesy of Toyota Motor Sales USA, Inc.)*

oppose centrifugal force (Figure 6-30). The output of this valve is a gradual fluid pressure increase that is roughly proportional to vehicle speed (Figure 6-31). The pressure produced by the governor is called *governor pressure.* Many transmissions use a *throttle valve* to produce a hydraulic pressure that is proportional to vehicle load (Figure 6-32). A throttle valve can be controlled either mechanically or by vacuum. Some transmissions use a rod or cable to make a mechanical connection to the engine's throttle linkage. Other transmissions use a **modulator valve** with a vacuum signal from the intake manifold that acts on the diaphragm of a vacuum motor. The valve is balanced between a mechanical pressure from a spring-versus-vacuum-diaphragm pressure at one end and fluid pressure at the other. The pressure produced by sensing engine load is known as throttle pressure or TV pressure.

The vacuum motor (modulator) has a spring that is always pushing against the hydraulic valve, and the engine manifold vacuum reduces the power of the spring. Throttle valve (TV) pressure is very low at idle speed and very high at wide-open throttle (WOT). A **detent valve** is used in some circuits

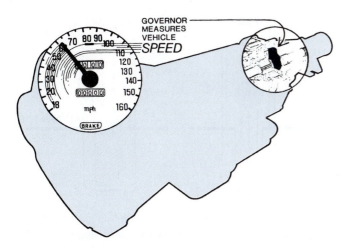

FIGURE 6-30 The governor valve produces a fluid pressure that is proportional to the speed of the vehicle. *(Courtesy of Nissan North America, Inc.)*

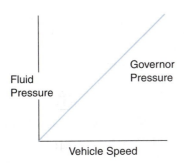

FIGURE 6-31 Ideally, governor pressure increases with speed so the pressure in psi matches the speed in mph. There should be about 40 psi at 40 mph.

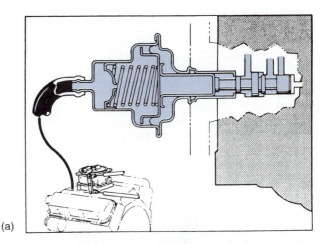

(a)

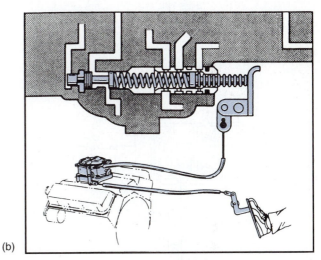

(b)

FIGURE 6-32 A vacuum-operated throttle valve uses a vacuum modulator to produce an engine-load-sensitive signal at the transmission (a). A mechanical-controlled throttle valve (in this case a cable) transfers an engine-load-sensitive signal through mechanical linkage (b). *(Reprinted with permission of General Motors)*

to increase TV pressure and force downshifts at WOT. The maximum pressure that a governor or a throttle valve can produce is line pressure.

Another way to control the position of a spool valve is to use an electric solenoid. The solenoid can be switched on or off by an electric switch or an electronic control module (ECM). The ECM can be programmed to react to inputs from many different sensors. Electronic transmissions use several solenoids to control the torque converter clutch, line pressure, and shift valve operation. The solenoid can control a shift valve by exhausting the fluid pressure at one end, and a spring or fluid pressure at the other end causes the spool valve to move and change the fluid path through the valve (Figure 6-33). Some valves are moved mechanically by the solenoid.

A *check ball* is the simplest method of controlling fluid flow. A *one-way check valve* resembles a steel bearing or plastic ball over a hole in the *separator plate.* The separator plate, also called a *transfer plate* or *restrictor plate,* is positioned between valve body sections or between the valve body and transmission case (Figure 6-34). An upward fluid flow moves the ball aside and fluid flows around it. A downward fluid flow forces the ball against the hole and stops the flow. The flow of fluid is only possible in one direction, upward.

Some transmissions use a *two-way check valve,* also called a *shuttle valve.* The ball is positioned above two side-by-side holes with another flow passage extending upward or to the side. Upward flow through one of the holes in the plate causes the ball to move over and seat against the other hole (Figure 6-35). Fluid flow upward through the second hole causes the ball to move over and seal the first hole.

A pressure relief valve resembles a check valve, but it is spring loaded (Figure 6-36). Sometimes a flat disc or spool

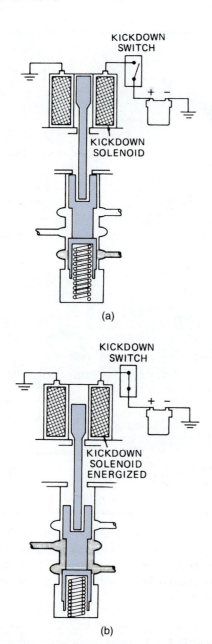

(a)

(b)

FIGURE 6-33 This kickdown valve is controlled by the electric solenoid and is closed when there is no electrical signal (a). The valve opens when the solenoid is energized (b). *(Courtesy of Nissan North America, Inc.)*

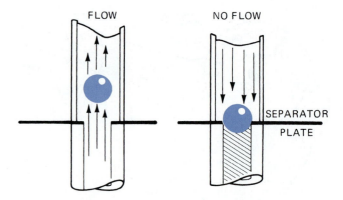

FIGURE 6-34 A check valve is opened by fluid flow in one direction (left) and closes when the fluid tries to flow in the other direction.

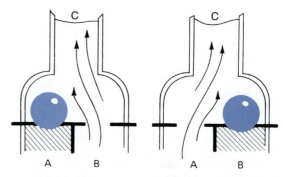

FIGURE 6-35 When fluid flows through this shuttle valve from port B to port C, the check ball moves over to close port A (left). Fluid flow from port A will close port B (right).

(a)

(b)

A X P = Spring Force

FIGURE 6-36 A pressure relief valve (a). When fluid pressure acting on the area of the ball exceeds the spring force, the ball will move off of its seat and allow excess pressure to escape (b).

valve is used in place of a ball. The fluid pressure required to unseat this valve is determined by the strength of the spring and the size of the opening at the seat. Fluid pressure acting on the exposed area of the ball pushes against the spring. When fluid pressure exceeds spring pressure, the ball moves off it's seat, the pressure is relieved through the opening, and the spring closes the passage again. This can happen many times a second. The rate of fluid flow can be controlled by a restriction called an orifice. Orifices are described more completely in a following section.

6.7.1 Valve Hydraulic Forces

Think of a valve as a hydraulic actuator. The hydraulic force exerted by a valve is simply the valve land area multiplied by fluid pressure. The valve area is determined using the formula for the area of a circle, πr^2.

Let us imagine a valve with a 2-lb (0.9-kg) spring pressing on one end and a 0.5-in. (12.67-mm) diameter land at the other end (Figure 6-37):

- The area of the 0.5-in. land is $0.25 \times 0.25 \times 3.1416 = 0.196$ in^2 (1.26 cm^2), and

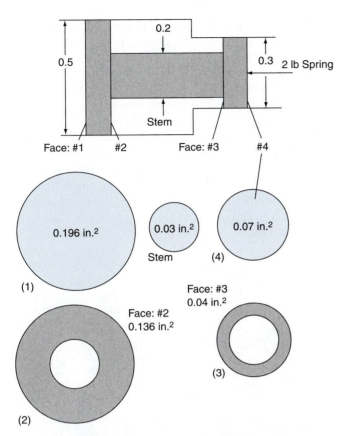

FIGURE 6-37 This valve spool has four possible hydraulic reaction faces. The areas are calculated like those of any other circular surface using the formula πr^2.

- a fluid pressure of 10.2 psi (70.33 kPa) acting on an area of 0.196 in² (1.26 cm²) generates a force of 2 lb.

Fluid pressure greater than 10.2 psi will cause the valve to move and compress the spring.

In some cases, pressure is exerted between two different-size land faces; fluid pressure acting on a larger face develops a greater force that will move the valve in that direction. If the diameter of one land is 0.5 in., the other land is 0.3 in. (7.6 mm), and the stem or shank of the valve is 0.2 in. (5.1 mm). There are three diameters and two important areas:

- Face 1: 0.5-in. diameter has an area of 0.196 in².
- Stem: 0.2-in. diameter has an area of $0.1 \times 0.1 \times 3.1416 = 0.030$ in².
- Face 2: has an area of 0.196 − 0.030 = 0.136 in².
- Face 4: 0.3 diameter has an area of $0.15 \times 0.15 \times 3.1416 = 0.070$ in².
- Face 3: has an area of 0.070 − 0.030 = 0.040 in².
- Area difference between Face 2 and Face 3: 0.136 − 0.040 = 0.096 in².
- A fluid pressure of 10 psi (68.95 kPa) will develop a force of 0.96 lb (0.75 kg) pushing in the direction of Face 2, the larger land.

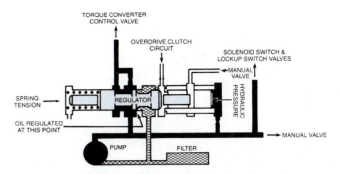

FIGURE 6-38 When fluid pressure at the right end of the regulator valve gets high enough, the valve will move toward the left and allow excess pressure to return to the pump suction passage. *(Courtesy of Chrysler Corporation)*

6.8 CONTROLLING FLUID PRESSURE

Fluid pressure in an automatic transmission is controlled by a variable pressure regulator valve. Fluid pressure must be high enough to apply a clutch or band tightly enough to prevent slippage. Excessive fluid pressure will produce heat and fluid foaming as well as more drag on the engine. Remember that fluid horsepower is a product of pressure and flow. In most transmissions, the pressure regulator valve is positioned close to the outlet of the pump. This valve is usually arranged so fluid pressure is at one end and a spring is at the other end. An additional passage from the pump enters the valve at one valley, and a passage leading back to the pump inlet is located at an adjacent valley (Figure 6-38).

When fluid pressure is multiplied by the reaction area of the valve, a force greater than that of the spring's strength is created, and the valve will move to allow flow back to the pump inlet. The valve finds a balanced position where the fluid pressure acting on the reaction area of the valve and working against the spring releases enough fluid to maintain the correct pressure.

Transmissions with a vane pump use a different style of pressure regulator. The pressure regulator valve works like those with other pumps, but the passage from the valve goes to the pump's vane housing instead of back to the pump inlet. This pressure moves the pump slide to reduce the displacement and output of the pump (see Figure 6-17). High fluid pressure causes the pressure regulator to send a calibrated pressure to the pump slide, which reduces pump output and thus pressure. When fluid pressure drops, the priming spring returns the pump slide back to the high-output position.

Regulator valves have additional lands and valleys or another valve in the same bore to provide boost pressures for medium- to full-throttle operation or while in reverse. Sometimes manual low and intermediate gear require additional pressure because of the probable increased torque requirement.

Usually a pressure regulator valve produces the correct pressure, but a valve that does not slide easily in its bore can stick and then overtravel. This can cause the pressure to drop; the valve then moves back to its original position, and the cycle soon repeats. A pressure regulator valve can move back and forth quite rapidly, probably several thousand times a second. This movement follows the pressure pulsations from the pump. At times this makes a whining or buzzing sound in some transmissions, especially when they are cold.

Boosted mainline pressure is used to provide additional holding power at the clutches and bands. A firmer shift occurs when operating under wider throttle openings (increased load).

PROBLEM SOLVING 6-2 Imagine that you are working in a shop that specializes in transmission repair, and these problems are brought to you:

Case 1 A 1996 Dodge Ram pickup drives okay in first and second gears, but there is no 2–3 shift. There is no third gear; it just stays in second. The fluid level is okay, but it is almost black. Would a worn band cause this problem? Could a sticking valve cause it? How about a worn third-gear clutch?

Case 2 A 1994 Ford Mustang has very harsh upshifts in all gears. The shifts are severe with all throttle positions. The fluid level is slightly low but within the range on the dipstick, and the fluid condition appears good. What do you think might be wrong with this transmission? What would you check next?

6.9 SEALING FLUID PRESSURE

The fluid passages run throughout the valve body, transmission case, shafts, and tubes of the transmission. Remember that fluid transmits pressure equally through a passage, regardless of its size or shape. The many passages in the valve body and the transmission case look like a bunch of *worm tracks* (a nickname used by transmission rebuilders; Figure 6-39). The passages in the transmission case can be worm tracks or simply holes drilled to form passages. Metal ball plugs are commonly used to seal unwanted openings. Some transmission shafts have several different passages for apply pressure for various clutches or lubrication (Figure 6-40). Gaskets and seals are

used to keep the pressure from escaping where fluid flows between parts. Seals fall into two categories: *static* and *dynamic.*

A static seal is used to seal the space between two parts that are stationary relative to each other. Static seals include *gaskets* and **O-rings** that are placed between the two parts and squeezed tightly as the parts are fastened together. A static seal must provide enough compression to fill any possible voids between the two surfaces (Figure 6-41). The compression needed for a seal to work properly depends greatly on the flatness and rigidity of the sealing surfaces. Wavy or weak surfaces need a thick, resilient seal or gasket. Aluminum transmission cases move quite a bit as they expand and contract during heating and cooling cycles, so a resilient gasket and seal material are required.

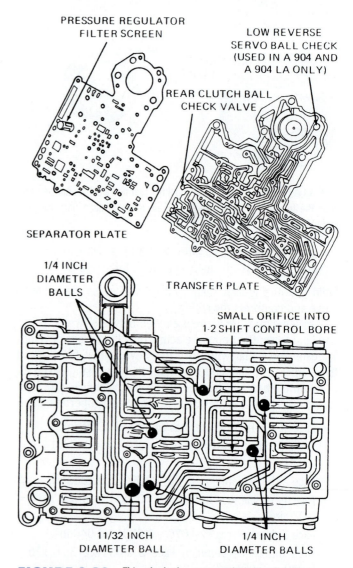

FIGURE 6-39 This valve body uses upper (at bottom) and lower sections (at top) that are separated by the separator plate. Note how the separator plate can restrict a passage so it becomes a port or orifice for flow into the other section. *(Courtesy of Chrysler Corporation)*

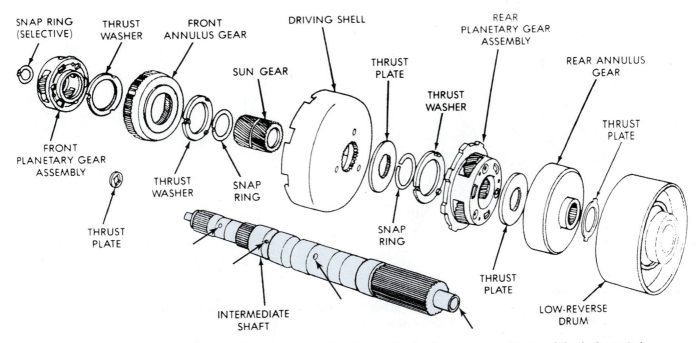

FIGURE 6-40 This intermediate shaft has fluid passages to transfer lubricating oil to the planetary gearsets. *(Courtesy of Chrysler Corporation)*

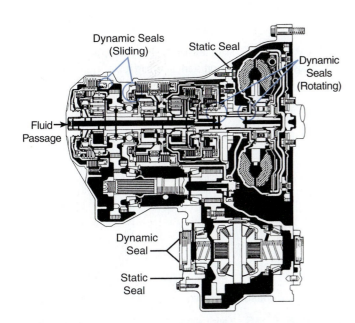

FIGURE 6-41 Static seals prevent fluid from passing between two stationary surfaces. Dynamic seals keep fluid from passing through when one of the surfaces is moving. *(Courtesy of Toyota Motor Sales USA, Inc.)*

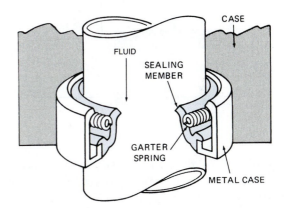

FIGURE 6-42 The sealing member of a metal-clad lip seal makes a dynamic seal with the rotating shaft while the metal case forms a static seal with the transmission case. *(Courtesy of Chrysler Corporation)*

A dynamic seal has a much harder job because one of the surfaces to be sealed is moving relative to the seal. The movement can be rotating (e.g., the torque converter enters the front of the transmission or the fluid flows from the pump housing into a clutch assembly) or a sliding motion (e.g., the stroking of a clutch piston; Figure 6-42).

At each end of the transmission, a rotating shaft enters or leaves the transmission, and the opening through which the shaft runs must be sealed to keep the fluid in and dirt and water out. At these openings the torque converter enters the front pump and the output shaft(s) leaves the extension housing. In both cases, a **metal-clad lip seal** is used. A lip seal has a flexible rubber sealing lip that rubs against the revolving shaft with enough pressure so fluid cannot flow between the shaft and the seal lip. A garter spring is often used to increase this sealing pressure. The lip is molded into the seal's case or outer housing, which forms a static seal with the transmission case or extension housing.

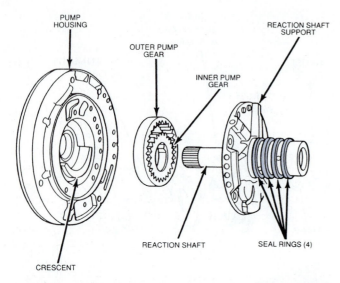

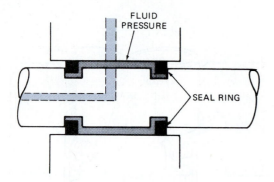

FIGURE 6-43   Sealing rings are used to seal the passages between stationary and rotating members. For example, the seal rings at the right keep the fluid flows from the pump to the front clutch from escaping. *(Courtesy of Chrysler Corporation)*

FIGURE 6-44   Fluid pressure forces a sealing ring outward in both directions to make firm contact with the side of the groove and outer diameter of the bore.

Another type of seal is used to seal the fluid passages where fluid leaves a stationary member and transfers to a rotating member such as the turbine shaft, front clutch assembly, or governor support (Figure 6-43). This seal is a metal, plastic, or Teflon ring that fits tight in its bore to make a seal while the side of the seal seals against the side of its groove (Figure 6-44). A seal with a small leak is sometimes desirable to lubricate a bearing area close to the sealing ring. Metal and plastic sealing rings can be a full-circle *hook ring* or a *butt-cut ring* with a small gap. Teflon rings can be *scarf cut* (have the ends cut at an angle so they overlap), *butt cut,* or *uncut* (Figure 6-45). Teflon seals can change size. When a Teflon ring is stretched over a shaft, it must be resized smaller to fit into the groove and bore. Special installing and resizing tools are recommended when installing Teflon sealing rings.

The sliding seals for the clutch and band servo pistons are made of rubber in an *O-ring, lathe-cut seal,* or *lip seal* shape.

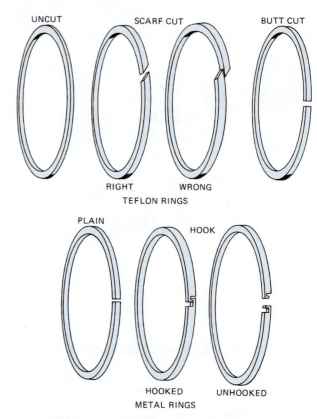

FIGURE 6-45   Metal seal rings (bottom) have plain or hooked ends. Teflon rings (top) are either uncut, scarf cut, or butt cut.

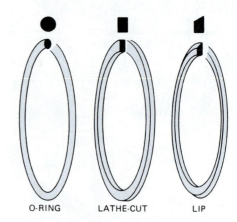

FIGURE 6-46   Clutch and servo piston seals are usually O-rings, lathe-cut rings, or lip seals.

An O-ring is a rubber ring with a round cross section. A lathe-cut seal, also called a *square-cut seal* or *quad-ring,* is a rubber ring with a square cross section. A lip seal has a sealing lip much like that of the metal-clad seal described earlier (Figure 6-46). The type of seal used on a piston is determined by the shape and size of the seal groove. By its nature, a lip seal provides the best pressure retention as well as the ability to adapt to piston-to-bore clearance (Figure 6-47). The lip seal is bonded to the

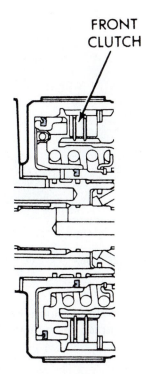

FRONT CLUTCH

FIGURE 6-47 Two lip seals (blue) form fluid-tight seals between the front clutch piston and its bore. *(Courtesy of Chrysler Corporation)*

piston in some transmissions to give more consistent operation and lower drag. The bore in the clutch assembly as well as the center seal area must have straight, smooth sides to provide a good sealing surface and keep seal wear to a minimum. The outer ends of the piston bores are normally chamfered to make piston and seal installation easier.

6.9.1 Special Notes on Elastomers

The rubber seal materials used for seals are called *elastomers* because of their elastic nature. A dynamic seal must remain flexible and maintain its size and shape in order to work properly. Plain rubber is not used in a transmission because it is adversely affected by heat and contact with ATF. Natural rubber has an operating range of −58°F (−50°C) to 212°F (100°C). Higher temperatures cause rubber materials to harden, and exposure to transmission fluid causes it to swell excessively. A hardened seal may leak and cause a pressure loss, which in turn will cause clutch slippage and failure.

Synthetic rubber compounds are blends of various rubber-like materials. Some of these that are used in automatic transmissions are *Buna N* or *nitrile rubber* (to 230°F), *polyacrylate* (to 320°F), *ethyleneacrylic* (to 375°F), *fluoroelastomer* (to 400°F), and *silicone* (above 400°F; Figure 6-48). Another major difference between these compounds is cost; as the operating temperature range increases, the cost of the material goes up many times. A manufacturer usually selects the lowest-cost

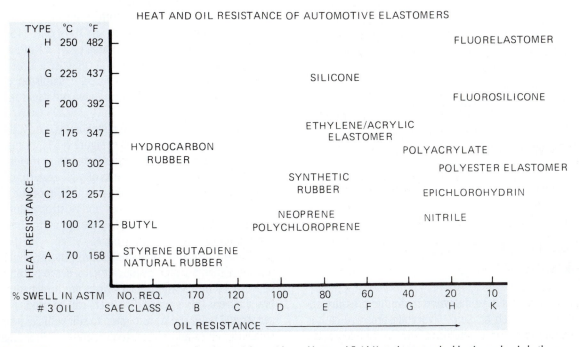

HEAT AND OIL RESISTANCE OF AUTOMOTIVE ELASTOMERS

FIGURE 6-48 This chart compares the ability of seal materials to withstand heat and fluid. Note that natural rubber is very low in both cases.

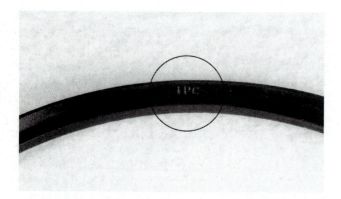

FIGURE 6-49 The code letters cast into the surface of this seal identify the manufacturer of the seal.

seal material that will do the job, and we should realize that different seals in a transmission have different working conditions. For example, the high-reverse clutch in a Simpson gear train transmission is subjected to about 30 to 35 times as much activity as the forward clutch. One seal material might work well in one clutch but not stand up to the load or movement requirements of another.

When a transmission rebuilder purchases a gasket and seal kit, cost should not be the only concern. The use of better-quality materials will lead to an overhaul that will perform better and last longer. The price of the correct seal material can be many times greater than a cheaper Buna N seal. Several methods can be used in the field to identify the quality of a particular seal:

- A letter code is molded into the seal surface. The code is registered with the Rubber Manufacturers Association (RMA) to identify the manufacturer. The original equipment manufacturer (OEM) of a transmission seal normally supplies the same OEM seal to the aftermarket (Figure 6-49). These are the best-quality seals.
- Ignite the seal with a match, let it burn for 2 or 3 seconds, and then extinguish the fire. If the smoke odor is like a burning tire, the material is Buna N; if it has a sweet smell, it is polyacrylic material. This destroys the seal, but it gives you a good idea of the material.
- Feel the material. Polyacrylic material is harder and less elastic than rubber.

6.10 APPLYING FLUID PRESSURE

An automatic transmission shifts when hydraulic pressure applies or releases a clutch or band. Hydraulic pressure causes the clutch or servo piston to stroke, taking up the clearance, and then squeezes the parts together. Both bands and clutches

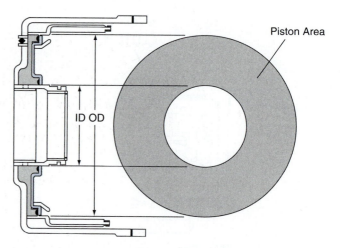

Piston Area: 6" OD = 28.27 in.^{2} $(3 \times 3 \times 3.1416)$
         3" ID = −7 in.^{2} $(1.5 \times 1.5 \times 3.1416)$
       Area = 21.27 in.^{2}

FIGURE 6-50 A typical clutch piston area is determined by subtracting the area of the inner diameter from the area of the outer-circle diameter.

are released by spring pressure. Band servos can also be released by hydraulic pressure.

The force that a clutch piston exerts on the clutch plates is a product of piston area multiplied by hydraulic pressure. A rotating, driving clutch has a piston with an outside diameter (OD) of about 6 in. (152 mm), and an inner diameter (ID) that can vary from 2 to 5 in. (102 to 127 mm; Figure 6-50). Most stationary, holding clutches have a larger diameter; the intermediate clutch piston in some transmissions has an OD of 10 in. (254 mm). A piston with an OD of 6 in. (152 mm) and an ID of 3 in. (76 mm) has an area of 21.27 in^2. A hydraulic pressure of 80 psi (551.6 kPa) will generate a force of 9,697 lb (4,408 kg), a fairly significant force. This piston will require about 2 cubic in. (in^3) of fluid to complete its stroke of 0.1 in. (0.254 mm).

Some clutches have two piston areas, and a lip seal is located between these two areas (Figure 6-51). In high gear, the inner, smaller area is used; it fills faster and provides sufficient force for the torque requirements of high gear. In reverse, fluid enters the outer area and leaks past the lip of the center seal to fill both areas. This produces a very strong clutch application force, and since reverse is a garage shift, there is ample time to fill the clutch.

Most bands use fairly small servo pistons, which generate less force than a clutch piston; a typical servo piston has an OD of a few inches. Some transmissions are designed so that several different servo piston diameters can be used. The different servos will tailor the transmission to suit vehicles with larger or smaller engines and torque requirements. More engine horsepower or heavier loads require more band application force.

Some servos are released by clutch apply pressure. For example, in some transmissions the intermediate servo is applied by hydraulic pressure in second gear. As the transmission shifts into third gear, it is released by third-gear oil pressure; when the vehicle slows for a stop, the servo is released by the spring.

6.10.1 Determining Piston Force

The force exerted by a piston is simply the piston area multiplied by fluid pressure. Like a valve, piston area is determined using the formula πr^2.

Piston A: A 5-in. diameter piston has a radius of 2.5 in.

- Radius squared: $2.5 \times 2.5 = 6.25$.
- 6.25 multiplied by π: $6.25 \times 3.1416 = 19.635$ (round up to 20 in^2).
- A fluid pressure of 80 psi acting on this piston will produce $80 \times 20 = 1,600$ lb of force.

- If this piston travels 0.100 in., it will require $20 \times 0.1 = 2$ in^3 of fluid.

Piston B: A clutch piston is slightly different because we must subtract the area of the center hole.

- If this piston has a 5-in. OD and a center hole diameter of 2.4 in., the center hole radius is 1.2 in.
- Radius squared (r^2): $1.2 \times 1.2 = 1.44$.
- The area of the center hole: $1.44 \times 3.1416 = 4.524$.
- 5-in. piston area: 19.635 in^2.
- 5-in. clutch piston area: $19.635 - 4.524 = 15.1$ in^2 (round off to 15 in^2).
- A fluid pressure of 80 psi acting on this piston will produce a force of $80 \times 15 = 1,200$ lb of force.
- If this piston travels 0.100 in., it will require $15 \times 0.1 = 1.5$ in^3 of fluid.

6.11 MODIFYING FLOW AND PRESSURE

During a shift , it is desirable to provide a gradual pressure increase to the clutch pistons or band servos. This improves the *shift quality,* producing the desirable *shift feel.* Shift feel is a "seat-of-the-pants" response the driver experiences during shifts. As the piston is stroking to take up the clutch or band clearance, the pressures in the circuit are relatively low. But the instant the clearance disappears and the piston stops moving, the pressure rises very rapidly, causing a sudden and possibly very harsh application. Shift quality can be adjusted mechanically by changing the friction material or hydraulically by controlling fluid pressure. There are many variables that affect shift quality (Figure 6-52).

The two commonly used devices to control band or clutch application are an **orifice** and an **accumulator.** Different versions of a particular transmission often have different orifice sizes and accumulator settings to adjust the transmission to the engine, vehicle weight, and intended use.

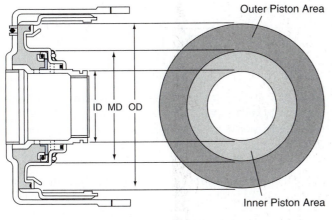

Outer Piston Area

ID MD OD

Inner Piston Area

Outer Piston Area:		Inner Piston Area:	
6" OD	= 28.27 in.^{2}	4" MD	= 12.56 in.^{2}
4" MD	= −12.56 in.^{2}	3" ID	= −7 in.^{2}
Area	= 15.71 in.^{2}	Area	= 5.56 in.^{2}

FIGURE 6-51 Some clutch pistons use a middle seal so the piston will have two working areas.

Variable	Softer	Firmer
Line pressure	lower	higher
Flow rate	slower	faster
Accumulator stroke rate	faster	slower
Clutch cushion springs	more	less
Friction plate grooving	less grooving less aggressive pattern	more aggressive pattern
Friction plate composition	less aggressive compound	more aggressive compound
Steel plate/drum surface	smoother	rougher
Fluid type	lower dynamic friction	higher dynamic friction

Shift quality can be modified by changing any of these variables.

FIGURE 6-52 Shift quality can be modified by changing any of these variables.

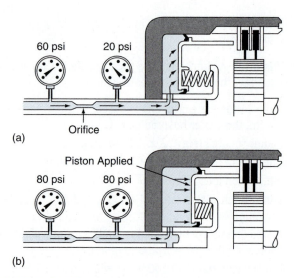

(a)

(b)

FIGURE 6-53   An orifice will cause a pressure drop as fluid flows through (a); when the flow stops, the pressure on both sides of the orifice will be the same (b).

An orifice is simply a small hole, usually in the separator plate (Figure 6-53). An orifice produces a resistance to fluid flow and therefore causes a pressure drop as long as fluid is flowing through it. The amount of pressure drop is relative to the size of the orifice and the flow volume. The smaller the orifice, the greater resistance to flow and the larger the pressure drop. As soon as the flow stops, the orifice no longer has an effect on the flow, and the pressure on both sides becomes equal. An orifice is also used to dampen fluid flow to the control valves. There is usually one in the passage between the pump and reaction land of the pressure regulator valve; this orifice helps soften pressure pulses from the pump that can cause the valve to overreact.

Fluid flow rate through an orifice requires a rather complex formula; calculating the actual flow is beyond the scope of this book, but understanding the effect of an orifice is important. Imagine a clutch with a piston that requires 1.5 in³ of fluid to apply. Transmission engineers will determine the orifice diameter that allows a flow of 1.5 in³ of fluid in about one-fifth of a second to apply the clutch at about 80 psi. Increased fluid pressure, from boost, will produce increased flow, quicker clutch filling, and a faster, firmer shift.

An orifice keeps the supply side of the circuit from having a pressure drop during a clutch or band application. In a simple shift circuit, when the shift valve moves to send fluid to a clutch piston, the fluid pressure will drop at the shift valve. It might also drop in the circuit that feeds the shift valve, which could cause an unwanted operation.

An accumulator is a piston or valve that is not attached to anything; all it does is stroke in its own bore (Figure 6-54). The pressure required to stroke the accumulator is controlled by a spring or by opposing fluid pressure. An accumulator is tied to an apply piston by a branch of the fluid passage used for apply pressure. It is adjusted to stroke at a pressure just

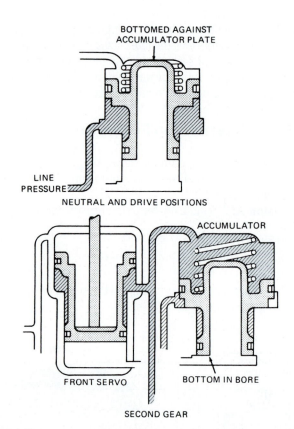

FIGURE 6-54   In neutral, the accumulator piston is moved to the top of its stroke by line pressure (top). Front servo apply pressure strokes the accumulator piston downward, delaying the pressure rise at the servo. *(Courtesy of Chrysler Corporation)*

above that needed to stroke the apply piston. Just after the apply piston takes up the clutch or band clearance and the fluid pressure starts to increase, the accumulator strokes and absorbs some of the fluid flow. This causes a lag in the pressure increase at the band servo and clutch (Figure 6-55). The effect is a slightly longer and smoother shift. If we were to add an accumulator with the capacity of 0.75 in³ to the circuit previously described, the clutch would now take 50% longer, about 3/4 second, to fill. Some transmissions vary the pressure behind the accumulator to provide different shift characteristics depending on the throttle position or load. Full-throttle shifts are usually firmer than part-throttle shifts.

6.12 AUTOMATIC TRANSMISSION FLUID

Automatic transmission fluid (ATF) is one of the most complex fluids used in a vehicle. It has to:

- transfer *hydrodynamic* energy in the torque converter;
- transfer *hydrostatic* energy at the clutch and servo pistons as well as the valve body;

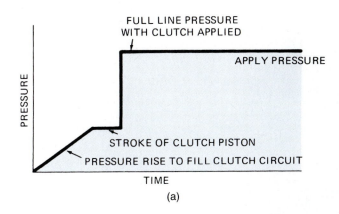

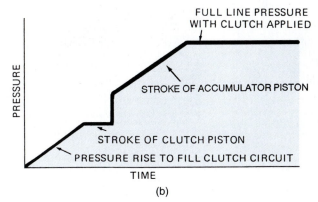

FIGURE 6-55 When a clutch applies, fluid pressure rises gradually until the circuit is filled and the piston strokes to take up the clearance; then there is a rapid increase to line pressure (a). An accumulator can be placed into the circuit to slow this pressure rise and soften clutch application (b).

- help transfer sliding friction energy as the clutches and bands apply;
- transfer excess heat away from high-temperature locations such as the torque converter's friction surfaces, gears, and bushings;
- lubricate the various moving parts.

Early automatic transmissions used engine oil for a transmission fluid. Since the internal operating conditions in an engine and automatic transmission are significantly different, a special transmission fluid was developed in the late 1940s. At first the ATF was simply a mineral oil much like motor oil but dyed red. Newer ATFs can be mineral oil or synthetic lubricant with a number of additives to make it more suited to the needs of a transmission. The first transmission fluid was developed by General Motors and was labeled *Type A* transmission fluid. As transmission fluid was improved, Type A was replaced with *Type A, Suffix A; Dexron;* and then *Dexron II, Dexron IIE,* and *Dexron III* (Figure 6-57). The Dexron fluids are compatible, and Dexron III can be used in older transmissions that specify one of the older fluid types.

Like other vehicle manufacturers, Ford Motor Company has developed fluids for use in its vehicles. *Types F, CJ, Mercon,*

General Motors	Ford Motor Company	Chrysler	Toyota
1940			
Type A			
1950			
Type A Suffix A	M2C33 A-B		
1960	M2C33 C-D		
Dexron	M2C33-F		
1970 -(Type F)-			
Dexron II	M2C33-G		Type F
1980 --M2C138-CJ----	----ATF+----		
M2C166-H	ATF+1		Dexron II
Mercon			Type T
1990 --Dexron IIE--			
Dexron III		ATF+2	Dexron III
		ATF+3	
Mercon V	ATF+4		
2000			
Dexron VI	Mercon SP		ATF-WS
2010			

FIGURE 6-56 The first special ATF was developed in the late 1940s. Since that date, advanced, special fluids have been developed by domestic as well as foreign vehicle manufacturers.

and *Mercon V* are required for various Ford transmission models. Mercon can be used in place of older Ford fluids. Mercon V should be used only in transmissions that specify its use (Figure 6-58). Some fluids meet both Mercon and Mercon V specifications. Other manufacturers have developed specific fluids to meet the needs of their transmissions. Always use the specified fluid when adding or replacing transmission fluid. At least one vehicle manufacturer has stated that it will not reimburse dealers for repair costs if the wrong transmission fluid was used. Many transmission shops are forced to keep a large variety of fluid types on hand, but they have discovered that the OEM-specified fluid makes the transmission operate the way that it was designed to operate.

Manufacturers introduce new transmission fluids as they develop new transmissions with more speed ranges, improved fuel economy, and reduced maintenance costs. The increased fluid durability has made it possible to eliminate or reduce scheduled fluid changes. General Motors introduced Dexron® VI. It has a more consistent viscosity to produce more consistent shift performance during extreme conditions and less degradation over time. This fluid has more than twice the durability and stability in tests compared to previous ATFs. Toyota uses world standard fluid (WS). It is formulated to provide lower viscosity at normal operating temperatures, which helps improve fuel economy. At higher temperatures, this ATF provides greater durability. Ford introduced Mercon SP fluid, which has the

(a)

(b)

(c)

FIGURE 6-57   The markings on ATF containers show the fluid types. *(b and c are courtesy of Pennzoil)*

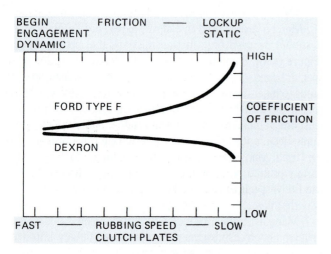

FIGURE 6-58   The dynamic coefficient of friction for these two fluids is almost the same, but the static friction is very different.

same characteristics as Dexron® VI and Toyota WS. Although these fluids are similar, they are not interchangeable.

All fluids are similar but have different friction characteristics. Normally a fluid has a *higher static coefficient of friction* than *dynamic coefficient of friction.* In a nonmodified fluid, the coefficient of friction increases as a clutch or band locks up. A *friction-modified* fluid does just the opposite. It has

a much lower static coefficient of friction than the dynamic coefficient of friction (Figure 6-59). A transmission designed for a friction-modified fluid must have more friction area in the clutches and bands or use higher apply pressure to compensate for the lower friction. But the lock-up portion of the shift is less harsh, and the shifts are smoother. Use of the wrong fluid can produce a harsh shift with higher shock loads to the drive line components or a slipping shift with possible transmission damage. Service information should be consulted when selecting the fluid for a particular transmission, and the fluid container should be checked to ensure that it meets the transmission's fluid requirements.

Transmission fluid is formulated with various additives to produce the favorable operating characteristics. A fluid contains about 10% to 15% additives. These additives are chemical compounds, and the reasons for their use are as follows:

Detergents-dispersants: Keep the transmission clean and the valves free from sticking by keeping foreign items in suspension until they are removed by the filter or by draining.

Oxidation inhibitors: Reduce oxidation and decomposition of the fluid, which can produce varnish and sludge.

Viscosity index improvers: Reduce the fluid viscosity change relative to temperature so fluid thickness and shift characteristics remain stable.

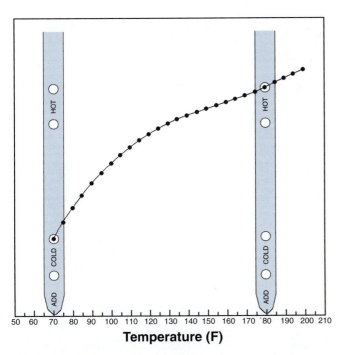

50 60 70 80 90 100 110 120 130 140 150 160 170 180 190 200 210

Temperature (F)

FIGURE 6-59 As the transmission warms up, the fluid level increases from the cold mark at 70°F to the hot mark at 180°F.

Friction modifiers: Change the fluid's coefficient of friction.

Foam inhibitors: Prevent formation of air bubbles and foam in the fluid.

Seal swellers: Produce a slight swelling of the elastomers to compensate for any wear that occurs.

Antiwear agents: Reduce friction and prevent scoring and seizure of metal parts running against each other.

Rust inhibitors: Prevent rust from forming on the iron and steel parts.

Corrosion inhibitors: Prevent corrosion of the nonferrous parts.

Metal deactivators: Form a protective film to inhibit oxidation of metal surfaces.

The transmission fluid that is blended by different companies must meet specifications established by the transmission manufacturers and the American Petroleum Institute (API). Fluids that meet a particular specification are allowed to show that specification or type label on the container. A listing of the more common fluids and their test is shown in Appendix C.

Synthetic fluids are man-made in that chemists have rearranged the oil molecule. Generally, synthetic fluids offer better high-temperature lubrication, better resistance to oxidization, and have a lower cold viscosity. They are more stabile with temperature changes with better cold and hot lubrication. Synthetic fluids often have a longer life. Some modern ATFs use a synthetic base.

Transmissions are expected to perform over a wide range of temperatures. Cold fluids are much thicker than hot fluids.

On a cold day, the first shifts tend to be sluggish because the fluid moves slowly through the orifices and small openings. The best operating temperature for an automatic transmission is in the range of 150 to 250°F (65 to 120°C). This produces good fluid viscosity without excessive fluid degradation. Some transmissions use fluid heaters to improve cold operation.

Like other fluids, ATF expands with heat (Figure 6-59). The coefficient of expansion is about 0.004% per degree F. This means that a temperature increase from 32°F (0°C) to 180°F (82°C) will cause the fluid to expand 148 × 0.0004 = 0.0592%. If the transmission holds 10 quarts (9.5 L) of fluid, the volume will increase to 10.592 qt (10 × 0.0592). This volume increase is slightly more than 1/2 qt (1 pint; 1/2 L), which is about the distance between the cold/low point on the dipstick to the higher hot point.

Probably the greatest problem for transmission fluid is heat. Excess heat significantly shortens the fluid's life. Excess temperatures cause the fluid to break down and form gum or varnish. This in turn can cause valve sticking or reduce the fluid flow in certain circuits. All transmissions use a cooler to help remove excess heat. The fluid should be changed more frequently than normal if it operates at temperatures above 175°F (79°C). Adverse driving conditions that produce higher fluid temperatures are trailer towing, driving on hills, and stop-and-go driving. The torque converter is the primary source of heat in an automatic transmission. The greater the speed difference between the torque converter input and output, the greater the temperature increase.

Experience has shown that a temperature increase of 17°F (8°C) will double the rate of fluid oxidation and cut the fluid life in half. A transmission operating at 250°F (121°C) should have a fluid life of about 75,000 miles (120,700 km). The same transmission operating at a temperature of 267°F (131°C) will have a fluid life reduced to about 37,500 miles (60,350 km).

Another heat-related problem occurs at contact areas between the friction surfaces of an applying band or clutch. The friction can cause the fluid temperature to increase to its oxidation point, and some fluids will burn and leave an abrasive ash on the friction surfaces.

PROBLEM SOLVING 6-3 Imagine that you are working in a shop that specializes in transmission repair, and these problems are brought to you:

Case 1 A 1986 Ford LTD has just had a fluid change (by the owner). It drives okay, but there is a very soft 2–3 upshift, almost a slipping condition. The owner says that it drove okay before the fluid change. Could a worn band cause this problem? Where should you begin to find the cause of this problem?

Case 2 A 1993 Chrysler New Yorker has a harsh 2–3 shift. It operates normally in all gear ranges, but the problem began one day and has been the same ever since. What do you think might be wrong with this transmission? Could this be a misadjusted throttle valve?

SUMMARY

1. The hydraulic system applies the band and clutches, transmits force and motion, maintains fluid flow to the torque converter, and provides lubrication and cooling to the moving parts of the transmission.

2. Pumps produce the fluid flow in a transmission and the restriction to the flow results in the system pressure.

3. The mainline pressure is controlled by a variable pressure regulator. Other valves and orifices are used to modify mainline pressure for various purposes.

4. The flow of fluid through a transmission is controlled by valves that are moved by hydraulic pressure, spring force, centrifugal force, and engine vacuum, electrically or manually.

5. Seals are used to confine the fluid to the appropriate passages. Metal, rubber, Teflon, and various synthetic materials are used for this purpose.

6. Automatic transmission fluid is the lifeblood of an automatic transmission, and only the specified fluid should be used.

REVIEW QUESTIONS

The following questions are provided to help you study as you read the chapter.

1. The important functions of the automatic transmission's hydraulic system are to _____ the clutches and bands, transmit _____ and _____, maintain _____ _____ through the torque converter, and cool and _____ the moving parts.

2. Pressure is defined as _____ pushing on a specified area and is commonly measured in _____.

3. Hydraulic systems usually have a _____ valve or a _____ _____ to prevent damage from excessive pressure.

4. The automatic transmission pump turns whenever the _____ is running.

5. Regulated pump output pressure is called _____ pressure.

6. Pump output volume changes relative to engine _____.

7. The main transmission filter is designed to trap _____, metal, and other foreign _____.

8. A micron is approximately _____ of an inch.

9. The position of a valve can be controlled by: (List five)

10. Identify a transmission valve that is controlled
    a. mechanically.
    b. by centrifugal force.
    c. by vacuum.

11. Older automatic transmissions use a _____ and a _____ _____ to control shift timing and quality.

12. Electronically controlled automatic transmissions use a _____ _____ _____ and a _____ _____ _____ to help the ECU determine when the shift should occur.

13. A typical application for a ball check valve is to act as a _____ relief valve.

14. Three types of seals are used to seal clutch pistons. Which one provides the best pressure retention?

15. Clutches are applied by a _____ in the clutch assembly and bands are applied by a _____ piston.

16. If a clutch piston has a diameter of 5 in. and 80 psi of pressure is applied, the apply force is _____ pounds.

17. The rate that pressure is applied to a clutch will affect shift _____ and shift _____.

18. Two devices that can be used to control shift feel and quality are an _____ and an _____.

19. Driving conditions that produce higher temperatures are _____ towing, driving up _____, and stop-and-_____ driving.

20. Always use the automatic transmission fluid that is recommended by the _____ when adding or replacing the fluid.

CHAPTER QUIZ

The following will help you check the facts you have learned. Select the answer that completes each statement correctly.

1. Fluid under pressure can be used to transmit motion and force because
   a. fluids cannot be compressed.
   b. fluid conforms to the shape of its container.
   c. fluids under pressure will apply pressure equally in all directions.
   d. All of these

2. Student A says that fluid pressure is measured in kilopascals or pounds per square inch. Student B says that 1 psi is equal to about 7 kPa. Who is correct?
   a. Student A
   b. Student B
   c. Both A and B
   d. Neither A nor B

3. If a fluid pressure of 50 psi is exerted on a piston area of 10 in^2, it will generate a force of _____ lb.
   a. 10
   b. 50
   c. 100
   d. 500

4. Student A says that to increase hydraulic force, the amount of fluid flow should be increased. Student B says that to increase hydraulic force, the length of the piston stroke should be increased. Who is correct?
   a. Student A
   b. Student B
   c. Both A and B
   d. Neither A nor B

5. The pressure regulator valve
   a. directs flow in the valve body.
   b. regulates flow to match the driving conditions.
   c. regulates pressure to match transmission requirements.
   d. controls the pump speed.

6. Positive displacement pumps
   a. maintain a constant pressure.
   b. move a constant volume of fluid.
   c. vary the flow with rpm.
   d. vary the flow with gear changes.

7. Fluid is forced through the pump intake by
   a. pump suction.
   b. inner case pressure.
   c. atmospheric pressure.
   d. gravity.

8. Student A says that some automatic transmissions use an internal/external pump. Student B says that some automatic transmissions use gerotor or a vane-type pump. Who is correct?
   a. Student A
   b. Student B
   c. Both A and B
   d. Neither A nor B

9. Variable displacement pumps change the output volume based on
   a. torque converter demands.
   b. transmission temperature.
   c. gear range and shift demands.
   d. engine speed.

10. Student A says that a depth filter can trap smaller particles than a surface filter. Student B says that depth filter has more filter capacity than a surface filter. Who is correct?
    a. Student A
    b. Student B
    c. Both A and B
    d. Neither A nor B

11. Excessive mainline pressure loss could be caused by
    a. too much fluid.
    b. a plugged filter.
    c. the wrong transmission fluid.
    d. a plugged cooler line.

12. The part of a spool valve where pressure is applied to cause the valve movement is called the
    a. land.
    b. bore.
    c. valley.
    d. face.

13. The throttle valve is designed to produce a fluid pressure signal that is proportional to
    a. the speed of the vehicle.
    b. the gear selector position.
    c. the load on the engine.
    d. All of these

14. A governor's output pressure increases gradually and in proportion to
    a. engine speed.
    b. vehicle speed.
    c. gear range.
    d. road conditions.

15. A shift valve is moved to the upshift position by

   a. throttle valve pressure.

   b. a spring.

   c. governor pressure.

   d. Any of these

16. The metal balls are used in a valve body to

   a. allow fluid flow in only one direction.

   b. close one passage while fluid is flowing in another.

   c. relieve excess pressure.

   d. Any of these

17. Student A says that an accumulator in a hydraulic circuit is used to increase the fluid flow through the circuit. Student B says that an accumulator in a hydraulic circuit is used to cushion a shift by absorbing some of the fluid flow. Who is correct?

   a. Student A

   b. Student B

   c. Both A and B

   d. Neither A nor B

18. An orifice in a fluid passage

   a. reduces the pressure in a servo while it is in the applied position.

   b. causes a servo to apply faster than normal.

   c. causes a pressure drop in the circuit while there is fluid flow.

   d. reduces the chance that a leak will develop.

19. Which type of seals require special tools to properly install and resize?

   a. lip

   b. O-ring

   c. Teflon

   d. square cut

20. Automatic transmission fluid contains additives designed to

   a. change the friction characteristics of the fluid.

   b. clean the transmission.

   c. reduce the rate of oxidation.

   d. All of these

21. Clutches are applied by hydraulic pressure and released by

   a. hydraulic pressure.

   b. a spring.

   c. centrifugal force.

   d. Neither A nor B

22. Bands are applied by hydraulic pressure and released by

   a. hydraulic pressure.

   b. a spring.

   c. centrifugal force.

   d. Both A and B

23. Student A says that all transmission fluids are the same and a universal type of fluid can be used in any automatic transmission. Student B says that all transmission fluids are not the same and only the fluid recommended by the manufacturer should be used. Who is correct?

   a. Student A

   b. Student B

   c. Neither A nor B

   d. Both A and B

24. When automatic transmission fluid is overheated,

   a. it will turn pink.

   b. nothing will happen.

   c. varnish will form.

   d. tar will form.

25. Using the wrong fluid could

   a. shorten the life of the transmission.

   b. cause shift-quality problems.

   c. cause the clutches to slip excessively.

   d. All of these

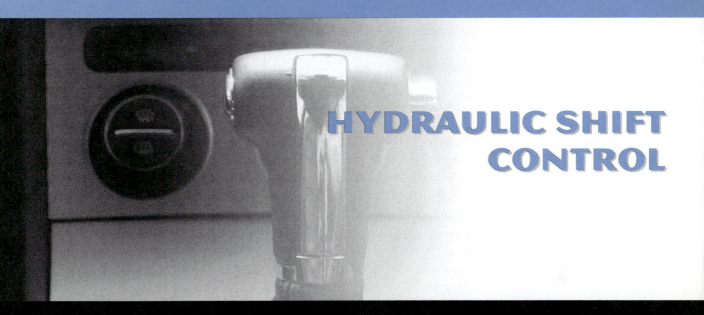

CHAPTER 7

HYDRAULIC SHIFT CONTROL

OBJECTIVES

After studying Chapter 7, the reader should be able to:

1. Explain how an automatic transmission hydraulic system operates.
2. List the valves used in an automatic transmission.
3. Describe the operation of the valves in an automatic transmission.
4. Describe how vehicle speed and load affect automatic shifts.
5. Follow an upshift or downshift sequence through a hydraulic schematic.

KEY TERMS

Accumulator (p. 182)
Detent Valve (p. 173)
Downshift Valve (p. 173)
Exhaust (p. 164)
Governor Valve (p. 177)
Kickdown Valve (p. 173)
Manual Valve (p. 175)
Nonsynchronous (p. 180)

Orifice (p. 182)
Rooster Comb (p. 175)
Servo Valve (p. 163)
Slide-Bump Shift (p. 182)
Supply Pressure (p. 164)
Switch Valve (p. 167)
Synchronous (p. 180)
Vacuum Modulator (p. 173)

7.1 INTRODUCTION

The hydraulic system enables an automatic transmission to operate automatically. It supplies the force to apply the clutches and bands and the valves that control pressure and direct the fluid for automatic shifts. Most of these valves are contained in the valve body (Figure 7-1). The valve body in most transmissions and many transaxles is attached to the bottom of the transmission case, inside the pan (Figure 7-2). Some transaxles mount the valve body in other locations. With experience, you will gain the ability to identify the valves, determine if they are working correctly, and repair any faults.

The basic function of the hydraulic control system is to:

- Schedule shifts to optimize engine performance,
- Provide the best gear ratio for the driving conditions,
- Safely shift into reverse when requested,

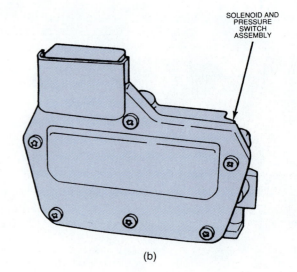

(b)

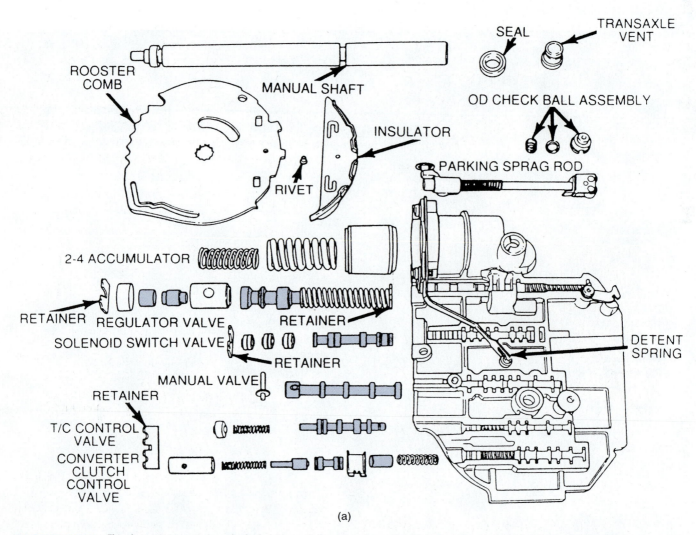

(a)

FIGURE 7-1 This electronic transmission valve body (a) has only five valves. Four solenoids in the solenoid assembly (b) control shifts and torque converter clutch (TCC) apply and release. *(Courtesy of Chrysler Corporation)*

- Provide driver control of the operating ranges,
- Provide engine braking to help control vehicle speed on downgrades,
- Lock or unlock the torque converter clutch.

Most of the valves used in an automatic transmission are spool valves, and each valve has a specific purpose. Most of the valves are controlled by fluid pressure. Some valves, like the manual valve, are operated mechanically. The mass/weight of a spool valve is kept as low as possible so the valve will move quickly. Most valves are made from aluminum for this reason, and they are anodized to reduce wear. Valves can be divided into three categories: switch, servo, and regulator. A switch valve controls fluid flow into the different circuits; it is also called a *flow control valve*. A **servo valve** is a valve that is used

to move another valve. Some servo valves operate switch valves, and some help control pressure regulator valves. Control of the fluid pressure at various locations in the transmission allows for shifts that are tailored to the driving conditions. Various types of pressure regulating valves handle this job.

Most switch- or servo-type valves are kept in one of two positions. For example, a shift valve (switch-type valve) is spring loaded in the downshift position, and when there is sufficient fluid pressure from the governor, the valve moves to the upshift position (Figure 7-3). There should be no in-between with a shift valve; a halfway shift can cause slippage and wear.

Regulator-type valves will operate anywhere along their bore. Some pressure regulator and throttle valves move to a balanced position to produce a modulated pressure. Some pressure regulators and most pressure relief valves cycle rapidly. Pressure builds up and causes the valve to open and release pressure, and as soon as this happens, the valve closes and the cycle soon repeats.

The hydraulic system begins at the filter and ends as pressure at the clutch and servo pistons or as lubricating oil. In this chapter, we trace the fluid flow through a hydraulic system. A hydraulic circuit diagram is a useful tool for this purpose. Later, when diagnosing transmission problems, you will use a hydraulic circuit diagram as a tool to locate fluid routes and the possible cause of a problem.

The hydraulic system is easier to understand if it is divided into subcircuits, as shown in Table 7-1. A flow control valve is the dividing point as supply pressure enters the different circuits. Also note that each circuit serves a particular purpose.

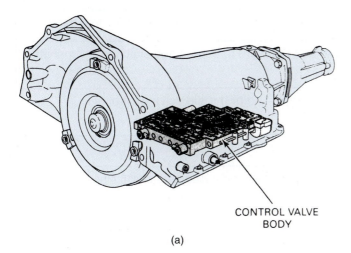

CONTROL VALVE
BODY

(a)

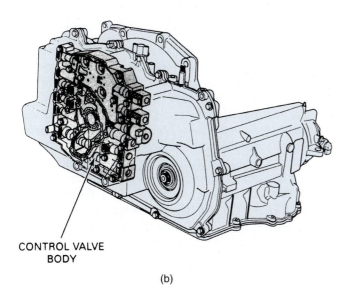

CONTROL VALVE
BODY

(b)

FIGURE 7-2   The valve body is mounted to the bottom of the main case of transmissions and some transaxles (a). It is also mounted at the end or top of some transaxles (b). *(Reprinted with permission of General Motors)*

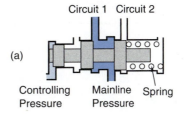

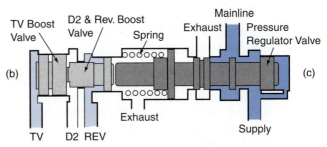

FIGURE 7-3   The switch valve (a) will shift the fluid flow from circuit 1 to circuit 2 when the controlling pressure increases. This regulator valve has two servo valves (TV boost, and D2 and rev. boost) (b), which cause a pressure increase when the throttle is opened or when the transmission is shifted into D2 or reverse. This regulator valve (c) controls supply pressure to become mainline pressure.

TABLE 7-1 Hydraulic System Subcircuits

Name of Circuit	Purpose
Supply	Provides fluid to pressure regulator valve and transmission.
Main control pressure	Supplies fluid at a controlled pressure to transmission and converter when the engine is running.
Converter and cooler	Regulates converter pressure; provides gear train lubrication and cooling of the fluid.
Drive	Applies forward clutch and supplies control systems in forward-gear ranges.
Manual-1	Applies low and reverse band and locks out second gear.
Manual-2	Prevents upshift from second-gear range.
Reverse	Increases control pressure and supplies reverse-high clutch and low-reverse band.
Shift valve	Controls switch pressure and exhaust pressure to servos and clutches for upshifts and downshifts.
Kickdown (downshift, detent)	Forces downshifts by overriding governor and/or throttle valve control of shift valves.
Governor	Provides a pressure proportional to road speed for upshifts.
Throttle valve (TV)	Provides a pressure proportional to engine load and vacuum for shift timing and quality.
Accumulator	Cushions shift by softening clutch or band apply.
Converter clutch	Controls the converter clutch to time clutch lock-up.

7.2 PRESSURE DEVELOPMENT AND CONTROL

As soon as the engine starts, the torque converter hub drives the transmission pump to produce fluid flow. Pressure is created by resistance to fluid flow. This pressure is called *line, mainline, supply,* or *control pressure.* Some sources identify *supply pressure* as the fluid in the passage between the pump and the pressure regulator valve. *Line pressure,* also called *mainline pressure,* usually refers to regulated fluid pressure. As soon as the supply passages fill with fluid, the fluid pressure acts on one end or one large land of the regulator valve acting in opposition to a spring positioned at the other end. When line pressure increases, the regulator valve moves and opens a passage that directs fluid back to the pump intake or sends a pressure signal to the housing of a vane pump to decrease pump volume (Figures 7-4 and 7-5). During start-up, the pressure will build up rapidly because the manual valve is blocking the flow to the clutches and bands; the only flow is to the *regulator valve,* a few other valves, and the torque converter. It should be noted that some transmissions do not build fluid pressure in park because the manual valve opens line pressure to exhaust; fluid flow is through the manual valve and back to the sump (Figure 7-6). The term *exhaust* refers to fluid flow back to the pan to empty or drain a circuit.

Pressure regulator valves balance line pressure against the strength of a spring. The spring has a predetermined strength to maintain fluid pressure at about 50 to 60 psi (345 to 414 kPa). In some transmissions, this spring is adjustable by turning a screw; in others it is adjustable by adding or removing shims (Figure 7-7).

Fluid pressure during mid-throttle to full throttle and reverse is boosted by one or more boost areas of the regulator valve. Some transmissions also *boost pressure* in manual low and intermediate gears (Figure 7-8). The throttle valve (TV) circuit produces a pressure signal relative to the throttle opening (engine load). *TV pressure* will be somewhere between

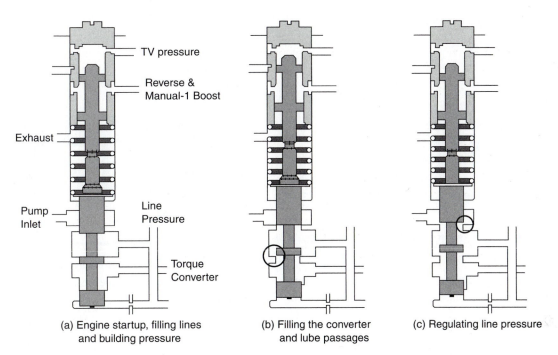

(a) Engine startup, filling lines and building pressure

(b) Filling the converter and lube passages

(c) Regulating line pressure

FIGURE 7-4   Many pressure regulator valves have three positions. (a) The spring has moved the valve to the bottom of the bore. (b) Line pressure is moving the valve upward, opening the passage to the torque converter (circle). (c) Increased line pressure has moved the valve upward to where it can release pressure to the pump inlet (circle). Note that boost pressure in either of the two upper ports can cause a pressure increase.

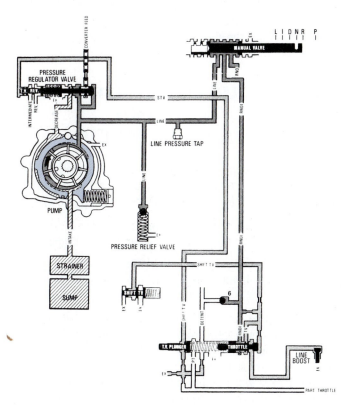

FIGURE 7-5   The pressure regulator of this variable displacement vane pump can send fluid pressure to the DECREASE passage. This pressure will move the pump slide to the right and reduce pump output. (*Reprinted with permission of General Motors*)

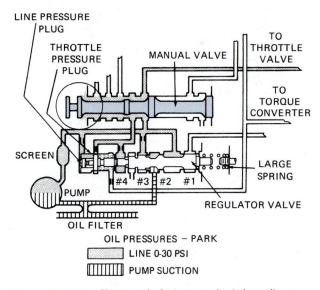

FIGURE 7-6   This manual valve is arranged so it dumps line pressure to the sump in park (circle). This reduces line pressure to below 30 psi. (*Courtesy of Chrysler Corporation*)

zero and line pressure depending on throttle position, and it acts on the regulator valve in the same direction as the valve's spring. This will increase spring pressure, causing the regulator valve to modulate to a higher pressure. Throttle boost is used to produce firmer shifts, improve shift feel, and increase clutch and band holding power at higher throttle openings.

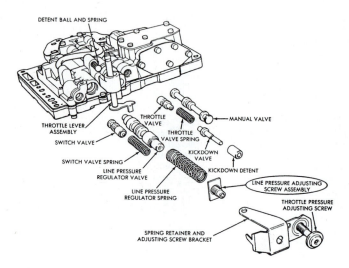

FIGURE 7-7 Some pressure regulators use an adjusting screw that allows adjustment of line pressure. Others use a shim/spacer to allow an adjustment.

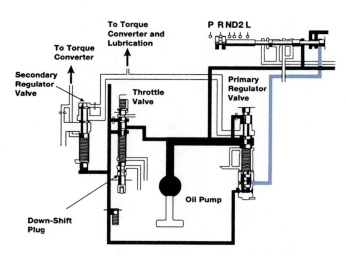

FIGURE 7-9 Fluid from the manual valve reverse circuit acts on the primary regulator valve to increase line pressure in reverse. *(Courtesy of Toyota Motor Sales USA, Inc.)*

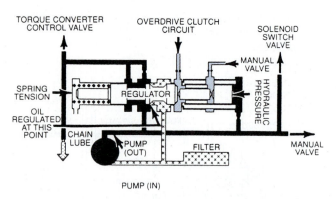

FIGURE 7-8 Hydraulic pressure moves this regulator valve to the left against spring tension. Pressure in the manual valve circuit will work against hydraulic pressure to increase/boost line pressure. Pressure in the overdrive clutch circuit will reduce/cut back line pressure. *(Courtesy of Chrysler Corporation)*

Full throttle in forward gears causes line pressure to increase to about 90 to 150 psi (621 to 1,034 kPa).

Line pressure is increased in reverse because the reverse passage at the manual valve sends pressure to the *reverse boost valve* (Figure 7-9). Line pressure acts with the spring to increase control pressure. Reverse boost produces line pressures of between 150 and 300 psi (1,034 and 2,068 kPa), depending on the transmission and the throttle opening. The purpose for boosting pressure in reverse is to ensure sufficient force to the clutch and band to prevent slipping.

Some transmissions boost pressure in manual-1 and sometimes manual-2 to ensure strong clutch and band application while operating in these gears. When used, another boost area of the regulator valve is pressurized by the manual valve in a manner similar to reverse boost. Low-gear boost increases line pressures to about 150 psi (1,034 kPa).

Electronic transmissions use an *electronic pressure control (EPC)* solenoid to control the pressure regulator valve. As we will see in Chapter 8, the EPC in most instances is controlled by either the transmission control module (TCM) or engine control module (ECM).

7.3 TORQUE CONVERTER, OIL COOLER, AND LUBRICATION CIRCUIT

As soon as the supply circuit begins to develop pressure, the regulator valve moves slightly and opens a passage to the torque converter. This fluid flow serves several purposes:

- It ensures that the torque converter is filled so it can transmit torque from the engine to the transmission's input shaft.
- It helps control converter fluid temperature.
- It provides lubrication for the moving parts inside the transmission (Figure 7-10).

It should be noted that this feature can shut off the fluid flow to the torque converter, cooler, and lubrication circuit whenever line pressure drops below the regulated pressure point. There are several possibilities in which a transmission with a slightly worn pump running at idle, very low engine speeds, or under conditions calling for high line pressures (full throttle, low vacuum, reverse gear, etc.) can be operated without converter, cooler, and lubrication flow. This can cause severe wear of the thrust washers, bushings, and gear train if it is allowed to continue for any length of time.

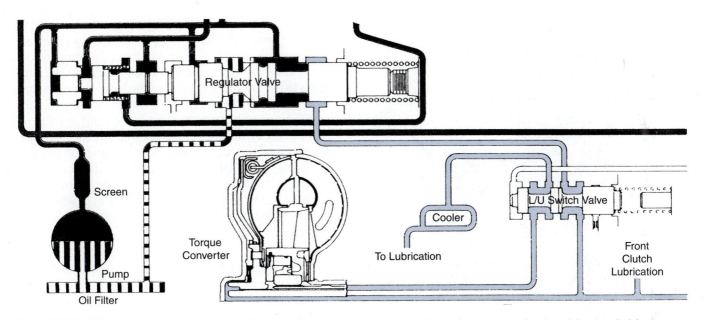

FIGURE 7-10   The converter and cooler feed circuit begins at the pressure regulator, goes through the converter and cooler, and then into the lube passages. Note that the cooler and the lines connecting it to the transmission are outside of the transmission. *(Courtesy of Chrysler Corporation)*

7.3.1 Torque Converter Pressure Control

A potential problem with torque converters is drain down or a partial emptying while the engine is off. This causes slippage and delay in power flow until the converter is refilled. The possibility of drain down is reduced by shutting the fluid passage to the converter at the regulator valve as soon as the pressure drops or when the engine is off (Figure 7-11). Some transmissions have an additional valve in the passage leaving the converter to prevent *drain down* through the cooler circuit. The simple, spring-loaded check valve, often called an anti-drain-back valve, closes off the passage as soon as fluid flow through the converter stops.

Pressure inside the converter is controlled by how fast the fluid enters and how fast it can leave. This flow is controlled by the sizes of the restrictions in the two passages. Since there is not much restriction on a converter's outlet passages, normal internal pressures do not get too high, about 15 to 75 psi (103 to 517 kPa; Figure 7-12).

Another potential converter problem is ballooning, which is a swelling of the outer shell of the converter that can result from excessive internal pressure. Some transmissions use a pressure relief valve or a torque converter pressure regulator valve to limit the pressure to about 100 psi (689 kPa) maximum.

7.3.2 Torque Converter Clutch Control

A torque converter clutch (TCC) is applied by redirecting the flow inside the converter. Depending on the transmission, this valve is called a *converter clutch control valve,* a **switch**

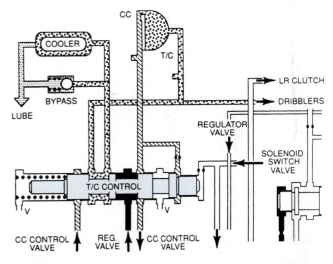

FIGURE 7-11   When the engine is not running, the regulator valve spring moves the T/C control valve to the right, blocking the cooler passage and reducing the chance of converter drain down. Note the bypass valve that will open if the cooler becomes plugged. *(Courtesy of Chrysler Corporation)*

valve, or a *converter clutch apply valve* (Figure 7-13). When the TCC valve moves, the fluid flow through the converter is reversed. In some transmissions, this valve is controlled completely by transmission fluid flow, but in most transmissions, it is controlled electronically by the ECM. The ECM uses input signals from the various engine sensors, vehicle speed sensor, and brake pedal switch to determine if the torque converter clutch should be applied or released. Electronic TCC control is described in Chapter 8.

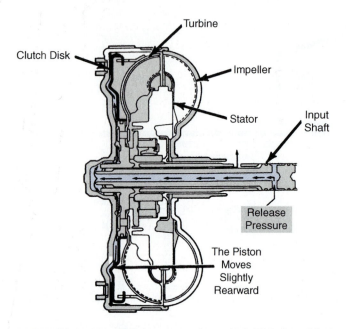

FIGURE 7-12 With the torque converter clutch (TCC) released, fluid enters this converter through the input shaft. It leaves through the area between the input shaft and the stator support. *(Courtesy of Chrysler Corporation)*

In older Chrysler Corporation transmissions, the switch valve is operated by fluid pressure from the drive circuit acting on one end of the valve and a spring at the other end that tries to hold the valve in a non-lock-up position. The valve moves to the lock-up position after the lock-up valve (moved by pressure in the governor circuit) and fail-safe valve (moved by pressure from the third-gear circuit) move to up-shift positions. In these transmissions, torque converter clutch lock-up only occurs above a certain speed and coolant temperature and after the transmission has shifted into third gear (Figure 7-14). It releases when the vehicle slows down, the transmission downshifts out of third gear, or when there is enough throttle pressure to move the fail-safe valve to a non-lock-up position.

7.3.3 Cooler Flow

The fluid leaving the torque converter is routed out of the transmission case and through a steel line to the *transmission cooler.* The cooler is positioned in the colder (outlet) tank of the radiator (Figure 7-15). Another steel line is used to return the fluid to the transmission. A *cooler* is often called a heat exchanger because it moves heat from one location to another. Heat from the transmission fluid is transferred to the engine coolant. The cooler is either a flat or a tubular-shape plate-type

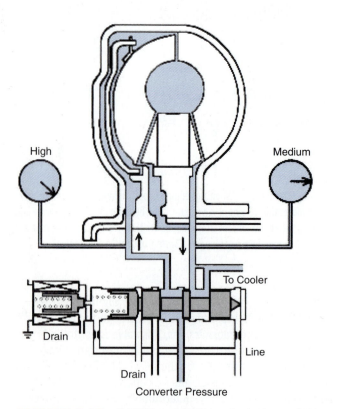

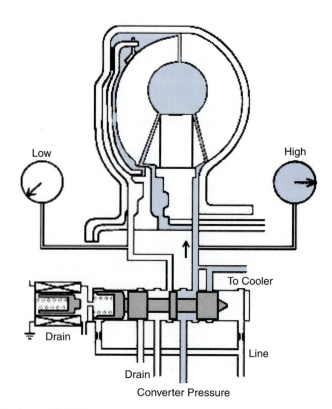

FIGURE 7-13 This TCC is controlled by a valve that is controlled by a solenoid that is controlled by the power train control module (PCM). When the solenoid is energized (right), the valve moves to the left, and this applies the TCC.

cooler that is simply two outer metal surfaces with a *turbulator* between them (Figure 7-16). The outer surfaces are in contact with the relatively cool coolant in the radiator tank. The screen-like turbulator causes a turbulence in the fluid flow to ensure constant mixing and thorough cooling of the fluid.

A plain-tube cooler is not very effective for cooling fluid because fluid tends to increase its viscosity and slow down as it cools. The cooler oil then tends to become stationary on the outer, cooler areas of the cooler while the hotter-, thinner-viscosity fluid flows through the center (Figure 7-17). The turbulator in a well-designed oil cooler continuously mixes

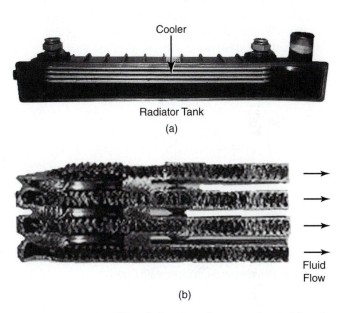

FIGURE 7-14   The lock-up valve and fail-safe valve control the switch valve. This in turn controls fluid flow through the converter and therefore converter lock-up. *(Courtesy of Chrysler Corporation)*

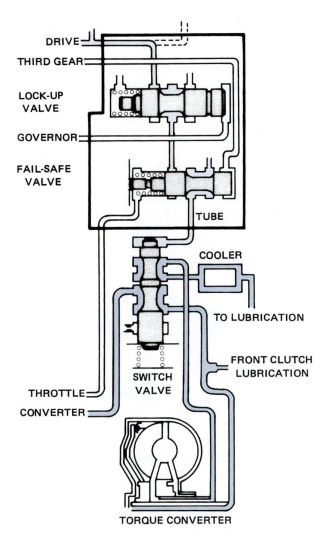

FIGURE 7-16   This cooler has a large, flat passage from its inlet to its outlet (a). The screenlike turbulator is shown (b).

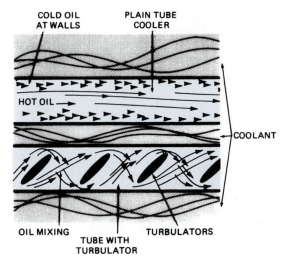

FIGURE 7-15   The transmission cooler is normally mounted in the colder, outlet tank of the radiator. Steel lines are normally used to connect the transmission to the cooler. *(Courtesy of Chrysler Corporation)*

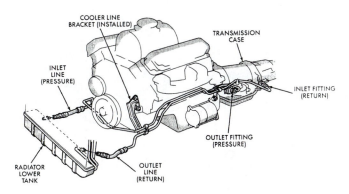

FIGURE 7-17   Cold fluid tends to stick to the walls of a plain tube cooler (top). The turbulator causes fluid turbulence to promote mixing so all of the fluid cools (bottom).

the fluid. It also causes some restriction to the fluid flow, but most coolers are sized properly to allow for this.

The transmission cooler tends to trap foreign particles and can become plugged, especially when the fluid is extremely dirty, contains metal particles, or there is a torque converter clutch mechanical failure. The procedure for checking cooler flow and cleaning of the cooler is described in Chapter 11. At least one aftermarket manufacturer markets a filter that can be installed in the transmission-to-cooler line (Figure 7-18). This filter provides added protection by removing foreign particles from the fluid and preventing cooler blockage; many filters contain a magnet to remove iron particles. If the filter gets plugged, fluid flow will be restricted or blocked completely, and this will shut off transmission lubrication. Supplementary filters must include a bypass valve to maintain fluid flow if the filter becomes plugged.

Supplementary coolers are also available that can be placed in series with the original equipment manufacturer (OEM) cooler to ensure adequate cooling. These are fluid-to-air coolers, whereas the OEM cooler is normally a fluid-to-coolant cooler. The heat in the supplementary cooler flows directly to the air passing through the cooler. The supplementary cooler is normally positioned where there is an adequate air flow, and this is often in front of the radiator or air-conditioning condenser. This location is not ideal because the new cooler tends to block the air flow through the other heat exchangers and increases their operating temperatures. The supplementary cooler is connected to one of the transmission's cooler lines and then to the OEM cooler. The hot fluid from the transmission can be routed through the supplementary cooler first, then through the OEM cooler and back to the transmission (Figure 7-19). Running the fluid through in this

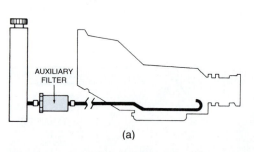

(a)

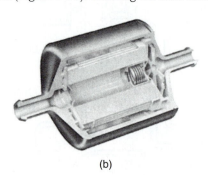

(b)

FIGURE 7-18   An auxiliary filter can be installed in one of the cooler lines to help trap contaminants (a). The cutaway view shows the internal magnet and folded paper filter element (b). *(Courtesy of SPX Filtran)*

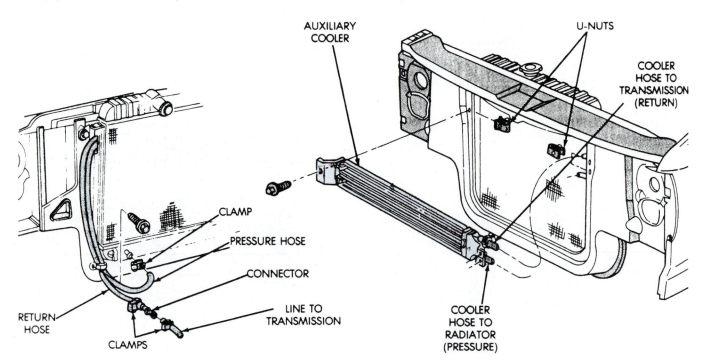

FIGURE 7-19   An auxiliary cooler is mounted so the fluid flows through it and then through the standard cooler in the radiator. *(Courtesy of Chrysler Corporation)*

manner improves the efficiency of the supplementary cooler by operating it at the highest possible temperature. When operating in very cold temperatures, the OEM cooler reduces the chance of overcooling the fluid by warming the fluid before returning it to the transmission. Raising the fluid's operating temperature helps ensure an adequate lubrication flow.

7.3.4 Lubrication Flow

In most transmissions, the fluid returning from the torque converter lubricates the transmission. The fluid from the cooler enters the lubrication passages at the case. It flows through holes drilled in the case to the main shaft bushings, where it passes into holes drilled in the input or output shaft (Figure 7-20). From here, it flows through the shaft to side holes that align with support bushings, thrust washers, planetary gearsets, clutch drum bushings, and clutch packs. The final drive gears and differential of a transaxle are also lubricated by this circuit.

A vehicle with an automatic transmission should not be towed or pushed very far because there will be no lubricating fluid flow without the engine running. The gearsets and bushings will run dry, wear, and overheat or burn out without a constant flow of lubricating oil (Figure 7-21). Most manufacturers recommend towing only when absolutely necessary. They caution that towing should be limited to a few miles with a

TECH TIP

At least one new transmission design has a lube scoop and through that allows lubrication while being towed. The vehicle can be towed with all four wheels on the ground at speeds up to 65 mph. All wheel drive (AWD) vehicles must be towed with all four wheels either on or off the ground.

maximum speed of 20 to 25 mph (32 to 40 km/h). If possible, the drive wheels should be lifted off the ground or the drive shaft removed from a rear wheel drive (RWD) vehicle. Special cautions should be taken when towing an AWD vehicle.

PROBLEM SOLVING 7-1 Imagine that you are working in a shop that specializes in transmission repair, and these problems are brought to you:

Case 1 A 1982 Corvette starts out okay in first gear; but the 1–2 shift is long and drawn out. A full-throttle shift has an engine speed flare with indications of slippage. What part of the transmission is faulty? What do you think is causing this problem?

Case 2 A 1995 Ford Thunderbird had a badly worn gear train; the gears were blue from overheating. The gearset was replaced while rebuilding the transmission. Are there any special checks that should be made before replacing this transmission into the car?

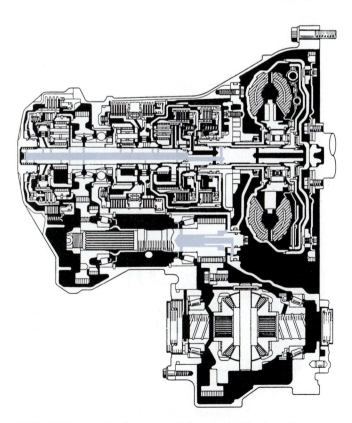

FIGURE 7-20 Transmission lube passages. Note how the passage leads to gears and bushings. *(Courtesy of Toyota Motor Sales USA, Inc.)*

FIGURE 7-21 This planet carrier burned out from lack of lubrication; note the excess clearance and dark coloration at the planet gear shafts.

7.4 THROTTLE PRESSURE

A circuit carrying a throttle pressure signal is always available while the engine is running in most transmissions. Throttle valves are pressure-regulating valves, and they provide a pressure signal that is proportionate to the load on the engine (Figure 7-22). This controlled, variable pressure is also called *modulated pressure.* The throttle signal can be brought to the transmission by three commonly used methods: mechanical, vacuum, and electrical.

Transmissions with hydraulic shift controls have hydraulic TV pressure working against governor hydraulic pressure to control shift valve movement (Figure 7-23). Shift feel is also controlled hydraulically with clutch or servo feed orifices and TV pressure modifying accumulator pressure. As you will learn in Chapter 8, electronic transmissions use electronic devices for these same purposes.

The transmission control system uses throttle pressure to reprogram or reschedule several areas of operation:

- **Shift quality:** The friction devices should apply firmly while under full throttle to handle the increased torque. This is accomplished by boosting line pressure.
- **Shift timing:** A full-throttle, full-load upshift should occur at a higher speed than a part-throttle, partial-load shift. This is accomplished by throttle pressure working against governor pressure at the shift valves.
- **Shift feel:** A full-throttle, high-load upshift should have a firmer, faster quality to reduce slippage during a shift. This is accomplished by changing the accumulator rate used to cushion a shift (Figure 7-24).

- **Torque converter clutch control:** The TCC should be released during full-throttle operation so the converter is able to multiply the torque needed for acceleration and power. This is accomplished by the throttle pressure acting on the TCC control valve.

Most older transmissions use either a double-throttle valve (mechanical operation) or two separate units (vacuum and mechanical or electrical) to sense engine load and throttle

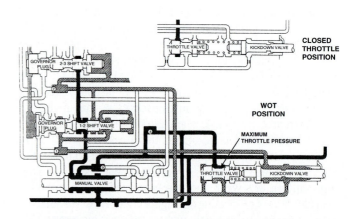

FIGURE 7-23   In this hydraulically controlled transmission, the shift valves are positioned by a spring and hydraulic pressures from the throttle valve and governor. *(Courtesy of Chrysler Corporation)*

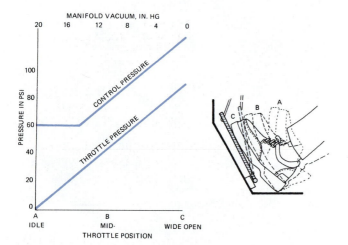

FIGURE 7-22   The throttle valve produces a pressure signal that is directly related to throttle opening or engine load. This pressure signal is used to control line pressure so that line pressure increases as the throttle is opened.

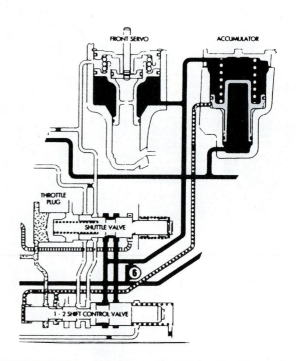

FIGURE 7-24   Application speed of this front band is controlled by the accumulator stroke rate, and this is controlled by the shuttle valve and the 1–2 shift control valve. *(Courtesy of Chrysler Corporation)*

position (Figure 7-25). The second throttle valve is called a **detent, downshift,** or **kickdown valve,** and it signals full-throttle operation, also called *wide-open throttle (WOT).* Other transmissions use a mechanical throttle and detent valve to control shift timing and a vacuum unit to control line pressure and shift feel.

TV pressure is modified in some transmissions by one or more of the valves in order to achieve precise shift timing. The 3–4 modified throttle valve (MTV) and 4–3 MTV act to reduce TV pressure at low throttle openings.

7.4.1 Mechanical Throttle Valves

A mechanical throttle valve and a detent valve are used in many transmissions. These valves are in the same bore, with the kickdown valve positioned by a spring to rest against the throttle lever assembly (Figure 7-26). The throttle valve is positioned at the opposite end of the kickdown valve spring. The throttle lever is connected to the throttle linkage by a metal rod or cable; the lever moves as the throttle is opened or closed. The throttle valve is also positioned by pressure in the throttle pressure passages. As throttle pressure moves the valve against the spring, the valve moves to cut off throttle pressure. The mechanical force of the throttle linkage tends to increase throttle pressure, but throttle pressure tries to reduce itself. The throttle valve will be balanced between the

mechanical throttle pressure (the strength of the spring controlled by the kickdown valve position) and the amount of throttle fluid pressure. At the wide-open throttle (WOT) position, the throttle valve is pushed to the end of the bore by an extension of the kickdown valve. At this time, throttle pressure increases to equal line pressure, and the kickdown valve opens the kickdown passages to allow fluid pressure to enter the valve.

7.4.2 Vacuum Throttle Valves

Many transmissions use a throttle valve operated by a vacuum unit called a **vacuum modulator.** The modulator is secured to the outside of the transmission case and is connected to the engine's intake manifold by a metal tube or rubber hose (Figure 7-27). The vacuum unit contains a flexible diaphragm and a spring. The spring pushes the diaphragm and its extension toward the transmission. Manifold vacuum acts on the diaphragm, compresses the spring, moving the diaphragm and its extension away from the transmission. A vacuum is simply a pressure that is lower than atmospheric, and atmospheric pressure pushes against the opposite side of the diaphragm to cause movement. Vacuum is commonly measured in inches of mercury (in. Hg).

The output of the vacuum modulator is a product of the area of the diaphragm, the pressure differential across the diaphragm (atmospheric pressure minus the lower vacuum pressure), and the strength of the spring (Figure 7-28). Vacuum modulators are made with different sizes of diaphragms and

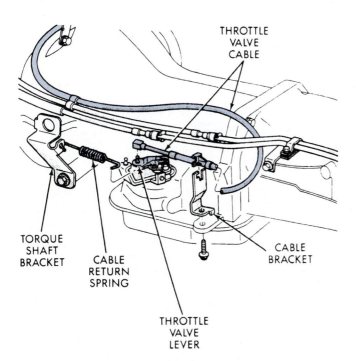

FIGURE 7-25   This mechanical throttle valve is operated by a cable that is connected to the engine throttle body and accelerator pedal. *(Courtesy of Chrysler Corporation)*

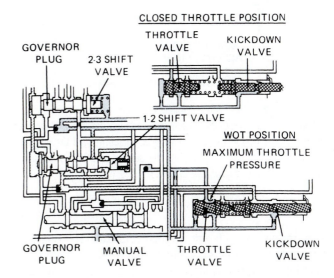

FIGURE 7-26   At wide-open throttle, the kickdown valve pushes the throttle valve to the end of the bore. At this position, TV pressure is equal to line pressure in both the TV and kickdown passages. *(Courtesy of Chrysler Corporation)*

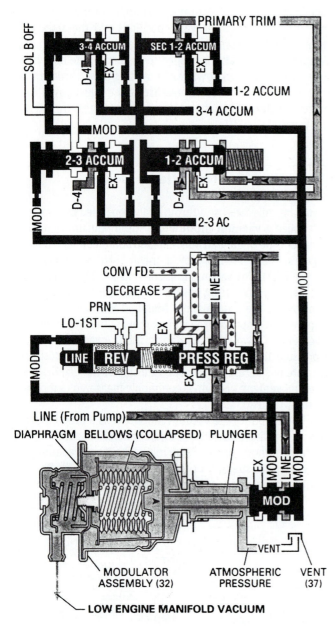

FIGURE 7-27 With high manifold vacuum, the modulator diaphragm and modulator valve are to the left, and modulator pressure is low. When manifold vacuum drops, the spring moves the diaphragm toward the right, and modulator pressure will increase. Note the bellows used in this modulator. *(Reprinted with permission of General Motors)*

with springs of different strengths to suit the operating conditions in vehicles of different sizes or engines with different torque outputs. A stronger spring or smaller diaphragm area produces a stronger outward force and higher TV pressure; a weaker spring or a larger diaphragm produces a weaker force and lower TV pressure. The stem of the vacuum modulator pushes against one end of the throttle valve while throttle

pressure acts against the opposite end, much like in a mechanical throttle valve.

Vacuum-operated throttle valves produce a throttle pressure that is more relative to engine load than a mechanically operated valve. Engine manifold vacuum is a product of throttle position, engine load, and engine speed. At idle speed and while operating at light throttle, intake manifold vacuum is relatively high, about 18 to 20 in. Hg. At this time, the pumping action of the pistons pulls air out of the manifold faster than it can flow in past the closed throttle plates (Figure 7-29). At WOT, manifold vacuum is usually lower than 1 in. Hg because air can easily flow past the open-throttle plates. During cruise conditions, the throttle is partially open, and manifold vacuum is somewhere in the range of 10 to 15 in. Hg. Cruise vacuum will vary greatly depending on engine size, vehicle weight, and gear ratio. During cruise conditions, an increase in engine load such as a head wind or going up an incline slows the engine relative to the throttle opening and thus causes a drop in vacuum, from 10 to 15 in. Hg down to 6 to 8 in. Hg.

Some vacuum modulators contain an evacuated bellows assembly. This unit acts against the spring to produce more consistent shift response at differing altitudes. When a vehicle is operated at higher altitudes, the air is thinner and atmospheric pressure is lower. This produces less torque in the engine, and the transmission pressures should be lowered slightly to prevent harsh shifts. At this time, the reduced atmospheric pressure acting on the bellows allows the bellows to lengthen and increase the pressure acting against the diaphragm spring. This has the effect of reducing the spring's strength, which reduces the force acting on the throttle valve and therefore the throttle pressure.

7.4.3 Wide-Open Throttle Kickdown Valve

A vacuum modulator cannot accurately indicate the exact throttle opening. The WOT signal can be brought to the transmission by a mechanical linkage, a rod or a cable, or an electric current. A WOT kickdown valve is also called a detent valve. A mechanical detent valve resembles the mechanical throttle and detent valve combination described earlier. Throttle movement is transmitted to the detent valve so it can produce a full pressure in the detent passages at WOT.

An electric detent valve is controlled by a switch in the throttle linkage and a solenoid at the valve body. When the throttle is opened to a point close to WOT, the switch is closed to complete the circuit. Battery voltage energizes the solenoid, causing it to stroke a metal rod or move a metal plate that either moves a valve or opens a passage. In either case, fluid pressure is sent to the detent passages.

Diaphragm Diameter (in.)	Diaphragm Area (SI)	Manifold Vacuum			(1.76 SI Diaphragm) Force (lb)
		in. Hg.	psia	Pressure Difference	
$1\frac{1}{4}$	1.227	0	14.7	0	0
$1\frac{9}{32}$	1.289	5	12.2	2.5	4.4
$1\frac{1}{2}$	1.767	10	9.7	5	8.8
$1\frac{9}{16}$	1.917	15	7.2	7.5	13.25
$1\frac{11}{16}$	2.23	20	4.7	10	17.7
2	3.1416				

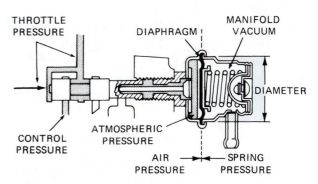

FIGURE 7-28   Vacuum modulators have different diameters, which change the relative strength of the modulator.

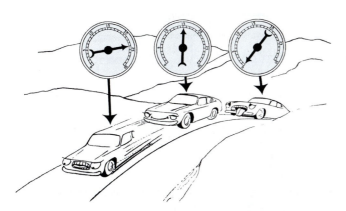

FIGURE 7-29   Manifold vacuum varies with load. Cruising at light load produces about 15 to 20 in. Hg. A high load produces zero vacuum, 0 in. Hg. *(Courtesy of Nissan North America, Inc.)*

PROBLEM SOLVING 7-2 Imagine that you are working in a shop that specializes in transmission repair, and these problems are brought to you:

Case 1 A 1982 Chevrolet pickup starts out okay in first gear, but the 1–2 shift is long and drawn out. A full-throttle shift has an engine flare. What part of the transmission is at fault? What do you think is causing this problem?

Case 2 A 1988 Dodge Diplomat (RWD) drives okay, but the shifts are very harsh. What could be wrong? How can you determine which part is faulty?

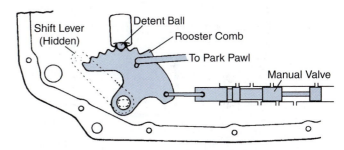

FIGURE 7-30   The manual valve is moved by the shift lever and held in position by the detent lever (cam).

7.5 MANUAL VALUE

The **manual valve** controls the fluid flow to the band servos, clutch apply pistons, and the shift valves for the various forward and reverse gears. This valve is also called a *selector valve*. It receives the fluid from the pump at line pressure. The manual valve is moved by mechanical linkage when the driver moves the shift lever. It is held in position by the detent cam at the valve body (Figure 7-30). This detent is a spring-loaded roller or ball that drops into notches in the cam to position the manual valve properly in its bore. The detent cam is commonly called a **rooster comb**.

When the gear selector is in neutral or park, fluid flow through the manual valve is blocked by a land or trapped between two lands. Many transmissions send line pressure to the throttle valve in neutral so the TV circuit is ready to

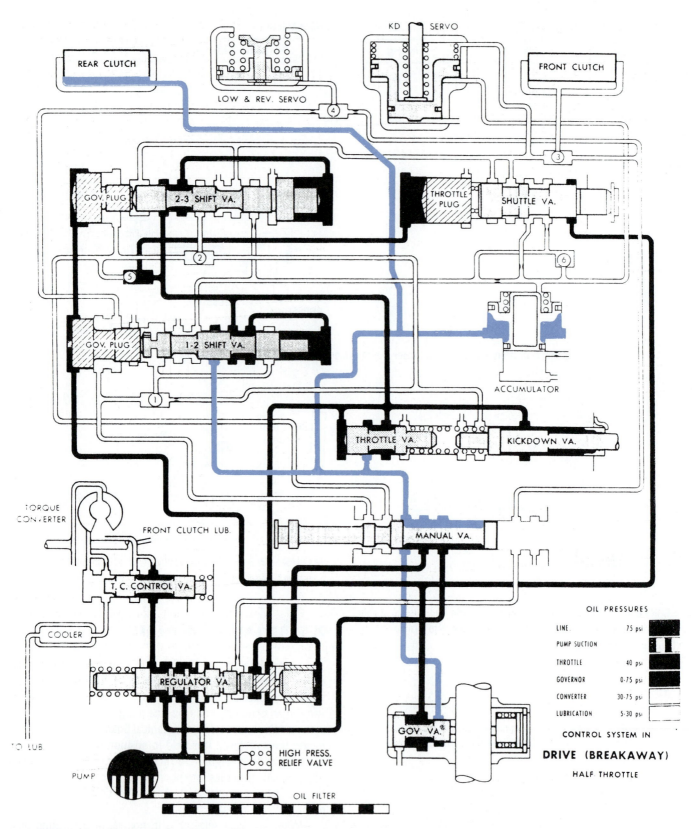

FIGURE 7-31 The manual valve is in drive and the transmission is in first gear. Fluid is being sent to the rear clutch, accumulator, 1–2 shift valve, throttle valve, and governor. *(Courtesy of Chrysler Corporation)*

operate as soon as the neutral–drive or neutral–reverse shift is made.

In the other gear selector positions, the valve is moved to allow fluid flow through the valve to various valves and friction-apply circuits. Most three- and four-speed transmissions have six gear selector positions. Some four-speed transmissions have seven positions that allow fourth-gear operation in overdrive and limit the transmission to first- through third-gear operation in drive. For simplicity, the following descriptions are for a three-speed transmission. In general, the fluid flows are as follows:

- **Drive:** Fluid is directed to the forward clutch, the 1–2 shift valve, and the governor (Figure 7-31). Automatic upshifts and downshifts will occur.
- **Intermediate:** Same as drive but the 2–3 shift valve is blocked from moving or fluid is not fed to it.
- **Low:** Fluid is directed to the forward clutch, the low-reverse clutch or band, and the governor; and the 1–2 shift valve is blocked from moving. A pressure signal may also be sent to the pressure regulator to boost line pressure.
- **Reverse:** Fluid is directed to the high-reverse clutch, the low-reverse clutch or band, and the pressure regulator to boost fluid pressures.

The various fluid flows leaving the manual valve are labeled drive oil, manual-2, manual-1, and reverse.

7.6 GOVERNOR VALVE

The transmission will begin transferring power and rotating the output shaft when the selector lever is moved to drive, intermediate, or low. When the output shaft starts turning, the governor spins with it. The governor is either shaft mounted (attached directly onto the output shaft) or case mounted (driven by a gear on the output shaft) (Figure 7-32).

The **governor valve** produces a pressure signal that is proportionate to the vehicle speed; it is used to move the shift valves to an upshift position. The governor pressure should be zero when the vehicle is at rest. When the vehicle is moving, governor output pressure should roughly equal vehicle speed. There should be a steady pressure increase as the vehicle accelerates (Figure 7-33). Governor pressure is routed to one end of each shift valve. It is also sent to any other valve that requires a speed-related input, such as a TCC control valve or a downshift inhibitor valve.

A governor uses the centrifugal force acting on a pair of weights to measure speed. The weights try to move outward as speed increases, moving the valve to increase governor pressure. Centrifugal force moves the governor valve, allowing drive oil into the governor oil passages. Somewhat like a throttle valve, governor pressure acts on a reaction area of the governor valve trying to reposition the valve and exhaust governor pressure. Governor pressure is balanced between output shaft rpm and governor pressure.

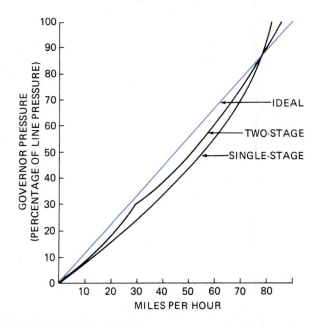

FIGURE 7-33 The ideal governor pressure signal increases in exact proportion to vehicle speed, but a simple governor produces a signal that is too low at intermediate speeds or too high at higher speeds. The pressure signal from a two-stage governor comes closer to matching vehicle speed.

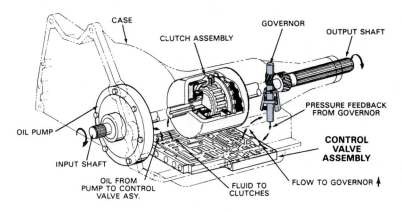

FIGURE 7-32 A case-mounted governor is driven by a gear on the output shaft. It provides a pressure signal relative to vehicle speed. *(Reprinted with permission of General Motors)*

All governor assemblies share the same basic engineering problem: Centrifugal force increases at an ever-increasing rate; the force more than doubles as rpm doubles. This produces an output that is not properly aligned with speed. Most governor assemblies use two or more stages to produce a more straight-line pressure increase.

Governor valve assemblies are manufactured in four basic styles. Two are shaft mounted, and two are case mounted:

- **Shaft mounted with the weight(s) opposing the valve** The valve is on one side of the shaft and the weight(s) on the other, and they are connected by a pin that passes through the shaft (Figure 7-34).

- **Shaft mounted with a primary and secondary valve** These two valves, which also act as the weights, are mounted so the output of one valve acts to help control the movement of the other valve (Figure 7-35).

- **Case mounted with a pair of primary and secondary weights** The valve is operated by a pair of levers (weights) that move the valve.

- **Case-mounted bleed-off system** Two governor pressure balls bleed off pressure. With the vehicle at rest, pressure escapes past these balls. They are seated by a pair of levers extending from the weights. An increase in governor pressure occurs as speed increases (Figure 7-36).

In all of these governor assemblies, governor pressure acts on the valve(s) or balls to allow the pressure to escape or bleed off to exhaust. This occurs as the vehicle slows to a stop. As the vehicle speed increases, the centrifugal force acting on the weights causes the exhaust flow to decrease. In the valve, a flow is opened between the drive oil and governor pressure passages. Governor pressure is a balance between governor pressure trying to open the valve to exhaust and centrifugal force trying to open the valve to drive oil as it closes the exhaust port (Figure 7-37).

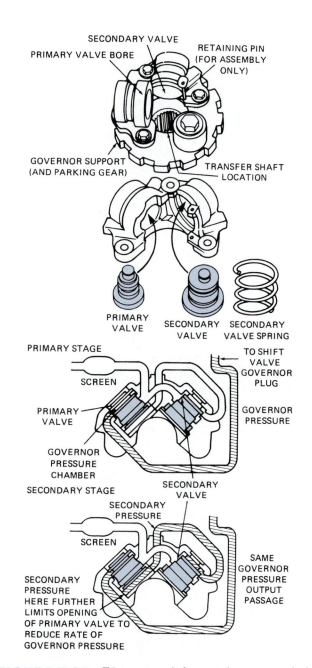

FIGURE 7-35 This two-stage, shaft-mounted governor uses both a primary and secondary valve. *(Courtesy of Chrysler Corporation)*

In two-stage governors, the primary governor weight is heavier so centrifugal force begins to act on it as soon as the vehicle starts moving. This weight is the major control for slow-speed operation. The primary weight is designed so it reaches a limit and bottoms out at middle operating speeds, and any further centrifugal force from that point is blocked. As the vehicle speed increases, the secondary weight becomes the controlling factor in the governor.

The governor valve is the least-reliable valve in a transmission because of its tendency to stick in its bore. This is

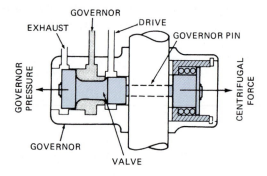

FIGURE 7-34 As the vehicle speeds up, centrifugal force acting on the governor weight tries to move the weight and valve toward the right to increase governor pressure. This is opposed by governor pressure at the valve, which tries to move the valve toward the left and reduce governor pressure. *(Courtesy of Chrysler Corporation)*

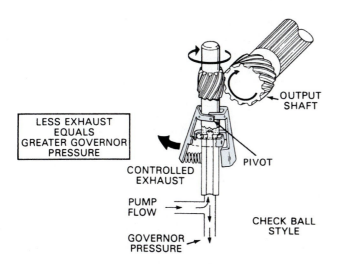

FIGURE 7-36   Centrifugal force will cause the two weights to move outward. This pushes the two balls against their seats, reducing the amount of exhaust and increasing governor pressure. *(Reprinted with permission of General Motors)*

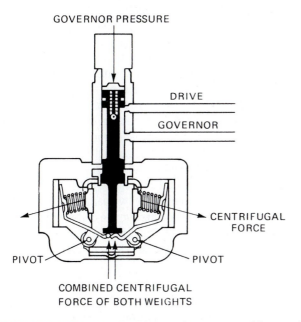

FIGURE 7-37   Centrifugal force produces an upward force on the valve that will increase governor pressure if the valve moves. Governor pressure at the top of the valve opposes this action. The governor valve is positioned between these two forces. *(Reprinted with permission of General Motors)*

basically a result of the very gradual movement of the valve in normal operation; most of the other valves in a transmission "snap" from one end of their bore to the other. A governor valve must move freely to respond to every change in speed. A very fine screen is normally placed in the fluid passage leading to the governor to trap dirt and debris that might cause a valve to stick. A stuck governor valve can cause a no-upshift condition or high gear starts.

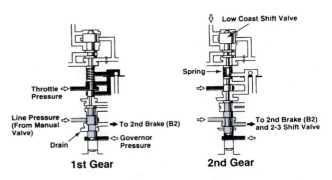

FIGURE 7-38   Governor pressure can move this 1–2 shift valve from the downshift position (left) to the upshift position.

7.7 SHIFT VALVES

An upshift or downshift occurs when the shift valves move. Shift valves are balanced between the governor pressure trying to move the valve to cause an upshift and the spring plus throttle pressure trying to resist an upshift (Figure 7-38). At rest or very slow speeds, the spring moves the valve to the downshift position. A typical shift valve has a land for the governor reaction area at one end and a spring at the other. Throttle pressure enters from the side, crosses through a valve valley, and reenters at the end with the spring. The controlled flow to the next gear's apply device also enters from the side and is blocked by a land or a closed valley while the passage to the apply device is open to exhaust.

As the vehicle is accelerating, governor pressure gradually increases until the force at that end of the shift valve becomes stronger than the spring plus the force created by throttle pressure. At this time, the shift valve should move, but we want the valve to snap from one end to the other to ensure a complete application of the controlled apply device. This happens in most shift valves because the first valve movement cuts off the throttle (TV or STV) pressure at the end of the valve and opens this chamber to exhaust. This unbalances the forces on the valve, and the valve then quickly completes its movement to an upshift position.

The governor land on the 1–2 shift valve is usually larger than the 2–3 shift valve governor land to guarantee that the 1–2 valve moves before the 2–3 valve. When the 1–2 shift valve moves to upshift, it opens a passage so that drive oil can flow through the valve and to the intermediate band or clutch applying second gear (Figure 7-39). When the 2–3 shift valve moves to upshift, it opens a passage sending pressure to the high-reverse clutch and the intermediate band. This pressure will release the band and apply the clutch (Figure 7-40).

Fluid flow into the shift valves also affects shift sequence. Most shift valves are *series fed* (Figure 7-41). With series-fed valves, the 2–3 shift valve receives its fluid for the upshift from

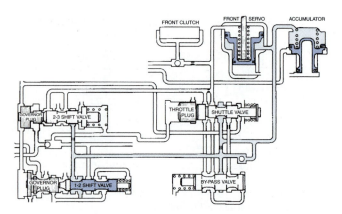

FIGURE 7-39 The 1–2 shift valve has moved to upshift, allowing drive oil to flow into the second-gear passages. Fluid pressure moves the front servo to apply the band and also strokes the accumulator piston. *(Courtesy of Chrysler Corporation)*

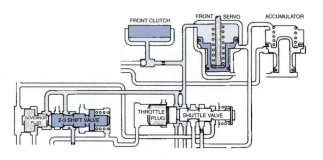

FIGURE 7-40 The 2–3 shift valve has moved to upshift. Fluid pressure will apply the front clutch and also move the front servo to release the band. *(Courtesy of Chrysler Corporation)*

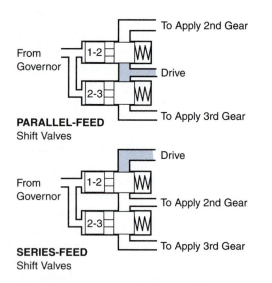

FIGURE 7-41 Both parallel-feed shift valves are connected to drive oil (top); an upshift will occur when governor oil moves either one to the right. With series-feed shift valves, drive oil feeds only the 1–2 shift valve, and the 2–3 shift valve is fed from the 1–2 valve (bottom).

the 1–2 shift valve; the 1–2 upshift must occur before the 2–3 shift. *Parallel-fed* shift valves are connected to the same fluid supply source. It is possible for the 1–2 and 2–3 shifts to occur at the same time, producing a 1–3 upshift.

PROBLEM SOLVING 7-3 Imagine that you are working in a shop that specializes in transmission repair, and these problems are brought to you:

Case 1 A 1982 Chevrolet Impala starts out okay in first gear, but the 1–2 and 2–3 shifts are late. What part of the transmission is faulty? What do you think is causing this problem?

Case 2 A 1986 Toyota Celica starts out okay in drive, but it stays in first, and at about 20 to 30 mph, it makes a 1–3 shift. There is no second gear. What do you think might be wrong? How can you determine what part is faulty?

7.7.1 Shift Overlap

To shift from one gear range to another, transmissions apply and release clutches or bands. This is often called *shift calibration.* Some transmissions are designed to apply a clutch or a band without having to release another one. These are called *non-synchronous* or *asynchronous* transmissions. **Synchronous** transmissions require a clutch or band to release during the clutch or band apply for the next gear range, and these must be carefully synchronized. For example, during a 2–3 shift in many Simpson three-speed transmissions, the intermediate band releases while the high-reverse clutch applies (Figure 7-42). The band must be released as the clutch is applied. An early application of the clutch or a late release of the band produces a "fight" or "bind" between these two parts, and this produces a harsh shift and probable damage to the clutch or band. A late application of the clutch or an early release of the band produces an engine over-speed (also called a "flare" or "buzzup")

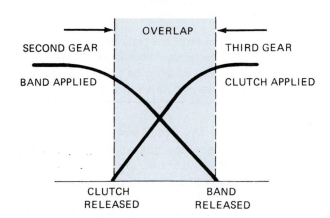

FIGURE 7-42 Shift overlap is the time period as the band releases and the direct clutch applies between second and third gears.

as the transmission falls back to first gear before the shift to third is completed.

Timing these two apply devices occurs by using the upshift fluid pressures from the shift valve to apply the clutch and also release the band. In some units, band-release fluid flow is used as an accumulator control for the clutch apply. Accumulators are also used to control shift quality, as described in the next section.

During a 3–2 downshift, the clutch must release as the band reapplies, and this action must be carefully coordinated, just like an upshift. An additional problem occurs at this time because centrifugal force in the spinning clutch tends to inhibit the fluid from flowing back to the entrance port at the center. The clutch exhaust check ball is designed to allow the fluid to leave from the outer area of the clutch chamber (Figure 7-43). When the clutch applies, fluid pressure seats the check ball to prevent losing pressure. When the clutch releases and the pressure drops, centrifugal force moves the ball outward to an un-

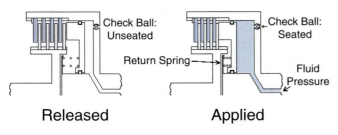

Released   Applied

FIGURE 7-43 When a clutch is applied, fluid pressure keeps the exhaust check ball tightly seated (right). When the pressure is released, centrifugal force moves the check ball off its seat and allows a fluid flow out of the clutch (left).

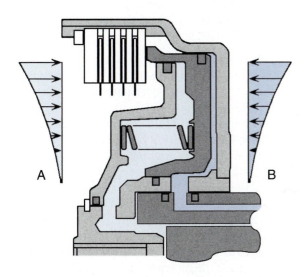

A   B

FIGURE 7-44 Centrifugal force in the balance/release cavity (a) generates the same fluid force as that in the apply chamber (b). This balanced force allows the springs to return the piston and release the clutch.

seated position. This allows the fluid in the clutch assembly to escape so the clutch can release quickly and completely.

Some newer transmissions use a *centrifugal force balanced clutch,* also called *centrifugal fluid pressure cancelling* (Figure 7-44). This clutch has a second fluid chamber on the spring/release side of the clutch piston. Fluid in this chamber develops the same pressure from centrifugal force as that on the apply side of the piston. The springs can now move the piston to release the clutch, and both the apply and release chambers stay filled with fluid. This style of clutch gives more precise clutch apply and release characteristics than a clutch that uses a check ball and is becoming more popular with electronic-shift control.

7.7.2 Shift Modifiers

Many automatic transmissions contain valves to adjust the quality (speed and firmness) of the shift. A light-throttle shift, made while the engine is not producing much torque, can be fairly slow and at a light pressure. At heavy throttle, the engine is producing more torque so higher pressures are needed for the shift in order to lock the band or clutch being applied and prevent excessive slippage. Too slow of a shift at pressures that are too low will cause slippage and burning of the friction material. Too fast of a shift at pressures that are too high produces an aggressive, harsh shift that can cause mechanical damage to the drive train. Several methods are used to tailor a shift to the throttle opening or speed of the vehicle (Table 7-2).

TABLE 7-2   Shift Quality

Variable	Change	Effect
Line Pressure	Increase	Firmer Shift
Flow Rate	Increase	Firmer Shift
Orifice Size	Increase	Faster Flow Rate
Accumulator Rate	Increase	Firmer Shift
Accumulator Spring	Softer	Faster Accumulator Rate
Accumulator Back Pressure	Reduce	Faster Accumulator Rate
ATF Type	More Aggressive	Firmer Shift

An **accumulator** is tied hydraulically to the clutch or band servo, and the accumulator absorbs fluid during the pressure buildup stage when a clutch or band applies. This has the effect of slowing the pressure increase and lengthening the time it takes for the friction device to lock up (Figure 7-45). As clutch or band apply pressure is entering the apply side of the accumulator, fluid must leave the opposite, exhaust side of the accumulator piston. The pressure on the apply side and rate of stroke can be controlled by how easily the fluid leaves the exhaust side. An accumulator valve or shift control valve is often placed in the accumulator exhaust passage. The accumulator valve is usually balanced between throttle pressure and accumulator pressure in such a way that high throttle pressure closes down the accumulator exhaust flow. This produces higher accumulator pressure and therefore a firmer, quicker shift. The shift must be completed before the accumulator completes its stroke. If the accumulator piston bottoms before the shift is complete, there will be a sudden pressure increase that will cause a **slide-bump shift.** This is a shift with poor quality that starts smooth, but ends harsh.

Another method of changing upshift speed relative to downshift speed is to use an **orifice** in parallel with a one-way check ball. During upshifts, the ball seats so the flow passes through the orifice, and the diameter of the orifice controls the apply rate. During a downshift, the fluid flow unseats the ball, allowing a fast release.

Still another method of changing shift speed is to position a valve to open a circuit bypassing an orifice (Figure 7-46). Under high throttle pressures, the valve opens the bypass so that a higher flow and pressure reaches the clutch or band apply piston, producing a faster shift. Low throttle pressures will close the bypass valve so the apply fluid must pass through the orifice and be controlled by the small size of the orifice opening.

7.7.3 Downshifts

The shift valves move to the downshift position under four operating conditions:

- **Coasting downshift:** What normally occurs as a vehicle is brought to a stop. The spring moves the valve as governor pressure drops.
- **Part-throttle downshift:** When the throttle is opened slightly to accelerate slowly and the rise in throttle pressure plus the spring can overcome governor pressure.
- **Detent downshift:** Full-throttle/kickdown operates the detent valve and sends pressure through the detent passages to the shift valve. This pressure plus the spring will overcome governor pressure (see Figure 7-23).

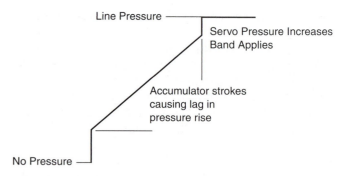

FIGURE 7-45   The pressure rise in this servo is delayed as the accumulator strokes.

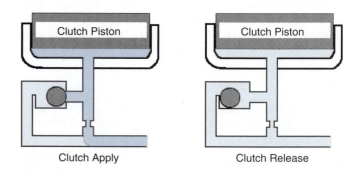

Clutch Apply   Clutch Release

FIGURE 7-46   Clutch apply pressure seats the check ball so apply fluid must pass through the orifice (left). When the clutch releases, the check ball moves off it's seat, allowing a faster clutch release because the fluid can bypass the orifice (right).

- **Manual downshift:** Movement of the shift lever to the manual-1 or M2 position sends pressure to a reaction area on the shift valve or governor plug that works against governor pressure (Figure 7-47).

Coasting downshift is 4–1 or 3–1, not 3–2–1. A 3–1 downshift cannot be felt because the one-way clutch (the first-gear reaction member) overruns. Under most driving conditions with easy stops, we do not really need the compression braking that a 3–2 shift provides because there is adequate power in the vehicle's braking system. A 3–2 shift causes more wear in the transmission and an unnecessary downshift "bump."

If the shift selector is moved to manual-1 at speeds above 30 mph (48 km/h), the 1–2 shift valve normally stays in the upshift position until the speed drops off. A downshift at too high of a speed causes the engine to overrev and possible engine damage. This delay in a manual downshift is obtained by the relative sizes of the governor and manual-1 reaction areas. Some transmissions include an *inhibitor valve* that blocks this type of action, which can cause unsafe conditions and possible damage.

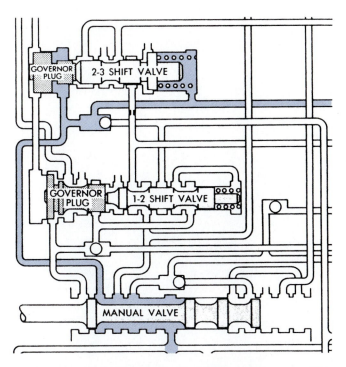

FIGURE 7-47   The manual valve has been moved to manual-2 to send line pressure to the 2–3 shift valve and governor plug. This moves both of them to the left and forces a downshift.

PROBLEM SOLVING 7-4   Imagine that you are working in a shop that specializes in transmission repair, and these problems are brought to you:

Case 1   A 1983 Ford Ranger pickup starts out in second gear. The 2–3 and 3–4 shifts are normal. What part of the transmission is faulty? What do you think is causing this problem?

Case 2   A 1993 Buick Regal drives okay most of the time, but the 3–4 part-throttle upshift is harsh. Could this be an accumulator or shift modifier valve problem? How can you determine if either of these parts is used in this transmission?

7.8 CVT HYDRAULIC CONTROL

Several hydraulic valves are used in a CVT to control the pulley positions and the fluid pressure for other systems:

- Ratio control valve
- Secondary pulley pressure
- Reverse and, if used, forward clutch apply pressure
- Torque converter clutch apply and release pressures
- Lubrication pressure

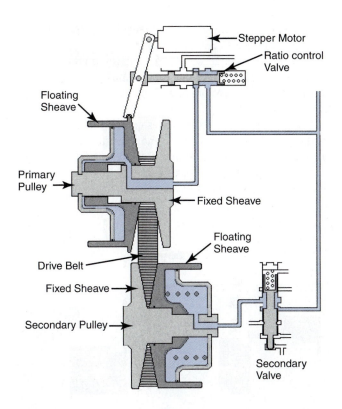

FIGURE 7-48   Movement of either the stepper motor or primary floating sheave will move the ratio control valve to add or remove fluid from the primary pulley. The secondary valve maintains the necessary pulley pressure on the drive belt.

The ratio control valve is a three-position valve that can feed fluid to the primary piston, hold that fluid, or bleed fluid from the piston. The valve is connected at the center of a link between the floating pulley side and a stepper motor. When the TCM desires a higher ratio, the stepper motor is commanded to move, and this moves the ratio control valve to feed fluid to the primary piston (Figure 7-48). The primary piston will then move, and the pulley movement will move the ratio control valve to a hold position. If the TCM desires a lower ratio, the stepper motor will be driven inward, and the ratio control valve will bleed fluid from the primary piston until the pulley moves to the proper position.

The drive belt must be clamped tight enough between the pulley sides and the two pulleys to prevent slippage. The primary pulley must be able to overcome the clamping force of the secondary pulley. This is done by giving the primary a larger piston area, higher fluid pressure, or both. The secondary pulley pressure valve controls the fluid pressure to the secondary piston, and this pressure provides belt-clamping pressure. Primary and secondary piston pressure can be as high as 900 psi (6.2 Mpa).

The forward and reverse clutches are hydraulically operated, multiplate clutches, like those used in other transmissions.

Their operation is controlled by a manual valve. Clutch apply pressure ranges up to 220 psi (1.5 Mpa)

Some CVTs use an offset, chain-driven pump to reduce transaxle length (Figure 7-49); others mount the pump in a normal position. A gerotor and a balanced vane-type pump can be used.

TCC and lube circuits are similar to those of other transaxles. TCC control is by a solenoid-controlled spool valve. These circuits have pressures from 0 to 145 psi (0.0 to 1 MPA).

CVT transmission requires a special fluid; even a small amount of another fluid, such as ATF, can cause belt-to-pulley slippage and serious damage (Figure 7-50).

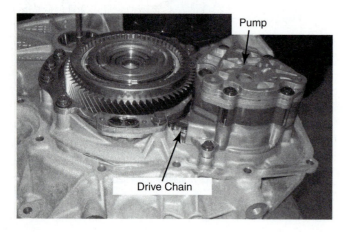

FIGURE 7-49   This pump is mounted off to the side and driven by a chain from the transmission input shaft.

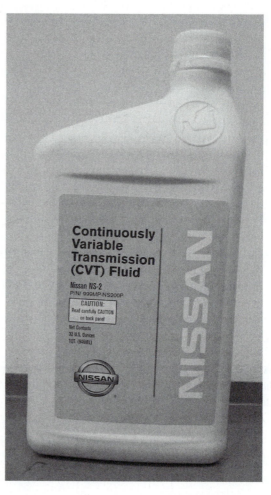

FIGURE 7-50   Always use the recommended CVT fluid in CVT transmissions.

SUMMARY

1. An automatic transmission monitors vehicle load and speed to determine shift timing and quality.

2. Various types of valves are used to direct the fluid flow and regulate the pressures used to operate the transmission.

3. The torque converter is a hydraulic coupling that connects the engine to the transmission. It also has a hydraulically operated lock-up clutch that, when applied, makes a mechanical connection between the engine and transmission.

4. A governor valve is used to monitor vehicle speed, and a vacuum or mechanically controlled throttle valve regulates pressure that is applied to the ends of the shift valves to control when the shifts will occur.

5. Additional valves are used to control the shifts needed for other driving conditions. A kickdown valve is used to force a downshift, and shift-modifying valves are used to improve the quality and timing of both the upshifts and downshifts.

REVIEW QUESTIONS

The following questions are provided to help you study as you read the chapter.

1. Valves can be placed into three categories. What are they?

2. Servo valves are used to _____ another valve and switching valves are used to _____ flow.

3. The term *exhaust* when used with an automatic transmission means that the fluid is being directed to the _____ to empty a circuit.

4. The typical spring-balanced pressure regulator valve maintains mainline pressure at about _____ to _____ psi.

5. Under certain driving conditions, _____ pressure will increase and be used to _____ mainline pressure.

6. Full-throttle pressure will increase mainline pressure to about _____ to _____ psi.

7. Mainline pressure in reverse should be between _____ and _____ psi.

8. The torque converter must have continual flow to maintain _____ temperature.

9. Typical torque converter pressure is _____ to _____ psi.

10. Most lock-up torque converters are controlled _____ by the ECM.

11. Fluid leaving the torque converter is directed to the _____ exchanger.

12. Fluid returning from the heat exchanger is used to _____ the transmission.

13. Throttle valves are _____ regulating valves that provide a pressure _____ relative to the vehicle _____.

14. Throttle valves can be controlled by _____, _____, or _____ connections to the throttle linkage.

15. As vehicle load _____, engine vacuum will _____, and throttle valve pressure will _____.

16. The detent valve is used to produce full-throttle pressure at _____ _____ _____.

17. The governor produces a signal that is proportionate to vehicle _____.

18. Shift valves are positioned by a spring and _____ pressure at one end and _____ pressure at the other end.

19. A coasting downshift results when _____ pressure drops.

20. A part-throttle downshift results because of a rise in _____ _____ pressure.

CHAPTER QUIZ

The following questions will help you check the facts you have learned. Select the answer that completes each statement correctly.

1. Automatic transmission hydraulic pressure is created by
   a. the pump.
   b. the pressure regulator valve.
   c. restrictions to fluid flow.
   d. All of these

2. Three categories of valves found in a hydraulic circuit are
   a. switching, servo, and pressure regulating.
   b. accumulator, flow control, and pressure regulating.
   c. switching, manual, and flow control.
   d. manual, shift, and accumulator.

3. Hydraulic diagrams are useful to
   a. trace the power flow.
   b. trace the fluid flow.
   c. understand the gear train.
   d. All of these

4. A switching valve can be moved
   a. hydraulically.
   b. mechanically.
   c. by another valve.
   d. All of these

5. Normal unboosted line pressure is about _____ psi.
   a. 10 to 15
   b. 25 to 35
   c. 50 to 60
   d. 125 to 135

6. Student A says that most pressure regulator valves are arranged so that line pressure tries to move the valve in one direction while a spring tries to move the valve in the other. Student B says that most pressure regulator valves are arranged so line pressure tries to move the valve in one direction while boost valve pressure tries to move the valve in the other. Who is correct?

   a. Student A

   b. Student B

   c. Both A and B

   d. Neither A nor B

7. An increase in mainline pressure is desirable to

   a. produce firmer shifts.

   b. improve shift feel.

   c. increase holding power.

   d. All of these

8. Fluid is directed to the torque converter by the

   a. pressure regulator.

   b. manual valve.

   c. pump.

   d. boost valve.

9. In many transmissions, torque converter clutch lock-up occurs when the

   a. fluid flow through the converter is reversed.

   b. fluid flow to the cooler is shut off.

   c. converter pressure is raised to 125 psi.

   d. All of these

10. The transmission cooler is usually located in the

    a. oil pan.

    b. coolest tank of the radiator.

    c. area in front of the air-conditioning condenser.

    d. hottest part of the radiator.

11. An automatic transmission can be damaged by towing a vehicle because

    a. it will not be lubricated unless the engine is running.

    b. the torque converter will seize up.

    c. the clutches and bands will not apply.

    d. All of these

12. A supplemental transmission cooler should typically be installed

    a. before the heat exchanger.

    b. after the heat exchanger.

    c. behind the radiator.

    d. behind the condenser.

13. The throttle valve is used to sense

    a. vehicle speed.

    b. engine load.

    c. engine speed.

    d. transmission load.

14. Higher throttle openings cause the transmission to

    a. shift at higher speeds.

    b. produce firmer upshifts.

    c. increase the line pressure.

    d. All of these

15. The governor valve is used to sense

    a. vehicle speed.

    b. engine load.

    c. engine speed.

    d. transmission load.

16. A vacuum modulator transmission also has a throttle-controlled valve that can produce

    a. reduced line pressure.

    b. full-throttle downshifts.

    c. slightly earlier shift timing.

    d. All of these

17. A stronger spring in the vacuum modulator produces

    a. less part-throttle line pressure.

    b. greater part-throttle line pressure.

    c. earlier upshifts.

    d. softer upshifts.

18. Student A says that the manual valve position is controlled by the shift lever. Student B says that the manual valve position is controlled by a detent cam and spring-loaded ball or roller. Who is correct?

    a. Student A

    b. Student B

    c. Both A and B

    d. Neither A nor B

19. The pressure signal from the governor is used to

    a. produce higher line pressure at higher speeds.

    b. move the shift valves to the upshift position.

    c. produce firmer shifts at higher speeds.

    d. move the shift valves with the vehicle stopped.

20. Student A says that as the speed increases, centrifugal force acting on the governor weights will move the valve to increase governor pressure. Student B says that as the speed increases, centrifugal force acting on the governor weights will balance the output shaft to prevent vibrations. Who is correct?

    a. Student A

    b. Student B

    c. Both A and B

    d. Neither A nor B

21. Most shift valves use _____ to move them to a downshift position when the vehicle stops.
    a. throttle pressure
    b. governor pressure
    c. spring pressure
    d. Any of these

22. When a shift valve moves against the spring pressure, the transmission will
    a. upshift.
    b. downshift.
    c. increase the line pressure.
    d. shift to neutral.

23. Student A says that an accumulator is used to reduce fluid pressure in a servo that is applying to produce a softer upshift. Student B says that an orifice is used to reduce fluid pressure in a servo that is applying to produce a softer upshift. Who is correct?
    a. Student A
    b. Student B
    c. Both A and B
    d. Neither A nor B

24. Student A says that an orifice will cause a fluid pressure drop when fluid is flowing through it. Student B says that an orifice will have no effect on fluid pressure if there is no flow. Who is correct?
    a. Student A
    b. Student B
    c. Both A and B
    d. Neither A nor B

25. A manual-1 downshift above 30 mph can cause the
    a. engine to overrev.
    b. transmission to shift into second.
    c. transmission to shift into neutral.
    d. vehicle to set off an alarm.

CHAPTER 8

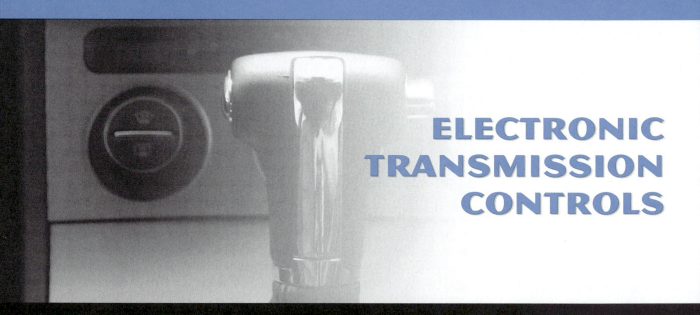

ELECTRONIC TRANSMISSION CONTROLS

OBJECTIVES

After studying Chapter 8, the reader should be able to:

1. Explain how electronic controls are used for transmission operation.
2. Identify the major automatic transmission electronic control components.
3. Describe the relationship between volts, amperes, and ohms.
4. Explain the circuit required for an electrical system to operate.
5. Describe the operation of an electronic transmission.

KEY TERMS

8.1 INTRODUCTION

Many years ago, automotive engineers discovered that electronic devices could be used to accurately control the ignition spark and timing. Since then, electronic controls have been used to operate and control almost every system used in a vehicle. The first electronic transmissions were introduced in the early 1980s. These were relatively simple applications that only controlled shift timing and quality, and the operation was similar to a typical nonelectronic transmission. A speed sensor was used in place of a governor and a throttle position sensor was used to detect vehicle load. An electronic control unit would process the sensor information and control solenoids that would cause the transmission to shift and the torque converter clutch to apply (Figure 8-1). Engineers continued developing electronic systems to improve the operation of the transmission and the way it interacts with the rest of the vehicle. Current electronic automatic transmissions are able to provide diagnostic information as well as accurately control:

- Shift timing and quality
- Mainline pressure
- Application and release of apply devices
- Apply-device pressures
- Clutch-apply fluid volume
- Application and release of the torque converter clutch
- Ignition timing during shifts

The accurate control of shift timing and quality provides a smoother driving experience. Improved performance, increased fuel economy, and superior vehicle durability are other benefits of electronic controls. In addition to improving shift quality, altering the ignition timing during the shift increases transmission life by decreasing the load on the transmission (Figure 8-2). This is called **torque management** or *torque reduction.* Another benefit is that the driver may not notice the shift occurring. Shift feel is also controlled by the transmission control module (TCM). By comparing the speed difference of the transmission

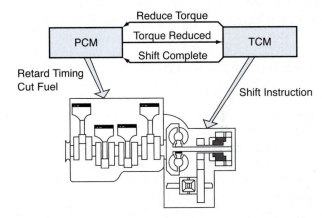

FIGURE 8-2 When the transmission control module (TCM) is ready to begin an upshift, it signals the power train control module (PCM) to reduce engine torque. This produces a smoother shift with less wear in the transmission.

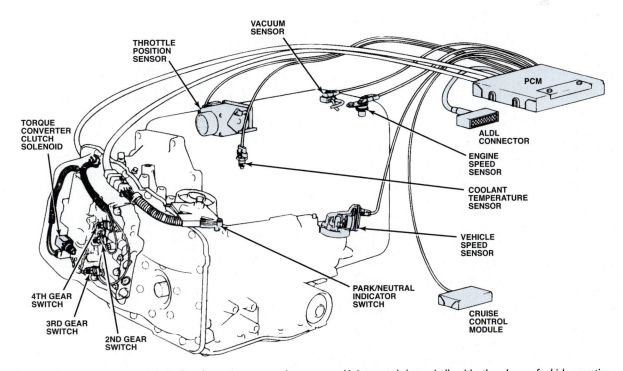

FIGURE 8-1 An electronic transmission has electronic sensors and actuators and is integrated electronically with other phases of vehicle operation.

input and output shafts a solenoid can be cycled (pulsed on and off). Fluid is then sent to an applying member at the rate needed to produce the desired shift quality. Some vehicles allow the driver to have limited control of the shift timing. The driver can choose economy mode, which causes the transmission to shift early with a smooth shift feel. When switched to power mode, the transmission shifts later and more firmly.

An automatic transmission can be controlled by its own computer, called a *transmission control module (TCM)* or a transmission control unit (TCU). The transmission can also be controlled through either the body control module (BCM) or the power train control module (PCM). Each manufacturer has its own design criteria and terminology. For consistency in this text, we will refer to the controlling unit as the TCM.

The TCM is normally located outside the transmission in a protected, relatively cool and clean location. Some transmissions have the TCM mounted on the valve body inside the transmission. The primary advantage is the reduction of wiring and the elimination of electrical connectors, both common sources of problems.

Electronic transmissions need to sense the same basic information for operation as a traditional hydraulic transmission: engine load and vehicle speed. The governor is replaced by a *vehicle speed sensor (VSS)*, and engine load is sensed using a *throttle position sensor (TPS)*, manifold air pressure (MAP) sensor, or a mass air flow (MAF) sensor. Electronic transmissions have a big advantage over hydraulically controlled transmissions that could only use mechanical, hydraulic, or vacuum to determine fluid pressure, shift timing, and quality. Additional information is available to the TCM that can be used to more precisely determine when and how the transmission will shift. Additional inputs to the TCM that are often used are:

- Mainline pressure
- Input shaft speed
- Fluid temperature
- Gear range
- Coolant temperature
- Engine speed
- Brake apply switch
- Air conditioning
- Cruise control

The additional sensors allow improved shift timing through a process referred to as *fuzzy logic*. In most situations, shifts simply match vehicle speed and throttle position. Fuzzy logic adapts shifts to driving conditions such as mountains, upgrades and downgrades, and while turning corners. The shifts will be delayed and firmer because of increased load and multiple changes in throttle position. Fuzzy logic and advanced electronics allow improved shifts for many different situations (Figure 8-3).

Another shift improvement is adaptive control that keeps shift duration within a certain time period as determined by the driver's habits. The TCM learns shift duration by monitoring

the input and output speed sensors and the pressure sensors. It can easily calculate the transmission gear ratio at any point in time. Some TCMs make this calculation every 4 milliseconds. It can correct a shift that is taking too long by increasing line pressure. It does this by adjusting the electronic pressure control (EPC) solenoid. One system can adjust a slipping shift in 400 milliseconds, which is less than half a second.

An electronic transmission controls the shift points by turning a **solenoid**(s) on and off. The solenoids in turn control the hydraulic pressure that moves the shift valves or operates the torque converter clutch (Figure 8-4). In some transmissions the solenoids completely replace the shift valves.

An automatic transmission technician needs a working knowledge of electricity and basic electronics as well as hydraulics. In the past, diagnosing and repairing the simple

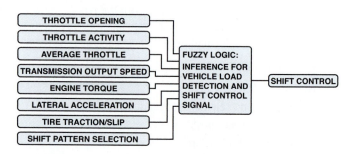

FIGURE 8-3   The fuzzy logic part of the TMC receives input signals, compares what the driver is doing with the throttle and what the vehicle is doing with normal operation, and adapts shift timing.

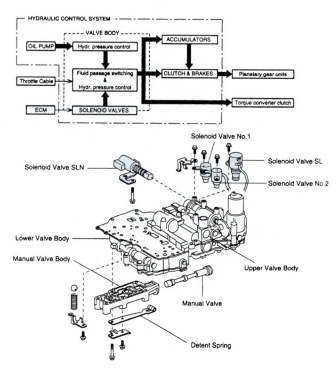

FIGURE 8-4   This electronic transmission valve body includes four solenoids.

electrical circuits that were used for detent, neutral start switch and backup light circuits could often be accomplished with a limited knowledge of electrical circuits and a simple test light. The introduction of solid-state computerized electronics presented the need to have an understanding of the system and electrical test procedures. The ability to measure electrical values and interpret their meaning has become very important. Specialized electronic test equipment and scan tools are required to diagnose some problem transmissions.

Solid-state electronics is at the heart of computerized circuits. Electronic components include transistors, diodes, and integrated microchips. These devices are quite fragile relative to other automotive components. They are also relatively trouble free and usually have a long life. They have no moving parts except electrons, so nothing should wear out.

8.2 BASIC ELECTRICITY

A course in basic automotive electronics is necessary to thoroughly understand electricity, how to measure it, and how to diagnose electrical problems. The following is a brief review of basic electricity.

In the future, vehicles are going to depend more on electricity for driving power and the operation of accessories (air conditioning, power steering, power brakes, etc.). Originally, vehicles used 6-volt electrical systems. These systems gave way to 12-volt systems to meet customer demands for more power and convenience. Now there are hybrid vehicles that are using 275-volt electrical systems. As a result of the changes in electrical power, it is becoming more important for every automotive technician to have at least a basic understanding of electrical circuit characteristics and Ohm's law.

The three measurable aspects of electricity that concern an automotive technician are: current flow (amperage), electrical pressure (voltage), and the resistance to current flow (ohms).

- **Voltage (volts)** is comparable to the pressure in a hydraulic system. Voltage is the force that causes electrical flow much like hydraulic pressure forces the fluid to flow in a hydraulic circuit (Figure 8-5). In a vehicle, the source of voltage is the battery or alternator.

- **Amperes (amps)** is the measurement of the current flowing through a circuit. One amp is equal to 6.28 billion electrons flowing past a point in one second. Current flow

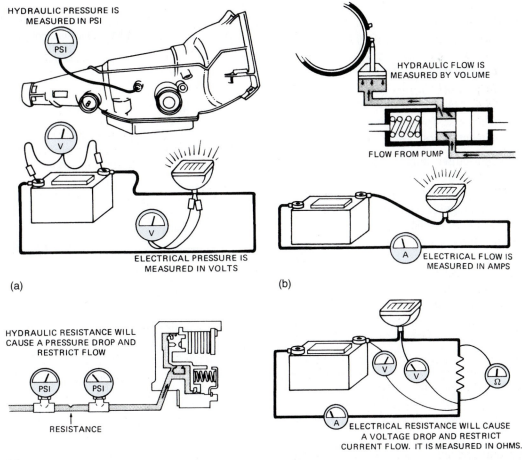

(a)

(b)

(c)

FIGURE 8-5   If we compare electricity with hydraulics, voltage and pressure (a), current flow and fluid flow (b), and a resistor and orifice (c) are very similar.

can be compared to the quantity of hydraulic fluid flowing into a clutch or servo.

- **Ohm** is the term used for the measurement of electrical **resistance.** The resistance in an electrical circuit controls how much current flows—much like an orifice restricts fluid flow in a hydraulic circuit. The higher the circuit resistance, the lower the current flow. The symbol Ω (omega) indicates ohms.

In order for current to flow, there must be a complete *circuit.* The circuit starts at the power supply, travels through the wires to the working component(s) (often called the load), and returns back to the power supply. The positive side of the circuit, often called battery positive (B+), is routed through wires. The negative side, *ground* (B−), can be run through wires or the metal parts of the vehicle can provide the ground (Figure 8-6). A component that is grounded by being bolted to the ground circuit is called case grounded.

Vehicles have many different electrical circuits. It is common for a vehicle to have over a mile (1.6 km) of wiring. Each circuit starts at the battery/alternator positive connection (B+) and ends at the battery/alternator negative connection (B−). A simple circuit has only one load. Other types of circuits are:

- Series: The loads are connected one after the other in a *series circuit.* This causes all the current to flow through all of the loads (Figure 8-7).
- Parallel: There are branches in a *parallel circuit.* Each branch is connected to the power source and ground, allowing the current to flow through separate paths.
- Series/parallel: The series/parallel circuit is a combination of the series and parallel circuits. All of the current will flow through the series loads and split as it passes through the parallel branches.

The vehicle manufacturers publish *wiring diagrams* that are the road maps of the electrical circuits. These maps help the technician understand the electrical circuits, the location of the components, and how the circuits are related. Wiring diagrams or *schematics* use symbols for the components to help simplify the drawings (Figure 8-8).

Automotive electrical circuits commonly use *direct current (dc)* systems. Direct current always travels in one direction. The flow of electrons in a dc circuit is believed to be from negative to positive. Household electricity is *alternating current (ac).* Alternating current switches direction many times a second. Most vehicles use 12-volt systems, which are actually 12.6 volts. Automotive engineers are working on 42-volt dc systems, and hybrid vehicles that use alternating current to operate some of their circuits.

Some automatic transmission technicians may find understanding electricity easy because it bears a strong resemblance to hydraulic systems.

- Hydraulic pressure and voltage are both forces that cause something to move.

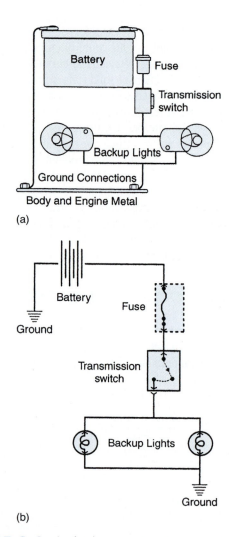

(a)

(b)

FIGURE 8-6   Insulated wires conduct electricity to the lights. The body metal forms the ground circuit to complete the circuit back to the battery. This is shown in a diagram (a) and a schematic (b).

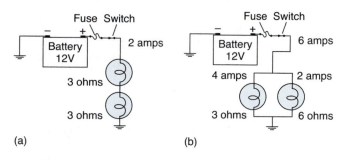

(a)   (b)

FIGURE 8-7   A series circuit (a) and a parallel circuit (b).

- The flow of hydraulic fluid and amperage are the movement in the circuits.
- The hydraulic circuit and the electrical circuit wiring are both the paths that the flow must follow.

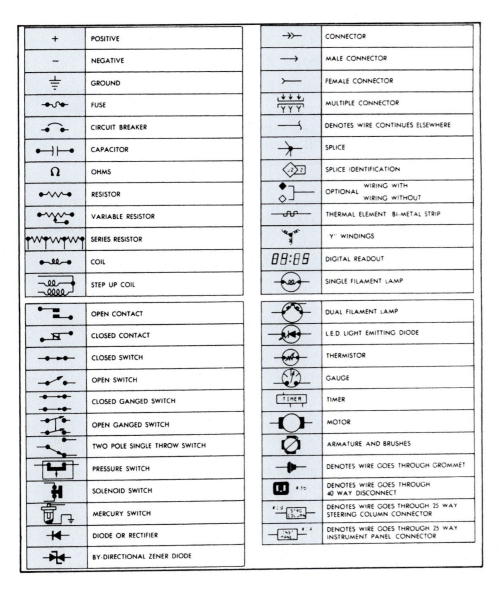

FIGURE 8-8 Wiring schematics use symbols to show the various components. *(Courtesy of Chrysler Corporation)*

- The orifice and the resistor both reduce the flow in the circuit.
- The hydraulic check valve and a diode are one-way check valves.
- An accumulator and a capacitor are used to absorb and hold some of the circuit flow.

8.2.1 System Components

A typical automotive circuit has the following components (Figure 8-9):

- Power source: the battery or alternator
- Circuit protection: fuse, fusible links, and circuit breakers
- Circuit control: switches
- *Conductor:* wires, connectors, and metal conductors
- Load: components that do the work

Power Source. The automotive power source is either the battery or the alternator. The battery is primarily used to start the engine. It also provides the electrical power when the engine is not running or the electrical demands exceed the ability of the alternator to provide the needed electricity. The alternator not only provides electrical power while the vehicle is running but must also be able to recharge the battery when necessary. A fully charged battery will measure 12.6 volts. When the engine is running, the alternator raises the system voltage to between 13.6 and 15.6 volts.

Circuit Protection. Circuit protection is the weak link in a circuit and will burn out or blow if excess current flows in the circuit. Serious damage can result if too much current is allowed to flow through a circuit. Circuit protection devices are used to stop the current flow in a circuit if the current exceeds the rated capacity of the circuit. The circuit protection devices used in vehicles are fuses, fusible links, and circuit breakers (Figure 8-10).

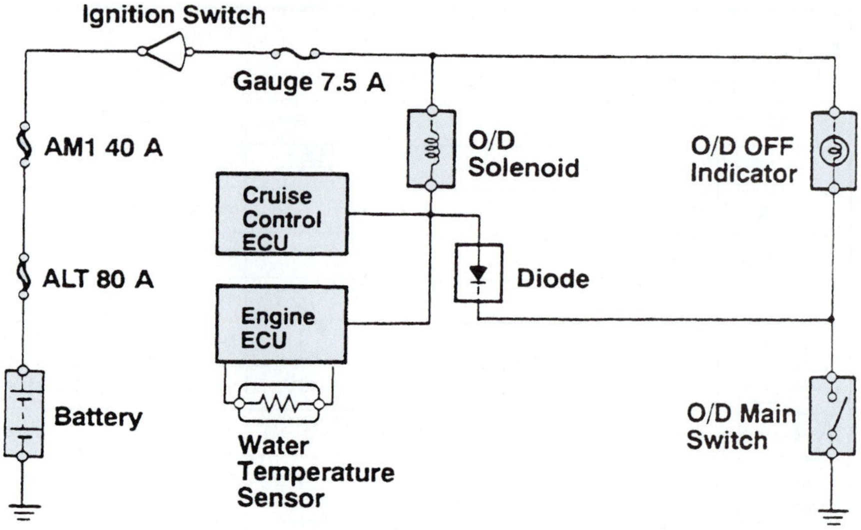

Ignition Switch

Gauge 7.5 A

AM1 40 A

ALT 80 A

Battery

Cruise
Control
ECU

Engine
ECU

Water
Temperature
Sensor

O/D
Solenoid

Diode

O/D OFF
Indicator

O/D Main
Switch

FIGURE 8-9 This wiring diagram of a transmission with electronic controls for fourth gear (O/D) shows the power source (battery), three fuses for protection, a control switch and two ECUs (electronic control units), two output devices (the O/D solenoid and indicator light), and the wires that connect them.

A *fuse* is a device that melts at a predetermined current flow. Fuses are designed to be easily tested and quickly replaced if they melt or blow. They are available in different shapes, sizes, and amp ratings to meet the requirements of the circuit. Color-coding provides a means for easy identification.

A *fusible link* is a short piece of wire that is about four wire gauge sizes smaller than the wire used in the circuit it is designed to protect. When the circuit is overloaded the fusible link will burn open, stopping the flow of current in the circuit.

A *circuit breaker* senses the current flow in a circuit; if the amperage (heat) becomes excessive a set of contacts cycles open, stopping the current flow. Some circuit breakers are designed to be self-resetting. They will reset automatically after the circuit breaker has cooled, allowing the circuit to operate again. Other circuit breakers must be reset manually.

A *PTC, positive temperature coefficient,* thermistor acts like a self-resetting circuit breaker. The circuit is opened by the temperature increase as the current reaches the maximum value. The circuit will reset when the cause of the excess current flow is corrected.

Switches. A **switch** is used to control a circuit. It will **break (open)** the circuit to stop current flow or *make (close)* the circuit to allow current to flow (Figure 8-11). An open switch has **infinite resistance** and will not allow electricity to pass through it. A closed switch should have no resistance to electrical flow. Switches come in many sizes and shapes but they all do the same job: control the circuit. Switches can be *normally open (NO)* or *normally closed (NC).* Normally open switches are open at rest and closed as needed to complete a circuit. Normally closed switches are closed at rest and opened as

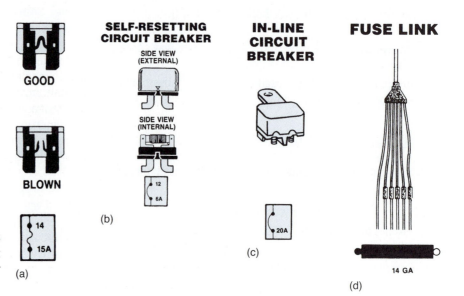

FIGURE 8-10 Circuit protection can be fuses with tubular or flat-blade connections (a), a circuit breaker (b and c), or a fusible link (d). *(Courtesy of Chrysler Corporation)*

needed to stop current flow. Automatic transmissions may have one or more switches that are opened or closed by fluid pressure, and they may be mounted on the inside or outside of the transmission. A switch can control a circuit directly or indirectly through a relay. Switches are also used as an input to the TCM.

A *relay* is an electromagnetic switch (Figure 8-12). It is made up of a switch and a coil. When current passes through the coil a magnetic field is produced, and the magnetic field can close or open the switch contacts. The horn circuit is a good example of how a relay is used. The horn button is the control switch. When the button is depressed, it closes and current passes through the relay coil, and the relay contacts close. This completes the circuit, allowing current to pass to the horn. Relays are used to reduce the current flow through the controlling switch.

Wiring. Wire is used to connect the components of the circuit. Automotive wire typically is a multistrand copper wire surrounded by a plastic *insulator*. Copper is a very good conductor, bends easily, and offers a relatively small resistance to the circuit. The size of the conductor in a wire determines the amount of current it can safely carry. A **gauge** number is used to identify the size of the wire conductor (Figure 8-13). The gauge number is inversely proportional to the wire size so the larger the conductor, the

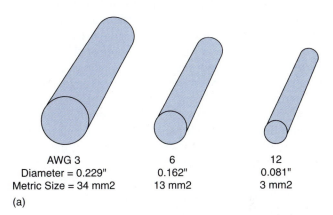

AWG 3	6	12
Diameter = 0.229"	0.162"	0.081"
Metric Size = 34 mm2	13 mm2	3 mm2

(a)

Wiring Color Code Chart					
Color Code	Color	Standard Tracer Color	Color Code	Color	Standard Tracer Code
BK	Black	WT	PK	Pink	BK or WH
BR	Brown	WT	RD	Red	WT
DB	Dark Blue				
DG	Dark Green	WT	VT	Violet	WT
GY	Gray	BK	WT	White	BK
LB	Light Blue	BK	YL	Yellow	BK
LG	Light Green	BK	•	With Tracer	
OR	Orange	BK			

(b)

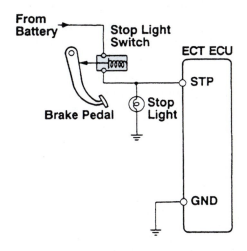

Brake Pedal	STP Terminal Voltage
Depressed	**12 V**
Released	**0 V**

FIGURE 8-11   This stop light switch is a normally open switch. When the brake pedal is depressed, battery voltage is sent to the ECT ECU. *(Courtesy of Toyota Motor Sales USA, Inc.)*

FIGURE 8-13   Electrical wire is sized by gauge sizes or cross section in millimeters; three American wire gauge (AWG) sizes are shown for comparison (a). Wire colors with tracers are used to identify particular wires (b). *(b is courtesy of Chrysler Corporation)*

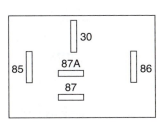

Bottom View of Relay

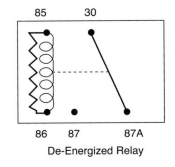

86   87   87A

De-Energized Relay

FIGURE 8-12   A de-energized relay. Relays use a magnetic coil to either close or open switch contacts. Note that terminals 85 and 86 are for control, terminals 30 to 87 are normally open, and terminals 30 to 87A are normally closed. *(Courtesy of Chrysler Corporation)*

smaller the gauge number. The conductor can also be identified by the cross-sectional diameter of the wire measured in inches or millimeters. The insulation keeps the electricity in that wire.

Electrical Loads. The electrical loads are the components that do the work. Typical loads are lights, motors, relay coils, and solenoids. Solenoids are the most common load in automatic transmission circuits (Figure 8-14). A solenoid is an electromagnet with a moveable core or plunger. When current passes through the solenoid windings, a magnetic field is produced that moves the core or plunger. The core or plunger, in turn, opens or closes a fluid passage. The strength of the solenoid magnet is determined by the amount of current flowing through the coil and the number of wire turns (length). The current flow is determined by the resistance of the wire in the coil, and increasing the wire size or making the wire shorter will increase the current flowing through the coil and the strength of the magnetic field.

A solenoid can be turned on and off many times a second. The cycle speed or on–off time can be used to control fluid pressure or how fast fluid moves to fill a clutch.

Electromagnetic devices cause a problem for electronic circuits that cannot handle large increases in voltage or current. When the current stops flowing in a coil of wire, the magnetic field collapses, and it will collapse inward, passing through the coil. The collapsing field induces a high voltage in the coil, and this voltage is high enough to damage electronic devices. To prevent this, a clamping diode, also called an isolation diode, is included in many circuits that use a coil. A diode is an electronic check valve that will only allow current to move in one direction. A clamping diode is connected to each end of the coil, and during operation, the diode will block current from bypassing the coil (Figure 8-15). When the system is shut off, the diode will allow the induced current to bleed off through the coil, eliminating the high-voltage spikes.

PROBLEM SOLVING 8-1 Imagine that you are working in a shop that specializes in automatic transmission repair. You are asked to repair vehicles with the following concerns:

Case 1 A 1985 Thunderbird has no backup lights. You find a blown fuse for the backup lights. You replace the fuse, but as soon as you shift into reverse, the new fuse blows. What do you think is the cause? Where would you begin checking the cause of the problem?

Case 2 A 1987 Citation has no TCC lockup. The converter clutch does not engage at any speed or under any driving condition. Could this be caused by a broken wire? How would you check for a broken wire?

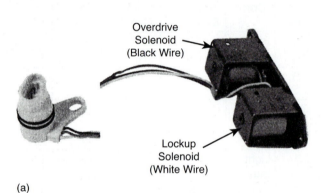

(a)

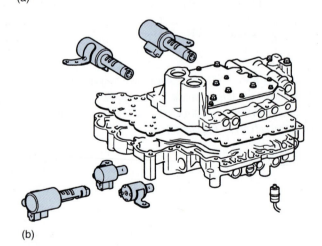

(b)

FIGURE 8-14 Transmission solenoids can take different shapes, but they all include an electromagnet and a valve. The style shown in (b) is the most common. *(a is courtesy of Chrysler Corporation; b is courtesy of Toyota Motor Sales USA, Inc.)*

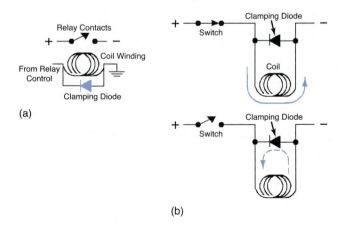

(b)

FIGURE 8-15 A clamping diode is wired parallel to the coil winding (a). It blocks current flow when the switch is closed, but it allows induced current to dissipate when the switch opens (b).

8.3 BASIC ELECTRONICS

Solid-state electronics is the basis of automotive computers and control modules. These devices are constructed from diodes, transistors, capacitors, resistors, integrated circuits, and microchips. Solid-state devices, for all practical purposes, do not wear out because there are no moving parts. A major difference between electrical and electronic circuits is the quantity of electrical flow. The current flow in electronic circuits is very small, thus the voltage requirement is low and circuit resistance must be kept to a minimum.

Electronic devices can, however, be easily damaged by rough handling, vibration, and high temperatures. Because of the small current capacity in electronic circuits, high current or voltage spikes will damage the electronics. Voltage spikes can result from circuit problems or *electrostatic discharge (ESD)*. High resistance can also limit the current to the point that the electronics will not operate. Well-maintained circuits and proper handling are essential for proper operation.

Electronic devices are used for sensing and controlling circuits. The automatic transmission is a good candidate for electronically controlled circuits (Figure 8-16). An electronically controlled system can be divided into three parts: *inputs (sensors), the electronic control module (ECM), the power train control module (PCM)* or *transmission control module (TCM),* and *outputs (actuators).*

8.3.1 Sensors

Sensors are the TCM inputs. They monitor the things that can affect transmission operation: *vehicle speed; input shaft speed; engine coolant temperature, rpm, and load; driver input; the selected gear range;* and *transmission fluid temperature.* In some vehicles, clutch *input and output shaft speed* are also TCM inputs. A typical transmission sensor can be a switch that is made to open or close at certain pressures, a transducer that senses pressure, a thermistor that senses temperature, or a speed sensor that measures vehicle speed or shaft rpm. The various sensor types (organized by the type of electrical signal) are as follows:

- frequency generators (creates an ac signal with a frequency relative to speed)
- voltage generator (creates a voltage signal that is relative to speed)
- potentiometer or variable resistor (alters the voltage or resistance)
- switches (an on–off signal)
- serial data (an on–off signal coming from another control module)
- thermistor (changes resistance relative to temperature)
- transducer (changes resistance relative to pressure)

The vehicle speed sensor is located off the output shaft, similar to the governor (Figure 8-17). One style of speed sensor consists of a normally open reed switch. The switch is mounted next to a rotor that has a magnet built into it or a gear-like reluctor (Figure 8-18). When the vehicle starts moving, the magnet passes by the reed switch and momentarily pulls the contacts closed. The TCM can accurately determine how fast the vehicle is going by "counting" how often the speed sensor switches on and off. Another style of speed sensor operates by using a coil of wire that is wrapped around a magnetic core. This sensor is mounted next to a toothed ring or wheel (Figure 8-19). As the toothed ring revolves, an alternating voltage is produced in the sensor. The rate or frequency of this pulsating voltage is used by the TCM to determine transmission speed. Most rpm or speed sensors are frequency generators; they produce an ac current that increases in frequency as the speed increases. Some transmissions use an input and an output speed sensor. By comparing the signals, the TCM can determine what gear is engaged and how long it

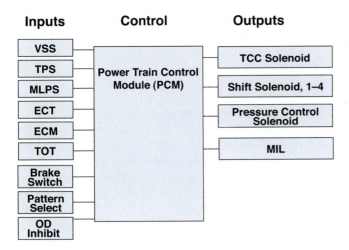

FIGURE 8-16   This PCM receives sensor input (at left) and controls actuators (outputs) inside the transmissions.

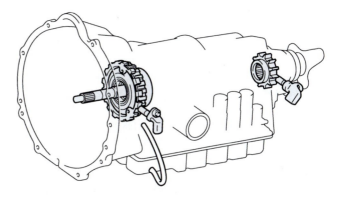

FIGURE 8-17   This transmission uses an input (left) and output (right) speed sensor. The sensors generate a signal frequency that is relative to the speeds of the reluctor rings. *(Courtesy of Toyota Motor Sales USA, Inc.)*

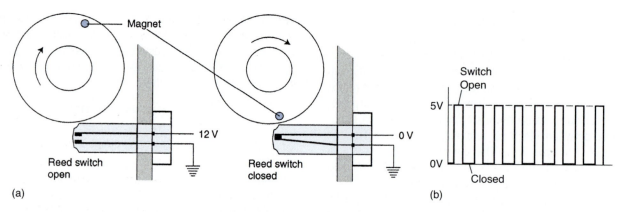

FIGURE 8-18   The speed sensor switch will close as the magnet moves past it (a). It will generate a square wave/on–off signal (b).

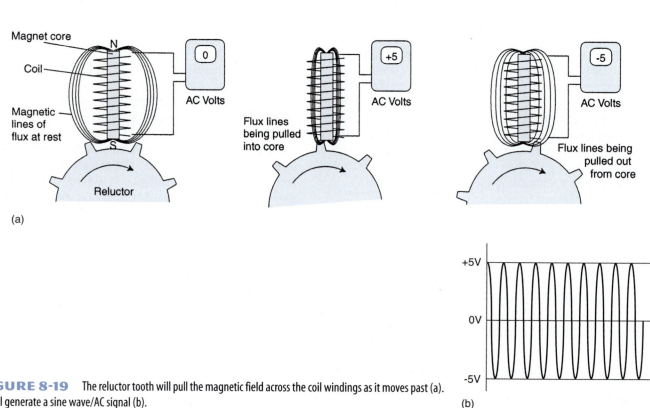

FIGURE 8-19   The reluctor tooth will pull the magnetic field across the coil windings as it moves past (a). It will generate a sine wave/AC signal (b).

takes to make a shift (Figure 8-20). Chrysler refers to this as the *clutch volume index (CVI);* this refers to the length of time it takes to fill the clutches with fluid.

The throttle position sensor (TPS) is attached to the throttle shaft (Figure 8-21). It changes resistance as the throttle is opened and closed. By measuring the voltage, the TCM can accurately determine the throttle position and produce correctly timed upshifts or downshifts. The TPS takes the place of the throttle/vacuum modulator valve in hydraulically controlled transmissions.

Most temperature sensors are thermistors, and these are a type of variable resistor that changes electrical resistance

relative to temperature. These are called negative temperature coefficient (NTC) thermistors. The signal from a thermistor is the inverse of the temperature; it has high resistance at low temperatures and a low resistance at high temperatures. For example, a particular transmission fluid temperature sensor has a resistance of 37 to 100 Ω at 32 to 58°F (0 to 20°C) and 1.5 k to 2.7K Ω at 195 to 230°F (91 to 110°C). The *engine coolant sensor (ECT)* tells the TCM when the engine is at operating temperature (Figure 8-22). The temperature signal is used to prevent TCC lockup while the engine is cold. In some transmissions, this signal is used to produce earlier-than-normal converter clutch lockup if the engine temperature rises too

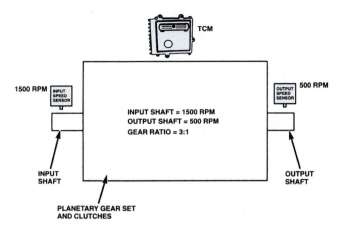

FIGURE 8-20 An input speed sensor along with an output speed sensor allows the TCM to calculate the gear ratio and determine how long it takes to complete a shift or if there is internal slippage in the gear train. *(Courtesy of Chrysler Corporation)*

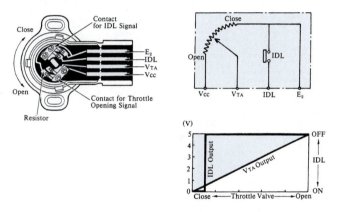

FIGURE 8-21 A TPS (throttle position sensor) is mounted at the throttle body. It provides an electronic signal of the throttle operation to the ECM.

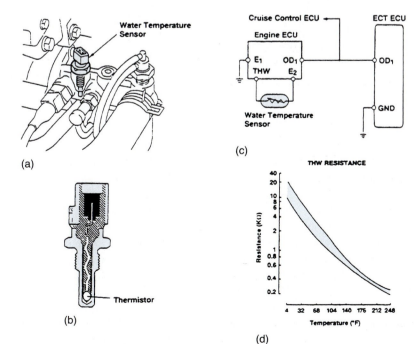

FIGURE 8-22 The ECT (engine coolant temperature) sensor is mounted close to the engine's thermostat (a). It is a thermistor (b) that provides a coolant temperature signal to the ECM (c and d).

high. A cold engine temperature signal can also be used to delay upshifts or prevent an upshift until the engine is at operating temperature.

A *transmission oil temperature (TOT)* sensor is used in some transmissions. The TOT can be a thermistor or a bimetal switch that opens or closes at a specific temperature (Figure 8-23).

A *transducer* is a variable resistor; it produces a variable signal that is relative to pressure, allowing the control module to monitor pressure. The *line pressure sensor (LPS)* is a transducer that converts line pressure to a variable resistance.

Many transmissions include pressure switches at the valve body (Figure 8-24). This signal tells the TCM that the circuit has pressure. The TCM uses this along with other information to determine TCC lockup and shift timing.

The *manifold air pressure (MAP)* sensor is a type of transducer that provides an "engine load" signal to the ECM.

A commonly used variable resistor found in automotive applications is the *potentiometer,* a type of variable resistor. The control module sends a low-voltage (about 5-V) signal to the potentiometer, and the sensor returns a voltage that is relative to the condition that the sensor is monitoring (see Figure 8-21). If sensor resistance increases, the voltage returning from the sensor to the control module will be lower, and the opposite is true if the resistance decreases. These sensors are normally used to monitor position; common examples are throttle position sensors (TPS) and the mass air flow sensor (MAF). These are often called three-wire sensors; a switch-type sensor or variable resistor needs only two wires.

Frequency and voltage generators develop an **analog** ac electrical wave that is continuously varying in frequency and intensity. The control module operates using a **digital** signal that

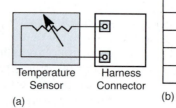

FIGURE 8-23 A transmission fluid temperature sensor can be checked by connecting an ohmmeter to the harness connector terminals (a). The resistance should change as the temperature changes (b).

Temperature Sensor   Harness Connector

(a)

Temperature		Resistance (Ohms)
°C	°F	
140	284	0.6 K
120	248	1.1 K
100	212	2.1 K
80	176	3.8 K
50	122	10 K
30	86	27 K
10	50	69 K
-10	14	193 K
-30	-22	600 K

(b)

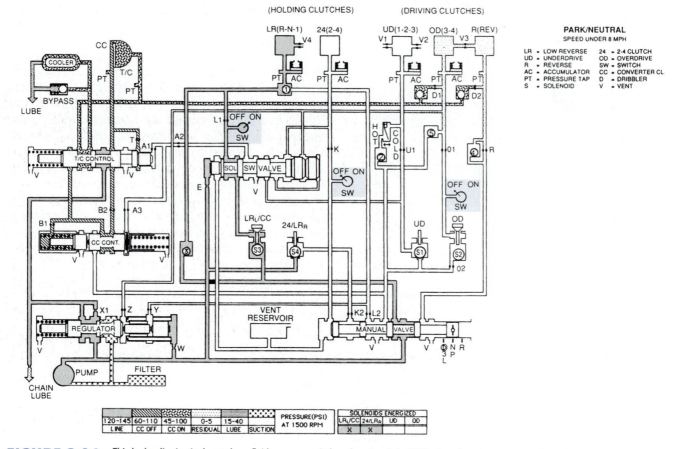

FIGURE 8-24 This hydraulic circuit shows three fluid pressure switches that signal the TCM when there is pressure in their circuits. *(Courtesy of Chrysler Corporation)*

is essentially an on–off pulse of electricity. It reads the signal by the length of time that the input is on or off (Figure 8-25). The ECM or TCM uses an analog-to-digital (AD) converter to modify the analog signal to a digital one.

The transmission *manual lever position (MLP)* switch, sometimes called a neutral start switch, is usually mounted

on the transmission (Figure 8-26). It is operated by the shaft connecting the gear selector and manual linkage to the manual valve. It is a multiposition switch that has multiple inputs to the TCM. As the gear range selector is moved, the MLP switch can make a variety of switch connections for each gear range. These inputs allow the TCM to determine which gear range has been selected. The MLP switch is used by the TCM to:

- Keep the engine from starting in any gear position except park or neutral.
- Allow a 1–2–3–4 shift sequence in drive.
- Limit upshifts in manual ranges.
- Operate the backup lights in reverse.

Another important switch is *brake on/off (BOO)* switch, commonly called the stop light switch. It is mounted at the brake pedal, and its signal is used to release the TCC when the brakes are applied (Figure 8-27).

Some vehicles use a comfort-power switch. This switch allows the driver to select one of two operating modes programmed into the TCM. In the "comfort" mode, the upshifts and downshifts are made at normal shift points, producing quiet, economical operation. This is also called the economy mode. In the "power" mode, the upshifts are made later and the downshifts occur at higher speeds. Delaying the shifts allows higher engine rpm at wider throttle openings for added performance.

The following sensors are used with transmission:

> **NOTE:** Sensor terminology can be confusing because different manufacturers use different names for similar items. The italicized terms show the terminology standardized by SAE J1930. A listing of SAE J1930 terminology pertaining to an automatic transmission is given in Appendix E.

Brake on/off (BOO) switch: A switch mounted at the brake pedal that provides a signal when the brake is depressed. It signals the TCM that the brake is applied, and the TCC should be released.

Engine coolant temperature (ECT): A variable resistor (thermistor) that monitors engine temperature. It signals the TCM that the engine is at operating temperature or approaching overheat temperatures.

Line pressure sensor (LPS): A transducer that monitors line pressure. It allows the TCM to determine the actual line pressure.

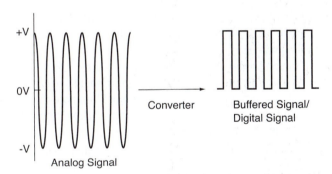

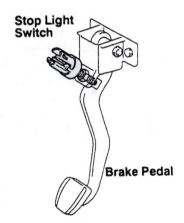

FIGURE 8-27 The stop light switch is mounted at the brake pedal. It provides a brake-apply signal to the TCM. *(Courtesy of Toyota Motor Sales USA, Inc.)*

FIGURE 8-25 Some systems include an AD (analog–digital) buffer to convert the ac analog speed sensor signal so it can be read by the ECM.

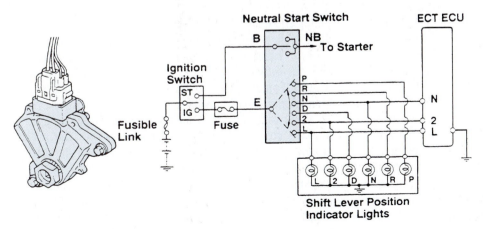

FIGURE 8-26 This MLP (manual lever position) sensor/neutral start switch is mounted at the transmission. It provides a shift lever position signal to the ECM.

Manifold absolute pressure (MAP), mass air flow sensor (MAF): It provides an engine load signal to the PCM.

Transmission control switch (TCS), park reverse neutral park/neutral position, (PNP) switch: A multicontact switch that provides a park or neutral gear range position signal. It signals the TCM of the driver's request for neutral or park.

Manual lever position (MLP) switch, park reverse neutral drive low (PRNDL) switch: A multicontact switch that provides a gear range position signal. It signals the TCM of the driver's request for a particular gear range.

Pressure sensor switch: A hydraulically operated switch or pressure transducer that allows the TCM to determine the fluid pressure in one or more circuits.

Power-economy switch: Allows the driver to raise or lower the shift points. Raising the shift points delays the shifts and increases power. Lowering the shift points produces earlier shifts to increase fuel economy.

Throttle position sensor (TPS): A variable resistor (potentiometer) that provides a voltage signal that is relative to throttle opening. It provides a throttle position signal to the TCM.

Transmission oil temperature (TOT): A variable resistor (thermistor) that monitors transmission temperature. It signals the TCM that the transmission is at operating temperature or approaching overheat temperatures.

Transmission range drive (TRD), transmission range low (TRL), transmission range overdrive (TROD), transmission range reverse (TRR), fourth-gear/OD lockout switch: Limits transmission operation to specific ranges. It signals the TCM of the driver's request for a particular gear operating strategy.

Transmission speed sensor (TSS), turbine speed sensor (TSS), output speed sensor: A magnetic pickup, frequency generator that determines the speed of the input and output shafts. It allows the TCM to determine what gear the transmission is in and if there is excessive slippage in that gear range.

Vehicle speed sensor (VSS): A switch (a digital, on–off) or sensor (AC frequency) that counts the revolutions of the output shaft. It provides a voltage or frequency signal that is relative to vehicle speed. The TCM uses this signal to determine vehicle speed.

8.3.2 Electronic Transmission Shift Controls

Automatic transmissions have been using a torque converter clutch (TCC) that is controlled by the engine control module (ECM) for many years. The TCM controls the transmission actuators, usually solenoids. There are one or more solenoids in the transmission valve body that are used to control fluid flow for torque converter lockup and gear changes. There may

also be solenoids that control fluid pressure, and these solenoids are pulsed on and off very rapidly. Some shift solenoids are also pulsed to obtain more precise shift quality. The basic operation of an electronic-shifted transmission is the same as that of a hydraulically controlled transmission. The major difference is that the shift valves are balanced between hydraulic pressure from the governor and throttle valve in a standard unit, and in an electronic-shifted unit, the shifts are controlled by the TCM.

A TCM is programmed to open or close the actuator circuits based on the signals from the various input sensors. The TCM is an electronic device that receives electronic signals from the sensors, and when these signals match the program stored in the TCM's memory, the TCM sends a signal to one or more actuators. The TCM can be programmed to incorporate several different operation strategies:

- Adaptive Learning/Shifts: With *adaptive learning,* the TCM learns how a driver operates the vehicle, and will adjust shifting to match the driver's style, driving conditions or transmission condition.

- Reverse/Drive Lockout: If the TCM detects a manual shift while the vehicle is rolling in the opposite direction, it can block the shift and go into neutral to prevent transmission damage.

- Rocking: If the TCM detects repeated shifts between drive and reverse, it can adjust the current to the EPC solenoid, raising the line pressure to prevent transmission damage.

- Failure Mode: If the TCM detects a sensor signal that is significantly out-of-value, it can ignore that signal and default to a programmed strategy. It will illuminate the MIL. The vehicle will operate, and the driver should be aware that service is required.

- Limp-Home Mode: If the TCM detects a condition that can cause transmission damage, it will illuminate the MIL and shut off the transmission, which will operate in only one forward gear with high line pressure. The driver should be aware that service is required.

Many features of an electronic transmission, such as shift timing and quality, torque converter clutch apply timing, and quality, are software driven. A vehicle manufacturer can use the same transmission and adjust the operating characteristics with the software for various types of vehicles with different engines. Some control modules allow calibration values to be reprogrammed by technicians in the field.

The electrical circuit for the TCM is fairly complex. It must be connected to the power source, B+, and a good ground, B−. The power feed is usually through the ignition switch and a fuse for protection (Figure 8-28). The TCM can switch on B+ power to a solenoid that is grounded at the transmission, and this is called *hot-side switching* or *feed-control* (Figure 8-29). With some designs, the solenoids

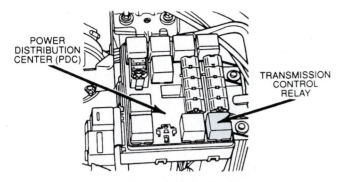

FIGURE 8-28 Power supply for the electrical circuits of a modern vehicle begins at the power distribution center. It usually includes major relays and the fuses. *(Courtesy of Chrysler Corporation)*

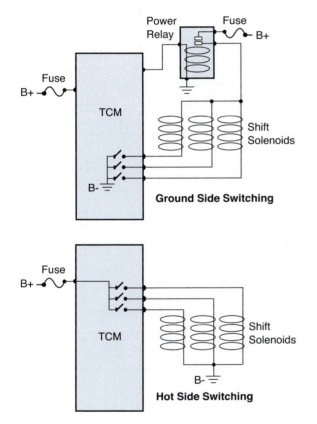

FIGURE 8-29 Solenoid control occurs when the ECM completes the circuit to ground (top) or switches on B+ (bottom). The ground connection is also B−.

receive B+ through a power relay. The TCM switches on the ground path to activate the solenoid, and this is called *ground-side switching* or **ground-control.** Because the TCM is unable to handle the high electric current needed for the solenoids, the control module can operate relays or transistors to turn the solenoids on. Units that use small current flows such as the *malfunction indicator light (MIL),* a *light-emitting*

diode *(LED),* or digital display operate directly from the control module (Figure 8-30).

Many control modules are programmed to run a test sequence at engine start-up. If out-of-range electrical values are found, the TCM will indicate a failure by turning on the MIL. The system is also monitored during operation, and if a failure should occur, it will revert to *default* or *limp-in mode.* In limp-in mode, the operation of most transmissions will be limited to one gear, often second gear, to protect the transmission. There will be no upshifts or downshifts, but the driver will not be stranded. At the same time, the TCM will set a *diagnostic trouble code (DTC).* A technician can read the DTC by following a prescribed procedure. A scan tool can be used to pull codes from the TCM. Service information is used to identify the code(s), the problem circuit, and what tests are needed to determine the exact cause of the failure (Figure 8-31).

Wire connections at the sensors and control module must be clean and tight to prevent any change in voltage. The connection is made when a round or square male pin/terminal enters a female terminal. Connectors have multiple cavities for the wire terminals. These cavities determine the "way" number for the connector; a four-way connector will make four connections. The cavities are often identified by a number or letter to help identify a particular wire or terminal. Quite often, all of the connection's cavities will not be used. A small amount of corrosion can produce enough resistance to cause a significant change in low-voltage, low-current circuits. Most manufacturers use mechanical-locking, *weathertight connectors.* Many also use waterproof conductive compound (dielectric silicon) on these connections (Figure 8-32). A multiterminal connector connects the external wiring harness to the transmission's internal harness. The internal harness is connected to each of the electrical components inside the transmission (Figure 8-33).

The TCM, like other automotive computers, is somewhat fragile and relatively expensive. It is normally mounted in a relatively clean and cool location where it is protected from possible damage. A fairly standard location is in the passenger compartment, under the instrument panel or the center console.

Serial Data. An advantage of electronic controls is that digital control modules can communicate with each other using *serial data streams.* The TCM can share information with other control modules such as the engine control module and the body control module. The data stream is a series of low-voltage, on–off electrical signals. The length of the on and off time becomes the message.

Multiplexing allows one sensor or wire to work for more than one circuit; in older vehicles, every circuit uses a separate wire or electronic device. Multiplexing uses a pair of wires to complete multiple circuits, which greatly reduces the number of wires in a vehicle. Multiplex circuits include the serial data stream between two control modules, for example, the PCM and the BCM. The two modules share the same sensors, and the output of one often affects the output of the other

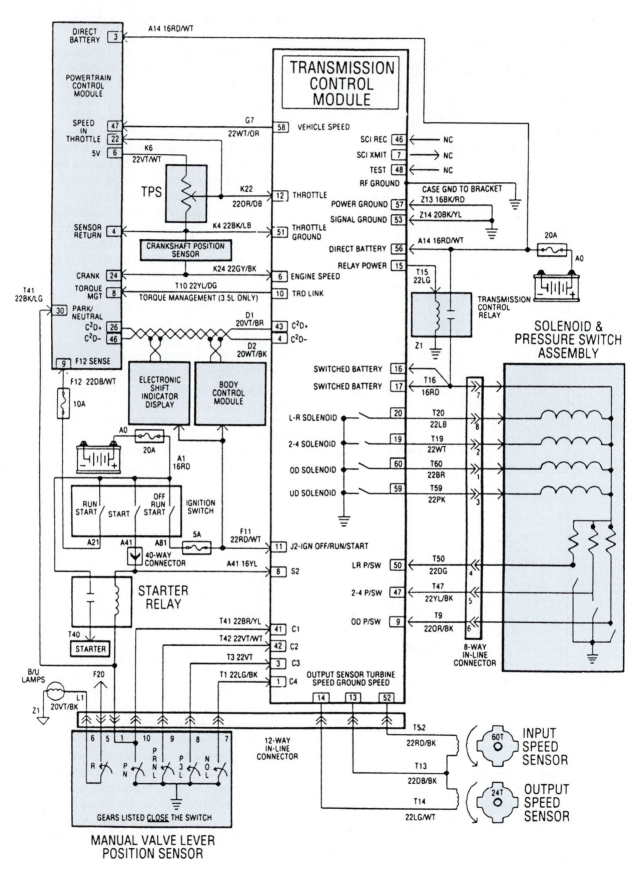

FIGURE 8-30 This electrical schematic shows the various inputs and outputs of the transmission control module for a 42LE transaxle. *(Courtesy of Chrysler Corporation)*

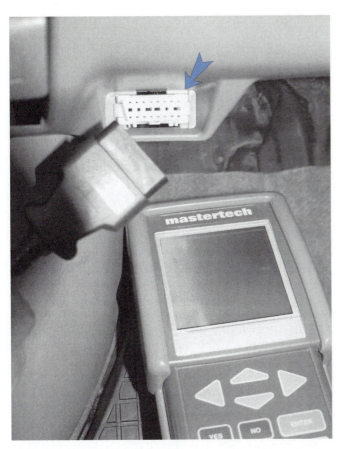

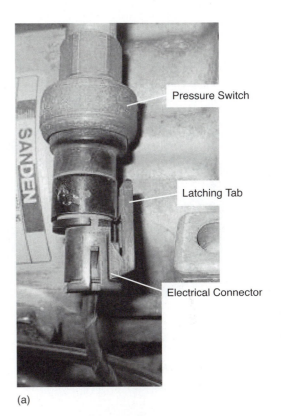

(a)

FIGURE 8-31 The scan tool is being plugged into the diagnostic connector (arrow) under the instrument panel. It can read any DTCs, sensor outputs, and operate the solenoids inside the transmission.

(Figure 8-34). For example, a transmission upshift or downshift will change the speed of the engine, and the power from the engine definitely affects the quality of the shift.

Multiplexing is also called a *bus information system*, and besides reducing the amount of wire and connections, it also eliminates some switching hardware, reduces current flow through the sensors, and improves diagnostics. A microprocessor is required in each control module and bus + and bus − wires connect the control modules. The bus + and bus − wires are twisted together to prevent stray electromagnetic signals from altering signal transmission. These wires are often called a twisted pair.

Probably the biggest impact of multiplexing on the transmission technician is that seemingly unrelated problems can affect the operation of the transmission. If the multiplex system does not operate properly, strange faults can occur. A technician has to be more aware than ever of all the branches of the circuit.

OBD-II. On-board diagnostics, second generation, commonly called **OBD-II,** is a set of standards required for all 1996 and newer vehicles. OBD standards were first established in 1988 by the California Air Resources Board (CARB) and the Society of Automotive Engineers (SAE) for vehicle

(b)

FIGURE 8-32 A weathertight connector is used at this pressure switch (a). Opening the latch allows the connector to be removed (b).

control systems. The purpose is to simplify and standardize vehicle diagnosis. These standards are designed to improve diagnosis and repair of malfunctioning vehicles in order to reduce vehicle emissions. Improper transmission operation can increase emissions. OBD-II standards require the following commonalities between vehicle manufacturers:

- terms and definitions (SAE J1930)
- diagnostic trouble codes and definitions (SAE J2012)

- diagnostic connector and connector location (SAE J1962)
- diagnostic scan tool (SAE J1978)
- diagnostic test modes (SAE J1979 and 2190)
- procedure for technicians to obtain service information (SAE J2008)

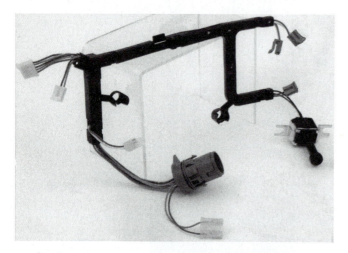

FIGURE 8-33 One of the solenoids is wired directly to this internal electrical harness. Note the case connecter near the bottom.

- an SAE-recommended serial data communication system (SAE J1850)
- an international serial data communication system (ISO 9141)

A technician reads the DTC of an OBD II vehicle by connecting a scan tool to the *diagnostic connector* and requesting the DTCs. The diagnostic connector is mounted in the instrument panel within reach of the driver. It should be visible when kneeling next to an open driver's door. This process is described in Chapter 13. A listing of the OBD-II power train DTCs is given in Appendix D.

Controller Area Network. A *controller area network (CAN)* is a system that determines how the various control modules communicate with each other, share sensor information, and determine which ECMs have operating priority. CAN was used on a few 2003 vehicles, and all new vehicles sold in the United States in the 2008 model year will use CAN. CAN is a very high-speed system, much faster than earlier multiplex systems. CAN also is better at operating the critical

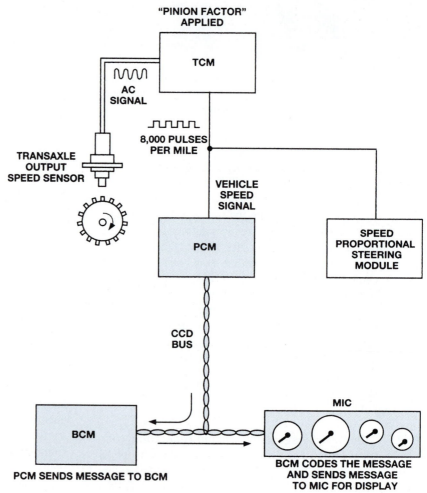

FIGURE 8-34 The CCD (Chrysler Collision Detection) bus allows the BCM (body control module) and PCM (power-train control module) to share information such as the signal from the transaxle output speed sensor. Among other things, this signal is used for the speedometer. *(Courtesy of Chrysler Corporation)*

safety systems such as ABS, electronic steering control, and stability and traction control systems.

The biggest impact on automatic transmission service will be the need for upgraded or enhanced scan tools or cartridges that will allow current scan tools to communicate with the system. One technician has found that some current scan tools will almost work with a CAN system by programming an earlier model vehicle, but the scanner connection will disable the ABS, traction control, and stability control systems—this was not good in this instance because the vehicle had a hard brake pedal with no brake operation while on a road test. The best practice is to always use the correct tool for the job.

8.3.3 Transmission-Based Control Module

Many vehicles using CAN electronics integrate the TCM into the transmission (Figure 8-35). This is called *control solenoid valve assembly, mechatronic,* and *solenoid body.* The assembly greatly reduces the number of wires entering the transmission because the:

- input and output shaft speed sensors,
- transmission range sensor,
- fluid pressure sensors,
- fluid temperature sensor, and
- shift and pressure control solenoids

are connected directly to the TCM. The wire connections to the rest of the vehicle are:

- Hi and Lo CAN bringing data from the ECM, BCM, and PCM
- ignition on
- diagnostic connection
- ground

The TCM in some transmissions is about the same size as a common credit card. To prevent overheating, the TCM must have good contact with a heat sink to transmit any excess heat from the electronics to the transmission case. Some TCMs will shut down at certain temperatures, and this will put the transmission into fail-safe until it cools down.

8.3.4 Actuators

The *actuators* are the outputs for an electronically controlled system. They do the mechanical work for the TCM. The various types of outputs are controller modules, diagnostics (MIL and DTCs), display and indicator lights, motors, relays, serial data (sent to another control module),

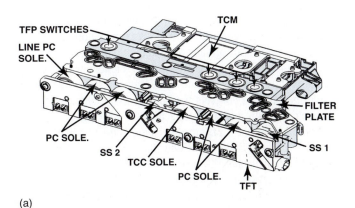

(a)

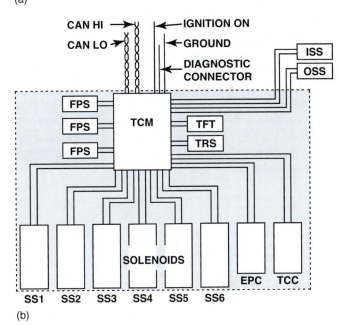

(b)

FIGURE 8-35   This control solenoid assembly (a) contains four transmission fluid pressure (TFP) switches, a line pressure control (PC) solenoid, four pressure control (PC) solenoids, two shift solenoids (SS), a torque converter clutch (TCC) solenoid, a transmission fluid temperature (TFT) sensor, and the transmission control module (TCM). It also has a vehicle harness connector and connectors to the shift position switch and the input and output speed sensors. A simplified view is also shown (b).

and solenoids. The primary transmission actuators are the solenoids.

Shift Solenoids.   Shift solenoids open or close an oil passage so fluid pressure will be trapped and increase, drain and escape, or pass through to apply a clutch or servo. A solenoid is a coil of wire that becomes an electromagnet when current flows through it. It loses its magnetism when the current flow is shut off. An iron plunger or plate is located inside the coil and is spring loaded to one position. When the solenoid is energized, the plunger moves to the other position (Figure 8-36). Plunger movement opens or closes a hydraulic valve. A solenoid valve can be normally closed and then opened or normally opened and then closed.

Depending on the transmission, the solenoid either directly controls the fluid flow to the apply device or controls a shift valve that in turn controls the flow to the apply device. The solenoids shown in Figure 8-37 have direct control. When a solenoid is energized (on), the check ball is held on its seat, and the fluid passage is closed. When the solenoid is de-energized (off), the ball leaves the seat, and fluid flows to apply the clutch. This arrangement also allows the solenoid to be cycled on and off to control how fast the pressure builds up in the circuit. This in turn controls how fast the clutch applies and therefore controls the shift quality.

Some solenoids are mounted so they open or close a passage that is fed through a small orifice from line or drive pressure. When the solenoid is off, fluid pressure drains from the passage, and when the solenoid is on, pressure builds (Figure 8-38). The orifice prevents a large pressure loss from the main circuits when the solenoid is open. The pressure controlled by the solenoid acts on one or more shift valve(s) while a spring acts on the other end. Shift valve position can be easily controlled with this arrangement.

Shift Solenoid Operation.   A shift solenoid is usually turned completely on or off. Some might cycle a few times during a shift to prevent a rapid clutch apply with a harsh shift. The example shown in Figure 8-39 shows an electronically controlled shift circuit. In first gear, it uses a normally closed solenoid valve (1) that is on while the normally closed solenoid (2) is off. This produces a pressure at the end of the 1–2 shift valve that compresses the spring and keeps the valve downshifted. This combination also allows the springs to hold the 2–3 and the 3–4 shift valves downshifted.

The 1–2, 2–3, and 3–4 shifts in this transmission occur as follows:

- *1–2 shift:* Activate solenoid 2 to drain shift pressure; the spring moves the 1–2 shift valve to upshift.
- *2–3 shift:* Turn solenoid 1 off. The shift pressure moves the 2–3 shift valve to upshift.
- *3–4 shift:* Turn solenoid 2 off. The shift pressure moves the 3–4 shift valve to upshift.

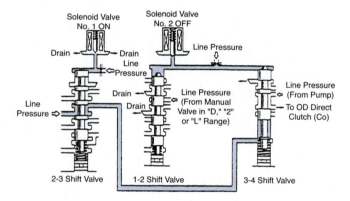

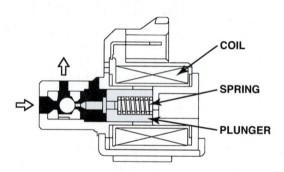

FIGURE 8-36   This solenoid is on. Magnetic force has pulled the plunger to the right. Fluid pressure has moved the metering ball off its seat, and fluid is passing through the valve. *(Courtesy of Toyota Motor Sales USA, Inc.)*

FIGURE 8-38   The No. 1 solenoid is on. Fluid pressure is exhausted at the drain, and the 2–3 shift valve is upshifted. The No. 2 solenoid is off, so fluid pressure has the 1–2 shift valve in downshift position. *(Courtesy of Toyota Motor Sales USA, Inc.)*

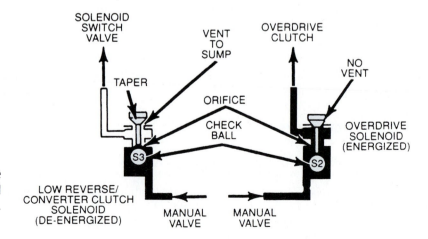

FIGURE 8-37   The tapered stems are connected to the shift solenoids. When the solenoids are on, they move downward to move the check balls off their seats and also close the vent. *(Courtesy of Chrysler Corporation)*

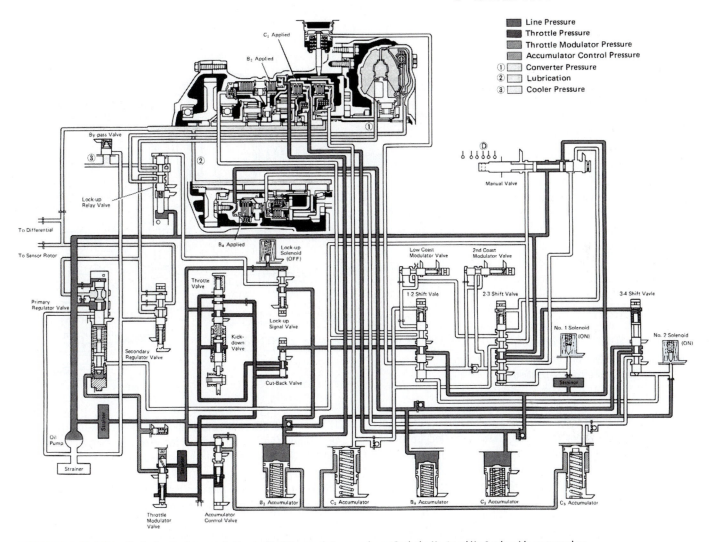

A240E

"D" RANGE SECOND GEAR

FIGURE 8-39   The hydraulic diagram of a Toyota A240E transaxle in second gear. Both the No. 1 and No. 2 solenoids are turned on.

A summary of the relationship of the transmission gear range and the solenoids for this transmission is as follows:

TCM

Commanded Gear	Solenoid 1	Solenoid 2
First	On	Off
Second	On	On
Third	Off	On
Fourth	Off	Off (limp-in gear)

Downshifts occur in exactly the reverse manner as upshifts. For example, a 4–3 kickdown occurs from fourth gear if solenoid 2 is turned on.

- *4–3 shift:* Turn solenoid 2 on. The 3–4 shift valve spring moves the valve to downshift.

- *3–2 shift:* Turn solenoid 1 on. The 2–3 shift valve spring moves the valve to downshift.

- *2–1 shift:* Turn solenoid 2 off. Fluid pressure moves the 1–2 shift valve to downshift.

Note that some transmissions will make a second- or third-gear start if a solenoid fails. The Toyota transmission shown in Figure 8-37 will make a third-gear start because the TCM has a fail-safe program that turns on solenoid 2 if solenoid 1 fails. If both solenoids fail, this unit will start out in fourth gear.

The Chrysler 41TE transaxle does not use shift valves. The relatively simple valve body contains only a pressure regulator valve, manual valve, solenoid switch valve, lockup (TCC) switch valve, and the T/C (torque converter) control valve (Figure 8-40). The gear ranges are controlled by the manual valve and the operation of four solenoids.

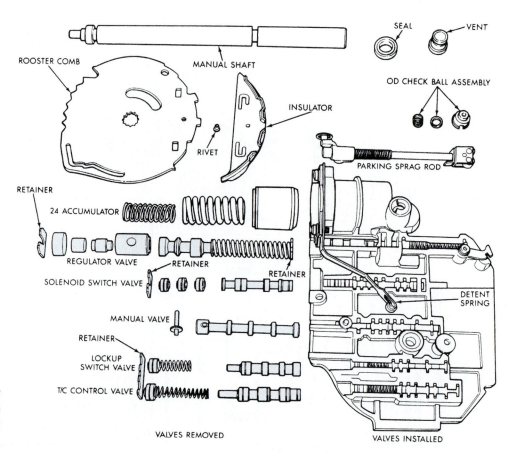

ROOSTER COMB

MANUAL SHAFT

SEAL

VENT

OD CHECK BALL ASSEMBLY

INSULATOR

RIVET

PARKING SPRAG ROD

RETAINER

24 ACCUMULATOR

REGULATOR VALVE

RETAINER

RETAINER

SOLENOID SWITCH VALVE

DETENT
SPRING

MANUAL VALVE

RETAINER

LOCKUP
SWITCH VALVE

T/C CONTROL VALVE

VALVES REMOVED

VALVES INSTALLED

FIGURE 8-40 The valve body for a 41TE transaxle. Note that there are no shift valves. *(Courtesy of Chrysler Corporation)*

Each of the four solenoids operates a check ball, and two solenoids also operate a vent valve. The low-reverse/lockup and the overdrive solenoids are *normally vented*. When they are not energized the check ball is allowed to operate in a normal manner, and the vent is opened. Opening the vent allows residual pressure to bleed from the circuit. When they are energized, the check ball is held open, off its seat, and the vent is closed. The 2–4/low-reverse and the underdrive solenoids are normally applied. When they are not energized, the check balls allow fluid to pass. When they are energized, the check balls are held closed, on their seats, preventing fluid from entering the clutch circuits (Figure 8-41). These solenoids are pulsed, rapidly cycled on and off, at a high frequency to control the rate of pressure rise and clutch apply. In this way, the TCM can control clutch application and therefore shift feel. Three pressure switches are used in the circuits controlled by the solenoid valves, and these pressure switches allow the TCM to monitor circuit pressure.

Depending on the position of the solenoid switch valve, the low-reverse/lockup solenoid controls the operation of either the low-reverse clutch (all gear ranges except second, third, or fourth) or the torque converter clutch (TCC) (second, third, or fourth gear). The low-reverse clutch or the TCC applies when this solenoid is energized. The overdrive solenoid controls the operation of the overdrive clutch; the clutch applies when this solenoid is operated. The 2–4/low-reverse solenoid controls the low-reverse clutch when the manual valve

is in reverse (the clutch applies when the solenoid is energized) and the 2–4 clutch is in forward-gear ranges (the clutch applies when the solenoid is *not* energized). The underdrive solenoid controls the underdrive clutch; the clutch applies when the solenoid is *not* energized. All of the solenoids are in a single unit mounted to the outside of the transmission case (Figure 8-42).

The solenoid operating strategy for this transmission is:

TCM

Commanded Gear Solenoids:	LR/LU	2–4/LR	UD	OD
Park/Neutral	ON	OFF	OFF	OFF
First	ON	ON	OFF	OFF
Second	OFF (limp-in gear)	OFF	OFF	OFF
Third	OFF	ON	OFF	OFF
Third (with TCC)	ON	ON	OFF	ON
Fourth	OFF	OFF	ON	ON
Fourth (with TCC)	ON	OFF	ON	ON
Reverse	OFF	ON	OFF	OFF

Faulty shift solenoid operation can cause a no-upshift condition, skipped gears, or stacked shifts.

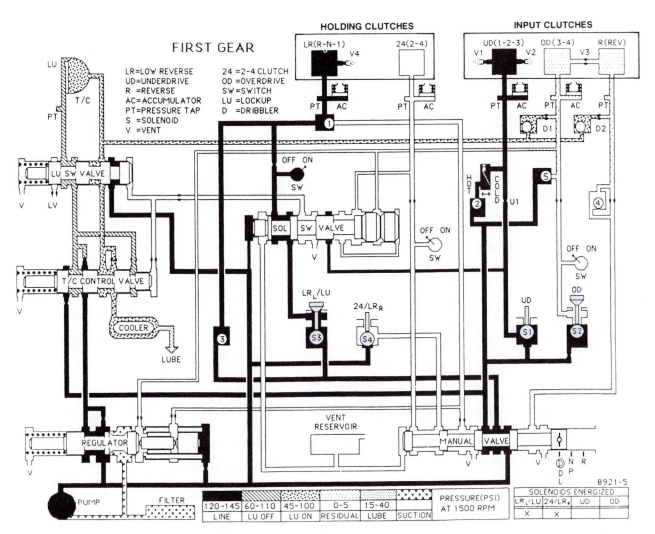

FIGURE 8-41 The hydraulic diagram of a 41TE transaxle in first gear. The shift to second occurs when the 2–4/LR solenoid is turned on to allow pressure to flow to the 2–4 clutch. *(Courtesy of Chrysler Corporation)*

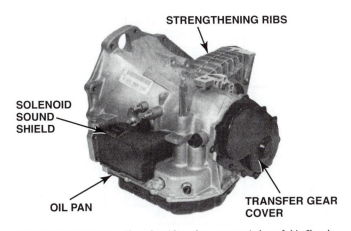

FIGURE 8-42 The solenoids and pressure switches of this Chrysler transaxle are mounted under the solenoid sound shield on the outside of the transaxle. *(Courtesy of Chrysler Corporation)*

Pressure Control Solenoids. Some transmissions control line pressure using an *electronic pressure control (EPC)* solenoid. It is also called a force motor. The pressure is controlled by the amount of current sent to the solenoid (Figure 8-43).

An EPC solenoid is constantly stroking when it goes into operation. Some EPC solenoids use pulse-width modulation; the current is pulsed on and off. This is also called *duty cycle*. A 100% duty cycle means the current is on all of the time. A duty cycle of 50% means the current is on for 50% of the time and off for 50% of the time. A longer duty cycle produces lower line pressure in most systems because the open solenoid releases line pressure. A longer duty cycle (say 75%) means the system is draining 75% of the time and holding pressure 25% of the time.

Some transmissions use **strategy-based** pressure control; line pressure is adjusted to control shift duration. EPC duty cycle is adjusted to keep the shifts within the proper time interval. Some of these transmissions use an adaptive strategy based on previous shift times, vehicle load, and throttle position. Calculations are programmed in the TCM to adjust fluid pressure

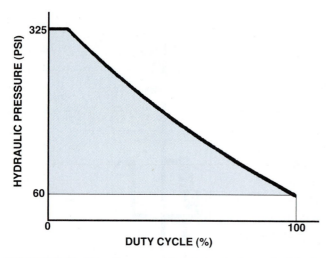

FIGURE 8-43   Line pressure increases as the duty cycle of the EPC solenoid increases.

to keep future shifts within the same parameters as a new vehicle. Other transmissions use *torque-based* or *pressure-based* control of line pressure. A line pressure sensor is used to measure the actual line pressure during a shift, and the TCM keeps line pressure at a preset level (100 to 120 psi) during shifts.

A serious potential problem is created when an electromagnet (solenoid) is mounted inside a transmission. The magnetism will attract fine metal particles worn from the moving parts, and this contamination can cause a sticking solenoid or a leaking valve. If this solenoid valve has problems, it can cause line pressure that is too low, with possible clutch and/or band slippage, or too high, causing harsh shifts. Some transmissions have a TCM strategy that pulses the solenoid completely open at regular intervals. The resulting full fluid flow should flush out any debris.

TCC Solenoid.   The TCC solenoid in most transmissions performs like a shift solenoid; it is either on or off. Some transmissions vary the TCC apply signal to gradually increase or *ramp* the apply and release pressures. Ramping produces a smoother operation and is done by using pulse-width modulation.

PROBLEM SOLVING 8-2   Imagine that you are working in a shop that specializes in transmission repair, and these problems are given to you:

Case 1   A 1997 Dodge van drops back into second gear when it gets hot and will not upshift or downshift in drive. The transmission MIL light begins blinking at this time. Reverse feels good. Is this a mechanical, hydraulic, or electrical problem? Where would you start looking for the cause?

Case 2   A 1987 Camry was driving down the freeway, and the transmission downshifted unexpectedly, and at the same time, the speedometer stopped operating. What could have caused this? Where would you start looking for the cause?

Problem solving and diagnosis are described more completely in Chapter 13.

8.3.5 CVT Electronic Controls

The TCM of a CVT uses direct and indirect inputs to monitor transmission and engine operation (Figure 8-44).

Direct inputs are as follows:

- Transmission range sensor (TRS), a multicontact switch operated by the manual shift lever.
- Input speed sensor (ISS), a Hall-effect sensor.

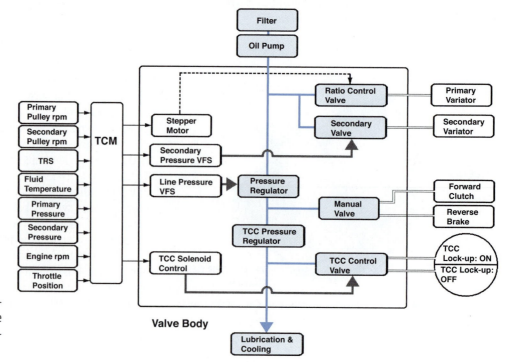

FIGURE 8-44   This block diagram shows the relationship between the TCM, electrical actuators, valve body, and hydraulic actuators for a CVT transmission.

- Output speed sensor (OSS), a Hall-effect sensor.
- Primary pressure sensor, a pressure transducer to monitor primary pulley pressure.
- Secondary pressure sensor, a pressure transducer to monitor secondary pulley pressure.
- Transmission temperature sensor (TTS), a NTC thermistor.

Indirect inputs (from CAN bus) are as follows:

- PCM requests
- Engine output torque
- Brake switch
- ABS status signals
- Charging system voltage
- Engine rpm
- Engine coolant temperature
- Accelerator pedal position
- Vehicle speed
- A/C system requests

TCM outputs include:

- Stepper motor to control ratio control valve
- Line pressure solenoid
- Secondary pressure solenoid
- TCC lockup solenoid

The TCM controls the drive ratio to match vehicle needs. It can adjust the ratio during vehicle cruise to produce the maximum fuel economy, best emissions, or maximum pulling power. It continuously monitors ISS and OSS signals to ensure that the speeds match the desired ratio.

The stepper motor, also called a ratio control motor, is a linear position motor that changes the position of the upper end of the pulley ratio link (Figure 8-45). The lower end of this link moves with the floating side of the primary/drive pulley; the ratio control valve is connected to the center of this link. Movement of the stepper motor or the floating sheave will move the ratio control valve to produce a ratio change.

The TCM also controls fluid pressure to the secondary/driven pulley and torque converter as well as TCC lock-up.

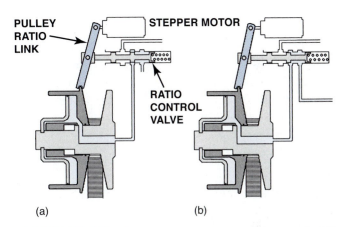

FIGURE 8-45   The stepper motor and pulley ratio link with the CVT in low ratio (A). The stepper motor has extended (B), moving the ratio link and ratio control valve; this should cause the primary pulley to become narrower to produce a higher ratio.

SUMMARY

1. Electronic controls are used for more accurate automatic operation of the transmission.
2. A basic understanding of electricity and electronic devices is essential to understanding and repairing electronically controlled transmissions.
3. Electronic controls use sensors to monitor various operational inputs that will be used to control the operation of the transmission.
4. The hydraulic operation of the transmission is controlled by solenoids that are switched to redirect pressurized fluid to move shift valves or change the operational pressures.
5. The TCM receives the signals from the sensors and operates the solenoids to produce upshifts and downshifts at the proper speed.
6. CVT transmissions use the same type of logic for transmission control as conventional electronic transmissions.

REVIEW QUESTIONS

The following questions are provided to help you study as you read the chapter.

1. Electronic control of the automatic transmission provides for accurate control of shift _____ and _____.

2. Electronic transmissions replace the governor with a _____ _____ _____ and the throttle valve with a _____ _____ _____.

3. Match the electrical terms with the appropriate definition

   a. Ohms   _____ controls flow

   b. Amp   _____ changes direction

   c. Volts   _____ plastic

   d. Battery   _____ flows in one direction

   e. Watt   _____ connected in a string

   f. Series   _____ conductor

   g. Parallel   _____ power source

   h. Ground circuit   _____ separate branches

   i. Direct current   _____ resistance

   j. Alternating current   _____ current flow

   k. Switch   _____ electrical work

   l. Copper   _____ pressure

   m. Insulator   _____ frame

4. A complete electrical circuit has a _____ source, circuit _____, _____, conductors, and an electrical _____.

5. Three types of electrical protection devices are _____, _____, and _____.

6. When the circuit is _____, current will stop flowing.

7. A _____ controls a switch by electromagnetism.

8. A _____ controls fluid flow by electromagnetism.

9. The three major parts that an electronic control system can be divided into are _____, _____, and _____.

10. Identify the six inputs that an electronically controlled transmission might use for each of these.

    a. Vehicle _____

    b. Input shaft _____

    c. Engine coolant _____

    d. Engine _____

    e. Driver _____

    f. Transmission _____ temperature

11. A thermistor is a _____ resistor that changes resistance relative to _____.

12. Identify each of the following abbreviations.

    a. BOO

    b. PRNDL

    c. ECT

    d. MAP

    e. MAF

    f. MLP

    g. PNP

    h. TOT

    i. TSS

    j. TPS

    k. VSS

    l. TCC

    m. ECM

    n. PCM

13. Good ground connections are essential for proper operation of _____ circuits.

14. A diagnostic _____ code (DTC) will set if an electrical problem is identified by the electronic control unit (ECU). DTCs can be read with a _____ tool.

15. Six actuators that are computer controlled are _____, _____, _____, _____, serial data, and _____.

16. Shift solenoids are controlled by the ECU to control the fluid pressure in the _____ valve circuits.

17. If both shift solenoids on a typical Toyota transmission are inoperative, what gear will the transmission be in?

18. If the shift solenoids fail in a Chrysler 41TE transmission, what gear will the transmission be in?

19. EPC solenoids use _____ _____ to cycle a circuit on and off.

20. Ramping a torque converter clutch (TCC) solenoid produces a _____ lockup clutch apply.

CHAPTER QUIZ

The following questions will help you check the facts you have learned. Select the answer that completes each statement correctly.

1. Student A says that it is important to have an understanding of electricity to understand an automatic transmission. Student B says that in most electronically controlled transmissions, the shift valves are controlled by solenoids. Who is correct?
   a. Student A
   b. Student B
   c. Both A and B
   d. Neither A nor B

2. Electrical pressure is measured in
   a. amperes.
   b. ohms.
   c. volts.
   d. watts.

3. The current flowing through a circuit is measured in
   a. amperes.
   b. ohms.
   c. volts.
   d. watts.

4. The resistance to electrical flow through a component is measured in
   a. amperes.
   b. ohms.
   c. volts.
   d. watts.

5. The controlling unit for an electronically shifted transmission is the
   a. vehicle speed sensor.
   b. TCM.
   c. throttle position sensor.
   d. None of these

6. A _____ is an electromagnetic device that can be used to control fluid pressure in a hydraulic circuit.
   a. neutral start switch
   b. TCM
   c. solenoid
   d. vehicle speed sensor

7. A normally vented solenoid _____ allow fluid to flow to the sump when it is not energized.
   a. will
   b. will, but at a reduced flow,
   c. will not
   d. Any of these

8. Student A says that a transmission with electronic shift controls uses a throttle position sensor in place of a throttle valve. Student B says that a vehicle speed sensor is used in place of a governor. Who is correct?
   a. Student A
   b. Student B
   c. Both A and B
   d. Neither A nor B

9. If the solenoids fail in a transmission with electronic shift controls, the transmission will
   a. be ruined if the car is driven.
   b. not have any forward gears.
   c. operate in reverse only.
   d. operate in only one gear.

10. Student A says that the neutral start switch in a transmission with electronic shift controls is the same as the ones in all other transmissions. Student B says that the neutral start switch in a transmission with electronic shift controls is operated by the manual shift linkage. Who is correct?
    a. Student A
    b. Student B
    c. Both A and B
    d. Neither A nor B

11. Student A says that if a transmission uses a comfort power switch, the switch will raise the shift points when it is in the power position. Student B says that if a transmission uses a comfort power switch, it will produce firmer shifts when it is in the comfort position. Who is correct?
    a. Student A
    b. Student B
    c. Both A and B
    d. Neither A nor B

12. The TCC should not apply if the
    a. brakes are applied.
    b. engine coolant sensor senses a cold engine.

    Which is correct?
    a. A
    b. B
    c. Both A and B
    d. Neither A nor B

13. An electrical circuit must have which of the following to operate?
    a. Power source, conductors, load
    b. Circuit protection, conductor, load
    c. Power source, switch, load
    d. Conductor, load, ground

14. Student A says that diagnostic trouble codes can be read from a light on the dash. Student B says that the diagnostic trouble codes will pinpoint the problem. Who is correct?
    a. Student A
    b. Student B
    c. Both A and B
    d. Neither A nor B

15. The vehicle speed sensor is driven by the
    a. front wheel.
    b. speedometer.
    c. transmission output shaft.
    d. drive shaft.

16. The throttle position sensor is located on the
    a. throttle cable.
    b. throttle body.
    c. gas pedal.
    d. transmission case.

17. The throttle position sensor is typically a
    a. thermistor.
    b. rheostat.
    c. potentiometer.
    d. switch.

18. A pulse-width modulated solenoid can be used to
    a. modulate the engine pulses.
    b. smooth the application of the clutches.
    c. signal the computer of a problem.
    d. give the technician information about a problem.

19. If a conductor has infinite resistance it is
    a. corroded.
    b. open.
    c. closed.
    d. grounded.

20. A _____ is used to prevent high-voltage spikes from a collapsing electromagnetic field.
    a. transistor
    b. relay
    c. diode
    d. potentiometer

CHAPTER 9

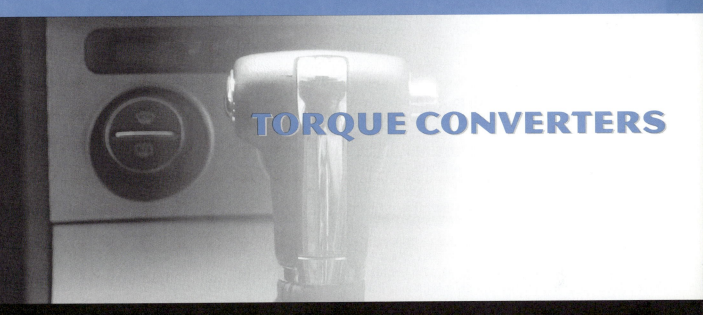

TORQUE CONVERTERS

OBJECTIVES

After studying Chapter 9, the reader should be able to:

1. Identify the components of a torque converter.
2. Explain the purpose for each torque converter component.
3. Describe the fluid flow inside a torque converter.
4. Explain the operation of a torque converter clutch.

KEY TERMS

9.1 INTRODUCTION

The torque converter, commonly called a *converter*, is a type of **fluid coupling** that transmits power from the engine's crankshaft to the transmission input (turbine) shaft. It has two important purposes as it transfers the engine torque to the transmission:

- It serves as an automatic clutch so the vehicle can be stopped with the engine running and the transmission in gear.
- It multiplies torque while the vehicle is accelerating to improve acceleration and pulling power (Figure 9-1).

A driver uses the throttle to control the converter's output. At idle, there is not enough power transfer through the torque converter to move the vehicle. This is especially true if the brakes are applied. Opening the throttle increases engine speed and causes the converter to begin transferring power. At this time the converter begins multiplying engine torque to move the vehicle. Since the power transfer is through fluid, it will be very smooth and free from the severe shocks sometimes found with standard transmissions and clutches. Note that the fluid coupling shown in Figure 9-2 has only two internal parts, a turbine and an impeller.

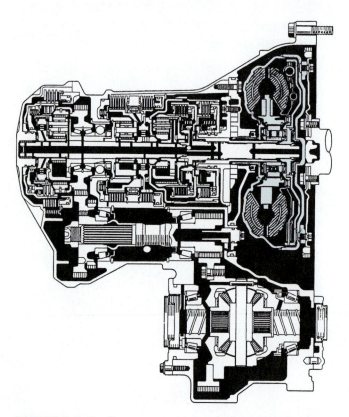

FIGURE 9-1   The torque converter is mounted on the engine's crankshaft and transfers power to the transmission. *(Courtesy of Toyota Motor Sales USA, Inc.)*

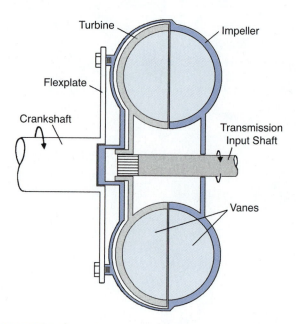

FIGURE 9-2   A fluid coupling transfers power through fluid, from one set of vanes to the other.

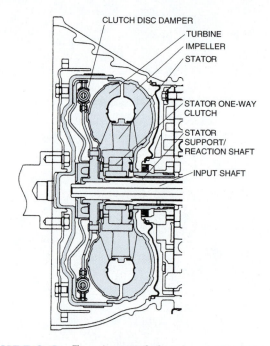

FIGURE 9-3   The major parts of a four-element torque converter are the clutch disc, turbine, stator, and impeller shown in this cutaway view. The turbine is splined to the transmission input shaft, and the stator is splined to the stationary reaction shaft at the front of the transmission. *(Courtesy of Chrysler Corporation)*

9.2 CONSTRUCTION

Most torque converters have four major elements: an **impeller, turbine, stator,** and *converter clutch* (Figure 9-3). Before the late 1970s, most torque converters had three elements

(Figure 9-4). Three-element converters did not have a lock-up clutch. Torque converter clutches were added to increase fuel economy. Each of the members in a three-element torque converter has a set of vanes that serve to control the fluid flow.

Some sources call the impeller a pump. To prevent confusion with the transmission's pump, the term *impeller* will be used.

The impeller is a converter's input. The vanes/fins are attached to the rear of the impeller, transmission end, of the converter housing or cover (Figure 9-5). This assembly is bolted to

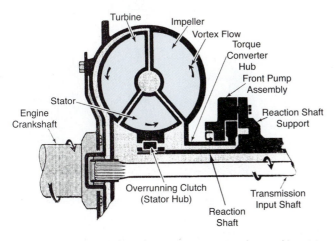

FIGURE 9-4   A three-element torque converter has a turbine, stator, and pump or impeller. *(Courtesy of Chrysler Corporation)*

the **flexplate,** which connects to the crankshaft. The flexplate and converter replace the flywheel used with standard transmissions. When the engine is running, the flexplate and converter rotate with the crankshaft (Figure 9-6). The flexplate is flexible enough to allow the front of the converter to move forward or backward if the converter expands or contracts slightly from heat or pressure. The pilot of the converter slides into the end of the crankshaft and centers the converter to the crankshaft.

The cross-sectional area of the impeller, turbine, and stator of most torque converters is round to give an efficient flow. The converter used with many newer transaxles has an elliptical cross-sectional shape that reduces the width of the converter (Figure 9-7). A shorter, low-profile converter, often called a *squashed* converter, makes the engine and transaxle shorter and easier to fit transversely in a vehicle.

The turbine is the converter's output member. The center hub of the turbine is splined to the transmission input shaft. The turbine is positioned in the front, engine end, of the converter housing so the turbine vanes face the impeller vanes.

The stator is the reaction member of the torque converter. The stator assembly is about one-half the diameter of the impeller or turbine. The outer edge of the stator vanes forms the inner edge of the three-piece fluid guide ring that is also part of the impeller and turbine vanes. The stator is mounted on a one-way clutch that is attached to the stationary reaction shaft splines. The reaction shaft extends from the front of the transmission, around the turbine shaft. The one-way clutch allows the stator to rotate clockwise but blocks counterclockwise rotation (Figure 9-8).

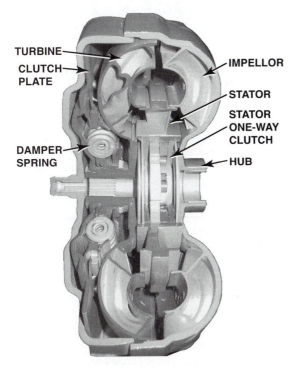

FIGURE 9-5   This cutaway view of a four-element torque converter shows the relationship of the internal parts.

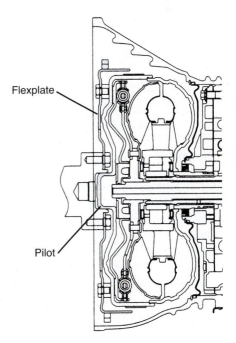

FIGURE 9-6   The flexplate connects the converter to the crankshaft. The pilot of the converter fits the end of the crankshaft to center the converter to the crankshaft. *(Courtesy of Chrysler Corporation)*

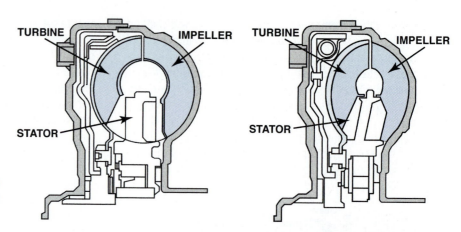

FIGURE 9-7   Most torque converters have a round cross section (left). Some new transmissions use a shorter, elliptical, squashed converter (right).

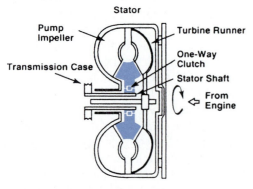

FIGURE 9-8   The stator one-way clutch allows the stator to rotate freely during the coupling phase, but stops counterclockwise rotation during torque multiplication. *(Courtesy of Toyota Motor Sales USA, Inc.)*

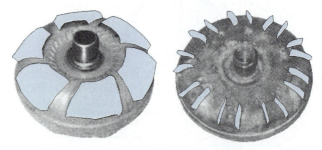

FIGURE 9-9   These air-cooled torque converters have shrouds that pump cooling air past the impeller.

FREQUENTLY ASKED QUESTION

WHAT DOES THREE- OR FOUR-ELEMENT MEAN?

In the late 1940s and 1950s, some transmissions used four- and five-element torque converters. The fourth or fifth part or element was either a second turbine, stator, or impeller assembly. In a few cases, the five elements were three separate turbines along with one impeller and stator. The reason for the additional elements was to obtain a torque converter with a wider range, a lower reduction ratio, with the ability to smoothly change ratios inside the converter.

9.3 OPERATION

A torque converter is a **hydrodynamic** unit. It transfers power through the dynamic motion of the fluid. Most other hydraulic units transfer power through the static pressure of

FREQUENTLY ASKED QUESTION

WHAT IS AN AIR-COOLED TORQUE CONVERTER?

Some early torque converters used with smaller engines are air cooled. They have a shroud with fins attached to the rear of the converter cover to force cooling air flow past the converter (Figure 9-9). Torque converters must be cooled because of the heat they generate during torque multiplication.

the fluid. When the engine is running, the converter impeller acts as a centrifugal pump. Fluid is thrown from the outer edge of the impeller vanes, and because of the curved shape of the converter cover, the fluid is thrown forward into the turbine. The impeller is turning in a clockwise direction, and the fluid also rotates in a clockwise direction as it leaves the impeller vanes (Figure 9-10). The mechanical power entering the converter is transformed in the fluid as fluid motion.

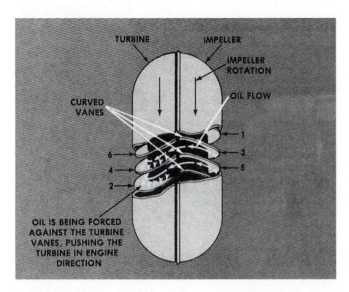

FIGURE 9-10 When the engine is running, fluid in the impeller is thrown outward and into the vanes of the turbine. *(Courtesy of Chrysler Corporation)*

FIGURE 9-11 The two major operating conditions of a converter are stall and coupling. These conditions shift back and forth depending on throttle opening and vehicle load.

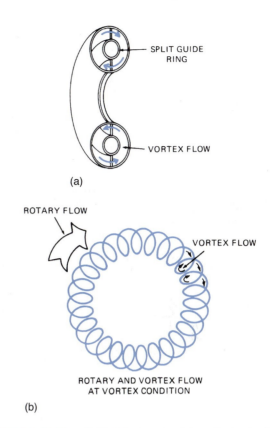

FIGURE 9-12 The fluid flowing around the guide ring is called vortex flow (a). The fluid flow around the converter is called rotary flow (b). *(Courtesy of Chrysler Corporation)*

The torque converter operates at two very different conditions: **stall** and *coupling* (Figure 9-11). Stall occurs with the turbine stopped and the impeller turning at engine speed. Coupling normally occurs while the vehicle maintains a steady speed and the turbine and impeller are turning at the same speed. A gradual shift from stall to coupling occurs as vehicle speed increases. The **torque converter clutch (TCC)** applies during the coupling phase.

At stall, the rotating fluid from the impeller tries to turn the turbine in a clockwise direction. If the turbine is stationary or turning at a speed substantially slower than the impeller, only part of the energy leaves the fluid to drive the turbine. Most of the fluid energy is lost as the fluid bounces off the turbine vanes. The fluid moves toward the center of the turbine, driven there by the continuous flow of fluid from the impeller. As energy leaves the fluid, the flow slows down and returns to the center of the impeller vanes, where the impeller will pick it up and keep it circulating. This flow is called a **vortex flow.** The vortex flow is a continuous circulation of fluid outward from the impeller, around the guide ring, inward into the turbine, through the stator, and back to the impeller (Figure 9-12). The guide ring directs the vortex flow, creating a smooth, turbulence-free flow. The clockwise flow of

fluid leaving the impeller, in the direction of engine rotation, is called **rotary flow.**

When the impeller is rotating substantially faster than the turbine, the fluid tends to bounce off the turbine vanes and change the rotary flow to a counterclockwise direction. The fluid flow still has quite a bit of energy. It can be compared with a tennis ball thrown against a wall. The ball bounces back and travels in a different direction, but it still has most of its energy of motion (Figure 9-13). A strong counterclockwise fluid flow from the turbine would tend to work against the clockwise rotation of the impeller.

9.3.1 Torque Multiplication

The stator redirects the fluid flow in the torque converter. It returns the fluid from the turbine back to the impeller in a clockwise direction. This action helps recover any energy remaining in the fluid. The curved shape of the stator vanes and a one-way clutch make this possible. Fluid leaving the turbine in a counterclockwise direction tries to turn the stator counterclockwise. This causes the stator one-way clutch to lock up and hold the stator stationary. The smooth, curved shape of

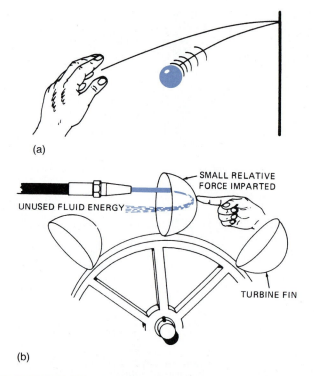

(a)

(b)

FIGURE 9-13 If a ball is thrown against a wall, kinetic energy in the ball will cause it to bounce back (a). The energy remaining in the fluid striking the turbine vanes will cause the fluid to bounce back in a similar manner (b).

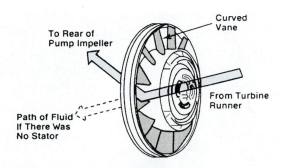

FIGURE 9-14 The fluid flow from the turbine is turned to the same direction as the impeller by the stator vanes.

the stator vanes redirects the fluid flow in a clockwise direction (Figure 9-14). This fluid leaving the stator is picked up by the impeller. The leftover energy in the fluid produces the torque increase in a torque converter. The term *K-factor* is used by automotive engineers as they match torque converter design to the amount of torque of the engine. The k-factor is calculated by dividing the square root of engine torque by the torque converter stall speed. Another engineering term is stall torque ratio (STR). STR is the torque converter's ability to multiply torque. Most passenger car converters have a STR between 1.68:1 and 2.1:1.

A physical rule states that for every action, there is an equal and opposite reaction. The action is the flow of fluid pushing on the turbine vanes; the reaction is the fluid bouncing back. A converter cannot multiply torque without the reaction of the stator.

A way to view the stator operation is to imagine what would occur if the stator was not in the converter. The fluid flow leaving the turbine would be in a counterclockwise direction, opposite that of the impeller. This flow would fight, not help, the impeller rotation, and the opposing fluid flows would cause a power loss and slow the impeller. Torque multiplication occurs because the stator redirects the fluid flow. This occurs only when the impeller is rotating faster than the turbine. As the turbine speed increases, the direction of flow becomes more rotary. The stator clutch overruns and the

converter becomes more of a coupling, transferring power from the engine to the transmission (Figure 9-15).

9.3.2 Coupling Phase

The vehicle starts moving when the turbine begins rotating. As the vehicle speed increases, the turbine speed increases relative to the impeller. The fluid flow is redirected as the turbine speed increases.

The rotation of the turbine causes the fluid to leave the turbine in a clockwise direction. This moves the fluid force from the front to the back of the stator vanes. The stator is now pushed in a clockwise direction. Because of this action, the stator one-way clutch releases (overruns), and the stator is now free to move along with the impeller and turbine. The fluid flow from the turbine back to the impeller is now smooth and undisturbed.

When the turbine speed reaches 90% to 95% of impeller speed, *coupling* occurs. The **coupling phase** occurs when the speeds of the impeller and turbine are nearly equal. Centrifugal force acting on the fluid in the spinning turbine is great enough to stop the vortex flow. At this point, there is no torque multiplication. It should be noted that this coupling speed is a relative point between the speeds of the impeller and turbine. Therefore, the coupling phase occurs at various vehicle speeds depending on throttle position and speed.

Some slippage occurs during the coupling phase. If power and load demands require it, the converter can return to the torque multiplication phase. In a non-lock-up converter, the turbine almost never turns at the same speed as the engine and impeller, and this is commonly referred to as converter slippage.

A torque converter is a relatively simple and inexpensive device for transferring power, but it is not a completely efficient device. In fact, at stall speeds it is totally inefficient; of the power that enters it, no power leaves to the transmission. At stall, all the power entering the converter is lost to the fluid as heat. The converter's efficiency steadily improves during torque multiplication and the coupling phases to about 90% to 95%.

Engine & Impeller Speed	1,800 rpm				
Turbine Speed	0	300	900	1,500	1,800
Vortex Flow	Very High	High	Low	None	None
Torque Multiplication	2.25:1	2:1	1.5:1	1:1	1:1
Efficiency	0%	40%	80%	90%	100%
	Torque Multiplication Phase			Coupling Phase	Lockup

FIGURE 9-15   The vortex flow, torque multiplication, and efficiency of a torque converter change as the turbine speed increases relative to the impeller.

9.4 TORQUE CONVERTER CLUTCHES

Since the late 1970s, most torque converters include an internal clutch called a torque converter clutch (TCC). The clutch is applied to eliminate the slippage during the coupling phase. Eliminating this slippage makes a significant improvement in fuel mileage. Most transmissions apply the clutch hydraulically, but a few used centrifugal force. When the TCC applies, the converter locks up, connecting the transmission input shaft directly to the engine, much like a vehicle with a standard transmission and clutch.

The converter clutch is a large clutch disc called a *pressure plate* or *clutch disc*. It has friction material and a damper assembly attached to it and it is splined to the turbine (Figure 9-16). When the friction material is forced against the torque converter cover, the turbine is driven mechanically by the engine.

The TCC is applied and released when the fluid entering the converter changes from the rear or front. Normal torque converter action occurs when the TCC is released, and the fluid flows from the front to the rear, past the clutch plate. TCC lock-up occurs when the fluid enters the rear of the torque converter and forces the clutch plate against the front cover. TCC apply forces the fluid in front of the clutch outward, and this fluid acts like an accumulator to soften clutch application (Figure 9-17).

TCC fluid flow is controlled by a TCC control valve that is in turn controlled by a solenoid. TCC apply blocks the flow of fluid through the torque converter and cooler. The torque converter does not generate heat when TCC is applied, but some heat is generated by the rest of the transmission. Some fluid will be directed past the TCC control valve to provide cool fluid for transmission lubrication.

Most TCCs use paper friction material. It can be secured to the front of the clutch disc, to the inside of the converter cover, or left free between the two. Some vehicles use a modulated or pulsed TCC apply pressure to smooth out TCC apply. This produces a lot of slipping that can burn out paper clutch lining fairly rapidly. These converters use graphite or paper-graphite lining material for greater endurance under these more severe operating conditions.

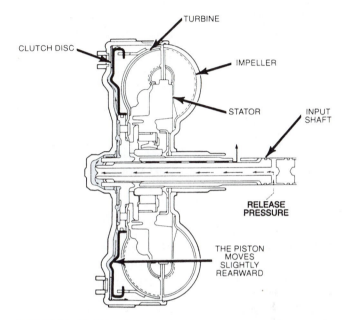

FIGURE 9-16   The clutch disc of a TCC has lining on the outer edge where it can contact the inner side of the cover. While released, there is a fluid flow between the disc and the cover. Note that the clutch disc is splined to the turbine. *(Courtesy of Chrysler Corporation)*

FREQUENTLY ASKED QUESTION

WHAT IS A CLC TORQUE CONVERTER?

Some torque converters used a centrifugally applied clutch with the friction material attached to a group of shoes arranged around the outer diameter of the clutch disc. Each shoe is spring loaded to move toward the center of the disc to release the clutch. As the turbine speed increases, centrifugal force pushes the shoes and friction material outward. The friction material contact produces a mechanical transfer of torque from the converter cover to the clutch disc. Ford Motor Company calls this converter a centrifugal lock-up converter (CLC).

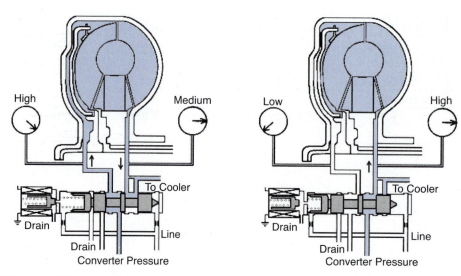

FIGURE 9-17   TCC release fluid flows through the center of the turbine shaft to the front of the clutch disc (left). Pressure to apply the clutch enters between the converter hub and the stator support (right).

Clutch discs include a **damper assembly** that transfers the power through a group of coil springs (Figure 9-18). In most converters, the damper springs are grouped at the center; in others they are grouped around the outer edge. These springs are used to dampen *torsional vibrations* from the engine. All automotive engines produce torsional vibration at some operating speed. Torsional vibrations are small speed increases and slowdowns as the crankshaft revolves. These vibrations can produce gear noise in the transmission and drive train as well as a noticeable vibration and harshness in the vehicle (Figure 9-19).

TCC application tends to be harsh in some vehicles. Some drivers dislike the bump that occurs during application. One method used to smooth TCC apply is to delay the rate of pressure increase by cycling or pulsing the TCC solenoid, as described in Chapter 8.

9.4.1 Controlled TCC Capacity

The TCC can be used to provide a gradual transition into higher gear ranges by slipping or easing into lock-up. Controlling TCC capacity has improved vehicle drivability. Early TCC lock-up improves fuel mileage but it can drop engine rpm to the point where misfire and vibration occurs.

A TCC solenoid controls TCC apply and release; this is a normally open solenoid that is either open (release) or closed (apply). Controlled-capacity systems use a pulse-width modulated (PWM) solenoid to control TCC apply pressure. When the TCC is first applied, the TCC PWM solenoid will operate at a duty cycle of about 25%. Apply pressure will be very low and the clutch will have a high slip rate. Depending on the vehicle speed and load, the duty cycle gradually increases, causing the slip rate to gradually reduce until full lock-up is achieved.

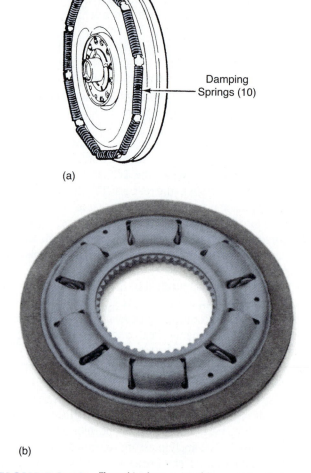

Damping Springs (10)

(a)

(b)

FIGURE 9-18   The turbine has a series of damper strings that connect to the clutch disc (a). Many clutch discs have a damper assembly at the center (b). *(a is courtesy of Chrysler Corporation; B is courtesy of Tribco, Inc.)*

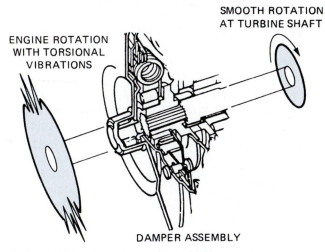

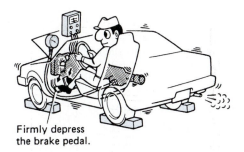

Firmly depress
the brake pedal.

FIGURE 9-20   A technician measures stall speed while testing a transmission. This test is performed using extreme caution because of the potentially dangerous conditions. The test period is limited to 5 seconds because of potential transmission damage.

FIGURE 9-19   A four-cylinder engine has two power impulses every revolution, and these impulses cause the crankshaft to speed up momentarily. During this time, the damper springs will compress to absorb the speed fluctuation.

converter clutch apply will occur at about 12 mph (20 kph) and stay locked until the vehicle comes to a stop.

Some small vehicles with CVTs do not use a torque converter. The forward and reverse clutches are released for stops and one will be applied to start the vehicle moving.

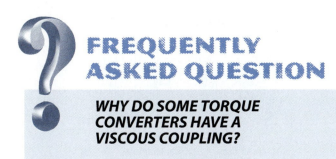

FREQUENTLY ASKED QUESTION

WHY DO SOME TORQUE CONVERTERS HAVE A VISCOUS COUPLING?

A *viscous converter clutch* was used in some vehicles to smooth TCC application. The operation is the same as the hydraulically applied converter clutch, except that a viscous element is built into the clutch disc. The viscous element, much like that in a cooling fan clutch, includes a rotor, a body, the clutch cover, and silicone fluid. The rotor and the body have a series of concentric, intermeshed ridges that provide two large surface areas. The viscous drag of the thick silicone fluid transfers power from the body to the rotor. The viscous clutch smoothly transfers power, minimizing engagement shock.

9.5 CVT TORQUE CONVERTER

Most CVT transmissions use a low-profile elliptical torque converter with a lock-up clutch. Since CVTs are infinitely variable, the torque converter is not needed once the vehicle is moving. Therefore the converter is used to multiply the torque to get the vehicle moving from a stop, and then becomes a mechanical connection between the engine and the CVT. The torque

9.6 STALL SPEED

Stall is when the turbine is held stationary while the converter housing and impeller are spinning. This is done by shifting the transmission into gear and applying the brakes to hold the drive wheels stationary. The importance of stall speed is that an engine must be able reach an rpm where enough torque is available to accelerate the vehicle, but not running so fast that there is poor fuel economy and excessive noise. Stall occurs to some degree each time a vehicle starts moving, either forward or backward, and each time a vehicle stops at a stop sign. **Stall speed** is the fastest rpm that an engine can reach while the turbine is held stationary (Figure 9-20).

A *stall test* measures stall speed in each of the gear positions. It is an important diagnostic test to determine transmission and torque converter condition. This test should be performed with caution because it operates the vehicle in a potentially dangerous situation: The vehicle is in gear with the throttle wide open. It is recommended that both the parking brake and the service brake be firmly applied, the wheels be blocked, and the throttle be held open for a maximum of 5 seconds.

A stall test can severely damage the transmission if done incorrectly. During a stall test, the dynamic fluid pressures inside a converter become very high because there is a lot of turbulence. Fluid temperatures also become very high. All of the power the engine can produce is going into the converter, and no mechanical power is being delivered to the transmission. The natural law of energy conservation says that energy cannot be created or destroyed. The energy going into the converter must go somewhere; it is converted to heat. Because so much heat is generated, stall tests should be no longer than 5 seconds and followed by a cooling period.

9.6.1 Stall Factors

The actual stall speed of a torque converter is determined by several factors:

- the amount of engine torque,
- the diameter of the converter,
- the angle of the impeller vanes,
- the angle of the stator vanes.

We will refer to a high stall speed as a *loose converter* and a low stall speed as a *tight converter*. When a vehicle is standing still, the turbine is not rotating. As the vehicle accelerates, the engine rpm rises quickly to the torque capacity of the converter (stall speed); then it stabilizes to a speed above turbine rpm. As the turbine speed increases, the engine speed also increases. A loose converter allows a higher engine rpm relative to the turbine rpm.

A high-torque engine has the ability to turn the impeller faster against a stalled turbine than a small or weak engine (Figure 9-21). A low-torque engine is normally equipped with a looser converter. If the converter is too tight, the engine rpm cannot increase to the point of usable power, and the vehicle would lose acceleration and overall performance. A converter that is too loose will cause the engine to operate at excessive speed. The result will be poor fuel economy, excessive noise, and reduced performance because of the excessive slippage. In production, the torque converter capacity/stall speed is matched to the engine size and vehicle weight to produce the best vehicle performance and fuel economy. Depending on the engine, different converters are used with a transmission model. One manufacturer uses eight different converters with one transmission model. The technician must ensure that the correct replacement converter is used.

Diameter is a major factor in determining converter stall speed. Passenger car converters vary in size from about 8 to 12 in. (20.3 to 30.5 cm) (Figure 9-22). The rotary speed of the fluid in the impeller is almost the same speed as the converter's outer diameter. The circumference of a circle is a product of the diameter times π (pi), which is equal to 3.1416. The circumference of an 8-in. converter is 25.1 in. (63.7 cm); the circumference of a 12-in. converter is 37.7 in. (95.8 cm), about 50% greater. From this, it should be fairly easy to see how a larger-diameter converter can put about 50% more speed and energy into the fluid. A 9-in. converter will have a stall speed that is about 30% faster than a 10-in. converter in the same vehicle. It should be noted that the increased fluid speed and energy requires more power from the engine. A larger converter is tighter and has a higher torque capacity.

The impeller vanes can be angled forward, straight, or backward relative to the direction of converter rotation (Figure 9-23). A forward or *positive fin angle* produces greater fluid speed and therefore a tighter converter. A rearward or *negative fin angle* increases the stall speed. Changing the

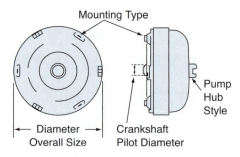

FIGURE 9-22   Converter diameter helps determine stall speed. Along with other factors, it is used to help select the correct replacement converter.

FIGURE 9-21   The stall speed of a torque converter must match the engine for good vehicle driveability.

COMPARING STALL SPEED				
Example	Engine Size	Maximum Torque: lb-ft @ rpm	Stall Speed: 11" Converter	Effect
#1	2L, I4	140 lb-ft @ 5,000	1,300 rpm	Engine stall speed is below power and; vehicle will show power loss
#2	3L, V6	202 lb-ft @ 3,800	1,600 rpm	Engine stall speed is below power band; vehicle will show power loss
#3	4.2L, V8	303 lb-ft @ 3,100	2,000 rpm	OK combination
#4	5.4L, V8	350 lb-ft @ 2,500	2,500 rpm	Engine stall speed is at maximum torque; good combination
#5	5.9L, I6, Diesel	610 lb-ft @ 1,600	3,100 rpm	Stall speed is too high, above engine power band; vehicle will show power loss and poor fuel economy

FIGURE 9-23 On some converters, it is possible to see the impeller fin angle from the outside. The converter on the right has rearward or negative fin angles that will produce a higher stall speed than the one on the left, which has forward or positive fin angle.

impeller fin angle is an easy method for a manufacturer to change converter torque capacity.

Another method of changing converter capacity is the angle of the stator vanes. The greater the curvature, the more the fluid will return to the direction of impeller rotation, and the stall speed and converter looseness will be increased. Straighter vanes produce a tighter converter.

PROBLEM SOLVING 9-1 Imagine that you are working in a shop that specializes in transmission repair, and these problems are given to you.

Case 1 A 1995 Ford van has a bump and shudder that occurs in drive at 20 to 40 mph. The shudder occurs once in every shift cycle. Could this be a torque converter problem? Would this be a mechanical, hydraulic, or electrical problem? Where would you start looking for the cause?

Case 2 A 1987 Chevrolet Citation transaxle was rebuilt, and a rebuilt torque converter was installed. Now the car has poor acceleration. The four-cylinder engine acts as if it has lost two of the cylinders. What could have caused this? Where would you start looking for the cause?

FREQUENTLY ASKED QUESTION

HOW IS A SUPER THM 400 DIFFERENT?

In the 1960s, the THM Super 400 and Super 300 transmissions were produced with variable-pitch stator vanes. A hydraulic piston was built into the stator assembly, and fluid to this piston was controlled by an electric solenoid-controlled valve. At very low vehicle speeds or high-throttle openings, the stator vanes are moved to a high angle for maximum stall speed, torque multiplication, and acceleration. Otherwise, the stator vanes are kept at a low-angle position for maximum fuel economy and quiet, smooth vehicle operation. The switch to control stator fin position is mounted in the speedometer or throttle linkage, depending on the vehicle application.

SUMMARY

1. A torque converter hydraulically connects the engine to an automatic transmission and will multiply the engine torque under certain conditions.

2. Torque converters utilize an impeller, turbine, stator, and lock-up clutch.

3. Stall and coupling are the extremes of torque converter operation. Stall occurs when the impeller and turbine are operating at different speeds, and coupling occurs when the impellers are turning at nearly the same speed.

4. Torque converter clutches are used to mechanically connect the engine to the transmission. During lock-up, torque converter slippage will be eliminated and fuel mileage will improve.

5. The factors that affect torque converter stall are converter diameter, angle of the vanes, and the torque of the engine.

REVIEW QUESTIONS

The following questions are provided to help you study as you read the chapter.

1. The two purposes for a torque converter are to serve as an automatic _____ and to multiply the engine's _____.

2. List the four elements of a typical torque converter.

3. The torque converter is bolted to the _____.

4. The torque converter's input member is the _____ and the output member is the _____.

5. The stator is the _____ member of the torque converter and is splined onto the reaction shaft through a _____ clutch.

6. The flow of fluid from the impeller to the turbine is called a _____ flow. The circular flow of fluid leaving the impeller is called _____ flow.

7. The stator _____ the flow from the turbine to the impeller. The effect of this is to increase _____.

8. The coupling phase occurs when the turbine and the impeller are rotating at nearly the _____ speed.

9. The purpose of the torque converter clutch is to eliminate torque converter _____ during the _____ stage of operation.

10. The torque converter clutch is similar to a _____ _____ for a standard transmission.

11. The torque converter clutch is splined onto the _____, and when applied, it is forced against the torque converter _____.

12. The torque converter clutch is released by directing fluid to the _____ of the clutch, and applied by directing fluid to the _____ of the clutch.

13. A torque converter clutch uses _____ springs to smooth out _____ vibrations.

14. Some torque converter clutches use a _____-filled clutch to smooth out torque converter clutch application.

15. Torque converter stall is when the _____ is held stationary and the _____ is spinning.

16. Stall speed is the _____ rpm that an engine can turn while the turbine is _____.

17. Stall testing can be used to check _____ and _____ condition.

18. Vehicles with small engines typically use a torque converter that has a _____ stall speed, and vehicles with a powerful engine use a torque converter with a _____ stall speed.

19. Four factors that affect torque converter stall speed are:
    a. Engine _____
    b. _____ diameter
    c. Impeller _____ angle
    d. Stator fin _____

CHAPTER QUIZ

The following questions will help you check the facts you have learned. Select the answer that completes each statement correctly.

1. Student A says that a torque converter is a hydraulic connection between the engine and transmission. Student B says that a torque converter clutch will increase the torque to the transmission. Who is correct?
   a. Student A
   b. Student B
   c. Both A and B
   d. Neither A nor B

2. The input member of the converter is the
   a. turbine.
   b. stator.
   c. impeller.
   d. All of these

3. Student A says that the flexplate connects the torque converter to the crankshaft. Student B says that the torque converter is considered part of the transmission. Who is correct?
   a. Student A
   b. Student B
   c. Both A and B
   d. Neither A nor B

4. Student A says that fluid motion inside a converter is controlled by the guide ring. Student B says that fluid motion inside a converter is controlled by the stator vanes. Who is correct?
   a. Student A
   b. Student B
   c. Both A and B
   d. Neither A nor B

5. The fluid flow from the impeller through the turbine and stator is called
   a. rotary flow.
   b. impeller flow.
   c. vortex flow.
   d. turbine flow.

6. The fluid flow around the circumference of the converter is called
   a. rotary flow.
   b. impeller flow.
   c. vortex flow.
   d. turbine flow.

7. A strong vortex flow will
   a. cause the stator clutch to lock.
   b. release the stator clutch.
   c. circulate through the guide ring.
   d. All of these

8. During the coupling phase the
   a. vortex flow nearly stops.
   b. stator clutch locks.
   c. rotary flow nearly stops.
   d. flow stops.

9. A torque converter is more efficient while
   a. stopped at a stop sign.
   b. accelerating hard.
   c. accelerating under a light throttle.
   d. cruising.

10. Student A says that at stall speed the impeller is spinning as fast as the engine can drive it. Student B says that at stall speed the turbine is stationary. Who is correct?
    a. Student A
    b. Student B
    c. Both A and B
    d. Neither A nor B

11. In most lock-up torque converters, lock-up occurs when the
    a. fluid flow in the converter is reversed.
    b. converter switch valve is moved by the lock-up solenoid.
    c. turbine speed reaches a certain rpm.
    d. converter speed reaches a certain rpm.

12. In a lock-up torque converter, the
    a. clutch plate is splined onto the turbine shaft.
    b. clutch lining transfers power through a mechanical connection during lock-up.
    c. fluid is passing through the torque converter.
    d. Both A and B

13. Lock-up torque converters use a damper assembly to dampen
    a. noise.
    b. torsional vibration.
    c. lateral force.
    d. spring oscillations.

14. Stall testing can be used to find
    a. problems with the torque converter.
    b. slipping clutches.
    c. slipping bands.
    d. All of these

15. A large-diameter torque converter will
    a. have a higher stall speed.
    b. have a lower stall speed.
    c. not have an effect on stall speed.
    d. All of these

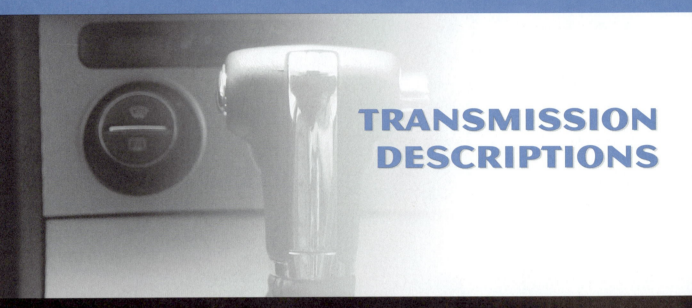

TRANSMISSION DESCRIPTIONS

OBJECTIVES

After studying Chapter 10, the reader should be able to:

1. Describe some of the transmissions used in domestic vehicles.
2. Describe some of the transmissions used in the more popular import vehicles.
3. Explain the operation of a particular transmission.
4. Identify which transmission is used in a particular vehicle.
5. Identify a particular transmission.

KEY TERMS

Cruise-O-Matic (p. 241)
Loadflite (p. 234)

Turbo Hydra-Matic (THM) (p. 247)

10.1 INTRODUCTION

Many different types of transmissions and transaxles have been used in domestic and imported vehicles. It is difficult to describe each one of these with the information provided in a book of this type. We will concentrate only on domestic transmissions and the transmissions installed in the more popular import vehicles.

The transmission technician's job is easier if he or she has a working knowledge of the transmission being diagnosed and/or repaired. It may seem to be a difficult task to learn the many different transmissions, but it is made easier by the fact that many transmissions have similar operating characteristics. We can place the more common transmissions and transaxles into the categories described in Chapter 5. Some of these categories are similar except for the apply devices. Most transmissions used in import vehicles fit into these same categories. Remember that most transmissions and transaxles have the following common characteristics:

- Planetary gearsets achieve the various ratios (Honda, older Saturn, and CVT transaxles are the exceptions).
- Multiple-disc clutches, bands, or one-way clutches control the power flow.
- Hydraulic pressure applies the application devices.
- Most use electronic shift controls.
- Most use a lock-up type of torque converter (CVTs with electromagnet clutches are the exception).

In the following sections, we will briefly describe the more common transmission and transaxles. They will be described by manufacturer and cross-referenced by the gear train types described in Chapter 5. The gear train categories are based on the type of gear train and the type of apply devices used.

A particular transmission design may have many small differences. In any single year, there may be many versions of the same transmission depending on the application. The differences might be the:

- number of lined and unlined plates in a clutch pack,
- ratio of the band levers,
- size of the band servos,
- programming of the valve body,
- strength of the spring in an accumulator,
- torque converter stall speed,
- location of the mounting pad bolts,
- shape of the torque converter housing (bell housing),
- ratio of the drive sprockets and chain, or
- exact number of teeth on the gears in the gearsets.

Each transmission must be matched to the weight of the vehicle, the strength of the engine, emission and fuel mileage requirements, and sometimes where the vehicle will be sold.

Links to online resources for identifying domestic and import transmissions are provided in Appendix B.

10.1.1 Transaxles

A transaxle is a combination of a transmission, either standard or automatic, and a final drive assembly. The final drive is typically a set of reduction gears and the differential. The differential is made up of two pairs of gears, the differential pinion gears mounted on the differential pinion shaft and the axle or side gears, which are attached to the axles or drive shafts (Figure 10-1). In a front wheel drive (FWD) vehicle, the axle shafts are often called *drive shafts* and occasionally called *half-shafts.* The purpose of the differential is to allow the drive wheels to be driven at different speeds while the vehicle is going around a corner.

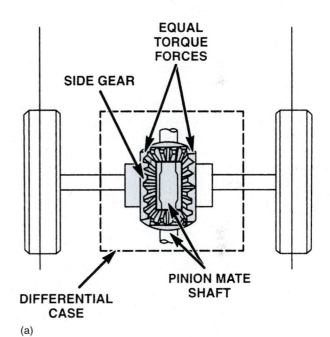

(a)

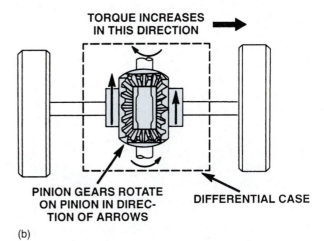

(b)

FIGURE 10-1 When a vehicle is driving straight, the differential gears rotate as a unit; equal load keeps the pinion gears stationary on the mate shaft (a). An unequal load causes the pinion gears to rotate on the mate shaft so one axle can turn faster than the other (b). *(Courtesy of Chrysler Corporation)*

There are essentially four types of final drive and differential combinations used in transaxles:

- The first type uses helical gears and an intermediate/idler gear or shaft to transfer power from the transmission planetary gear assembly to the differential case (Figure 10-2). The helical gears provide the necessary reduction ratio and are relatively efficient, quiet, and inexpensive. Older Chrysler transaxles and the Ford ATX are examples.

- The second type uses a planetary gearset mounted to the output of the transmission gearset for the final drive reduction gears (see Figure 3-35). The output of the transmission is a sun gear that is also the input for the final drive reduction gears. In this set, the ring gear is splined into the transaxle case so it is always a reaction member and the planet carrier is part of the differential case so it is always the output. The short, right-side drive shaft exits almost directly out of the case, and the longer, left drive shaft runs through the center of the transmission gearset. Examples are the General Motors transaxles and the Ford AX4N, AX4S, and AXOD.

- The third type uses a planetary gear final drive that is driven by a chain and sprockets from the transmission section (Figure 10-3). An example of this is the Ford CD4E.

- Some FWD vehicles use an engine mounted lengthwise in the vehicle so the crankshaft and the transaxle shafts run *longitudinal* (fore and aft) instead of *transverse* or *lateral* (side to side) relative to the vehicle. In these units, the power must make a right-angle turn as it goes from the transmission to the differential. These units use either a spiral bevel or a hypoid gearset that is similar to the gears in the rear axle of a RWD vehicle. The hypoid gearset is the most common. It changes the power flow 90 degrees and provides the gear reduction. Examples of these transaxles are the Acura Legend and Chrysler 42LE. The 42LE uses a chain and sprocket set to transfer power from the transmission output to the transfer shaft, and the transfer shaft becomes the pinion gear of the hypoid final drive (Figure 10-4).

Remember that the gear ratio through a transaxle is a product of at least two gear ratios, and in some cases, three gear ratios. In many units, the gearset ratio times the final drive ratio equals the overall ratio (Figure 10-5). In units using a chain and sprockets, multiplying the chain and sprocket ratio times the gearset ratio times the final drive ratio equals the overall ratio. The overall ratio is the actual operating ratio between the engine and the drive wheels. The chain and sprocket ratio can vary between models. This becomes important when transaxles are replaced with a used or remanufactured transaxle. If the overall gear ratio does not match the ratio of the original

FREQUENTLY ASKED QUESTION

WERE THE THM 325, 325-4L, AND 425 MODELS TRANSMISSIONS OR TRANSAXLES?

Another approach to providing FWD was used in the THM 325, THM 325-4L, and THM 425 transmissions installed in Cadillac Eldorados, Oldsmobile Toronados, and later Buick Rivieras. They were replaced by the THM 440-T4 (4T60) in the mid-1980s. These transmissions are mounted alongside the engine and use a pair of sprockets and a drive chain to transfer power from the torque converter turbine shaft to the transmission input shaft (Figure 10-6). A final drive gear assembly is bolted to the output of these transmissions, and this unit contains the reduction ring and pinion gears and the differential. Technically, since the final drive gears can be separated from the transmission, these units are not transaxles. This final drive gearset uses a hypoid gearset for the final drive ratio and to turn the power flow 90 degrees.

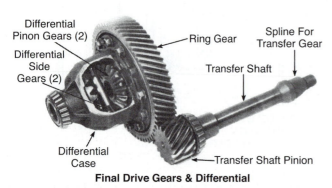

Differential Pinon Gears (2)
Differential Side Gears (2)
Ring Gear
Spline For Transfer Gear
Transfer Shaft
Differential Case
Transfer Shaft Pinion

Final Drive Gears & Differential

(a)

TRANSFER SHAFT GEAR
OUTPUT SHAFT GEAR
SPLINED TO TRANSFER SHAFT
SPLINED TO OUTPUT SHAFT

TRANSFER GEARS

(b)

FIGURE 10-2   The 41TE transaxle uses a set of helical final drive gears (a) to transfer power from the transfer shaft to the differential and drive shafts. A set of helical transfer gears (b) is used to transfer power from the transmission gears to the transfer shaft. *(Courtesy of Chrysler Corporation)*

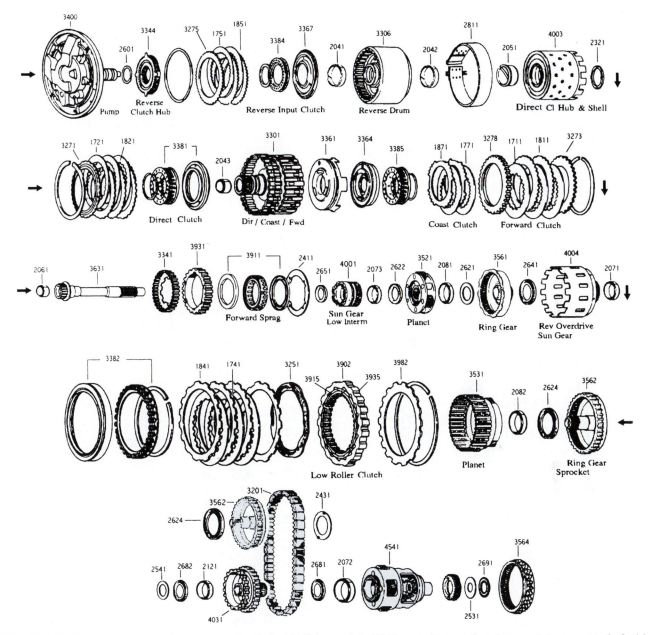

FIGURE 10-3   An exploded view from a parts catalog of a Ford CD4E shows a chain (3201) to transfer power from the transmission gearset to the final drive and differential. *(Courtesy of Aceomatic Recon)*

transaxle, the transmission control module (TCM) will note the difference and may set a diagnostic trouble code (DTC). Also, the customer might be dissatisfied with the performance, drivability, and fuel economy of the vehicle.

10.1.2 New-Generation Transmissions and Transaxles

Vehicle manufacturers are working to improve vehicle efficiency, performance, and fuel mileage. Transmissions and transaxles are being introduced that are smaller, lighter, and have additional gear ranges. The authors are trying to keep

this chapter current, but it must be realized that it is not practical to include all transmissions and transaxles.

10.2 CHRYSLER

Torqueflites are three-speed, Simpson gear train transmissions of two basic sizes. The A-904 was introduced as a Torqueflite 6 (TF6) in 1960 for use with 6-cylinder engines. The A-727 was introduced in 1962 for use with 8-cylinder engines. The A-727 is called the Torqueflite 8 (TF8). Both transmissions used an aluminum case. A cast-iron-case Torqueflite was used from 1956 to 1961. A two-speed unit called the Powerflite

FREQUENTLY ASKED QUESTION

WHAT IS A TORQUEFLITE?

In the past, Chrysler Corporation, now Chrysler LLC, has traditionally used the terms *Torqueflite* for passenger car transmissions and **Loadflite** for transmissions intended for pickups, SUVs, and light trucks.

was used from 1954 to 1960. Its operation was similar to the Powerglide transmission produced by General Motors.

In 1992, Chrysler adopted an alphanumeric system for identifying and describing its transmissions. The system used for these units is as follows:

1st character: Number of forward speeds
2nd character: Relative torque capacity—0 is the smallest and 10 the highest
3rd character: Wheels driven or transmission position: A = AWD, R = RWD, L = longitudinal, T = Transverse
4th character: Type of shift control: H = Hydraulic control, E = Electronic control, FE = Fully electronic

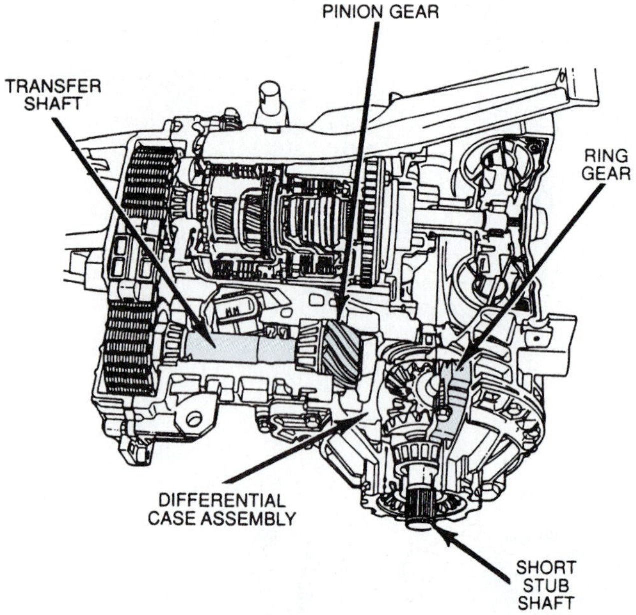

FIGURE 10-4 The Chrysler 42LE transaxle uses hypoid final drive gears. Note the transfer chain to connect the transmission gearset to the final drive pinion gear. *(Courtesy of Chrysler Corporation)*

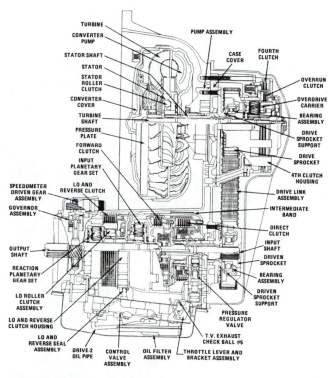

FIGURE 10-6 A THM 3254L transmission is mounted alongside of the engine. The front axle assembly is attached directly to the output shaft (lower left) to drive the front wheels. *(Reprinted with permission of General Motors)*

Chain & Sprocket	Final Drive	Transmission
0.98:1 or 0.91:1	3.85:1 or 4.31:1	1st = 2.89:1, 2nd = 1.57, 3rd = 1:1, 4th = 0.69:1

The overall gear ratio in 1st gear when used with the 2.0 L engine is:
1st gear ratio × chain & sprocket ratio × final drive ratio
2.89 × 0.91 × 4.31 = 11.33:1

The overall gear ratio in 1st gear when used with the 2.5 L engine is:
1st gear ratio × chain & sprocket ratio × final drive ratio
2.89 × 0.98 × 3.85 = 10.9:1

FIGURE 10-5 The overall gear ratio in a transaxle is a product of multiplying the transmission gear ratio by the final drive ratio. This should be multiplied by any transfer gear/chain ratio.

Interpreting the code for a Chrysler 45RFE transmission identifies the transmission as a four-speed, relatively high-torque-capacity, rear wheel drive transmission that is controlled fully by electronics.

Detailed descriptions of each Chrysler transmission and how it operates is available in the manufacturer's service information, transmission service manuals, and trade publications. The gear ratios of the Chrysler transmissions and transaxles are shown in Figure 10-7.

10.2.1 Chrysler Rear Wheel Drive Transmissions

Several RWD transmissions are currently in production. They can be identified by the transmission code on the vehicle body plate (Figure 10-8). When the transmission is out of the vehicle, it can be identified by a transmission identification number stamped on the left side of the case, just above the pan gasket surface, or by an identification label attached to the transmission (Figure 10-9). The size, shape, and appearance of the case along with the shape of the pan also help identify a unit (Figure 10-10).

30RH-32RH Transmissions. These transmissions are three-speed units that use a Type 1 gear train (Figure 10-11). The 30RH was formerly called a TF6 or A904; the 31RH was formerly called a 998; and the 32RH was formerly called a 999. These are similar units with slight internal variations.

Electronic controls are used for torque converter clutch operation in models from 1978 on.

36RH-37RH Transmissions. The 36RH and 37RH are also three-speed transmissions that use a Type 1 gear train. They are larger transmissions than the 30RH-32RH units, and are designed to handle the higher torque loads for larger engines and heavier vehicles. They were formerly called a TF8 or A727. Electronic control for the torque converter clutch began in 1978.

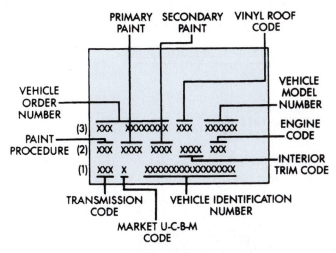

FIGURE 10-8 This body decal identifies the transmission as well as other important features of this vehicle. *(Courtesy of Chrysler Corporation)*

Model	First	Second	Third	Fourth	Fifth	Sixth	Reverse
TRANSAXLE GEAR RATIOS							
31TH	2.69	1.55	1				2.1
40TE	2.84	1.57	1	0.69			2.12
41AE/TE, 42LE	2.842	1.575	1	0.69			2.21
62TE	4.11	2.84	2.27	1.57	1	0.68	3.22
F4A33	2.554	1.488	1	0.685			2.17
F4A42	2.842	1.529	1	0.712			2.48
W4A33	2.551	1.488	1	0.685			2.176
TRANSMISSION GEAR RATIOS							
30RH, 32RH, 36RH	2.74	1.54	1				2.22
42RE, 44RE	2.74	1.54	1	0.69			2.21
42RLE	2.84	1.57	1	0.69			2.21
46RE, 47RE, 48RE	2.45	1.45	1	0.69			2.21
45RFE	3.0	1.67/1.5	1	0.75			3.0
545RFE*	3.0	1.67/1.5	1	0.75	0.5/0.67		3.0
AW4	2.80	1.53	1	0.75			2.39
W5A580	3.59	2.19	1.41	1	0.83		3.0

*** These transmissions have two second gear ratios, called second and second prime.
Second prime is used as the transition between 4th and 2nd during kickdown.**

FIGURE 10-7 The gear ratios for Chrysler transmissions and transaxles.

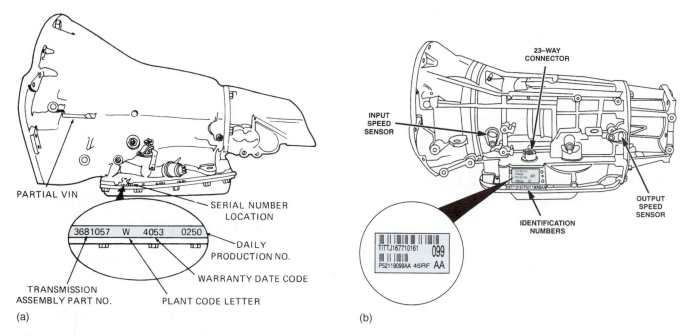

(a)

(b)

FIGURE 10-9   Older Torqueflite transmissions can be identified by a code stamped in the case (a). Newer units use a label attached to the case (b). *(Courtesy of Chrysler Corporation)*

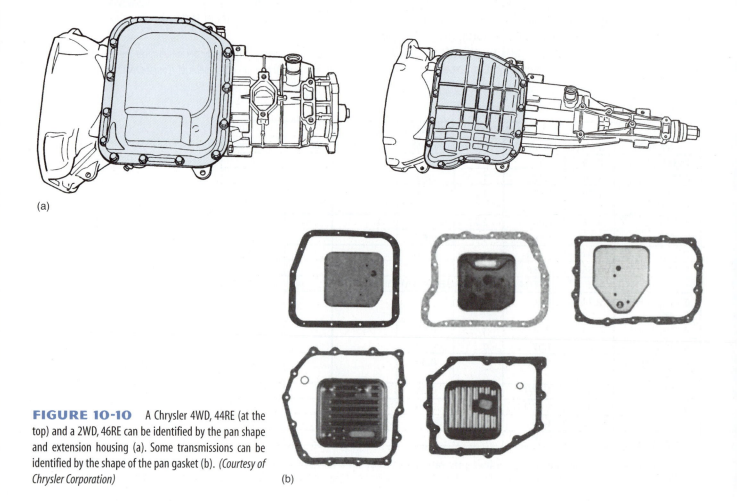

(a)

(b)

FIGURE 10-10   A Chrysler 4WD, 44RE (at the top) and a 2WD, 46RE can be identified by the pan shape and extension housing (a). Some transmissions can be identified by the shape of the pan gasket (b). *(Courtesy of Chrysler Corporation)*

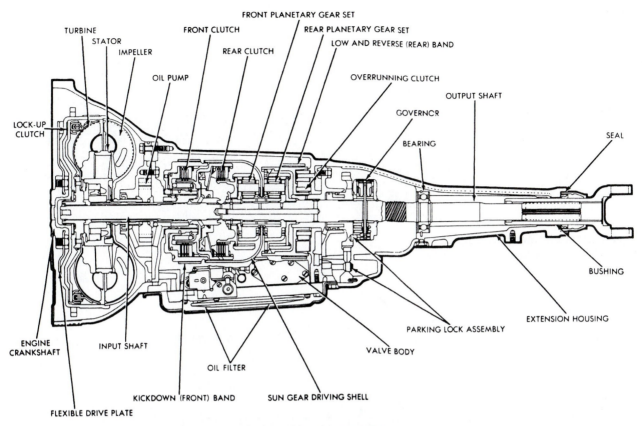

ELEMENTS IN USE AT EACH POSITION OF THE SELECTOR LEVER

LEVER POSITION	START SAFETY	PARKING SPRAG	CLUTCHES			BANDS	
			FRONT	REAR	OVER-RUNNING	(KICKDOWN) FRONT	(LOW-REV.) REAR
P—PARK	X	X					
R—REVERSE				X			X
N—NEUTRAL	X						
D—DRIVE First Second Direct			X	X X X	X	X	
2—SECOND First Second				X X	X	X	
1—LOW (First)				X			X

FIGURE 10-11   A cutaway view of a 30RH (A940) transmission with a clutch and band application chart. *(Courtesy of Chrysler Corporation)*

40RH-42RH, 42RE-44RE Transmissions. These transmissions are Type 5 units that combine a three-speed Type 1 transmission (30RH-32RH) with an overdrive gearset positioned at the rear of the transmission (Figure 10-12). They were previously called the A500. These units are used in pickups, SUVs, vans, and light trucks with 6-cylinder engines. In the 40RH/42RH, the torque converter clutch, 3–4 shift, and 4–3 shift are hydraulically controlled. They are electronically controlled in the 42RE/44RE.

42RLE Transmission. This transmission is used in 2WD and 4WD vehicles. It is a redesign of the 42LE transaxle. It uses the same Type 14 gearset and transmission controls. Because there is no final drive, a redesigned transmission case and output shaft are used.

45RFE Transmission. The 45RFE transmission is a four-speed transmission that uses three simple planetary gearsets. The gearsets are called the reaction gearset (at the front of the

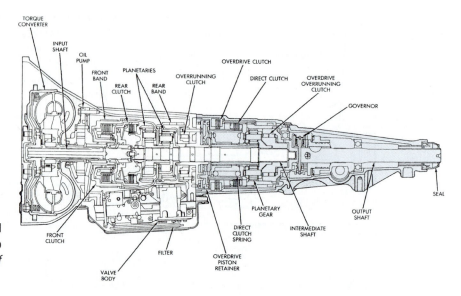

FIGURE 10-12   A cutaway view of a 42RH transmission; note that the overdrive unit attaches to the rear of the main transmission section. *(Courtesy of Chrysler Corporation)*

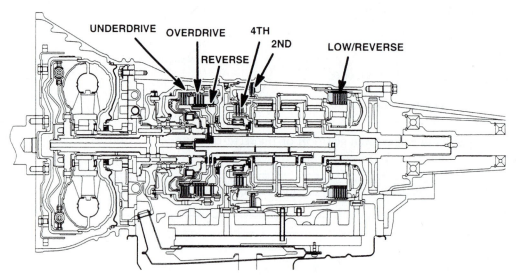

FIGURE 10-13   A cutaway view of a 45RFE transmission showing the three driving clutches, the three reaction clutches, and the complex gearset. *(Courtesy of Chrysler Corporation)*

transmission), reverse gearset (center), and input gearset (at the rear) (Figure 10-13). It uses seven control devices, as shown by the clutch and band chart (Figure 10-14). With the exception of the freewheel/overruning clutch, these are all mulitplate clutches; there are no bands. Two devices are applied in each gear range, and these are controlled by seven solenoids. These fully electronic units are used in pickups, SUVs, vans, and light trucks.

46RH-47RH, 46RE-47RE-48RE Transmissions.

These transmissions also use two planetary gearsets like the 40RH/42RH units. They are larger, stronger units—note the higher torque capacity, as indicated by the second character. They also combine a three-speed Type 1 transmission (36RH-37RH) with an overdrive unit at the rear. The 46RH and 47RH, formerly called the A518, are used with 8-cylinder engines. Electronic controls are used for the 3–4 and 4–3 shifts and torque converter operation in the RH versions.

W5A580/722.6 Transmission.

This five-speed transmission combines a simple planetary gearset with a compound gearset that connects a ring gear of one set with the carrier of the second set. Two overrunning clutches, three multiplate clutches, and three multiplate brakes/reaction clutches control the power flow (Figure 10-15). This transmission was developed jointly with Mercedes-Benz.

10.2.2 Chrysler Transaxles

Chrysler transaxles can be identified by the transmission code on the vehicle body plate. When the transaxle is out of the vehicle, it can be identified by an identification tag on the case (Figure 10-15). The size, shape, and appearance of the case and the shape of the pan are also useful when identifying these transaxles.

Shift Lever Position	Park Sprag	Under Drive	Overdrive	Reverse	2nd	4th	Low–Reverse	Over–running Clutch
CLUTCHES APPLIED								
P–Park	X						X	
R–Reverse				X			X	
N–Neutral							X	
D–Overdrive First		X					X*	X
Second		X			X			
Second Prime		X				X		
Third		X	X					
Fourth			X			X		
Limp–in		X	X					
2–First		X					X*	X
Second		X			X			
Limp–in		X			X			
1–Low		X					X	X

FIGURE 10-14   This clutch chart shows the active control devices for each gear range of a 45RFE transmission.

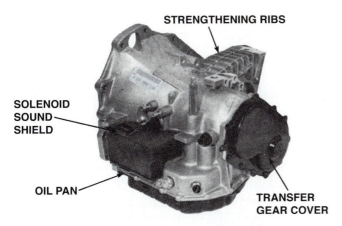

FIGURE 10-15   The 41TE transaxle can be identified by an identification label attached to the converter housing and by the shape of the case with the solenoid sound shield, transfer gear cover, and strengthening ribs over the final drive section. *(Courtesy of Chrysler Corporation)*

30TH–31TH Transaxle.   The 30TH and 31TH transaxles are three-speed units that use a Type 1 gear train. They are used with a transverse-mounted engine (Figure 10-16). They were formerly called the A404, A413, A414, A470, and A670. The transmission section of these units is very similar to the TF6/A904 transmission. The major exterior difference between these units is the bell housing, which is designed to fit a particular engine. Internally, the final drive ratios may be different.

41TE Transaxle.   The 41TE transaxle is a four-speed unit with a transverse engine mounting. It uses a Type 14 gear train and was formerly called an A604 (Figure 10-17). This unit uses no bands or one-way clutches. It is a fully electronic transaxle.

42LE Transaxle.   The 42LE transaxle is a four-speed unit similar to a 41TE with a longitudinal-mounted engine (see Figure 10-4). It is a fully electronic unit.

62TE Transaxle.   The 62TE is a six-speed transaxle with a transverse-mounted engine. The transmission is very similar to the 41TE with the addition of a compounder gearset on the transfer shaft. The compounder has a 1:1 and 1.45:1 ratio, so the transaxle gear ratios are as follows: first—4.11:1 (2.84 × 1.45), second—2.84:1, third—2.27:1 (1.57 × 1.45), fourth—1.57:1, fifth—1:1, sixth—0.68:1, and reverse—3.2:1 (2.21 × 1.45). The compounder is a simple planetary gearset with two multiplate clutch packs and an overrunning clutch.

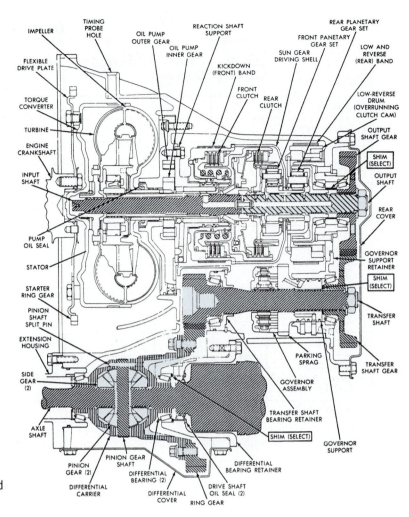

FIGURE 10-16 A cutaway view of a 30TH three-speed transaxle. *(Courtesy of Chrysler Corporation)*

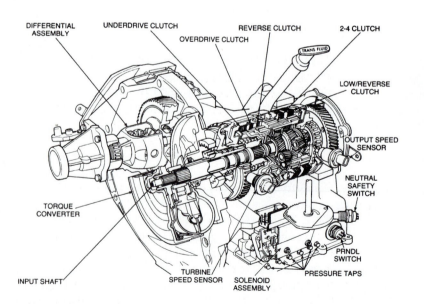

ELEMENTS IN USE SHIFT LEVER POSITION	Start Safety	Park Sprag	CLUTCHES				
			Underdrive	Overdrive	Reverse	2/4	Low/Reverse
P — PARK	X	X					X
R — REVERSE					X		X
N — NEUTRAL	X						X
OD — OVERDRIVE							
First			X				X
Second			X			X	
Direct			X	X			
Overdrive				X		X	
D — DRIVE*							
First			X				X
Second			X			X	
Direct			X	X			
L — LOW*							
First			X				X
Second			X			X	
Direct			X	X			

*Vehicle upshift and downshift speeds are increased when in these selector positions.

FIGURE 10-17 A cutaway view of a 41TE transaxle with a clutch application chart. *(Courtesy of Chrysler Corporation)*

10.3 FORD MOTOR COMPANY

Ford now uses an alphanumeric code. Like other vehicle manufacturers, Ford transmissions are manufactured all over the world. Some are from Ford-owned production lines in the United States and France; others are produced by manufacturers in Japan (JATCO and Aisin [AW]) and in Europe (ZF).

Ford Motor Company also uses an alphanumeric model designation system as follows:

1st character: Number of forward speeds
2nd character: Transmission features: A = Automatic, C = Vehicle application size, Production year, Chain or Close ratio, D = Drive, E = Electronic, F = FWD, H = Taurus SHO, HD = Heavy duty, L = Lock-up, M = Manual, N = Nonsynchronous, O = Overdrive, S = Synchronous, T = Transmission, W = Wide ratio, X = Transaxle
3rd and 4th characters: Torque capacity (maximum input from torque converter): 44 = 440 ft-lb, 55 = 550 ft-lb, 70 = 700 ft-lb

Detailed descriptions of each Ford Motor Company transmission and how it operates are available in the manufacturer's service information, transmission service manuals, and trade publications. The gear ratios for Ford Motor Company transmissions and transaxles are shown in Figure 10-18.

10.3.1 Ford Motor Company Rear Wheel Drive Transmissions

Ford transmissions can be identified by the vehicle's label located on the door pillar (Figure 10-19). When the transmission is out of the vehicle, it can be identified with a service identification tag attached to the case (Figure 10-20). The size, shape, and appearance along with the shape of its pan can also be used to identify a transmission (Figure 10-21). Five RWD transmissions that are out of production will also be described (Section 10.3.1).

FREQUENTLY ASKED QUESTION

WHAT IS A FORD-O-MATIC?

In the past, the Ford Motor Company has traditionally used the terms **Cruise-O-Matic,** *Ford-O-Matic,* and *Merc-O-Matic* for its automatic transmissions. The "C" in C4 and C6 stood for Cruise-O-Matic.

TRANSAXLE GEAR RATIOS							
Model	First	Second	Third	Fourth	Fifth	Sixth	Reverse
4F20E	2.78	1.54	1	0.69			2.27
4F27E	2.8	1.49	1	0.73			2.65
4F50N/AX4N/ AX4S/AXOD	2.77	1.54	1	0.69			2.26
ATX	2.79	1.61	1	0.69			1.97
CD4E	2.89	1.57	1	0.69			2.31
F4E/4EAT	2.8	1.54	1	0.7			2.33
6F50	4.84	2.87	1.84	1.41	1	0.74	2.88
TRANSMISSION GEAR RATIOS							
4R44E/A4LD	2.47	1.47	1	0.75			2.1
4R70W	2.8	1.55	1	0.7			2.32
4R100/E4OD	2.71	1.54	1	0.71			2.18
5R55E	2.47	1.87	1.47	1	0.75		2
5R55N	3.25	2.44	1.55	1	0.75		3.07
5R110/ TORQSHIFT	3.09	2.2	1.54	1.09/cold 1/hot	0.71		2.9
6R60/6R80	4.17	2.34	1.52	1.14	0.87	0.69	3.4
C4/C5	2.47	1.47	1				2.11
C6	2.46	1.46	1				2.18

Some transmission models made by other manufacturers have been omitted.

FIGURE 10-18 The gear ratios for Ford Motor Company transmissions and transaxles.

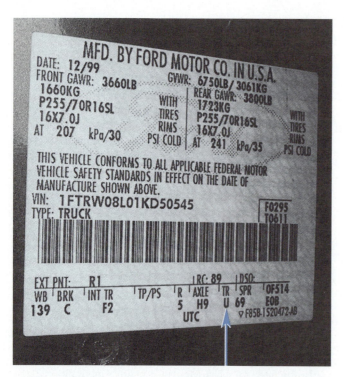

FIGURE 10-19 This body decal identifies the transmission and other important features of this vehicle. The transmission type U (arrow) indicates a 4R70W transmission.

FIGURE 10-20 A 4F50N (AX4N) transaxle can be identified by the tag attached to the top of the case, the stamping on the valve body cover, and the overall shape of the unit.

4R44E Transmission. The 4R44E transmission is the updated version of the A4LD introduced in 1986 (Figure 10-22). It is a four-speed that uses a Type 6 gear train. This is another dual gearset design that combines an overdrive unit at the front and a three-speed Simpson gearset at the rear. Electronic controls determine the shift strategy. It was used in compact pickups.

5R55E Transmission. The 5R55E transmission is essentially a stronger version of the 4R44E that uses a different electronic

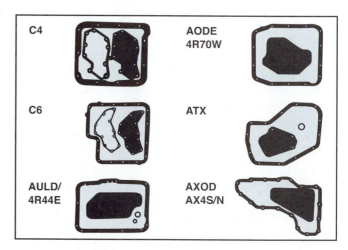

FIGURE 10-21 Many technicians use the shape of the oil pan gasket and filter to identify a transmission.

shift strategy to get the five speeds (see Table 5-8). It is currently used in compact pickups and SUVs.

4R70W Transmission. The 4R70W transmission is an updated version of the AOD that was introduced in 1980. It is a four-speed that uses a Type 12, Ravigneaux gear train. Electronic controls are used to determine the shift strategy. It is used in RWD passenger cars, midsize pickups, and SUVs (see Figure 5-40).

4R100/E4OD Transmission. The E4OD transmission was introduced in 1990 (Figure 10-23) for use in larger pickups, SUVs, and commercial vehicles. It is a four-speed unit that uses a Type 6 gear train. The dual gearset design combines an overdrive unit at the front and a three-speed gearset at the rear. Electronic controls are used to determine the shift strategy.

5R110W Transmission. This transmission is a five-speed called the "TorqShift" and is a redesigned 4R100. It was introduced in F-Series trucks and Excursions equipped with the 6.0-L diesel engine. This transmission actually has six speeds available with two different five-speed strategies. When cold, below 5°F (−15°), it will shift 1–2, 2–3, 3–4, and 4–6 (skipping fifth); when hot, it will shift 1–2, 2–3, 3–5, and 5–6 (skipping fourth). The TorqShift uses a new fluid, Mercon Sp. It is not interchangeable with other Mercon fluids.

6R60, 6R80 Transmission. This is an electronically controlled six-speed transmission. It features clutch-to-clutch shifts, with adaptive shift patterns and timing. It is a Type 13 transmission that combines one simple planetary gearset with a Ravigneaux gearset. This is a wide-ratio transmission with a 4.17:1 first gear and a 0.69:1 sixth gear for a 6.04:1 gear ratio spread. The very low first gear provides rapid starts and the two overdrive gears allow economical low engine speed when cruising. This transmission model is similar to the ZF 6HP26.

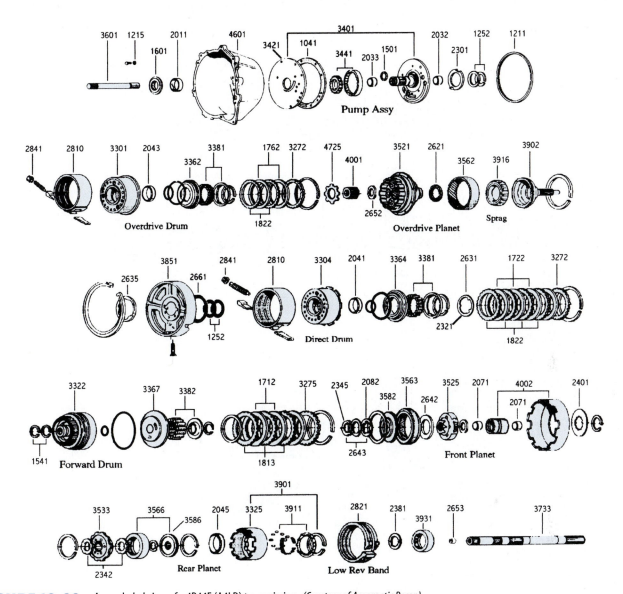

FIGURE 10-22 An exploded view of a 4R44E (A4LD) transmission. *(Courtesy of Aceomatic Recon)*

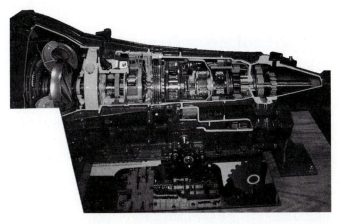

FIGURE 10-23 A cutaway view of a 4R100 (E40D) transmission. Note the mirror at the bottom showing the valve body.

FREQUENTLY ASKED QUESTION

WERE THE C3, C4, AND C5 DIFFERENT?

These transmissions were all based on the C4 transmission (Figure 10-24). They are three-speed units that use a Type 1 Simpson gear train. They were used in small and midsize passenger cars, pickups, and SUVs.

The C4 was one of the most widely used Ford transmissions. It was used in various configurations from 1964 to 1981. It was upgraded with a centrifugal lock-up torque converter and renamed the C5. The C3 was a European-built transmission used in the Pinto, Bobcat, and Capri. These transmissions were used in small and midsize passenger cars, pickups, and SUVs up to 1986.

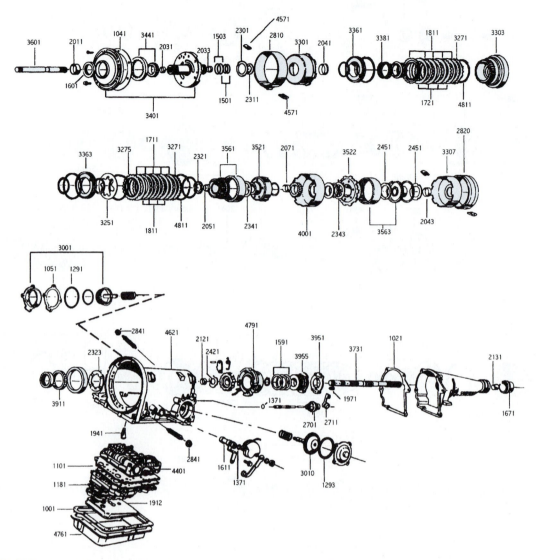

FIGURE 10-24 An exploded view of a C4 and C5 transmission. *(Courtesy of Aceomatic Recon)*

C6 Transmission. The C6 transmission was used between 1966 and 1983 (Figure 10-25). It is a three-speed unit using a Type 2 Simpson gear train. The C6 was a larger, more refined transmission than the C4 and was used in medium to large-size passenger cars, pickups, SUVs, and commercial vehicles.

JATCO L3N71B. This transmission was produced by the Japanese Automatic Transmission Company and used in Ford products between 1977 and 1980. It is a three-speed unit that uses a Type 2 Simpson gear train, similar to the C6. It was used in smaller passenger cars.

FM, FMX, HX, MX. These transmissions were also called Ford-O-Matic or Cruise-O-Matic. They were all based on a Borg-Warner transmission design and were used between 1951 and 1980. They are three-speed units that use a Type 10 Ravigneaux gear train. They were used in vehicles throughout the product line.

Two Speed. This transmission was used between 1960 and 1964. It was a two-speed unit that used a Ravigneaux gear train similar to the Type 9. It was used in the Falcon, one of the early compact passenger cars.

10.3.2 Ford Motor Company Transaxles

Ford transaxles can be identified by the vehicle's production label located on the driver's side door pillar. When the transaxle is out of the vehicle, it can be identified by a service identification tag attached to the case. The size, shape, and appearance along with the shape of its pan can be used for identification. At this time, all Ford transaxles are used with transverse engine and transaxle mounting.

4F50N/AX4N Transaxle. The 4F50N was originally named the AX4N. It is an electronically controlled version of the AXOD introduced in 1986 (see Figure 10-20). It is a four-speed

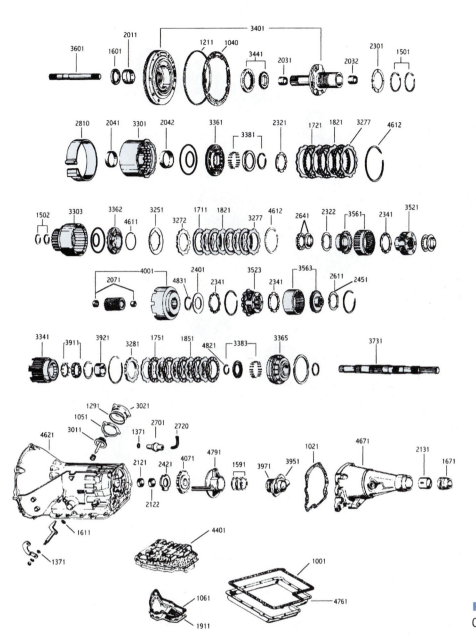

FIGURE 10-25 An exploded view of a C6 transmission. *(Courtesy of Aceomatic Recon)*

unit that uses a variation of a Type 15 gear train (Figure 10-26). The low/intermediate band of the AXOD has been replaced with a low/intermediate clutch and low/intermediate one-way clutch to make the AX4N a nonsynchronous gear train. This gives better shift feel with no hesitation between gears. Electronic controls determine the shift strategy. It is currently used in full-size, FWD cars.

AX4S Transaxle. This transaxle is another electronically controlled version of the AXOD, but it retains the low/intermediate band, making it a synchronous transmission (Figure 10-27). During the 2–3 shift, the release of the intermediate/low band must be synchronized with the application of the direct clutch. Electronic controls determine the shift strategy. The 3–4 shift also requires synchronization of the friction members. It is currently used in full-size, FWD vehicles and vans.

CD4E Transaxle. The CD4E transaxle was introduced in 1995. It is a four-speed unit that uses a Type 16 gear train. A centrally located chain and sprocket connects the transmission gearset with the final drive planetary gearset. Electronic controls are used to determine the shift strategy. It is currently used in midsize FWD vehicles (see Figure 10-3).

F4E Transaxle. The F4E is a modern version of the 4EAT transaxle. It is a four-speed unit that uses a Type 12 gear train. Electronic controls determine the shift strategy. It is used in compact, FWD cars.

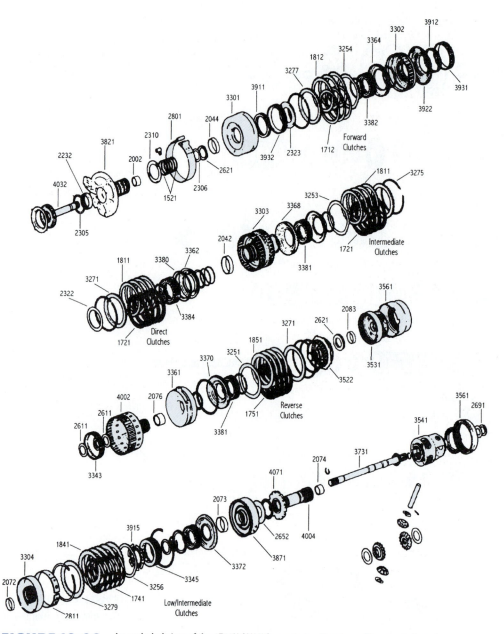

FIGURE 10-26 An exploded view of the 4F50N (AX4N) gear train. *(Courtesy of Aceomatic Recon)*

4F20E Transaxle. The 4F20E transaxle is built by JATCO. It is used in a joint-venture vehicle, the Mercury Villager van, that is coproduced with Nissan. See Section 10.8 for more information.

4F27E Transaxle. The 4F27E is a four-speed transaxle that is used in the Focus. It uses a gear train that is similar to a Type 16 gear train. Electronic controls determine the shift strategy.

6F50, 6F35. The 6F50 is the Ford version of a very compact, six-speed transaxle that was developed jointly with General Motors. About 40 parts will interchange between the 6F50 and 6T70 transaxles. The gear ratios of these transaxles range from a 4.48:1 first gear to 0.74:1 sixth gear. This gives a gear ratio spread of 6.05. They use a hyper-elliptical torque converter and an offset, chain-driven pump to help shorten the overall length. The gear train uses three simple planetary sets that have the carriers and ring gears interconnected. The transmission module is located inside the transmission, where it has a contact temperature sink in a controlled environment. It has adaptive shift controls, and the driver has the option of tap-up/tap-down shift control.

The 6F35 is a smaller version designed for use with the 2.5 l I-4 and 3.0 l V-6 engines.

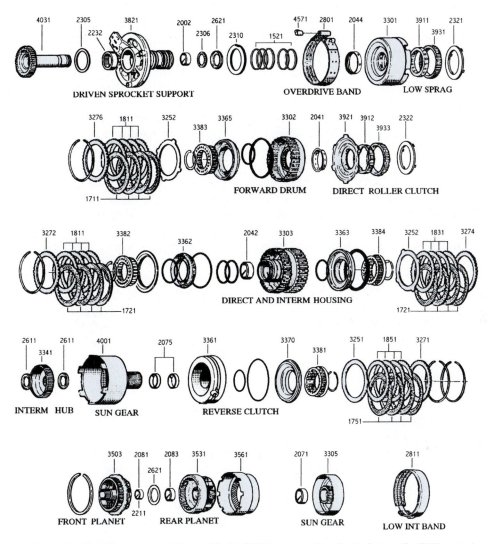

FIGURE 10-27   An exploded view of the Ford AX4S gear train. Note the similarity to the AX4N gear train with the addition of a low sprag and a direct roller clutch. *(Courtesy of Aceomatic Recon)*

ATX Transaxle. The ATX three-speed transaxle was used in compact cars from 1981 to 1997. Power was transmitted through a Type 10 Ravigneaux gear train. The ATX was first built using a unique planetary torque converter that split the gearset input between hydraulic and mechanical connections. Later units used conventional and centrifugal lock-up converters.

10.4 GENERAL MOTORS CORPORATION

Like other manufacturers, General Motors uses transmissions produced in various parts of the world, and supplies other manufacturers with General Motors transmissions. The most notable are Rolls Royce and Jaguar.

FREQUENTLY ASKED QUESTION

WHAT IS A HYDRAMATIC?

General Motors has traditionally used the terms *Hydramatic,* or **Turbo Hydra-Matic (THM)** for its automatic transmissions. The Hydramatic transmission was the first mass produced automatic transmission for passenger cars; it went into production in 1939 to be introduced in the 1940 Oldsmobiles.

General Motors previously identified its transmissions as Turbo Hydra-Matic (THM) followed by an alphanumeric code that described the relative size of the unit. Currently, General Motors uses an alphanumeric model designation system, introduced in the mid-1980s, as follows:

1st character: Number of speeds
2nd character: L = Longitudinal, T = Transverse, M = Manual
3rd character: Relative torque capacity, 10 = smallest
Optional digit: A = AWD, E = Electronic, HD = Heavy duty

Detailed descriptions of each General Motors transmission and how it operates are available in the manufacturer's service information, transmission service manuals, and trade publications. The gear ratios for General Motors transmissions and transaxles are shown in Figure 10-28.

10.4.1 General Motors Rear Wheel Drive Transmissions

General Motors has produced many different automatic transmissions. Six popular, out-of-production transmissions will also be described in this text. General Motors transmissions can be identified by the identification tag on the vehicle. When the transmission is out of the vehicle, it can be identified by a service identification tag attached to the case (Figure 10-29). The size, shape, and appearance of the case and the shape of the pan also can be used to identify a unit (Figure 10-30).

3L30 Transmission. The 3L30 is a three-speed, relatively low-torque-capacity unit that uses a Type 11 Ravigneaux gear train (see Figure 5-35B). The 3L30 was formerly called a THM 180 or THM 180C if it had a lock-up torque converter (Figure 10-31). It is used in small RWD SUVs.

4L30-E Transmission. The 4L30-E is a four-speed dual planetary design that combines a Type 11 gear train with an overdrive unit at the front (see Figure 5-42). This combination is similar to Types 6, 7, and 8 transmissions, but it uses a Ravigneaux (Type 11) gear train. It uses electronic shift controls and is currently used in various RWD vehicles. The Cadillac XLR uses the 5L50E adapted from the 4L30-E and 5L40E.

4L60-E Transmission. The 4L60-E is a four-speed, electronically controlled transmission that uses a Type 13 gear train. It was formerly called a THM 700-R4 or M30 (Figure 10-32). It is currently used in the F- and Y-cars (Camaro and Corvette) as well as pickups, SUVs, and RWD vans. The low first gear and overdrive fourth gear have made this transmission popular with hot-rodders. The 4L65 is a renamed version of a 4L60E HD.

4L80-E Transmission. The 4L80-E is a four-speed dual planetary design that combines a three-speed gear train (3L80) with an overdrive unit at the front (Figure 10-33). The gear train used is similar to a Type 4 Simpson gear train. The four-speed combination is similar to Types 6, 7, and 8 transmissions, but it uses the different rear unit. The 4L80-E was formerly called the MT1 or THM R2. It uses electronic shift controls and is currently used in pickups, SUVs, and light trucks.

TRANSAXLE GEAR RATIOS							
Model	First	Second	Third	Fourth	Fifth	Sixth	Reverse
3T40	2.84	1.6	1				2.07
4T40	2.96	1.626	1	0.681			2.13
4T60, 4T65E	2.921	1.568	1	0.705			2.38
4T80E	2.96	1.626	1	0.681			2.13
6T70, 6T75	4.48	2.87	1.84	1.41	1	0.74	2.88
AF33-5	4.69	2.94	1.92	1.3	1		3.18
TRANSMISSION GEAR RATIOS							
3L30, 3L80	2.4	1.48	1				2.0
4L30-E	2.4/2.86	1.48/1.62	1	0.723			2.0
4L60E/4L65E	3.059	1.625	1	0.696			2.29
4L80E/4L85E	2.482	1.482	1	0.75			2.08
5L40E/5L50E	3.46	2.21	1.59	1	0.76		3.03
6L45/6L50	4.06	2.37	1.55	1.16	0.85	0.67	3.2
6L80/6L90	4.02	2.36	1.53	1.15	0.85	0.67	3.06
ALLISON 1000	3.1	1.18	1.41	1	0.71		4.49
HM 200	2.74	1.57	1				2.07
HM 200-4R	2.74	1.57	1	0.67			2.07
HM 350	2.52	1.52	1				1.93
HM 400	2.48	1.48	1				2.08

FIGURE 10-28 The gear ratios for General Motors transmissions.

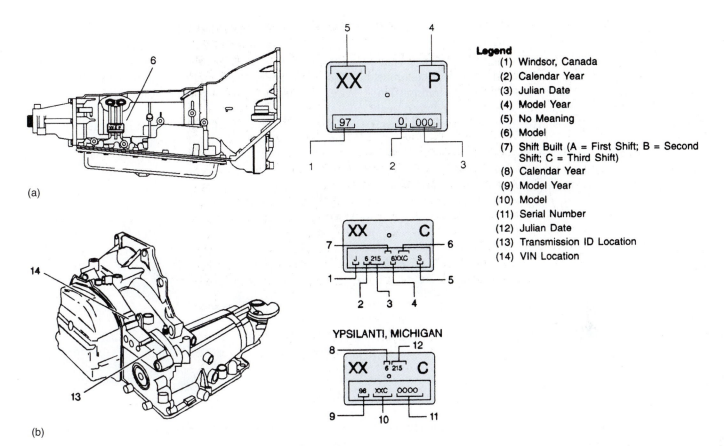

Legend
(1) Windsor, Canada
(2) Calendar Year
(3) Julian Date
(4) Model Year
(5) No Meaning
(6) Model
(7) Shift Built (A = First Shift; B = Second Shift; C = Third Shift)
(8) Calendar Year
(9) Model Year
(10) Model
(11) Serial Number
(12) Julian Date
(13) Transmission ID Location
(14) VIN Location

YPSILANTI, MICHIGAN

FIGURE 10-29 General Motors transmissions (a) and transaxles (b) can be identified by a label or tag on the case. *(Reprinted with permission of General Motors)*

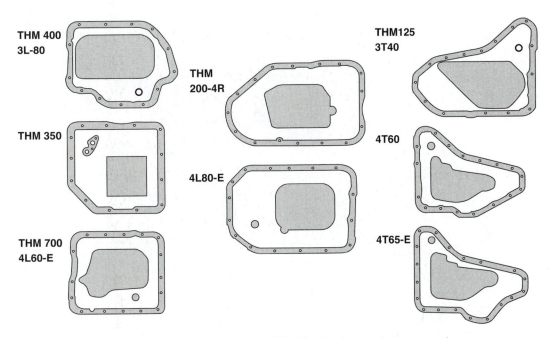

THM 400
3L-80

THM 350

THM 700
4L60-E

THM
200-4R

4L80-E

THM125
3T40

4T60

4T65-E

FIGURE 10-30 The shape of the pan gasket can be used for a general identification of a transmission or transaxle.

THM 200, THM 200C, THM 325 Transmissions.

These are three-speed transmissions that use a Type 2 Simpson gear train. The THM 200 was used from 1976 to 1987 in compact to midsize cars. Later versions that used a lock-up torque converter used the THM 200C designation. This transmission was the first unit built in the United States with stamped steel clutch drums, sintered/powdered iron one-way clutch races, and metric dimensions.

The THM 325 used the same gear train in a manner similar to the THM 425 (see Figure 10-6). It was longitudinal mounted alongside of the engine, and was combined with a hypoid final drive assembly and used in FWD cars. A chain and sprocket assembly coupled the torque converter to the transmission input shaft. With the exception of the pan covering the chain and sprockets, the THM 325 appears identical to the THM 325-4L (see Figure 10-35). The THM 325-4L has a much deeper pan to enclose the overdrive unit.

THM 200-4R, THM 325-4L Transmissions.

The THM 200-4R is a Type 7 four-speed transmission used in a dual-unit

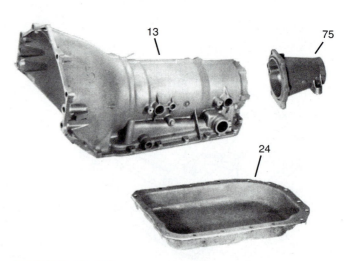

FIGURE 10-33   4L80E transmission. *(Courtesy of Slauson Transmission Parts, www.slauson.com)*

FIGURE 10-31   A 3L30 transmission. *(Courtesy of Slauson Transmission Parts, www.slauson.com)*

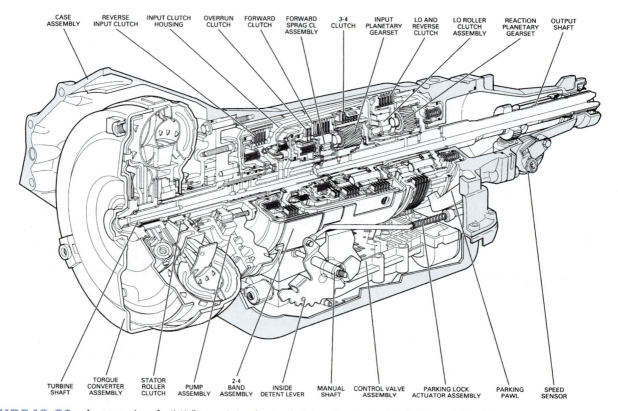

FIGURE 10-32   A cutaway view of a 4L60-E transmission showing the internal parts. *(Reprinted with permission of General Motors)*

design that combined a Type 2 gearset with an overdrive planetary at the front (see Figure 5-26). It was used from 1981 to 1990 in smaller and midsize vehicles (Figure 10-34).

The THM 325-4L is the FWD version of the THM 200-4R (Figure 10-35). It is similar to the THM 325 with an overdrive unit located at the torque converter output. In all gears but fourth, the drive chain transfers power at a 1:1 ratio. In fourth gear, power is transferred at an overdrive ratio.

THM 250, THM 250C Transmissions.
The THM 250 is a three-speed, Type 2, Simpson gear train transmission that is a light-duty version of the THM 350 (see Figure 10-36). A band is used for the second gear reaction member, making the THM 250 have a synchronous 2–3 shift. A THM 250 transmission can be identified by the exterior band adjustment. It was used in the early 1970s in inexpensive vehicles. The THM 250C uses a lock-up torque converter.

THM 350, THM 350C, THM 375B Transmissions.
These are three-speed transmissions that use a Type 3 Simpson gear train (Figure 10-36). They have a nonsynchronous 2–3 shift because an intermediate roller clutch is used for second gear (see Figure 4-22). Later versions with a lock-up torque converter used the THM 350C designation. The THM 375B was a heavy-duty version with increased clutch pack capacity. At one time, there were more THM 350s on the road than any other automatic transmission.

3L80, THM 400, THM 375, THM 425 Transmissions.
These three-speed transmissions use a similar gear train to the Type 4 (Figure 10-37). Like the 4L80-E, the Simpson gear train is turned end-for-end. This transmission was used from 1964 to

FIGURE 10-35   A THM 325 transmission. A 325-4L will have a larger chain cover to enclose the overdrive gearset. *(Courtesy of Slauson Transmission Parts, www.slauson.com)*

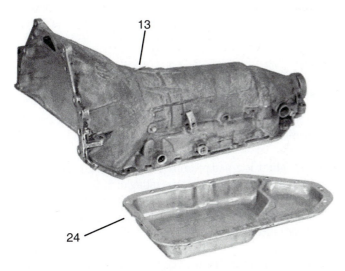

FIGURE 10-34   A THM 200-4R transmission. It has the appearance of a stretch THM 200C. *(Courtesy of Slauson Transmission Parts, www.slauson.com)*

FIGURE 10-36   A THM 350C transmission. The similar THM 250C has a band adjustment screw in the other side (right) of the case. *(Courtesy of Slauson Transmission Parts, www.slauson.com)*

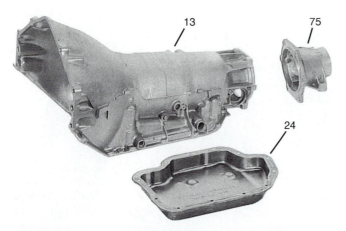

FIGURE 10-37 A 3L80 (THM 400) transmission. *(Courtesy of Slauson Transmission Parts, www.slauson.com)*

1990 in larger passenger cars, pickups, vans, and light trucks. The TH-375 was a light-duty version using smaller clutch packs.

The THM 425 version of this transmission was combined with a final drive assembly and used in FWD cars (see Figure 10-6). A chain and sprocket assembly was used to couple the torque converter to the transmission input shaft.

Two-Mode Hybrid Transmission. This transmission, also called the 2ML70, was developed for full-size hybrid cars, SUVs, and pickup in cooperation with Chrysler Corporation and BMW. It includes two 60 kilowatt, three phase, 300 volt motors, four multidisc clutches, and three simple planetary gearsets. These produce four fixed gear ratios: First: 3.69:1, Second: 1.7:1, Third: 1:1, and Fourth: 0.74:1 and two variable ratios: EVT Mode 1: infinity to 1.7:1 and EVT Mode 2: 1.7:1 to 0.74:1. A torque-dampener is used in place of a torque converter.

6L80E Transmission. This is an electronically controlled six-speed transmission. It features clutch-to-clutch shifts, with adaptive shift patterns and timing. It is a Type 13 transmission that combines one simple planetary gearset with a Ravigneaux gearset. This is a wide-ratio transmission with a 4.03:1 first gear and a 0.67:1 sixth gear for a 6.04:1 gear ratio spread. The very low first gear provides rapid starts, and the two overdrive gears allow economical low engine speed when cruising. The transmission module is located inside the transmission; it is attached to the control solenoid assembly for temperature control. It has adaptive shift controls, and the driver has the option of tap-up/tap-down shift control.

6L50E Transmission. This transmission is a smaller, lighter version of the 6L80E.

Allison 1000 and 2000 Transmissions. Allison produces medium- and heavy-duty transmissions used in many trucks, busses, and various types of off-highway vehicles. The 1000 and 2000 series transmissions are used in some General

(a)

(b)

FIGURE 10-38 This Allison transmission has an external fluid filter and plates covering the areas where a power take-off (PTO) can be mounted.

Allison Transmission Gear Ratios

Gear	1000	2000
1st	3.10:1	3.51:1
2nd	1.81:1	1:90:1
3rd	1.41:1	1:44:1
4th	1:1	1:1
5th	0.71:1	0.74:1
Reverse	4.49:1	5.09:1

FIGURE 10-39 The gear ratios for Allison 1000 and 2000 transmissions.

Motors light trucks and pickups (Figure 10-38). These are five-speed units with an input torque rating of 520 ft-lb (705 N-m) of torque. They have a screw-on fluid filter, much like an engine oil filter, and mounting pads for a power take-off (PTO). The gear ratios are shown in Figure 10-39.

Ravigneaux Gear Train. The Powerglide was used only by Chevrolet and was produced in two versions: a cast-iron-case unit from 1950 to 1960 and a redesigned, aluminum-case unit

from 1960 to 1973 (see Figure 5-33). The TH 300 was used by other divisions from 1964 to 1969 in smaller cars. The lightweight aluminum case and its simplicity make this unit popular for racing applications.

The Powerglide was built into a transaxle that was used in the 1960 and later Corvairs and Pontiac Tempests, making it the first domestic automatic transaxle.

10.4.2 General Motors Transaxles

With the exception of the THM 325, THM 325-4L, and THM 425 transmissions used from 1966 to 1985, all FWD transaxles are used with a transverse-mounted engine.

With each of the transaxles, the valve body, which contains the pump, is located in the upper pan at the left end of the transaxle. Most of these units use a variable-displacement vane pump.

Currently, General Motors has five transaxles in production. When the transaxle is out of the vehicle, it can be identified by a service identification tag attached to the case. Like other units, the size, shape, and appearance of the case and the shape of the pan can be used for identification (see Figures 10-29 and 10-30).

3T40 Transaxle. The 3T40 is a three-speed transaxle that uses a Type 2 Simpson gear train. The 3T40 was formerly called a THM 125, M34, THM 125C, HM3T40, or MD9 transaxle and was introduced in 1980 for the X-body car line (Citation). The transmission section is similar to that of a THM 200 transmission with a chain and sprocket assembly connecting the torque converter to the transmission input (Figure 10-40). It was used with four-cylinder engines in the J-cars (Cavalier and Sunfire).

4T40-E Transaxle. The 4T40-E is a four-speed transaxle that uses a gear train that is similar to the Type 16. The appearance is similar to a 4T60 and 4T65-E (see Figure 10-41). It uses electronic controls for shift timing and quality. It is currently used with four-cylinder engines in the J- and N-car lines (Cavalier and Malibu).

4T60-E Transaxle. The 4T60-E is a four-speed transaxle that uses a Type 16 gear train (Figure 10-41). The 4T60-E was formerly called a THM 440 or M13. It is currently used with the smaller V6 engine in the N-car, W-car, and U-body van (Malibu, Grand Prix, and Venture).

4T65-E Transaxle. The 4T65-E is a redesigned version of the 4T60-E and uses the Type 16 gear train. Upgrades were made to the case, second gear, and torque converter to improve durability and performance. It uses advanced electronic controls allowing the PCM to control line pressure. It is used in the larger V6 engines in the G-, H-, and W-cars (Riviera, Le Sabre, and Grand Prix).

4T80-E Transaxle. The 4T80-E is a four-speed unit that uses a gear train that is similar to the Type 16. It uses full electronic controls (Figure 10-42). The 4T80-E uses three pumps to move fluid. A primary gerotor pump supplies fluid for the basic needs of the transaxle, and a secondary gerotor pump helps meet demands for fluid pressure during shifts. The third pump is a scavenger, gear-type pump that is used to move fluid from the bottom pan to the side cover. All three pumps are mounted at the valve body and are driven by a drive shaft from the torque converter. The 4T80-E is used with high-torque engines found in the E-, G-, and K-cars (Eldorado, Aurora, Seville, Concours, and Deville).

6T70 and 75. The 6T70 is the General Motors version of a very compact, six-speed transaxle that was developed jointly with Ford. About 40 parts will interchange between the 6T70 and 6F50 transaxles. The gear ratios of these transaxles range from a 4.48:1 first gear to 0.74:1 sixth gear. This gives a gear ratio spread of 6.05. The 6T75 is a high-torque, 300-lb-ft version of the 6T70 (280 lb-ft). It uses a hyper-elliptical torque converter and an offset, chain-driven pump to help shorten the overall length. The gear train uses three simple planetary sets that have the carriers and ring gears interconnected. The transmission module is located inside the transmission, where it has a contact temperature sink in a controlled environment.

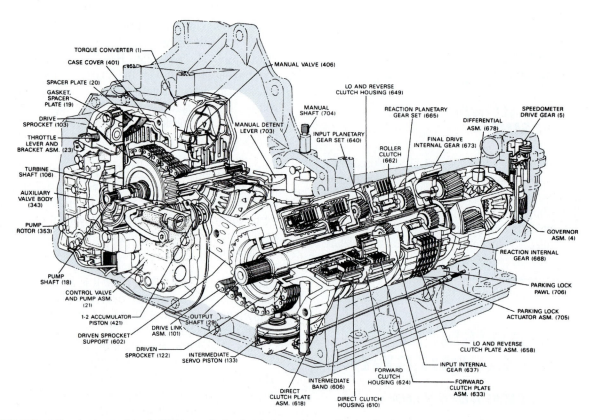

FIGURE 10-40 A cutaway view of a 3T40 transaxle showing the internal parts. *(Reprinted with permission of General Motors)*

It has adaptive shift controls, and the driver has the option of tap-up/tap-down shift control.

10.5 SATURN TRANSAXLE

Saturn began as an independent division of General Motors, and these vehicles use a FWD transverse engine and transaxle of their own design. This transaxle is called the TAAT. It is an electronically controlled, Type 19, nonplanetary gear train, similar to the transaxle used in Hondas (see Figure 5-65). Year 2000 and later Saturn vehicles use General Motors transaxles.

10.6 IMPORT TRANSMISSIONS/ TRANSAXLES

The transmissions and transaxles used in import vehicles are very similar to the domestic units. They use planetary gears (with the exception of the Honda transaxles), multiple-disc clutches, bands, one-way clutches, hydraulic control systems, and lock-up torque converters. A detailed description of their operation is normally available in the manufacturer's service manual, transmission service manuals, and trade publications.

In some cases, the import vehicle manufacturer will design and build its own transmissions, much like the domestic manufacturers. In other cases, they use units built by another manufacturer, such as Aisin-Seiki, Aisin-Warner, JATCO, or ZF. These companies are typically subsidiaries of major manufacturers; for example, Toyota owns a large share of both Aisin-Warner and Aisin-Seiki. These two companies build transmissions for Toyota and other Asian and American companies. Companies that have used these transmissions include Chrysler, General Motors, Isuzu, Mitsubishi, Subaru, and Suzuki.

The Japanese Automatic Transmission Company (JATCO) is jointly owned by Mazda and Nissan. JATCO builds transmissions for Asian, American, and European companies such as BMW, Chrysler, Ford, Infinity, Isuzu, Mitsubishi, Nissan, Subaru, and Suzuki.

Zahnradfabrik Friedrichshafen (ZF) is a German transmission manufacturer that builds transmissions for many high-end vehicle manufacturers (Figure 10-43). Some companies that have used or are currently using ZF transmissions are Alfa Romeo, Audi, BMW, Chrysler, Citroen, Ford, Jaguar, Peugot, Porsche, Range Rover, Saab, and Volvo.

There are too many import transmissions to describe in a book of this type. We will limit the description to the three most popular vehicle manufacturers. The transmissions that are most commonly encountered by technicians are those used in Honda, Nissan, and Toyota vehicles. A brief description of the more common units follows.

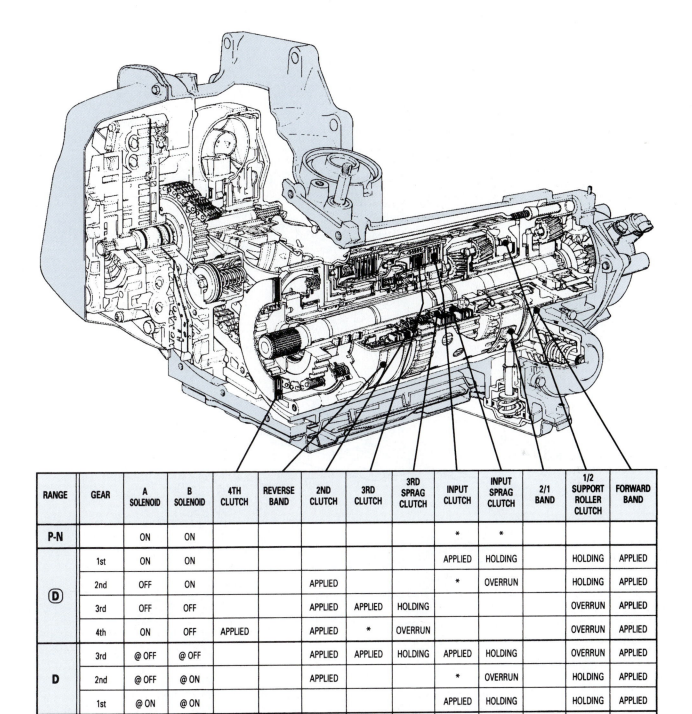

RANGE	GEAR	A SOLENOID	B SOLENOID	4TH CLUTCH	REVERSE BAND	2ND CLUTCH	3RD CLUTCH	3RD SPRAG CLUTCH	INPUT CLUTCH	INPUT SPRAG CLUTCH	2/1 BAND	1/2 SUPPORT ROLLER CLUTCH	FORWARD BAND
P-N		ON	ON						*	*			
Ⓓ	1st	ON	ON						APPLIED	HOLDING		HOLDING	APPLIED
	2nd	OFF	ON			APPLIED			*	OVERRUN		HOLDING	APPLIED
	3rd	OFF	OFF			APPLIED	APPLIED	HOLDING				OVERRUN	APPLIED
	4th	ON	OFF	APPLIED		APPLIED	*	OVERRUN				OVERRUN	APPLIED
D	3rd	@ OFF	@ OFF			APPLIED	APPLIED	HOLDING	APPLIED	HOLDING		OVERRUN	APPLIED
	2nd	@ OFF	@ ON			APPLIED			*	OVERRUN		HOLDING	APPLIED
	1st	@ ON	@ ON						APPLIED	HOLDING		HOLDING	APPLIED
2	2nd	@ OFF	@ ON			APPLIED			*	OVERRUN	APPLIED	HOLDING	APPLIED
	1st	@ ON	@ ON						APPLIED	HOLDING	APPLIED	HOLDING	APPLIED
1	1st	@ ON	@ ON				APPLIED	HOLDING	APPLIED	HOLDING	APPLIED	HOLDING	APPLIED
R	REVERSE	ON	ON		APPLIED				APPLIED	HOLDING			

* APPLIED BUT NOT EFFECTIVE

ON = SOLENOID ENEGERIZED
OFF = SOLENOID DE-ENEGERIZED

@ THE SOLENOID'S STATE FOLLOWS A SHIFT PATTERN WHICH DEPENDS UPON VEHICLE SPEED, THROTTLE POSITION AND SELECTED GEAR RANGE.

FIGURE 10-41 A cutaway view of a 4T60-E transaxle showing the control devices. *(Reprinted with permission of General Motors)*

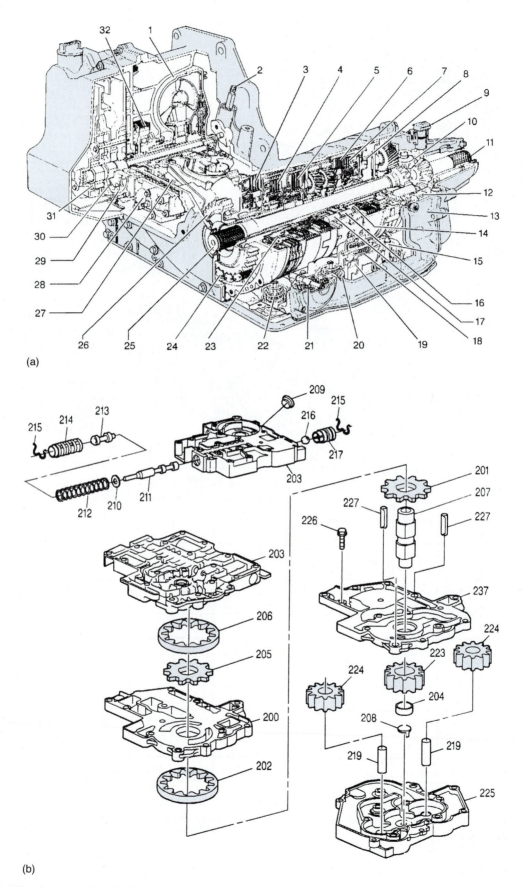

(a)

(b)

FIGURE 10-42   A cutaway view of a 4T80-E transaxle showing the internal parts (a) and an exploded view of the pump (b) showing the primary pump (200 and 201), secondary pump (205 and 206), and the scavenge pump (223 and 224). *(Reprinted with permission of General Motors)*

FIGURE 10-43 The 6HP26 transmission is the first six-speed automatic transmission produced for passenger cars. *(Courtesy of ZF Group North American Operations)*

10.7 HONDA/ACURA

Honda produces the transmissions used in Honda and Acura vehicles. These units do not use planetary gears like most other automatic transmissions; they use constant-mesh, helical gears like those in a standard transmission. Hydraulically operated multiple-disc clutches are used in place of the synchronizer assemblies of a standard transmission.

The early Honda transaxles were two-speed units (1973 to 1980), then three-speed (used from 1981 to 1985), and now four-speed units (since 1983). Honda transaxles are coded to specific vehicles by a small tag on the side of the transmission case. A two-part number is used, with the first part being the transmission model number and the second part being the serial number. The model number should always be used when purchasing parts or locating service information; it can also be used to match a transaxle to a vehicle (Figure 10-44).

10.7.1 Honda Three-Speed Transaxles

Honda three-speed transaxles were used in the 1981 to 1985 Civic and 1979 to 1982 Accord. These units have two parallel shafts: the mainshaft and the countershaft (Figure 10-45). The mainshaft is inline with the crankshaft, and the countershaft provides the output to the final drive and differential. The gears on the mainshaft and countershaft are in constant mesh. Three clutches are used, one for each of the gear ranges. For first gear, the first clutch applies to lock first gear to the mainshaft to drive the first countershaft gear. Second and third gears are very similar, but use gears of different sizes for the higher ratios. All shifts are hydraulic and have to be carefully synchronized. One clutch must be released as the next clutch is applied.

An idler gear is used to obtain reverse. Reverse is achieved by engaging the reverse selector mechanically and applying the reverse clutch.

10.7.2 Honda Four-Speed Transaxles

A variety of four-speed units have been produced in both transverse and longitudinal models. Their operation is very similar to the three-speed transmissions with an additional pair of gears along with another clutch for fourth gear. A lock-up torque converter clutch was used, with the exception of the 1983 Prelude. These units are commonly identified by the number of clutches and shafts used in the unit. For ease of discussion, they will be grouped into two-shaft and three-shaft versions.

Two-Shaft Versions. These four-speed transaxles, like the three-speed unit, have the mainshaft inline with the engine crankshaft and a countershaft connected to the final drive and differential (Figure 10-46). The first, second, and fourth clutches are mounted on the mainshaft, and the second clutch is mounted on the countershaft. A one-way clutch under first gear is also on the countershaft. This one-way clutch allows first gear to drive the countershaft in first gear. When the transmission shifts into second, third, or fourth gear, the one-way clutch overruns.

Three-Shaft Versions. There are two variations of this design: a short shaft and a full shaft.

The short-shaft variation has an additional subshaft with a first-hold clutch for a total of five clutches (Figure 10-47). These provide a means to hold the transmission in manual-low for compression braking. The first-hold clutch is applied only in manual-1.

A second design, short-shaft variation, uses four clutches, and second gear is mounted on the short subshaft (Figure 10-48). This transaxle does not have a manual-1 gear selector position; manual-2 is the lowest manual range available. First gear is mounted on a one-way clutch so it will overrun in all of the higher gears and during deceleration.

The full-shaft variations have three parallel shafts. The mainshaft is the power input from the engine and is inline with the crankshaft. The countershaft is the output to the final drive and differential, and the secondary shaft is parallel to the other two shafts (Figure 10-49). The third and fourth clutches and third, fourth, and reverse gears are on the mainshaft. The countershaft has gears for first, second, third, fourth, and reverse along with idler gears and park gear. The secondary shift has the first and second clutches along with first, second, and idler gears. The latest versions of these transaxles use electronic shaft controls to improve shift quality and transaxle durability.

10.7.3 Honda Longitudinal Designs

These transaxles are used in the Acura product line. They are two-shaft designs with the mainshaft in line with the engine crankshaft. The countershaft is below the mainshaft and

TRANSAXLE GEAR RATIOS						
Model	First	Second	Third	Fourth	Fifth	Reverse
4-SPEED	2.61	1.55	1.02	0.68		1.91
	2.68	1.54	1.08	0.74		2.0
	2.72	1.52	0.98	0.67		1.95
5-SPEED	2.56	1.55	1.02	0.73	0.52	1.85
	2.65	1.52	1.04	0.74	0.57	2.0
	2.69	1.56	1.02/1.07	0.73/0.69	0.53/0.48	1.89
	2.7	1.57	1.07	0.69	0.48	1.89
	2.7	1.61	1.07	0.77	0.54	1.89

FIGURE 10-44 The gear ratios for the current-model Honda and Acura automatic transaxles.

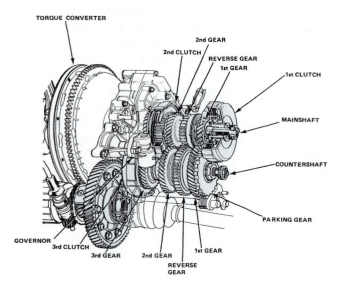

FIGURE 10-45 This Honda three-speed gearset shows the arrangement of the gears and controlling clutches. *(Courtesy of America Honda Motor Company)*

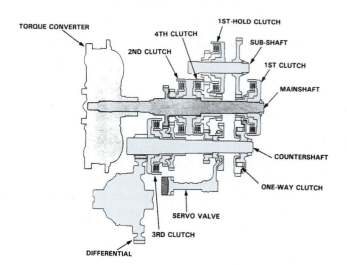

FIGURE 10-47 A cutaway view of a short-shaft version of a three-shaft, four-speed Honda transaxle that uses five clutches. *(Courtesy of America Honda Motor Company)*

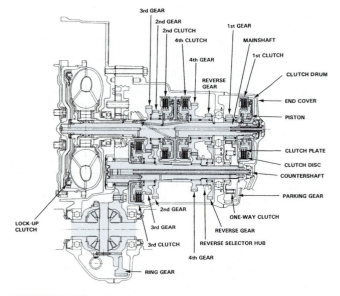

FIGURE 10-46 A cutaway view of a two-shaft, four-speed Honda transaxle. *(Courtesy of America Honda Motor Company)*

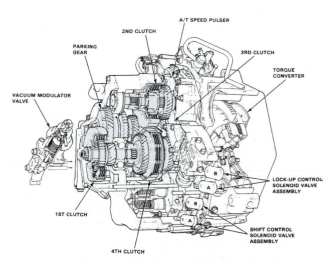

FIGURE 10-48 A cutaway view of a short-shaft version of a three-shaft, four-speed Honda transaxle that used four clutches. *(Courtesy of America Honda Motor Company)*

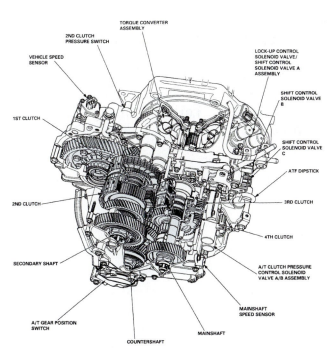

FIGURE 10-49   A cutaway view of a long-shaft version of a three-shaft, four-speed Honda transaxle that uses four clutches. *(Courtesy of America Honda Motor Company)*

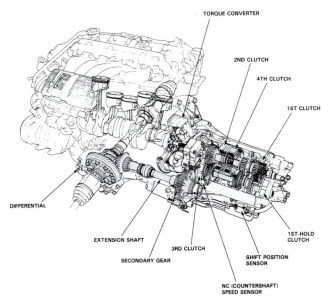

FIGURE 10-50   A longitudinal, two-shaft, four-speed Honda transaxle that uses five clutches. *(Courtesy of America Honda Motor Company)*

transfers power through the secondary gears to the extension shaft that drives the hypoid ring and pinion final drive gears at the differential (Figure 10-50).

There are two versions of this unit. The five-clutch version has clutches for first, second, third, fourth, and first-hold. The hydraulically operated servo moves the reverse gear into

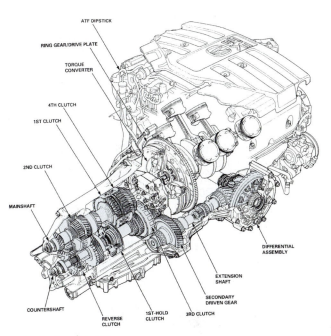

FIGURE 10-51   A longitudinal, two-shaft, four-speed Honda transaxle that uses six clutches. *(Courtesy of America Honda Motor Company)*

position, similar to the transverse transaxles. The six-clutch version has a clutch for first, second, third, and reverse plus first-hold for manual-1 (Figure 10-51).

10.8 NISSAN

JATCO is the major supplier of Nissan transmissions. Like other manufacturers, Nissan has used several different coding systems (Figure 10-52). The latest system uses a seven-character, alphanumeric system:

1st letter: E = Electronic TCC, L = Hydraulic TCC, and R = Remote shift
2nd letter: E = Electronic control, L = Hydraulic TCC, and N = Nissan (JATCO trans.)
1st digit: Number of forward speeds
3rd letter: F = Front wheel drive (FWD), R = RWD
2nd and 3rd digits: Transmission style/unit
4th/final letter: Series A = First version, B = Second, and so on; can be V = Viscous coupling in the differential

10.8.1 Nissan RWD Transmissions

The JATCO/Nissan four-speed transmissions use a dual planetary gear train. The SUV Pathfinder and pickups use the smaller RE4R01A (Figure 10-53). 4WD versions are connected to a transfer case, and 2WD versions use a drive shaft for the rear axle. The Infiniti Q45 uses a larger RE4R03A that has four-gear planetary assemblies.

Transaxle Gear Ratios						
Model	First	Second	Third	Fourth	Fifth	Reverse
RE4F04A, B, V & W	2.785	1.545	1	0.694		2.27
RL4F03A, B & V	2.861	1.562	1	0.697		2.23
RE5F22A	4.657	3.032	1.982	1.341	1.018	5.11
Transmission Gear Ratios						
RE4R01A/ RE4R04A/ RL4R01A	2.785	1.545	1	0.694		NA
RE5R05A	3.827	2.368	1.519	1	0.834	2.61
	3.540	2.264	1.417	1	0.834	
	3.84	2.35	1.53	1	0.834	2.76

FIGURE 10-52   The gear ratios for Nissan transaxles and transmissions.

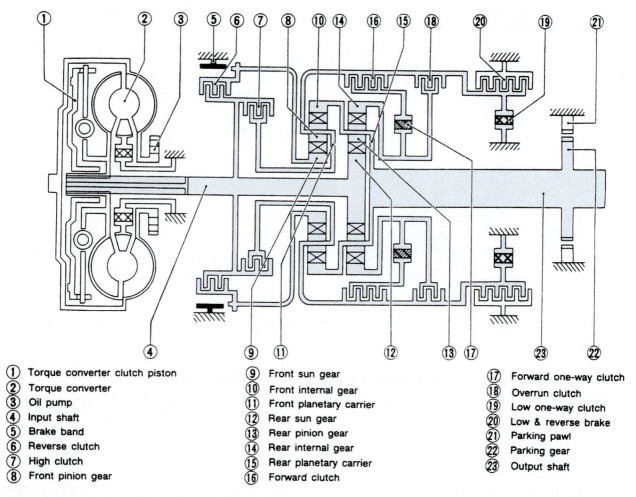

① Torque converter clutch piston	⑨ Front sun gear	⑰ Forward one-way clutch
② Torque converter	⑩ Front internal gear	⑱ Overrun clutch
③ Oil pump	⑪ Front planetary carrier	⑲ Low one-way clutch
④ Input shaft	⑫ Rear sun gear	⑳ Low & reverse brake
⑤ Brake band	⑬ Rear pinion gear	㉑ Parking pawl
⑥ Reverse clutch	⑭ Rear internal gear	㉒ Parking gear
⑦ High clutch	⑮ Rear planetary carrier	㉓ Output shaft
⑧ Front pinion gear	⑯ Forward clutch	

FIGURE 10-53   A schematic view of a Nissan RE4R01A four-speed transmission gearset, torque converter, and apply devices. *(Courtesy of Nissan North America, Inc.)*

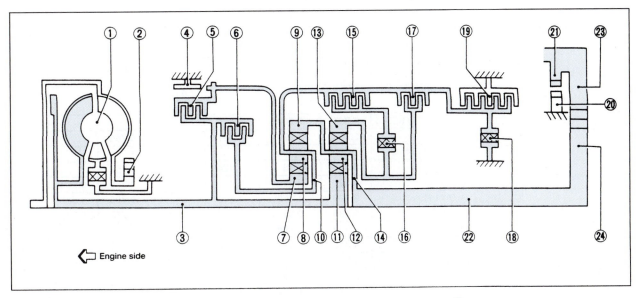

◀ Engine side

① Torque converter	⑨ Front internal gear	⑰ Overrun clutch
② Oil pump	⑩ Front planetary carrier	⑱ Low one-way clutch
③ Input shaft	⑪ Rear sun gear	⑲ Low & reverse brake
④ Brake band	⑫ Rear pinion gear	⑳ Parking pawl
⑤ Reverse clutch	⑬ Rear internal gear	㉑ Parking gear
⑥ High clutch	⑭ Rear planetary carrier	㉒ Output shaft
⑦ Front sun gear	⑮ Forward clutch	㉓ Idle gear
⑧ Front pinion gear	⑯ Forward one-way clutch	㉔ Output gear

FIGURE 10-54   A schematic view of a Nissan RE4F02 four-speed transaxle gearset, torque converter, and apply devices. *(Courtesy of Nissan North America, Inc.)*

10.8.2 Nissan FWD Transaxles

The JATCO/Nissan four-speed transaxles also use a dual planetary gear train (Figure 10-54). The major difference is the transaxle output to the final drive gears and differential. The RE4F02, 03A, 03B, and 04A series transaxles are in current production.

10.9 TOYOTA

Toyota has used a variety of transmissions beginning with the two-speed Toyoglide. It was replaced with three- and then four-speed designs. Most of these designs are very similar. Toyota seems to have a large number of different models, because the case might have been changed to suit a particular vehicle model or the hydraulic or electronic shift controls may have been changed (Figure 10-55).

Toyota uses an alphanumeric coding system to identify the various models and configurations as follows:

1st character: Transmission type: A = Automatic
2nd character: Transmission family
3rd character: Family generation

This system was modified to add another digit plus a suffix. The current system is as follows:

1st character: Transmission type: A = Automatic
2nd character digit: Transmission family
3rd character digit: Number of forward speeds
4th character digit: Family generation

Suffix: D = Overdrive, E = Electronic, F = Four wheel drive/mechanical transfer case, H = Four wheel drive/electronic transfer case, L = Lock-up converter, I = Intelligence

A typical transmission code of A140E tells us that it is an automatic transmission. It is family number 1. It is a four-speed that uses electronic controls.

Toyota transmissions can be divided into transverse and longitudinal drive arrangements:

Transverse series (all FWD): A130, A140, A240, and A540
Longitudinal series: A20, A30, A40, A340

10.9.1 Toyota RWD Transmissions

The A20 and A30 were early Toyota automatic transmissions used in the 1950s and 1960s. The A20 is a two-speed Ravigneaux unit similar to a Type 9 gear train. The A30 is

TRANSAXLE GEAR RATIOS							
Model	First	Second	Third	Fourth	Fifth	Sixth	Reverse
A131/132	2.81	1.549	1				2.296
A140E/240E	2.81	1.549	1	0.706			2.977
A242L/245E/241E	3.643	2.008	1.296	0.892			2.977
A244E/246E	4.005	2.208	1.425	0.981			3.272
A350E	2.804	1.978	1.531	1	0.705		2.393
A540E/541E	2.81	1.549	1	0.73			2.296
A650E	3.357	2.18	1.424	1	0.753		3.431
A760H	3.52	2.042	1.4	1	0.716	0.586	3.224
A761E	3.296	1.958	1.348	1	0.725	0.582	2.951
A960E	3.538	2.06	1.404	1	0.713	0.582	3.168
U140E & F	3.938	2.194	1.411	1.019			3.141
U151E & F	4.235	2.36	1.517	1.047	0.756		3.378
U240E/241E	3.943	2.197	1.413	1.02			3.145
U250E	3..93	2.197	1.413	0.975	0.703		3.145
U340E/341E/341F	2.847	1.552	1	0.7			2.343
U660E	3.3	1.9	1.42	1	0.713	0.608	4.148
TRANSMISSION GEAR RATIOS							
A43D	2.452	1.452	1	0.688			2.212
A44D	2.826	1.493	1	0.688			2.703
A46DE/46DF	2.452	1.452	1	0.73			2.212
A340E & F	2.804	1.531	1	0.705			2.393
A343F	2.804	1.531	1	0.753			2.393
A440F/A 442F	2.95	1.53	1	0.717			2.678
AB60E	3.333	1.960	1.353	1	0.728	0.588	3.061
A750E & F	3.52	2.042	1.4	1	0.716		3.224

FIGURE 10-55   The gear ratios for Toyota and Lexus transaxles and transmissions.

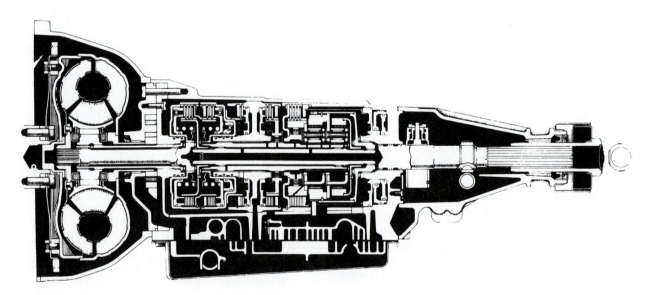

FIGURE 10-56   A cutaway view of a Toyota A40, three-speed transmission. *(Courtesy of Toyota Motor Sales USA, Inc.)*

a three-speed Ravigneaux gear train, similar to a Type 10 gear train. These designs were followed by the A40 transmission, a three-speed design using a version of the Simpson gear train. This design is similar to a Type 3 gear train, but it is unique in that it uses no bands

(Figure 10-56). This gear train design is the basis for many Toyota transmissions.

The A40D is a dual planetary gearset, four-speed design that combines the A40 gear train with an overdrive unit (Figure 10-57). This design is similar to the Type 8 gear train.

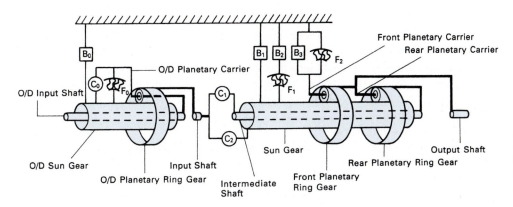

FIGURE 10-57 A schematic view of the gearset and apply devices for a Toyota A40D, four-speed transmission. *(Courtesy of Toyota Motor Sales USA, Inc.)*

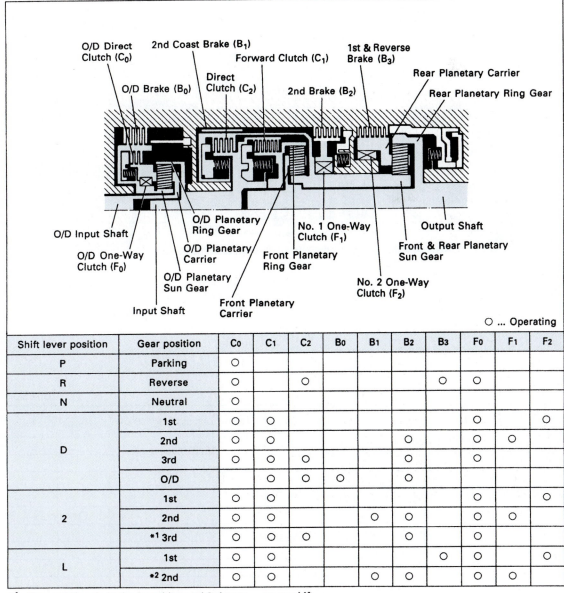

○ ... Operating

Shift lever position	Gear position	C₀	C₁	C₂	B₀	B₁	B₂	B₃	F₀	F₁	F₂
P	Parking	○									
R	Reverse	○		○				○	○		
N	Neutral	○									
D	1st	○	○						○		○
D	2nd	○	○				○		○	○	
D	3rd	○	○	○			○		○		
D	O/D		○	○	○		○				
2	1st	○	○						○		○
2	2nd	○	○			○	○		○	○	
2	*¹ 3rd	○	○	○			○		○		
L	1st	○	○					○	○		○
L	*² 2nd	○	○			○	○		○	○	

*¹ Down-shift only in the 2 position and 3rd gear — no up-shift.

*² Down-shift only in the L position and 2nd gear — no up-shift.

FIGURE 10-58 A cutaway view of a Toyota A340 four-speed transmission gearset with a clutch application chart. *(Courtesy of Toyota Motor Sales USA, Inc.)*

The newer version, the A340, is very similar; the clutch arrangement has been changed and modified to simplify the design and increase the torque capacity (Figure 10-58). This transmission is currently used with six-cylinder engines in pickups and SUVs and with the eight-cylinder engine in Tundra pickups.

Toyota has introduced a high-torque, five-speed transmission called the A750. It is electronically controlled, has three planetary gearsets (one Ravigneaux and two simple), seven clutches (three driving and four holding) and three one-way clutches. It also uses an ATF warmer and optional ATF cooler to increase transmission performance and fluid life.

Another new electronically controlled six-speed transmission is called the AB60E. It uses a Ravigneaux and two simple planetary gearsets controlled by eight clutches (four driving and four holding) and four one-way clutches. This transmission utilizes advanced electronic controls that include TCC flex lock-up control, tow/hauling programming, cooperative power train control, artificial shift intelligence, coast downshift, and multi-mode controls.

10.9.2 Toyota FWD Transaxles

The A130 is a three-speed transaxle, Simpson gear train unit that uses no bands (Figure 10-59). Currently, it is being used in the Corolla.

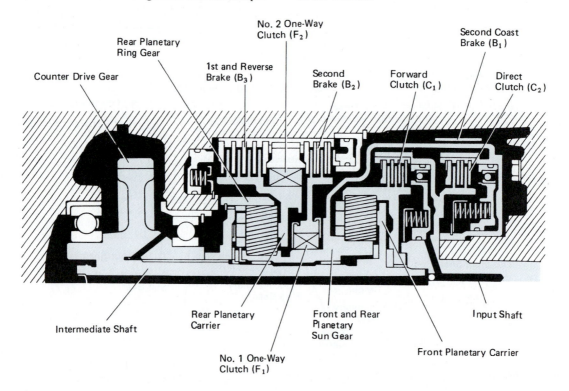

Shift lever position	Gear position	C_1	C_2	B_1	B_2	B_3	F_1	F_2
P	Parking							
R	Reverse		◯			◯		
N	Neutral							
D	1st	◯						◯
	2nd	◯			◯		◯	
	3rd	◯	◯		◯			
2	1st	◯						◯
	2nd	◯		◯	◯		◯	
L	1st	◯				◯		◯
	*2nd	◯		◯	◯		◯	

◯ .... Operating

*Down shift in L range, 2nd gear only — no up-shift.

FIGURE 10-59   A cutaway view of a Toyota A130 three-speed transaxle with a clutch application chart. *(Courtesy of Toyota Motor Sales USA, Inc.)*

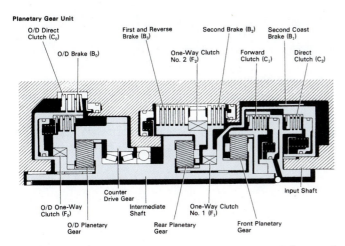

Planetary Gear Unit

O/D Direct Clutch (C₀)

O/D Brake (B₀)

First and Reverse Brake (B₃)

One-Way Clutch No. 2 (F₂)

Second Brake (B₂)

Forward Clutch (C₁)

Second Coast Brake (B₁)

Direct Clutch (C₂)

Counter Drive Gear

Intermediate Shaft

One-Way Clutch No. 1 (F₁)

Input Shaft

O/D One-Way Clutch (F₀)

O/D Planetary Gear

Rear Planetary Gear

Front Planetary Gear

FIGURE 10-60 A cutaway view of a Toyota A140E four-speed transaxle. *(Courtesy of Toyota Motor Sales USA, Inc.)*

Toyota uses three basic designs for its four-speed transaxles. The first was the A140E series. Introduced in mid-1983, it was the first electronically controlled transmission. It is a dual planetary gearset design, combining the Simpson gear train with an overdrive unit (Figure 10-60). The A540 series transaxles are very similar; they are modified to provide better driveability and increased torque capacity for 6-cylinder engines.

The A240L series is also similar to the A140E units. The overdrive unit was relocated to the countershaft to reduce the overall length of the transaxle and improve durability (Figure 10-61).

Toyota has two new transaxles, the U660E and the U250E. The U250E is an electronically controlled five-speed transaxle. It uses three-simple planetary gearsets that are controlled by seven clutches (four driving and three holding) and two one-way clutches. The U660E is an electronically controlled six-speed transaxle with two planetary gearsets, one Ravigneaux and one simple. Four clutches (two driving and two holding) and one one-way clutch control the power flow through the planetary gearsets. Both the U250E and the U660E have advanced electronic controls that provide TCC flex lock-up control, tow/hauling programming, cooperative power train control, artificial shift intelligence, coast downshift, and multi-mode controls.

Front & Rear Sun Gear

U/D Planetary Gear Unit

Rear Planetary Gear Unit

Front Planetary Gear Unit

Intermediate Shaft

Input Shaft

Ring Gear

Counter Shaft

Range (i.e.,) Shift Lever Position	Gear	No. 1 Solenoid Valve	No. 2 Solenoid Valve	C₁	C₂	C₃	B₁	B₂	B₃	B₄	F₁	F₂	F₃
P	Park	ON	OFF							●			
R	Reverse	ON	OFF		●				●	●			
N	Neutral	ON	OFF							●			
D	1st	ON	OFF	●						●		●	●
D	2nd	ON	ON	●				●		●	●		●
D	3rd	OFF	ON	●	●			●		●			●
D	O/D	OFF	OFF	●	●	●		●					
2	1st	ON	OFF	●						●		●	●
2	2nd	ON	ON	●			●	●		●	●		●
2	3rd *	OFF	ON	●	●			●		●			●
L	1st	ON	OFF	●					●	●		●	●
L	2nd *	ON	ON	●			●	●		●	●	●	●

● : Operating
* : Down-Shift only in the 3rd gear for the 2 range and 2nd gear for the L-range - no up-shift

FIGURE 10-61 A schematic view of a Toyota A244E four-speed transaxle and its clutch application chart. *(Courtesy of Toyota Motor Sales USA, Inc.)*

SUMMARY

1. There are many different automatic transmissions. They are easier to understand if the operation of the planetary gears and the application of the clutches and bands are understood.
2. Transaxles combine the transmission and final drive into one unit.
3. Each manufacturer uses specific transmissions and transaxles to meet the requirements of the vehicle it is used in.
4. Some companies specialize in automatic transmissions and supply many vehicle manufacturers with their products.
5. Most automatic transmissions use planetary gearsets, but some vehicle manufacturers use CVT or constant-mesh transmissions.

REVIEW QUESTIONS

The following questions are provided to help you study as you read the chapter.

1. In any single year a transmission may have many variations. List eight possible differences between the variations.

2. The purpose of the differential is to allow the drive wheels to turn at _____ _____ speeds while the vehicle is turning a corner.

3. Transaxles that are mounted longitudinally in the vehicle use a _____ or _____ gearset to transfer the power to the drive wheels.

4. Use Chrysler's code to describe the following transmissions.
   a. 37RH _____
   b. 44RE _____
   c. 47RE _____
   d. 42LE _____

5. The Chrysler 44RE transmission is similar to the 32RH, with a(n) _____ unit positioned at the rear of the transmission.

6. The gear ratios for a Ford E40D transmission are:
   1st _____
   2nd _____
   3rd _____
   4th _____
   Rev. _____

   The gear ratios for a Ford CD4E are:
   1st _____
   2nd _____
   3rd _____
   4th _____
   Rev. _____

7. Use Ford's code to describe the following transmissions.
   a. 4R44E _____
   b. 5R55E _____
   c. AX4S _____
   d. AX4N _____

8. The gear ratios for a General Motor's 4L80 transmission are:
   1st _____
   2nd _____
   3rd _____
   4th _____
   5th _____
   Rev. _____

9. Use General Motor's code to describe the following transmissions.
   a. 3L30 _____
   b. 4L80-E _____
   c. 4T65-E _____

10. Name four foreign companies that manufacture automatic transmissions.

CHAPTER QUIZ

The following questions will help you check the facts you have learned. Select the answer that completes each statement correctly.

1. Student A says that many transmissions have similar operating characteristics. Student B says that all transmissions of a particular type are identical. Who is correct?

    a. Student A

    b. Student B

    c. Both A and B

    d. Neither A nor B

2. Student A says that transaxles use helical gears for the final drive reduction gears. Student B says that transaxles use hypoid gears for the final drive reduction gears. Who is correct?

    a. Student A

    b. Student B

    c. Both A and B

    d. Neither A nor B

3. Gearsets that are used in transaxles to turn the power flow 90 degrees are called

    a. constant mesh.

    b. helical.

    c. hypoid.

    d. hilipoid.

4. Student A says that a Chrysler 37RH transmission is a heavy-duty, four-speed transmission. Student B says that the 40RH is a stronger unit than the 37RH transmission. Who is correct?

    a. Student A

    b. Student B

    c. Both A and B

    d. Neither A nor B

5. Student A says that the Chrysler 30RH and 30TH are the same transmission. Student B says that the 30RH is a rear wheel drive transmission and the 30TH is a transaxle. Who is correct?

    a. Student A

    b. Student B

    c. Both A and B

    d. Neither A nor B

6. Student A says that the General Motors 4L60-E was formerly known as the THM 700-R4. Student B says that the 4L80-E is the smallest transmission made by General Motors. Who is correct?

    a. Student A

    b. Student B

    c. Both A and B

    d. Neither A nor B

7. Student A says that all automatic transmissions use planetary gears. Student B says that all automatic transmissions use multiple-disc clutches. Who is correct?

    a. Student A

    b. Student B

    c. Both A and B

    d. Neither A nor B

8. Student A says that import vehicles use automatic transmissions that are nothing like the transmissions used by domestic manufacturers. Student B says that all planetary automatic transmissions are basically similar. Who is correct?

    a. Student A

    b. Student B

    c. Both A and B

    d. Neither A nor B

9. Student A says that all manufacturers build the automatic transmissions used in their vehicles. Student B says that some manufacturers buy transmissions built by other companies. Who is correct?

    a. Student A

    b. Student B

    c. Both A and B

    d. Neither A nor B

10. Honda and Saturn use automatic transmissions that have constant-mesh, helical gear trains similar to standard transmissions. In place of synchronizers used in standard transmissions, they use

    a. planetary gears.

    b. accumulators.

    c. servos.

    d. multiple-disc clutches.

11. Honda has built a variety of transmissions. They can be described by the number of

    a. shafts.

    b. speeds.

    c. clutches.

    d. All of the above

12. Student A says that the Nissan RE4R03A is an electronically controlled, rear wheel drive, four-speed automatic transmission. Student B says that it is an electronically controlled, transverse, rear wheel drive, three-speed automatic transmission. Who is correct?

    a. Student A

    b. Student B

    c. Both A and B

    d. Neither A nor B

13. Student A says that all current Toyota transmissions use a band for compression braking. Student B says that all current Toyota transmissions do not use bands. Who is correct?

    a. Student A

    b. Student B

    c. Both A and B

    d. Neither A nor B

14. Toyota's heavy-duty RWD transmission is the

    a. A140E.

    b. A40D.

    c. A340E.

    d. A540E.

15. Which Toyota transmission has the overdrive planetary gearset mounted on the countershaft?

    a. A240E

    b. A130

    c. A540E

    d. A140E

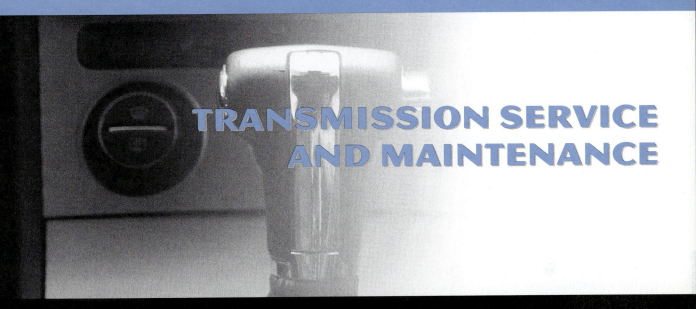

CHAPTER 11

TRANSMISSION SERVICE AND MAINTENANCE

OBJECTIVES

After studying Chapter 11, the reader should be able to:

1. Check the fluid level in an automatic transmission.
2. Check automatic transmission fluid condition.
3. Change the fluid in an automatic transmission.
4. Adjust manual shift linkage.
5. Adjust throttle linkage.
6. Adjust a band in an automatic transmission.
7. Complete the SAE tasks related to transmission/transaxle maintenance and adjustment (see Appendix A).

11.1 INTRODUCTION

Automatic transmissions and transaxles can operate properly for many miles while being totally neglected. Some that fail could have had a longer service life if they had been properly maintained. Several surveys of transmission shops have produced responses that over 80% of transmission failures were the result of neglecting to change the fluid. Newer transmissions require very little maintenance.

Maintaining the correct fluid level and changing the fluid is the primary maintenance task. Other maintenance checks should be performed occasionally, and problems corrected if necessary; these include:

- **Manual linkage:** To ensure that the manual valve and the internal park mechanism are positioned properly relative to the gear selector.
- *Throttle linkage:* To ensure that the throttle or detent valve provides the correct fluid pressures relative to the throttle position.
- *Band adjustment:* To ensure the correct band clearance. Note: adjustable bands are found only on older transmissions.

11.2 FLUID CHECKS

The operator of a vehicle should check the fluid level in an automatic transmission periodically. A good time is right after every engine oil change. If the level is low, fluid of the correct type should be added. It usually takes one pint (0.5 L) to move the fluid level from low to the full mark on the dipstick. The fluid should be changed if it looks deteriorated.

Most transmission dipsticks are marked for both cold and **hot fluid** temperatures (Figure 11-1). The most obvious markings are for the hot level, which is the normal operating temperature, about 150 to 170°F (66 to 77°C). Some manufacturers use a higher operating range of 180 to 200°F (82 to 93°C). Room temperature of about 65 to 85°F (18 to 29°C) is considered cold for transmission fluid. When the fluid is cold, use the cold

markings on the dipstick. Some transaxles use a thermostatic valve to raise the fluid level in the upper valve body pan as the transaxle warms up. These units have a lower hot level and a higher cold level. The exact procedure for checking the fluid level can be found in the vehicle owner's manual, or occasionally it is printed on the dipstick.

Some transmissions are sealed units without dipsticks. These are commonly called *sealed* or *overflow-type* transmissions. A special fluid-checking procedure is required for these units; always refer to the appropriate service information.

It is never a good idea to operate a transmission with the fluid level too high (an *overfill*) or too low (an *underfill*). An

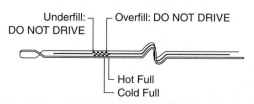

FIGURE 11-1 Most dipsticks have fluid-level markings for various temperatures. The vehicle should not be operated if the level is below the underfill or above the overfill marks.

TECH TIP

Many technicians use this rule of thumb: The fluid is hot if the end of the dipstick is too hot to hold between your fingers.

SAFETY TIP

Vehicle fires have occurred soon after a transmission service. These fires were probably caused by ATF leaking or spilling onto a hot exhaust system. Other causes could have been a high fluid level, a leaking cooler line, or a plugged transmission vent.

REAL WORLD FIX

A 1998 Dodge Durango (89,000 miles) transmission slips when taking off and during the 1–2 shift when cold. The fluid level is okay.

Fix. Following advice, the fluid level was checked in neutral, not park, and found to be 1 1/2 quarts low. Adding the correct amount of fluid fixed this problem.

underfill is below the low, cold level on the dipstick; it is sometimes marked "Do not drive." An underfill condition can allow air to enter the filter and pump intake, which can cause mushy operation, lack of engagement, slipping, or failure of the TCC to lock up and unlock properly.

Overfilling can cause slippage and mushy operation because of the air in the foamy fluid. An overfill can bring the fluid level up to the point where it contacts the spinning gearsets. This in turn causes foaming of the fluid and a loss of the foamy fluid out of the vent or filler pipe. There have been cases of vehicle fires caused by the fluid spilling out of the filler pipe and onto a hot exhaust manifold.

To check transmission fluid, you should:

1. Park the vehicle on a level surface, apply the parking brake securely, and place the gear selector in park or neutral as required by the manufacturer. Start the engine, and let the transmission come up to operating temperature.
2. Apply the service brakes firmly, and move the gear selector to each of the operating ranges. Leave the selector in each position long enough for each gear to become completely engaged.
3. Return the selector lever to park or neutral, depending on the transmission. Leave the engine running at idle speed.
4. Clean any dirt from the dipstick cap, and remove the dipstick (Figure 11-2).
5. Wipe the dipstick clean and return it to the filler pipe, making sure that it is fully seated.

6. Pull the dipstick out again and read the fluid level. Carefully grip the end of the dipstick between your fingers to get an indication of the fluid temperature.
   a. If it feels cold, use the COLD marks.
   b. If it feels warm and you can hold onto it, the correct fluid level will be between the HOT and COLD marks.
   c. If it is too hot to hold onto without burning yourself, use the HOT marks.
7. Replace the dipstick completely into the filler tube. Note that some dipsticks are threaded and must be rotated to lock them in place.

When checking sealed units, a general procedure is to bring the transmission to operating temperature, and then remove the fluid level plug. Fluid will trickle or weep out of the plug if the level is correct. If it runs out, the level is high; if there is no fluid, the level is low.

Some manufacturers require a special procedure or tool in order to check the fluid level of their sealed transmissions, so it is wise to review their fluid-checking procedure. A general procedure follows.

To check sealed transmission fluid level, you should:

1. Check the service information for the correct checking procedure.
2. Make sure the vehicle is level.

TECH TIP

If the fluid is fairly new, it appears almost transparent and can be very difficult to read on the dipstick. You can rub the dipstick with ordinary carbon paper, and recheck the fluid level. This will darken the fluid and make it easier to see.

TECH TIP

It is a good practice to read both sides of the dipstick and believe the lower level. Occasionally, fluid suspended in the filler pipe causes a false high or normal reading. If there is any sign of fluid above the correct range, repeat steps 5 and 6 several times and believe the lowest reading.

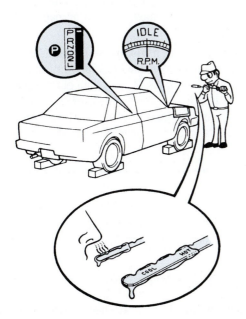

FIGURE 11-2   When checking the fluid level, the engine should be at idle speed, the fluid hot, and the gear selector should be positioned as required by the vehicle manufacturer. Note the fluid level and compare it with dipstick markings. It is also a good practice to note any unusual fluid color or odor.

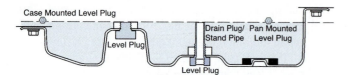

FIGURE 11-3 Fluid level on sealed units (without a dipstick) is checked by removing the level plug, which can be mounted in the bottom or side of the pan or in the case.

TECH TIP

If the vehicle has just been operated under heavy loads or at high speeds, it is a good idea to let it sit for about 30 minutes to cool before checking the fluid level.

3. Check the transmission temperature using a contact thermometer, infrared thermometer, or scan tool.
4. Make sure the transmission is at operating temperature range. If specifications are not available, use 120 to 160°F (49 to 71°C).
5. Locate and carefully remove the fluid level plug. Note that the level plug can be small, like a pressure check plug, or large, like a conventional plug. The plug can be located in the transmission case or in the bottom or side of the pan (Figure 11-3).
6. If fluid drips or seeps from the hole, the level is correct. If fluid runs out, the level is too high; allow the excess fluid to drain out. If no fluid comes out, the level is low; add additional fluid of the correct type until the level is correct.
7. If necessary, add additional fluid by pumping it through the fill port located at the side of the case or up through the fluid level checking plug opening.

CAUTION: Any fluid that comes out of the fluid level opening will be extremely hot.

11.2.1 Transaxle Final Drives and Differentials

Some transaxles separate the final drive assembly from the transmission section and use gear oil for the lubricant. These units may have a separate fluid-checking requirement for the transaxle and final drive (Figure 11-4). The vehicle will

REAL WORLD FIX

The shop changed the filthy transmission fluid and filter in the VW Passat and then noticed that there was no dipstick to check the fluid level. The problem was how to properly adjust the fluid level.

Fix. On this vehicle, the recommended fluid level is to install 2 quarts of the proper fluid, start the engine, and monitor the transmission fluid temperature. At 96°F (35°C), fluid should flow from the fluid level port. If no fluid flows, the level is low and more should be added. The exact procedure published by the manufacturer for each transmission should be followed.

REAL WORLD FIX

The 1996 Pontiac Grand Am (130,000 miles) transmission slips and loses speed when hot. After a few minutes, it will operate normally again. The fluid level is okay. An inspection shows a clean oil pan, and a scan tool check shows no DTCs.

Fix. A decision was made to change the fluid and filter to help loosen a possible sticking shift valve. While removing the filter, the filter seal fell out; normally, this seal has a tight fit. Replacement of the filter with a new seal and the fluid fixed this problem. Apparently, the poor-fitting seal allowed an air leak into the fluid pickup.

still operate with a low final drive lubricant level, but expensive wear and damage can result.

11.2.2 Fluid Condition

Fluid condition should always be checked when checking fluid level. A transmission technician will normally smell the fluid and check the color for unusual characteristics. We normally expect the fluid to be a bright reddish color with a smell that is similar to new fluid. It should be noted that some fluids will normally darken and take on a definite odor after a few hundred

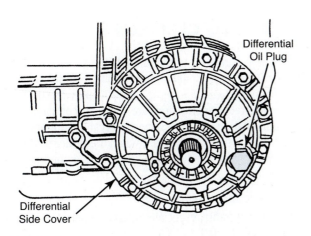

FIGURE 11-4   Some transaxle differentials have a plug to allow checking of the fluid level in the final drive section. *(Courtesy of Chrysler Corporation)*

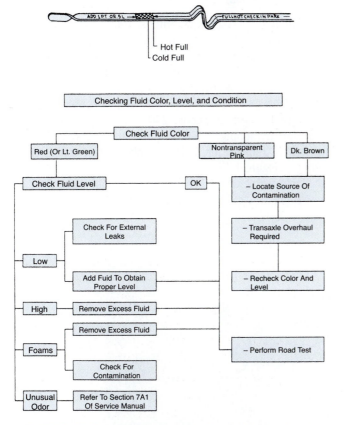

FIGURE 11-5   A useful chart for checking fluid level and condition. *(Reprinted with permission of General Motors)*

miles. One manufacturer states that a smokey odor with light brown color is normal (Figure 11-5). Do not confuse this normal occurrence with the signs of fluid breakdown.

If the fluid has signs of grit or foreign particles in it or a dirty appearance, it is a good practice to check for solid contaminants. Put a fluid sample onto a clean, white paper towel or blotter. The wetness of the fluid will slowly spread through the paper, leaving a stain. Clean fluid will make a

TECH TIP

If you suspect the fluid contains water, place a drop from the dipstick on a hot exhaust manifold. The oil will spread and burn off while the water droplets sizzle and move around. One manufacturer recommends that fluid with water contamination should be changed immediately. Then change the fluid two more times, running the engine so all of the old fluid and the water it contains will be mixed with the fluid to be drained.

TECH TIP

Coolant or water contamination, a strawberry-milkshake-colored fluid, can ruin a transmission in several ways:

- It can weaken the bond holding the lining to the friction plates.
- It can cause rust on iron components.
- It can soften nylon thrust washers.
- The water can boil, turn to steam, and force fluid out of the dipstick tube, which might cause a fire.

reddish ring. Contaminated fluid will leave specks or deposits of the very fine solid material on the paper as the fluid spreads (Figure 11-6).

Indications of fluid breakdown are:

- Dark brown or black color indicates dirt or burned friction material.
- A definite burned odor indicates slippage or overheating.
- *Pink fluid* or a **milky color** indicates a coolant leak at the heat exchanger in the radiator.
- A varnishlike odor indicates fluid oxidation and breakdown. This is often accompanied by a gold-brown *varnish* coating on the dipstick.
- Metallic appearance or very fine metal particles indicate wear.
- Foam might indicate a leak in the pump intake system or incorrect fluid level.

TECH TIP

Dirty or contaminated fluid should be changed, the filter should also be changed, and the inside of the pan and transmission case should be checked for contamination, varnish, metallic particles, or other signs of possible transmission problems.

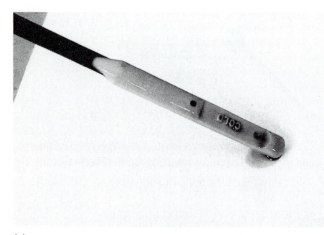

(a)

11.3 FLUID CHANGES

Most manufacturers recommend fluid changes every 100,000 miles (160,000 km) under normal driving conditions. Some recommend a *fluid change* at 50,000 miles (80,000 km). Fluid change recommendations are usually accompanied with a recommendation that the change interval be shortened to as low as 15,000 miles (24,000 km) when the vehicle is used under severe driving conditions. Severe driving conditions are described as:

- Frequent trailer pulling.
- Heavy city traffic, especially in areas where the temperature exceeds 90°F (32°C).
- Very hilly or mountainous conditions.
- Commercial use such as taxi or delivery service.
- Police or ambulance usage.

The main factor that determines transmission fluid life is heat or how hot the fluid is during vehicle operation. If the fluid temperature is kept below 175°F (79°C), the fluid should easily last 100,000 miles. At higher temperatures the fluid oxidizes, causing it to break down at a rate of one-half its expected life for every increase of 20°F (11°C). Varnish begins forming at temperatures above 240°F (116°C), and the rubber seals start hardening at temperatures above 260°F (127°C). A chart of transmission fluid life relative to temperature is shown in Figure 11-7.

Fluid temperature is related to the torque converter's operating efficiency. Remember that a converter is not efficient

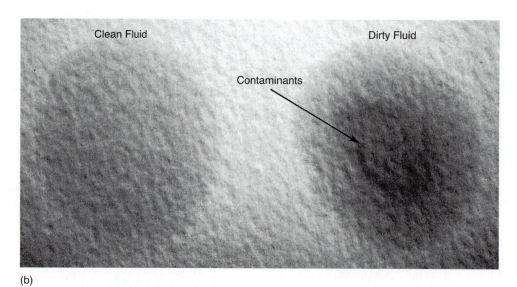

(b)

FIGURE 11-6   Fluid condition can be checked by placing a sample on clean, white, absorbent paper (a). Clean fluid will spread out and leave only a wet stain (b). Dirty fluid will leave deposits of foreign material.

at stall. Mechanical power is going into the converter, but no power is coming out. All mechanical energy is being transformed into heat, which increases the fluid temperature. Heat is generated whenever the converter is slipping and multiplying torque. A transmission also generates heat because of internal friction: At the bushings, bearings, and gears, additional heat is generated as the pressurized fluid is forced through the passages and orifices. The heat generated by friction is fairly small compared with the heat generated by the converter. It can be safely said that the fluid life is shortest in a vehicle that has a lot of torque converter slippage.

The fluid should be changed when it starts to break down, which is best indicated by the fluid appearance and smell. It is wise to change the fluid early, before transmission damage occurs. Dirty fluid may cause the valves to start sticking, which

in turn can cause sluggish shifts and slippage and thus more fluid heat, breakdown, contamination, and damage.

11.3.1 Fluid Changing, Dropping the Pan

The procedure for changing the fluid in a specific vehicle can be found in the manufacturer's service manual or aftermarket service information sources.

Transmission Fluid

Fluid Life (miles)	Temperature (°F)
100,000	175
50,000	195
25,000	215
12,500	235
6,250	255
3,125	275
1,560	295
780	315
390	335
195	355
97	375
48	395

FIGURE 11-7   In many transmissions, the fluid is expected to last 100,000 miles if the fluid temperature can be kept below 175°F (80°C); but the life will be cut in half for every 20°F increase in temperature.

REAL WORLD FIX

The 1994 Honda Accord (165,000 miles) transmission whines badly, making the car essentially undriveable. Shifts are normal (except there is no fourth gear), and the fluid level is okay. The vehicle was recently taken to a "quick oil change" shop for an engine oil change, and at the shop's advice, the transmission fluid was also changed.

Fix. Following advice, the technician checked the fluid, and it appeared to be Dexron. He then replaced the transmission with a good used unit, and replaced the fluid in it using the proper Honda transmission fluid. This fixed the problem. The best policy is to always use the fluid recommended by the vehicle manufacturer.

TECH TIP

If the old transmission fluid is extremely dirty, be aware that when the fluid is changed, the new ATF contains a fresh supply of detergents and dispersants, and these will:

- Loosen varnish and other deposits that have accumulated inside the transmission.
- Carry this material throughout the transmission, including valves and solenoids.
- Possibly remove varnish that has formed over worn seals and open up a leak.

The supply of new friction modifier will increase the "slippery" level of the fluid, which might increase slipping on upshifts.

TECH TIP

Some transmissions contain very expensive *lifetime fluid* that does not need to be changed. If drained, any solid particles can be allowed to settle, and the clean oil is skimmed off to be reused.

SAFETY TIP

The material safety data sheets (MSDS) for most transmission fluids indicate that there are few safety hazards when working with new fluid. Some indicate a possible skin reaction. Used fluid, however, goes through an unknown change inside the transmission that might cause it to be more of a hazard. The following is recommended:

- Wear goggles or a face shield to protect your eyes.
- Wear gloves or barrier cream to protect your skin.
- Clean any skin contact with ATF using soap and water.
- Change clothing that has contacted ATF.
- Wash any clothing that has contact with ATF.

If ATF under pressure breaks the skin, medical attention should be sought; consult your doctor.

TECH TIP

Most transmissions do not have a drain plug in the oil pan. The fluid is drained by allowing it to spill over the side of the pan as it is removed. The pan is first lowered at an angle to allow the fluid to spill and then removed completely (Figure 11-8).

TECH TIP

Fluid section pumps are available that can suck the fluid from the transmission. A small plastic hose is inserted down the dipstick tube, and the pump is connected to shop air pressure. Operation of the pump creates the suction. This removes much of the mess of removing a pan full of hot fluid.

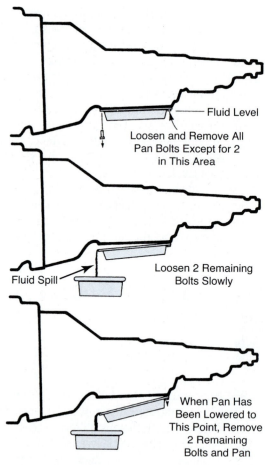

Fluid Level

Loosen and Remove All Pan Bolts Except for 2 in This Area

Fluid Spill

Loosen 2 Remaining Bolts Slowly

When Pan Has Been Lowered to This Point, Remove 2 Remaining Bolts and Pan

FIGURE 11-8 Since most transmissions do not have drain plugs, the fluid must be spilled in a controlled fashion by lowering the pan at an angle. To do this, all but two bolts are removed. As the last two bolts are loosened, the pan will lower and fluid will spill over the edge.

To change transmission fluid, you should:

1. Raise and securely support the vehicle. This is normally done on a hoist to allow complete access to the transmission pan.
2. Select the best direction for fluid to spill from the pan. Place a large drain pan in this area, and remove all but two of the pan bolts. The remaining two bolts should be at the end away from the drain pan; they will serve as the "hinge" for lowering the pan.
3. Loosen the two remaining bolts about two turns (Figure 11-9).
4. If the oil pan does not come loose and start dropping on its own, carefully tap on the sides of the pan. The jarring should loosen the pan from the transmission. If the pan is sealed using form-in-place gasket/sealant, it may be necessary to cut the sealant that tends to glue the pan to the transmission case (Figure 11-10).
5. Loosen the remaining two bolts as needed to get a continuous and controlled spill into the drain pan.

FIGURE 11-9   Fluid is draining from this transmission pan. Note how the pan is hanging from two front bolts.

FIGURE 11-10   A gasket splitter is used to break the seal between the pan and transmission case. It is tapped in between the pan and case and then tapped sideways, around the pan.

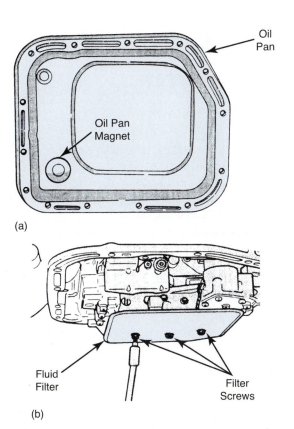

Oil Pan

Oil Pan Magnet

(a)

Fluid Filter

Filter Screws

(b)

FIGURE 11-11   The filter is normally located in the oil pan (a); note the magnet inside the pan to trap ferrous metals. The filter is held by three screws (b). *(Courtesy of Chrysler Corporation)*

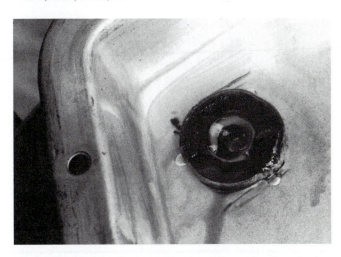

FIGURE 11-12   This pan magnet has a thin coating of very fine iron particles and the pan is fairly clean. This is normal transmission wear.

6. When the pan lowers to an angle of about 30 to 45 degrees, support it by hand; remove the remaining two bolts and finish draining the pan.
7. Remove the filter, which is usually attached to the valve body (Figure 11-11). Watch for any small parts that may come loose with the filter.
8. Inspect the pan, filter, and pan magnet for debris and varnish buildup (Figure 11-12). A few metal particles are

TECH TIP

Some technicians will cut the old filter open so they can inspect for foreign particles (Figure 11-13). Many filters can be quickly broken open by covering them with a shop cloth and striking them on the edge with a hammer. Be cautious of flying plastic parts.

TECH TIP

Many transmissions are shipped to the vehicle assembly line wet (full of fluid) and a sealing device is used to close the openings for the drive shaft(s) and dipstick tube. When the transmission is installed, the sealing device(s) is pushed into the transmission, where it remains harmlessly inside the pan (Figure 11-14).

TECH TIP

Rubber or neoprene seals must be lubricated when they are slid into place. Most greases will cause problems inside a transmission. ATF is always a safe lubricant. Transmission assembly gel and petroleum jelly have more holding or sticking power, and both of these will melt and dissolve harmlessly into the ATF.

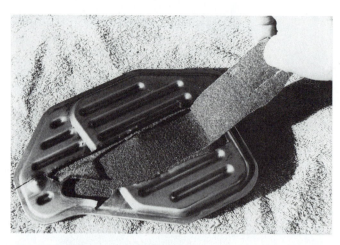

FIGURE 11-13   This depth filter has been cut open, and there are only a few small metal particles caught in the fold.

FIGURE 11-14   This "popcycle" was found laying in the transmission pan. It was used to plug the dipstick opening while the transmission was shipped to the vehicle assembly line.

TECH TIP

If the flange surface is bent or has dimples, it should be flattened using a hammer and block of wood, vise, or anvil (Figure 11-15). Failure to straighten the pan can result in a fluid leak.

considered normal. These are the result of wear and transmission break-in. Inspect the inside of the transmission for any visible damage or varnish buildup.

9. Install a new filter using a new gasket or O-ring, and tighten the mounting bolts to the correct torque. If an O-ring is used, it should be lubricated with transmission assembly gel, petroleum jelly, or automatic transmission fluid (ATF) before installation.

10. Clean the oil pan and dry it with compressed air. Check the flanges for dimpling or bends at the pan bolt holes. Repair the damaged flanges as necessary.

11. Install a new gasket on the pan, and install the pan on the transmission. The bolts should be tightened in a back-and-forth, across-the-pan sequence to the correct torque. Overtightening can cause a future leak by compressing the gasket too tightly and bending the flange.

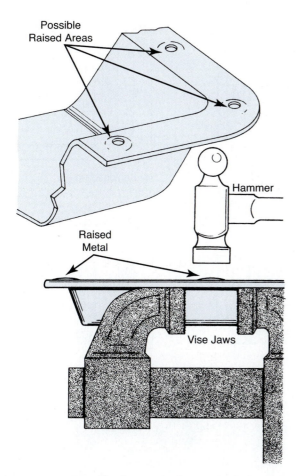

FIGURE 11-15   The flange area of a pan should be checked for distortion from overtightened bolts. These can be corrected by tapping down the raised areas as shown.

TECH TIP

The only thing that should be put on a rubber or neoprene gasket is "gasket stick" or assembly lube to hold it in place. Other sealants might affect the gasket or work their way into the hydraulic circuits, where they can cause problems.

12. Lower the vehicle, and add the proper amount of fluid. A rule of thumb is 4 quarts.
13. Start the engine and check the fluid level as described earlier. Add additional fluid to correct the level if necessary (Figure 11-16).
14. Dispose of the old transmission fluid in an approved manner.

REAL WORLD FIX

The 1997 Honda Civic CVT (17,000 miles) came in with a bad shudder. The clutches were rebuilt because they appeared to be burned, but the shudder was still there.

Fix. Following advice, the technician drained the fluid and replaced it with the proper CVT fluid. This fixed the shudder problem.

TECH TIP

Some technicians have made a transmission fill pump using a Honda remote-reservoir power steering pump that uses hoses for the pump inlet and outlets, 5/16-in. rubber hose, a drill motor for power, and a small metal tube to fit through the fluid level opening.

Note that this procedure only changes the fluid in the pan. This is about one-quarter to one-third (1/4 to 1/3) of the fluid in the transmission. The remaining fluid stays in the torque converter, clutches and band servos, accumulators, cooler, and fluid passages.

It is possible to drain the converter by drilling a hole in it and installing a plug when finished. Most technicians do not do this because of the time involved and the possible damage that can occur to the converter. The procedure to drill a converter is described in Chapter 19. For very dirty transmissions, it is best to change the fluid in the pan as just described; then operate the transmission long enough to thoroughly mix the new and old fluid; and then change the fluid again.

In cases of very dirty fluid, it is good practice to check for a plugged oil cooler. Debris can plug up the cooler, causing severe gear train and bushing wear because of the reduction of lubrication oil flow. The procedure used to check fluid flow through a cooler is described in Section 12.6.2.

Another recommendation for very dirty fluid is to change the fluid, change the filter, and inspect the pan, as just described, and then flush the fluid remaining in the transmission as described in the next section.

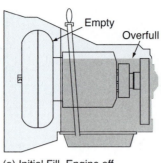
(a) Initial Fill, Engine off

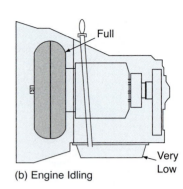
(b) Engine Idling

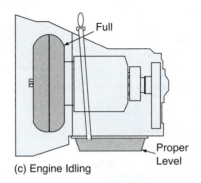
(c) Engine Idling

(d) Engine Off

FIGURE 11-16   If the transmission fluid and filter are replaced, the proper amount of fluid will overfill the transmission (a). The fill procedure should add fluid to a full level and then start the engine (b). Add additional fluid as needed to bring it to the proper level (c). Checking the engine with the engine off can show an overfill if the converter drains down (d).

REAL WORLD FIX

The 1993 Mercury Villager van (147,000 miles) will go into neutral under varying conditions. During a test drive it operated normally in all gears until accelerating from a stop; it then went to neutral and after a short period of time, back into gear. The fluid appears and smells good. The transmission electrical connections were checked, and these were good.

Fix. The pan was checked—it was bent upward, apparently blocking flow to the filter. The pan was removed, bent back to the proper shape, and replaced. This repair fixed the problem.

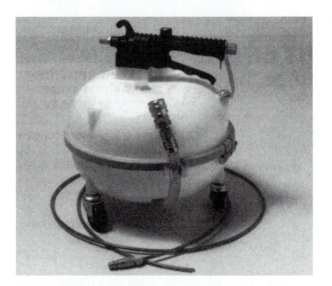

FIGURE 11-17   This fluid evacuation system has a small tube that can be inserted into the transmission dipstick tube. A connection to shop air is used to create a vacuum that sucks the fluid into the container. (Courtesy of ATEC Trans-Tool and Cleaning Systems)

11.3.2 Fluid Changing, Fluid Evacuator

Fluid changing by dropping the pan (described in the previous section) is often messy. Fluid spills onto the floor and is absorbed into the concrete, and if not attended to, the fluid can pass through the concrete and into the groundwater. This can create an environmental hazard. Some shops have stopped dropping the pan of an automatic transmission for this reason. Transmission fluid can be changed by sucking the fluid out through the filler tube using an evacuating/extraction tool (Figure 11-17). It should be noted that the pan must be dropped to change the filter and inspect any debris that might be in the pan.

To change transmission fluid using an evacuating tool, you should:

1. Operate the vehicle to bring the fluid up to operating temperature.
2. Insert the evacuating tool hose into the filler tube until it contacts the transmission pan.
3. Operate the evacuating tool to remove as much of the old fluid as possible.
4. Remove the evacuating tool and dispose of the old fluid in an approved manner.

Optional Step: Remove the pan for inspection or replacement of the filter.

5. Refill the transmission using the correct fluid for the vehicle.
6. Start the engine and check the fluid level as described earlier. Add additional fluid to correct the level if necessary.

11.3.3 Fluid Exchange and Flush Units

A complete transmission fluid change can be very time-consuming. Several different pieces of equipment have been designed to make this operation faster and more efficient.

Fluid flushing usually involves using a chemical to dissolve varnish and other deposits. **Exchange** usually means taking out the old fluid and replacing it with new fluid of the correct type.

It should be remembered that most vehicle manufacturers specify a filter replacement and pan inspection during the fluid change. At least one flushing machine allows fluid exchange with the pan removed (Figure 11-18).

Fluid exchange machines are usually connected into the transmission cooler lines so that the machine can pump new fluid to the return line as it captures the fluid leaving the transmission (Figure 11-19). Running the engine will pump the old fluid out of the transmission, and a pump in the fluid exchange machine will pump new fluid into the return line. When new, clean fluid starts leaving the transmission, the fluid exchange is complete.

Always follow the manufacturer's instructions when using a fluid exchanger.

To change fluid using a transmission fluid exchange unit, you should:

1. Identify the cooler lines so you know which one is the return line.
2. Disconnect the return line from the cooler, and connect the line to the NEW FLUID connector of the machine. Connect the USED FLUID connector of the machine to the cooler.
3. Apply the parking brake and shift the transmission into park. Start the engine and observe the fluid flow at the machine. To prevent starving the transmission of fluid,

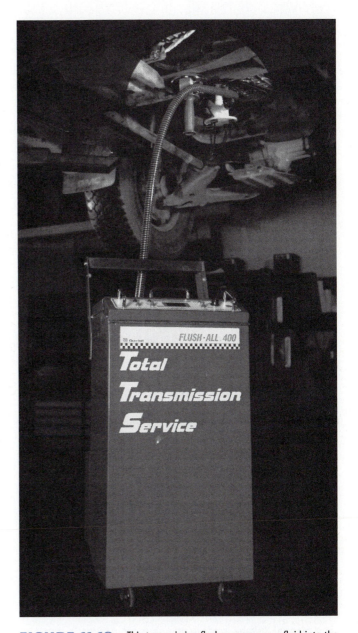

FIGURE 11-18 This transmission flusher pumps new fluid into the transmission pump intake. It is operated until the old, dirty fluid is forced out. *(Courtesy of Goodall Manufacturing)*

TECH TIP

Either line can be used when flushing, but using the return line allows you to check for a plugged cooler. A rule of thumb is that the flow through a cooler should be 3 quarts per minute (1 quart per 20 seconds) or greater.

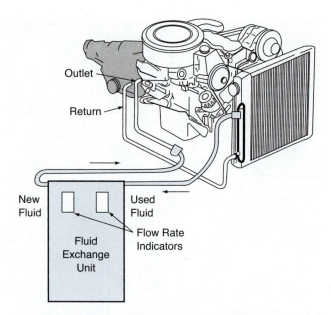

FIGURE 11-19 A fluid exchange unit is normally connected to the cooler return line, and it sends new fluid to the transmission to replace the old fluid being captured from the cooler.

new fluid should leave the machine at the same rate that used fluid enters.

4. When the used fluid has the same appearance as new fluid, stop the engine.
5. Disconnect fluid connections to the machine, and reconnect the cooler return line.
6. Start the engine and check the line connection for leaks.
7. Check the transmission fluid level and adjust as necessary.
8. Dispose of the used transmission fluid in an approved manner.

11.4 MANUAL LINKAGE CHECKS

The manual linkage is adjustable on most automatic transmissions. This ensures the manual valve is positioned correctly relative to the gear selector. Linkage position should be checked periodically because a misadjusted linkage can cause the manual valve to leak oil pressure into the wrong passage (Figure 11-20). Imagine if a small amount of line pressure were able to leak into the drive passages while in neutral. This might cause a clutch to partially apply and produce a slight creep condition. But even worse, this slippage will produce overheating and eventually burn the clutch out.

A detent is a spring-loaded device that causes the notchy feel and clicking sound as the gear selector is moved. Since the detents act on the transmission's internal linkage, they normally stay correctly aligned with the valve position.

The manual linkage adjustment for a specific vehicle can be found in the manufacturer's service manual or aftermarket

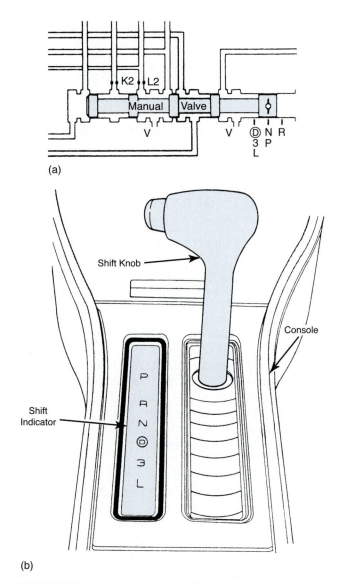

(a)

(b)

FIGURE 11-20 Proper manual linkage ensures that manual valve position (a) matches correctly with the position of the manual shift lever and shift indicator (b). *(Courtesy of Chrysler Corporation)*

TECH TIP

A serious problem related to manual linkage adjustment is for the transmission to shift into park without the gear selector entering the locking gate. If the vehicle is left with the engine running, the selector level may slip out of park and the transmission may shift into reverse gear, creating a highly dangerous condition. There have been serious accidents with some fatalities as a result of this happening.

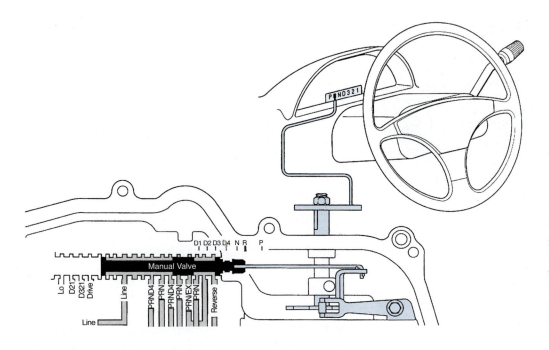

FIGURE 11-21 As the shift selector is moved across the quadrant, you should be able to feel the detents inside the transmission. The detent feel should correspond with the gear position. *(Reprinted with permission of General Motors)*

REAL WORLD FIX

The 1995 Volkswagen Golf (55,000 miles) had the transmission rebuilt. The transmission was installed, but there was no engagement in drive. The car would move in M3 and all shifts were good.

Fix. Following advice, the technician checked the shift linkage adjustment and found the problem. A shift linkage adjustment fixed this problem.

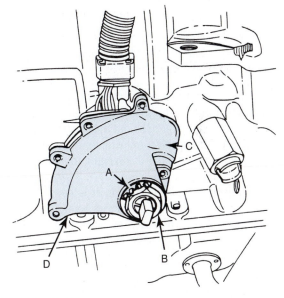

FIGURE 11-22 This neutral safety switch is mounted in the transmission and operated by the manual lever cam. It always stays in proper adjustment. *(Courtesy of Chrysler Corporation)*

service information. Following is a general procedure for linkage adjustment.

To check manual linkage adjustment, you should:

1. Firmly set the parking brake and leave the engine off.
2. Move the selector lever lock or the selector lever to the unlocked or ungated position to allow moving the selector lever freely through the different ranges (Figure 11-21). Move the lever through its travel as you feel for the detents inside the transmission.
3. Move the selector level through the ranges, and observe the range pointer as you note the position of the internal detents. You should feel the detent engage as the pointer aligns with the gate for each gear position indicator.
4. Move the selector lever to park, and release the lever/lock. The parking pawl should freely engage to

lock the transmission, and the lever lock should freely enter the gate and be locked.

5. Check that the starter operates in park and neutral but not in other gear positions.

The neutral start switch in some transmissions is activated by the manual lever quadrant inside the transmission, so it will always be positioned correctly relative to the manual valve (Figure 11-22). Improper starter operation on these

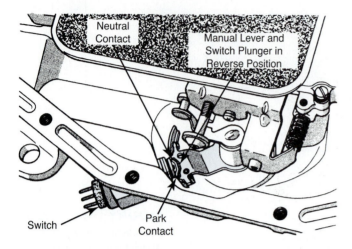

FIGURE 11-23 This neutral safety switch is mounted to the outside of the transmission case. If the starter operates with the gear selector in a position other than park or neutral, the switch position should be adjusted. *(Courtesy of Chrysler Corporation)*

vehicles indicates a misadjusted shift linkage. Other transmissions mount the neutral start switch on the outside of the case, or at the shift lever. These switches are adjusted differently; consult the appropriate service information for the proper procedure (Figure 11-23).

The range pointer in some vehicles is operated by a cable controlled by a lever on the shift column. On these vehicles, it is possible for the pointer to be out of adjustment relative to the linkage and manual valve. Adjustment of the pointer position is usually a simple matter of changing the pointer or connecting link position.

While checking the adjustment, it is good practice to also watch for any binding or hard movement. This indicates a shift cable that is dirty, rusty, or beginning to fail. Also check for excessive lever slide or vertical movement or sloppy motion, which indicates failure of the selector lever bushings.

11.4.1 Manual Linkage Adjustment

The manual linkage should be adjusted if the starter engagements occur in the wrong position or the transmission detents do not align correctly relative to the gear range pointer. The procedure will vary with vehicle makes and models. Check a service manual for the exact procedure for a particular vehicle (Figure 11-24). The description that follows is general.

To adjust manual shift linkage, you should:

1. Shift the gear selector into park, making sure the selector lever is correctly positioned and the lever pawl has completely entered the park gate.

2. Raise and securely support the vehicle on a hoist or jack stand.
3. Locate the manual linkage and the adjustment in the linkage. The adjustment is a slot in the shift rod or cable, a swivel clamp, or a long, threaded portion using a bracket and two nuts (Figure 11-25). Loosen the clamping nut or bolt.
4. Move the transmission lever to park, making sure that the detent and the parking pawl are completely engaged. Test this by trying to rotate the drive shaft(s); it should be securely locked. Adjust the linkage to the proper length.
5. Tighten the clamping nut or bolt, making sure that the transmission lever and/or the shift rod do not move out of adjustment.
6. Repeat the linkage check described earlier (Section 11.4) to ensure correct adjustment.

Shift Lock Mechanism. The shift interlock mechanism locks the shifter in park position when the ignition key is removed. The brake pedal must be depressed before the shifter can be moved, and the ignition key cannot be removed unless the lever has been shifted into park. These systems operate either electrically or through a mechanical linkage (Figure 11-26). The mechanical systems usually have an adjustment to ensure proper positioning. These systems vary so service information for that particular vehicle should be consulted when diagnosing problems or checking adjustments.

A shift interlock can get out of adjustment or fail to release. Vehicle manufacturers have incorporated a fail-safe mechanism so the vehicle can be operated. Located near the shift lever is a small lever or button that can be used to override the shift lock and release the lever. The release is often located under a cover that must be removed for access. This procedure is normally described in the vehicle owner's manual.

11.5 THROTTLE LINKAGE CHECKS

Nonelectronic transmissions may have a throttle rod or cable that connects the engine's throttle linkage to the transmission's throttle valve. This linkage is commonly called a *TV linkage.* The TV linkage controls a valve that produces a rise in TV or line pressure that is matched to the throttle position (Figure 11-27). This pressure controls the timing and quality of the shifts.

Sticky, binding, or improperly adjusted TV linkage will cause incorrect TV pressure and the following problems:

- Sticky or binding, erratic, irregular shifts.
- High TV pressure causes higher than normal shift points, overly sensitive downshifts, and excessively firm, harsh shifts (cable is too tight).

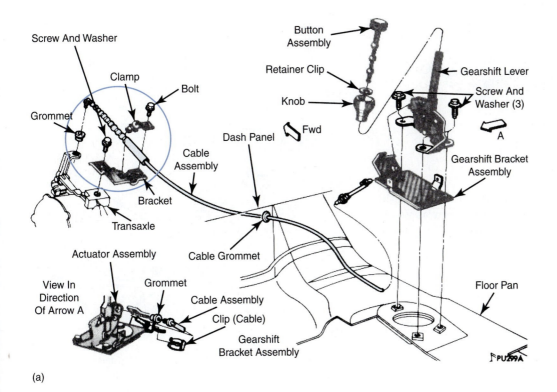

(a)

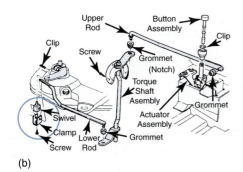

(b)

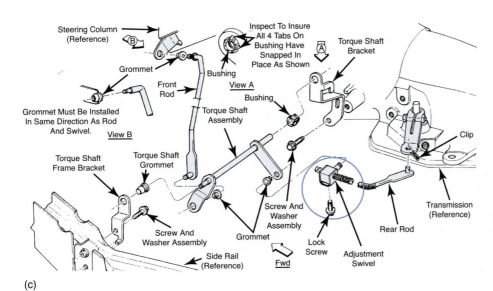

(c)

FIGURE 11-24   A floor-mounted shift linkage using a cable (a); a floor-mounted shift linkage using rods (b); and a column-mounted shift linkage using rods (c). Each one has a method of adjusting the length for proper gear positioning (circled). *(Courtesy of Chrysler Corporation)*

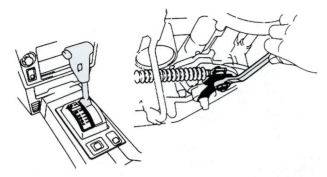

FIGURE 11-25   This neutral safety switch is mounted to the outside of the transmission case. If the starter operates with the gear selector in a position other than park or neutral, the switch position should be adjusted. *(Courtesy of Chrysler Corporation)*

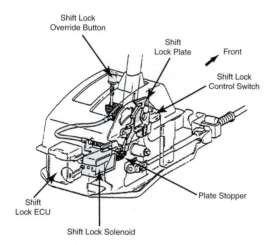

FIGURE 11-26   The manual shift lever is in park. The linkage adjustment is being tightened to lock the adjustment after making sure that the transmission is in park.

- Low TV pressure causes lower shift points, late or no downshifts, and soft, mushy shifts (cable is too loose).

On non-fuel-injected vehicles, it should be noted that the TV linkage movement begins at idle speed with the engine at normal operating temperatures. Most manufacturers provide a fail-safe in case the TV linkage breaks or comes loose. The fail-safe will cause very high TV pressure that will cause late and harsh upshifts.

Electronically controlled transmissions can use either a throttle cable or an ECM-controlled solenoid to modify mainline pressure based on engine load.

TV linkage checks are fairly easy and are normally made with the engine off. In some cases, the linkage binds only with the engine running. If symptoms indicate this is happening, some of the checks should be repeated with the engine running.

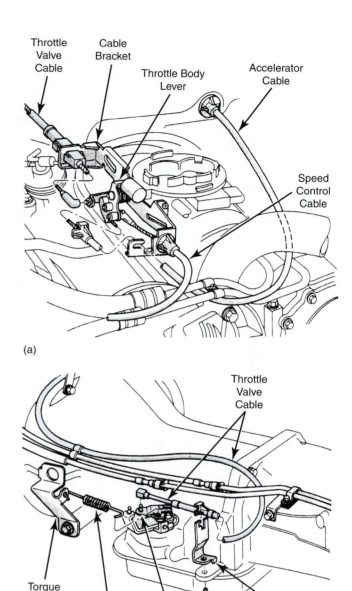

(a)

(b)

FIGURE 11-27   This TV cable connects the throttle body (a) to the transmission (b). The adjustment is at the throttle body cable bracket. *(Courtesy of Chrysler Corporation)*

Check service information for the proper adjustment procedure for a specific vehicle.

To check TV linkage, you should:

With the engine off:

1. Make sure that the throttle is closed against the idle stop (idle-speed adjusting screw). Check the cable or rod for any slack or free movement; in most cases, there should be none.

2. Move the throttle to the WOT position and, while doing this, check the cable or rod for free or sloppy movement, binding, or sticking.
   The TV linkage should move to the WOT position and release freely and smoothly.
3. With the throttle at WOT, pull on the TV linkage. It should be able to move a very small amount before contacting its stop inside the transmission.

With the engine running:

1. Firmly set the parking brake, and shift the gear selector to neutral.
2. Pull on the end of the TV cable or move the TV rod so it moves through its travel and then release it. During the linkage movement, check for free or sloppy movement, sticking, or binding. There should be none.

Improper TV operation should be corrected by readjusting, rerouting, repairing, or replacing the linkage.

REAL WORLD FIX

The 1989 Bronco (74,000 miles) has a harsh 4–3 downshift. On the road test, it was noted that the TCC was not applying. A remanufactured transmission was installed, but this did not fix the problem.

Fix. Following the advice of other technicians, the TV cable was checked and found to be out of adjustment. Adjusting the TV cable fixed this problem. A lot of time and money could have been saved if the proper diagnostic procedure had been followed.

TECH TIP

On vehicles using carburetors, it is good practice to ensure that the idle speed is correct and the carburetor fast idle cam is off before making a linkage adjustment. Also, the throttle should reach its wide-open throttle (WOT) position before the transmission's throttle valve bottoms in its bore.

REAL WORLD FIX

The 1990 Honda Accord (186,000 miles) has an engine flare on hard-throttle 2–3 shifts; light-throttle shifts are okay. The transmission was removed, and the clutches appeared good when inspected. There were no DTCs.

Fix. The technician was advised to adjust the TV cable so throttle pressure would begin increasing as soon as the throttle starts moving. This adjustment fixed this shift flare problem.

TECH TIP

A more exact check for proper TV operation can be made using a pressure gauge. With a gauge installed and the engine running, you should be able to see a pressure increase as you move the linkage toward WOT. This procedure is described in Chapter 12.

TECH TIP

Remember that many customers will be dissatisfied with harsh shifts caused by TV linkage that is too short, and the transmission can be ruined if the cable is too long.

11.5.1 Throttle Linkage Adjustments

Like the manual shift linkage, TV linkage is adjustable. Always consult the service manual for that particular vehicle when making an adjustment. The descriptions that follow are examples of some of the methods used. All adjustments are made with the engine off and the throttle at normal idle position unless specified otherwise.

To adjust TV linkage, you should:

"Threaded mounting" adjustment:

1. Measure the cable position as required in the service information (Figure 11-28). Some vehicles require measurements in both idle and WOT positions.
2. If adjustment is required, loosen the adjustment nuts on the cable housing, and move the cable housing to the proper position. Retighten the locking nuts after making the adjustment.

"Sliding swivel" adjustment:

1. Loosen the swivel lock screw; the TV rod should slide in the swivel.
2. Move the TV linkage forward against its internal stop, and retighten the lock screw.

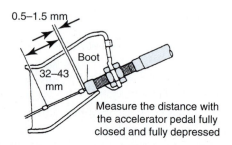

FIGURE 11-28   This throttle linkage is adjusted by turning the two adjusting nuts until the cable stopper ring is the correct distance from the housing end.

"Snap lock" adjustment:

1. Lift the snap lock to the unlocked position; the cable housing should be free to slide in the assembly (Figure 11-29).
2. Rotate the throttle to WOT, and push the snap lock inward to lock.

"Self-adjusting" adjustment:

1. Depress the readjusting tab, and move the slider inward against the base of the adjuster housing and release the tab (Figure 11-30).
2. Rotate the throttle to WOT. As this occurs, the cable slider should move at least three "clicks" or about 1/8 inch.

"Self-adjusting at transaxle" adjustment:

1. Depress the adjuster button, and extend the adjuster to its longest position by pulling on the cable housing.
2. Using the proper special tool, rotate the throttle to the WOT position using a torque of 50 in-lb (Figure 11-31). The adjuster should automatically change to the proper length.

"Gauge" adjustment:

1. Install a 0 to 300 psi pressure gauge in the proper transmission port (see Figure 12-10).
2. Start the engine and note the gauge pressure.
3. Adjust the linkage as necessary to correct the pressure.
4. Remove the gauge and reinstall the plug.

Throttle Position Sensor Position Adjustment. The TV signal on electronically controlled systems originates at the throttle position sensor (TPS) that is mounted on the throttle body (Figure 11-32). In some cases, the vehicle will run with an improperly adjusted TPS, but the transmission shift quality could be affected. TPS adjustment varies between vehicles; service information should be consulted when checking or making this adjustment. This adjustment could also affect engine operation and vehicle emissions. The TPS cannot be adjusted on some vehicles.

Manual Type T.V. Cable

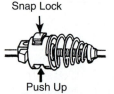

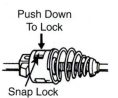

FIGURE 11-29   This throttle cable uses a "snap lock" adjuster that is adjusted using the procedure shown. *(Reprinted with permission of General Motors)*

Stop engine.

Unlock T.V. cable "snap-lock" button.

Rotate throttle lever by hand to wide open throttle and hold open.

Engage T.V. cable "snap-lock" button.

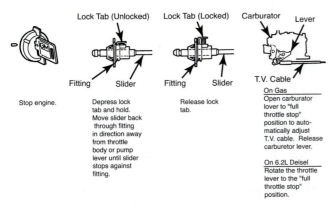

FIGURE 11-30 This "self-adjusting" TV cable is adjusted using the procedure shown. *(Reprinted with permission of General Motors)*

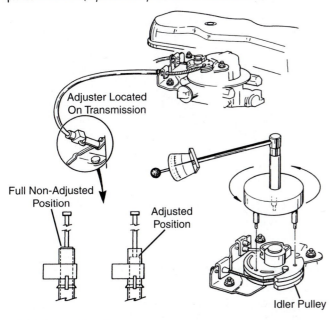

FIGURE 11-31 This "self-adjusting" TV cable used with some transaxles is adjusted using the procedure shown. *(Reprinted with permission of General Motors)*

REAL WORLD FIX

The 1996 Honda Accord (57,000 miles) came in with a shudder at 25 mph when warm. The tires were balanced and rotated, but this did not help. The shudder felt like a torque converter clutch was applying early, so the TCC solenoid was disconnected and the shudder disappeared.

Fix. Following advice, the technician adjusted the TV cable and changed the transmission fluid. The TV cable adjustment fixed this shudder complaint.

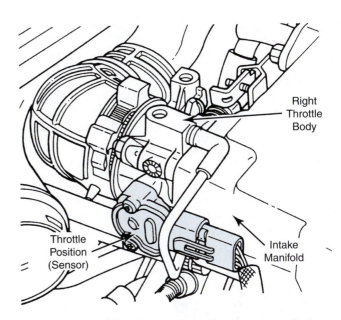

FIGURE 11-32 The throttle position sensor normally has an adjustment so it is positioned correctly on the throttle body. *(Courtesy of Chrysler Corporation)*

11.6 BAND ADJUSTMENTS

At one time, a common transmission maintenance procedure was to readjust the band clearance. Wear of the friction material would increase the clearance to the point where engagement would not be complete and slippage would occur (Figure 11-33). Modern fluids and friction materials have reduced the need for regular band adjustments. Also, the band in many modern transmissions is used only in manual ranges for compression braking. The band is expected to last the life of the transmission. Most new transmissions have no provision for in-car adjustments; any adjustment is made during transmission overhaul.

Some older transmissions have threaded adjusters extending through the case to allow an easy readjustment of the band. Some band adjustments are made inside the transmission and it is necessary to drop the pan to gain access to the adjuster.

It is good practice to check the band adjustments during a fluid change or if there is a shift problem related to a band. Service information should be checked to determine the exact adjustment procedure for each particular vehicle. The following procedure is very general.

To readjust a band, you should:

1. Loosen the lock nut on the adjuster screw several turns (Figure 11-34).
2. Tighten the adjuster screw to the specified torque. Special adjuster wrenches with preset torque settings are available for this operation.

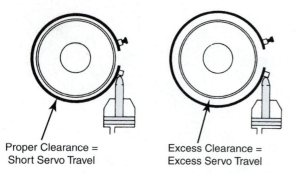

Proper Clearance =
Short Servo Travel

Excess Clearance =
Excess Servo Travel

FIGURE 11-33   When a band is new, the servo piston travels only a short distance to apply it. As the lining wears, servo piston travel increases; if there is too much wear, the band might not tighten completely.

TECH TIP

When adjusting a band using a threaded adjuster, it is good practice to count the number of turns as the adjuster is turned inward. For example, if the adjuster is turned three complete turns and then backed off two and one-half turns, the difference gives an indication of the amount of lining wear.

TECH TIP

With some transmissions, it is recommended to replace the lock nut with a new one. These transmissions use a rubber sealing ring formed in the nut to prevent a fluid leak.

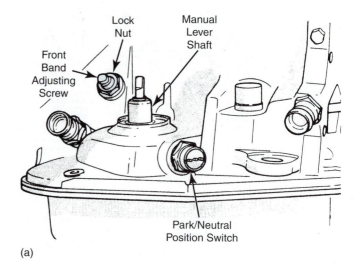

(a)

Lock Nut

Manual Lever Shaft

Front Band Adjusting Screw

Park/Neutral Position Switch

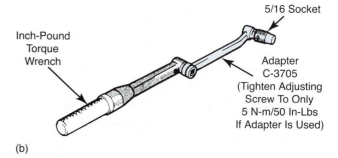

5/16 Socket

Inch-Pound Torque Wrench

Adapter C-3705 (Tighten Adjusting Screw To Only 5 N-m/50 In-Lbs If Adapter Is Used)

(b)

FIGURE 11-34   This band is adjusted by holding the adjuster screw while the lock nut is loosened (a). Step 2 turns the adjuster screw inward to 72 in-lbs (8 N-m) of torque. The special adapter is used if there is tight access (b). Step 3 is to back off the adjusting screw the proper number of turns and tighten the lock nut to the correct torque. *(Courtesy of Chrysler Corporation)*

3. Mark the adjusting screw position; back it off the specified number of turns. Hold the adjuster screw stationary and retighten the lock nut to the specified torque.

4. Road test the vehicle to check your adjustment. For example, a loose intermediate band (on a Simpson three-speed transmission) can cause a long, drawn-out 1–2 shift; a tight intermediate band will cause a drag in reverse, first, and third.

SUMMARY

1. Automatic transmissions require periodic service and maintenance.
2. Transmission fluid should be regularly checked for correct level and good condition.
3. The transmission fluid should be changed at the required intervals or if the condition indicates the need for a change.
4. The manual shift linkage and the throttle linkage need to be checked and adjusted if necessary.
5. Some transmissions have one or more bands that may need to be adjusted.

REVIEW QUESTIONS

The following questions are provided to help you study as you read the chapter.

1. Servicing and maintaining an automatic transmission includes:
   a. Checking the _____ level.
   b. Changing the _____.
   c. Cleaning or replacing the _____.
   d. Checking and adjusting the _____ and _____ linkages.
   e. _____ the bands if required.

2. It usually takes _____ _____ to change the fluid level from low to full on the dipstick.

3. Mushy operation, lack of engagement, or slipping can be caused by a transmission that has a fluid level that is too _____.

4. Before checking the fluid level, the vehicle should
   a. be on _____ ground.
   b. be in _____.
   c. be at normal operating _____.
   d. have the engine _____.

5. All transaxles share fluid between the differential and the transmission. True or False?

6. When checking the fluid level, the _____ and _____ should also be checked.

7. The normal color of automatic transmission fluid is _____.

8. What is indicated by these fluid conditions?
   a. Dark brown color
   b. Burned odor
   c. Pink or milky color
   d. Gold or brown coating on the dipstick
   e. Metallic appearance
   f. Foamy

9. An automatic transmission can be ruined by contaminated _____.

10. Severe driving conditions include:
    a. Frequent _____ pulling.
    b. Heavy _____ and _____ traffic.
    c. _____ weather conditions.
    d. _____ service.
    e. _____ or _____ police usage.

11. The major factor that affects transmission fluid life is _____.

12. To change fluid in most automatic transmissions, the _____ must be removed.

13. Before installing the clean pan after draining the fluid, check the pan for _____ and _____ sealing surface.

14. The notchy feel and clicking sound when a gear is selected is caused by the spring-loaded _____.

15. To properly adjust the manual linkage, always check the manufacturer's _____ procedures.

16. A sticking, binding, or out-of-adjustment throttle valve cable can cause _____ shifts, _____ shifts, or late, soft, mushy or no downshifts.

17. An exact check for proper throttle valve operation is made using a _____ gauge.

18. It is always necessary to consult a _____ _____ when making a throttle linkage adjustment.

19. Throttle position sensor adjustment will affect _____ operation, vehicle _____, and transmission _____ quality.

20. Many modern automatic transmissions use a band that does not require adjustment because the band is only used for _____ braking and in _____ ranges.

CHAPTER QUIZ

The following questions will help you check the facts you have learned. Select the answer that completes each statement correctly.

1. Student A says that you should check the transmission fluid level with the engine idling in park. Student B says that if the end of the dipstick is too hot to hold, the fluid can be considered hot. Who is correct?

   a. Student A

   b. Student B

   c. Both A and B

   d. Neither A nor B

2. Student A says that on most dipsticks, the distance from the bottom of the cross-hatched area to the top is equal to 1 pint of fluid. Student B says that too much fluid in a transmission can cause poor shifts. Who is correct?

   a. Student A

   b. Student B

   c. Both A and B

   d. Neither A nor B

3. The transmission fluid should be changed if it has

   a. black or brown coloration.

   b. a definite burned smell.

   c. gone the limit of miles recommended by the manufacturer.

   d. Any of these

4. Student A says that too high a fluid level can cause foamy fluid to spill out of the vents or filler pipe. Student B says that too low a fluid level can cause this same problem. Who is correct?

   a. Student A

   b. Student B

   c. Both A and B

   d. Neither A nor B

5. Student A says that all ATF is a bright medium-red color. Student B says that all ATF has the same burnt, oily smell. Who is correct?

   a. Student A

   b. Student B

   c. Both A and B

   d. Neither A nor B

6. A pink transmission fluid color indicates

   a. normal operation.

   b. too high a level and air in the fluid.

   c. water in the fluid.

   d. None of these

7. Student A says that transmission fluid life is dependent on the transmission's operating temperature. Student B says that driving conditions that increase fluid temperature, such as trailer towing or delivery-type operations, shorten fluid life. Who is correct?

   a. Student A

   b. Student B

   c. Both A and B

   d. Neither A nor B

8. Student A says that most transmissions can be drained by removing the drain plug. Student B says that you should also change the filter when the fluid is changed. Who is correct?

   a. Student A

   b. Student B

   c. Both A and B

   d. Neither A nor B

9. Student A says that you normally have to start the engine as you refill a transmission with fluid. Student B says that a torque converter can be refilled with the engine off. Who is correct?

   a. Student A

   b. Student B

   c. Both A and B

   d. Neither A nor B

10. Student A says that if an engine cranks while the gear position indicator is in drive, the manual shift linkage is out of adjustment. Student B says that this problem can be caused by a misadjusted neutral safety switch. Who is correct?

    a. Student A

    b. Student B

    c. Both A and B

    d. Neither A nor B

11. You can quickly check the adjustment of the manual shift linkage by

    a. trying the operation of the starter in the various gear positions.

    b. feeling for the transmission internal detents as you move the gear selector from park to low.

    c. feeling for complete engagement of the lever pawl into the park gate.

    d. Any of these

12. Student A says that a misadjusted manual linkage can cause vehicle creep in neutral. Student B says that a gear selector can slip out of park if the linkage is not adjusted correctly. Who is correct?

    a. Student A

    b. Student B

    c. Both A and B

    d. Neither A nor B

13. Student A says that most manual linkages can be easily adjusted by repositioning the adjustable end of the rod or cable. Student B says that the selector lever should be positioned in reverse while adjusting the linkage. Who is correct?

    a. Student A

    b. Student B

    c. Both A and B

    d. Neither A nor B

14. If the throttle linkage is too short, the transmission will probably

    a. shift early.

    b. have very late shifts.

    c. have soft, mushy shifts.

    d. Both a and b

15. Student A says that sticky throttle linkage can cause erratic shifts. Student B says that passing gear engagement is affected by the throttle linkage adjustment. Who is correct?

    a. Student A

    b. Student B

    c. Both A and B

    d. Neither A nor B

16. Student A says that the bands in modern transmissions can be adjusted using an adjuster screw that extends out at the side of the transmission case. Student B says that if the intermediate band (three-speed transmission) is too tight, there will be a drag in reverse. Who is correct?

    a. Student A

    b. Student B

    c. Both A and B

    d. Neither A nor B

17. To drain the fluid from the differential of a transaxle,

    a. remove the transaxle pan.

    b. drain the differential separately from the transmission.

    c. check the service manual for the proper procedure.

    d. There is no need to check the differential fluid.

18. The shift lock mechanism is used to prevent the shifter from being moved out of park unless

    a. the brakes are applied and/or the key is in the ignition.

    b. the doors are closed and the key is in the ignition.

    c. the seat belts are on and the doors are closed.

    d. the doors are closed and the brakes are applied.

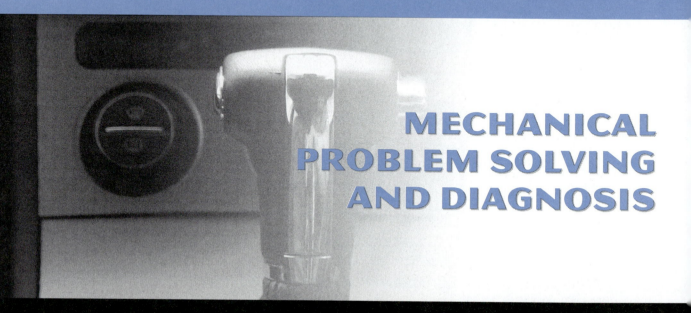

CHAPTER 12

MECHANICAL PROBLEM SOLVING AND DIAGNOSIS

OBJECTIVES

After studying Chapter 12, the reader should be able to:

1. Perform and analyze the tests that are used to diagnose transmission problems.
2. Determine the root cause of the transmission's problem.

3. Recommend the proper repair procedure.
4. Perform the SAE tasks for general transmission/transaxle diagnosis and the mechanical/hydraulic system.

KEY TERMS

Electrical System Check (p. 295)
Known-Good (p. 314)
Modulator Check (p. 295)
Modulator Weight (p. 313)

NVH (Noise, Vibration, and Harshness) Check (p. 295)
TCC (Torque Converter Clutch) Test (p. 295)
Technical Service Bulletins (TSBs) (p. 296)
Vacuum Supply/Source (p. 312)

12.1 INTRODUCTION

An automatic transmission is a complicated device, and there are many possible reasons for complete or partial failure. When experienced technicians are given a problem, they often go directly to the solution by basing their diagnosis on their experience. If they are not absolutely sure of the cause, they will perform the necessary tests to locate the specific cause of the problem.

A sound knowledge of automatic transmission operation helps greatly when diagnosing transmission failures. An example is a transmission that does not move in drive but starts in manual-1 and then, if shifted back into drive, operates normally. The power flow is the same in drive-1 and manual-1 with one exception. In drive-1, a one-way clutch is the reaction member; in manual-1, the one-way clutch is assisted by a band. In this case, the problem is probably caused by a faulty one-way clutch. Another example is a transmission that moves in drive but does not upshift. Knowledge of this transmission indicates that the intermediate band is not applying, but why? In this case, there are several possible faults besides the band, for example, no governor pressure, a modulator or throttle valve fault, or a stuck 1–2 shift valve. Additional tests are needed to determine the exact cause of this problem.

The following is a series of tests and checks that can be used to determine the exact cause of automatic transmission problems:

- *Visual inspection:* Involves a quick, preliminary overall check of external factors that affect operation.
- *Fluid check:* Ensures the correct level and condition (described in Chapter 11).
- *Road test:* Gives the technician the opportunity to: check the actual operation of the transmission, confirm the original concern, check shift timing and quality under different throttle openings, monitor torque converter clutch operation, and listen to unusual noises and vibrations.
- **Electrical system check:** Ensures that the electronic controls are operating correctly (described in Chapter 13).
- **Torque converter clutch (TCC) test:** Determines if the TCC is operating properly and isolates the cause of the problem.
- *Hydraulic pressure test:* Checks the hydraulic system pressures, which give a good indication of the condition of the pump, pressure control and shift valves, various seals, and gaskets.
- **Modulator check:** Checks the operation of the modulator and vacuum throttle valve system.
- *Stall test:* Loads the apply devices to check for slippage; also checks the torque converter stator one-way clutch.
- *Leak check:* Locates the source of a fluid leak.
- *Oil pan debris check:* The oil pan is inspected to determine if an abnormal amount of debris is present and, if so, the type nature of debris.

- *Air test:* Determines if the seals, sealing rings, and gaskets in the hydraulic circuits are operating correctly.
- *Wet air test:* A more precise air test locates the exact location or severity of a leak.
- **Noise, vibration, harshness (NVH) check:** Checks to locate the cause of a noise or vibration.

When diagnosing a transmission problem, a technician will perform only the checks appropriate for the problem. A technician relies on experience to determine which tests are needed, and will perform the checks in the most logical order for the particular problem.

12.2 PROBLEM-SOLVING PROCEDURES

One of the difficulties in describing a diagnostic procedure is caused by the varied types of problems that are encountered. There is no single diagnostic procedure. The process of finding and curing a leak or noise problem is different from the procedure to locate a faulty upshift. With experience, a technician makes the checks or tests that will identify the cause of a particular problem. It is recommended that a sequence similar to that shown in Figure 12-1 be followed.

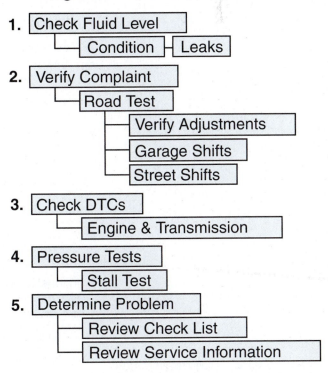

Diagnostic Test Procedure

1. Check Fluid Level
    Condition — Leaks
2. Verify Complaint
    Road Test
        Verify Adjustments
        Garage Shifts
        Street Shifts
3. Check DTCs
    Engine & Transmission
4. Pressure Tests
    Stall Test
5. Determine Problem
    Review Check List
    Review Service Information

FIGURE 12-1 *A general diagnosis procedure flow chart is used to locate automatic transmission problems.*

Problem solving should always begin with identifying the problem. This starts with the person who brings the problem to you. It is important to realize that the customer feels there is something wrong with the vehicle and may not understand automatic transmissions or automotive drive trains. In most cases, it is helpful to go for a road test with the customer; during the road test, the customer can explain the problem to you or demonstrate what he or she is experiencing. Taking notes while discussing the concern with the customer may prove helpful later in the diagnosis. Some manufacturers recommend that you follow a check sheet like the one shown in Figure 12-2. This gives the technician a more professional appearance and prevents skipping important checks.

An experienced technician will check all available diagnostic service information for any *technical service bulletins (TSBs)* for the vehicle. Some vehicles have known problems, and their repair is described in a TSB. These are called *pattern*

failures. Diagnostic information is also available on the Internet through several different organizations, such as the Automatic Transmission Rebuilders Association (ATRA), Automatic Transmission Service Group (STG), and International Automotive Technicians Network (IATN).

12.3 DIAGNOSTIC PROCEDURE

All transmission problem solving should begin with a check of the fluid level and fluid condition. Many problems can be caused by low or high fluid level or poor fluid condition. Fluid level and condition will often give you a clue as to the cause of the problem. Many technicians make it a practice to check the manual shift linkage and the throttle linkage at this time. Linkage checks are not difficult and take little time to complete. Several problems can result if the linkages are not working or adjusted correctly.

Vehicle _____

Driver _____   Recorder _____

Tach Reader _____   Speedometer Reader _____

1. D Range Upshifts: NORMAL   POWER

   Quarter Throttle   1-2 _____ mph   1-2 _____ mph
                        2-3 _____ mph   2-3 _____ mph
                        3-4 _____ mph   3-4 _____ mph

   Half Throttle   1-2 _____ mph   1-2 _____ mph
                        2-3 _____ mph   2-3 _____ mph
                        3-4 _____ mph   3-4 _____ mph

   Shift Quality: ☐ Normal   ☐ Excess Shock   ☐ Slippage

2. 2-Range Upshifts:

   Quarter Throttle   1-2 _____ mph
   Half Throttle   1-2 _____ mph

   Shift Quality: ☐ Normal   ☐ Excess Shock   ☐ Slippage

3. 2-Range Engine Braking: ☐ OK   ☐ NG

4. L Range Engine Braking: ☐ OK   ☐ NG

5. D Range Kick-Down:

	OK	NG
OD to 3	_____	_____
OD to 2	_____	_____
3 to 2	_____	_____
2 to 1	_____	_____

6. Manual Down-Shifts:

   ECT Transmission—At 35 mph in OD, press OD OFF button; record engine rpm change.   _____ rpm

   At 35 mph, shift from D to 2; engine speed increases.   _____ rpm

   At 25 mph, shift from 2 to 1; engine speed increases.   _____ rpm

Comments: _____

_____

_____

FIGURE 12-2 A diagnostic guide/concern checklist leads the technician through a series of systematic checks and provides a place to record the findings. *(Courtesy of Toyota Motor Sales USA, Inc.)*

REAL WORLD FIX

The 1994 BMW 740i (50,000 miles) will not move forward without full throttle or setting the program switch to winter mode. A scan tool check showed a selector signal fault, so the neutral safety switch was replaced. The car operated okay, but it came back in a few days with the original problem. A check showed no electrical fault codes. For some reason, the car moves backwards while idling in neutral. With the control unit disconnected, the transmission operates with a normal neutral.

Fix. A fellow technician provided a TSB describing a similar problem for this transmission. When making the checks described in the TSB, the technician found that a check ball had worn through the transfer plate. Replacing the 0.236-in. ball with a larger, 0.250-in. ball as directed by the TSB fixed this problem.

Poor engine performance can affect transmission operation. It is a good practice to check for recent engine or transmission service. While checking the fluid, look at the engine. Is it idling smoothly? Does it show signs of recent work? Does it appear to be well maintained? Are all the sensors, actuators, and controls connected? If the answer is no to any of these questions, make the necessary corrections before proceeding.

The next check varies with the nature of the problem, which can involve over a dozen different areas. The normally encountered problems and the checking procedure are shown in Table 12-1.

The diagnostic procedure for electronically controlled transmissions will be slightly different from nonelectronic units. For example, a problem in the electronic controls is indicated if the transmission malfunction indicator light (MIL) is illuminated. The technician should follow a diagnostic routine to solve electrical/electronic faults, as described in Chapter 13. If the transmission MIL is not illuminated, a hydraulic/mechanical system diagnostic routine as described in this chapter should be followed.

12.4 VISUAL INSPECTION

Before beginning any of the complex diagnosis checks, make a quick visual inspection of the vehicle and transmission to

TABLE 12-1 Diagnostic check procedure

Problems	Checks to Perform	Diagnostic Checks
1. Noise	A, G, H, I, L	A. Fluid level and condition
2. Vibration	A, G, O	B. Manual linkage
3. Smell	A, G, N	C. Throttle linkage
4. Leaks	A, N	D. Engine idle speed
5. Blows fluid out of vent or filter	A, J, M, N	E. Electronic controls
6. No forward or reverse gears	A, B, H, J, M	F. Modulator
7. Slips in any gear	A, B, E, H, I, J, K, L, M	G. Road test
8. Slow initial engagement	A, B, C, E, F, J	H. TCC
9. Harsh initial engagement	A, C, D, E, F	I. Band adjustment
10. No upshifts or downshifts	A, C, E, F, H, I, M	J. Hydraulic pressure test
11. Harsh shifts	A, C, E, F, H, I, J	K. Stall test
12. Engine flare during shift	A, C, E, F, H, I, J	L. Oil pan debris
13. Surge while driving	A, E, G, H	M. Air test
14. Converter clutch does not engage	A, E, G, H, J	N. Oil leak test
15. Stalls at stops	A, E, G, H	O. Vibration check
16. Creeps at stops	A, D, H, L	
17. Creeps in neutral	A, B, H	
18. Early, late, or irregular shifts	A, C, E, F, H, J	
19. Skips intermediate gear	A, B, E, H, I	
20. Drags or locks up on shifts	A, B, H	
21. No power, poor accelerations	A, H, K	

avoid overlooking the obvious. These checks should include the following:

- Fluid level and condition
- Fluid leaks
- Engine running condition
- Signs of past repair or tampering
- Motor/transmission mount condition
- Electrical connections to the transmission
- Vacuum connections to the transmission and engine
- If the vehicle does not move, the drive shaft(s), final drive, and differential condition

REAL WORLD FIX

The 1988 Ford F150 pickup (300,000 miles) AOD transmission was rebuilt for the second time because there is no reverse. The clutches and bands all appear okay.

Fix. Following advice, the technician checked the reverse sun gear drive shell and found a broken weld. Replacement of the reverse sun gear and drive shell fixed this vehicle.

NOTE: It is a good practice to review the power flow through the gearset when trying to determine the cause of a problem.

REAL WORLD FIX

The C4 transmission in the 1982 Mustang was just rebuilt, but it has a long, drawn-out, part-throttle, 2–3 shift. Full-throttle shifts are good. The band adjustments were checked, and they were also okay. The valve body was removed and inspected. No problem was found. The servos were checked, and they were okay.

Fix. Fellow technicians advised checking the modulator. Replacement of the modulator pin with one that was 1/16 in. longer fixed this shift problem.

12.5 ROAD TEST

A road test is used to verify the customer's concern and check the general overall condition of the transmission. The vehicle should be road tested at the start of the diagnosis and after the repair. The first road test helps the technician understand the customer's concern as well as the nature of the problem. The road test after repairs have been completed confirms that the repairs were successful. A road test may involve simply driving the vehicle and mentally reviewing the transmission operation (Figure 12-3). Depending on the problem, a technician may install one or more of the following: a hydraulic pressure gauge to measure line, governor, shift circuit, or cooler line pressure; a tachometer to measure engine speed; a vacuum gauge to indicate engine load; a test light or voltmeter to monitor electrical circuits; an electronic scan tool to monitor engine or transmission operation; or a special electronic transmission analyzer (Figure 12-4).

Following are items normally checked during a road test:

- Quality of the garage shifts (neutral–drive and neutral–reverse)
- Engagement time for the garage shifts
- Quality of each upshift and downshift at various loads
- Timing of each upshift and downshift at various loads
- Any busyness (hunting) between gear ranges
- Operation of the torque converter and TCC
- Slipping in any gear range

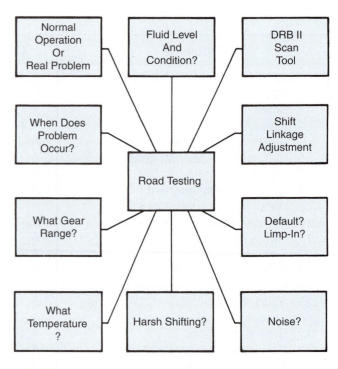

FIGURE 12-3 A road test is performed to verify the customer's concern and provide the technician information that can be used to determine the proper repair. *(Courtesy of Chrysler Corporation)*

- Binding or tie-up in any gear range
- Noise or vibration in any gear range
- Compression braking during deceleration in drive and manual gear ranges
- Speedometer operation (shows output from VSS)
- Engine operation

There are many shift quality and timing problems that can occur; the common terms used to describe abnormal shifts are described in Table 12-2.

A technician will often use a check sheet like the one shown in Checklist 12-1. This helps to make sure that no important points are skipped during the road test. It is also a good way to keep a record of the findings. The checklist

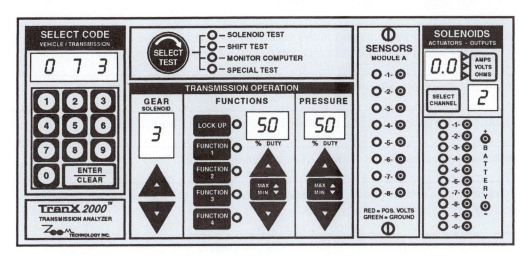

FIGURE 12-4 This transmission analyzer allows the technician to check the operation of electronic components. *(Courtesy of Zoom Technology)*

TRANSMISSION PRESSURE CHECKLIST

CHECKLIST 12-1 Checklists allow a technician to quickly record observations so they can be referred back to or shown to the vehicle owner. The code letter (from the center) is simply placed in the proper square if an improper operation should occur.

Vacuum Modulator Transmission

Engine Speed	Vacuum	Park	Neutral	Drive	Manual-1	Manual-2	Reverse
Idle	+15 in. Hg						
1,000 rpm	+15 in. Hg						
Idle	0 in. Hg						
1,000 rpm	0 in. Hg						

Mechanical Throttle Valve Transmission

Engine Speed	Throttle	Park	Neutral	Drive	Manual-1	Manual-2	Reverse
Idle	Closed						
1,000 rpm	Closed						
Idle	WOT						
1,000 rpm	WOT						

E = early, L = late, H = harsh, M = miss, N = noisy, S = slip, SO = soft

TABLE 12-2   Shift problem terms

Term	Meaning
Binding	A very noticeable drag that causes the engine to slow down and labor.
Bump	A sudden, harsh application of a clutch or band.
Chuggle	A bucking or jerking condition, similar to the sensation of clutch chatter or acceleration in too high of a gear with a standard transmission (could be engine related).
Delayed shift	The shift occurs sometime after normally expected. This is also called a "late shift."
Double bump	Two sudden, harsh applications of a clutch or band, also called "double feel."
Dropout	An unexpected shift to neutral or a lower gear, also called "fallout."
Early	The operation occurs before normally expected. An early shift results in a laboring engine, poor acceleration, and sometimes chuggle.
End bump	A shift feel that becomes noticeably firmer as it is completed, also called "end feel" or "slip bump."
Firm shift	A quick, easily felt shift that is not harsh or rough.
Flare	A rapid increase in engine speed usually caused by slippage.
Harsh shift	An unpleasantly firm band or clutch application.
Hunting	A repeated up-and-then-down shifting sequence that produces noticeable repeated engine rpm changes.
Initial feel	The feel of the beginning of the shift.
Late shift	See *Delayed shift.*
Rough	See *Harsh.*
Shudder	A more severe form of chuggle.
Slipping	A noticeable loss of power transfer that results in an increase in engine rpm.
Soft shift	A very slow shift that is barely noticeable.
Stacked shifts	An upshift that occurs immediately after another upshift.
Surge	An engine condition that is a very mild form of chuggle.
Tie-up	The result of being in two gears at once. See also *Binding.*

becomes a valuable tool when identifying the exact cause of the problem, explaining the nature of the problem to the customer, and in cases of warranty repairs, meeting the requirement for warranty documentation.

On the test drive, the technician will drive the vehicle in a normal manner while evaluating each upshift or downshift by sound and feel. He or she will note the timing and quality of each shift as the vehicle is operated in various driving conditions. A tachometer is a helpful tool when checking shift timing and TCC operation. If the vehicle is not equipped with a tachometer, a scan tool or tachometer can be used. Since the 1980s, important engine and transmission operating information can be obtained from a scan tool. A scan tool can be used to access and record the data as the vehicle is driven (Figure 12-5). This operation is described in Chapter 13.

The technician operates the vehicle at various throttle positions during the road test. Light-, medium-, full-throttle, and through detent or wide-open throttle (WOT) upshifts are made to check shift quality and timing under each of these conditions. The vehicle is also operated under different closed-throttle conditions. The various throttle positions used are defined as follows:

- **Minimum:** The least throttle opening that produces acceleration.
- **Light:** The throttle is about one-fourth open.
- **Medium:** The throttle is about one-half open.
- **Heavy:** The throttle is about three-fourths open.
- **Wide-Open Throttle (WOT):** Fully opened throttle without forcing a downshift.
- **Detent:** WOT, which forces a downshift.
- **Closed:** A complete release of the throttle, which results in coasting.
- **Engine Braking:** A closed-throttle manual downshift to produce a condition where engine compression slows the vehicle.

Manufacturers publish shift points for their vehicle drive train combinations. These are the vehicle speeds at which upshifts and downshifts should occur relative to the different throttle openings. It is easy to check the shift points. Accelerate

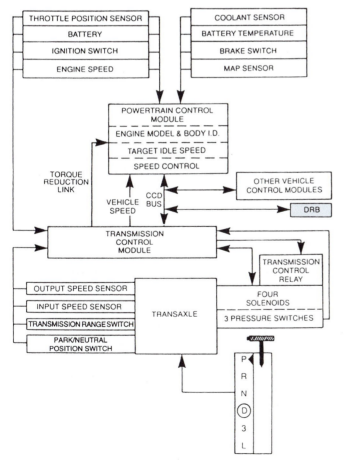

(a)

(b)

FIGURE 12-5 The DRB (Diagnostic Readout Box) is a scan tool that can communicate with the transmission electronic controls (a). It plugs into the diagnostic connector that is usually located under the instrument panel (b). *(a is courtesy of Chrysler Corporation)*

the vehicle using different throttle openings, and watch the tachometer or listen for the engine speed change that indicates a shift. Note and record the speed for comparison with the specifications. Remember that shift points are related to tire diameter and drive axle ratio. A change in either of these will affect the shift points. If no specifications are available, the approximate shift points are shown in Table 12-3.

Observe all speed limits and traffic regulations during a road test to ensure your safety and that of those around you. A road test is not a reason to violate any traffic law or regulation. Experienced technicians use the same test route for every test drive. This route includes all of the necessary driving conditions. Since the route is familiar, any malfunction becomes more obvious.

It is good practice to make sure that park works and will hold the vehicle stationary on a grade in both forward and reverse. While on the road test, stop the vehicle on a hill, shift into park, and carefully release the brake. It should only roll a short distance to completely engage park and then stop securely. Next, you should turn the vehicle around and repeat this test in the opposite direction.

TECH TIP

When diagnosing a "vehicle does not move forward problem," it may be possible to cause the transmission to operate by tightening a band all the way so there is no clearance. This should apply the band, and the operation of the transmission working or binding up should give you an idea of what might be causing the problem.

12.6 TORQUE CONVERTER CLUTCH TESTS

Possible TCC problems are failure to apply, failure to release, hunting or busyness, early application, or harsh application. These problems can be confirmed on a road test by using a

TECH TIP

On some vehicles, the governor weights can be held in the open position by placing a short section of rubber hose under the weights. This should cause the vehicle to make high-gear starts when shifted into drive because the shift valves should be upshifted by the increased governor pressure.

TECH TIP

TCC application is felt as a rather mild upshift with less engine speed change than a part-throttle upshift. Depending on the throttle opening, TCC application will cause the engine speed to drop about 50/100 rpm.

TABLE 12-3   Shift points

Closed Throttle	Speed	Part Throttle	Speed	WOT	Speed
1-2	5–10	1-2	15–30	1-2	35–45
2-3	15–25	2-3	25–45	2-3	55–65
3-4	30–45	3-4	40–55	3-4	Above 55–65
4-3	30–40	4-3	35–45	4-3	Above 55–65
3-2	10–15	3-2	30–40	4-3	55–65
2-1	5–10	2-1	10–20	2-1	25–40

scan tool or tachometer to note the engine speed change during clutch application.

To test an electronically controlled TCC, light application of the brake pedal should cause the converter clutch to release. An increase in engine speed of 50 rpm or more should be noticed as the clutch releases.

There are different procedures for troubleshooting each type of TCC. The description that follows will cover the most common electronically controlled systems. There are essentially two areas to check: hydraulic pressure and electrical control circuit; the electrical checks are described in Chapter 13.

12.6.1 Converter Clutch Hydraulic Checks

Most torque converter clutches apply when the oil flow through the converter is reversed. If a pressure gauge is installed in the oil cooler line, a slight momentary drop (or, in a few transmissions, a slight increase) in oil pressure can be observed during clutch apply.

TECH TIP

When diagnosing problems on a 4WD vehicle that uses an electrically shifted transfer case, remember that this type of transfer case can cause problems such as delayed or no engagement in forward or reverse and/or slipping in forward or reverse.

TECH TIP

The recommended TCC test procedure is to operate the transmission in its highest gear and then repeat it at the same speed in the next highest gear range. A greater rpm drop should occur in the higher gear because of the greater load on the converter. The greater load produces more slippage and therefore a greater rpm change during lock-up. Converter lock-up testing cannot be made on a hoist because of the very small rpm change that occurs when the vehicle has no road load.

To test converter clutch apply pressure, you should:

1. Install a 0 to 100 psi (0 to 689 kPa) oil pressure gauge in the transmission-to-cooler feed line at the radiator (Figure 12-6). A tee fitting should be used to prevent blocking the flow to the cooler. Carefully route the pressure gauge hose from under the vehicle, and tape the gauge to the windshield in view of the driver.

SAFETY NOTE: Make sure that the hose is not next to a hot exhaust or a location where it can be cut. At least one vehicle was destroyed by fire from transmission fluid spraying on a hot exhaust. This occurred while on a road test with a pressure gauge connected to the transmission.

TECH TIP

Poor engine operation has an adverse effect on TCC application. A rough-running or weak engine can cause a chuggle, busy feeling, or jerky TCC application. When the TCC applies, especially at low vehicle speeds, the engine speed can drop below the power band. Any engine malfunction becomes very evident as the engine struggles against the load. Adjust or repair all engine problems before condemning a torque converter.

REAL WORLD FIX

The 2000 Buick LeSabre (47,000 miles) came in with a misfire DTC and the transmission would not upshift unless the accelerator pedal was lifted. A scan tool shows a DTC for a shorted TCC. The fuses tested good. An exhaust rattle is noticed on the road test.

Fix. Following advice, the technician checked the exhaust system and found a back pressure of 2.5 psi at idle and 5 to 6 psi at half-throttle. This indicated a plugged catalytic converter, and replacement of the catalytic converter fixed the shift problem.

REAL WORLD FIX

The 1993 Jeep Cherokee (83,000 km) stalls the engine when shifted into reverse. This occurs after the engine and transmission are warmed up. If the engine does not stall, it bogs down, showing a severe load. When this occurs, the only test port with fluid pressure is the rear servo, and this pressure is normal. There are no DTCs.

Fix. Following advice, the transmission was removed and disassembled. The front pump was found to be severely worn. The customer decided to install a remanufactured transmission.

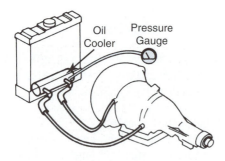

FIGURE 12-6   Converter clutch hydraulic operation can be checked by installing a pressure gauge in the transmission-to-cooler line. A change in pressure will be seen as the clutch applies or releases. Note that the gauge can be connected to the most accessible location in the cooler circuit.

2. Securely support the vehicle on a hoist or jack stands with the drive wheels raised.
3. Operate the vehicle in drive range until the 2–3 shift occurs and maintains a speed of 45 to 55 mph (72 to 88 km/h) as you watch the pressure gauge. A momentary drop of 5 to 10 psi (35 to 70 kPa) indicates operation of the TCC control valve.

TCC Test Results:

If the pressure changed and the converter clutch applied: This is normal operation.
If the pressure changed and the converter clutch did not apply: There is a problem inside the converter, a worn input shaft, or a cut O-ring on the input shaft (Figure 12-7).
If the pressure did not change: There is a problem in the converter clutch valve, control solenoid, or solenoid control circuit.

SAFETY NOTE: When running a vehicle with the drive wheels off the ground, never exceed 60 mph (96 km/h) on the speedometer. The differential can allow one tire to overspeed to 120 mph (193 km/h). At these speeds, the centrifugal force can cause the wheel cover to fly off or the tire could fly apart.

TECH TIP

NOTE: If a pressure gauge is reading near the maximum, stop the engine immediately, and replace it with a gauge of greater capacity.

TECH TIP

When measuring fluid pressures, always use a pressure gauge that has the capability to read higher pressures than you expect. A pressure gauge will be damaged if subjected to higher pressures than it was designed to measure. In other words, a 0 to 100 psi (0 to 690 kPa) pressure gauge does not have the capability of reading pressures over 100 psi, and it will be ruined if you try.

TECH TIP

NOTE: If you miss the pressure change while testing a TCC, lightly tap the brake pedal; this should cause the converter clutch to release and then reapply. The gauge pressure should fluctuate as this occurs.

12.6.2 Cooler Circuit Flow Check

A flow meter has been developed that can be installed into the cooler line (Figure 12-8). This tool is much more accurate than the old test method of disconnecting a cooler line and measuring the time it takes to pump a quart of fluid into a bucket. The flow meter allows measuring cooler flow in different gears as well as on a road test. It can be used to identify:

- a restricted cooler,
- a worn pump with low capacity,
- TCC apply and release,
- worn control valves.

To measure cooler line flow, you should:

1. Disconnect the cooler line at a convenient location. Connect the flow sensor into the cooler line using adapters as needed.
2. Connect the display unit to the flow sensor and plug it into the vehicle's power receptacle.
3. Start the vehicle, and observe the cooler line flow rate (Figure 12-9).
4. To check the TCC, drive the vehicle at a moderate speed while observing the flow rate.

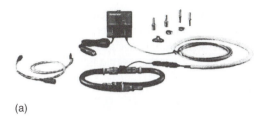

(a)

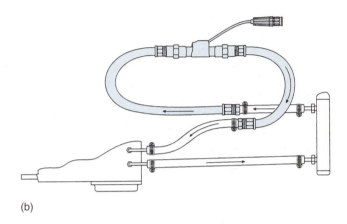

(b)

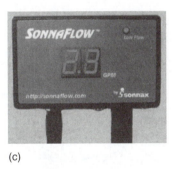

(c)

FIGURE 12-8   A flow meter (a) can be connected into the cooler line (b) and the vehicle's power supply. The vehicle can be road tested and the rate of fluid flow through the cooler line can be read on the display (c). *(Courtesy of Sonnax)*

FIGURE 12-7   This badly worn turbine shaft caused TCC pressure loss and improper operation. A cut or damaged O-ring would have a similar effect.

TIP: The traditional flow check of 1-quart-in-20-seconds corresponds to a flow rate of 0.7 to 0.8 GPM.

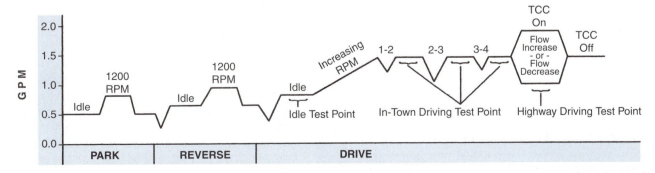

FIGURE 12-9   This graph shows the recommended flow through the cooler lines during different operating conditions. Note the flow change during TCC apply and release. *(Courtesy of Sonnax)*

This tool can also be used as a quality control check when road testing a transmission that has been rebuilt. If there is poor cooler flow, the unit will not have good lubrication, and it will probably fail much earlier than would normally be expected.

12.7 HYDRAULIC SYSTEM PRESSURE TESTS

The operation of an automatic transmission is dependent on hydraulic pressure. A technician uses a gauge pressure to check the condition of the hydraulic system. Some hydraulic system problems can be cured with the transmission still in the vehicle. For example, it is not a good business practice to remove and replace (R&R) a transaxle if the problem was caused by a loose valve body, faulty governor, or electrical problems.

All transmissions have a pressure test port, and some have more than one. If there is only one port, it will usually be for line pressure. The additional ports provide the apply or release pressure of a particular clutch, servo, governor, or throttle valve pressure (Figure 12-10). Most automatic transmission

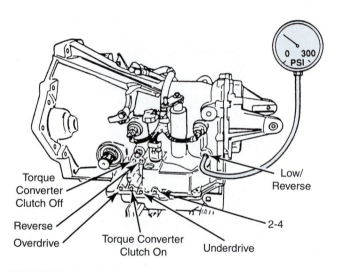

FIGURE 12-10 The pressure test ports for a 42LE transaxle are used for testing the various hydraulic circuits. *(Courtesy of Chrysler Corporation)*

TECH TIP

A common analog hydraulic pressure gauge is normally dampened, so minor pressure fluctuations are lost. The electrical transducer of an electronic gauge can be connected to a scope, which will allow you to watch small pressure changes and find an important clue as to the cause of a problem.

TECH TIP

If using a hydraulic pressure gauge, it is recommended that the gauge is 0–300 psi (0–2 Kpa) to prevent gauge damage while testing reverse gear pressure.

TECH TIP

An electronic pressure gauge uses a transducer installed at the test port and a wire to connect the transducer to the gauge. This eliminates the potential danger of a hose being damaged, causing a fluid leak and possible fire (Figure 12-11).

service manuals include illustrations to identify these test ports.

To test the transmission hydraulic pressures, you should:

1. Raise and securely support the vehicle on a hoist or jack stand.
2. Locate the pressure ports, remove the plugs, and connect the gauge(s) to the ports (Figure 12-12). Note that most domestic transmission ports use female, 1/8-in. National Pipe Threads (NPT).
3. If the tester is equipped with a vacuum gauge and the transmission uses a vacuum modulator, remove the vacuum hose from the modulator, and connect a tee to the vacuum gauge, vacuum supply line, and modulator.
4. Connect a scan tool or tachometer to the vehicle to monitor engine speed.
5. Route the various lines and wires so they can be read while the vehicle is operated. Be sure to keep them away from the hot exhaust system and rotating parts. Do not run the hydraulic lines or gauge inside the vehicle.
6. Place the gear selector in park, securely apply the brakes, start the engine, and note the readings on the various gauges. Some transmissions will not read line pressure in park; most will. The vacuum gauge should read about 15 to 20 in. Hg, and the tachometer should be reading idle speed.

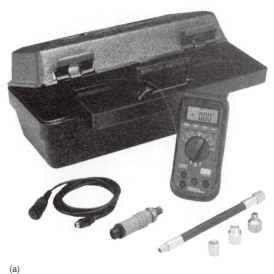

(a)

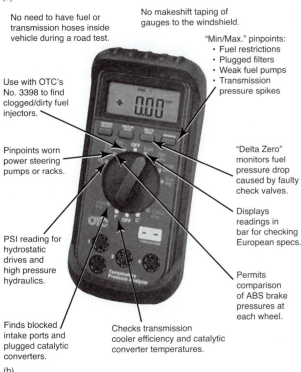

No need to have fuel or transmission hoses inside vehicle during a road test.

No makeshift taping of gauges to the windshield.

"Min/Max." pinpoints:
• Fuel restrictions
• Plugged filters
• Weak fuel pumps
• Transmission pressure spikes

Use with OTC's No. 3398 to find clogged/dirty fuel injectors.

Pinpoints worn power steering pumps or racks.

"Delta Zero" monitors fuel pressure drop caused by faulty check valves.

Displays readings in bar for checking European specs.

PSI reading for hydrostatic drives and high pressure hydraulics.

Permits comparison of ABS brake pressures at each wheel.

Finds blocked intake ports and plugged catalytic converters.

Checks transmission cooler efficiency and catalytic converter temperatures.

(b)

FIGURE 12-11 An electronic pressure gauge set (a) includes a pressure transducer(s) to convert pressure to an electronic signal that is displayed on the gauge (b). Note that the gauge can use four different pressure/transducer inputs. *(Courtesy of SPX/OTC)*

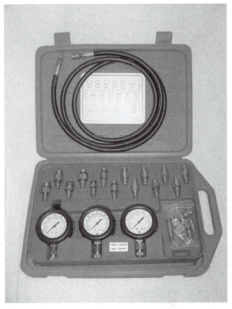

(a)

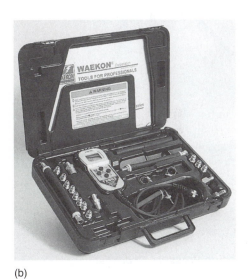

(b)

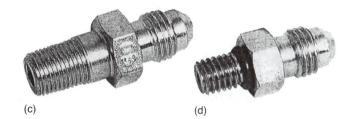

(c)   (d)

FIGURE 12-12 Pressure test kits have adapters to connect to the test ports of various transmissions. Adapter (a) uses a standard oil pressure gauge; (b) uses an electronic digital gauge that can also measure temperature. Adapter (c) uses self-sealing, tapered threads; adapter (d) uses straight threads that require an O-ring seal. *(Courtesy of Waekon Corporation)*

7. Run the engine at idle speed; shift the gear selector through each of the gear ranges and record the pressure readings (Checklist 12-2). On vacuum modulator transmissions, vacuum reading should be at least 15 in. Hg.

8. Make sure the brakes are securely applied; increase the engine speed to 1,000 rpm and repeat step 7.

9. *On mechanical throttle valve linkage transmissions,* disconnect the transmission TV linkage from the throttle and pull it to the WOT position. Repeat step 7.
10. *On vacuum modulator transmissions,* disconnect the vacuum line and plug the engine end to ensure normal engine operation. Repeat step 7.

TECH TIP

Always double-check that the fitting has the same threads as the transmission port. They usually have a good match if you can turn the adapter inward several turns using only your fingers.

TECH TIP

While testing pressure during a road test, watch the gauge pressure before, during, and after a shift. The pressure should drop and then come back; a lower pressure after a shift indicates a leaking fluid circuit.

12.7.1 Interpreting Pressure Readings

A technician compares the pressure readings to specifications to determine if the system is operating correctly.

The most likely cause for a pressure problem in park or neutral is the pump, intake filter, and pressure regulator because the fluid flow path is usually through the filter, valve body, transmission case, pump assembly, and back through the transmission case to the valve body. These are the circuits that are supplying fluid or are under pressure in that gear range. In park and neutral, the throttle valve, torque converter, and

REAL WORLD FIX

The 1990 Buick (130,000 miles) transmission was rebuilt, but at speeds above 45 mph, it will not downshift. The TV cable is adjusted properly, and the vacuum modulator is getting good engine vacuum. The line pressure is 69 psi in all gears, with or without the vacuum modulator connected. If the TV cable is pulled toward WOT, the line pressure will quickly jump up to 140 psi.

Fix. A careful recheck revealed that the modulator was removed to make transmission removal and installation easier. The modulator valve had fallen out, and the modulator was replaced without the valve. Installation of the modulator valve fixed this problem.

CHECKLIST 12-2 This checklist allows the technician to quickly record pressure readings.

Transmission Pressure Checklist

Mechanical Throttle Valve Transmission

Engine Speed	Throttle	Park	Neutral	Drive	Manual-1	Manual-2	Reverse
Idle	Closed						
1000 rpm	Closed						
Idle	WOT						
1000 rpm	WOT						

Vacuum Modulator Transmission

Engine Speed	Vacuum	Park	Neutral	Drive	Manual-1	Manual-2	Reverse
Idle	+15 in. Hg						
1000 rpm	+15 in. Hg						
Idle	0 in. Hg						
1000 rpm	0 in. Hg						

cooler are open to flow but the flow to the rest of the transmission is shut off at the manual valve. High or low pressures in neutral are usually caused by a problem in the throttle valve, torque converter, and cooler circuits.

The throttle valve and modulator circuits are tested by making pressure checks at high and low vacuum to the modulator or normal and full TV linkage movement. If line pressure increases in step 9 (neutral range), the throttle/modulator valve is working (Figure 12-13).

Clutch and band apply pressures are checked by moving the gear selector to the different gear ranges. For example, normal pressure in every range except drive-3 and reverse indicates leakage in the clutch that is applied for the drive-3 and reverse circuits. This pressure loss can cause slippage in high and reverse. It should be noted that you cannot check all of the servos with the drive wheels stationary. Some technicians take the pressure gauge on a road test or raise the drive wheels to allow upshifts to second, third, and fourth gear.

When a transmission has test ports for individual apply circuits as well as line pressure, the condition of that circuit can be easily determined by comparing its pressure with line pressure. For example, if line pressure is 75 psi (517 kPa) and third-gear pressure is also 75 psi, you know that the third-gear

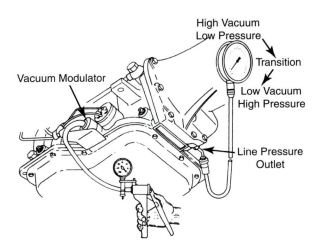

FIGURE 12-13   A properly operating modulator and TV circuit produces line pressure that is inversely proportional to the vacuum modulator. *(Reprinted with permission of General Motors)*

TECH TIP

If no specifications are available, the approximate pressures in most transmissions will be as follows:

- Neutral, park, and drive at idle: 50 to 60 psi (345 to 414 kPa)
- Neutral, park, and drive with the TV linkage at wide-open throttle or 0 in. Hg to modulator: 75 to 125 psi
- Manual-1 and M2: 50 to 60 psi; in some transmissions: 100 to 125 psi
- Reverse: 150 to 250 psi

TECH TIP

Any transmission that develops normal pressure in reverse is sure to have a good pump and pressure control circuit.

TECH TIP

If a transmission has an external servo cover that is retained by a snap ring, you can test for pressure by prying the cover inward slightly and shifting into the gear range that uses that servo. If the cover pops outward, there is fluid pressure in that circuit.

TECH TIP

Control pressure test results:

If okay in any range, the pump and pressure regulator pressure control solenoid and circuit are okay.

If okay in reverse, the pump and pressure regulator valve or pressure control solenoid and circuit are okay.

If low in all ranges, there is probably a clogged filter, defective pump, or defective pressure regulator valve, or faulty pressure control solenoid or circuit.

If low in any gear range, there is a problem in that circuit, probably defective seals or sealing rings.

circuit, all of the piston seals, and sealing rings are in good condition. If any circuit is more than 10 psi (69 kPa) lower than line pressure, there is a sealing problem in that gear circuit that must be corrected.

12.7.2 Fluid Flow Diagrams

Manufacturers provide *hydraulic schematics/fluid diagrams* of the fluid passages and valves (Figure 12-14). They are used to locate the cause of a problem such as low fluid pressure or no upshift. The diagrams are used to trace the fluid flow through a circuit in the same way that you would use a street map to locate the roads between two points.

The symbols (such as for check valves or exhaust ports) vary between manufacturers. These are shown in Figure 12-15.

12.7.3 Checking Governor Pressure

When a nonelectronic transmission fails to upshift and stays in first gear or starts out in third gear, the problem may be caused by a stuck governor or shift valve. Some transmissions provide a governor test port. Connect a pressure gauge to this port, raise the drive wheels, run the vehicle in drive, and watch the gauge. A steadily increasing pressure relative to wheel speed indicates a good governor and circuit.

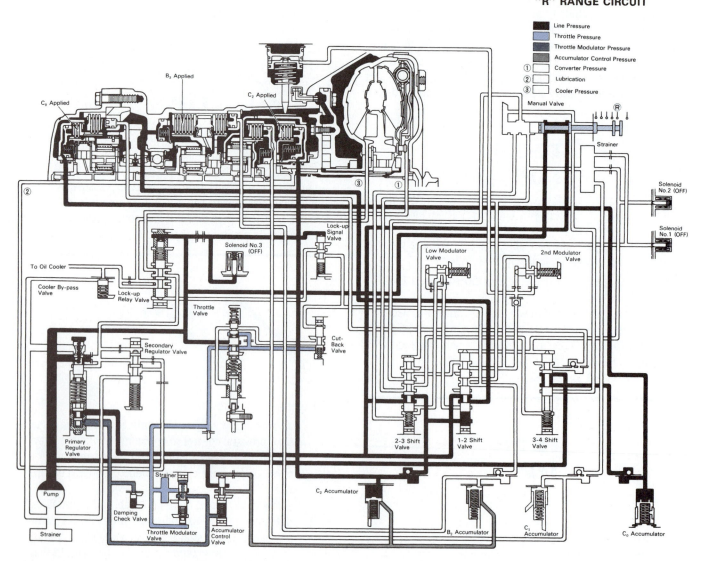

FIGURE 12-14   This A140E hydraulic diagram shows the fluid path for reverse; note the position of the manual valve. Also note the legend (upper right) indicating the color code used to show the circuit pressures. *(Courtesy of Toyota Motor Sales USA, Inc.)*

Many transmissions do not have a governor pressure port, but many have a governor cutback of line pressure as the vehicle is moving at 10 to 20 mph. This cutback can be seen on a pressure gauge connected to the line pressure port.

To check governor pressure, you should:

1. Raise and support the vehicle.
2. Connect a pressure gauge to the governor pressure port.
3. Disconnect and plug the vacuum line to the modulator.
4. Start the engine, place the gear selector in drive, and slowly accelerate the drive wheels. During acceleration, carefully note the gauge pressures. The pressure should increase at the same rate as vehicle speed.

To check governor cutback pressure, you should:

1. Raise and support the vehicle.
2. Connect a pressure gauge to the line pressure port.
3. Disconnect and plug the vacuum line to the modulator.

4. Connect a vacuum pump to the modulator, and maintain a constant 2-in. Hg vacuum during the test.
5. Start the engine, place the gear selector in drive, and slowly accelerate the drive wheels. During acceleration, carefully note the gauge pressures. At some point above 10 mph (16 km/h), the pressure should decrease.
6. Repeat this check with the gear selector in manual second and with 10-in. Hg vacuum. Pressure cutback should occur at some point above 5 mph (8 km/h).

If line pressure decreases, the governor is working. Governor cutback is also indicated by a pressure increase as the vehicle coasts down through these same speeds.

Some students have difficulty the first time they try to interpret a hydraulic schematic. After a little practice, though, they find it is not hard, and the schematic becomes a useful tool. Here are some tips that make them easier to read:

- When first looking at a diagram, do not try to read it all at once. Look for the circuit you need, and concentrate on it.
- Most manufacturers provide a separate fluid schematic diagram to illustrate the fluid flow path for the different gears. If you need to identify a gear position, look at the position of the manual valve and the shift valves.
- Many fluid diagrams are color-coded, and a legend normally identifies the various colors.
- A circuit is easiest to locate by starting from the servo or clutch and following it backward through the valves going toward the pump.
- Fluid passages often have a different name after they pass through a valve.
- The passages in and out of a valve are normally arranged in the same position as the real passages at the valve.
- The valves are normally shown in their actual position for the gear status of the diagram. For example, in drive-1, the shift valves should be in a downshift position.

	Chrysler	Ford	General Motors
1. Check Valve, Open			
2. Check Valve, Closed			
3. Shuttle Valve, Open			
4. Shuttle Valve, Closed			
5. Orifice			
6. Exhaust Port			
7. Screen			

FIGURE 12-15   Some of the hydraulic symbols used by the domestic vehicle manufacturers.

A rule of thumb is that the governor pressure should be about the same as the speed; governor pressure at 20 mph should be about 20 psi.

12.8 MODULATOR CHECKS

Some transmissions use a vacuum modulator to control shift points and feel. Engine vacuum is used to adjust TV, line, accumulator, or shift valve pressure. Modulator checks should include diaphragm leakage, vacuum supply, sleeve/stem alignment, spring pressure, and on-car operation. The on-car checks are similar to those described in Section 12.7. The modulator should be checked whenever there is a concern about shift timing or quality and when a transmission is overhauled.

12.8.1 Modulator Diaphragm Leakage

There are several ways to check the modulator. The easiest is to remove the vacuum hose from the modulator and inspect the inside of the hose for automatic transmission fluid (ATF). Any sign of ATF on the vacuum side of the modulator indicates a faulty modulator diaphragm.

12.8.2 Modulator Vacuum Supply

A modulator must have a good **vacuum supply/source** in order to operate correctly. Many technicians check the vacuum source first when they suspect a modulator problem. This is checked by installing a tee and a vacuum gauge at the modulator port (Figure 12-18). Start the engine, and let it idle in park (parking brake applied). With the engine at operating temperature, the vacuum reading at the modulator should be about

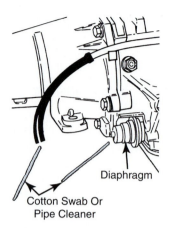

FIGURE 12-16 A cotton swab or pipe cleaner is used to wipe the inside of the modulator port or vacuum hose, and it should show no sign of ATF.

FIGURE 12-17 Applying a vacuum to the modulator should cause the pin to move inward about 1/4 in. The modulator should hold the vacuum for at least 30 seconds.

TECH TIP

Some technicians wipe the inside of the vacuum hose with a cotton-tipped swab or pipe cleaner (Figure 12-16). Any red ATF easily shows up on the white cotton.

A hand-operated vacuum pump can be used to check the modulator diaphragm. Connect the vacuum pump to the modulator port and apply 20-in. Hg of vacuum (Figure 12-17). The vacuum should hold and not leak down for at least 30 seconds. This check can be made with the modulator on or off the vehicle. If this test is made with the modulator off the vehicle, the sleeve/plunger should move smoothly inward as the vacuum is applied and smoothly out again as the vacuum is released.

TECH TIP

If the modulator is off the vehicle, a quick way to check the diaphragm is to push the sleeve/plunger all the way inward; it should move smoothly inward against the spring pressure. With the sleeve all the way in, place your finger over the vacuum port and release the plunger/sleeve. The sleeve/plunger should remain inward, and a vacuum should be felt at the port. Release your finger, and the sleeve/plunger should pop out. This is a fast, simple check, but is not as accurate as using a vacuum pump.

A modulator with a leaky diaphragm must be replaced.

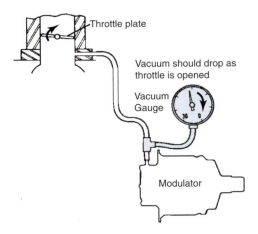

FIGURE 12-18   A vacuum gauge can be connected into the vacuum modulator line using a tee fitting. A good, strong vacuum signal that varies with throttle opening should be present when the engine is running.

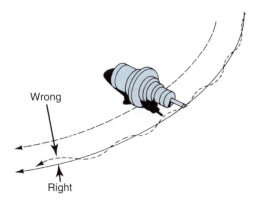

FIGURE 12-19   If a modulator is rolled across a bench top, the stem section of a good modulator should not wobble up and down. A wobble motion indicates a bent stem.

TECH TIP

Some technicians disconnect the vacuum line from the tee fitting while the engine is running to check for restricted lines. The vacuum leak created should cause the engine to stall or at least pick up speed and run rough. If the engine speed stays the same, there is a restriction.

TECH TIP

An alternate check is to place the modulator so only the stem is contacting the bench top and, again, roll the modulator (Figure 12-19). If the body wobbles up and down, the stem is bent, and the modulator should be replaced.

15 to 20 in. Hg. This reading is affected by altitude and engine condition. Higher altitudes produce lower readings; 10 to 15 in. Hg is normal for an elevation of 5,000 ft. Worn or out-of-tune engines also produce weaker vacuum signals. While checking the vacuum, the throttle should be opened and closed quickly while watching the vacuum gauge. The gauge needle should quickly drop as the throttle is opened and then rise as it is closed. A small change in the engine speed or sluggish movement of the vacuum needle as the throttle is operated indicates a restricted or kinked vacuum supply line. Fluctuating vacuum readings indicate an engine problem. A vacuum reading that drops while the engine is at 2,000 rpm indicates a plugged exhaust system.

12.8.3 Modulator Stem Alignment

The body of the modulator must be aligned with the stem or else the plunger will bind. The modulator is in a fairly well-protected location, but when a transmission is removed or replaced, there is a possibility of bumping the modulator and bending the stem. The simplest way to check for a bent modulator is

to roll it across a bench top and watch for a wobble motion of the stem, which indicates a problem (Figure 12-19). You can expect it to roll in a circle. A bent modulator will produce an easily seen up-and-down wobble.

12.8.4 Modulator Spring Pressure

Modulator spring pressure is also called **modulator weight** by some technicians because it is measured by "weighing" the modulator. Place the modulator with the stem end down on a 0- to 20-lb scale that is graduated in pounds (Figure 12-20). With some modulators, an extension made from a 1/8-in. rod, a small bolt, or an old modulator valve must be used.

Next, simply push downward on the modulator as you watch the extension and the scale. At about 10 to 15 lb of pressure, you should be able to see the extension start to move into the modulator as the spring compresses. This is the minimum spring pressure, and as you push harder, the extension will move farther inward. At some point if you keep pushing, the spring will be fully compressed, and the inward movement of the extension will stop. This is the maximum spring pressure.

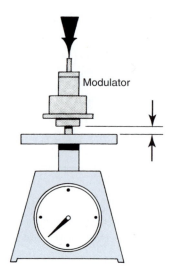

FIGURE 12-20 Modulator spring strength is checked by weighing the modulator. Push downward until the stem starts to retract into the modulator sleeve, and note the reading on the scale.

TECH TIP

A modulator with a higher spring pressure produces higher hydraulic pressures at a given vacuum than one with a weaker spring. This in turn produces firmer shifts. A heavier vehicle with a stronger engine generally needs a stronger, heavier modulator, whereas a lighter vehicle or one with a weaker engine needs a weaker, softer, lighter one.

TECH TIP

Some manufacturers use different sizes of modulators, and the strength of the modulator is affected by its diameter (see Figure 7-27). Remember that a modulator has atmospheric pressure on one side of the diaphragm and the vacuum manifold and the spring on the other. A larger diaphragm makes atmospheric pressure stronger relative to the spring.

TECH TIP

Some modulators are adjustable. Try turning the adjustment screw after you have weighed the modulator. Turning the screw inward should increase the weight. This causes the modulator-controlled pressures in the transmission to increase and should produce firmer shifts. Turning the screw outward should lower the modulator weight, which should produce softer shifts.

TECH TIP

With modulators that use a pin between the vacuum diaphragm and the throttle valve, modulator pressure can be adjusted by changing the length of the pin. A longer pin will increase pressures, and a shorter pin will decrease the pressure.

A similar modulator check is called the *load check* or *bellows comparison check*. It compares the strength of a "known-good" modulator with the one you are checking. A **known-good** modulator is one that you know is operating correctly; it must be of the same type and part number as the one you are checking. This check requires a special gauge that can be either purchased or made. The gauge is placed in the stem ends of the two modulators; then the modulators are pushed slowly toward each other (Figure 12-21).

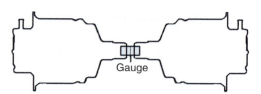

FIGURE 12-21 A modulator load check requires a special gauge and a known-good modulator. The two modulators are pushed together, and the gauge is read to determine if the one being tested is faulty.

If the modulators compress at the same rate while they come together, the one you are checking is good. If the modulator being checked compresses easier so that the center of the gauge disappears while it is 1/16 in. or more from the other modulator, the questionable modulator is bad.

12.9 STALL TESTS

Stall tests are used to check the stator one-way clutch and the strength of the apply devices. A band and clutch application chart is used when making a stall test to verify which clutch or band is applied in each gear range (Figure 12-22).

Caution should be exercised when performing a stall test for several reasons: personal safety, the safety of those around you, and the chance of possible damage to the vehicle and transmission. You will be operating the vehicle with the transmission in gear and the throttle wide open. There is a possibility that the vehicle can get away from you. All four wheels must be on the ground, the brakes must be in good operating condition, and the parking and service brakes must be firmly applied while performing a stall test. Many technicians place blocks at the front and rear tires.

Stall testing the transmission creates high pressure, a lot of heat inside the torque converter, and severe loads to the drive train. The period during which the transmission is at stall should be kept as short as possible, never over 5 seconds.

A stall test also places a heavy load on the engine's mounts. It is good practice to have the hood open and keep an eye on the engine while doing a stall test. If the engine appears to lift or rotate too far, stop the test immediately and check the condition of the mounts (Figure 12-23).

It is a good practice to shift into neutral between the checks and run at fast idle for 30 seconds or so to allow a change of fluid inside the converter.

Faulty mounts usually cause a heavy clunk or knock when you close the throttle and allow the engine to drop down on the mounts.

Shift Lever Position	Transmission Clutches And Bands					Overdrive Clutches		
	Front Clutch	Front Band	Rear Clutch	Rear Band	Overrun. Clutch	Overdrive Clutch	Direct Clutch	Overrun. Clutch
Reverse	X			X			X	
Drive Range First Second Third Fourth	 X X	 X	 X X X X		 X	 X	 X X X	 X X X
2-Range (Manual) (Second)		X	X		X		X	X
1-Range (Manual) (Low)			X	X	X		X	X

FIGURE 12-22   A clutch and band apply chart shows which units are applied during the different gear ranges. For example, with this 42RH/46RH transmission, the rear band and the front clutch are applied in reverse. *(Courtesy of Chrysler Corporation)*

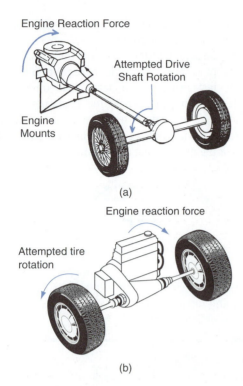

(a)

(b)

FIGURE 12-23 During a stall test, torque reaction tries to lift the left side of an RWD vehicle's engine (a). It tries to rotate the top of an FWD vehicle's engine toward the rear (b).

Most manufacturers publish stall speed specifications for their engine-transmission combinations. This allows for an easy comparison between your readings and the specifications. If specifications are not available, you can compare the readings between gear ranges; stall speed should be the same in each gear. Remember that the brakes of the vehicle hold the transmission output shaft stationary, and the clutches and bands should hold the transmission and the torque converter turbine stationary. Slipping of these parts allows the turbine shaft to rotate and therefore the engine speed to increase. Too high of a stall speed indicates slippage inside the transmission.

To perform a stall test, you should:

1. Connect a tachometer to the engine following the directions for the tachometer.
2. Position the vehicle with all four wheels securely on the ground. It is a good practice to place blocks in front and in back of the drive wheels (Figure 12-24).
3. Start the engine and note the tachometer reading.

SAFETY NOTE: Direct any bystanders away from the front or back of the vehicle.

4. Apply the brakes firmly, move the gear selector to reverse, move the throttle to wide open, and watch the tachometer. The speed should increase to somewhere between 1,500 and 3,000 rpm. As soon as the speed stops increasing or goes higher than 3,500 rpm, quickly note the reading and close the throttle. Record the speed.

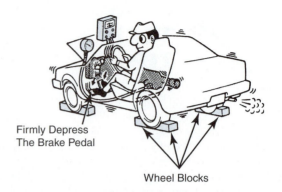

FIGURE 12-24 The wheels should be blocked, and both the parking and service brakes should be firmly applied during a stall test. A tachometer is used to measure engine speed, and if needed, a pressure gauge is used to measure system pressure.

TECH TIP

It is recommended that you mark the upper and lower stall speed limits on the face of your tachometer using a grease pencil or nonpermanent marker. This allows you to quickly note the tachometer reading and determine if the stall speed is good, low, or high.

TECH TIP

During a stall test, the throttle should not be held open longer than 5 seconds.

5. Shift to neutral, and run the engine at fast idle for 30 to 60 seconds to cool the converter.
6. Repeat steps 4 and 5 with the gear selector in drive.
7. Repeat steps 4 and 5 with the gear selector in low.

12.9.1 Interpreting Stall Test Readings

If all of the stall speeds were within the specification range: The apply devices for the three gear ranges are all sound and in good shape. The apply devices for some gear(s) cannot be applied with the vehicle at rest so they cannot be stall tested.

A stall check of a Type 2 transmission shows the stall speed is too high only in drive-1. The clutch and band chart indicates that the forward clutch and the one-way clutch are the apply devices for drive-1. The forward clutch must be good because it is also applied in manual-1, and the stall speed is okay in manual-1. Therefore, the high stall speed in drive-1 is caused by a faulty one-way clutch. If the stall speed was too high in both drive-1 and manual-1, the forward clutch would be the cause of the problem.

If all of the stall speeds were equal but low: The engine is weak, out of tune, or the stator one-way clutch is slipping. Checking engine performance will let you know which is at fault.

If the stall speeds are normal, but the vehicle has normal acceleration and has reduced performance at higher speeds: The stator one-way clutch could be seized in a locked-up condition.

If the stall speed is high in one or two of the gear ranges: One or more of the apply devices is slipping. Consult a clutch and band application chart to determine which apply devices are at fault.

12.10 OIL PAN DEBRIS CHECK

When it has been determined something is wrong with the transmission, the next step is to drain the oil and remove the pan for inspection. The debris in the pan can give a good indication of what is occurring in the transmission.

- A small amount of debris with a blackish oil film is normal. A small amount of metal can be attributed to the wear that occurs during break-in and normal operation.
- An excess of loose, black material is burned lining material from a slipping band or clutch. It usually has a burned smell.
- A heavy golden brown coating is from badly oxidized, old fluid. The lower part of the case and valve body will also have this varnish coating. It usually has a strong odor similar to varnish and indicates that the transmission ran hot.
- An excess of metal is from a gearset, thrust washers, bushings, or the transmission case. Steel and iron are usually from the gears, needle bearings, a spring, or a spring retainer. Aluminum is from the case, a carrier, or a clutch piston. Brass or bronze is from a bushing or thrust washer.
- Any plastic debris (broken or melted) is from a thrust washer, spacer, or clutch spring retainer.

It is a good practice to inspect the pan while the transmission is still in the vehicle. If you wait until it has been removed and placed on a bench, the debris might move around inside the unit. This could cause a misdiagnosis of the problem.

Transmissions that use internal input and/or output speed sensors will attract iron or steel particles to the magnetic tip of the sensor. Removing the sensor provides an easy check for debris.

12.11 AIR TESTING

Air testing is a valuable diagnostic tool and is also used as a final quality-control check during transmission assembly. Air tests are used to tell if a clutch or band servo operates, if a governor can operate, and if the passages are properly sealed.

SAFETY NOTE: You must wear eye protection when making air tests.

Air tests often are made with the valve body removed. With it removed, the passages to the apply devices are easily accessible. Many manufacturers provide illustrations in their service information that identifies these passages (Figure 12-25).

A rubber-tipped air gun is normally used when making air tests. It is merely pushed against the end of the passage to make a seal (Figure 12-26).

To perform an air test, you should:

1. Remove the pan and valve body and identify the fluid passages to be tested.
2. Adjust the air pressure to 30 to 50 psi. Apply air pressure to the passages one at a time. As you air test the different components, you should get the following results:
   a. Band servos: operation of the band with a very small amount of air leakage. Removal of the air gun from the passage should result in band release. Some bands

FIGURE 12-25   The passages in this Torqueflite transmission are identified so the different components can be air checked. They are exposed when the valve body is removed. *(Courtesy of Chrysler Corporation)*

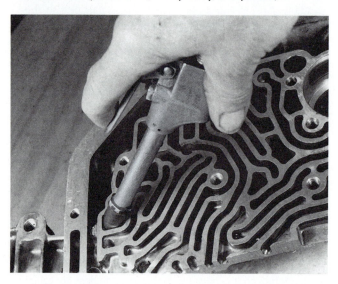

FIGURE 12-26   A rubber-tipped air gun is commonly used for air checks. Pushing it against the port opening usually makes an airtight seal. It must be removed from the opening to allow air to escape and release the component.

TECH TIP

If the passage ends in a long slot, a shop cloth can be forced into part of the opening to close it down to a manageable size (Figure 12-27).

FIGURE 12-27   When the test port is a long slot, part of the slot can be closed off by forcing a shop cloth into the slot.

TECH TIP

When air testing through an irregularly spaced hole, a common washer can be placed over the hole, and the air is applied through the washer's hole (Figure 12-28).

FIGURE 12-28   A common washer can be used to air test irregularly shaped passages to close oversize or odd-shaped holes.

require that air be used to apply the band and a second air nozzle be used to release the band. When the second air nozzle is removed, the band will reapply, and when the first air nozzle is removed, spring pressure will release the band.

b. Clutches: a "kachunk" noise indicates the clutch applied. Removal of the air gun should result in the sound of a clutch release. If the air nozzle is kept in place, good clutch seals should hold air pressure for about 5 seconds or more after the air is turned off.

Some technicians use an air gun that is modified with a piece of tubing for hard-to-reach locations (Figure 12-29). Special test plates are also available to provide air-pressure access to difficult passages (Figure 12-30).

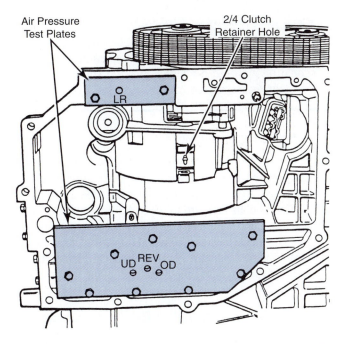

FIGURE 12-29 The tip of this air gun has been replaced with an adapter and short length of 1/4-in. tubing. The tubing can be bent for difficult-to-reach locations.

Pressures of about 50 psi (345 kPa) should be used while air checking. Very high pressures (over 90 psi/621 kPa) can cause normal seepage to appear as a major leak. Remember that air passes through openings easier than ATF. In some cases, the air pressure should be dropped to 20 psi (138 kPa).

Some clutches have two piston areas—an inner and an outer. When air is applied to one chamber, it can normally leak into the other and pass out through the other apply port. You can cover this second port with your finger while testing.

   c. Governor: air tests will vary between makes. There are two governor ports to check: one is the feed from the drive circuit and the other is the return from the governor. Check both of them. In some cases, you will get a "click" or "snap" and then a very small leak, a "click" and an open exhaust leak, or a rather heavy "buzz" sound. The exact sound depends on the type of governor, the position of the governor shaft, and whether you blow air into the inlet or outlet passage. The response should change if you plug the second passage with your finger. As you gain experience, you will learn the correct response from the governor for a particular transmission.

12.11.1 Wet Air Checks

At times, it is difficult to determine excessive leakage during an air test. You hear or feel an air leak, but is it bad enough to condemn a part or cause the problem? Sometimes, you hear the leak, but you cannot locate the exact location. When you need to detect a small leak or determine if valve or bore wear is excessive, you can make a wet air check. This is the same as an air test with a small amount of ATF put into the passage

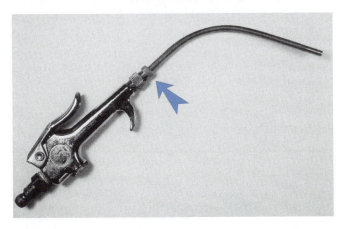

FIGURE 12-30 The two air pressure test plates have been installed to help make the air checks of the LR, UD, REV, and O/D circuits of the 42LE transaxle easier. The 2–4 clutch can be checked without a plate. *(Courtesy of Chrysler Corporation)*

TECH TIP

It is also possible to air check the whole transmission or an individual circuit by blowing air into the pressure test ports. If checking the whole transmission, insert the rubber tip of the air gun into the "line" test port, set the air pressure to about 90 psi (621 kPa), and apply air pressure (Figure 12-31).

Depending on the location of the test port in the hydraulic circuit, the air flow can be controlled using the manual valve. In some cases with the transmission on the bench, the pump will rotate, but it can be held stationary by installing the torque converter. With some transmissions, the governor weights can be blocked outward, and the shift valves will operate in an upshift position. This allows pressure checking of each of the gear positions, which you can control by shifting the manual valve. If the transmission has pressure test ports for the different circuits, each of these circuits can be checked by pressurizing each port. Note that this pressure will try to exhaust at the shift valve, but you can often block this flow with your finger. In this case, you might have to drop the air pressure to about 40 psi (275 kPa). While performing these checks, you should be listening for escaping air that indicates leaks.

FIGURE 12-31 A transmission can be air checked by blowing air into the pressure test ports. In this case air is being blown into the 2–3 pressure port to check the third-gear circuit. Air leaks can be heard through the filter tube.

prior to the check. It is recommended to regulate the air pressure to 30 to 50 psi when making a wet air test. Any leaks show up easily because of the escaping red ATF. With experience you will learn how to tell if the leak is excessive.

REAL WORLD FIX

The 1994 Chevrolet C-1500 pickup (162,000 miles) makes a 1–3 shift, skipping second gear. The 4L60E transmission was disassembled, and the 2–4 band and input drum were worn out, metal to metal. The transmission was rebuilt using a new band, input drum, shift solenoids, and torque converter. The transmission was reinstalled, but the road test showed the same problem. A scanner showed the 1–2 shift occurring, but the transmission shifts 1–3.

Fix. The 2–4 servo was rechecked and found to be leaking. Replacement of the seals in the 2–4 servo fixed this shift problem. Air checks during assembly could have found this servo problem and prevented the come-back and extra time locating the problem.

TECH TIP

Teflon rings or seals lubricated with Vaseline or Door-Ease may take more pressure or temperature before normal operation. You can increase the pressure, but you should be prepared for a high-pressure spray of fluid. You must wear eye protection.

To perform a wet air test, you should:

1. Put a small amount of ATF into the suspected passage to be checked. A pump assembly or valve body is usually assembled, and all plugs should be installed in the passages.
2. Adjust the air pressure to 30 to 50 psi, apply air to the passage, and carefully check for escaping air and ATF (Figure 12-32). Be careful when removing the air nozzle from the passage, as ATF can blow back. Turn off the air and let the pressure drop before removing the nozzle.

12.11.2 Isolating Valve Body Problems

A hydraulic circuit analyzer is available to test valve body operation, while it is off the transmission (Figure 12-33). The valve body is connected to a series of gauges, and fluid

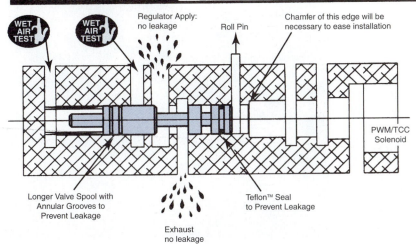

WET AIR TEST INFO

Regulator Apply:
no leakage

Roll Pin

Chamfer of this edge will be
necessary to ease installation

PWM/TCC
Solenoid

Longer Valve Spool with
Annular Grooves to
Prevent Leakage

Exhaust
no leakage

Teflon™ Seal
to Prevent Leakage

FIGURE 12-32 A wet air test is performed by putting a small amount of ATF into the passage before a low-pressure air test. Fluid leaking from the regulator apply or exhaust passages indicates a worn valve. *(Courtesy of Sonnax)*

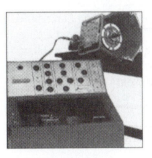

Tests Units
On Bench

Tests Units
In Vehicle

FIGURE 12-34 The Answermatic can be connected to transmissions that are on the bench or in a vehicle. This allows pressure checking the hydraulic circuits using pressurized ATF. *(Courtesy of Zoom Technology)*

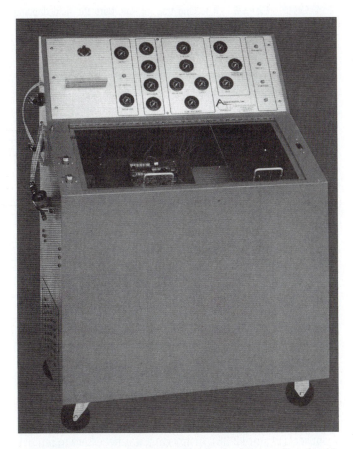

FIGURE 12-33 The valve body under the clear cover (near front) is connected to the diagnostic machine through a series of pressure lines. Fluid under pressure can be directed to the valves, and their operation can be observed on the pressure gauges. *(Courtesy of Zoom Technology)*

pressure can be sent into the system to simulate the flow from a transmission. The operator can cause the valve body to perform shifts while watching the pressure change. This unit can also be connected to a transmission that is either on the bench

or in a vehicle. This allows pressure testing the transmission using fluid pressure (Figure 12-34). If testing a transmission that is in the vehicle, the technician can operate the transmission using the machine controls.

12.12 OIL LEAK TESTS

There are several tests that can be made to locate the cause of oil leaks. Most leaks originate at the joints or connections between the various parts of the transmission; between the cooler line connections; at the front-torque converter seal, rear extension housing/universal joint seal; or with transaxles, the two CV (constant velocity) joint seals (Figure 12-35).

The cause of a leak can often be found by raising the vehicle on a hoist and making a visual inspection. You can usually follow the red ATF upward and often forward to the source (Figure 12-36). A *fluorescent dye* is available that can

REAL WORLD FIX

The 1997 Dodge R1500 pickup (90,000 miles) came in with a delayed 2–3 shift. The shift solenoids were replaced, and this seemed to fix the problem. However, the vehicle returned with the same problem, and the customer said there was also a slip into third gear under a hard load. The technician felt that a direct clutch seal was failing.

Fix. Following advice, the technician told the customer that the seal was probably leaking and that DOT 3 brake fluid will cause the seals to swell. The customer added 6 oz of brake fluid to the transmission, and this seemed to fix the slipping problem. Adding brake fluid to an automatic transmission can be considered a diagnostic step. Since this temporarily fixed the problem, we know that the seal was leaking. The seals should be replaced to correctly fix the problem.

A. Pump gasket
B. Front seal
C. Pump O-ring
D. Cover gasket
E. Level plug seal
F. CV joint seal
G. Pan gasket
H. Case
I. Cover gasket
J. Vent tubes
K. Shift shaft seal

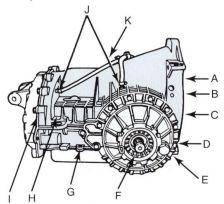

FIGURE 12-35 Possible leak locations for most transmissions are the pump seal and gasket, output shaft seal(s), pan gasket, manual shift shaft, vent(s), and case porosity. A cover gasket, drain, or fill plug is another possibility.

be added to the transmission fluid. The blacklight causes the dye to glow, making the leak visible (Figure 12-37).

A leak coming from inside the torque converter housing usually indicates a bad front seal, but this can also be caused by a leaking torque converter, faulty pump gasket, or faulty

FIGURE 12-36 A leaking transmission. Note the fluid dripping off the governor cover and the washed area at the rear of the pan. This fluid probably came from above and forward of these points.

FIGURE 12-37 Fluorescent dye has been added to the transmission fluid. The dye will glow when the blacklight (arrow) shines on it, showing the location of the leak.

front seal (Figure 12-38). In any case, it is necessary to remove the transmission for a closer inspection and repair.

12.13 NOISE, VIBRATION, AND HARSHNESS (NVH)

NVH has become the automotive repair trade term for noise, vibration, and harshness problems. Unpleasant noise and vibration problems can be caused by automatic transmissions.

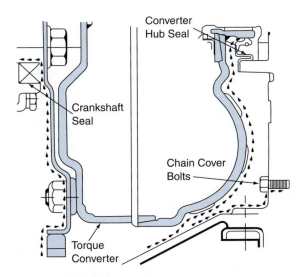

FIGURE 12-38 Fluid from a leaking front seal or pump gasket tends to move down the front of the transmission. Fluid leaks from a converter drain plug or bad welds tend to come from the outer surface of the torque converter. A leak from the back of the engine will move across the flexplate. *(Courtesy of Chrysler Corporation)*

TECH TIP

The vent of some transmissions is located in the bell housing. A fluid overfill can cause what appears to be a leak in this area.

TECH TIP

When there is so much fluid that you cannot locate the source of the leak, it is necessary to steam clean the transmission and vehicle underbody. After cleaning the transmission, drive the vehicle briefly to dry things off. Operate the transmission in all gear ranges at high-throttle openings to move the high-pressure oil so the source of the leak can be seen. Then raise the vehicle on a hoist, and using a good, strong light, carefully check the transmission area for the red ATF.

TECH TIP

Some vehicles, including all recent General Motors vehicles, use Dex-Cool antifreeze, and Dex-Cool is dyed orange. Old Dex-Cool antifreeze can appear much like ATF. Make sure of the source for the leak you are trying to locate and fix.

TECH TIP

If you have located a leak in a general area but cannot find the specific location, thoroughly clean the area and dry it. Next, coat the area using an aerosol-applied foot powder. Most foot powders dry quickly and leave a white, powder coating. Any leak under this coating will show as an obvious red stain (Figure 12-39).

REAL WORLD FIX

The 1989 GMC C1500 pickup (292,000 km) has a fluid leak with an unknown source. The leak is not apparent with the engine running in the shop, but it will leak a quart of ATF after a few miles on the road. Fluid is sprayed all over the vehicle's front suspension.

Fix. Following advice, the technician put the vehicle on a lift and ran it through all of the gears. The leak was coming from some pin holes in the 2–4 servo cover. A new servo cover fixed this leak problem.

Harshness is defined as an unpleasant motion, above 20 Hz, that can be felt. Harshness is not a major concern for transmission technicians.

NVH problem diagnosis normally begins with a road test, and the technician notes when the noise or vibrations occur. The speed and gear range are varied to note their effect on the problem.

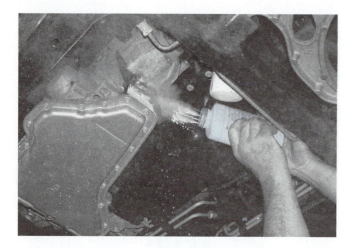

FIGURE 12-39 Foot powder is being spread on the suspected leak area. Next, the transmission will be operated, and the leak should be obvious as a red stain on the white powder.

TECH TIP

To locate those difficult-to-find leaks, it is possible to pressurize the transmission case with air and then locate the escaping air. This requires that you close off the oil filter and vent openings if the transmission is in the vehicle, and the converter, extension housing, and cooler line openings if the unit is out of the vehicle. Caps and plugs can be fabricated for this purpose, as shown in Figure 12-40.

TECH TIP

Leaks can be caused by a fluid level that is too high, excess fluid pressure, plugged vents, plugged drainback holes in some transmissions, improperly tightened fasteners, warped sealing surfaces, and cracked or porous castings.

To make an NVH road test, you should:

1. Make sure the vehicle is at normal operating temperature, start the vehicle, and accelerate the vehicle in drive, using a moderate throttle, to the problem speed or the speed limit. Note any unusual noises or vibrations.

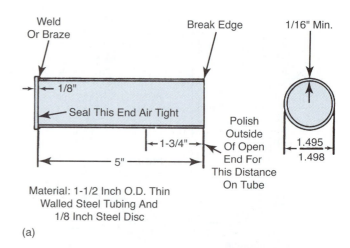

(a)

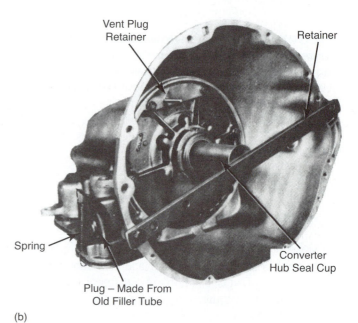

(b)

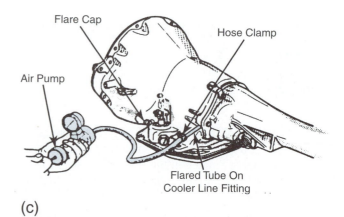

(c)

FIGURE 12-40 When the openings into the transmission are plugged, air can be pumped into the transmission through the cooler return line. Soapy water can now be sprayed onto the transmission, and bubbles will expose the exact location of any leaks. *(Courtesy of Chrysler Corporation)*

REAL WORLD FIX

The 1998 Ford Econoline E350 (91,000 miles) came in with several oil leaks. The easy leaks were repaired using the proper parts, but a small leak in the pump area was still evident.

Fix. The technician added dye to the fluid, and he was then able to locate a cracked pump housing. Replacing the pump assembly fixed this problem.

2. Let up on the throttle, and allow the vehicle to decelerate to a stop or a speed below the problem speed.
3. Repeat step 1 using full throttle. Do not exceed the speed limit.
4. Repeat step 2, shifting into neutral to allow the vehicle to coast.
5. Repeat step 1, using different gear ranges or throttle positions to give you a better idea of the origin of the problem.
6. An FWD vehicle can have a drive shaft, CV joint, or differential problem that is sensitive to turns. With these vehicles, it is recommended to repeat these steps while making gradual or sharp turns to cause a speed difference between the drive shafts.

12.13.1 Noise Checks

Noise problems are closely related to vibration; they often accompany each other. The sources of most objectionable noises in automatic transmissions can be the transmission mounts, torque converter, flexplate, drive chain and sprockets (in some transmissions), planetary gearset, band application, and transaxle final drive. Noise concerns are usually confirmed on a road test, and it is good practice to have the customer identify the exact noise. Remember that the engine, suspension system, tires, exhaust system, and drive line are also causes of objectionable noises.

The three most common sources of transmission noise are the bearings, gears, and hydraulic system. Bearings, both ball and roller, consist of three parts: the bearing element (rollers or balls with cage), and the inner and outer races. The races can be separate parts or a hardened portion of a shaft, gear, or carrier. Bearing noise, often described as a *whine,* is caused by damage, pits, or scoring that makes the bearing surface rough.

TECH TIP

Transmission mounts are designed to isolate transmission noises from the vehicle. The first check when looking for the cause of transmission noises should be a thorough check of the mounts.

TECH TIP

A bearing or gear is quiet when the parts are stationary or rotating at the same speed. A loaded bearing will make a noise only when the bearing elements are rotating.

TECH TIP

A damaged gear is noisier when it is being used to transmit power. For example, a damaged rear planet gear in a Simpson gear train will be quiet in second and third gears; it will be noisy only in first and reverse gears. A gearset will be quieter when it is a 1:1 ratio (usually third gear) and the gearset is locked up.

Gear noise is usually the result of a rough gear surface or a worn bearing that allows the gear to change position. Gear noise usually shows up as a whine in a certain gear or multiple gears. Another type of gear noise is a *clack* or *clunk* that occurs when there is a change in power flow; it is the result of excessive clearance in the gear train. Worn differential gears and differential pinion shaft are a major cause of neutral-to-drive or neutral-to-reverse clunk.

Hydraulic noise, often described as a *buzz,* is the result of rapid fluid pressure pulsations. With many transmissions, it will occur for a short time period while the fluid is cold and then go away.

TECH TIP

Hydraulic noise can be seen as a rapidly pulsating pressure gauge needle. Another tip is that the noise will change if the pressure changes. With some transmissions, shifting into or out of reverse will cause a pressure change because of the increased reverse boost, and this will change the noise level or frequency. On transmissions with a throttle rod or cable, move the lever toward full-throttle position, or on units using a vacuum modulator, disconnect the vacuum hose; this should change the TV boost and change the noise level or frequency.

TECH TIP

An NVH diagnostic tool, ChassisEar, consists of a headset and six sensors that can be attached to various locations under the vehicle. The vehicle can be driven on a road test while the technician listens to the six locations. This should help locate the exact source of the noise (Figure 12-41).

When troubleshooting noise problems, it helps to determine how the noise fits into the following categories:

- *Speed relation:* Related to engine or vehicle speed
- *Gear range:* Related to gear range
- *Pitch/frequency:* Low (rumble), medium (growl), or high (squeal)
- *Load sensitive:* Heavy throttle, light throttle, or coast
- *Direction:* Straight or right or left turn

To locate the cause of a transmission noise, you should:

1. Raise the vehicle so you have access to the transmission mounts. Visually check their condition, and if the mounts appear weak, pry upward on the transmission to check for possible separation of the mounts.
2. Start the engine and shift the transmission through its gear ranges while observing for any mount problems.
3. With the engine running and the gear selector in P or N, listen for the noise problem. Shift into D, and with the brake firmly applied, listen for the noise problem. A torque

(a)

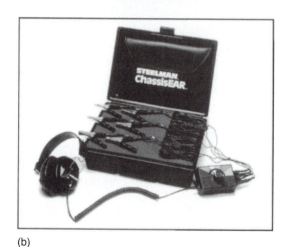

(b)

FIGURE 12-41 A ChassisEar has a microphone built into each of the clamps that are connected to various points under the vehicle. During a road test, the technician can switch between them and listen for the problem noise through the headset. *(Courtesy of Steelman)*

converter problem is indicated if the noise occurs with the transmission in gear but not in P or N. A pump problem is indicated if the noise occurs in both D and P or N. A faulty input drive chain and sprockets can also cause this problem (Table 12-4).

REAL WORLD FIX

The 1995 Neon (87,000 miles) has a bad, tinny rattle noise coming from the torque converter area. The noise occurs whenever the engine is running. Visual inspection through the inspection cover area does not show a problem. A cracked flexplate is suspected.

Fix. Removal of the transaxle allowed inspection of the torque converter and flexplate. Visual inspection showed that a balance weight had come loose. Replacement of the torque converter fixed this noise problem.

TABLE 12-4 Noise Isolation

Quiet	Noisy	Problem
In park or neutral	In gear with wheels stopped	Torque converter/input shaft/input drive chain
In park or neutral	In reverse with wheels stopped	Pump
In third gear (1:1 ratio)	In all other gears	Gearset
With wheels stopped	While moving and increases with speed	Final drive or chain drive

4. With the engine running, shift from N to R while listening for the noise. A hydraulic noise is indicated if the noise increases when shifted into R. Shift into D and pull on the TV cable, disconnect the vacuum hose from the modulator or alter the signal to the EPC solenoid to boost line pressure. A hydraulic noise is indicated if the noise increases.

5. Perform a road test and listen for noise changes as the transmission shifts through its gear ranges. A transmission gearset problem is indicated if the noise changes depending on the gear range, especially if it is quiet during the range with a 1:1 ratio.

6. Repeat step 5 and listen for a noise that increases as the vehicle speed increases. A final drive problem is indicated if the noise intensity or frequency increases with

TECH TIP

Sometimes transmission mounts can be neutralized to reduce noise transfer. Loosen the mounting bolts, lift the weight off of the mounts, and retighten the bolts so the mounts are in their natural position.

TABLE 12-5 Noise problems

Noise	Probable Cause
Chain noise	A whine or growl that increases in frequency and amplitude with vehicle speed. Most noticeable under light acceleration. Input chain noise can be heard in park and neutral.
Final drive	A hum related to vehicle speed. Usually torque sensitive.
Gear noise	A whine or growl related to vehicle speed. Usually torque and gear-range sensitive.
Pump noise	A high-pitched whine that increases in amplitude with engine speed. Most noticeable in park or neutral with cold transmission fluid.

vehicle speed. Note that the final drive can include transfer gears or chain drives depending on the transaxle.

Transmission noise problem areas usually fit into the categories shown in Table 12-5. The next step is disassembly and careful inspection of the suspected component. The exact cause might be a rough bearing, a loose drive chain, a cracked flexplate, or any number of other defects. Some manufacturers recommend the use of a diagnostic guide to locate the source of noise problems (Figure 12-42).

12.13.2 Vibration Checks

Occasionally a transmission repair or replacement results in a vibration, or a vehicle vibration diagnosis leads to the possibility of the transmission as the cause. Most transmission vibrations are caused by an unbalanced torque converter, an

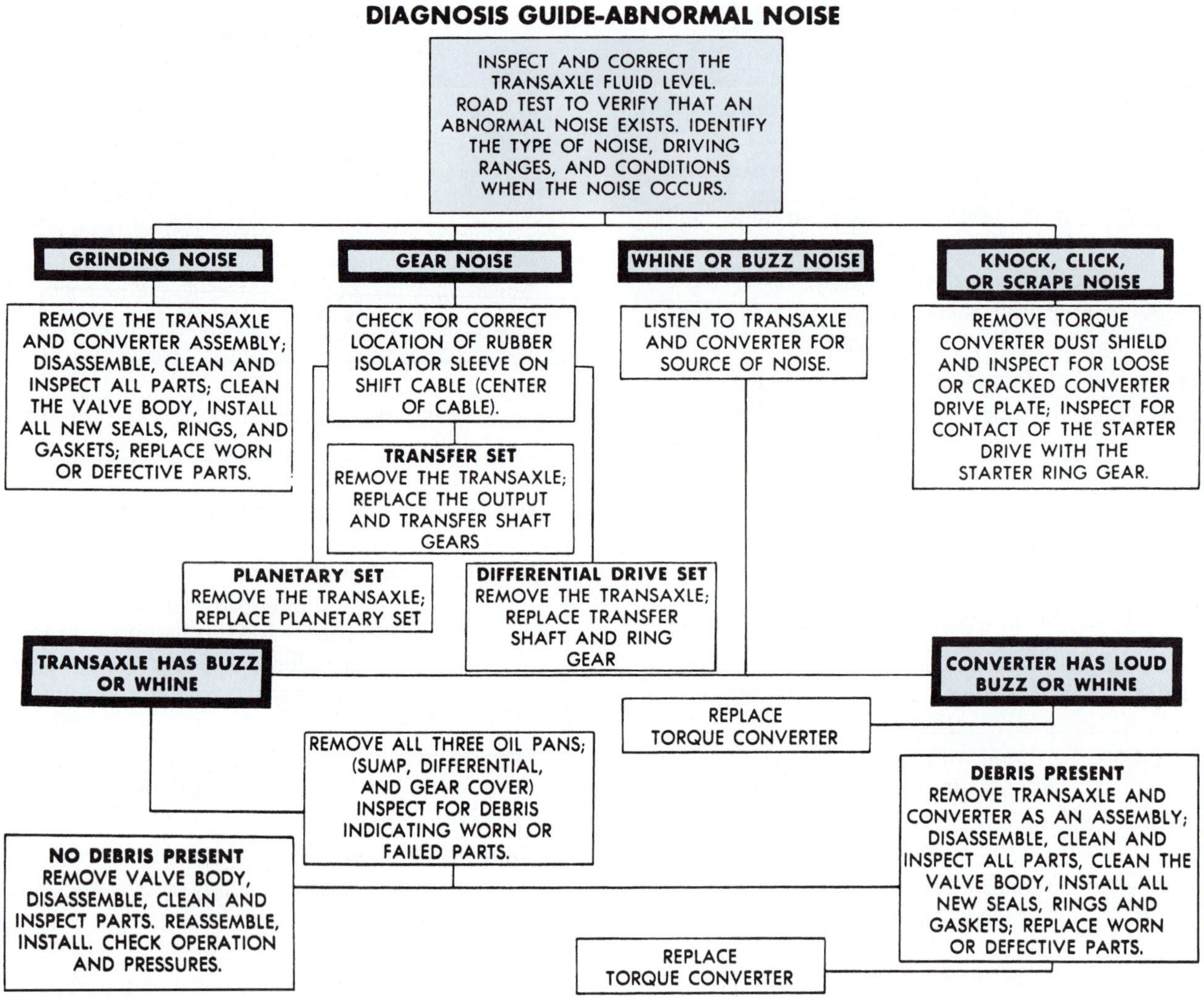

DIAGNOSIS GUIDE-ABNORMAL NOISE

INSPECT AND CORRECT THE TRANSAXLE FLUID LEVEL. ROAD TEST TO VERIFY THAT AN ABNORMAL NOISE EXISTS. IDENTIFY THE TYPE OF NOISE, DRIVING RANGES, AND CONDITIONS WHEN THE NOISE OCCURS.

GRINDING NOISE

REMOVE THE TRANSAXLE AND CONVERTER ASSEMBLY; DISASSEMBLE, CLEAN AND INSPECT ALL PARTS; CLEAN THE VALVE BODY, INSTALL ALL NEW SEALS, RINGS, AND GASKETS; REPLACE WORN OR DEFECTIVE PARTS.

GEAR NOISE

CHECK FOR CORRECT LOCATION OF RUBBER ISOLATOR SLEEVE ON SHIFT CABLE (CENTER OF CABLE).

TRANSFER SET
REMOVE THE TRANSAXLE; REPLACE THE OUTPUT AND TRANSFER SHAFT GEARS

PLANETARY SET
REMOVE THE TRANSAXLE; REPLACE PLANETARY SET

DIFFERENTIAL DRIVE SET
REMOVE THE TRANSAXLE; REPLACE TRANSFER SHAFT AND RING GEAR

WHINE OR BUZZ NOISE

LISTEN TO TRANSAXLE AND CONVERTER FOR SOURCE OF NOISE.

KNOCK, CLICK, OR SCRAPE NOISE

REMOVE TORQUE CONVERTER DUST SHIELD AND INSPECT FOR LOOSE OR CRACKED CONVERTER DRIVE PLATE; INSPECT FOR CONTACT OF THE STARTER DRIVE WITH THE STARTER RING GEAR.

TRANSAXLE HAS BUZZ OR WHINE

CONVERTER HAS LOUD BUZZ OR WHINE

REPLACE TORQUE CONVERTER

REMOVE ALL THREE OIL PANS; (SUMP, DIFFERENTIAL, AND GEAR COVER) INSPECT FOR DEBRIS INDICATING WORN OR FAILED PARTS.

DEBRIS PRESENT
REMOVE TRANSAXLE AND CONVERTER AS AN ASSEMBLY; DISASSEMBLE, CLEAN AND INSPECT ALL PARTS, CLEAN THE VALVE BODY, INSTALL ALL NEW SEALS, RINGS AND GASKETS; REPLACE WORN OR DEFECTIVE PARTS.

NO DEBRIS PRESENT
REMOVE VALVE BODY, DISASSEMBLE, CLEAN AND INSPECT PARTS. REASSEMBLE, INSTALL. CHECK OPERATION AND PRESSURES.

REPLACE TORQUE CONVERTER

FIGURE 12-42 This diagnosis guide is designed to help technicians locate the cause of abnormal noises in a 41TE transaxle. *(Courtesy of Chrysler Corporation)*

REAL WORLD FIX

The 1997 Pontiac Montana van (28,000 miles) has a noise problem on right turns. The CV joints check out okay.

Fix. Following advice, the starter was checked. The return spring was loose, allowing contact with the flywheel during right turns.

off-center torque converter, or a faulty output shaft–universal joint connection. Misaligned engine or transmission mounts can produce vibrations or noise caused by improper U-joint or CV joint clearance. An exhaust system contacting body parts will also produce vibrations that can be felt throughout the vehicle.

Torque converter problems cause an engine-speed-related vibration problem. Output shaft vibration problems are vehicle-speed related. These often are accompanied by drive line clunk. FWD output shaft problems will usually be most noticeable on turns because of the increased differential and CV joint action.

Engine-speed-related vibrations occur at a particular engine speed range; these vibrations change when the transmission shifts gears. There are several causes, for example, belt-driven

TECH TIP

Drive line clunk usually occurs during garage shifts, neutral–drive, or neutral–reverse. It can often be confirmed by looseness as you shake the universal joint side to side. The cure for this is usually a replacement of the rear extension housing bushing and seal or universal joint.

TECH TIP

Engine and transmission mounts are usually checked visually by inspecting them for deterioration or breakup of the rubber.

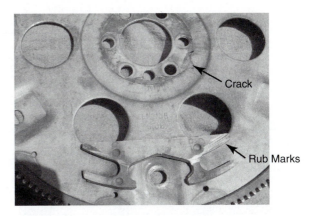

FIGURE 12-43 A cracked flexplate. Note the fine crack near the mounting bolts and the rub marks where the balance weight has been contacting the engine. *(Courtesy of Tony Jewell)*

REAL WORLD FIX

The 1991 Mazda B2600 4WD pickup (131,000 km) has a vibration at 1,300 rpm in neutral. The vibration occurs at the same engine speed while driving. The technician feels it might be a bad harmonic balancer.

Fix. The technician checked the transmission skid plate and saw where the plate was bent and was rubbing on the transfer case. Straightening out the skid plate fixed this vibration problem.

accessories such as the fan, alternator, air-conditioning compressor, or internal engine unbalance. Belt-driven problems can be identified by running the engine with the belt removed; if the vibration is gone, you have located the vibration source. Identifying a torque converter problem begins with removing the converter cover and carefully inspecting the torque converter and flexplate. Look for a wobble (called runout) of the converter during engine rotation. Torque converter runout can be caused by:

- Improper tightening of the torque-converter-to-flexplate bolts.
- A damaged flexplate (Figure 12-43).
- Improper mounting of the torque converter into the crankshaft.

If there is no runout, the next thing to do is to remove the torque converter and either check its balance or replace it.

12.14 TROUBLESHOOTING CHARTS

Another important diagnostic tool is the troubleshooting chart or diagnostic guide (Figure 12-44). These charts are published for each transmission and normally found in service manuals. They normally list the more common problems encountered. For each problem, there is a list of the most probable causes and what should be done to repair or correct the problem. The causes are normally listed in descending order starting with the most common or easiest to check.

As mentioned earlier, it is a good practice to determine what is wrong with a transmission before you disassemble it for repairs. This allows you to make the necessary checks during disassembly to locate the exact cause of the original problem and helps ensure that you cure all problems for the first time repairs are made.

DIAGNOSIS CHART "B"

POSSIBLE CAUSE	Harsh Engagement From Neutral to D	R	Delayed Engagement From Neutral to D	R	Poor Shift Quality	Shifts Erratic	Drives in Neutral	Drags or Locks	Grating, Scraping, Growling Noise	Knocking, Noise	Buzzing Noise	Buzzing Noise During Shifts Only	Hard to Fill, Oil Blows Out Filler Tube	Transaxle Overheats	Harsh Upshift	No Upshift Into Overdrive	No Lockup	Harsh Downshifts	High Shift Efforts	Harsh Lockup Shift
Engine Performance	X	X			X										X			X		
Worn or faulty clutch(es)	X	X	X	X		X	X	X							X	X		X		
—Underdrive clutch	X		X			X	X	X										X		
—Overdrive clutch						X	X	X							X	X				
—Reverse clutch		X		X		X	X													
—2/4 clutch						X		X							X			X		
—Low/reverse clutch	X	X				X		X										X		
Clutch(es) dragging							X													
Insufficient clutch plate clearance							X							X						
Damaged clutch seals			X	X														X		
Worn or damaged accumulator seal ring(s)	X	X	X	X														X		
Faulty cooling system														X						
Engine coolant temp. too low																X	X			
Incorrect gearshift control linkage adjustment			X	X		X	X							X						
Shift linkage damaged																				X
Chipped or damaged gear teeth									X	X										
Planetary gear sets broken or seized									X	X										
Bearings worn or damaged									X	X										
Driveshaft(s) bushing(s) worn or damaged									X											
Worn or broken reaction shaft support seal rings			X	X	X	X												X		
Worn or damaged input shaft seal rings			X	X													X			
Valve body malfunction or leakage	X	X	X	X	X	X	X				X							X	X	X
Hydraulic pressures too low			X	X	X	X								X	X			X		
Hydraulic pressures too high	X	X														X		X		
Faulty oil pump			X	X		X										X		X		
Oil filter clogged			X	X	X	X							X							
Low fluid level			X	X	X	X					X			X				X	X	
High fluid level													X	X						
Aerated fluid			X	X	X	X					X		X	X				X	X	
Engine idle speed too low			X	X																
Engine idle speed too high	X	X												X				X		
Normal solenoid operation												X								
Solenoid sound cover loose												X								
Sticking lockup piston																				X

CONDITION

FIGURE 12-44 This diagnostic chart is designed to help technicians locate the cause of improper operation of a 41TE transaxle. *(Courtesy of Chrysler Corporation)*

SUMMARY

1. Before removing a transmission from a vehicle or disassembling a transmission, the problem should be evaluated to determine the exact fault with the transmission.

2. There are many tests and checks that can be used to determine the exact cause of an automatic transmission problem.

3. A technician should become familiar with how and when to perform the transmission tests to determine the cause of common problems.

4. Experienced technicians determine which tests are needed for a particular problem and will perform the checks in the most logical order.

5. Following a systematic diagnostic approach to a problem quickly leads to the correct repair.

REVIEW QUESTIONS

The following questions are provided to help you study as you read the chapter.

1. The following is a series of tests and checks that can be used to help determine the exact cause of problems. Fill in the blanks to complete the description of the tests or checks.

   a. A visual inspection is a quick, preliminary overall check of _____ factors that affect operation.

   b. A fluid check is an inspection of the fluid to ensure the correct _____ and _____.

   c. A _____ _____ gives the technician the opportunity to check the actual operation of the transmission.

   d. A torque converter clutch test is used to determine if the _____ is operating properly.

   e. Hydraulic _____ tests are used to check the hydraulic system pressures.

   f. Modulator checks are used to check the operation of the vacuum _____ valve system.

   g. _____ system checks are used to check the proper operation of the electronic controls.

   h. The _____ test loads the clutches and bands to check for slippage and also checks the torque converter stator one-way clutch.

   i. Leak checks are used to locate the source of a _____ leak.

   j. Debris checks determine if an abnormal amount of debris is present in the _____ _____ and, if so, the nature of the debris.

   k. Air tests are made to determine if the seals, _____, and gaskets in the hydraulic circuits are operating correctly.

   l. A more precise air test to locate the exact location or severity of a leak is called a _____ _____ _____.

   m. Checks to locate the cause of a noise, vibration, or harshness are known as _____ checks.

2. Diagnosing a problem with an automatic transmission should always begin by _____ the problem.

3. All transmission diagnosis should begin with a check of the _____ _____ and _____.

4. It is advisable to always _____ drive a vehicle before and after any repairs.

5. Below are the throttle positions that a technician should use while test driving a vehicle. List the term that fits the description of the driving condition or the throttle position.

   a. The throttle is about three-fourths open.

   b. A complete release of the throttle, which results in coasting.

   c. The least throttle opening that produces acceleration.

   d. WOT, which forces a downshift.

   e. A manual downshift with zero throttle to produce a condition where engine compression slows the vehicle.

   f. The throttle is about one-fourth open.

   g. Fully opened throttle without forcing a downshift.

   h. The throttle is about one-half open.

6. A student is testing a torque converter using a pressure gauge. The pressure changed when the clutch was to apply, but the clutch does not apply. The problem is in the _____ _____.

7. A transmission only has one pressure test port. When checking hydraulic pressure at that port you would be monitoring _____ pressure.

8. A technician is testing line pressure and notices that line pressure reads lower in some of the gear ranges. His or her diagnosis is that there is a _____ problem in the hydraulic circuit for the ranges with low pressure.

9. A good-operating governor is indicated during a governor pressure check by a steadily rising pressure that is relative to _____ _____.

10. If a transmission does not have a governor pressure test port, governor operation can be monitored by watching mainline pressure for a _____ in pressure due to governor _____.

11. When testing a vacuum modulator, the modulator should have _____ inches of mercury available to it, and it should be able to hold a vacuum for _____ seconds.

12. A stall test can be used to detect problems with the torque converter _____ _____ and for _____ apply devices.

13. If all of the stall speeds during a stall test are equal but low, the _____ _____ clutch has failed or the _____ is weak. If they are all high, the problem is _____ apply devices.

14. Brass or bronze debris in the transmission oil pan indicates that a _____ or _____ has failed.

15. Air tests are used to check operation of the _____, _____, and/or _____.

16. When doing an air pressure test on an automatic transmission, air pressure used for testing should be set to _____ psi.

17. To locate those hard-to-find leaks, a _____ light and a special _____ can be used.

18. *NVH* is the trade term for _____, _____, and _____.

19. The three most common sources of noise in most automatic transmissions are _____, _____, and the _____ system.

20. A drive line clunk during garage shifts is most likely the _____ _____ bushing or the _____ joint.

CHAPTER QUIZ

The following questions will help you check the facts you have learned. Select the answer that completes each statement correctly.

1. Student A says that you should begin by checking the fluid when you are diagnosing a transmission problem. Student B says to use a pressure gauge to start diagnosing a transmission problem. Who is correct?
   a. Student A
   b. Student B
   c. Both A and B
   d. Neither A nor B

2. Student A says that when diagnosing an automatic transmission you should do only the diagnostic checks that are necessary to locate the problem. Student B says that you need to do all of the diagnostic tests to fully evaluate the transmission before starting any repairs. Who is correct?
   a. Student A
   b. Student B
   c. Both A and B
   d. Neither A nor B

3. Student A says that you should verify the customer concern before making any check of the vehicle. Student B says that you should check the fluid level and condition before going on a road test. Who is correct?
   a. Student A
   b. Student B
   c. Both A and B
   d. Neither A nor B

4. Student A says that ATF in a modulator vacuum hose is a sign of a bad modulator. Student B says that the engine should run differently if you pull the vacuum hose off the modulator. Who is correct?
   a. Student A
   b. Student B
   c. Both A and B
   d. Neither A nor B

5. When making a road test, particular attention should be paid to
   a. the quality of the garage shifts.
   b. the timing of the upshifts and downshifts.
   c. any unusual noises that might occur.
   d. All of these

6. Student A says that a minimum-throttle 1–2 upshift should be smooth and soft and occur at about 20 mph. Student B says that a harsh light-throttle upshift could be caused by a sticky modulator. Who is correct?
   a. Student A
   b. Student B
   c. Both A and B
   d. Neither A nor B

7. Student A says that both a tachometer and an oil pressure gauge are necessary to diagnose torque converter clutch problems. Student B says that a tap of the brake pedal causes the converter clutch to release. Who is correct?
   a. Student A
   b. Student B
   c. Both A and B
   d. Neither A nor B

8. If a transmission has a single pressure test port, it will be for

a. governor pressure.

b. modulator pressure.

c. line pressure.

d. None of these

9. Student A says that low fluid pressure in all forward ranges could be caused by a faulty pump or plugged filter. Student B says that fluid pressures should increase when the gear selector is moved to reverse. Who is correct?

a. Student A

b. Student B

c. Both A and B

d. Neither A nor B

10. When making a stall test, you should

a. connect a tachometer to the engine.

b. completely apply the parking and service brakes.

c. make sure there is no one in front of or behind the vehicle.

d. Do all of these

11. During a stall test, the stall speed is high in drive-1 but normal in manual-1 and reverse. Student A says that this indicates a faulty forward clutch. Student B says that it could be caused by a bad one-way clutch. Who is correct?

a. Student A

b. Student B

c. Both A and B

d. Neither A nor B

12. A Simpson gear train transmission has a slipping second gear but the fluid pressures are normal. Student A says that this problem could be caused by a loose intermediate-band adjustment. Student B says that it is a leaking intermediate servo. Who is correct?

a. Student A

b. Student B

c. Both A and B

d. Neither A nor B

13. A transmission has no high gear or reverse, but all other gears are normal. Student A says you could confirm the problem by dropping the pan and valve body to air check the high-reverse clutch. Student B says that you could make a complete oil pressure check before removing the pan to confirm the problem is in the high/reverse clutch circuit. Who is correct?

a. Student A

b. Student B

c. Both A and B

d. Neither A nor B

14. When checking the pan contents,

a. a small amount of metal particles is considered normal.

b. a golden-brown coating is a sign of a needed fluid change.

c. metal or melted plastic debris indicates a need for a transmission overhaul.

d. All of these

15. Student A says that you should be able to hear a clutch apply and release when you apply air pressure to test it. Student B says that an excessive air leak is an indication of bad seals. Who is correct?

a. Student A

b. Student B

c. Both A and B

d. Neither A nor B

16. Student A says that you can use foot powder to trace the location of a transmission leak. Student B says that the actual location of a leak is usually slightly forward of where the fluid is found. Who is correct?

a. Student A

b. Student B

c. Both A and B

d. Neither A nor B

17. Which of the following is a handy tool for locating transmission leaks?

a. Foot powder

b. Blacklight and dye

c. Air test

d. All of the above

18. A vehicle vibrates rather violently just before a full-throttle 1–2 or 2–3 shift. Student A says that this can be caused by a faulty extension housing bushing or universal joint. Student B says that this can be caused by an engine problem or unbalanced torque converter. Who is correct?

a. Student A

b. Student B

c. Both A and B

d. Neither A nor B

19. When diagnosing transmission noise problems, it is important to note

a. when the noise occurs.

b. the frequency or pitch of the noise.

c. if the noise changes with the load on the car.

d. All of these

20. Student A says that troubleshooting noise-related problems can be done on a road test. Student B says that noise and vibration problems are not normally a concern of the automatic transmission student. Who is correct?

a. Student A

b. Student B

c. Both A and B

d. Neither A nor B

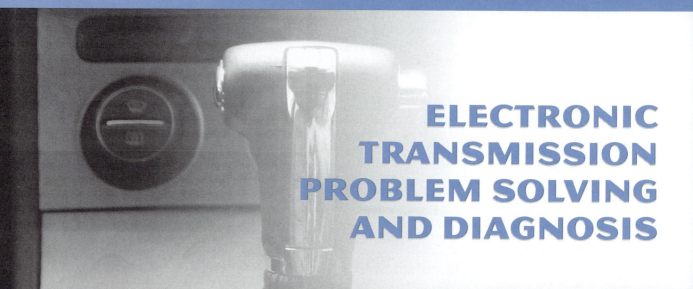

ELECTRONIC TRANSMISSION PROBLEM SOLVING AND DIAGNOSIS

OBJECTIVES

After studying Chapter 13, the reader should be able to:

1. Describe the problems that can occur in electrical circuits.
2. Test electrical circuits.
3. Explain what a diagnostic trouble code (DTC) is and how it can be used by the service technician.

4. Retrieve DTCs.
5. Perform the ASE tasks related to electronic problem diagnosis and repair.

KEY TERMS

Digital Meter (p. 338)
Excessive Resistance (p. 336)
Transmission Control Module (TCM) (p. 335)

Out of Limits (OL) (p. 343)
Shrink Tube (p. 353)
Soft Codes (p. 358)

13.1 ELECTRONIC TRANSMISSION DIAGNOSIS

Electronic shift controls require the transmission technician to learn additional diagnostic and test procedures. When diagnosing an electronic transmission, it must be determined if the cause is faulty electronic controls, a hydraulic system problem, or a mechanical system malfunction (Figure 13-1). Electrical/electronic problems can usually be repaired with the transmission in the vehicle. Mechanical or hydraulic problems usually require transmission removal.

Shift timing and quality are computer controlled in electronic transmissions. The **transmission control module (TCM),** also called an *electronic control module (ECM),* can be an independent control module or a part of another control module such as the *power train control module (PCM).*

REAL WORLD FIX

The 2001 Chevrolet Silverado 2500 HD pickup (55,000 miles) does not shift correctly. A scan tool check shows these DTCs: P0708, transmission range sensor circuit, and a P0722, output speed sensor circuit. The shift problems began after the customer removed, recharged, and reinstalled the battery. Following diagnostic procedure, the technician was led to a bad TCM, but replacement of the TCM did not fix the problem.

Fix. Following advice, the technician replaced the black neutral safety switch with a revised, brown switch. After clearing the codes and a test drive, a code check showed that the new switch fixed this problem.

REAL WORLD FIX

The 1992 GMC C3500 pickup (95,000 miles) had a torque converter clutch that was cycling on and off. At 65 mph the TCC would cycle rapidly. A scan tool check revealed no DTCs, with all scan data normal. The TCM was replaced, but this did not help.

Fix. Following advice, the technician checked the engine distributor and found a bad shaft bushing. This worn bushing caused a variable ignition signal that the TCM interpreted as changing engine load. A new distributor bushing fixed this problem. Vehicles that incorporate electronics may have problems that seem to be unrelated, but they can cause transmission problems.

REAL WORLD FIX

The 1990 BMW 520i (197,000 km) came in with only second gear, limp-in mode. The customer said the car would operate normally one day and have only second gear the next day. The fluid level is correct and appears in good condition.

Fix. A dealership checked for fault codes and found two: gear position switch and speed sensor. Testing revealed faults in the gear position switch and speed sensor circuits (Starbucks syndrome). Replacement of these two components fixed the problem. *Starbucks syndrome* is a name given to the results of coffee and food spills onto the center console control switches. Corrosion caused by the spills increases resistance at the wire connections.

1. Will the vehicle move forward and backward? → NO → Severe Hydraulic or Mechanical Fault
   ↓ YES
2. Is the vehicle operating in Fail-Safe Mode? → YES → NO
   ↓
3. Is a MIL illuminated or flashing? → YES → NO
   ↓
4. Are there any DTCs? → NO → Check control module and transmission power and ground circuits
   ↓ YES
5. Are they electrical DTCs? → NO → Check hydraulic and mechanical systems
   ↓ YES
6. Repair electrical fault, clear DTCs, and road test vehicle to insure that the fault does not return.

FIGURE 13-1   A diagnostic procedure for an electronically controlled transmission.

A PCM controls both engine and transmission functions. The transmission control module will be referred to as the TCM for uniformity.

Electrical/electronic service requires an understanding of basic electricity as well as the use of electrical testers and meters.

Transmissions with integrated TCMs (control solenoid valve assembly, Mechatronic, and solenoid body) require scan tool diagnostics because you do not have access to the TCM connections to the various transmission sensors and solenoids.

13.2 ELECTRICAL CIRCUIT PROBLEMS

There are three common types of electrical problems: opens, high-resistance, and low-resistance (short or ground). These problems can occur either continuously or intermittently. Intermittent problems are usually much harder to locate, and are often the result of the vehicle's movement, vibration, or changes in temperature. With the proper equipment and knowledge, most electrical components can be easily diagnosed.

13.2.1 Open Circuits

An unwanted **open circuit** is an incomplete, broken circuit in which no current can flow. A switch is an example of a wanted open circuit. When the switch is closed, current flows and the circuit operates. When the switch is open, no current will flow and the circuit is off. An unwanted open is usually caused by a broken wire, damaged connecter, broken light bulb filament, or a blown fuse or fusible link (caused by an overloaded circuit). An open circuit can occur at any point between the B+ and the ground connections (Figure 13-2). Source voltage will be present up to the point of the open.

13.2.2 High-Resistance Circuits

Circuit resistance controls the amount of current flow. An increase in resistance will reduce current flow. **Excessive resistance** is often caused by corroded, loose, or dirty connections. Remember that voltage forces current through the resistance. Ideally, the only resistance in a circuit is the load, which is the electrical component to be operated. Unwanted *high resistance* uses some of the available voltage to force current through the extra resistance. The result is less voltage to move the current through the intended load(s). Unwanted resistance causes an unwanted *voltage drop,* also called a *wasted voltage drop.* Excess circuit resistance can be identified by measuring the voltage drop at various connectors, wires, and components. A high-resistance circuit can be compared with a cooler fluid line that is kinked and restricting the fluid flow.

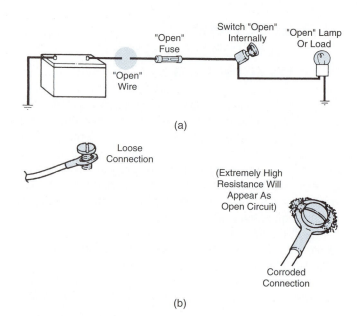

(a)

(b)

FIGURE 13-2 An open circuit is a break in the circuit that will stop the current flow (a). Corroded or loose connections will cause high resistance that will reduce the current flow (b). *(Courtesy of Chrysler Corporation)*

REAL WORLD FIX

A 1996 S-10 pickup drops out of fourth gear. It makes a 4–3 shift on its own. There are no diagnostic trouble codes (DTCs).

Fix. On the road test, the technician found intermittent loss of power to the transmission fuse caused by a failing ignition switch. Replacement of the ignition switch fixed the transmission problem.

13.2.3 Shorted Circuits

A *short circuit* means that the current is taking a shorter path than normal and has bypassed part of the intended circuit. Shorts occur when the insulation breaks down and two bare wires touch or a bare wire touches chassis ground. This gives the current an alternate path back to its source. As a result, the amount of current flow will increase relative to the decrease in circuit resistance.

A short can occur in a coil winding and bypass some of the coils. The effect of the short is a lower coil resistance because of the shortened path, allowing an increase in current flow. The strength of the magnetic field will also be reduced due to the fewer turns in the coil.

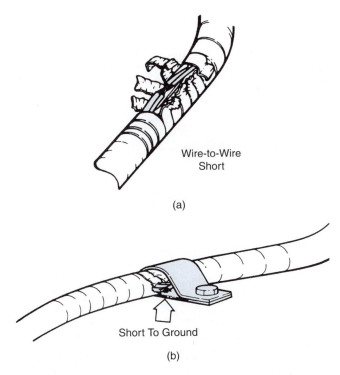

Wire-to-Wire Short

(a)

Short To Ground

(b)

FIGURE 13-3 A short circuit is a wire-to-wire connection that can reduce magnetic coil strength or allow current to flow to the wrong circuit (a) or a short to ground. *(b is courtesy of Chrysler Corporation)*

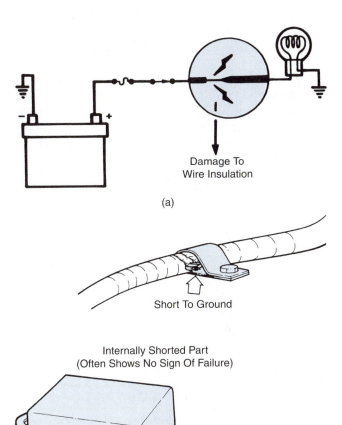

Damage To Wire Insulation

(a)

Short To Ground

Internally Shorted Part
(Often Shows No Sign Of Failure)

(b)

FIGURE 13-4 A ground or short-to-ground circuit occurs when damage to the insulation allows an electrical path to the metal of the vehicle (a). It can occur at a wire or inside a component (b). *(Courtesy of Chrysler Corporation)*

REAL WORLD FIX

The 1991 Taurus had a very hard 1–2 shift. The transmission had 2,400 miles on a rebuild and was working properly except for the 1–2 shift.

Fix. A resistance check showed the turbine shaft speed sensor to have a resistance of 0.3 Ω with a specification of 108 to 146 Ω. This test revealed shorted windings in the sensor coil. Replacement of this faulty sensor repaired this transmission.

A short can also occur between the wires of two separate circuits if their insulation is damaged. A short will allow an unwanted current flow between the circuits (Figure 13-3).

13.2.4 Grounded Circuits

A *grounded circuit* is a short where a bare wire touches ground. This is commonly called a *short to ground.* The grounded circuit completes a path directly back to battery ground (B–),

bypassing the rest of the circuit. Most of the current will follow the path of least resistance. A grounded circuit can have zero resistance, and the current flow will instantly increase to the limit of the fuse, wire, or battery. This usually causes a very rapid burnout, and the resulting smoke and burned wires are often easy to locate (Figure 13-4).

13.3 MEASURING ELECTRICAL COMPONENTS

In the past, technicians used a *test light, jumper wire,* and *analog volt-ohmmeter* or *multimeter* (a combination ammeter, ohmmeter, and voltmeter) for troubleshooting automotive electrical problems. Today, the weathertight connectors make the use of a jumper wire very difficult (Figure 13-5). A jumper wire should only be used to check switches and unloaded parts of the circuit. Never use a jumper wire to bypass a load. A *test light* and analog meter should not be used on solid-state circuits

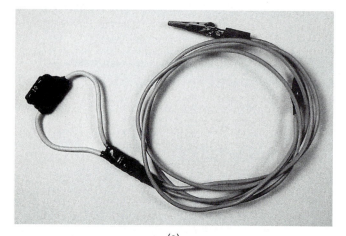

(a)

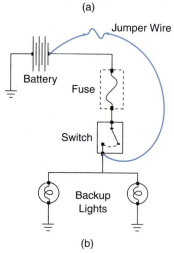

(b)

FIGURE 13-5 A fused jumper wire can be used to bypass portions of a circuit to determine where the problem is located (a). If the lights come on with the jumper wire installed, the problem is the fuse, switch, or wires to the battery (b).

because they can cause too much current through the ECM. This current overload can cause erroneous meter readings and possible sensor or ECM damage. The meter must have an internal resistance of 10 megohms (10,000,000 Ω) or greater. LED test lights and most *digital multimeters (DMMs)* can be safely used on any automotive electrical or electronic circuit.

Test lights are simple, inexpensive, durable, and easy to use. They have one wire that is normally connected to ground, and when the probe contacts B+, the test light lights up (Figure 13-6). Some test lights are self-powered and use an internal battery. Self-powered lights can be used to check *continuity* (a continuous, complete circuit) through a component such as a relay. Most test lights indicate either a pass or fail; they cannot make measurements, so they will not tell us the condition of a circuit or component.

Meters make accurate measurements. There are two types: *analog* (a needle sweeps across a scale) and **digital** (actual value is displayed in a series of digits). Analog meters should not be

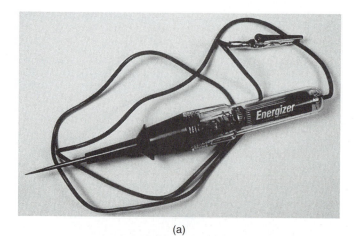

(a)

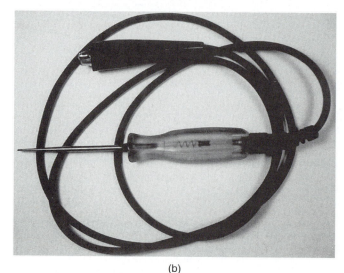

(b)

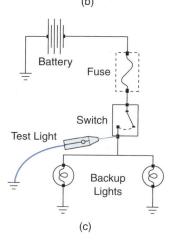

(c)

FIGURE 13-6 A self-powered test light includes a battery and can be used to check for continuity (a). A nonpowered test light (b) can be used to determine if a point in a circuit has voltage (c).

used on electronic circuits because they can cause the circuit to draw too much current, resulting in a damaged circuit. The DMM is more accurate, easier to read, and can be used on all computer circuits. On circuits with changing values, however,

(a)

(b)

(c)

FIGURE 13-7   Analog (a) and digital (b) multimeters. Do not use analog meters when testing electronic circuits unless instructed to do so. The bar graph and digital display are shown in (c).

the sweep of an analog needle is much faster and easier to follow than the rapidly changing display of digits (Figure 13-7). For that reason, some digital multimeters include a *bar graph* for a continuous response to value changes. A service manual may direct you to use an analog meter for some tests.

Multimeters have a selector switch that must be set to the desired function before connecting the meter to a circuit. Some meters also have a range switch that is set to the range where the readings are expected to fall. The range selector should always be set above the highest reading expected and then reset downward until readings occur. Many DMMs are *self-ranging* or *auto-ranging*. The technician should always check the range indicator on the display.

Weathertight connectors present a difficult problem when probing for electrical values (Figure 13-8). You can disconnect a connector and probe the ends, but without normal circuit load this can be an inaccurate reading. It is also possible to damage the connector pins. Thin probes are available

TECH TIP

Fingernail polish or battery sealant spray can be safely used to seal wire insulation; the coating prevents corrosion and resistance problems caused by water leaking into the connector or component.

that allow backprobing a connection by sliding the probe into a connector, through the weathertight seals. Probes that pierce the wire's insulation are also used. Caution should be taken to not damage wire insulation. Some manufacturers suggest that the hole left by the piercing pin should be filled with a sealant when testing is completed.

FIGURE 13-8 Many electrical components, like this TPS, use weathertight connectors with latches to keep contacts clean and tight.

TECH TIP

The common test probes are larger than the small female wire connectors. Forcing the probe into the connector will make it too large to make a good connection with the male wire connector. You can test a female wire connector using a Number 60, 0.040″ drill bit; there should be a snug fit between the drill bit and connector.

TECH TIP

When probing female wire connections, T-pins can be used to prevent distorting the connectors. T-pins can be purchased at a sewing or hobby store.

REAL WORLD FIX

The 1986 BMW 535i (86,000 miles) came in with a complaint of fourth-gear dropout. This occurs when it is hot with the A/C on. Normal operation returns after the car is shut off for a while.

Fix. The technician checked the A/C evaporator drain and found that it was dripping water onto the transmission hardness connector. Sealing/waterproofing this electrical connector fixed this problem.

REAL WORLD FIX

The 2002 Mazda Tribute AWD (9,000 miles) came in with the AWD MIL intermittently illuminated. Electrical pin checks were made with no problems found. The oil temperature switch and TCM were replaced, but this did not help.

Fix. Following advice, the technician performed the wiggle testing by wiggling the wires while making voltage checks. A faulty terminal crimp was found at one of the connectors into the TCM. Repairing this terminal crimp fixed this problem.

13.3.1 Measuring Voltage

A voltmeter is used to measure circuit voltage and voltage drop. Voltage is measured by connecting the negative (−) lead to ground and probing various points along the circuit with the positive (+) lead (Figure 13-9). The meter will display the actual voltage at that point in the circuit. Depending on the circuit and its components, this reading should be B+ (around 12.6 V) or some lesser value. A zero (0) reading indicates an open circuit between the probe and B+. A reading less than B+ indicates a voltage drop and possible problem. If there is full battery voltage to the component and full battery voltage drops across the component, the component is either using all the electrical power or has an open circuit.

Voltage drop can be measured by connecting the negative lead to the ground side of a component and the positive lead to the B+ side. The reading will be the amount of voltage dropped across that component. Remember that voltage drop only occurs while the circuit is on and under load. *The total voltage drop in a series circuit is equal to the sum of each voltage drop, which is equal to the source voltage.* Ideally, all of the voltage drop should occur across the circuit loads, a light bulb, actuator, or output device. A voltage drop equal to source voltage across the load may be okay, or it may indicate that the load is open (Figure 13-10). If there is source voltage available and the component is not working, the component (load) is open.

In a solenoid circuit, there should be B+ voltage at the solenoid's insulated connection, and there will be a voltage drop equal to B+ across the solenoid. A very small drop across a connection or switch is allowed, but this is usually limited to 0.2 or 0.3 volts per connection and a circuit total drop of 0.5 V.

Any drop greater than 0.5 V indicates a high-resistance problem that will cause a circuit to function below normal, and should be corrected (Figure 13-11).

To measure voltage, you should:

1. Adjust the voltmeter control to DC volts.
2. Connect the negative, black or −, lead of the voltmeter to a good, clean ground.
3. Determine the point where you want to measure, and touch or connect the positive, red or +, lead to the connector.
4. Read the voltage on the meter.

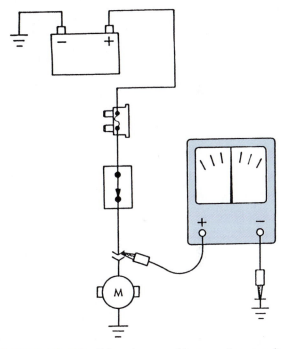

FIGURE 13-10   Voltage is measured by connecting one voltmeter lead (normally the negative) to ground, and probing the wire connections with the other lead. *(Courtesy of Chrysler Corporation)*

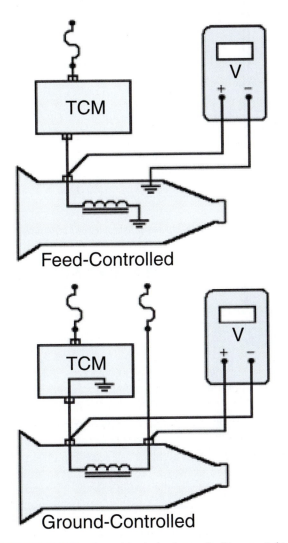

FIGURE 13-9   The positive (+) voltmeter lead is connected to the positive (+) solenoid terminal, and the negative (−) lead is connected to ground. With ground-controlled solenoids, the negative (−) lead is connected to the solenoid TCM terminal.

TECH TIP

Ohm's law includes a formula that shows the relationship of the three important electrical values. A modernized version of Ohm's law memory triangle is shown in Figure 13-12. If you know two of the values, you can easily calculate the third. This becomes handy if one value, resistance, is hard to measure but two other values, volts and current, can be easily measured.

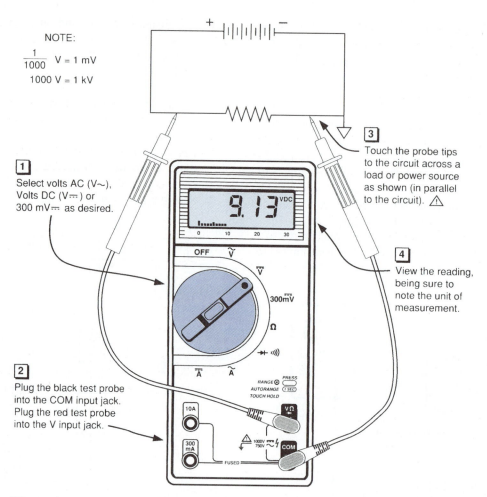

NOTE:

$\dfrac{1}{1000}$ V = 1 mV

1000 V = 1 kV

1 Select volts AC (V~), Volts DC (V⎓) or 300 mV⎓ as desired.

2 Plug the black test probe into the COM input jack. Plug the red test probe into the V input jack.

3 Touch the probe tips to the circuit across a load or power source as shown (in parallel to the circuit). ⚠

4 View the reading, being sure to note the unit of measurement.

FIGURE 13-11   This meter is connected to measure the voltage drop across the resistor. *(Courtesy of Fluke Corporation; reproduced with permission)*

V (Volts) = C × R
C (Current) = V R
R (Resistance) = V C

FIGURE 13-12   This modernized version of Ohm's law memory triangle shows the relationship between volts, current (amps), and resistance.

To measure voltage drop, you should:

1. Select DC volts.

Total B+side voltage drop is measured by:

2. Connect the positive, red or +, lead of the voltmeter to the positive, or +, battery post.
3. Touch or connect the negative, black or –, lead to the B+ side of the component.
4. Read the voltage drop on the meter.

Total ground side voltage drop is measured by:

5. Connect the positive, red or +, lead of the voltmeter to the ground side of the component.
6. Touch or connect the negative, black or –, lead to the negative, –, battery post.

REAL WORLD FIX

The 1987 Chevrolet Astro (100,000 miles) has a hunting condition with the TCC going in and out of lock-up at 60 mph.

Fix. A voltage check of the wire harness found an open circuit caused by a broken wire between the frame and transmission. Repair of this wire fixed this problem. The hunting condition was probably the result of an intermittent connection at the wire break.

7. Turn the circuit on.
8. Read the voltage drop on the meter.

Component voltage drop:

9. Connect the positive, red or +, lead of the voltmeter to the B+ side of the component.

10. Touch or connect the negative, black or −, lead to the ground side of the component.
11. Turn the circuit on.
12. Read the voltage drop on the meter.

13.3.2 Measuring Resistance

An ohmmeter is used to measure the resistance of electrical components. When the two ohmmeter leads are connected to the ends of a wire or connections of a component, the meter will display the resistance value. Ohmmeters are self-powered by an internal battery. *They must never be connected to a circuit that has power,* because the usually higher voltage from the circuit will damage the ohmmeter. Some meters have a protective fuse that will burn out to save the meter if it is connected incorrectly. Always turn the circuit power off or disconnect the power lead when checking a circuit or component using an ohmmeter. Disconnecting the component from the circuit will also keep the meter from reading other parts of the circuit. When checking components with parallel circuits, remember that the meter does not know which path you wish to measure. It will include all possible paths. To be safe, disconnect one end of the component you are measuring from the circuit. Most DMMs are designed not to affect solid-state components when making resistance measurements.

Many DMMs are self-ranging and give a reading of any resistance value within their ability (Figure 13-13). Analog meters require setting the meter to the desired range (1 K or 1000 Ω, 10 K or 10,000 Ω, 1 M or 1,000,000 Ω) and recalibrating the meter each time the range is changed. An analog ohmmeter is calibrated by connecting the leads and rotating the calibration knob until the meter reads zero.

An ohmmeter is perfect for checking a component like a solenoid coil when it is off the vehicle. Connect the ohmmeter leads to each end of the coil. If the resistance value matches the specifications, the component does not have a short circuit and has continuity. If the coil includes a diode, reverse the two ohmmeter leads and the resistance should change. Moving one of the leads to the component's mounting point checks for a grounded coil; at this time the reading should be infinite ($\infty\,\Omega$) (see Figure 13-41). A DMM displays **OL (out of limits)** to indicate infinite resistance.

An ohmmeter is also ideal for checking a transmission oil temperature (TOT) sensor, also called a transmission fluid sensor (TFT). It has a resistance that is inversely proportionate to temperature; if the temperature increases, the resistance will decrease. Measure the resistance at the specified temperatures, and if the resistance matches the specifications, it is good. One commonly used TOT sensor should have a resistance of 20 to 40 K Ω at 32 to 58°F (0 to 20°C), 16 to 37 K Ω at 59 to 104°F (21 to 40°C), and 5 to 16 K Ω at 105 to 158°F (41 to 70°C).

REAL WORLD FIX

The 1994 Buick Century had an erratic shift problem. A scan tool check revealed three DTCs: P0502: VSS low, P0705: PRNDL switch, and P1650: Quad driver module error. The VSS was inspected and bad connector pins were found and replaced. The shift solenoid resistance was checked and all were within specification.

Fix. The technician measured solenoid voltage at the TCM connector and found these voltages: SSA: 7.5 V, SSB: 0.38 V, TCC: 11.45, and PWM: 11.45. Replacing shift solenoid "A" and shift solenoid "B" fixed this problem.

REAL WORLD FIX

The 1988 Ford Aerostar (95,000 miles) came in with no 3–4 shift or TCC lock-up. The B+ power and grounds checked out fine. The 3–4 and TCC solenoids were replaced, but this did not help. The band adjustment and servo were checked and these were good.

Fix. The technician did a voltage drop check at the case connector. There was 12.5 V at the outside, but only 4.5 V at the solenoids. Replacing the internal electrical harness and case connector fixed this problem.

TECH TIP

It is possible for the coil of a relay to have a weak internal connection and test showing continuity and correct resistance with an ohmmeter. Ohmmeters measure resistance while the component is disconnected. Circuit load generates heat that in turn increases the resistance. An internal weak connection (resistance) will cause reduced current flow. Many technicians prefer to check circuit resistance using an ammeter. If a circuit has the correct current flow with the correct input voltage, it has the proper resistance, and it is good.

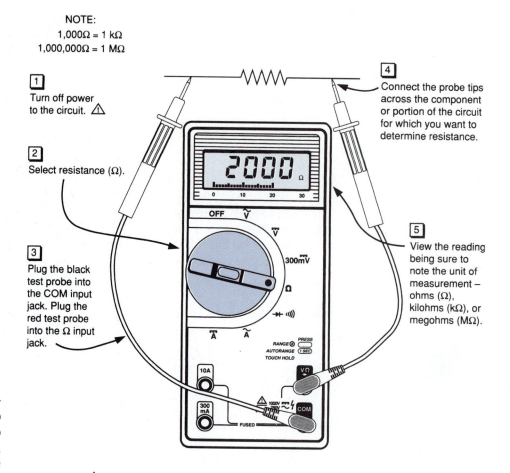

NOTE:
1,000Ω = 1 kΩ
1,000,000Ω = 1 MΩ

1 Turn off power to the circuit. ⚠

2 Select resistance (Ω).

3 Plug the black test probe into the COM input jack. Plug the red test probe into the Ω input jack.

4 Connect the probe tips across the component or portion of the circuit for which you want to determine resistance.

5 View the reading being sure to note the unit of measurement — ohms (Ω), kilohms (kΩ), or megohms (MΩ).

FIGURE 13-13 A digital multimeter being used to measure resistance. Be sure to turn off or disconnect the electrical power to the circuit when using ohmmeter functions. *(Courtesy of Fluke Corporation; reproduced with permission)*

⚠ Make sure power is off before making resistance measurements.

REAL WORLD FIX

The 1994 GMC pickup (126,000 miles) will not shift. A shift could be forced by grounding the solenoid leads at the transmission. There was 12.6 V at the transmission. The solenoids were removed and tested, and would allow flow when activated. The resistance checked out okay.

Fix. The technician was advised to check the current flow through the solenoids. The 2–3 solenoid would draw 2.5 amps and its specification is 0.75 amp. Replacement of the solenoids fixed this shift problem.

To measure resistance, you should:

1. Disconnect at least one lead of the component, and make sure that all electrical power to the component is shut off.
2. Adjust the ohmmeter or DMM to ohms, Ω.

3. Connect the positive, red or +, lead to one side of the component.
4. Touch or connect the negative, black or −, lead to the other side of the component.
5. Read the amount of resistance on the meter.

To check a diode:

6. Measure the resistance of the diode using steps 3 and 4.
7. Reverse the two connections in steps 3 and 4.
8. Read the amount of resistance on the meter. A change in resistance indicates the diode has more resistance in one direction.

13.3.3 Measuring Amperage

An ammeter measures amperage (current flow). The circuit is opened and the ammeter is connected in series with the circuit (Figure 13-14). Some ammeters use a transformer-type, inductive pickup that is simply placed over or around the wire (Figure 13-15). Most technicians prefer the inductive pickup because it is much easier to connect, and it does not change the circuit in any way. If the current readings measured in the

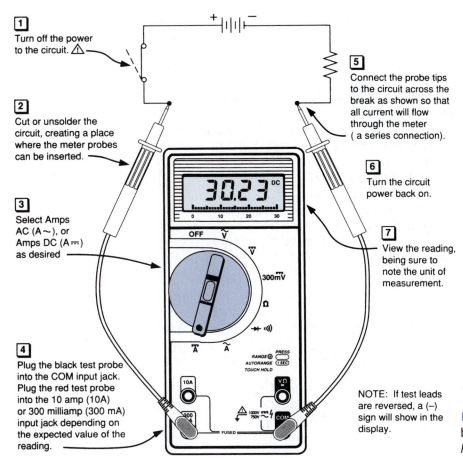

1 Turn off the power to the circuit. ⚠

2 Cut or unsolder the circuit, creating a place where the meter probes can be inserted.

3 Select Amps AC (A∼), or Amps DC (A⎓) as desired

4 Plug the black test probe into the COM input jack. Plug the red test probe into the 10 amp (10A) or 300 milliamp (300 mA) input jack depending on the expected value of the reading.

5 Connect the probe tips to the circuit across the break as shown so that all current will flow through the meter (a series connection).

6 Turn the circuit power back on.

7 View the reading, being sure to note the unit of measurement.

NOTE: If test leads are reversed, a (−) sign will show in the display.

FIGURE 13-14 A digital multimeter is being used to measure current flow. *(Courtesy of Fluke Corporation; reproduced with permission)*

TECH TIP

Measuring the resistance of a shift solenoid with the solenoid mounted inside the transmission pan can be difficult, but measuring voltage and solenoid current flow can be easy. If the voltage measures 13.9 V and there is a 3-amp current draw, use Ohm's law to find the solenoid resistance: $13.9 \div 3 = 4.6\ \Omega$.

TECH TIP

When using an induction ammeter, the readings can be multiplied by forming a loop (if there is enough slack in the wire), and connecting the inductive pickup over the multiple wires. Two wires will double the reading, three wires will triple it, and so on.

circuit are less than specifications, excessive resistance is indicated. If the current readings are higher than specifications, a shorted or grounded circuit is indicated.

A current probe is a handy tester that is used with electronic circuits (Figure 13-16). This tool combined with a scope allows the technician to watch the current flow to a solenoid. Figure 13-17 shows the current increasing about six vertical divisions, then dipping a couple of divisions, and then increasing again to the maximum value. The increases are

called *ramping*. The dip shows a reduction in the current flow that is caused by the counterelectromotive force that is created when an inductor moves through the solenoids' magnetic lines of force. This is the normal movement of the solenoid plunger. The maximum value is the total current flow through the solenoid, and the dip should occur at about 2/3 to 3/4 of the maximum value. The current probe uses an inductive pickup so it can be clipped over the wire feeding the solenoid. When troubleshooting a problem like a shift failure, the technician can easily connect the current probe, perform a road test, and watch for a solenoid operation. This will help

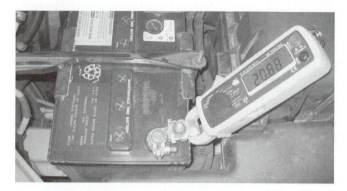

FIGURE 13-15 Inductive ammeters can be clipped over a wire to measure the current flow without disturbing the wire connections.

FIGURE 13-16 The jaws of the amp probe are around the wire, and the probe is connected to the DMM. The circuit is drawing 2.85 amps, which is read on the volts scale of the DMM.

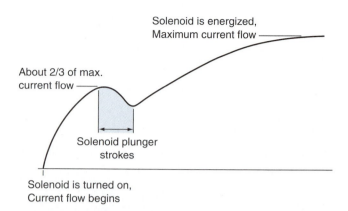

FIGURE 13-17 This graph shows the current flow to a solenoid. The dip near the center shows that the solenoid plunger has actually moved.

TECH TIP

Current flow is the same at all points through a simple circuit, so current can be measured at a common point of the circuit. A common point and convenient location of measuring current is at the fuse. Remove the transmission fuse and substitute a modified fuse. This is an old, burned-out fuse with a wire attached to each blade of the fuse (Figure 13-17). Connect the ammeter leads to the two fuse connections to read current and operate the transmission using a scan tool. Current flow for each solenoid will be displayed as each solenoid is activated. Use caution if activating low-resistance solenoids such as some PWMs or EPCs with a resistance as low as $2\ \Omega$; these can draw $14\text{ V} \div 2\ \Omega = 7$ amps.

the technician to quickly determine whether the problem is electrical or of a hydraulic or mechanical nature.

To measure amperage/current flow using an inductive pickup, you should:

1. Connect the inductive pickup to the DMM, and set the meter to DC amps.
2. Open the inductive pickup jaws, and place them completely around the current-carrying wire.
3. Turn the component on and read the amperage on the meter.

To measure amperage/current flow using the meter leads, you should:

1. Select DC amps on the meter control.
2. Disconnect one connector for the circuit being tested at a convenient location.
3. Connect the positive, red or +, lead to the wire or connector that is the most positive or closest to B+.

4. Connect the negative, black or −, lead to the other side (most negative) of the open connection. The ammeter leads should now be in series with the circuit being tested.
5. Turn the component on and read the amperage on the meter.

13.3.4 Measuring Duty Cycle

Many electronic pressure control (EPC) and torque converter clutch (TCC) solenoids are pulse-width modulated (PWM) and operate with a variable duty cycle. The duty cycle rate at which they operate is used to control transmission line pressure and/or TCC apply pressure. Most digital meters have a duty cycle function and can display both positive (+) and negative (−) pulse readings. Voltage/feed-controlled solenoids use a + pulse, whereas ground-controlled solenoids use a − pulse. If the duty cycle is measured along with line pressure, a shift into reverse will produce a change in both duty cycle and line pressure.

The meter reads an upward electrical pulse as a positive pulse. A negative pulse is downward. If the meter is set for the wrong polarity, it will provide an inverse reading. An 80% duty cycle will be displayed instead of an actual 20% signal.

To measure the duty cycle, you should:

1. Select the duty cycle function on the meter.
2. Note the meter display to determine if a + or − is displayed, and select the proper polarity to match the solenoid control (Figure 13-19).

TECH TIP

A convenient tool for measuring current is a fuse buddy (Figure 13-18). It can be inserted into a fuse holder in place of a fuse and the amperage can be read as the vehicle is operated.

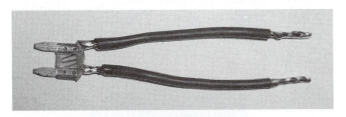

(a)

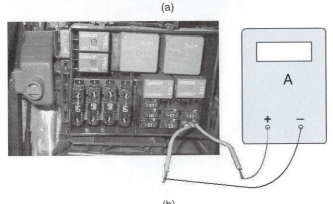

(b)

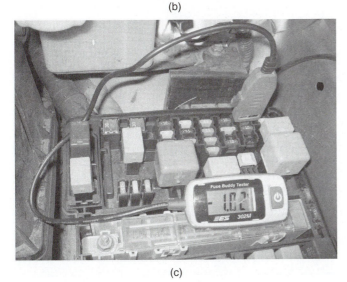

(c)

FIGURE 13-18 A blown fuse has been modified by soldering a short wire to each test point (a). Replacing a circuit fuse with a modified fuse provides an easy location to check the circuit's current flow (b). This handy ammeter, called a Fuse Buddy, can be easily inserted into the fuse box (c). Note the system fuse has been inserted into the tool to protect the circuit.

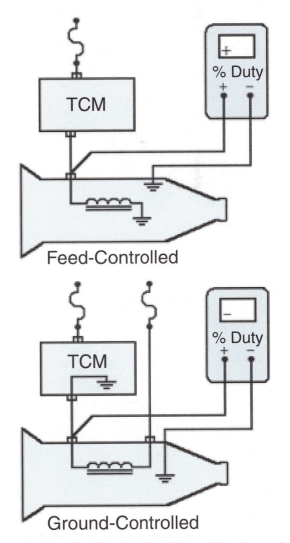

FIGURE 13-19 Measuring solenoid duty cycle is similar to a solenoid voltage check. Note that feed-controlled circuits should be read at + duty cycle while ground-controlled circuits use a − duty cycle.

3. Connect the negative (−) meter lead to a good ground.
4. Connect the positive (+) meter lead to the solenoid wire.
5. Operate the transmission and read the duty cycle on the meter.

13.3.5 Scan Tools

Special tools to scan data from the vehicle computers have been developed by most vehicle manufacturers. Generic scanners are available from aftermarket sources that work on more than one make of vehicle if they have the proper data cartridge (Figure 13-20). These units can be used only on specific circuits for which they have been designed or for which special adapters are available. Scan tools are fairly expensive but can save considerable time when trying to locate a computer circuit electrical fault.

Scan tools are connected to the vehicle's data link connector (DLC) (Figure 13-21). They are bidirectional testers that can display the diagnostic trouble codes (DTCs), solenoid off and on signals from the transmission control module (TCM), or scan the various input signals to the TCM. They also allow the technician to request information from the TCM or command the TCM to perform different operations. Scan tools allow the technician to:

- read DTCs.
- read signals from the input devices.
- read TCM signals to the output devices.
- operate the output devices.

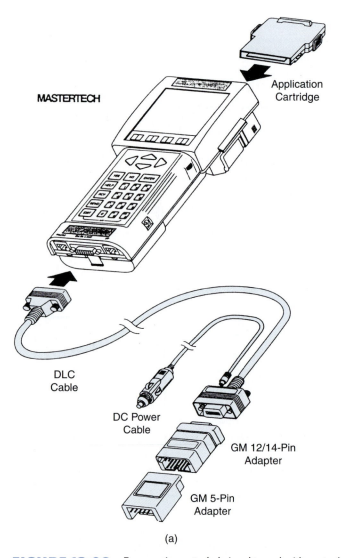

(a)

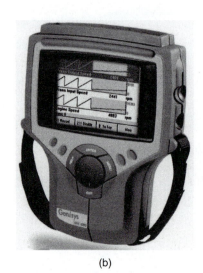

(b)

Shift Error 2-3	-2.42	sec
Shift Error 3-4	-2.42	sec
Shift Sol A Open Ckt	Yes	
TCC Duty Cycle	62	%
TCC En Fbk	No	
TCC Enable Open Ckt	Yes	
TCC Enable Short Ckt	Yes	
TCC Open Ckt	Yes	
TCC Short Ckt	Yes	
TCC Slip Speed	-3148	rpm
Trans Input Speed	5075	rpm
Trans Output Speed	5043	rpm

Frame: 0   Press Left Arrow for Freeze Frame

● Record | ⎍ Graph | ↑ To Top | More

(c)

FIGURE 13-20 Two generic scan tools designed to work with most vehicles. The Mastertech (a) uses adapters to connect to the diagnostic connector and an application cartridge to provide data for a particular vehicle. The Genisys scan tool (b) has software cartridges for many vehicles. Note that the screen of (b) is showing the engine, transmission input, and transmission output rpm; transmission operating data can also be shown (c). *(a is courtesy of Vetronix; b and c are courtesy of OTC)*

(a)

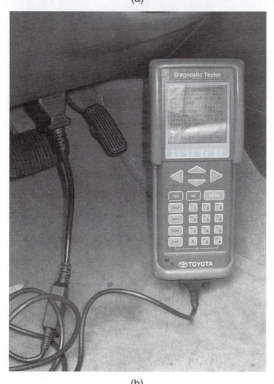

(b)

FIGURE 13-21 This DLC (diagnostic link connector) is under the instrument panel (a). Connecting a scan tool to the DLC allows it to display and operate vehicle functions (b).

- record a snapshot of a problem occurrence showing both the input and output signals.
- clear DTCs.
- recalibrate a TCM.

The *OBD-II* DTCs are five-character codes (Figure 13-22). Transmission codes begin with the letter "P," indicating a power-train code, followed by four numbers. If the first number is zero, the code was created by SAE; if it is 1, the code was created by the vehicle manufacturer. The second number tells

Example: P0781: 1-2 Shift Malfunction

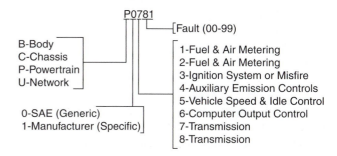

FIGURE 13-22 The first letter of an OBD-II code identifies the function of the fault code area; transmission faults will begin with P. The first digit indicates if the DTC is generic or manufacturer specific. The second digit indicates the power train system; a 7 or 8 would indicate a transmission fault. The last two digits indicate the fault.

Scan tools are limited by the software they contain or in their available software cartridges. Always use the newest available software. Some shops use more than one scan tool because of the limitations of various units.

When trying to locate the cause of intermittent problems, an important feature available in some scan tools is the ability to store the electronic events that occur during short time periods. This allows the technician to review these events at a more convenient time.

what system the problem is in; numbers 7 and 8 indicate the transmission. The last two digits indicate the nature of the problem. The OBD-II DTCs for transmissions are given in Appendix D.

Scan tools can only display electrical/electronic signals and can only indicate if a problem occurs in a particular circuit such as a solenoid or speed sensor. Further checks of the affected circuit are required to locate the exact cause of the problem.

TECH TIP

While checking for codes with a scan tool, do not cycle the key off (starting the engine will become a key cycle). Cycling the key may cause the codes to be lost.

13.3.6 Oscilloscopes

An *oscilloscope,* or scope, displays a voltage signal over a period of time. This allows the technician to observe the voltage change as an electrical device operates. A scope displays voltage on the vertical scale and time on the horizontal scale (Figure 13-23). Scopes are expensive and more difficult to use than multimeters. They are normally used to find the cause of difficult-to-locate problems that cannot be found using the other types of meters. Some scopes can display more than one electrical signal, and these are called *dual-trace* or *multiple-channel scopes.* Oscilloscopes, like multimeters, can be either analog or digital. Analog scopes allow real-time viewing of the electrical circuit. Digital scopes have the advantage of being able to store the patterns for later viewing.

A scope is ideal for observing electrical events and operations of circuits with changing values, such as the output of a speed sensor or a pulse-modulated solenoid.

13.3.7 Interpreting Measurements

The technician must be familiar with the circuit and its components so he or she knows what to expect while measuring electrical values. Wiring diagrams can be used to follow the current flow through a circuit, much like a road map shows us how to get from one point to another. At one time electrical circuits were quite simple and easy to follow. Power train controls have improved greatly, and customers demand more convenience, so today's vehicles have much more complicated circuits. A technician must study the electrical diagram and any additional information that is available on that particular circuit to understand how the circuit operates before trying to diagnose a problem (Figure 13-24).

Exact specifications are often not available for automotive circuits. Sometimes the resistance value or current draw for a solenoid coil is given, but not always. When testing with a meter, the technician needs a good understanding of the circuit and what to expect from the meter readings. In most circuits, B+ voltage is available to the switch of an output device (load) except for an allowance for slight voltage drop at the connectors.

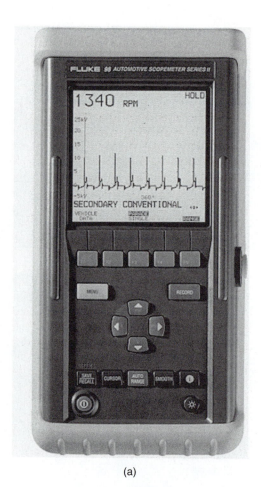

(a)

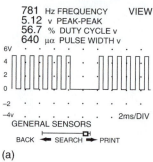

(a)

FIGURE 13-23   The scope is displaying a secondary ignition pattern in which most spark plugs are firing at about 10 kV; one is at 25 kV (a). A digital-style speed sensor pattern is shown in b; note the gap indicating a possible problem in the center of the pattern. *(Courtesy of Fluke Corporation; reproduced with permission)*

13.4 ELECTRICAL/ELECTRONIC SYSTEM REPAIR

A faulty electrical component such as a switch, relay, blower motor, or clutch is usually repaired by removing and replacing (R&R) it with a new unit. The R&R operation is usually a relatively simple process of disconnecting the wires or connectors,

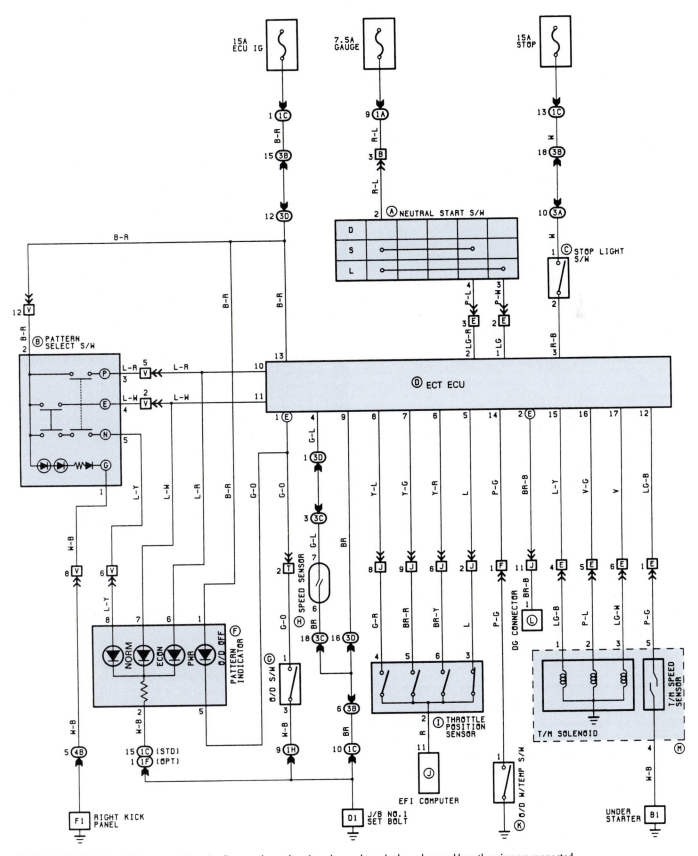

FIGURE 13-24   This transmission wire diagram shows the wire colors and terminal numbers and how the wires are connected.

TECH TIP

Operating voltage at a transmission should be the same as battery voltage (within 0.2 V). If it is lower, check for a voltage drop: Connect the + voltmeter lead to the + battery post and the − lead to the B+ connector at the transmission. The reading should be 0.2 V or less. Next, connect the − voltmeter to the − battery post and the + lead to the ground connection at the transmission. Again, the reading should be 0.2 V or less. Excessive voltage drop indicates a problem in that part of the circuit.

TECH TIP

A known-good similar component can be measured to find the electrical value.

TECH TIP

A rule of thumb for a shift solenoid coil is about 20 to 40 ohms of resistance and a current flow of about 0.5 amp. Solenoid resistance values can vary, so the manufacturer's specifications should be used.

removing the component, installing the new component, and reconnecting the wires and connectors (Figure 13-25).

Occasionally a technician must replace a faulty connector or wire by *splicing* the wire. A few connectors have the wires molded into them, so replacing the connector requires splicing the new connector to each wire. In most cases, however, individual wires can be removed from the connector. These wires have an end terminal that has a locking tang that expands to hold the terminal into the connector. Various special terminal disconnecting tools are available. The tool is pushed

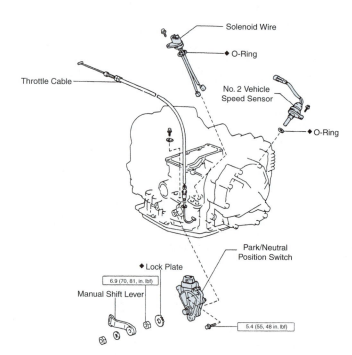

FIGURE 13-25 The No. 2 VSS and park/neutral position switch on this transaxle can be replaced rather easily.

TECH TIP

The green or white corrosion that is found on wire connectors can be cleaned using effervescent denture cleaner and hot water.

against the locking tang, and depresses the tang so the terminal can be pulled out of the connector (Figure 13-26).

To splice a wire, you should:

1. Make sure the new wire is the same gauge size or larger than the original. Strip insulation slightly longer than the splice clip or about 3/8 to 1/2 in. (10 to 13 mm) long (Figure 13-27).
2. Push the two wire ends together so the bare wires overlap inside a splice clip.
3. Use a crimping tool to firmly squeeze the splice clip onto the connection (Figure 13-28). Or, if a splice clip is not being used, twist the connection so the wires are tight (Figure 13-29).
4. Use a soldering gun or iron to heat the wires enough to melt the solder, and apply 60/40 rosin-core solder to the hot wires until the solder flows through the joint. *Do not use acid-core solder* (Figure 13-30).

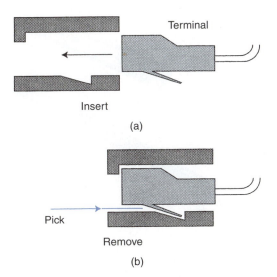

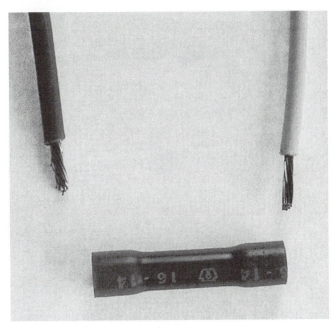

FIGURE 13-26   A terminal is usually pushed into a connector until it locks into place (a). A pick tool is used to unlock the terminal for removal (b).

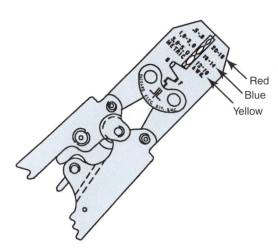

FIGURE 13-27   A wire stripping/crimping tool has an area designed to crimp wire terminals. A cutting area is used to cut insulation and pull it off the wire.

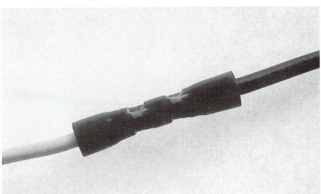

FIGURE 13-28   A splice can be made quickly by crimping a wire connector to the two wires.

5. Insulate the splice either by wrapping it with plastic electrical tape or installing a *shrink tube*. A shrink tube is a plastic tube that is slid over the splice and heated so it shrinks tightly in place.

13.5 ELECTRONIC CONTROL SYSTEM CHECKS

A technician's diagnostic routine will determine if the problem is *inside the transmission* (faulty hydraulic or mechanical operation) or *outside the transmission* (linkage or electrical problems). Systematic diagnosis should locate the problem and/or faulty part(s) that need to be repaired or replaced.

Many technicians begin their diagnosis by making a visual check of the battery and wiring. Green, corroded battery

TECH TIP

The wire stripper can be used as a gauge: The smallest opening that cleanly strips the insulation without nicking or cutting the wire strands is the wire gauge size.

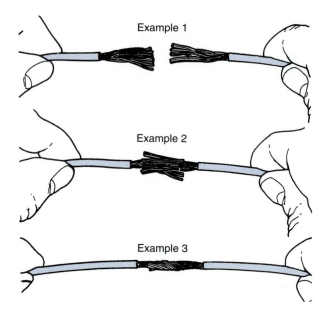

Example 1

Example 2

Example 3

FIGURE 13-29 A wire splice can be made by sliding the bared ends of the wires together, and then twisting them to hold them together. This connection should be soldered for security. *(Courtesy of DaimlerChrysler Corporation)*

FIGURE 13-30 A wire connection is soldered together using rosin-core solder.

TECH TIP

If using a shrink tube, slide a piece of tube about 1/2 in. longer than the splice over the wire before connecting it in step 2. Slide the tube away from the connection while soldering. After soldering the connection, slide the tube to the proper location. Heat the tube to shrink it, locking it in place. *If using tape,* make sure the tape is wrapped tightly, smoothly, and looks neat (Figure 13-31).

terminals or loose terminals can easily cause improper electrical operation. Modified or altered wire connections also lead to unsuspected problems. This quick inspection gives the technician insight into the vehicle's maintenance and repair history.

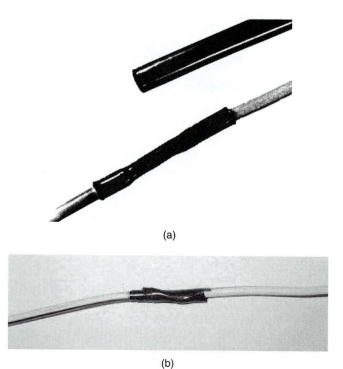

(a)

(b)

FIGURE 13-31 (a) A repaired wire connection should be insulated by wrapping it tightly with tape or using shrink tubing (b). The tubing will shrink tightly in place when heated using a hot air gun.

TECH TIP

Splicing wires is not recommended by some manufacturers because it might change circuit resistance, or improper insulating might lead to future corrosion problems. The recommended repair is to replace the wire or harness.

The Automatic Transmission Rebuilders Association (ATRA) recommends a three-step procedure for electronic transmission diagnosis:

Step 1   Check for codes.
Step 2   Check for signals (electrical signals between the TCM and solenoids).
Step 3   Force the shifts (mechanically and electrically). A checklist can be followed to record your findings and verify that important checks are not skipped (Checklist 13-1).

These steps are easy to follow and are very effective.

The code check identifies an electrical problem recorded in the TCM's memory. You should access and then record the

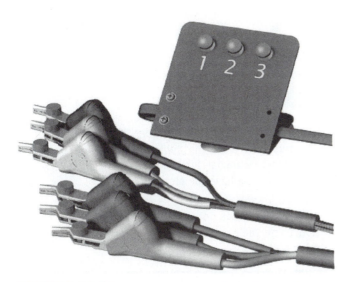

FIGURE 13-32   A signal monitor has three LEDs and wire connections for the transmission harness. On a road test, the LEDs show the electrical signals, and these should occur in the proper order. *(Courtesy of J. S. Popper Inc., www.jspopper.com)*

codes. The codes are then cleared, and if they return during the remaining checks, a problem is present. The check for signals is made using a scan tool or simple shop-made signal monitor (Figure 13-32). (Signal monitor use is described in Section 13.5.4.) These tools allow the technician to watch the signals between the TCM and the transmission. The technician can force the shifts mechanically during the road test by shifting into the different gear ranges. The shifts can be forced electrically by providing the proper electrical signal to operate the solenoids. If step 2 or 3 provides proper operation, the problem is in the electronic controls.

A quick way to start isolating the problem area is to road test the vehicle. The road test gives you the opportunity to verify and experience the problem. Next, remove the fuse that supplies power to the transmission control unit, and conduct a second road test. Without power, the TCM and the electronic controls will shut down, causing the transmission operation to revert to a limp-in mode. In this mode, forward operation in the drive range is limited to a single gear, usually second or fourth. Gear operation is controlled by the manual valve, and there will be no automatic upshifts or downshifts. The transmission's operation will be purely hydraulic and mechanical, so it will start in a higher gear than first, and not upshift. If the second road test has the same problems as the first, you can be sure the problem is not in the electronic controls. It should be noted that a few vehicles will not run if the transmission fuse is removed. Also, some vehicles will turn on the MIL and set a DTC that will need to be cleared after your road test.

13.5.1 Recalibration

Occasionally there is a concern that a transmission has improper shift points, delayed shifts, or just does not work right,

and a thorough diagnosis fails to locate any problems. The problem could be in the calibration or programming of the TCM. Many transmission control modules use an electronically erasable program read-only memory (EEPROM) that determines the operating parameters of the TCM. The TCM determines when the transmission upshifts or downshifts, when the TCC applies or releases, and the hydraulic system pressures in some transmissions. This memory function can be changed by connecting a computer interface to the TCM that will erase the old instructions and send new instructions to the vehicle TCM. *Recalibration* is normally done with a scan tool acting as an interface between a computer with the new program and the TCM. The vehicle dealer will have the equipment needed to perform this operation. Check the service information or TSBs for the need to or possibility for recalibration.

A speedometer that is reading incorrectly can be recalibrated in some vehicles.

Recalibration is often necessary when a new TCM is installed. The process must be performed exactly as directed by the manufacturer. The TCM can be recalibrated outside of the vehicle in some cases. The TCM in some vehicles has a learn strategy that can compensate for some transmission faults such as low line pressure. These units should be recalibrated after a major repair or overhaul.

TECH TIP

Line pressure is software driven, and it affects shift quality and clutch strength. Recalibrating a TCM can change both of these shift characteristics.

TECH TIP

Some shops obtain used control modules from auto dismantlers to use for diagnosis. This allows them to substitute the TCM and note changes that occur in vehicle operation. If this fixes the problem, they know that the problem should be cured using a new TCM. If using a substitute TCM, be careful that the TCM is the same as that in the vehicle being tested.

TECH TIP

If it becomes necessary to correct electronic speedometer readings when there is no recalibration process built into the vehicle's operating system, an aftermarket device is available (Figure 13-33). It can be spliced into the wiring to the VSS, and the speedometer correction can be programmed through a set of dip switches.

REAL WORLD FIX

The 1995 Chrysler Cirrus (87,000 miles) would go into limp mode intermittently with very erratic scan data (extremely high fluid temperatures and voltages). The control module was replaced with a new OE part. The transmission now worked well, but the speedometer would not work. A second new module was installed with the same results.

Fix. After doing some research, the technician learned that it is necessary to program "pinion factor" into the new module. When this was done, the vehicle worked properly.

REAL WORLD FIX

The battery in the 1999 Mercedes 200E (93,000 km) was replaced. Now the vehicle is locked in limp-in mode. The technician feels the TCM needs to be reset, but he does not have the proper tool.

Fix. Following advice, the technician took the vehicle to a Mercedes dealer. Resetting the transmission using their special scan tool fixed this programming problem.

REAL WORLD FIX

The TCC on the 1997 GMC pickup (61,000 km) will not engage. Scan tool data shows TCC duty cycle is 0%, VSS is 95 kph, brake switch is closed, TPS is 10%, coolant temperature is 90°C, and transmission temperature is 75°C. A comparative test on a similar pickup under the same conditions revealed the same data except the TCC duty cycle was 97% and the TCC was engaged.

Fix. It was found that the PCM was programmed with software for trailer towing. Reprogramming it with the correct software allowed the TCC to apply.

FIGURE 13-33 This recalibrator device can be connected into the wire connections to the VSS. The internal setting switches can be used to increase or decrease the rpm signal to correct the speedometer readings. *(Courtesy of Autotrans)*

Adaptive Function Relearn. The TCM of a transmission that uses *adaptive function relearn* will adjust shift control operations to compensate for changes that occur within the transmission as it wears. Worn transmissions tend to have weak, slow shifts because of fluid pressure loss through worn seals. If a worn transmission is repaired, rebuilt, or replaced, the shifts could be harsh until the TCM relearns and readjusts strategy. Repair or replacement of any faulty shift-related component can produce this problem. Unless the technician reprograms or recalibrates the TCM, the customer will notice unacceptable shifts.

TCMs are programmed with default settings; these are the shift values that were used when the vehicle was new. They were changed by the TCM as it learned the new requirements as the transmission wore. Some TCMs can be reset to the original default settings by using a scan tool; others can be reset by disconnecting the TCM from the battery for a short period of time.

The transmission will readapt shift strategy after repair, and if the shifts are too soft, the change will occur fairly fast. But, if the shifts are too harsh, adaptation is usually very slow going in a softer direction.

Many transmissions have a *fast learn* program that uses a scan tool. Fast learn only takes a few minutes as the transmission applies each of the clutches and calculates the clutch volume.

13.5.2 Electronic Control System Cautions

Electrostatic discharge (ESD) is the electrical shock that is felt after sliding across the seat and touching the vehicle's door handle. Sometimes we see small sparks as we take off a shirt made from synthetic fibers. Static electricity is generated when we rub one material across another under the right conditions.

Computer-controlled circuits require care because of possible ESD damage. The shock we feel or the spark that we see is about 10,000 V or greater. An ESD voltage as low as 60 V can easily damage solid-state electronic devices. The symbol shown in Figure 13-34 is placed on some components and wiring diagrams to indicate components that can be damaged by ESD. Unless you are connected electrically to the vehicle's ground, do not touch that component or its electrical connections. Do not make electrical measurements or checks on these components unless instructed to do so, and always follow directions exactly. If directed to make voltage checks, always connect the negative probe to ground first.

The TCM should never be disconnected while the ignition is on. Also, you should wait for a minimum of 5 seconds before disconnecting a TCM after turning the power off. Some control modules electronically send information to the EEPROM during this time, and interrupting the power flow can cause faults in this information.

Other problems can occur if the battery is disconnected for too long, and these problems can occur in any of the vehicle's

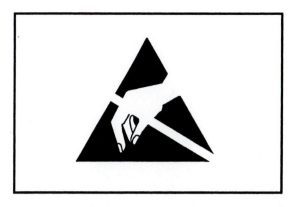

FIGURE 13-34 Extreme care should be used when testing components displaying the electrostatic discharge (ESD) symbol. These components can be damaged by ESD.

Do not touch any of the terminals of a TCM or any part of the circuit board unless you are wearing an ESD safety strap that is properly grounded.

At least one transmission with an integrated TCM will shut down the TCM when the TCM temperature reaches 288°F (142°C). The transmission will go into fail-safe operation until the TCM cools down.

electronically controlled circuits. For example, one vehicle requires that the HVAC (heating, ventilation, and air conditioning) air flow control doors must be recalibrated if the battery is disconnected. This vehicle will set a trouble code, and the rear wiper switch light will flash to indicate a problem.

13.5.3 Diagnostic Trouble Codes (DTCs)

Most electronic systems use a control module that can perform a self-diagnosis on the electrical/electronic components, its sensors, and its output circuits each time it starts up. It

Diagnostic Trouble Codes

The 42LE transmission control module may report any of the following diagnostic trouble codes:

11	Internal Control Module		37	Solenoid Switch Valve Latched in CC Position
12	Battery Was Disconnected		38	Torque Converter Clutch
13	Internal Control Module		41	LR Solenoid Circuit
14	Relay Output Always On		42	2-4 Solenoid Circuit
15	Relay Output Always Off		43	OD Solenoid Circuit
16	Internal Control Module		44	UD Solenoid Circuit
17	Internal Control Module		45	Internal Control Module
18	Engine Speed Sensor		46	UD Solenoid Circuit
19	C²D Bus Communication With PCM		47	Solenoid Switch Valve Latched In LR Position
20	Switched Battery		48	Torque Management Request
21	OD Pressure Switch Circuit		50	Output and Input Speed Checks: Speed Error in Reverse
22	2-4 Pressure Switch Circuit		51	Speed Error in 1st
23	2-4/OD Pressure Switch Circuit		52	Speed Error in 2nd
24	LR Pressure Switch Circuit		53	Speed Error in 3rd
25	LR/OD Pressure Switch Circuit		54	Speed Error in 4th
26	LR/2-4 Pressure Switch Circuit		56	Output and Input Speed Checks: Input Sensor Error
27	All Pressure Switch Circuits		57	Output Sensor Error
28	Check Shifter Signal		58	Sensor Ground Error
29	Throttle Position Signal		60	Low Element Volume: LR
31	OD Hydraulic Pressure Switch		61	2-4
32	2-4 Hydraulic Pressure Switch		62	OD
33	OD/2-4 HydraulicPressure Switch			
36	Fault Immediately After Shift			

FIGURE 13-35   These DTCs are vehicle-model specific. They indicate the nature of the faults for a 42LE transmission. *(Courtesy of Chrysler Corporation)*

measures circuit voltage, looking for insufficient resistance caused by shorts or grounds or excessive resistance caused by open or poor connections. If an electrical problem is identified, it will turn on the malfunction indicator light (MIL) or flash the overdrive (O/D) indicator light and set a DTC (Figure 13-35). The DTC is displayed on a special tester or scan tool, and the code number indicates the electrical component or circuit that is functioning improperly. The DTC does not tell exactly what is wrong, but will indicate a problem such as *Shift Solenoid 1 Circuit Failure,* which indicates that the solenoid 1 circuit is open or shorted. Additional testing is required to pinpoint the exact cause of the problem. These tests usually involve measuring voltage or resistance at different points of the circuit. A good service manual or circuit information is essential for the proper test routine.

The DTC can be either **soft** (temporary) or *hard* (semipermanent). A soft code is erased from the control module's memory when the ignition key is turned off. A hard code is erased by performing a special operation, pressing certain control head buttons, removing the fuse for the control module, or by using a scan tool. This is called *clearing codes.* Some systems can record and display the history of past failures. Self-diagnosis is vehicle-model specific. Carefully follow the directions given by the vehicle manufacturer. If using a scanner, follow the scanner manufacturer's directions.

Not all transmission electrical problems will set a trouble code. Without a trouble code, the technician must check all the circuits, one at a time, using an ohmmeter, voltmeter, test light, or scanner. Checking a circuit requires a wiring diagram as well as a good understanding of the circuit. Understanding the circuit often leads the technician close to the source of the problem. For example, if an electronically controlled transmission operates normally but has no third or fourth gear, a shift control solenoid is probably not allowing the clutches to operate properly. The technician should check both the electrical and hydraulic operation of the fourth-gear shift circuit.

TECH TIP

Some technicians have found that they can use a non-CAN scan tool on a CAN vehicle by inputting an earlier-model vehicle. This can disable critical vehicle operating systems. In one case, the scan tool connection disabled the ABS brakes during a road test; the brake pedal was very hard and would not apply.

REAL WORLD FIX

The 1993 Volvo 850 (132,000 miles) has shift problems. A scan tool check shows codes 114, 222, and 313.

Fix. The technician checked the S1 and S2 shift solenoid resistance and found both to be out of specification. Vacuum hose routing was also checked and three were found to be improperly connected. Installing new shift solenoids and connecting the vacuum hoses properly fixed this problem.

REAL WORLD FIX

The 1996 Ford Windstar (50,000 miles) had a remanufactured transaxle installed. It drives and shifts well, but after a few miles the O/D (MIL) light begins flashing. Reading the DTCs shows a P0730 code, incorrect gear ratio.

Fix. The transaxle has the wrong internal ratio. The fix was to install the correct transaxle for this vehicle.

NOTE: This is an extremely difficult problem to avoid. The only way to determine the internal gear ratios is to count the teeth on the sprockets or gearset members. Many remanufactured transmissions are painted, hiding any identification marks, which makes exact identification difficult.

REAL WORLD FIX

The 1994 Toyota 4 Runner (104,000 miles) will not shift into fourth gear most of the time. The shop has limited test equipment. They believe the problem is caused by a faulty overdrive solenoid, but they are not sure which one is the overdrive solenoid.

Fix. A check of the iATN information network informed the shop to check the engine thermostat. Someone had removed it. Replacement of the thermostat allowed the engine to come up to proper temperature and go into normal operation. This fixed the transmission problem.

Understanding of the proper operation of the transmission is essential to diagnosis. This transmission will not allow overdrive (fourth gear) until normal engine operating temperature is reached. Remember that electronic transmission problems can come from outside the transmission. It is essential to completely understand the system.

Self-diagnosis is usually entered (started) by manipulating the scan tool or a transmission control switch. The codes resulting from self-diagnosis will be displayed (1) on the instrument panel, (2) on a handheld scanner, or (3) on a voltmeter or test light. The DTC is read as a multidigit or alphanumeric number; some systems display the code by a pattern of pulses from a voltmeter or flashes of a light on the instrument panel (Figure 13-36).

When checking electrical circuits, it is wise to remember that the most probable faults are wire connectors or moving mechanical parts. These include all wire connectors, switches, speed sensors, and solenoids. When checking wire connectors, look for loose, corroded, dirty, or bent and misaligned prongs (Figure 13-37).

The least probable cause of failure will be the TCM. It is fairly well protected, and since there are no moving parts, there is nothing to wear out. However, the TCM can be damaged by excessive current flowing through it or a high-voltage spike occurring in one of its circuits. The wrong tester can cause excessive current flow. Testing a circuit using a test light or voltmeter is discussed in Section 13.3. The most common causes for a high-voltage spike are using a solenoid with an open diode, disconnecting the TCM while the ignition switch is on, and touching the prongs of the TCM with your fingers

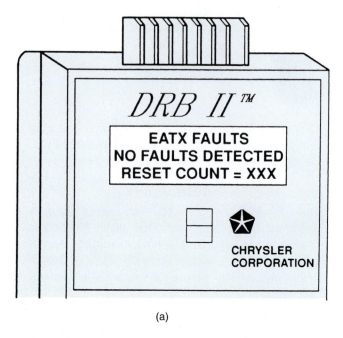

(a)

Fault ID:

Code 60 — Low L-R Element Volume

Code 61 — Low 2-4 Element Volume

Code 62 — Low OD Element Volume

(b)

FIGURE 13-36 This DRB II screen shows that no fault codes are stored in the TCM memory (a); it would display a screen similar to b if there were fault codes. *(Courtesy of Chrysler Corporation)*

TECH TIP

Incorrect chain and/or differential ratios can create a DTC. A way of confirming incorrect ratios is to drive the vehicle while streaming data from the scanner. If the TCC lock command reaches 100% and you feel lock-up, but the slip ratio is over 50 rpm, you have a transmission with the wrong internal ratio.

(ESD). Some simple rules to follow while testing and working on electronic-controlled transmissions are:

- Make sure the ignition is off before disconnecting or connecting the TCM.
- Make sure the ignition is off before disconnecting any TCM-related circuits or components.

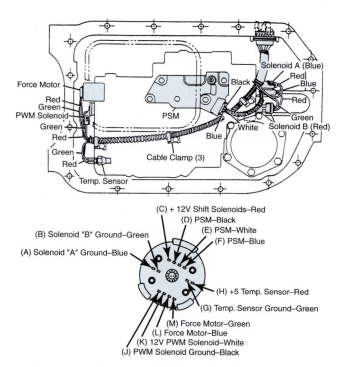

FIGURE 13-37 A visual inspection of the transmission electrical connector ensures that the terminals are clean and in good shape as well as being completely engaged.

- Never touch the TCM or electrical components without first connecting yourself to the vehicle's ground.
- Use the proper test equipment.

Following are general descriptions of some test procedures to give you an idea of the diagnostic process. However, you should always follow the procedure described in the service manual for a particular transmission.

After the fault is located and repaired, the codes must be cleared. With soft codes, this is easily done by turning off the key. Hard codes are cleared by performing certain operations with the scan tool, or by removing the control module fuse(s).

After the problems have been repaired and the codes erased, drive the vehicle through the basic road test. Recheck for any DTC to make sure that all faults have been corrected.

13.5.4 Signal Monitor

A simple but effective transmission test tool is a shop-made *signal monitor* containing a series of LED lights. By watching the LEDs, you can see when the electrical signal is sent to the solenoids (see Figure 13-32). This unit can be made using a few dollars' worth of parts purchased at most electronic stores (Appendix F).

The monitor is connected to the solenoid feed wires at the transmission connector and also to either B+ or ground

A DTC does not always indicate a faulty electrical value. A P0755, Shift Solenoid B malfunction, will set if the 1–2 shift takes longer than the prescribed period of time. A P0756, Shift Solenoid B Performance or Stuck Off, will set if fluid pressure does not increase in a circuit at the correct time. A P0758, Shift Solenoid B Electrical, will set if an improper electrical signal passes through that circuit.

Repair of a worn or faulty electronically controlled transmission will often result in harsh shifts. The electronic controls have been compensating for excessive clutch clearance or low fluid pressures by increasing the line pressure. The TCM must be recalibrated or the vehicle can be driven, 45 minutes or longer, until the TCM relearns how the repaired transmission operates and shifts. Always check the service information for the proper relearn procedure.

A scan tool will erase codes without affecting any other electrical circuits. Disconnecting a fuse or the battery could erase all of the electronic memories, including clock settings and radio station presets. The result could be an irate vehicle owner. Removing the control module fuse(s) erases the memory of only that control module, but can also cause other problems. Some electronic transmissions are controlled through the engine control module (ECM). Some of these have adaptive learning for the engine controls. These ECMs adjust certain engine operating functions to particular geographic locations or driving styles. If you pull the fuse on these vehicles, it can take about 100 miles of driving before operating strategies are relearned and switched from a default setting to the owner's location and driving style. During this time the vehicle can run poorly.

depending on whether the solenoids are computer or internally grounded. When the vehicle is driven on a basic road test, the monitor LEDs should light up in a pattern that matches the transmission's shift pattern. If the signals differ from the proper pattern, the problem is electronic in nature. If the signals occur, but the transmission does not shift properly, the problem is mechanical or hydraulic and is inside the transmission.

13.5.5 Forcing Shifts Electrically

Forcing a shift requires disconnecting the transmission electrical connector and connecting a special tool to provide the proper electrical signal to the shift solenoids. Most scan tools have this ability when connected to the DLC. Remember that when the special tool or scan tool forces a shift, it provides either the B+ or ground signal to the shift solenoid. It takes the place of the TCM and, in some cases, provides a redundant or its own ground. Providing power to the solenoids lets you determine if they are working properly. If they are, then the problem is in the wiring, the TCM, or the inputs to the TCM.

13.5.6 Clutch Volume Index

Some vehicles include a code for *clutch volume index (CVI)*. This monitors the time needed to fill a clutch as it applies. Each clutch should fill and stroke the clutch in a specified time. This time period usually increases with normal wear.

The TCM determines CVI from the speed differential between the input and output speed sensors. The TCM can determine the actual ratio and how long it takes to complete a shift from the speed differential of the two speed sensors. A high CVI usually indicates a clutch with excessive slippage.

If it is necessary to disconnect a battery, it is recommended that you first write down the station numbers for the radio presets. After reconnecting the battery, reset the radio stations and the vehicle's clock. Also perform any "relearn" steps for the ECM and the TCM.

The 1990 Plymouth Caravan (152,000 miles) transmission was rebuilt, and it worked well for a while. Now, it will not shift. A check for DTC showed code 24. The DTC was cleared, and the transmission operated properly for 3 weeks, then the problem and code returned.

Fix. A check showed the underdrive clutch volume (CVI) was high. The transmission was disassembled, and an air check of the underdrive clutch showed a leak. Repair of the clutch seals fixed this problem.

The 1991 Ford Explorer (158,000 miles) shifts in and out of overdrive erratically, and when this occurs, the speedometer shows speed changes, from 140 mph to 0 mph. A scan tool check revealed no DTCs, the VSS output is very erratic, and the park–neutral switch output changes between park and neutral. The VSS and park–neutral switch have been replaced using OEM parts, but this did not help.

Fix. Careful inspection revealed that the number 5 spark plug wire was wrapped around the wiring harness for the park–neutral switch. Rerouting of these wires fixed this problem.

13.5.7 EMI Electronic Problems

Electronic circuits can be influenced by *electromagnetic induction (EMI)* and *radio frequency interference (RFI)*. RFI is a form of EMI. This is the interaction between ferrous metal objects and the magnetic field around a current-carrying wire. Vehicle manufacturers twist electrical wires together, use shielded coaxial cable, and install metal shielding to protect some circuits from EMI interference.

EMI can cause strange electronic circuit malfunctions and a TCM to set a DTC when there is no real fault. If this is encountered, first check the vehicle for improperly installed aftermarket electronic accessories. These include a cellular telephone, radar detector, remote starter system, radio, or any other non-OEM electrical accessory. Discarded shields or misrouted wires from an improperly performed repair can also cause EMI problems.

13.6 ELECTRONIC COMPONENT AND CIRCUIT CHECKS

After the nature of the problem has been determined, the faulty circuit or components should be checked to locate the exact cause. These are often fairly simple voltage, resistance, or current flow checks. These checks can often be made with the components mounted in their normal position. A *breakout box* or *test box* can be connected into the circuit to allow the technician to check voltage or resistance (Figure 13-38). It is also possible to check internal transmission electrical components at the breakout box (Figure 13-39).

When checking a circuit, make sure that all connectors are properly latched. Disassemble the connector and check for loose, bent, or pushed-back pins, cracked connectors, and water intrusion that will cause corrosion.

The valve body with integrated TCMs (called control solenoid valve assembly, Mechatronic, and solenoid body) can be removed from the transmission and reconnected to the vehicle using a special harness. A signal generator can be used to input ISS and OSS signals, and if the TCM responds properly, the speed sensor in question must be faulty.

FIGURE 13-38 This 100-pin breakout box can be connected to a wiring harness to provide convenient points to make electrical checks. *(Courtesy of SPX/OTC)*

REAL WORLD FIX

The 1995 Lincoln Towncar (160,000 km) was towed in because it would not shift out of park. Pressing the brake does not help. Another problem is that the brake lights are not working.

Fix. The technician checked the brake light circuit and found a broken wire at the switch. Repairing this wire fixed both problems.

13.6.1 TCM Power Checks

An electronic system cannot function without adequate power or a good ground. The power and ground connections are often overlooked by the technician who is eager to solve a transmission problem. After determining there is a problem in the electronic system, an experienced technician will check B+ voltage at the battery and then at the TCM and transmission power relay if there is one. There should be at least 12.6 V with the engine off and 13.6 to 15 V with the engine running. There should also be a minimum voltage drop between the TCM ground (B–) terminal and ground, 0.2 V or less (Figure 13-40).

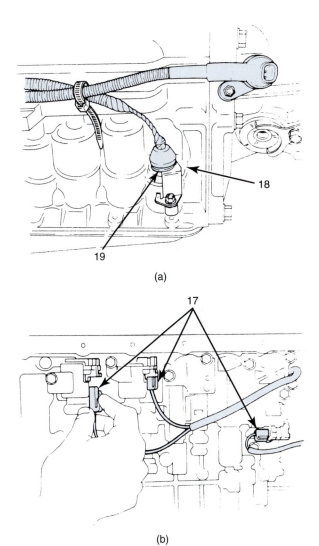

(a)

(b)

FIGURE 13-39 The external (a) and internal (b) wiring harnesses connect to the transmission electrical components.

A relay is a coil of thin wire with an iron core and switch contacts. When current flows through the coil, a magnetic field is produced, and the switch is pulled closed. The amount of resistance in the wire coil can be easily checked using an ohmmeter. First disconnect the solenoid, and then connect one ohmmeter lead to each of the relay electrical coil connectors, read the resistance, and compare the reading to the specifications (Figure 13-41). Solenoids should also be checked for a grounded coil. Relays with a diode should be checked to make sure the diode is good; this is done by reversing the ohmmeter leads at the coil connections. The resistance should be higher in one direction than it is in the other.

Battery. An electronic system cannot function properly without a good battery. This should be the first item to check, and there are two battery checks: state of charge and load test. State of charge is measured by simply connecting the two voltmeter

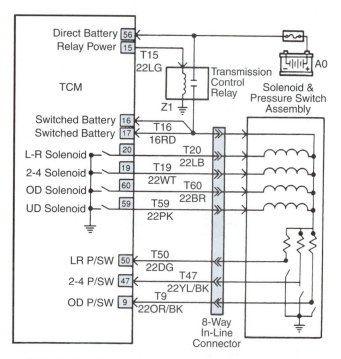

FIGURE 13-40 TCM terminals 16 and 17 receive B+ when the transmission relay is energized. This also sends B+ to the solenoid and pressure switch assembly.

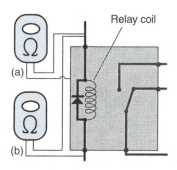

FIGURE 13-41 Ohmmeter A is connected to check for a grounded circuit: it should read infinite resistance. Ohmmeter B is measuring the resistance of the coil; if the leads are reversed, it will show a different resistance because of the diode.

TECH TIP

Wiggling the wire connectors and tapping the TCM sharply with your finger while testing may reveal the cause of an intermittent problem.

TECH TIP

When diagnosing a problem that has set an MIL, shut down the TCM, and will shut down the electrical functions, use the following procedure to get circuit values: (1) clear the codes, (2) connect your test equipment, and (3) turn the key on and measure the electrical values while the TCM is performing its self-check.

TECH TIP

A TCM is considered a nonserviceable component; a faulty TCM is removed and replaced. However, an experienced technician will check to determine what caused the failure. Checking a TCM follows this procedure: (1) remove the TCM from the vehicle, (2) give the TCM a gentle shake as you listen for rattles that indicate loose parts, (3) remove the cover, and (4) make a visual inspection for white or green corrosion, black or burned overheated parts, leaky capacitors, and cracked or broken solder joints. A faulty solder joint can usually be resoldered, saving the TCM.

REAL WORLD FIX

The 1995 Buick Skylark (63,000 miles) engine stalls when shifted into reverse. When a scan tool is connected, it momentarily quits reading as the shift is made. With the engine off, the scan tool acts normally.

Fix. Careful inspection showed that the engine harness ground wires had broken, but would make contact. Engine movement during the reverse shift would break the contact and open the circuits. Repair of these wires fixed this problem.

REAL WORLD FIX

The 1992 BMW 325 (164,000 miles) stays in first gear unless it is manually shifted into third and then during third gear, shifted back into D for fourth. The circuits were checked using a test light, the solenoids using an ohmmeter, and the sensors using a lab scope. Everything checked out fine. The TCM was replaced with no change.

Fix. A further check of the selector switch using a DMM showed a leakage of 8 V into a circuit that was off and should have had 0 V. This was enough to stop the TCM from operating. Replacement of the gear range selector switch fixed this problem.

REAL WORLD FIX

The 1995 Chevrolet S10 (54,000 miles) had no TCC lock-up. Use of an electronic tester showed a lock-up signal from the TCM, and the TCC will apply from the tester. Voltage checks show proper voltages.

Fix. A check of the ground circuit between the frame and transmission showed a bad connection. Cleaning the connections fixed this problem. The transmission tester provided a redundant ground for the TCC solenoid to operate during the tests. The technician should have made the voltage checks with the tester disconnected.

REAL WORLD FIX

The 1994 Dodge Intrepid (126,000 miles) transmission does not shift until warmed up. A scan tool check shows a code 66: No ETAX to CCD Messages Received. The instrument panel gauges do not work until the engine comes up to temperature. These problems are intermittent and the vehicle will work okay for several days.

Fix. The technician inspected all of the grounds plus the ignition switch. One of the ignition switch B+ circuits checked had 0.5 V. A new ignition switch fixed this problem.

TECH TIP

If battery testing a late-model vehicle with fuel injection, some technicians prevent starting by pushing the gas pedal all the way to the floor; this should shut off the fuel injectors.

leads to the two battery posts. A voltage of 12.6 V indicates a full charge; 12.4 V indicates a charge level of about 75%. A low battery should be charged before continuing to the next check.

The most accurate battery load test is made using a load tester; this unit applies a discharge load to the battery while observing the battery's drop in voltage. A load test can also be made by using the vehicle's starter to apply the load.

To make a battery load test, you should:

If a battery load tester is available:

1. Determine the CCA (cold cranking amperes) rating of the battery. Connect the current and the voltage leads to the battery posts.

2. Adjust the amperage load to one-half that of the battery's CCA rating, and allow the battery to discharge for 15 seconds while watching the voltage. Stop the test if voltage drops below 9.5 V; this indicates that the battery has failed the test.

If a load tester is not available:

1. Disable the vehicle's ignition system so it will not start.
2. Connect the voltmeter leads to the battery posts, and crank the engine for 30 seconds while watching the voltage. Stop the test if voltage drops below 9.5 V; this indicates that the battery has failed the test.

13.6.2 TCC Checks

TCC operation can be checked using a functional test. If it fails, further tests will be needed to find the exact cause.
To perform this test, you should do the following:

1. Perform a road test, and drive the vehicle about 40 mph (65 km/h) using a light throttle. Tap the brake lightly,

REAL WORLD FIX

The 1994 Ford Taurus (135,000 miles) came in with a TCC dropout after the vehicle gets to operating temperature. A scan tool check shows DTC 628: TCC circuit slippage. After the code is set, the EPC sets line pressure at 60 psi and the transmission upshifts and downshifts are harsh from that point. The valve body and EPC solenoid have been replaced twice and the TCM once, but this did not help.

Fix. Following advice, the technician learned that this is the normal strategy programmed for this transmission. When excessive TCC slippage is sensed by the ECM, the fluid pressure will be increased to a certain point, and then the TCM will turn off the TCC and lock line pressure to 60 psi. This set of symptoms indicates that this transmission has more severe internal problems.

just enough to turn on the stop lights but not enough to start brake application.

2. Observe the tachometer, if the vehicle has one, and feel for a soft, slight downshift indicating TCC release. This should be followed by a soft reapplication of the TCC.

If you notice the release and reapplication: This is normal operation.

If nothing happens: a faulty converter clutch or a stuck converter clutch control valve or a faulty solenoid, internal transmission switch, TCC circuit, or control module is indicated.

Some TCC problems will set a DTC, and this code may indicate the nature of the problem. There are several checks that can be made on the circuit, the solenoid, and its diode. These are described in the following section. The TCC hydraulic circuit checks are described in Section 12.6.

13.6.3 Solenoid Checks

A solenoid is a coil of thin wire with an iron plunger. When current flows through the coil, a magnetic field is produced and the plunger moves to the center of the magnetic field. The resistance in the coil can be easily checked using an ohmmeter. A solenoid can be checked either in the transmission or on the bench. Disconnect the solenoid connector and connect one ohmmeter lead to each of the solenoid electrical terminals. Read the resistance, and compare the reading to the specifications (Figure 13-42). Follow this by moving one of the leads to the solenoid body or base to check for a ground circuit. A two-wire solenoid should not have a circuit to the

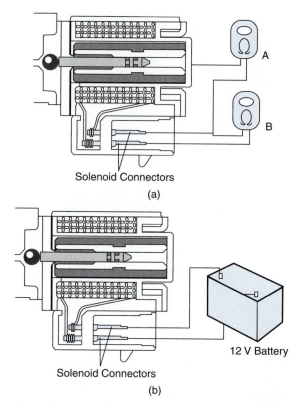

FIGURE 13-42   Ohmmeter A is checking for a grounded solenoid coil; the reading should be infinite. Ohmmeter B is measuring the coil resistance; it should be within the specifications for this solenoid (a). Connecting a solenoid to a 12-V battery should cause it to operate (b). Make sure the battery is connected using the correct polarity in case the solenoid has an internal diode.

TECH TIP

A quick check for a shift solenoid is to complete the solenoid circuit. Use a jumper wire to the battery for a single-wire solenoid or jumper wire to ground for a two-wire solenoid. A shift solenoid should click, indicating that the coil windings are complete and the plunger is moving. *Do not* use this quick check on a PWN solenoid; the lower internal resistance will allow excessive current flow that can damage the solenoid.

ground, the solenoid mounting point. If the first reading is within specifications and the second one is infinite or OL (out of limits), the solenoid should operate. A single-wire solenoid will be grounded through the solenoid case, and it should have continuity when one of the ohmmeter leads is connected to the case and the other to the solenoid terminal.

TECH TIP

A PWM solenoid draws enough current to overheat and burn out if connected directly to a battery. If testing with jumper wires, limit the connection to 1 second, just enough time to hear it click.

TECH TIP

If testing a solenoid using a special tester, use the same voltage and frequency/duty cycle settings that are used in the vehicle.

TECH TIP

Many technicians consider solenoids, especially PWM solenoids, to be "wear items" and automatically replace them if the transmission experiences problems after about 70,000 miles. Some PWM solenoids operate at 30 to 50 Hz while the vehicle is in drive.

TECH TIP

Early solenoid failure can be caused by excessive vehicle electrical system voltage.

Some solenoids include a diode to eliminate any voltage spikes that might occur as the solenoid is de-energized. As the solenoid is tested, the diode is also checked to see if it allows a flow in one direction but not the other. You can check the diode and the solenoid coil by connecting an ohmmeter lead to each of the terminals. With the solenoid out of the transmission and on the bench, you should connect the positive (+) ohmmeter lead to the positive (+) solenoid lead and the two negative (−) leads together. If checks are made with the solenoid in the transmission, be aware that some transmission circuits include a pressure switch between the solenoid negative terminal and the case connector.

With the ohmmeter connected to the solenoid as just described, the reading should be about 20 to 40 Ω depending on the temperature. If the reading is less than 20 Ω, the coil or diode is shorted. If the reading is greater than 40 Ω or infinite, there is an open or broken circuit. In either case, the solenoid is faulty.

Next, reverse the meter leads so they are connected positive to negative and negative to positive. The meter reading should now be lower than it was before, usually about 2 to 15 Ω. If the reading does not change, the diode is open, and the solenoid is faulty.

A solenoid can also be checked by connecting it to a 12-V battery, but take care when making this test. The diode will be destroyed if you connect the solenoid backwards. As the

solenoid is connected to the power source, you should be able to feel and hear it "click" as it changes position.

The mechanical operation of a solenoid also should be checked. Since solenoids are basically electromagnets operating in an area that might have some metal debris, they tend to attract metal particles. These can cause sticking or binding of the solenoid plunger or blocking of the fluid passage. Test the solenoid by blowing air through it while energizing and de-energizing the coil. When the solenoid is connected to the power source, you should be able to blow through a normally closed solenoid. The passage should close so air flow will be blocked when it is not energized. Other solenoids are normally open; they will test just the opposite. You should be able to blow through a normally open solenoid when it is not energized, but not when it is energized. Specialized testers are available that provide a power source and use air pressure to test solenoid operation (Figure 13-43). Some testers will also test switch operation. Another tester checks solenoid operation using fluid flow.

13.6.4 Switch Checks

A control switch is checked by removing it from the circuit and checking it with an ohmmeter. The meter leads are connected to the two terminals of the switch. If there is only one terminal, one meter lead is connected to it, and the other lead is connected to the switch body. Some switches are normally open, and the reading should be very high—infinite or OL. Some switches are normally closed, and the reading should be

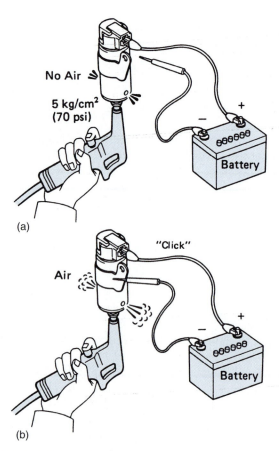

No Air

5 kg/cm² (70 psi)

Battery

(a)

"Click"

Air

Battery

(b)

FIGURE 13-43 You should not be able to blow through this solenoid if it is not activated (a). If it is connected to a 12-V battery, it should make a "click," and you should be able to blow through it.

TECH TIP

Solenoid tests can identify if a solenoid is plugged or clear and if it has good coil windings under shop conditions. Most tests cannot duplicate the heat and vibration that occur inside of a transmission, and they will not predict the solenoid's remaining useful life. Some technicians heat the solenoid using a heat gun while making solenoid checks.

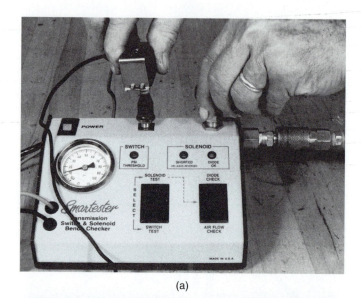

(a)

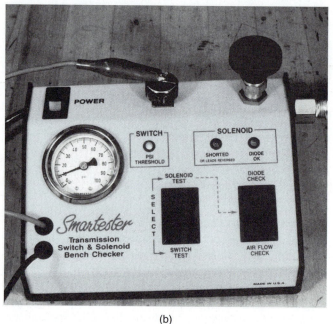

(b)

FIGURE 13-44 A special tester being used to check a solenoid (a) and a pressure switch (b). The switch should either open or close when air is supplied. The solenoid should allow or block an air flow when activated.

zero ohms. When the switch is operated, the reading should change to the opposite value. A pressure switch can usually be operated using a specialized tester or air pressure and a rubber-tipped air gun (Figure 13-44).

A mechanically operated switch can also be checked on the vehicle using a voltmeter. Connect the negative meter lead to a good ground or the switch body and the positive lead to the B+ wire entering the switch. Voltage should be available to the switch. Next, move the positive meter lead to the second switch terminal, and operate the switch. As the switch is operated, the output voltage should change from zero to the same as the input voltage or vice versa. If the voltage readings are not close to the same value, there is a voltage drop, and high resistance in the switch is indicated.

Pressure switches can also be checked at the transmission electrical connector.

REAL WORLD FIX

The 1991 Chevrolet Suburban R2500 (154,000 miles) goes into limp-in mode intermittently. Another shop has replaced all of the shift solenoids. A scan tool check shows code 81: Shift Solenoid B. The solenoid resistance checks are within specifications. The connections to the speed sensors have been checked and they are clean.

Fix. The technician checked solenoid resistances again and found out-of-specification and open circuit readings. A visual inspection of the solenoids showed that the locking tabs of the solenoid connectors were all broken, and solenoid B was almost unplugged. A new internal wire harness fixed this problem.

REAL WORLD FIX

The 1992 Subaru SVX (115,000 miles) came in with a burned transmission, and the O/D hub was torn off of the output shaft. The transmission was rebuilt, but it came back in one week with a slipping problem on the 2–3 and 3–4 shifts. Disassembly of the transmission showed a burned-up high clutch pack and 2–4 band. The unit was rebuilt again, and a shift kit was installed. A road test shows a good 1–2, mushy 2–3, and slipping 3–4 shifts.

Fix. Following advice, line pressure was checked and found to be low. The line pressure solenoid was rechecked and found to be stuck open, causing the low line pressure. This solenoid had been checked, and it had good electrical values. Replacement of this solenoid fixed this transmission.

A good road test before repairs should have indicated that the original problem was caused by low line pressure so it could have been cured. A good road test after the first rebuild should have caught this uncured problem earlier and saved a lot of time and expense.

TECH TIP

An external switch that has fluid leaking through it has failed and should be replaced.

REAL WORLD FIX

The 1993 Dodge Caravan (58,000 miles) goes into neutral after driving about 20 miles. Road testing with a scan tool connected shows the PRNDL switch going to neutral when this occurs. The gear select switch and the neutral safety switch were replaced, but this did not help. There are no transmission or engine DTCs.

Fix. Following advice, a redundant ground was added between the transmission case and battery ground. The connectors on the gear select switch were also replaced, and one or both of the operations cured this problem.

NOTE: A voltage drop check on the ground circuit would have determined if the redundant ground was needed.

The transmission range (TR) switch, manual lever position (MLP) switch, or neutral start switch has several circuits and multiple terminals. These switches are checked using an ohmmeter and service information to determine which terminals should have continuity as the switch is moved through its travel. For example, using the switch connections shown in Figure 13-45, there should be no resistance between three of the terminals and ground in park. There should be infinite resistance between the B/U lamp switch feed terminal and ground in all gear positions except reverse. Some MLP switches will have continuity between various terminals in some gear positions.

13.6.5 Speed Sensor Checks

Two styles of speed sensors are commonly used in automatic transmissions. One style is a switch that opens and closes as a

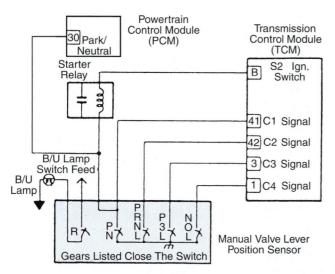

FIGURE 13-45 The five switches inside this MLP switch complete a connection to ground in the various gear positions. *(Courtesy of DaimlerChrysler Corporation)*

TECH TIP

Access to a VSS is very limited on some vehicles. The VSS can be checked at the TCM, where there may be more room.

magnet on the transmission output shaft rotates past it. The other style is a unit that generates an alternating voltage signal as a specially designed transmission part rotates next to it.

The switch-type speed sensor normally has a single-wire connector and is tested using an ohmmeter (Figure 13-46). Connect one lead of the ohmmeter to a good ground and the other lead to the switch's connector. Next, rotate the transmission output shaft while watching the ohmmeter. The reading should change from very low (zero to a few ohms) to very high (infinite or OL) as the output shaft rotates.

The voltage-generating unit in a speed sensor normally uses a two-wire connector and is checked using both an ohmmeter and a voltmeter. First, disconnect the sensor, and connect the ohmmeter leads to the sensor terminals. There should be a complete circuit through the unit, and the amount of resistance should fall within the range given in the specifications. Excessive or infinite resistance indicates a high resistance or open circuit; too low of a reading indicates a short circuit. The next check is to connect the two leads of a voltmeter to the two sensor connectors, set the meter to AC volts, and then rotate the transmission output shaft. As the shaft rotates, the

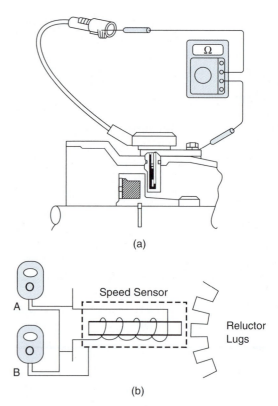

(a)

(b)

FIGURE 13-46 A single-wire VSS can be checked by connecting one ohmmeter lead to the output terminal and the other lead to ground (a). Rotating the transmission output shaft should cause the ohmmeter to fluctuate from zero to infinite ohms. A two-wire VSS is checked as shown in (b). Ohmmeter A is measuring the speed sensor coil resistance; it should be within the specifications. Ohmmeter B is checking for a grounded coil; the reading should be infinite. *(a is courtesy of Chrysler Corporation)*

TECH TIP

Switches and sensors provide the data that a TCM uses to determine how and when pressure control or shift solenoids operate. Figure 13-47 illustrate when these are required.

voltmeter should show a fluctuating ac voltage reading, first + and then − to the same value.

13.6.6 Throttle Position Sensor Checks

A throttle position sensor (TPS) can be checked using an ohmmeter or voltmeter. Disconnect the TPS electrical connector,

Sensor	Phase of Operation				
	Line Pressure Control	Shift Control	TCC Control	Fail-Safe	Self Diagnosis
VSS	X	X	X	X	X
ISS	X	X	X	X	X
TRS/PNP	X	X	X	X	X
TFT	X		X	X	X
TPS	X	X	X	X	X
Engine rpm	X	X	X		X
TCM Power	X				X

FIGURE 13-47 Switch and sensor operation can affect different phases of transmission operation.

REAL WORLD FIX

The 1995 Ford Windstar (109,000 miles) had a harsh shift complaint. A scan tool check showed DTC P0500: VSS missing input. The VSS signal is intermittent, sometimes good and sometimes not there.

Fix. The technician checked the VSS and found the heat shield was missing. When the VSS got hot, the signal would drop out. Replacing the VSS heat shield fixed this problem.

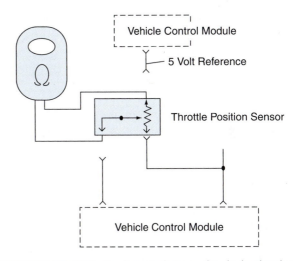

FIGURE 13-48 An ohmmeter being used to check a throttle position sensor. After disconnecting the 5-V reference, a lead is connected to the two TPS terminals. As the throttle is opened, the needle should deflect between no resistance and high resistance.

REAL WORLD FIX

The 1996 Ford E-350 van (107,000 miles) downshifts to second gear after reaching 35 to 40 mph; at this same time, the speedometer works erratically, reading up and down. A manual downshift will hold the transmission in that gear.

Fix. The VSS for this vehicle is in the rear axle; when removed for inspection, the sensor had a lot of metal filings stuck to it. Further inspection of the rear axle showed badly worn carrier bearings. The worn bearings allowed the sensor air gap to change, causing an erratic signal.

TECH TIP

Most TPS inputs are 5 V, and the output voltage should vary smoothly between 0.5 and 4.5 V.

connect the ohmmeter leads to one of the TPS terminals (called ECV signal and ground, in Figure 13-45), and rotate the throttle (Figure 13-48). As the throttle is opened and closed, the ohmmeter reading should change from a low to a high reading and vice versa.

When using a voltmeter, leave the TPS connector connected. Turn the ignition to the ON position. Connect the negative lead to a good ground, and use the positive lead to probe the input voltage at the connector (Figure 13-49). It should be the specified voltage indicated in the service manual. Next, move the positive voltmeter lead to the TPS output voltage lead, and measure the voltage as you open and close the throttle. The output voltage should increase and decrease smoothly as the throttle is opened and closed.

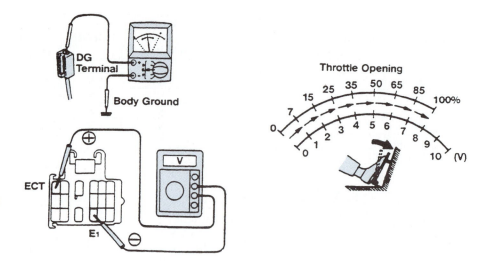

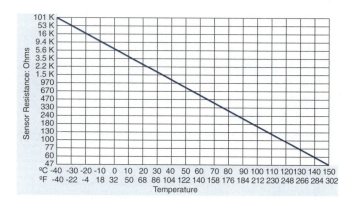

FIGURE 13-49   A TPS can be checked by connecting a DC voltmeter to the output terminal and ground. The signal should increase as the throttle is opened and stay within specifications.

REAL WORLD FIX

The 1990 Taurus runs well except for a 2–3 shift that slides and ends with a hard bump at high-throttle openings. Part-throttle operation is okay. The shift points are good, and the TV adjustment is okay.

Fix. A faulty TPS was found, and its replacement fixed this shift problem.

FIGURE 13-50   An ohmmeter connected to the two temperature sensor terminals should show that resistance will vary with the temperature. This sensor should have about 400 Ω at 70°C.

13.6.7 Temperature Sensor Checks

Temperature sensors are checked by measuring the resistance using an ohmmeter while changing the temperature. The resistance is compared with the specifications for the particular temperature (Figure 13-50). For accuracy, technicians can immerse the sensor into boiling water during the resistance check; the temperature of boiling water is 212°F (100°C). The resistance should now correspond to the specification for 212°F. A sensor with improper values should be replaced.

13.7 ELECTRONIC REPAIR JOB COMPLETION

Road test the vehicle after any repair to verify proper operation. This test drive is similar to the diagnostic test drive. You should also check to verify that all of the old DTCs were cleared and no new DTCs were set. Any problems found must be corrected before returning the vehicle to the customer.

SUMMARY

1. An understanding of electrical circuits is essential for diagnosing and repairing electronic transmissions.

2. The tools used to diagnose transmission electrical failures include test lights, digital multimeters, scan tools, oscilloscopes, and specially designed testers.

3. When diagnosing an electrically controlled automatic transmission, one of the first steps is to determine if the trouble is mechanical, hydraulic, or electrical.

4. Electrically controlled transmissions store a trouble code if a problem is identified by the PCM.

5. Testing the sensors and actuators involves basic electrical testing that can be done with a multimeter.

REVIEW QUESTIONS

The following questions are provided to help you study as you read the chapter.

1. The three major types of electrical problems are:
   a. _____
   b. _____
   c. _____

2. Electrical problems can show up as either _____ problems or be _____.

3. When a circuit is open, no _____ will flow.

4. An increase in resistance will cause a _____ in current flow.

5. Excess resistance problems are located by measuring the _____ _____ at the various parts of the circuit.

6. When current bypasses the intended path, the problem is known as a _____.

7. A short where a bare wire touches ground is commonly called a _____ to _____.

8. The most practical meter for testing electrical components is a _____ _____.

9. Voltage drop is the amount of _____ used to move _____ through a load.

10. An _____ would be used to test a component that is out of the circuit.

11. A technician would use a _____ _____ to read the DTCs from an ECM.

12. An _____ would be an ideal tool to observe the operations of a circuit with changing electrical values.

13. When making solder connections, always use _____-core solder.

14. The recommended three-step procedure for checking an electronically controlled transmission is:
   a. _____
   b. _____
   c. _____

15. The most probable causes of electrical problems are _____ _____ and _____ _____ that move.

16. Four simple rules to follow when testing or working on electronically controlled transmissions are:
   a. Make sure that the ignition is _____ before disconnecting or connecting the ECM.
   b. Make sure that the ignition is off before disconnecting or connecting any _____ controlled components.
   c. Never touch the _____ or _____ components without first grounding yourself.
   d. Use the proper _____ equipment.

17. The ECM must have a good _____ source and a good _____ to operate properly.

18. The transmission solenoid must be tested both for _____ and _____ operation.

19. Throttle position sensors are checked for a _____ increase or decrease in meter reading as the throttle is opened and closed.

20. The temperature sensor can be checked by measuring the _____ at a known temperature.

CHAPTER QUIZ

The following questions will help you check the facts you have learned. Select the answer that completes each statement correctly.

1. Student A says that a short can occur if the internal wires in a component make contact. Student B says that a short causes a fuse to open, shutting off the current flow. Who is correct?
   a. Student A
   b. Student B
   c. Both A and B
   d. Neither A nor B

2. Student A says that a check to determine if there is voltage at a component can be made using a voltmeter. Student B says that a test light is the best way to measure voltage at a component. Who is correct?
   a. Student A
   b. Student B
   c. Both A and B
   d. Neither A nor B

3. When checking electronic transmission controls, you should not use an analog voltmeter or ordinary test light because they
   a. are obsolete.
   b. are slow and clumsy.
   c. draw too much current and can change or damage the circuit.
   d. All of these

4. Student A says that high resistance in a circuit can be located with a voltmeter. Student B says that excessive resistance can cause a circuit to work improperly. Who is correct?
   a. Student A
   b. Student B
   c. Both A and B
   d. Neither A nor B

5. When checking electronic transmission controls, you should use a digital meter that has at least
   a. 100 ohms of resistance.
   b. 10 M ohms of internal resistance.
   c. 10 M ohms of external resistance.
   d. Any of the above

6. Student A says that the only difference between an analog meter and a digital meter is the readout. Student B says that an analog meter could damage an electronic circuit. Who is correct?
   a. Student A
   b. Student B
   c. Both A and B
   d. Neither A nor B

7. Student A says that it is not a good practice to pierce wire insulation during testing. Student B says that if a wire is pierced during testing, it should be sealed to prevent corrosion problems. Who is correct?
   a. Student A
   b. Student B
   c. Both A and B
   d. Neither A nor B

8. Student A says that a voltmeter is used to check for unwanted resistance in an operational circuit. Student B says that an ohmmeter is used to check resistance in an operational circuit. Who is correct?
   a. Student A
   b. Student B
   c. Both A and B
   d. Neither A nor B

9. Student A says that a scan tool can be used in place of a voltmeter. Student B says that a scan tool is used to communicate with the vehicle's ECM. Who is correct?
   a. Student A
   b. Student B
   c. Both A and B
   d. Neither A nor B

10. Student A says that during a road test if the electronic controls are disabled and the problem does not change, the problem is not the electronic controls. Student B says that the solenoids can be operated by a special tool to check their operation during a road test. Who is correct?
    a. Student A
    b. Student B
    c. Both A and B
    d. Neither A nor B

11. Student A says that all electrical problems will set a code. Student B says that when the trouble codes are cleared, the problem is repaired. Who is correct?
    a. Student A
    b. Student B
    c. Both A and B
    d. Neither A nor B

12. A common problem with electronically controlled transmissions is a bad
    a. electronic control unit.
    b. throttle position sensor.
    c. vehicle speed sensor.
    d. electrical connection.

13. Student A says that you can ruin an electronic control unit by touching its terminals with your finger. Student B says that you can ruin a solenoid by connecting it to a battery backward. Who is correct?

    a. Student A

    b. Student B

    c. Both A and B

    d. Neither A nor B

14. When testing a pressure switch, it should show

    a. an open circuit without pressure at the switch.

    b. a complete circuit with pressure at the switch.

    c. a complete circuit without pressure at the switch.

    d. All of the above, depending on the switch

15. Student A says that the voltage to the ECM is not as important as the voltage to the output solenoid. Student B says that the ECM must have a good ground connection. Who is correct?

    a. Student A

    b. Student B

    c. Both A and B

    d. Neither A nor B

16. Student A says that torque converter clutch operation can be easily checked on a road test by lightly stepping on the brake pedal and watching the tachometer for a change in speed. Student B says that the torque converter clutch can be tested using a scan tool to operate the circuit. Who is correct?

    a. Student A

    b. Student B

    c. Both A and B

    d. Neither A nor B

17. Student A says that a solenoid can be tested by checking the current flow. Student B says that a solenoid can be tested using an ohmmeter. Who is correct?

    a. Student A

    b. Student B

    c. Both A and B

    d. Neither A nor B

18. When testing a solenoid with an ohmmeter, reversing the test leads will check the

    a. transistor.

    b. triode.

    c. diode.

    d. winding.

19. Student A says that all transmission pressure switches are the same. Student B says that transmission pressure switches can be either normally open or normally closed. Who is correct?

    a. Student A

    b. Student B

    c. Both A and B

    d. Neither A nor B

20. When electrical or electronic repairs are completed the vehicle should be

    a. taken for a complete test drive.

    b. returned to the customer.

    c. held for several days to confirm the repair.

    d. All of the above

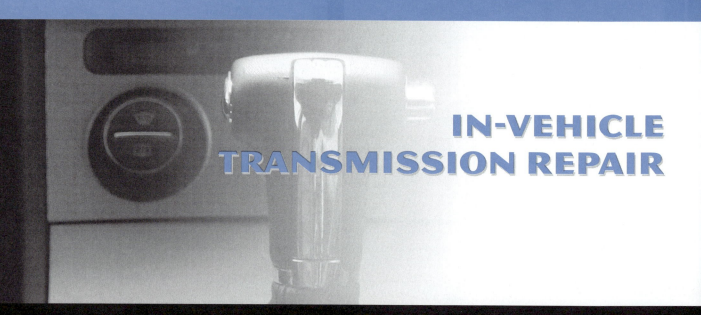

IN-VEHICLE TRANSMISSION REPAIR

OBJECTIVES

After studying Chapter 14, the reader should be able to:

1. Describe the repair operations that are performed with the transmission in the vehicle.

2. Determine the correct procedure for the in-vehicle repairs.

3. Make in-vehicle repairs in an approved manner.

4. Repair damaged threads in an aluminum casting.

5. Perform the ASE tasks related to in-vehicle transmission/transaxle repair.

KEY TERMS

Bench Repair (p. 377)
Off-Vehicle Repair (p. 377)

Stopoff Tool (p. 393)

14.1 INTRODUCTION

A technician should repair a transmission problem in a thorough manner, but also as quickly and efficiently as possible. Many transmissions require **off-vehicle** or **bench repair;** the transmission must be removed from the vehicle, repaired, and then replaced. Remove and replace *(R&R)* time for a FWD transaxle is about 4 to 10 hours depending on the vehicle. When possible, transmission repairs are made with the unit in the vehicle to save time.

The California Bureau of Automotive Repair (BAR) requires a complete inspection before removal to determine if the problem can be repaired in-vehicle, and the customer must be informed if in-vehicle repairs will resolve the problem.

In-vehicle service operations include those described in Chapter 11, plus other repairs depending on the make and model. The service to be done depends on the access to the component. In most cases, the following are considered in-vehicle repair tasks:

- Oil pan, gasket, filter, and magnet removal, inspection, and replacement
- Manual shift linkage adjustment and seal replacement
- Shift lever assemble and interlock replacement
- TV linkage or cable adjustment and seal replacement
- Vacuum modulator replacement
- Electrical/electronic component and wiring harness inspection, adjustment, repair, and replacement
- Cooler line and fitting replacement or repair
- Neutral start switch replacement
- Valve body removal, repair, and replacement
- Servo piston and cover seal replacement (when accessible)
- Accumulator piston and cover seal replacement (when accessible)
- Speedometer/speed sensor, gear, and seal replacement
- Governor removal, repair, and replacement
- Extension housing seal, bushing, or gasket replacement, RWD
- Parking pawl, shaft, and spring inspection and replacement (when accessible)
- Drive shaft seal replacement, FWD
- Engine and transmission mount alignment and replacement

Some of these tasks will be described in Chapter 18 with other subassembly repair procedures.

Remember that the exact procedure for in-vehicle service operations varies between transmission makes and models. Service information should always be consulted before transmission service. The tasks described in this chapter are normally found under the heading "Service (in vehicle)" or "On-Vehicle Service." In this text, they are described in as general a manner as possible.

14.2 MANUAL SHIFT LINKAGE, INTERLOCK, AND SEAL

The manual shift linkage attaches to a lever on the outside of the transmission case. A series of rods, levers, or a cable and housing assembly may be used. The cable connects to a shift lever using a metal clip or plastic grommet (Figure 14-1). The cable housing is secured to a bracket on the transmission case. The other end of the cable and housing is connected to the gear selector in a similar manner. The removal of a cable is usually done by disconnecting each end of the cable and removing any brackets. As the cable is removed from the vehicle, carefully note the routing so the new cable will be in the same location. Cable replacement is the reverse of the removal procedure and should be followed by an adjustment to ensure correct manual valve positioning.

The shift linkage interlock is the safety mechanism that prevents removal of the ignition key unless the vehicle is shifted into park. It also prevents shifting out of park unless the key is in the ignition and, in some cases, the brakes are applied. Interlocks are vehicle specific, so service information should be consulted before attempting repairs.

A lip seal is used to prevent fluid leaks where the manual selector shaft passes through the transmission case (Figure 14-2). This seal is easier to R&R if the manual selector shaft is removed, but that would require valve body removal in most cases. It is possible to remove this seal using either a slide hammer and self-tapping screw or a sharp chisel (Figure 14-3). Be careful that you do not damage the seal bore. The new seal can be driven into the bore using a seal driver or, in some cases, a correctly sized socket can be used as a driving tool (Figure 14-4).

REAL WORLD FIX

The 1992 Honda Accord (109,000 miles) is very hard to shift from park to reverse and back. The other shifts are okay.

Fix. The technician inspected the shift cable and found corrosion. A new shift cable fixed this problem.

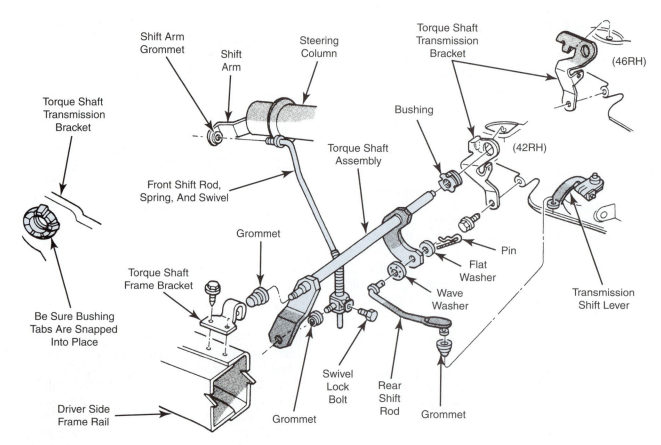

FIGURE 14-1 Shift linkage, both rod and lever and cable styles, can be adjusted, repaired, or replaced as necessary. *(Courtesy of Chrysler Corporation)*

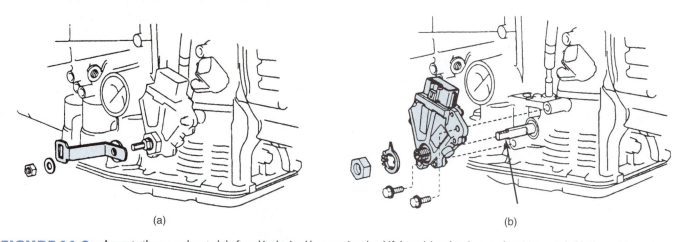

(a)

(b)

FIGURE 14-2 Access to the manual control shaft seal is obtained by removing the shift lever (a) and park-neutral position switch (b). The seal (arrow) can now be removed and replaced. *(Courtesy of Toyota Motor Sales USA, Inc.)*

14.3 LIP SEAL REPLACEMENT

A standard metal-backed lip seal must seal against two different surfaces: a dynamic seal with the moveable shaft at the inner bore and a static seal where it fits into its bore (Figure 14-5). The static seal is made when the slightly oversize seal backing is driven into the bore. A dry coating on the seal case helps prevent leakage (Figure 14-6). A leak can occur if the bore for the seal is scratched or damaged or if the seal case is bent or distorted. A driver that fits completely against the seal should always be used when installing a seal (Figure 14-7). This ensures that the seal is not damaged and driven in straight into its bore.

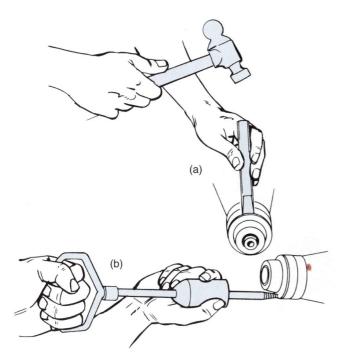

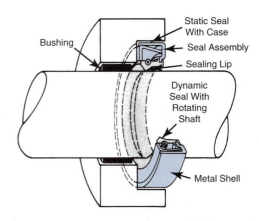

FIGURE 14-5 A cutaway view of a metal-clad seal. Note that the seal must make a static seal with the case and a dynamic seal with the shaft.

FIGURE 14-3 A seal can be driven out by catching the edge with a sharp chisel. Another removal method is to use a slide hammer that is threaded into the seal's metal cage. Be careful to not damage the seal bore when using either method.

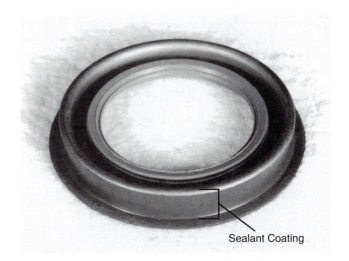

FIGURE 14-6 This lip seal has a coating of sealant on its metal backing. Before installing an uncoated seal, a sealant should be applied to this area.

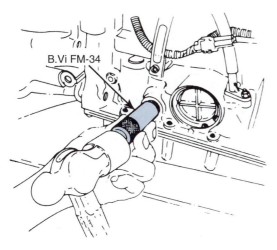

FIGURE 14-4 After the manual lever is removed, the manual shaft seal can be removed and replaced. The new seal should be driven in using a seal driver (B.Vi FM-34) to prevent damage. *(Courtesy of Chrysler Corporation)*

TECH TIP

When installing a seal over a shaft, it is good practice to protect the sealing lip with a seal protector, especially if there are any rough or sharp edges on the shaft. A piece of slick paper wrapped around the shaft will work as a seal protector in many cases (Figure 14-8).

The inner sealing lip is a flexible, elastic compound. It must remain flexible and resilient in order to maintain a fluid-tight seal against the moving shaft. Use care when installing the seal over a shaft or a shaft into a seal. The sharp lip of the seal is easily cut or torn.

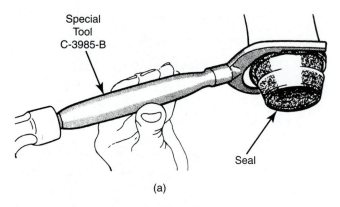

Special Tool C-3985-B

Seal

(a)

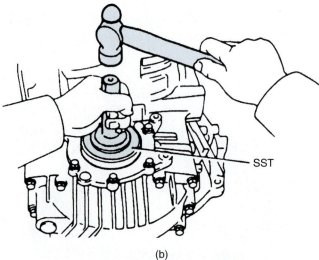

SST

(b)

FIGURE 14-7 A special tool is used to remove the extension housing seal (a), and a seal driver is used to install the seal (b). Note how the driver fits the seal so it can be driven straight into the bore with no damage to the sealing surfaces. *(a is courtesy of Chrysler Corporation; b is courtesy of Toyota Motor Sales USA, Inc.)*

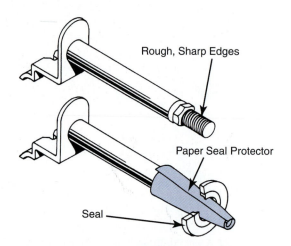

Rough, Sharp Edges

Paper Seal Protector

Seal

FIGURE 14-8 The sealing lip should be protected when installing a seal over a shaft. A piece of slick paper or plastic can be used to cover the sharp edges on the shaft.

TECH TIP

The lip of the seal should always be lubricated to prevent wear. Automatic transmission assembly lube, petroleum jelly, or automatic transmission fluid (ATF) can be used for a lubricant.

TECH TIP

Some seals include a garter spring to increase sealing lip pressure. This garter spring can be dislodged as the seal is driven into position. Filling the recess with assembly lube or petroleum jelly will keep the garter spring in place during installation.

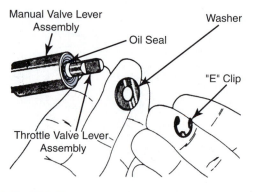

Manual Valve Lever Assembly

Washer

Oil Seal

"E" Clip

Throttle Valve Lever Assembly

FIGURE 14-9 Removal of this exterior throttle lever, E-clip, and washer allows access to the small seal at the throttle shaft. *(Courtesy of Chrysler Corporation)*

14.4 TV LINKAGE AND SEAL

In most transmissions, the throttle valve (TV) cable is a cable and housing assembly, and its replacement is essentially the same as a shift cable. In other transmissions, the TV cable is attached to a lever on a shaft that extends into the transmission, just like the shift lever and shaft. Also like the shift lever, a seal fits over the shaft (Figure 14-9).

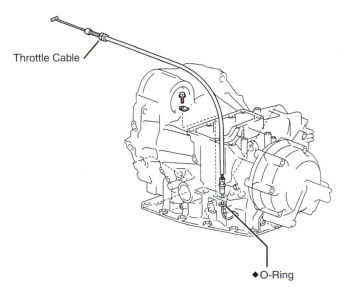

FIGURE 14-10   An O-ring seals the throttle cable where it enters the transmission case. *(Courtesy of Toyota Motor Sales USA, Inc.)*

The TV cable on some transmissions is attached directly to the case, and it extends into the transmission where it connects to the throttle valve. The transmission end of the cable is disconnected by unbolting the mounting bracket, removing the pan, and disconnecting the cable from the throttle valve linkage (Figure 14-10). The seal can be easily replaced while the bracket and cable are loose.

14.5 VACUUM MODULATOR REMOVAL AND REPLACEMENT

Most vacuum modulators are held in the transmission by a bolt and retaining clamp. Removing the clamp allows the modulator to be pulled out of the transmission case. Some transmissions use a control rod or pin to connect the modulator stem to the valve (Figure 14-11). The control rod and modulator valve can usually be removed once the modulator is removed.

In some older transmissions, the modulators are threaded into the case.

To R&R a vacuum modulator, you should:

1. Disconnect the vacuum hose and remove the retaining bolt and clamp.
2. Pull the modulator out of the transmission case.
3. If necessary, remove the control rod, modulator valve, or both. Note the position of the valve as it is removed. Perform the necessary service and replace them.
4. Install a new seal on the modulator stem, wet the seal with ATF, and push the modulator into the case.
5. Replace the retaining clamp and bolt and tighten the bolt to the correct torque (Figure 14-12).

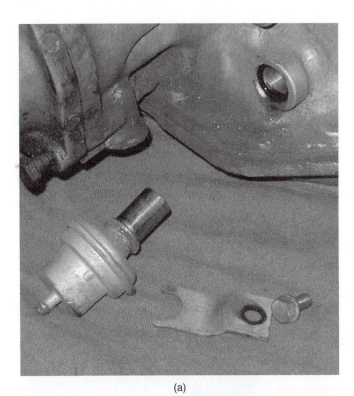

(a)

(b)

FIGURE 14-11   This modulator is secured using a clamp. Removing the bolt and clamp allows the modulator to be removed (a). The modulator valve can be removed using a magnet (b).

14.6 ALUMINUM THREAD REPAIR

Transmission cases and extension housings are made from relatively soft, cast aluminum. Bolt threads begin to wear after a

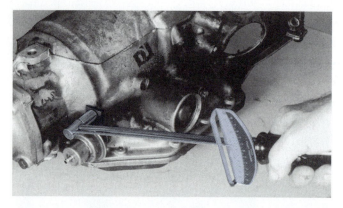

FIGURE 14-12 When a modulator is replaced, the retaining bolt should be tightened to the correct torque.

FIGURE 14-13 This bolt was too short for the job, and when it was tightened, it pulled the threads out of the aluminum case.

REAL WORLD FIX

The 1994 Ford Explorer (113,000 miles) transmission uses about two quarts of ATF each week, but the shop cannot find a leak.

Fix. The technician removed the vacuum line from the vacuum modulator, and ATF poured out of it. A new vacuum modulator fixed this leak problem.

few uses, and aluminum threads easily pull out if the bolt is overtightened or if too short of a bolt is used (Figure 14-13). The most commonly used thread repair method is to install a special steel coil *thread insert.* Thread inserts are commonly called a *Heli-Coil.* Some thread inserts are solid, like a tube with internal and external threads. These thread inserts provide a stronger and much longer-lasting thread. Another repair method is to form new threads using an epoxy compound.

TECH TIP

It is a good practice to lightly lubricate bolt threads going into a blind hole with ATF. Bolts going through holes can be dipped into transmission assembly lube. Using the thicker assembly lube in a blind hole could cause a hydrostatic lock and improper tightening or damaged threads.

TECH TIP

A bolt is usually designed to enter the threaded hole a distance that is about 1 1/2 to 2 times the bolt diameter (Figure 14-14). In other words, a 0.25-in. (6.35 mm) bolt will have about 2 × 0.25 in., or 0.5 in. (12.7 mm) of thread contact.

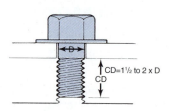

FIGURE 14-14 The thread contact distance (CD) of a bolt should equal about twice the diameter of the threads (D) to prevent thread stripping.

This method is not recommended for threads that will be in contact with ATF.

Thread damage is often caused by the use of a bolt or cap screw that is too long or too short. Too long of a bolt will bottom in the hole before it is tight, and too short of a bolt will grip fewer threads than needed. Use of a bolt with damaged threads or the wrong threads will produce damaged threads in the casting. Check all bolts before starting them into the threaded hole, and replace any that are questionable.

To install a coil-type thread insert, you should:

1. Drill out the worn threads, if necessary, using a drill of the correct size for the special tap (Figure 14-15).
2. Use the special tap to cut new threads slightly longer than the length of the insert.

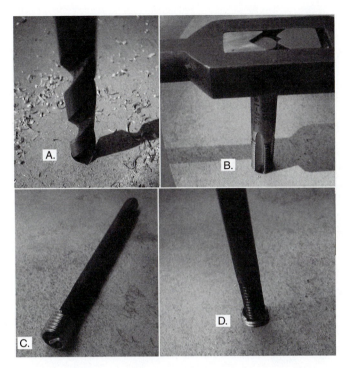

FIGURE 14-15   Step 1 in repairing damaged threads is to drill a properly sized hole for the special tap (a). Step 2 is to use the special tap to cut new threads (b). Step 3 is to put the thread insert on the installing tool (c). Step 4 is to screw the insert into the new threads (d). The final step (not shown) is to break off the insert's installing tang.

Damaged Threads   Repaired Threads

FIGURE 14-16   The damaged threads (left) have been repaired (right) by installing a thread insert. They are better than new because of the hardness of the insert.

3. Install the thread insert onto the installing tool, and thread the insert completely into the hole. The end of the last thread should enter into the hole.
4. Break off the installing tang or resize the insert as required by the manufacturer (Figure 14-16).

14.7 ELECTRICAL COMPONENT REMOVAL, REPAIR, AND REPLACEMENT

The testing procedures for electronic components are described in Chapter 13. Most of these components can be replaced in the

TECH TIP

Joint Venture transaxles with integrated TCMs use the transmission range sensor to position the park pawl operating rod. When the TRS is removed, the park rod can fall out of position if it is moved, and the transaxle must be disassembled to get it back in the correct position.

vehicle (Figure 14-17). With some transaxles, it can be challenging to remove and replace the upper pan where most of the electrical components are located. It might be necessary to lower the engine support cradle. Most of the electrical components are mounted either outside of the case or on the valve body with fairly easy access after the pan is removed (Figure 14-18).

14.8 COOLER LINE AND FITTING REPAIR

A crushed or leaking cooler line must be repaired or replaced (Figure 14-19). A leaking fitting is often fixed by merely tightening it. A cooler line is steel tubing that usually ends at a tube nut that is threaded into an adapter that in turn is threaded into the transmission case or radiator cooler (Figure 14-20). The adapter often uses tapered NPTs (National Pipe Threads) to form a seal. Some adapters use straight machine threads that require a gasket or a seal. Many vehicles now use a quick-disconnect-style cooler line fitting (Figure 14-21).

TECH TIP

Steel cooler lines have been successfully repaired by cutting out the damaged portion, flaring the cut ends, and using a flare union to rejoin the lines (Figure 14-22). Compression fittings can also be used to join tubing. If a section of the line has been cut away, an additional piece of tubing can be added. Steel tubing should be used; it is available in various sizes and lengths at automotive parts stores. If you make your own flare on the tubing, remember that steel tubing must have a double flare.

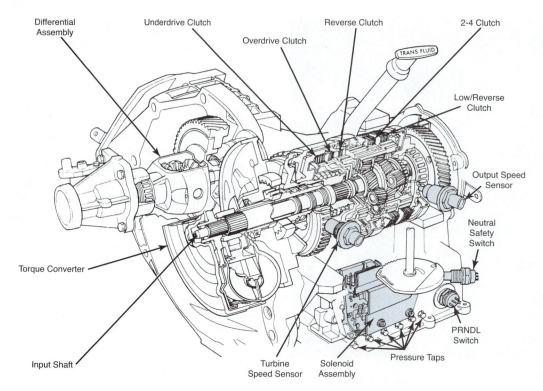

FIGURE 14-17 Electronic components (both speed sensors, both switches, and the solenoid assembly) can be removed and replaced in-vehicle. *(Courtesy of Chrysler Corporation)*

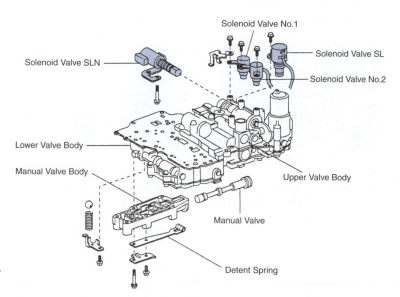

FIGURE 14-18 Solenoids can be attached to the valve body. *(Courtesy of Toyota Motor Sales USA, Inc.)*

The best repair for a damaged steel cooler line is replacement, but the replacement line has to be the correct length and have the correct bends. Replacing cooler lines can be labor intensive, so technicians have developed various repair methods for damaged lines. Cooler lines do not wear out, but they do get damaged. Remember to always repair the problem that caused the failure. Never use copper tubing for replacement because it has a tendency to fatigue, crack, and break.

14.9 VALVE BODY REMOVAL AND REPLACEMENT

There are many possibilities for valve body problems, and the valve body is removed for repairing these problems. This task is rather messy because removing the valve body opens many fluid passages that will begin draining. Depending on the transmission, you may find check balls, one or more filter screens,

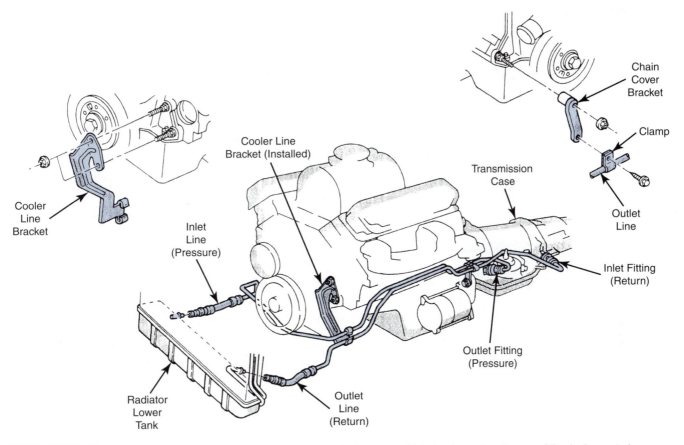

FIGURE 14-19 If replacing the cooler lines, use care to not bend them. The fit in some vehicles is quite precise. *(Courtesy of Chrysler Corporation)*

(a)

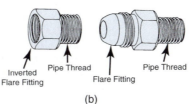

(b)

FIGURE 14-20 The cooler line fittings thread into the case (a). These fittings normally have a National Pipe Thread (NPT) where they thread into the case and a flare or other style of fitting for the line connection (b).

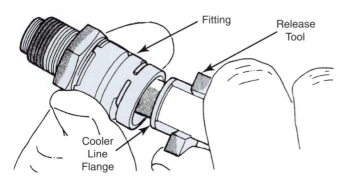

FIGURE 14-21 This cooler line fitting uses a push connector. Note the release tool. *(Courtesy of Chrysler Corporation)*

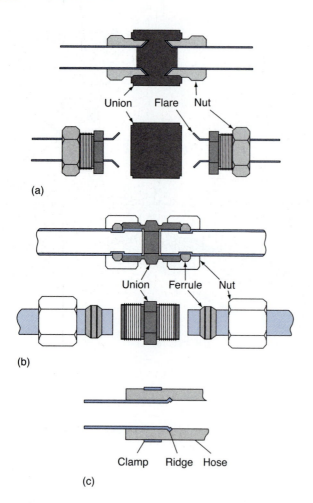

Union   Flare   Nut

(a)

Union   Ferrule   Nut

(b)

Clamp   Ridge   Hose

(c)

FIGURE 14-22   Cooler line damage can be repaired by removing the damaged section. A piece of steel tubing can be installed using flare (a) or compression unions (b). A hose can also be used; it is a good practice to make a small ridge at the ends of the metal tube to keep the hose from slipping off the tube (c).

TECH TIP

Another cooler line repair method is to cut out the damaged section and replace it with a rubber hose that is clamped onto the tubing. With this repair method, hydraulic hose or reinforced fuel hose of the correct size is used. The hose must be clamped securely onto the tubing, and it must be located so it will not be cut, burned, or otherwise damaged. It is recommended to keep the length of the rubber hose as short as possible to reduce possible damage.

SAFETY TIP

Should a cooler line repair fail, it might allow hot ATF to spray on a hot exhaust pipe and cause a fire.

TECH TIP

When removing and replacing a cooler line, two flare-nut or tube-nut wrenches should be used (Figure 14-23). If a single wrench is used, the tube nut and the adapter often turn together, which causes twisting and damage to the tubing. If the tube nut is tight, a common open-end wrench will tend to round off the corners on the tube nut; a flare-nut wrench has a much better grip that prevents damage to the nut.

TECH TIP

According to some technicians, it is important that a valve body be removed from a transmission at room temperature, especially with aluminum valve bodies. Removal of a hot valve body might produce warpage, which might cause sticky valves.

a servo piston and spring, or an accumulator assembly above the valve body. Be prepared for these as the valve body is removed so they are not lost or damaged (Figure 14-24).

To remove a valve body, you should:

1. Raise and support the vehicle on a hoist so you have access to the transmission pan.
2. Loosen the pan and drain the fluid as described in Chapter 11. Remove the pan and filter (Figure 14-25). Draining the fluid in the transmission is not necessary on transaxles with the valve body mounted inside the upper pan.

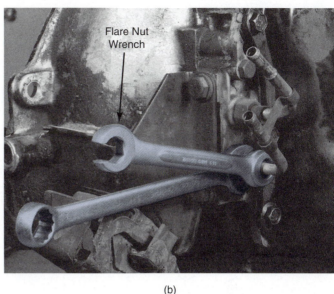

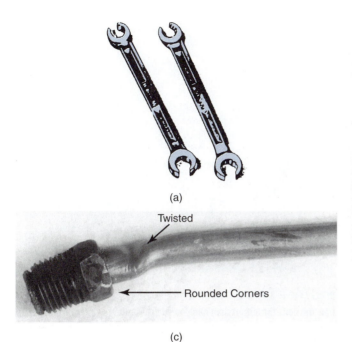

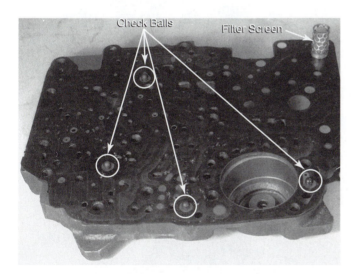

FIGURE 14-23 Two flare-nut wrenches (a) should be used to loosen a tube nut (b). Use of a standard open-end wrench can result in a rounded-off tube nut; using a single wrench can result in a twisted line (c). *(a is courtesy of Snap-on Tools)*

FIGURE 14-24 As the valve body is removed, you should be ready to catch some check balls, filter screens, or accumulator springs.

3. Disconnect the wires from any switches or solenoids that are attached to the valve body.

4. If necessary, remove any modulators and valves or servo covers and piston assemblies that interfere with valve body removal.

5. Remove the valve-body-to-case bolts. Carefully note the size and length of each bolt to make sure you can re-place them in the correct location. As the last bolts are

removed, carefully lower the valve body, disconnecting any linkages as required (Figure 14-26).

The valve body can be repaired or exchanged as necessary. Valve body service and repair is described in Chapter 18. A sep-arator plate is often used to align the hydraulic passages between the valve body and the case, and a gasket is usually used above and/or below the separator plate. A new gasket(s) should be used when reinstalling the valve body. Always compare the new and old gaskets to ensure the correct replacement. Often several gaskets are provided in the gasket set. They may look identical, but there are slight differences. These extra gaskets are intended for different applications, and a shift timing or quality problem may be the result if the wrong gasket is used (Figure 14-27).

To replace a valve body, you should do the following:

1. If used, position a new gasket or any check balls on top of the valve body or separator plate. The check balls can be held in place with assembly lube or petroleum jelly (Figure 14-28).

2. Carefully position the valve body, making sure to cor-rectly install the manual and TV linkage as necessary. It is recommended that two guide pins or bolts be threaded into the case to hold the transfer plate and gasket(s) in proper alignment. Loosely install a few bolts to hold the valve body in position (Figure 14-29).

3. Reinstall all of the valve body bolts, making sure the correct lengths and sizes are in the proper position (Figure 14-30). Remember that the bolts should thread into the case a distance that is about twice the bolt diameter.

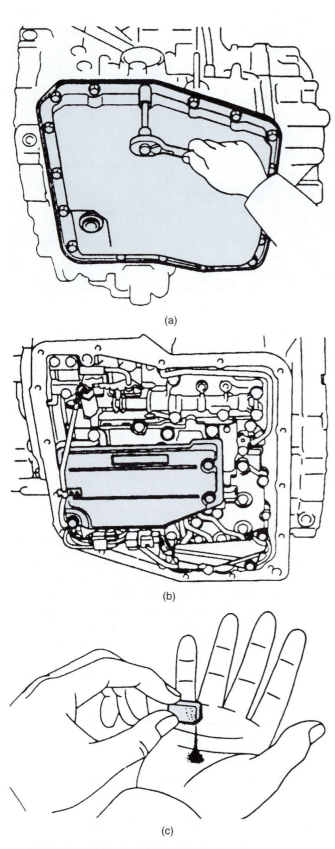

(a)

(b)

(c)

FIGURE 14-25   The oil pan (a) and filter (b) are removed from many transmissions to gain access to the valve body. Examine the pan magnet (c) for metal chips and particles. *(Courtesy of Toyota Motor Sales USA, Inc.)*

FIGURE 14-26   As the valve body is removed from many Torqueflite transmissions, the output shaft might need to be rotated so you can pull the park control rod (arrow) past the park pawl.

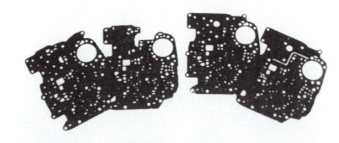

FIGURE 14-27   Save the old valve body gasket to compare it with the new to ensure that you install the correct gasket.

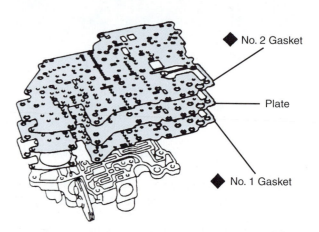

No. 2 Gasket

Plate

No. 1 Gasket

FIGURE 14-28   The No. 1 gasket, transfer plate, and No. 2 gasket, along with any check balls, screens, and springs, must be positioned properly as the valve body is installed. *(Courtesy of Toyota Motor Sales USA, Inc.)*

FIGURE 14-29 Two guide pins are used to ensure alignment of the gaskets, spacer plate, and valve body.

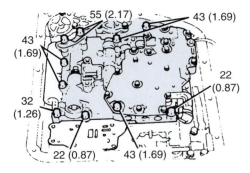

FIGURE 14-30 This valve body is secured with bolts of four different lengths; bolts of the correct length must be placed into the proper hole.

4. Evenly tighten the bolts to the correct torque. Normally, you should start at the center bolts and work to the outer bolts using a spiral pattern (Figure 14-31). Check the manufacturer's recommendation.
5. Replace the filter.
6. Check the pan rails for straightness and repair as necessary.
7. Refill the transmission with fluid as described in Chapter 11.

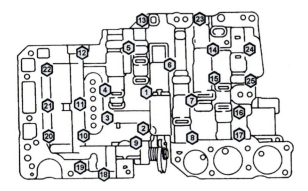

FIGURE 14-31 Valve body bolts should be tightened in the correct order. Note that this is a spiraling pattern that goes outward from the center.

REAL WORLD FIX

The 1997 Chevrolet Silverado (52,000 miles) had a P1870 DTC (transmission component slipping), and a lot of brass was found in the pan. The input housing and worn stator bushing were replaced, and new seals were also installed. The vehicle returned after 3,000 miles with the same problem, and disassembling the transmission showed the same problems. The unit was repaired again, but it still had a slippage problem. The PWM and PC solenoids were replaced, but this did not help. The technician was suspicious of the valve body, but could see no problem with it from a visual inspection.

Fix. The technician was advised to recheck the valve body by moving the valves out of the bore far enough to grab them and then trying to move them vertically. The excessive movement showed that the bores in the aluminum valve body were worn. Replacement of the valve body fixed the problem.

Aluminum valves are anodized to harden the surface and reduce wear. The bores in an aluminum valve body are not anodized; they will wear faster than the valves.

REAL WORLD FIX

The 1996 GMC pickup (132,000 miles) came in with a slipping transmission. A scan tool check showed code 1870, so the valve body was replaced. Now the transmission works okay in all forward ranges, but there is no reverse. There are no new DTCs.

Fix. Following advice, the technician raised the vehicle. With the transmission in neutral, he tried turning the drive shaft, and it only would rotate in one direction. This indicated that the valve body bolts were improperly installed. Placing the bolts in the correct holes fixed this problem.

14.10 SERVO AND ACCUMULATOR PISTON, COVER, AND SEAL SERVICE

A faulty servo piston or cover seal can cause a loss of servo apply pressure and band slippage. A faulty accumulator piston or cover seal can cause poor shift quality. A bad cover seal will leak. The service procedures for servos and accumulators are similar. A leaking servo or accumulator cover can be removed and the seal replaced. With the cover removed, the piston and spring can be easily removed and serviced.

A service manual should be checked before disassembling the servo or accumulator. In some cases, the valve body serves as the cover so servo or accumulator service becomes an easy operation once the valve body is removed (Figure 14-32). In others, a separate cover is used above the valve body so cover removal is done after the valve body is removed. Some servos are rather complex and have two or more pistons and up to four or five fluid passages and fluid control orifices or check balls. In some cases, a strong return spring is under the piston.

The servo or accumulator cover seal is either a gasket or an O-ring; it is fairly easy to R&R once the cover is removed. The servo or accumulator piston seal is either a metal or rubber ring. Seal ring checks are described in Chapter 17.

TECH TIP

Depending on the transmission, a special tool is sometimes required to keep the spring compressed so the cover can be removed (Figure 14-33).

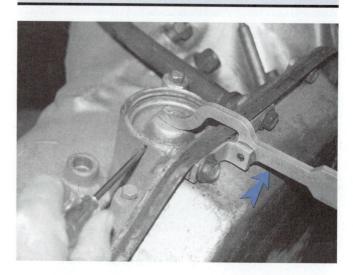

FIGURE 14-33 The special tool (arrow) compresses the servo spring and holds the cover inward while the retaining ring is removed. The punch is inserted through a hole to help remove the retaining ring.

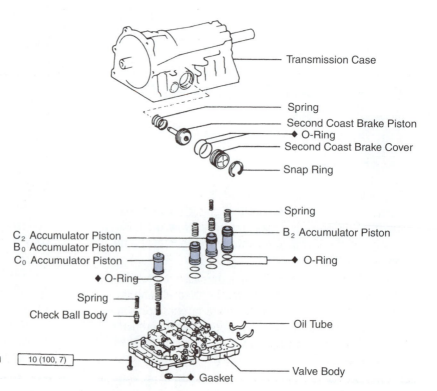

FIGURE 14-32 These four accumulators are held in the case by the valve body.

REAL WORLD FIX

The 1998 Ford Taurus (88,000 miles) was towed in because the engine stalls as soon as it is shifted into gear. Disconnecting the transmission electrical power did not help. The technician felt that this was a valve body problem but was not sure if he had access to the valve body on this AXOD transmission.

Fix. Following advice, the technician removed the battery tray, and this allowed removal of the valve body cover. A blown valve body gasket was found, and gasket replacement fixed this problem.

REAL WORLD FIX

The 1992 Dodge Caravan (115,000 miles) came into the shop in limp-in mode. A scan tool check shows code 22, 2–4 pressure switch circuit. A bad 2–4 driver in the EATX controller was found, so the ETAX controller was replaced. This fixed the electronic problem, but now the van starts in second gear.

Fix. Following advice, the technician checked the valve body and found a badly worn solenoid switching valve. A valve body replacement fixed this vehicle.

REAL WORLD FIX

The 1994 Volkswagen (135,000 miles) came in for service. This included a fluid change, and the shop was careful to use the correct fluid. The vehicle returned with harsh shifts. A scan tool check revealed no electronic faults.

Fix. Following advice that this transmission is sensitive to contaminants, the technician checked the fluid pressure and found high pressure. The EPC solenoid was removed, tested, and cleaned to remove contaminants. Cleaning the EPC solenoid fixed this vehicle.

REAL WORLD FIX

The 2002 Ford Ranger (104,000 km) came in with no second gear. A scan tool check reveals DTC P0733: gear 3 incorrect ratio. The technician thought this fault could be caused by a bad intermediate band, but he was not sure of this diagnosis and requested advice.

Fix. Following advice, the pan was dropped, and the valve body gaskets were checked. A faulty gasket was found and replaced, and this fixed the problem. The band adjustment was also checked and found to be slightly out of adjustment.

REAL WORLD FIX

A 2000 F350 Ford pickup (124,700 miles) works well until it backs up. Then it slips in all forward gears. After the vehicle is parked and the transmission cools down, it returns to normal operation until the next operation in reverse. There are no DTCs.

Fix. The technician removed the pan and checked the valve body bolts, and they were loose. After replacing the valve body gaskets and tightening the bolts to the correct torque, the problem was fixed.

REAL WORLD FIX

The 1999 Ford Taurus (42,000 miles) came in with a flashing MIL (no O/D) and an overdrive that was not working. A scan tool check shows two DTCs: P0761, shift solenoid C performance/stuck, and P0734, incorrect gear ratio 4. The shift solenoids check out fine, and a visual check of the valve body revealed no problems.

Fix. The technician checked the overdrive servo and found a torn piston seal. Replacement of the servo piston fixed this problem.

14.11 REMOVE, REPLACE, AND ALIGN POWER-TRAIN MOUNTS

Faulty power train (engine and transmission) mounts are replaced by lifting the engine and/or transmission slightly to remove the weight, and then removing the mounting bolts. The old mount is then removed and the new mount is installed.

The mount for an RWD transmission is aligned by the bolts through slotted holes in the mount. Alignment is required so the engine, transmission, and exhaust system do not contact the frame or body. A FWD transaxle must be aligned to the two front drive shafts. The alignment check is accomplished by completely compressing both inboard CV joints, and measuring the distance between the joint and the transaxle (Figure 14-34). The position

of the transaxle is then adjusted so that both distances are equal. Adjustment is accomplished by loosening the mounts and sliding the engine and transaxle sideways.

14.12 EXTENSION HOUSING SEAL AND BUSHING SERVICE

The extension housing seal and bushing can be removed and replaced with the transmission in the vehicle. In some cases the entire extension housing is removed for bearing, seal, governor, speedometer gear, or park mechanism service. A similar procedure is used to R&R the output shaft seal and bushing of a transaxle.

A faulty seal can be removed using a special puller that fits over the output shaft and into the seal. It can also be removed using a slide hammer and self-tapping screw or sharp chisel and hammer. Be careful to not damage the seal bore. A special puller and installation tool is usually required for on-vehicle bushing replacement.

To remove and replace a transmission extension housing seal, you should:

1. Raise and support the vehicle on a hoist that allows access to the transmission and drive shaft.
2. Place alignment marks on the rear universal joint and rear-axle pinion flange.
3. Disconnect the drive shaft from the rear axle (Figure 14-35). Do not let the drive shaft hang from the transmission; either remove it completely or support it until removal. Check the drive shaft slip yoke for wear at the seal and bushing surfaces.

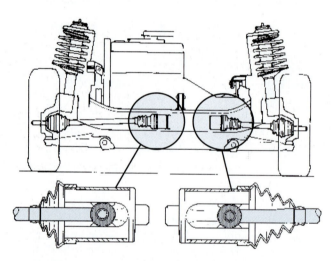

FIGURE 14-34　The enlarged views of the inner CV joints show that the engine and transaxle are misaligned; they should be moved toward the right.

REAL WORLD FIX

The 1993 Oldsmobile Ninety-Eight (195,000 km) has a severe drive-line clunk. The engine/transmission mounts along with upper dog bone mount were replaced. This cured the problem for about a week, but the clunk came back.

Fix. Following advice, the technician checked the cradle mount bushing and found that the two rear bushings had failed. Replacement of these bushings fixed this problem.

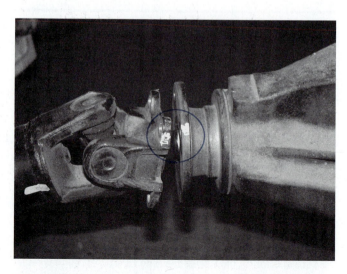

FIGURE 14-35　It is a good practice to place alignment marks on the axle flange and rear U-joint so they can be installed in the same position.

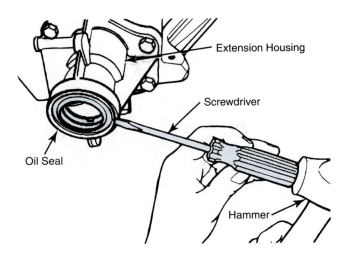

FIGURE 14-37   This seal is being removed using an old screwdriver. A chisel is a better tool for this. *(Courtesy of Chrysler Corporation)*

(a)

(b)

FIGURE 14-36   This set of plugs is used to close transmission drive shaft openings (a). A different set of plugs is used for FWD transaxles (b). *(Courtesy of ATEC Trans-Tool and Cleaning Systems)*

FIGURE 14-38   Several styles of pullers are available to remove the rear bushing with the transmission in the vehicle. *(Courtesy of OTC)*

4. Pull or pry out the rear seal using a suitable tool (Figure 14-37).
5. If necessary, remove the rear bushing using a suitable tool (Figure 14-38).
6. If the bushing is removed, use a suitable tool to drive the new bushing completely into place (Figure 14-39).
7. Use a correctly sized driver to drive the new seal into place. If the replacement seal does not have an outer sealant coating, a film of sealant should be spread around the outer surface of the seal case.
8. Lubricate the seal lip and drive shaft slip yoke with ATF. Slide the yoke into place in the transmission. Align your index marks, connect the universal joint to the rear axle flange, and tighten the retaining bolts to the correct torque.
9. Check and correct the transmission fluid if necessary.

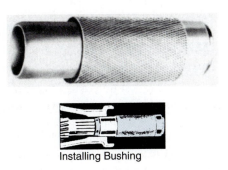

FIGURE 14-39   This tool will hold the bushing so it can be easily driven into place using a hammer. *(Courtesy of OTC)*

TECH TIP

When driving a seal into place, it is possible for the seal's garter spring to pop out of position. Some technicians fill the seal cavity with petroleum jelly to help hold the spring in position (Figure 14-40).

FIGURE 14-40 The cavity of this seal has been filled with petroleum jelly to hold the garter spring in position during installation. TransJel™ and petroleum jelly will melt and mix with ATF when the transmission gets hot.

The procedure for removing a FWD drive shaft varies with vehicle makes and models. Service information should be consulted for the proper procedure. A generic procedure is described in Section 15.4.2. Once the drive shaft has been removed, seal replacement is essentially a process of removing the old seal and installing the new one.

14.13 EXTENSION HOUSING REMOVAL, RWD TRANSMISSION

The extension housing is removable on most RWD transmissions. Depending on the transmission, extension housing removal allows replacement of the extension housing gasket, seal, and bushing. The governor, speedometer gear, and park mechanism are also accessible for service with the extension housing removed. Parts of the exhaust system may need to be removed on some vehicles. In the case of the Chrysler 42RH

REAL WORLD FIX

The 1988 Dodge Caravan (131,000 miles) has a leak at the left axle shaft. The axle can be moved up and down, indicating a worn bearing. The customer could not afford a complete transmission overhaul.

Fix. It was possible to remove the differential by removing the front engine mount and rotating the engine. With the differential removed, the worn carrier bearing was removed and replaced. After adjusting the bearing and installing a new seal, the transaxle was reassembled.

TECH TIP

A transmission jack is normally used to prevent damage to the transmission pan. If a conventional jack is used, blocks of wood should be placed in a position (under the stronger areas) so the pan will not be dented. Also check the transmission mount at this time.

and 46RH transmissions, extension housing removal allows service of the overdrive gear train.

To remove an extension housing, you should:

1. Raise the vehicle and remove the drive shaft.
2. Disconnect the speedometer cable/speed sensor connector. If necessary for access, remove the parking brake equalizer and move the cables out of the way.
3. Remove the bolts securing the engine-transmission mount to the transmission support/center cross-member.
4. Place a jack under the transmission pan and lift the transmission just enough to clear the transmission support (Figure 14-41).
5. Remove the transmission support.
6. Place a drip pan under the transmission and lower the transmission just enough to gain access to the upper extension housing bolts.
7. Remove the retaining bolts, the extension housing, and gasket (Figure 14-42). On some transmissions, it is necessary to expand a bearing retainer in order to remove the extension housing.

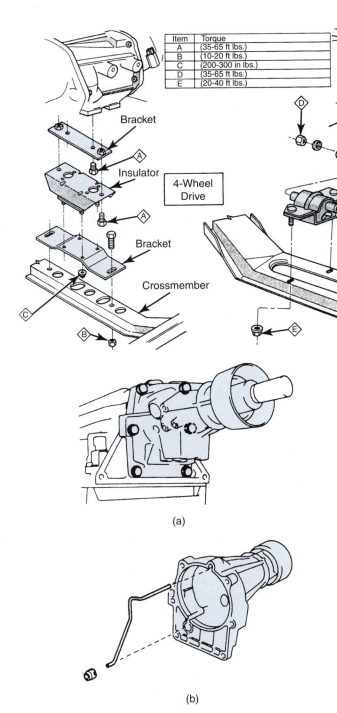

Item	Torque
A	(35-65 ft lbs.)
B	(10-20 ft lbs.)
C	(200-300 in lbs.)
D	(35-65 ft lbs.)
E	(20-40 ft lbs.)

FIGURE 14-41 A transmission jack can be used to support the transmission so the rear transmission mount and cross-member can be removed. *(Courtesy of Chrysler Corporation)*

(a)

(b)

FIGURE 14-42 After the extension housing bolts have been removed (a), the extension housing can be removed from the transmission (b).

Extension housing replacement is essentially the reverse of the procedure used to remove it.

To replace an extension housing, you should:

1. Clean off all traces of old gasket and sealant from the gasket surfaces.
2. Place the new gasket and extension housing in position. Install the bolts and tighten them to the correct torque.

TECH TIP

When a threaded hole extends through the transmission case, it is recommended that a sealant be placed on the bolt threads.

If necessary, petroleum jelly can be used to stick the gasket in position.
3. Raise the transmission, place the transmission support in position, install the bolts, and tighten them to the correct torque.
4. Lower the transmission onto the cross-member as you install the attaching bolts and tighten the bolts to the correct torque. Remove the jack.
5. Reconnect the speedometer cable and the parking brake mechanism if necessary.
6. Reinstall the drive shaft to complete the reassembly.

14.13.1 Speedometer Gear Replacement

Speedometer gear problems show up as a nonoperating speedometer. The cause can be a faulty cable, driven gear, or drive gear. On some transmissions, the speedometer drive gear is a set of teeth cut into the output shaft. On these transmissions, a rough drive gear can sometimes be cured using a

REAL WORLD FIX

The 1999 Dakota pickup (3,000 miles) will shift into overdrive only once, but not again unless the engine is shut off and restarted. The O/D solenoid was replaced, but this did not help. The wiring checked out fine.

Fix. The technician noted that the scan tool indicated that the transmission was shifting into O/D. The overdrive unit was removed and inspected. A torn inner seal was found and replaced. The transmission now operated normally. The overdrive unit of 42RH and 46RH transmissions is at the rear and can be removed with the transmission in the vehicle.

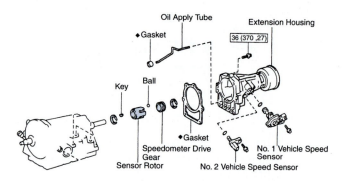

FIGURE 14-43 The speed sensor is driven through a key while a ball is used to drive the speedometer gear; these are positioned between the two retaining rings. Note that a new gasket should be used when the extension housing is replaced. *(Courtesy of Toyota Motor Sales USA, Inc.)*

three-corner file. Scale on the gear teeth usually can be removed using a wire brush. The other choice is to dismantle the transmission for output shaft replacement. On most transmissions, the drive gear is slid over the output shaft. It can be easily removed and replaced once the extension housing has been removed.

The speedometer drive gear in some transmissions is held in place by a special clip. To remove the gear, simply push inward on the clip and slide the gear over the clip and down the shaft (Figure 14-43). Other transmissions drive the gear using a steel ball that is halfway into the output shaft and halfway into the gear. To remove the gear, remove the retaining ring and slide the gear off the shaft and drive ball.

Speed sensor diagnosis and repair is described in Chapter 13.

14.13.2 Park Gear and Pawl Service

On some transmissions, the park pawl and spring are mounted in the extension housing, and the park gear is mounted on the output shaft (Figure 14-44). On these units, service such as inspection or replacement of the parking pawl, return spring, or park gear can be done. The operating rod coming from the transmission case can also be checked for correct movement.

14.14 GOVERNOR SERVICE

If the governor is shaft driven, removal of the extension housing allows access to the governor for inspection or disassembly and cleaning (Figure 14-45). Some transmissions use gear-driven governors. These units have a separate cover that retains the governor in the transmission (Figure 14-46). Removal of this cover allows the governor to be removed.

In-vehicle governor service includes disassembly of the valve and weights to cure sticking, replacement of the assembly, or replacement of the drive gear.

To remove a gear-driven governor, you should:

1. Raise and support the vehicle on a hoist.
2. Remove the governor cover attaching bolts or retaining ring and the cover (Figure 14-47). In some cases, it is necessary to lower the transmission as described in Section 14.13, steps 1 to 6.
3. Remove the governor. In some cases, it will slide out as the cover is removed; in others, turning the output shaft will move the governor outward.

To replace a gear-driven governor, you should:

1. Slide the governor into position in its bore. Some governors use a seal ring at one end; make sure this seal is in good condition before installing.

TECH TIP

If there is gear damage, the governor drive and driven gears should be inspected. If there is a problem with low governor pressure, inspect the governor bore in the transmission to make sure it is in good condition. A faulty governor gear will stop governor operation (Figure 14-48). Reaming and installing a bushing in a worn bore is described in Chapter 18.

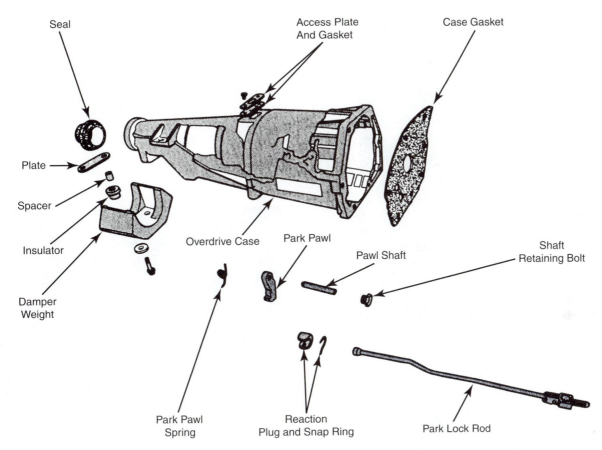

FIGURE 14-44   This park pawl, spring, and shaft are mounted in the extension housing. The park lock rod connects to the manual linkage at the valve body. *(Courtesy of Chrysler Corporation)*

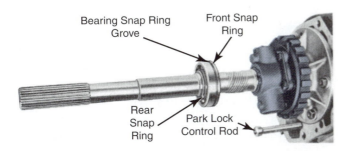

FIGURE 14-45   The governor is mounted onto the governor support/park gear of this Torqueflite transmission. *(Courtesy of Chrysler Corporation)*

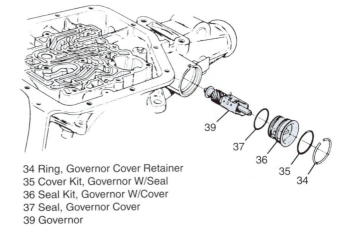

34 Ring, Governor Cover Retainer
35 Cover Kit, Governor W/Seal
36 Seal Kit, Governor W/Cover
37 Seal, Governor Cover
39 Governor

FIGURE 14-46   This gear-driven governor (39) is held in the transmission by its cover (36). *(Reprinted with permission of General Motors)*

14.14.1 Governor Disassembly

A shaft-driven governor usually consists of the governor body, valve(s), weight(s), support, and sometimes a spring or shaft/pin is used to connect the weight to the valve (Figure 14-50).

2. Install a new gasket or O-ring for the governor cover and place the cover in position. In cases where the cover slides into the transmission and O-ring, wet the O-ring with ATF and carefully tap the cover into place using a brass drift or suitable driver (Figure 14-49).
3. Install the retaining ring or bolts. If bolts are used, tighten them to the correct torque.
4. Check and adjust the fluid level.

(a)

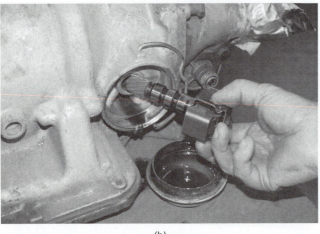

(b)

FIGURE 14-47   After the cover has been removed (a), this governor can be slid out of its bore (b).

Governor service includes operations: disassembly, cleaning, inspection to ensure the valve(s) and weight(s), move freely, and reassembly. It should be noted that some transmissions use a gasket between the governor body and support. On units where the

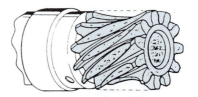

FIGURE 14-48   An apple-cored governor gear can cause erratic or no governor operation. This is usually caused by a rough or damaged drive gear or a governor that is trying to seize in the bore. *(Reprinted with permission of General Motors)*

FIGURE 14-49   This governor cover is a force-fit. An old C6 servo cover is the right size to use as a driving tool for a THM 350 governor cover.

REAL WORLD FIX

The 1993 Mitsubishi Montero (240,000 miles) starts out in second gear after coming to a stop. It will start in first if you shift to M-1. The governor and valve body were replaced, and the transmission shifted properly for two stops before the second-gear starts began again.

Fix. The technician checked the new governor and found a stuck valve. Inspection also found a faulty oil screen. Replacing the filter screen and cleaning the governor solved this problem.

body fits completely around the output shaft, it is good practice to tighten the body-to-support bolts after the two have been placed onto the output shaft.

A gear-driven governor can also be disassembled for service or replacement of the drive gear (Figure 14-51). Correct movement of the valve can be checked by holding the governor

REAL WORLD FIX

The 1993 Nissan Sentra would not shift out of first gear; reverse was fine. Inspection of the pan shows a black film with no sign of burning or varnish. The TV cable was adjusted properly and seems to operate the valve.

Fix. The technician removed the governor cover and found that the plastic governor was stripped. The replacement (OE) governor came with a metal gear. Replacement of the governor fixed this problem.

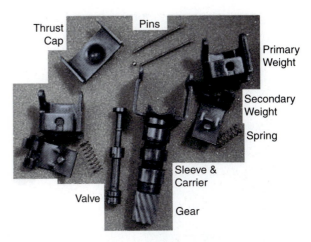

FIGURE 14-51 A typical early General Motors governor that has been disassembled for cleaning or repair.

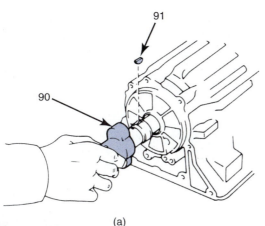

(a)

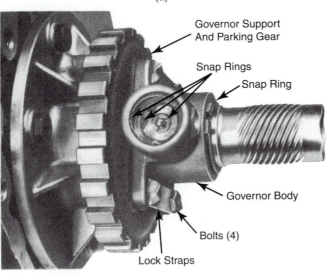

(b)

FIGURE 14-50 This speed sensor rotor (90) is held in place by a retaining ring and is driven by a key (91) in the output shaft (a). Some governors use a pin that passes through the output shaft to connect the weight to the valve (b). *(Courtesy of Chrysler Corporation)*

TECH TIP

An old connecting rod with a wrist pin hole slightly larger than the governor makes a handy holding fixture. Clamp in a vise and use it to support the governor during service.

with the gear end upward and squeezing and releasing the weights, as shown in Figure 14-52.

To disassemble a gear-driven governor, you should:

1. Cut the retaining pins and remove the thrust cap, weights, springs, and valve (Figure 14-53).
2. Support the governor and drive out the gear retaining pin (Figure 14-54).
3. Support the governor using two 7/64-in. (2.7-mm) plates positioned in the exhaust slots and press the gear off the sleeve.

To reassemble a gear-driven governor, you should:

1. Support the governor as just described and press the new gear completely into position.
2. Drill a new hole, 0.125 in. (3.17 mm) in diameter, through the new gear and the sleeve. This new hole should be at a right (90-degree) angle to the original hole.
3. Support the governor and install a new retaining pin. Stake both ends of the retaining pin hole to prevent the pin from coming out.
4. Wash the assembly thoroughly in solvent and air dry.

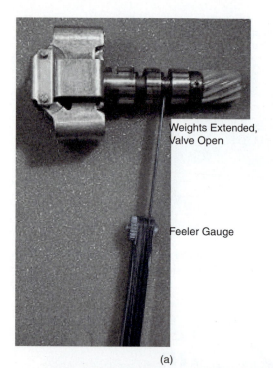

Weights Extended, Valve Open

Feeler Gauge

(a)

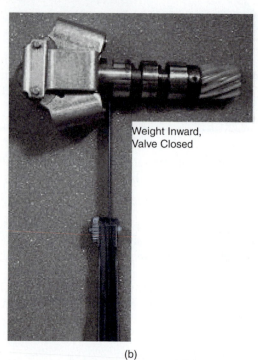

Weight Inward, Valve Closed

(b)

FIGURE 14-52 With the governor weights fully extended, there should be a minimum opening of 0.020 in. at the entry port (a). With the weights fully inward, there should be a minimum opening of 0.020 in. at the exhaust port (b).

FIGURE 14-53 The pins are cut so this governor can be disassembled.

FIGURE 14-54 A governor gear can be replaced after driving out the retaining pin. Note the old connecting rod being used as a support fixture.

5. Install the valve, weights, springs, and thrust cap; position new retaining pins in place; and crimp both ends of the pins.

Gear-driven governors that use check balls in place of a spool valve should be carefully inspected for missing check balls, damaged springs, a blocked oil passage, binding weights, or a damaged seal.

SUMMARY

1. Many transmission problems can be repaired without removing the transmission from the vehicle.

2. The pan should be removed and its contents carefully checked before removing a transmission from a vehicle.

3. Components that can be serviced without removing the transmission include linkage adjustment and repair, seal replacement, governor service and replacement, valve body repair, and transmission mounts, to name a few.

4. After making any repair, carefully check your work and road test the vehicle for proper operation.

REVIEW QUESTIONS

The following questions are provided to help you study as you read the chapter.

1. The replacement of the manual linkage cable or the throttle cable is always followed by a cable _____.

2. Shift linkage _____ is a safety mechanism that prevents a vehicle from being shifted out of park unless the key is in the ignition and the brake is applied.

3. To prevent damage to a seal during installation, a _____ driver should be used.

4. A handy trick to keep a seal spring from coming out on installation is to fill the recess with _____ _____.

5. Thread damage can be caused by using a bolt that is _____ _____ or _____ _____.

6. When removing a cooler line, a _____ wrench must be used.

7. It is important that the _____ of each bolt be noted as a valve body is removed.

8. A special _____ and _____ tool is usually required for on-vehicle bushing replacement.

9. A governor can be serviced by carefully _____, cleaning the parts, and _____.

10. The actual procedures of removal and replacement of various transmission components varies between manufacturers. Always check the _____ manual if in doubt about a service procedure.

CHAPTER QUIZ

The following questions will help you check the facts you have learned. Select the answer that completes each statement correctly.

1. Student A says that a faulty governor can be repaired with the transmission in the car. Student B agrees, but says that gear-driven governors require removal of the extension housing. Who is correct?
   a. Student A
   b. Student B
   c. Both A and B
   d. Neither A nor B

2. Which of these operations cannot usually be done with the transmission in the car?
   a. Valve body removal and replacement
   b. Manual shift linkage seal replacement
   c. Torque converter seal replacement
   d. Vacuum modulator replacement

3. Student A says that a seal can be pried out of a bore using a sharp chisel. Student B says that smaller metal-backed seals can often be driven into place using a standard socket. Who is correct?
   a. Student A
   b. Student B
   c. Both A and B
   d. Neither A nor B

4. Student A says that a metal-backed seal has to seal against two surfaces, the housing bore and shaft. Student B says that a sealing lip is used to seal the backing to the housing bore. Who is correct?
   a. Student A
   b. Student B
   c. Both A and B
   d. Neither A nor B

5. Student A says that a new seal will be ruined if the lip is cut during installation. Student B says that the seal lip should be lubricated with petroleum jelly or ATF before installing. Who is correct?

   a. Student A

   b. Student B

   c. Both A and B

   d. Neither A nor B

6. Student A says that all throttle/kickdown linkages pass into the case through a metal-backed lip seal. Student B says that all the cable or rods connect to a lever on the outside of the case. Who is correct?

   a. Student A

   b. Student B

   c. Both A and B

   d. Neither A nor B

7. Student A says that stripped threads in an aluminum case can be repaired by installing a thread insert. Student B says that a 1/4-in. bolt should have at least 3/8 in. of thread contact. Who is correct?

   a. Student A

   b. Student B

   c. Both A and B

   d. Neither A nor B

8. Student A says that the best repair for a kinked, leaky cooler line is to cut out the damaged section and replace it with copper tubing. Student B says that you should always use two wrenches to loosen a tube nut. Who is correct?

   a. Student A

   b. Student B

   c. Both A and B

   d. Neither A nor B

9. Student A says that you need to be careful not to lose any of the check balls when you remove a valve body. Student B says that a transmission must be upside down before removing the valve body. Who is correct?

   a. Student A

   b. Student B

   c. Both A and B

   d. Neither A nor B

10. Some valve bodies have a spring pressure from a (the) _____ that will move them when the bolts are loosened.

    a. servo or an accumulator

    b. servo or a relief valve

    c. shift valves or a servo

    d. pump relief valve or an accumulator

11. Student A says that you should carefully place the bolts with the correct length into the proper holes as a valve body is replaced. Student B says that the valve body bolts should always be carefully torqued. Who is correct?

    a. Student A

    b. Student B

    c. Both A and B

    d. Neither A nor B

12. Student A says that all servo covers are held in place by a group of three or four bolts. Student B says that many servos contain a spring that must be kept compressed while the cover is removed. Who is correct?

    a. Student A

    b. Student B

    c. Both A and B

    d. Neither A nor B

13. Which of the following is not a reason for removing an extension housing on a General Motors RWD vehicle?

    a. Speedometer driven-gear replacement

    b. Governor replacement

    c. Park pawl or spring replacement

    d. Extension housing bushing replacement

14. Student A says that you need to lift the transmission slightly in order to remove the rear mount and extension housing. Student B says that all transmissions use a paper gasket between the extension housing and case. Who is correct?

    a. Student A

    b. Student B

    c. Both A and B

    d. Neither A nor B

15. Student A says that a faulty governor gear can keep a transmission from upshifting. Student B says that it is possible to disassemble a governor so it can be thoroughly cleaned and repaired. Who is correct?

    a. Student A

    b. Student B

    c. Both A and B

    d. Neither A nor B

CHAPTER 15

TRANSMISSION/ TRANSAXLE REMOVAL AND REPLACEMENT

OBJECTIVES

After studying Chapter 15, the reader should be able to:

1. Remove an automatic transmission or transaxle.
2. Replace/install an automatic transmission or transaxle.
3. Complete the ASE tasks related to transmission/transaxle removal and replacement.

KEY TERMS

Engine Support (p. 406)
Flywheel Turner (p. 405)

15.1 INTRODUCTION

A badly worn or damaged transmission is removed from the vehicle for repair, replacement, or a complete overhaul. The repairs can be for specific problems such as a noisy gearset, worn-out band, or leaking front seal. A faulty transmission with considerable mileage, damage, or wear is a candidate for overhaul or replacement.

When choosing between overhaul or replacement, the following should be considered:

- Cost of overhaul (parts and labor)
- The skill of the technician
- Availability of special tools
  - Availability of the needed parts
- Cost of the replacement transmission
- Availability of the replacement transmission

Many shops install remanufactured transmissions because they are often less expensive than rebuilding or updating the original transmission.

The California BAR regulations require that if a transmission is "exchanged," a descriptive term such as *new, used, rebuilt, remanufactured, reconditioned,* or *overhauled* shall accompany the exchange.

The transmission in a rear wheel drive (RWD) vehicle can be removed without removing the engine. In some vehicles, the engine will balance and remain in place on its mounts. In other vehicles, the engine should be supported to prevent damage to the engine or surrounding components. The engine must be supported when the transaxle is removed from a front wheel drive (FWD) vehicle (see Figure 15-10). This is especially true if the front cradle is removed.

The torque converter is removed with the transmission. Leaving the converter in the transmission will prevent a fluid spill as the transmission is removed from the engine. The torque converter must be installed into the transmission during replacement to ensure proper alignment with the pump, stator, and input shaft.

15.2 TRANSMISSION REMOVAL

Transmission removal varies between vehicle makes and models. Transmissions and transaxles have slightly different removal procedures. The procedures outlined here are very general and are meant to provide an overview of what is involved. Service information should be consulted to determine the exact procedure for a particular vehicle.

To remove an RWD transmission, you should:

1. Open the hood, and disconnect the battery ground cable. Remove the dipstick and TV linkage if necessary.
2. Raise and support the vehicle on a hoist that allows access to the transmission and drive shaft. Remove the exhaust

REAL WORLD FIX

The 1997 Dodge Caravan (123,000 miles) transmission was bucking and slipping under a load. A scan tool check revealed no DTCs. A remanufactured transmission was installed, but this did not help. A new transmission controller was installed, but this did not help.

Fix. Following advice, the technician removed the flexplate so it could be thoroughly inspected. The flexplate was checked visually when the transmission was replaced, but this vehicle has a large washer that hides the inner portion. The flexplate appeared fine, but the center was broken, allowing the outer portion to rotate. A new flexplate fixed this problem. The technician recommendation: When replacing the transmission on this vehicle, remove the flexplate so it can be completely inspected.

REAL WORLD FIX

The 1971 Chevrolet pickup (200,000 miles) had an engine swap; the 400-ci engine was replaced with a 350-ci engine. The vehicle now has a bad vibration at speeds over 2,500 rpm. The technician then remembered that the 400 is an externally balanced engine, and the 350 is balanced internally.

Replacement of the flexplate with the proper part solved this problem.

system as needed to gain access to the transmission and transmission support.
3. Remove the transmission pan and drain the fluid as described in Chapter 11. Be sure to check the pan for debris that would indicate internal problems. Replace the pan and install three or four bolts to hold it in place.
4. Disconnect the electrical connectors (Figure 15-1). The harness on some vehicles is disconnected and removed with the transmission. Disconnect the fluid fill tube if necessary.
5. Remove the torque converter dust cover. Place match/index marks on the converter and flywheel/flexplate/drive plate. Remove the converter-to-flexplate bolts (Figure 15-2). You will need to turn the engine to get access to all of the

bolts. The engine can be turned using a **flywheel turner** or a wrench on the vibration damper bolt (at the front of the crankshaft; Figure 15-3). Slide the converter into the transmission as far as possible. It may be necessary to remove the starter on some vehicles.

6. Remove the drive shaft as described in Section 15.4.1.
7. Disconnect the manual shift linkage, TV linkage (if necessary), speed sensor connection or speedometer cable, and fluid cooler lines (Figure 15-4).
8. Support the transmission using a transmission jack. The jack should be positioned so it does not damage the pan. Attach the safety chain around the transmission. Remove the bolts securing the transmission mount to either the transmission or to the cross-member.
9. Raise the transmission and remove the center cross-member/transmission support (Figure 15-5).

TECH TIP

To stop ATF from leaking out of the lines, compress foam ear plugs and insert them into the cooler lines.

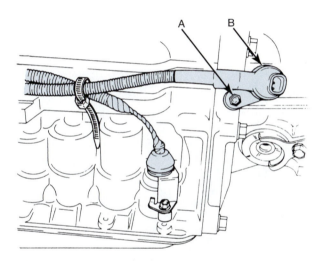

FIGURE 15-1 The external wiring harness is disconnected from the transmission speed sensor (A and B) and any other connections. *(Courtesy of Chrysler Corporation)*

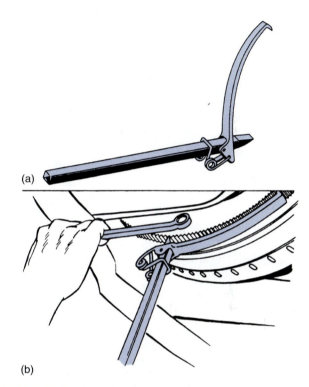

FIGURE 15-3 A flywheel turner (a) can be used to turn the flywheel or hold it while the converter bolts are loosened. *(Courtesy of Snap-on Tools)*

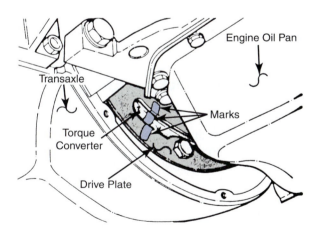

FIGURE 15-2 The converter should be disconnected from the flexplate by removing the flexplate-to-converter bolts. *(Courtesy of Chrysler Corporation)*

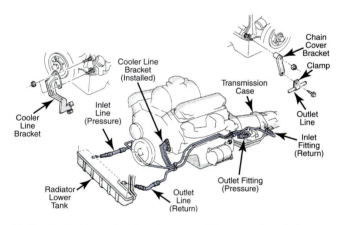

FIGURE 15-4 Position a drain pan and disconnect the cooler lines. Do not bend them any more than needed to remove the transmission. *(Courtesy of Chrysler Corporation)*

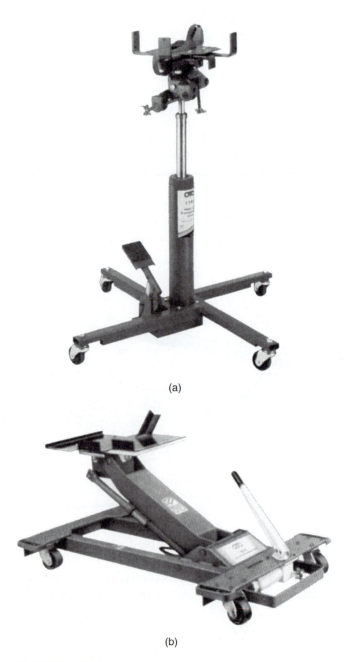

(a)

(b)

FIGURE 15-5 A transmission jack is positioned under the transmission pan so it can lift the transmission to allow removal of the mount and crossmember. A high lift jack (a) is used when the vehicle is on a lift; a low lift jack (b) is used when the vehicle is supported on jack stands. *(Courtesy of OTC)*

10. Lower the transmission just enough to gain access to the upper transmission-to-engine bolts and remove these bolts (Figure 15-6). It may be necessary to install an engine support fixture on some vehicles (Figure 15-7).
11. Pull the transmission back far enough to clear the converter housing alignment dowels, converter pilot, and lower the transmission and converter out of the vehicle.

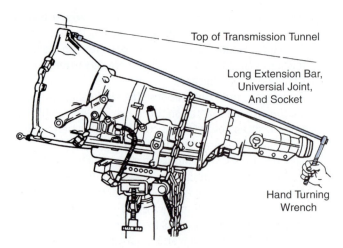

FIGURE 15-6 Many transmissions can be lowered enough to remove the upper transmission-to-engine bolt(s).

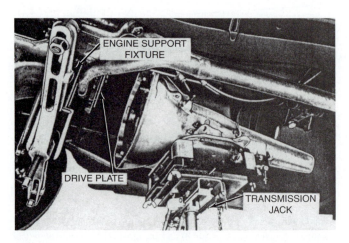

FIGURE 15-7 The engine support fixture is supporting the rear of the engine while the transmission and converter are removed. *(Courtesy of Chrysler Corporation)*

15.3 TRANSAXLE REMOVAL

The engine should always be supported when removing a transaxle. Special **engine support** fixtures are available that provide a safe, secure support without damaging the vehicle. These tools are usually placed on the fender flanges and radiator support.

The drive shafts are secured to the transaxle in different ways. Different removal methods are required to remove them, as described in Chapter 15. Some front suspension disassembly is also required. Vehicle service information should be checked to determine what is required. In some cases, only the right drive shaft will need to be removed. The other can

REAL WORLD FIX

The engine of the 1999 Subaru Forester (123,000 miles) was removed and replaced to repair the head gaskets. When the vehicle was started, the transmission temperature light flashed on and off. A check revealed a code P0748. An inspection showed all the transmission wiring to be correct, with correct internal resistance at the solenoid connectors.

Fix. The technician checked the transmission pan, and discovered that the jack, used under the transmission pan to lift the engine, had bent the pan and damaged a solenoid and connector. Replacement of the damaged solenoid fixed this problem.

TECH TIP

There is a possibility that the converter can slide off its splines and fall as the transmission is being removed. It is heavy and can cause injury or damage if it falls. Some manufacturers recommend installing a converter retaining bracket (Figure 15-9). Some technicians run a bungee cord or a piece of mechanics wire to hold it in place.

TECH TIP

When removing the transmission from a 4WD vehicle, it is often recommended to remove the transfer case before removing the transmission (Figure 15-8).

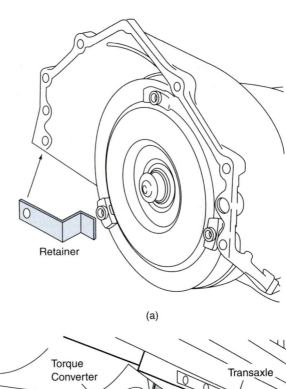

(a)

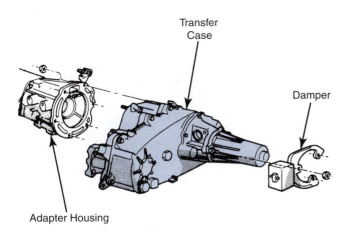

FIGURE 15-8   The transfer case is removed before the transmission is removed from most 4WD vehicles. *(Courtesy of Chrysler Corporation)*

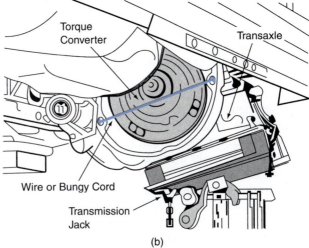

(b)

FIGURE 15-9   After disconnecting the torque converter from the flexplate, slide it into the transmission and install a retainer (a) or run a wire or bungee cord across the front of the transmission (b).

TECH TIP

Some shops have made support fixtures using a length of pipe or square tubing and a piece of threaded rod. A pair of thick phone books or catalogs can be placed on the fenders to prevent damage.

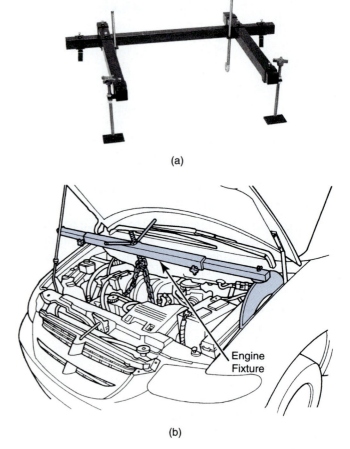

(a)

(b)

FIGURE 15-10 An engine support bar has been installed on this vehicle and adjusted to lift the engine slightly (a). These fixtures are designed to fit various FWD vehicles (b). *(a is courtesy of ATEC Trans-Tool and Cleaning Systems; b is courtesy of Chrysler Corporation)*

be disconnected from the transaxle as the transaxle is removed from the engine.

To remove a transaxle, you should:

1. Open the hood, and disconnect the battery ground cable. Disconnect the cooler lines, shift linkage, TV linkage, speed sensor connector or speedometer cable, and any accessible electrical connectors.
2. Install an engine support fixture and adjust it to support the engine's weight (Figure 15-10).
3. Remove any accessible transaxle-to-engine bolts.
4. Loosen the front hub nuts. The front wheels should remain on the ground with the parking brake applied, and the transmission should be in park while loosening the lug nuts (Figure 15-11).
5. Raise and support the vehicle so you have access to the transaxle and front suspension.
6. Remove the pan, and drain the fluid as described in Chapter 11. Be sure to check the pan for debris that would indicate internal problems. Replace the pan and install only three or four bolts to hold it in place.
7. Remove the drive shaft(s) (Figure 15-12).
8. Remove the torque converter cover/dust shield, place index marks on the converter and flexplate, and remove the converter-to-flexplate bolts. Slide the converter into the transaxle.
9. Disconnect any remaining oil cooler lines, shift linkage, speedometer cable, or electrical connectors. It may be necessary to remove the starter on some vehicles.
10. Place a suitable transmission jack under the transaxle, adjust it to support the transaxle, and attach the safety chain (Figure 15-13).
11. Remove any transaxle support mounts. On some vehicles, it is necessary to remove the engine cradle (Figure 15-14).
12. Remove any remaining transaxle-to-engine bolts.
13. Pull the transaxle away from the engine far enough to clear the engine-to-transaxle alignment dowels and torque converter pilot, and lower the transaxle and converter from the vehicle.

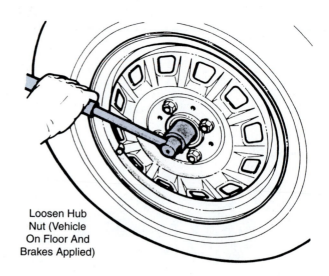

Loosen Hub Nut (Vehicle On Floor And Brakes Applied)

FIGURE 15-11 Before removing an FWD drive shaft, the front hub nut must be removed. It is usually necessary to have the tire on the floor and the brakes applied to loosen it. *(Courtesy of Chrysler Corporation)*

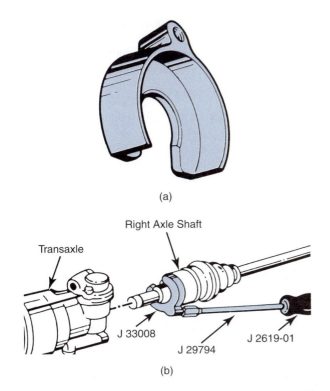

(a)

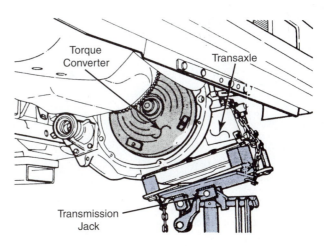

 FIGURE 15-13   A transmission jack has been positioned under the pan to support the transaxle as it is removed. *(Courtesy of Chrysler Corporation)*

FIGURE 15-12   A special tool is attached to the slide hammer (a) so that the slide hammer can be used to remove the drive shaft from a transaxle (b). *(Courtesy of Kent-Moore)*

TECH TIP

A special tool or a short section of heater hose may be required with some transaxles to hold the differential pinion gears from rotating out of position when both drive shafts are removed.

FIGURE 15-14   The lower ball joint (circled) is disconnected to allow the drive shaft to be removed. Some vehicles require the engine transaxle support/cross-member (arrow) to be removed to allow transaxle removal.

TECH TIP

FWD vehicles should not be moved with weight on the front wheels while the drive shafts are removed. Special dollies are available to support the front end so the vehicle can be moved (Figure 15-15).

15.4 DRIVE SHAFT REMOVAL AND REPLACEMENT

As a drive shaft is removed, technicians are advised to not allow it to hang from one end, bending a still-connected U-joint or CV joint to its limit. If necessary, support the shaft using mechanic's wire or an old V-belt until both joints can be disconnected (Figure 15-16).

FIGURE 15-15 A support dolly can be positioned under the front of an FWD vehicle so it can be easily moved while the drive shafts are out. *(Courtesy of The Mighty Mover)*

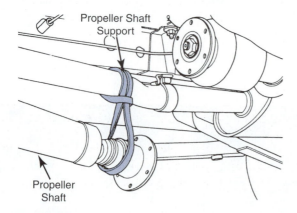

FIGURE 15-16 An old V-belt can be looped around the exhaust pipe to support the drive shaft. *(Courtesy of Chrysler Corporation)*

TECH TIP

RWD drive shafts with damaged tubes or worn, dry, or tight U-joints and FWD drive shafts with torn boots or worn, dry, or tight CV joints should be repaired before replacement.

15.4.1 RWD Drive Shaft Removal and Replacement

Most drive shaft slip joint splines float on the transmission mainshaft rear bushing. When the drive shaft is removed, it will slide out of the transmission, and lubricant will run out of the unsealed opening. To prevent leakage, some technicians raise the vehicle so that the back end is lifted higher than the front. Many

technicians use a stop-off tool or an old slip yoke to plug the opening (see Figure 14–36). A plastic bag and rubber band can also be used. When replacing a drive shaft, be sure to put some transmission oil on the slip yoke to lubricate the seal.

To remove a RWD drive shaft:

1. Raise and securely support the vehicle so the drive shaft is free to turn.
2. Place index marks at the rear U-joint flange and rear U-joint so the shaft can be replaced in the original position (Figure 15-17).
3. Remove the bolts securing the rear U-joint to the flange, being ready for the two bearing cups to fall off the U-joint cross.
4. Slide the slip yoke out of the transmission, plug the back of the transmission, and remove the drive shaft from the vehicle.

To replace a RWD drive shaft:

Most RWD drive shafts are replaced by sliding the slip yoke into the transmission, aligning the index marks as the

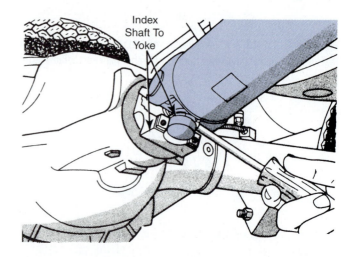

FIGURE 15-17 Before removal, make sure there are index marks at the rear U-joint so the shaft can be replaced in its original position. An old screwdriver is being used to scratch a mark onto the U-joint cross. *(Courtesy of Chrysler Corporation)*

TECH TIP

Many technicians will wrap tape around the joint or slide an old stocking over the U-joint and shaft to hold the bearing cups in place (Figure 15-18).

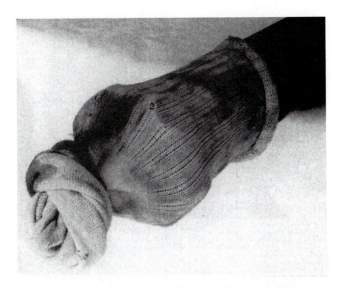

(a)

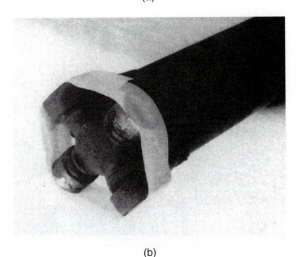

(b)

FIGURE 15-18   An old sock (a) has been slid over this drive shaft to hold the bearing cups in position. Tape (b) can be used for the same purpose.

rear U-joint is connected to the rear axle companion flange, and tightening the bolts to the correct torque. With the bearing caps held by a U-bolt or strap, make sure that the bearing cups are properly seated inside the locating lugs.

15.4.2 FWD Drive Shaft Removal and Replacement

Most FWD drive shafts are held in place at the outer end by the nut securing the outboard CV joint to the front hub. After removing the nut, which is normally very tight, the hub and steering knuckle must be moved outward and off the end of the splined section of the CV joint. This usually requires disassembling part of the suspension system (Figure 15-19). The drive shaft, along with the front hub and bearing, on General Motors

W series cars (which include the Chevrolet Lumina), can be removed through the steering knuckle; the hub and bearing can then be removed from the outer CV joint if desired.

Inboard joints are usually held into the differential side gears by a *circlip* that usually pops free when enough outward pressure is exerted on it. This style is sometimes called a *plugin* type of connection. Some inboard joints are bolted to a flange and shaft extending from the differential. Chrysler products from 1981 and earlier retained the CV joint in the differential using a snap ring that must be removed from inside the differential side gear (Figure 15-20). A problem that can be encountered on some vehicles is that the differential side gears can roll out of position when both CV joints are removed. Normally, the right drive shaft is removed first, then the left shaft is driven out using a special tool or 1/4-in. (6.3-mm) rod that is 12 in. (305 mm) long going through the differential (Figure 15-21). This tool, rod, or short hose section is left in the differential to hold the gears in place until one of the drive shafts is replaced.

A FWD vehicle should not be moved while the drive shafts are removed unless the weight is lifted off the front wheels. Damage to the front wheel bearings can result. After the drive shaft is replaced, it may be necessary to check the front end alignment.

The following description is very general. It is recommended that you follow the procedure given in a service manual for the vehicle you are repairing.

To remove an FWD drive shaft:

1. Remove the wheel cover and hub nut locking device, and loosen the front hub nut (Figure 15-22). For nuts that have been staked or bent to lock them in place, merely unscrew the nut. Most manufacturers recommend that you replace this nut with a new one during drive shaft replacement. Using an air impact wrench for removal is not recommended.
2. Raise and securely support the vehicle, and remove the front wheel. Finish removing the hub nut (Figure 15-23). If the vehicle has ventilated brake rotors, a pin can be placed into one of the ventilation slots to keep the drive shaft from turning as you remove the nut.
3. Remove the lower ball joint clamp bolt (Figure 15-24). Many manufacturers recommend using a new nut and bolt during reassembly.
4. Pry the lower control arm downward to separate it from the steering knuckle as you pull the steering knuckle outward to separate the front hub from the CV joint (Figure 15-25). It is may be necessary to install a puller to push the CV joint through the hub (Figure 15-26). Never hammer on the end of the CV joint.

   As you separate the hub and CV joint, be careful not to stretch the brake hose. On some vehicles it will be necessary to disconnect the brake caliper and hang it

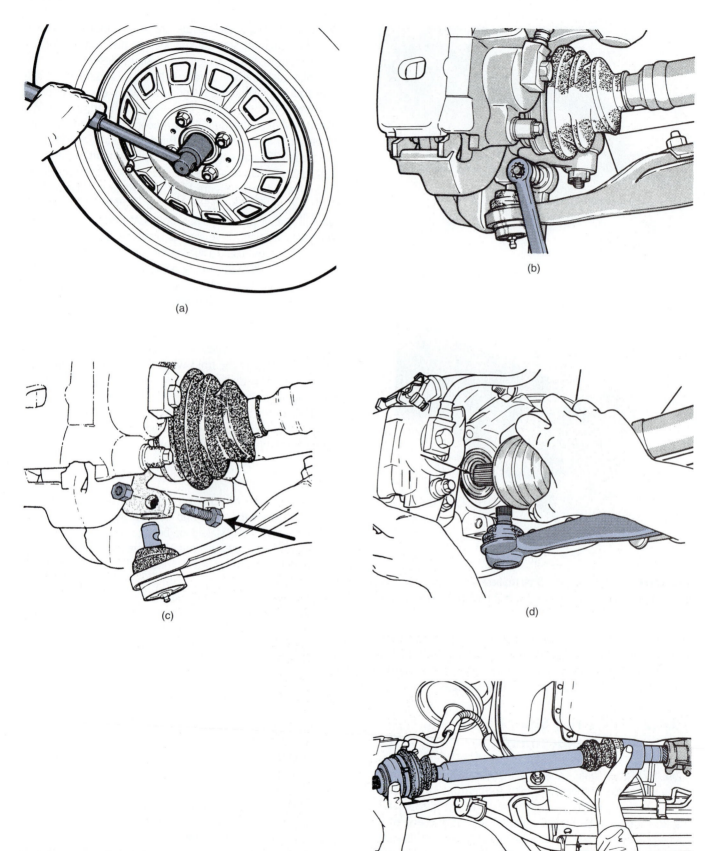

(a)

(b)

(c)

(d)

(e)

FIGURE 15-19   The procedure to remove the drive shaft on an FWD vehicle.

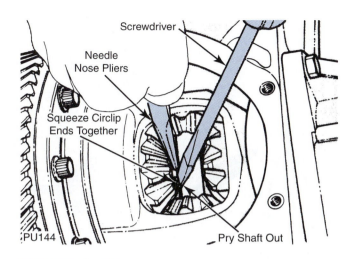

Screwdriver

Needle
Nose Pliers

Squeeze Circlip
Ends Together

Pry Shaft Out

PU144

FIGURE 15-20   This transaxle has a circlip inside the differential that must be removed before removing the drive shaft. *(Courtesy of Chrysler Corporation)*

FIGURE 15-21   The differential rotator is used to drive the left-side CV joint from this transaxle. It also keeps the differential side gears in alignment. *(Courtesy of OTC)*

FIGURE 15-22   Most hub nuts are very tight so a long wrench is usually required. The tire must be on the ground and brakes applied to keep it from rotating. *(Courtesy of NEAPCO)*

FIGURE 15-23   With the hub nut loosened and the vehicle raised, the wheel can be removed to allow access to remove the hub nut and other parts. Note the pin to hold the rotor from turning (arrow). *(Courtesy of NEAPCO)*

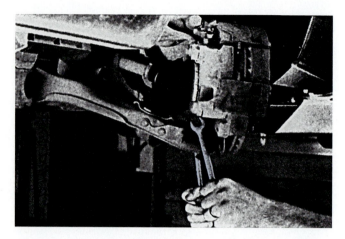

FIGURE 15-24   On many vehicles, removing the clamp bolt allows the ball joint stud to slide out of the steering knuckle. This allows the steering knuckle to be swung outward far enough for the CV joint splines to slide out of the hub. *(Courtesy of NEAPCO)*

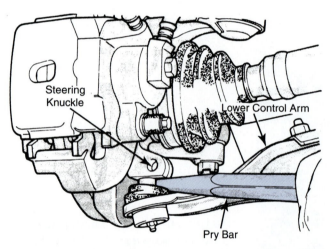

Steering Knuckle

Lower Control Arm

Pry Bar

FIGURE 15-25   A pry bar is being used to force the lower control arm downward far enough to remove the ball joint stud from the steering knuckle. *(Courtesy of Chrysler Corporation)*

from the strut assembly using a hook or wire. Be ready to support the drive shaft so that it does not drop.

5. The inner CV joint on some vehicles can be removed from the differential with a quick jerk using a prying tool, but do not put excessive force on the transaxle case (Figure 15-27). An attachment for a slide hammer can be used to jerk the CV joint out of the differential. Do not use the drive shaft as a slide hammer.

6. Remove the drive shaft, being careful not to damage the CV joint boots and keeping the shaft horizontal so the plunge joint will not be stressed (Figure 15-28).

To replace an FWD drive shaft (Figure 15-29):

1. Lubricate the seal area on the inboard CV joint. Slide the CV joint completely into the transaxle, being

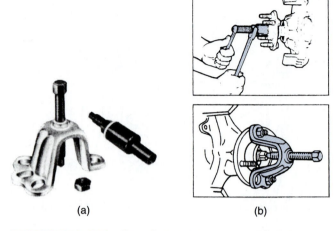

(a)   (b)

FIGURE 15-26   This puller (a) is being used to pull the hub outward and off the CV joint splines. The remover (b) is used to push the CV joint through the hub. *(Courtesy of OTC)*

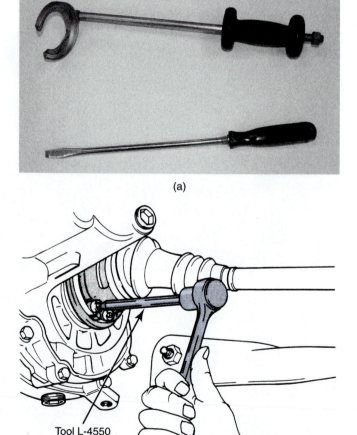

(a)

Tool L-4550

(b)

FIGURE 15-27   Most inboard CV joints can be pulled from the transaxle using a slide hammer and special adapter or by prying them out using a pry bar (a). Some inboard joints are bolted onto a flange at the transaxle (b). *(Courtesy of Chrysler Corporation)*

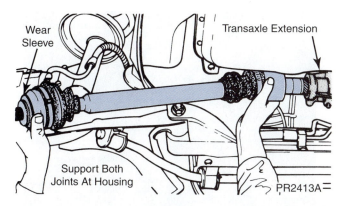

FIGURE 15-28   After the shaft has been disconnected, it should be removed carefully to prevent damaging the CV boots. Support both CV joints and hold the shaft horizontally while carrying it. *(Courtesy of Chrysler Corporation)*

careful not to damage the seal. Test the installation by pulling outward on the CV joint housing; it should not pull free.

2. Pull the hub and steering knuckle outward as you insert the spline of the outboard CV joint through the hub. Rotate the hub, if necessary, to line up the splines.

3. Thread a new hub nut onto the threads, and tighten the nut just enough to pull the CV joint into place. A special tool is required to pull the CV joint into place on some domestic and imported vehicles; do not use the hub nut for this purpose.

4. Reinstall the lower ball joint using a new bolt where required, and tighten the nut to the correct torque. If the ball joint stud is notched, be sure to align the notch with the clamp hole.

5. Tighten the hub nut to about 50 ft-lb (70 N-m), install the wheel and tire, and lower the vehicle. Set the parking brake, and finish tightening the hub nut to the specified torque.

6. Install the hub nut locking device, raise the vehicle, and check to ensure that the tire rotates freely.

15.5 TRANSMISSION INSTALLATION

Installing a transmission is the reverse of the removal procedure. The last operation in the removal is usually the first step in the installation.

To install a transmission or transaxle, you should:

1. Make a final check to ensure that the transmission is ready to be installed, and the wiring harness is in place and all the connectors are clean and properly connected (Figure 15-30).

2. Raise the transmission into position. Watch for wires or hoses that may be damaged as you move the transmission in place (Figure 15-31). Slide the transmission into place against the engine. Something is wrong if it does not go completely into place. Correct this problem before continuing. Never force the transmission up to the engine.

3. Install the transmission-to-engine bolts and tighten them to the correct torque.

4. Place the transmission supports into position, lower the transmission onto the mounts, and tighten the mounting bolts to the correct torque.

5. Slide the converter forward to align with the flexplate. Install the bolts and tighten them to the correct torque.

6. Connect the cooler lines and tighten them to the correct torque.

7. Replace the drive shaft(s) and tighten any retaining bolts to the correct torque.

8. Reconnect all linkage and wire connections that were disconnected, making sure they are routed properly. Tighten all retaining bolts to the correct torque.

TECH TIP

Before installing the transmission, make sure that the transmission alignment dowels are in place.

TECH TIP

The proof of correct converter installation is that you should be able to slide the converter forward as it is rotated into alignment with the flexplate. If the converter is jammed in place, it is stacked, and the transmission must be removed so the converter can be aligned and installed correctly. Don't forget to align the converter to the flexplate using the marks you made during removal.

(a)

(b)

(c)

(d)

STEERING KNUCKLE

GROOVE IN STUD

STEERING KNUCKLE

SLOT IN STUD

(e)

(f)

(g)

FIGURE 15-29 An FWD drive shaft is replaced by installing the inboard joint into the transaxle (a); swinging the steering knuckle outward and over the splines on the outboard CV joint (b) (in some cases a puller is used to pull the CV joint into the hub [c]); correctly installing the ball joint stud and retaining bolt (d); tightening the ball joint retaining bolt (e); replacing the hub nut (f); and tightening the nut to the correct torque (g). *(a, b, c, e, f, and g are courtesy of NEAPCO; d is courtesy of Moog Chassis Parts, a brand of Federal-Mogul Corporation)*

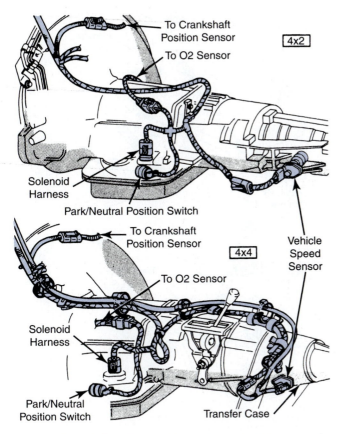

FIGURE 15-30 The external wiring harness should be connected to the transmission and should be properly routed through the brackets. *(Courtesy of Chrysler Corporation)*

REAL WORLD FIX

The 1992 Explorer (86,000 miles) transmission was just rebuilt, and a rebuilt torque converter was installed. The A4LD transmission worked well on the first test drive, but during a second, early morning drive to check cold operation, the transmission would not upshift. It would only make a whine noise and then quit working. A teardown revealed broken pump gears.

Fix. An ATRA TSB indicated a problem with the A4LD transmission breaking pump gears if the bell housing is warped. Replacement of the bell housing and pump gears fixed this problem.

TECH TIP

As you slide the transmission against the engine, make sure there are no electrical wires, vacuum lines, or other items caught between them. Expensive damage can result.

REAL WORLD FIX

The 5.7-L engine in the 1995 Suburban was replaced at 85,000 miles with a reputable remanufactured engine. After 7,000 miles, it came back with a knock. Inspection revealed a broken flexplate, which was replaced. It returned again after another 7,000 miles with a knock, and another broken flexplate. A new GM flexplate was installed. Now it has returned a third time with the same problem.

Fix. It was discovered after the transmission was removed that the replacement engine did not come with the alignment dowels, and this omission was overlooked three times. Installation of the alignment dowels and a new flexplate solved this problem.

After installation, the transmission should be filled with the correct amount of ATF and the engine started. If you are unsure of how much ATF is needed, add enough fluid to read slightly high on the dipstick. Adjust the fluid level after starting the engine and operating the transmission in the different gear ranges. Next, complete your transmission overhaul with a road test to ensure proper operation.

15.6 TRANSAXLE INSTALLATION

Transaxle installation is essentially the same as for a transmission. The major difference is that the transaxle should be centered between the two drive shafts; both of the inner, plunge-type CV joints should have been compressed the same amount (see Section 14.11). Another difference is that the front wheel alignment should be checked on those vehicles that require suspension or cradle removal.

Item	Torque
A	27-54 N•m (20-40 ft. lbs.)
B	8-15 N•m (75-130 in. lbs.)
C	3-6 N•m (30-50 in. lbs.)
D	47-88 N•m (35-65 ft. lbs.)

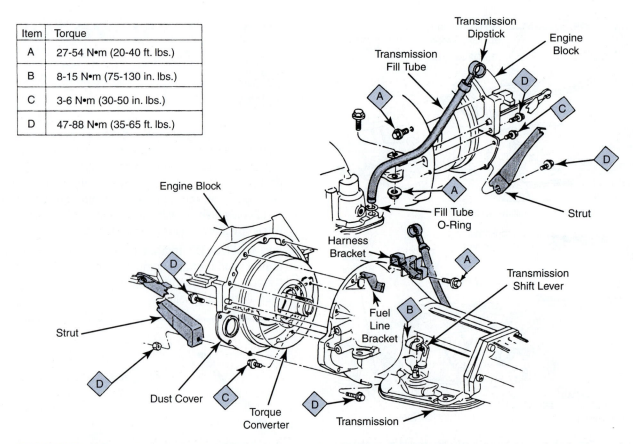

FIGURE 15-31 As the transmission is installed, the converter is aligned and secured to the flexplate; the transmission is aligned and secured to the engine; and all brackets, struts, and other necessary parts will be replaced. (Note that the converter must be installed into the transmission first.) *(Courtesy of Chrysler Corporation)*

TECH TIP

Some FWD vehicles will have a vibration problem if the engine is not centered. If no other information is available, compress the inner CV joints and note the amount of clearance to the transaxle case. Move the engine side to side until the clearance is equal before tightening the motor mount bolts.

TECH TIP

The engine cradle of some FWD vehicles also attaches to the front suspension. Improper installation can adversely affect the wheel alignment. The cradle should be replaced in exactly the same position as it was before removal.

REAL WORLD FIX

The 1988 Volkswagen Jetta (128,000 miles) came in with the transaxle in the trunk to be resealed and installed. After running it, the front seal was leaking so the transaxle was pulled, and a new seal was installed. This did not fix the problem, so another new seal was installed, but the same problem came back.

Fix. The next time the transaxle was removed, the alignment pins were checked; they were missing. Installation of the alignment pins allowed the transaxle to be centered properly and this fixed the problem.

SUMMARY

1. Transmissions are removed to make repairs, overhaul, or replacement.
2. The removal and replacement procedures are similar for most transmissions and transaxles.
3. Always check the service information before removing an automatic transmission.
4. Never force the transmission onto the back of the engine during installation.
5. It may be necessary to check the wheel alignment after installing a transaxle.

REVIEW QUESTIONS

The following questions are provided to help you study as you read the chapter.

1. A special _____ support is used when removing a front wheel drive transaxle.
2. A _____ manual should be consulted for the suggested removal and installation procedures for a particular transmission.
3. The first thing removed when removing an RWD transmission from a vehicle is the _____ ground _____.
4. Before unbolting the torque converter, put match marks on the converter and the _____ to aid installation.
5. As the transmission is removed from the vehicle, install a bracket to the _____ _____ to prevent it from sliding out of the transmission.
6. The first thing removed when removing an FWD transmission from a vehicle is the _____ ground _____.
7. To prevent leakage once the drive shaft has been removed from an RWD vehicle, the _____ _____ needs to be plugged.
8. When removing a drive shaft, always put _____ marks on the drive shaft and the differential flange to aid in reassembly.
9. When removing the drive shafts from an FWD vehicle, it is not advisable to let the brake _____ or the _____ hang free.
10. Since the front suspension is removed during removal of an FWD transaxle, it may be necessary to check the _____ of the front end at completion of the job.
11. After the transmission or transaxle is installed in the vehicle, check that the torque converter will rotate freely to ensure that the converter is not _____ into the pump or pump drive and the flexplate.
12. During installation, the transmission should fit easily up against the engine. Never use _____ to connect the transmission to the engine.
13. A _____ converter housing or other serious problem could result if anything is caught between the converter housing and the engine.
14. After the installation of the transmission or transaxle is complete, check the _____ level after shifting the transmission through its gear ranges.
15. After the installation of the transmission or transaxle is complete, the last step is to _____ _____ the vehicle.

CHAPTER QUIZ

The following questions will help you check the facts you have learned. Select the answer that completes each statement correctly.

1. Student A says that the torque converter is usually left on the engine when removing a transmission. Student B says that it is more difficult to remove a transaxle than a transmission. Who is correct?
   a. Student A
   b. Student B
   c. Both A and B
   d. Neither A nor B
2. Student A says that you should be able to rotate the converter to align the bolt holes with the flexplate after the transmission has been bolted to the engine. Student B says that a transmission overhaul is not complete until it passes a road test. Who is correct?
   a. Student A
   b. Student B
   c. Both A and B
   d. Neither A nor B

3. Student A says that the torque converter should be marked for proper installation. Student B says that the brake hoses are strong enough to support the weight of the calipers. Who is correct?

   a. Student A
   b. Student B
   c. Both A and B
   d. Neither A nor B

4. Student A says that a special fixture is required to support the engine on FWD cars when the transaxle is removed. Student B says that it is easier to remove the transaxle than it is to remove an RWD transmission. Who is correct?

   a. Student A
   b. Student B
   c. Both A and B
   d. Neither A nor B

5. Student A says that it is necessary to shift the transmission through the gears when checking the fluid after installing a transmission. Student B says that the last thing to connect when installing a transmission is the battery ground cable. Who is correct?

   a. Student A
   b. Student B
   c. Both A and B
   d. Neither A nor B

6. Student A says that the transmission alignment dowels are not necessary. Student B says that if the alignment dowels are not installed, a serious vibration or damage could result. Who is correct?

   a. Student A
   b. Student B
   c. Both A and B
   d. Neither A nor B

7. Student A says that the torque converter should be removed with the transmission. Student B says that it is easier to leave the torque converter attached to the engine. Who is correct?

   a. Student A
   b. Student B
   c. Both A and B
   d. Neither A nor B

8. Student A says that when removing the drive shaft on an RWD vehicle, match marks should be made to prevent a vibration after reassembly. Student B says that the front wheel bearings could be damaged if an FWD vehicle is moved while the drive shafts are removed. Who is correct?

   a. Student A
   b. Student B
   c. Both A and B
   d. Neither A nor B

9. Student A says that the axle nuts on an FWD car are reusable. Student B says that the drive shafts on an FWD car are usually removed with a pry bar or special puller. Who is correct?

   a. Student A
   b. Student B
   c. Both A and B
   d. Neither A nor B

10. Student A says that it is necessary to remove the engine cradle in order to remove the transaxle on some FWD vehicles. Student B says that it is permissible to let the FWD drive shaft hang down during removal and installation of the transaxle. Who is correct?

   a. Student A
   b. Student B
   c. Both A and B
   d. Neither A nor B

CHAPTER 16

TRANSMISSION OVERHAUL: DISASSEMBLY AND REASSEMBLY

OBJECTIVES

After studying Chapter 16, the reader should be able to:

1. Describe the automatic transmission overhaul procedures.
2. Perform the automatic transmission disassembly inspection procedure.
3. Properly disassemble and reassemble an automatic transmission.
4. Complete the ASE tasks related to off-vehicle transmission/transaxle repair.

KEY TERMS

Aftermarket (p. 422)
Anticlunk Spring (p. 438)
End Play (p. 430)
Exchange/Used (p. 422)
Rebuild (p. 422)

Remanufactured (p. 422)
Stacked Converter (p. 451)
Teardown (p. 422)
Update (p. 424)

16.1 INTRODUCTION

A badly worn or damaged transmission is removed from the vehicle for repair, and there are essentially four repair choices: (1) repair or replace the worn/damaged component, (2) *overhaul* the transmission, (3) replace the transmission with an **exchange/used,** or (4) install a **remanufactured** transmission. An exchange unit is a used unit usually from a wrecking yard. It is usually sold "as is" or with a very limited guarantee.

When the overhaul is done by a technician working at an automotive repair facility, it will be guaranteed by the shop. If the transmission fails, the shop will be responsible for any needed repairs. As transmissions become more complex and expensive, remanufactured units are gaining in popularity. If these units fail, the remanufacturer is responsible for the repairs. A remanufacturing plant is also better able to update a transmission and make necessary modifications.

16.1.1 Overhauled Transmissions

Most transmission shops are equipped to perform all repairs needed to the vehicle's transmission. Repairing the original transmission ensures that the transmission will be the proper one for the vehicle. The repairs can be for a specific problem such as a noisy gearset, worn band, or leaky front seal. An overhaul implies a **rebuild,** which is generally considered to include the following:

- transmission teardown or disassembly
- replacement of all gaskets and seals
- replacement of all the friction materials
- replacement of worn bushings
- replacement of the filter and modulator
- cleaning and inspection of the planetary gears
- cleaning and inspection of the valve body and all related components
- cleaning and inspection of the torque converter
- reassembly with a check of all necessary clearances

Some states have rules and regulations that define what an automatic transmission rebuild or overhaul must include. The California Bureau of Automotive Repair (BAR) states that a rebuilt, remanufactured, reconditioned, or overhauled transmission must include the following:

- cleaning and inspection of all internal and external parts
- valve body disassembly, cleaning, and inspection
- front and intermediate bands that have been replaced with new or relined units
- replacement of the following parts: lined frictions, internal and external seals, rotating metal sealing rings, gaskets, and organic media filters

- all worn or defective parts repaired or replaced with new, rebuilt, or good parts
- torque converter inspected or replaced with a new or rebuilt unit

16.1.2 Remanufactured Transmissions

An alternative to repairing a vehicle's transmission is to install a remanufactured unit. A remanufactured transmission is a unit that has been disassembled, cleaned, inspected, and reassembled using new or like-new parts. It will have any necessary modifications and updates. These units are commonly used by dealerships to repair transmission problems that occur while a vehicle is still under its new-vehicle or extended warranty.

Remanufacturing is done on a production line, with many transmissions of the same model being rebuilt at the same time. The procedure is essentially the same as that described in this text, except that each worker does a specific task such as **teardown,** clutch assembly, or valve body assembly. Special tools are at each workstation so each worker can do his or her job in a most efficient manner. As each transmission is assembled, the transmission code moves with the unit so it will be built to the proper specifications (Figure 16-1).

Many smaller shops will use remanufactured transmissions when the vehicle's unit is so badly damaged that the cost of the parts comes close to or exceeds the cost of a remanufactured unit. Repairing a transmission in some states means there will be a minimum parts cost to meet the requirements for a "rebuild." Another reason for choosing a remanufactured unit is that the shop lacks the special tools, service information, or expertise to repair that particular transmission.

16.1.3 Transmission Parts

Major transmission components such as the pump, a clutch drum, or a gearset are called *hard parts. Soft parts* are parts that are normally replaced during an overhaul. These include the gaskets, seals, and friction material.

The parts needed to overhaul a transmission are available from various sources (Figure 16-2). The vehicle manufacturer can supply all parts needed to repair or overhaul a transmission. Soft parts can be purchased from **aftermarket** sources (a supplier other than the vehicle manufacturer). These parts are usually available as individual components or as part of a kit. Kits are available in several forms, and the contents of a kit will vary between suppliers (Figure 16-3).

A kit is more convenient and often less expensive than buying individual parts. A variety of kits are available to fit the needs of the particular job. Some of the kits are as follows:

- **Banner Kit:** an overhaul kit plus the friction clutch plates
- **Bearing Kit:** all bearings for the transmission

(a)   (b)

FIGURE 16-1   A remanufacturing assembly line. The valve bodies are moving from left to right as they are being assembled; the computer identifies which parts are to be installed and their location (a). The transmissions also move along an assembly line; each station has a monitor to show the operation, the parts to be installed, and the special tools to install them (b). *(Courtesy of Williams Technologies Inc., Div. of Delco Remy International, Inc.)*

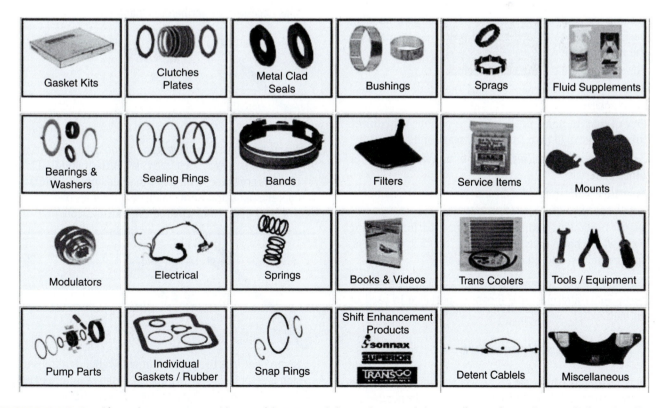

FIGURE 16-2   Aftermarket sources can provide most of the parts needed to repair a transmission as well as supplemental parts and information. *(Courtesy of Slauson Transmission Parts, www.slauson.com)*

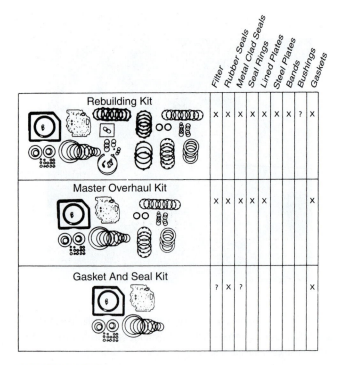

FIGURE 16-3 The soft parts required to rebuild a transmission are available as kits. The contents of a kit will vary with different suppliers.

- **Compliance Kit:** includes all parts that must be replaced as required for a rebuilt transmission in particular states
- **Deluxe or Super Kit:** a master kit plus filter, band(s), bushings, modulator, and bonded pistons as required for the transmission
- **Filter Kit:** the filter and pan gasket
- **Master Kit:** an overhaul kit plus the friction and steel clutch plates
- **Overhaul Kit, sometimes called a paper and rubber kit:** all gaskets, O-rings, metal-clad seals, and lip seals
- **Sealing Ring Kit:** all seals made from Teflon, metal, or other materials
- **Solenoid Kit:** shift, PWM, and force motor solenoids, which may include the wiring harness
- **Valve Body Kit:** additional parts needed for replacing worn valve body parts, can include check balls, filters, springs, valves, and other needed parts

New hard parts are generally available only from the manufacturer. Some aftermarket companies specialize in used or rebuilt hard parts.

16.1.4 Overhaul Procedure

The overhaul procedure varies between transmissions and transaxles. Each vehicle manufacturer has a recommended repair procedure for its transmissions. Service information should always be followed as you overhaul an automatic transmission. Following a service manual makes the job easier and quicker.

It also ensures that important checks and procedures are followed. The repair procedures were developed by experts for that particular transmission. Service information is available in the form of printed manuals, CDs, and on the Internet. Service information can be obtained from vehicle manufacturers and aftermarket automotive publishers (Alldata, Chilton's, Identifix, Mitchell, and Motors). Automatic transmission trade organizations such as the Automatic Transmission Rebuilders Association (ATRA) and the Automatic Transmission Service Group (ATSG) provide service information and advice to their members and partners.

The following procedure can be used as a guide for overhauling an automatic transmission.

To overhaul or rebuild an automatic transmission, you should:

1. Remove the transmission from the vehicle (see Chapter 15).
2. Remove any heavy deposits of dirt and oil residue.
3. Measure of input shaft end play.
4. Disassemble while making any additional end-play checks.
5. Repair subassemblies: pump, valve body, each clutch assembly, each gearset, and the differential in transaxles (described in Chapter 18).
6. Inspect the case and make any needed repair.
7. Replace worn bushings (described in Chapter 17).
8. Reassemble, including air checks, band adjustments, clearance checks, and end-play adjustments.
9. Inspect the torque converter; replace, rebuild, or service as necessary (described in Chapter 19).

Many transmissions have gone through a series of improvements after their original introduction. These changes are made to improve the transmission's durability, reliability, and performance. During an overhaul, it is a good practice to **update** the transmission.

Remember that the technician who rebuilds a transmission is responsible for the quality of the rebuild. There is no valid excuse for incomplete repairs. As the transmission is assembled, each new or used part should be thoroughly checked to ensure that it will operate correctly.

FIGURE 16-4   These special tools are used when rebuilding a THM 350. *(Courtesy of ATEC Trans-Tool and Cleaning Systems)*

16.2 TRANSMISSION DISASSEMBLY

The disassembly procedure for a transmission varies between makes and models. Special tooling or procedures are often required (Figure 16-4). It is always recommended to consult service information during disassembly. The descriptions given here cover the commonly used procedures and equipment. The disassembly procedure is known as a teardown.

16.2.1 Predisassembly Cleanup

Cleanliness is a must during a transmission overhaul. Many shops steam clean or pressure wash the outside of the transmission as soon as it is removed from the vehicle (Figure 16-5). Precleaning removes all exterior dirt and other debris and helps keep the work area clean. An alternate cleanup method is to use solvent or an engine degreaser with a parts-cleaning brush and scraper. Always dispose of hazardous waste following the appropriate disposal procedures and requirements.

FIGURE 16-5   This transmission is being cleaned using a hot, high-pressure washer. A thorough cleaning makes it easier to locate and remove bolts and retaining rings and keeps the work area cleaner.

TECH TIP

A clean work area is a must, and intrusion of dirt from outside the transmission can cause a misdiagnosis of the problem. This can result in an incomplete repair. It can also cause plugging of small passages and change precision measurements, leading to an early failure.

After the transmission is disassembled, the individual parts can be cleaned using an approved solvent. For many years technicians used petroleum-based solvent. This solvent type evaporates, releasing harmful hydrocarbons into the atmosphere. These vapors contribute to air-quality problems. The use of cleaning solvent is controlled in areas with serious air-quality problems. In the Los Angeles area, shops are required to use nonpetroleum solvents for parts cleaning. Read the material safety data sheets (MSDS) to learn about any personal health problems and special handling requirements for the cleaning agent being used.

16.2.2 Torque Converter Removal

The converter is removed from the vehicle with the transmission. It is then removed from the transmission by sliding it out the front of the transmission. Be ready to support its weight because converters are full of fluid and tend to be heavy. Tilt the converter, front downward, as it is removed to reduce the fluid spill. The converter should be either set aside for cleaning and inspection or sent out for rebuilding. Torque converter service is described in Chapter 19. Some transmissions use a turbine shaft O-ring seal, which should be removed at this time.

16.2.3 Disassembly Fixtures

Automatic transmission disassembly can be fairly messy. Fluid drains out as each hydraulic component is removed or disassembled. Many shops use a teardown bench that has a steel top designed to catch the fluid and drain it into a catch pan. During disassembly, the transmission is placed on the bench and torn down. It is usually placed upside down and rolled over as needed. Some shops use transmission holding fixtures during overheal (Figure 16-6). Holding fixtures allow the unit to be easily rotated to the best working position, which makes the work faster and easier. When using a holding fixture, a drain pan should be placed under the transmission to catch the dripping fluid.

TECH TIP

Some shops use a simple fixture that resembles a three-legged stool; other shops simply use an old transmission case in a rear-side-up position (Figure 16-7).

(a)   (b)

FIGURE 16-6   A transmission-holding fixture (arrows) has been mounted onto this transmission. It will allow the transmission to be rotated to the best working position. The round stem at the left will be slid into a bench fixture.

| (a) | (b) | (c) |

FIGURE 16-7 This simple, shop-made stool (a) has a hole for the transmission output shaft (b). The output shaft of this transmission being repaired has been placed through the rear opening of an empty case (c). Caution should be exercised if using either support method. Because of the narrow bases, they can tip over.

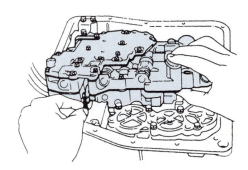

FIGURE 16-8 The valve body can be removed after the pan. Some valve bodies have a throttle cable or fluid tubes that need to be disconnected.

16.3 PRELIMINARY DISASSEMBLY

The first teardown step is to remove the oil pan, filter, and valve body. Many technicians use the oil pan to store the retaining rings, screws, bolts, and other small parts removed during disassembly. The procedure is to remove the pan, inspect the debris (if it has not been done already), wash the pan in solvent, and air dry it (see Figure 14-25). Next, the filter and gasket are removed and set aside for comparison with the new filter. The valve body is then removed and set aside for cleaning and inspection (Figure 16-8).

Watch for check balls as the valve body is removed, and note their location. Save the valve body gasket (if used) so

TECH TIP

Many experienced technicians prefer to use hand tools during disassembly. Hand tools enable the technician to feel how tight the bolts were as they are loosened. An air wrench is much faster, but it is very difficult to feel bolt tension. Improperly tightened bolts could have been the cause of the transmission's failure. Using hand tools takes a little longer to complete the repair, but it is an important technique to ensure a thorough, high-quality rebuild.

TECH TIP

Valve body bolts are often different lengths. Either identify where they belong or leave them in the valve body holes after they are loosened.

TECH TIP

It is recommended to make a simple wiring diagram for electronic transmissions showing the necessary connections needed during assembly.

TECH TIP

When prying a tube out of the case, place a piece of wood on the case to prevent damaging the case.

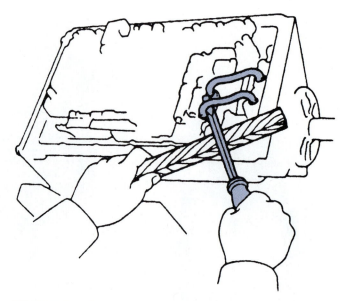

FIGURE 16-9 Oil tubs/pipes are removed by gently prying upward. Note the block of wood to protect the case. *(Courtesy of Toyota Motor Sales USA, Inc.)*

it can be compared with the replacement gasket. Remove any check balls and screens under the valve body.

Some transmissions use steel tubes to transfer a fluid passage from one location to another. These tubes normally use an O-ring to seal each end and are held in place by a retaining bracket (Figure 16-9). The tubes will often lift out after the retaining bolt is removed; sometimes it is necessary to pry them out. If a tube does not come loose, check the service information. Some tubes are secured using epoxy and will be damaged if removed.

The valve body of some transmissions can serve as the cover for the accumulator or servo piston(s). Note the position of the piston(s) and spring (if used), and remove them (Figure 16-10). In other transmissions, a separate cover is used for the accumulator or servo. Each accumulator has its own spring and piston configuration. They may look alike, but there are slight differences. Improper assembly will cause shift timing and quality problems.

Retaining rings are used to hold many parts in the proper position. One style is like a standard snap ring; another looks like a round wire. A handy tool for removing the first style is a thin screwdriver or scribe, which is commonly called a seal pick (Figure 16-11). The second style of ring may have a hole that allows a pin punch to be used to start ring removal (Figure 16-12). Use caution during servo cover removal because some servos use a strong piston spring. These require a

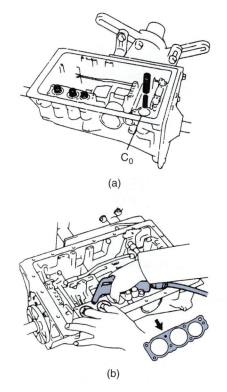

FIGURE 16-10 This transmission has four accumulators under the valve body (a). Note the differences in the springs and pistons and remove them. Compressed air can be used to lift the piston out of its bore (b).

REAL WORLD FIX

The 1992 Lincoln Town Car (96,000 miles) had no reverse and the fluid was badly burned. Severe wear became evident during disassembly, so the transmission was rebuilt using many new parts. But when the unit was reinstalled in the car, it had no O/D, delayed reverse engagement, and low pressure (less than 50 psi). There were no DTCs, and the EPC solenoid checked out okay on the bench. The transmission was torn down and reinspected. No problems were found. The EPC solenoid was replaced, but this did not help.

Fix. Some advice led to a more careful inspection that revealed the 1–2 and 3–4 servo covers had been installed on the wrong bores. The 3–4 cover has a hole in it that caused an internal leak. Replacement of the 1–2 accumulator seals and swapping the covers to the proper place fixed this problem.

REAL WORLD FIX

The 1992 Plymouth Voyager van (80,000 miles) with an A604 transaxle was rebuilt because the overdrive clutch pack was slipping, and the clutch plates were badly burned. When the unit was reinstalled, it had a ratcheting-type noise, almost a buzz, while operating in forward gears. The proper Chrysler –7176 fluid was used. The solenoid pack was replaced, but this did not help.

Fix. On advice from other technicians, the valve body was removed, and the accumulators were checked. They were installed upside down. Correct positioning of the pistons and springs eliminated the noise problem.

ACCUMULATOR

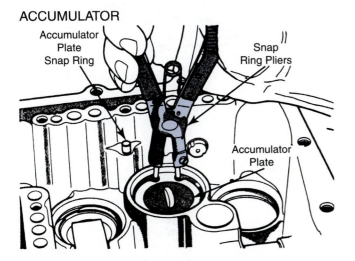

FIGURE 16-11 This accumulator cover retaining ring is being removed using a pair of snap ring pliers. Some can be pried out of the groove and bore using a small screwdriver or seal pick. *(Courtesy of Chrysler Corporation)*

TECH TIP

SPECIAL NOTES ON RETAINING RINGS

A retaining ring is commonly used to hold a part in place. It can hold a gear in position on a shaft or a servo cover in a bore. There is a variety of retaining rings; some examples are shown in Figure 16-14. All types come in different sizes as required to fit the shaft or bore diameter.

The two types of retaining rings are external and internal. External rings fit over a shaft and need to be expanded for removal or installation. Internal rings fit into a bore and are contracted or compressed for removal or installation. Many retaining rings can be removed by prying them free with a tool such as a scribe, seal pick, or screwdriver. Snap ring pliers are often used to remove and install retaining rings; specially designed snap ring pliers are sometimes required for snap rings that are hard to remove. The correct type and size of snap ring pliers must be used (Figure 16-15). Once removed, it is recommended that the retaining ring be replaced with a new one.

special tool to hold the spring compressed during retainer ring removal and then allow the spring to be safely extended (Figure 16-13).

On transmissions with gear-driven governors, remove the governor cover and governor.

16.3.1 End-Play Check

It is standard practice to measure the input shaft **end play** before removing the pump. End play is the in-and-out movement of the shaft (Figure 16-16). If there is no end play, there will be drag and a possible bind. Too much end play allows misalignment and damage from the excess movement. If the end play is correct, the internal thrust washers are probably in good shape. If the end play is excessive, there is internal wear, which must be corrected during the rebuild.

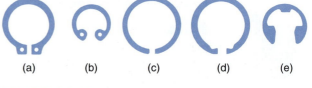

FIGURE 16-14 The most common styles of retaining rings are external, pin type (a), internal pin type (b), plain external (c), plain internal (d), and E-clip (e).

FIGURE 16-12 The punch is passing through a hole in the case to push the retaining ring out of the groove. This allows a seal pick or small screwdriver to pry the retaining ring out.

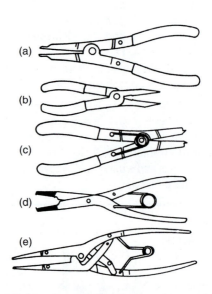

FIGURE 16-15 Snap ring pliers for external pin type (a), internal pin type (b), and three different styles for plain external snap rings (c–e). The bottom pliers have jaws that open in a parallel action. *(Courtesy of Snap-On Tools)*

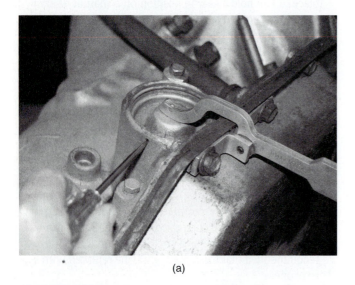

(a)

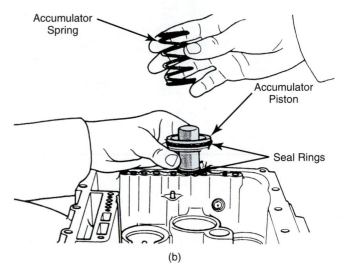

(b)

FIGURE 16-13 This accumulator plate/cover is retained by a retaining ring, and the accumulator spring is pushing upward on the cover (a). With the cover removed, the piston and spring can be removed (b). *(Courtesy of Chrysler Corporation)*

End play is normally measured using a dial indicator.

To measure input shaft end play, you should do the following:

1. Place the transmission in a vertical position with the input shaft pointing up. Some transmissions require that a special fixture be used to hold the output shaft in during end-play checks.
2. Attach a dial indicator onto the case or front pump, and position the measuring stylus against the end of the input shaft (Figure 16-17). Some units require special tools to lift the turbine shaft and/or to properly position the dial indicator (Figure 16-18).

TECH TIP

The measuring stylus must be parallel to the input shaft. The indicator body should be adjusted to load the stylus about one full needle rotation (Figure 16-19).

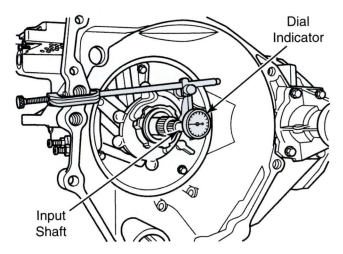

FIGURE 16-16   Input shaft end play is an important check for internal wear in a transmission. Note that a more accurate check is made if the input shaft is vertical. *(Courtesy of Chrysler Corporation)*

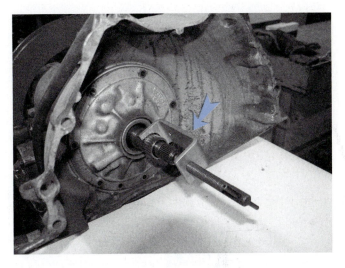

FIGURE 16-18   This special tool is used to pull the pump. It can also be attached to the input shaft to allow the shaft to be lifted so end play can be measured.

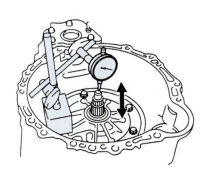

FIGURE 16-17   The dial indicator can be attached to the transmission case or pump (left) or to the input shaft (right). Moving the input shaft will show the end play on the indicator dial.

3. Pull the input shaft upward slightly and then push it inward as far as it will go. Now adjust the indicator to read zero.
4. On most transmissions, pull up on the input shaft and read the movement on the dial indicator. This is the amount of input shaft end play.
5. Repeat steps 3 and 4 until you get consistent, reliable readings. Then make three more measurements and, if there is a slight difference, average them.
6. Record your reading and compare it to the specification.

Some manufacturers specify gear train end-play checks at the output shaft or other locations (Figure 16-20).

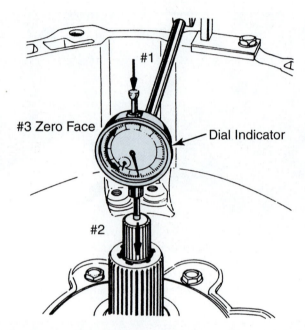

FIGURE 16-19   A dial indicator should be set up with the indicator stem parallel to the input shaft and the stem is loaded about one revolution of the indicator dial (1). Next, move the input shaft completely into the transmission (2), and rotate the dial to zero the needle (3). When the input shaft is lifted, the amount of end play can be read on the indicator dial.

TECH TIP

On some transmissions, the input shaft is not attached and can be easily pulled out of the transmission. On these units, end play is checked by measuring the distance from the end of the stator support to the end of the turbine shaft. End play on some of these units can be measured by prying upward on the gear train.

Some transmissions require additional end-play checks. This helps locate excessive wear in specific areas or to determine if the correct selective thrust washers or spacers are being used. For example, a transmission with a center support should have end play on each side of the center support. Manufacturers will specify end-play checks between various components of the gear train. *Selective* washers or snap rings are produced in various sizes (Figure 16-21). This lets the technician select the proper size thrust washer for the best end play or clearance.

16.3.2 Other Predisassembly Checks

Depending on the transmission design, other checks should be done before disassembly. An example is the 2–4 band apply pin check for a GM 4L60E. This check requires a special tool that is attached to the transmission case and operated using a torque wrench. This check determines if the intermediate-band apply

TECH TIP

To find the average measurement, add the three measurements and divide the result by 3. For example, if the measurements were 0.018, 0.020, and 0.019, add the three measurements (0.057), and divide by 3 for an average measurement of 0.019 in.

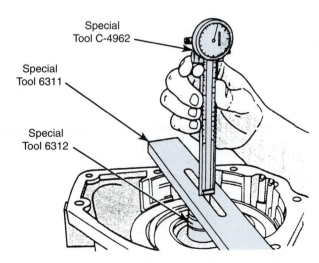

FIGURE 16-20   These special tools allow measuring gear train end play so that it can be properly adjusted. *(Courtesy of Chrysler Corporation)*

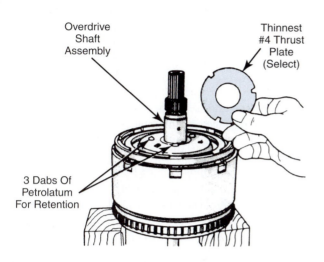

SHIM THICKNESS		PART NUMBER
mm	inch	
0.93-1.00	.037-.039	4431662
1.15-1.22	.045-.048	4431663
1.37-1.44	.054-.057	4431664
1.59-1.66	.063-.066	4431665
1.81-1.88	.071-.074	4431666
2.03-2.10	.080-.083	4431667
2.25-2.32	.089-.091	4431668
2.47-2.54	.097-.100	4431669
2.69-2.76	.106-.109	4446670
2.91-2.98	.114-.117	4446671
3.13-3.20	.123-.126	4446672
3.35-3.42	.132-.135	4446601

FIGURE 16-21   This transmission uses 12 different selective thrust plates for the No. 4 position. The proper thrust plate is selected to adjust the input shaft end play. *(Courtesy of Chrysler Corporation)*

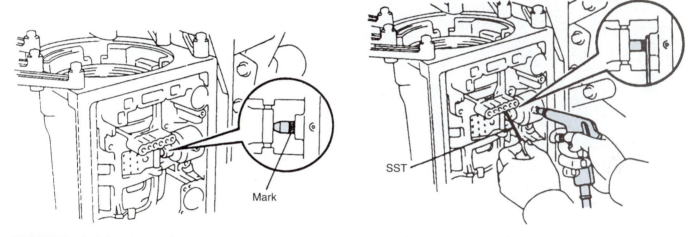

FIGURE 16-22   This special tool is used to measure the servo piston rod stroke as the servo is applied. A different piston rod can be installed if needed. *(Courtesy of Toyota Motor Sales USA, Inc.)*

TECH TIP

Some transaxles using tapered roller bearings will have no input shaft end play. Transmission end-play specifications will vary and be as little as 0.004 in. (0.102 mm) and as much as 0.91 in.(2.31 mm).

pin is the correct length for the band. If the check indicates that the apply pin is correct, there is probably not much band wear. If the check indicates the apply pin is too short, either the pin,

band, or both will need to be replaced during the overhaul (Figure 16-22).

16.4 PUMP REMOVAL

The pump assembly is the front cover that holds the gear train inside the case on RWD transmissions. Its removal allows the disassembly of the rest of the internal parts. The pump is held in place by a set of bolts. The close fit between the outer pump diameter and the case plus a rubber sealing ring and/or gasket makes pump removal a little difficult. Several methods can be used to remove the pump. These include slide hammers, special screw-type pullers, and prying on the gear train. Using slide hammers or prying the gear train is sometimes limited by transmission design.

To pull a pump using slide hammers, you should do the following:

1. Remove the pump-retaining bolts.
2. Check the pump body bolt holes for threads (Figure 16-23). These threads are one size larger than the pump-retaining bolts. Only two of the holes are threaded and they are on opposite sides of the pump.
3. Thread the slide hammer bolts into the two threaded holes (Figure 16-24). Adapters are available for different thread sizes.
4. Using the slide hammers along with a lifting action, remove the pump assembly.

One manufacturer makes a special tool that threads into these holes, and turning a center screw/bolt lifts the pump assembly (Figure 16-25).

To pull a pump using a screw-type puller, you should do the following:

1. Check the end of the input shaft for a check valve that can be damaged by the puller screw. If one is found, a protection device must be positioned between the puller and the end of the shaft.
2. Remove the pump-retaining bolts.
3. Attach the puller to the stator support shaft. Some pullers slide over the unsplined part of the shaft; others clamp onto the shaft (Figure 16-26).
4. Tighten the puller screw to pull the pump assembly.

FIGURE 16-23 This section of a front pump shows a hole that has internal threads to accept a slide hammer.

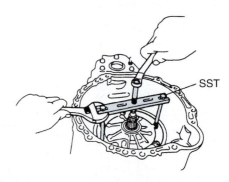

FIGURE 16-25 This special service tool is attached to the front pump. Turning the center bolt will push against the input shaft to lift the pump from the transmission.

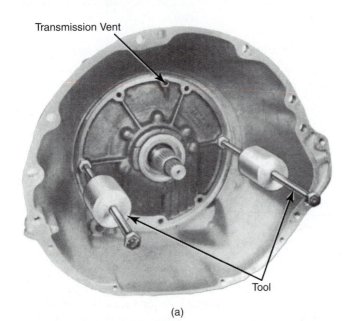

(a)

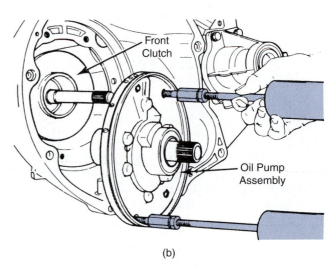

(b)

FIGURE 16-24 A pair of slide hammers has been threaded into the pump assembly (a). After the pump has pulled free, the tools are used to lift the pump out of the transmission (b). *(Courtesy of Chrysler Corporation)*

To pull a pump by prying, you should:

1. Lay the transmission upside down on the bench.
2. Remove the pump-retaining bolts.

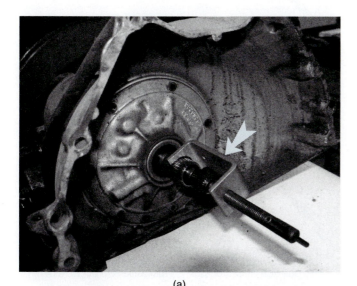

(a)

(b)

FIGURE 16-26   Tool J24773-A is connected to the front pump, turning the center bolt will lift the pump (a). A similar tool is attached to this pump (b). An aftermarket tool will serve the same purpose on a variety of pumps; note the valve protector (arrow) to prevent damage to the check valve at the end of some input shafts.

3. Place a large screwdriver between the sun gear input shell and the reaction carrier, and pry the input shell forward to remove the pump.

16.4.1 Transaxles Using Input Chain Drive

Some transaxles use a chain and sprockets for gear train input. The main gear train is behind the valve body; case cover, channel plate, or chain cover; and drive chain and sprockets (Figure 16-27). Removal of these parts provides access to the driven sprocket support, which supports the input end of the gear train.

The drive chain and sprockets are exposed after the valve body and case cover/channel plate assembly have been

TECH TIP

Occasionally, a badly worn or burnt transmission will have a seized pump or gear train. These can usually be disassembled by placing two wood blocks on the floor, lifting the transmission several feet, and dropping it front downward, onto the blocks. These units often have internal damage that is beyond repair so there is not much loss if they are damaged during disassembly.

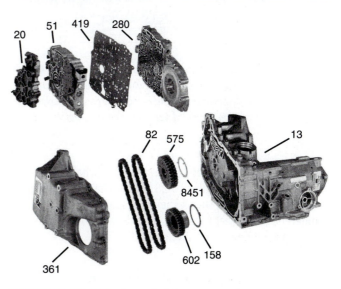

FIGURE 16-27   Removal of the upper pan/chain cover (361), valve body and pump (419 and 320), and the channel plate (280) allows access to the sprockets (575 and 602) and drive chain (82) along with the other parts of the gear train. *(Courtesy of Slauson Transmission Parts, www.slauson.com)*

FIGURE 16-28 Drive chain and sprocket wear is normally checked by moving the chain inward and outward. Excess movement indicates excessive wear. *(Courtesy of BergWarner, Morse TEC)*

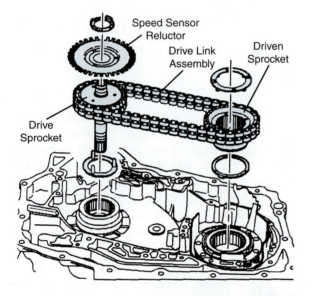

FIGURE 16-29 The drive chain and the sprockets can be lifted off the case. Note the position of the master link, where the thrust washers are, and how they fit onto the sprockets as you remove them. They must be replaced correctly in this same position. *(Reprinted with permission of General Motors)*

removed. It is recommended to check for chain wear/link stretch at this time (Figure 16-28). If the chain has stretched, it should be replaced. Locate the chain's master link; it may be a different color. After noting which side is up or down, lift the chain and sprockets from the transaxle (Figure 16-29).

16.5 MAJOR DISASSEMBLY

A service manual should be followed for the disassembly procedure. Some transmissions almost fall apart after the pump is removed; others come apart one piece at a time.

TECH TIP

The case cover will probably be stuck onto the case by the gasket. A sideways blow from a soft hammer should break it loose.

TECH TIP

If the chain is replaced with the master link in the opposite position, it can be noisy. This noise will occur whenever the engine is running, even in park and neutral.

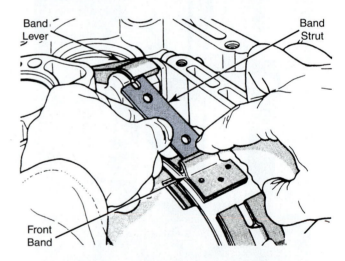

FIGURE 16-30 Removal of the band strut frees this band so it can slide out of the case. *(Courtesy of Chrysler Corporation)*

To complete transmission disassembly, you should:

1. To remove a band, carefully note the position of the band struts, loosen the band adjusting screw, and remove the servo cover and piston. Remove the band struts and band (Figure 16-30).

   On transmissions using a clutch mounted next to the pump, remove the clutch friction, steel, and pressure plates. Be sure to note the position of the various clutch plates.
2. Remove the driving clutch assemblies (Figure 16-31).

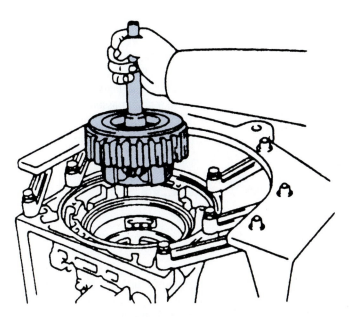

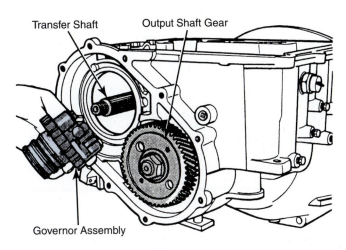

Transfer Shaft Output Shaft Gear

Governor Assembly

This governor assembly is being removed from the transfer shaft of this transaxle. *(Courtesy of Chrysler Corporation)*

FIGURE 16-31 This input shaft and clutch hub with planetary gears is lifted out of the case. *(Courtesy of Toyota Motor Sales USA, Inc.)*

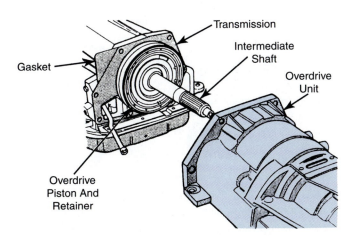

Transmission

Intermediate Shaft

Overdrive Unit

Gasket

Overdrive Piston And Retainer

FIGURE 16-32 Removal of the retaining bolts allows the extension housing and overdrive unit to be removed from this 42RH transmission. *(Courtesy of Chrysler Corporation)*

3. Remove the bolts retaining the extension housing. It may be necessary to remove a snap ring and remove the extension housing (Figure 16-32).
4. Remove the governor and its support on transmissions with shaft-mounted governors (Figure 16-33).
5. The planetary gear train can be slid out of the case as one assembly on some transmissions (Figure 16-34).

   On other transmissions, remove the retaining rings to disassemble the gear train; a seal pick or snap ring pliers are used. Note exactly where each retaining ring is located. As each part of the gear train is removed, note if a thrust washer is used and how it is positioned

TECH TIP

Many transmissions use a drive shell that is connected to a clutch through a set of lugs, and a wear pattern will be established between them. On reassembly, it is important to assemble them in the original position. During disassembly, it is a good practice to place index marks on both parts (Figure 16-36). Some technicians use a permanent felt marker or a small die grinder to make index marks on the parts.

TECH TIP

A special screwdriver-like tool is available to remove large snap rings. Some technicians modify a large screwdriver, as shown in Figure 16-37b, to remove large snap rings.

(Figure 16-35). The condition of each part should be checked as it is removed. Keep a list of the parts that need to be replaced.

6. If the transmission uses a center support, remove the retainer, usually a large snap ring, and lift the center support

TECH TIP

Pay attention to one-way clutch assemblies as you remove them. Note the free-wheel and lock-up directions, and record this for use when you assemble the unit.

out of the case. The low-reverse clutch assembly in some transmissions is the center support. A special tool may be required to remove the center support. In some cases, lifting the output shaft will push the center support and the rest of the gear train from the case (Figure 16-37).

7. On transmissions that use a clutch assembly in the end of the case, remove the retaining ring, pressure plate,

TECH TIP

Some center supports use an **anticlunk spring** that loads them in a counterclockwise direction (Figure 16-38). Look for this spring and how it is positioned before removing the center support.

(a)

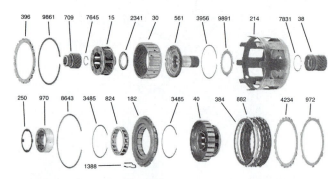

FIGURE 16-35   Parts 7376, 2341, 9891, and 250 are thrust washers that keep parts properly separated. Parts 9861, 7645, 3956, 7831, 8643, and 3485 are retaining rings that hold components in the proper position. *(Courtesy of Slauson Transmission Parts, www.slauson.com)*

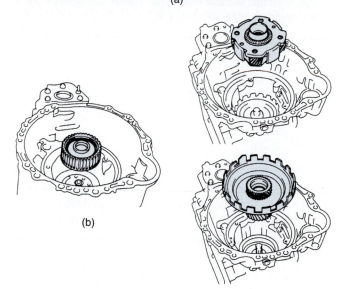

(b)

FIGURE 16-34   The entire gear train of some transmissions is removed as an assembly (a). The gear train of other transmissions is removed one section at a time (b).

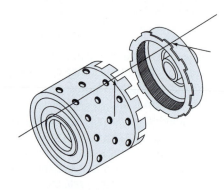

FIGURE 16-36   It is a good practice to place index marks on the driving lugs (arrows) so the direct clutch shell and the low/intermediate ring gear can be assembled in the original position.

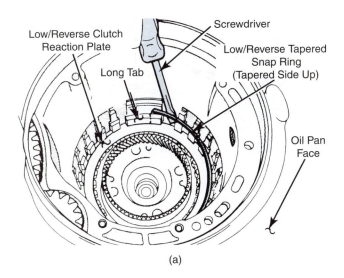

Low/Reverse Clutch
Reaction Plate

Screwdriver

Long Tab

Low/Reverse Tapered
Snap Ring
(Tapered Side Up)

Oil Pan
Face

(a)

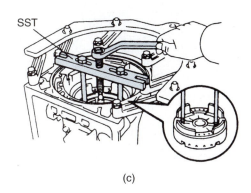

SST

(c)

(b)

FIGURE 16-37   Like a center support, this clutch pack is retained by a large retaining ring (a). A large screwdriver can be modified to hook the retaining ring for quick and easy removal (b). The special tool is being used to lift the overdrive support assembly (c). *(a is courtesy of Chrysler Corporation)*

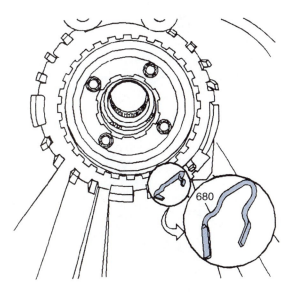

680

FIGURE 16-38   The low/reverse support/anticlunk spring (680) is removed with the low/reverse support. *(Reprinted with permission of General Motors)*

and clutch plates (Figure 16-39). Note the position of each of these parts and if a wave or Belleville plate is used. To remove the retaining ring, a spring compressor is required to compress the piston return springs. Remove the retaining ring, return springs, and clutch piston. The piston can be removed by blowing air into the apply passage (Figure 16-40).

**SAFETY
TIP**

When using a spring compressor, compress the springs just enough to allow the snap ring to be removed. Be careful that the compressor is positioned correctly so it will not slip, allowing the springs to fly out. Make sure there is enough travel to allow the springs to extend completely, and watch to ensure that the retainer does not catch on the snap ring groove during removal (Figure 16-41).

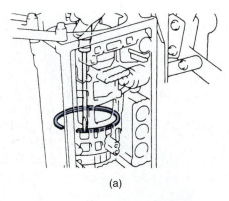

(a)

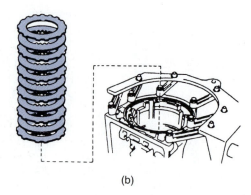

(b)

FIGURE 16-39 The retaining ring (a) locates the clutch pack in the rear of this case (b).

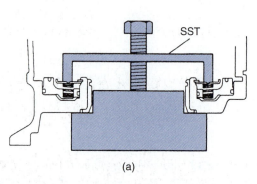

(a)

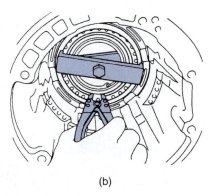

(b)

FIGURE 16-40 The special tool is used to compress the clutch piston return springs (a) so the retaining ring can be removed (b).

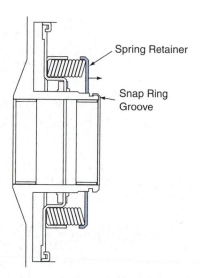

FIGURE 16-41 With the retaining ring removed, slowly release the spring compressor; make sure that the spring retainer does not catch on the snap ring groove.

8. As the park gear is removed, the gear and park pawl should be inspected for wear and damage. Also, the pawl return spring should be checked to ensure that the park pawl is moved completely away from the gear when released (Figure 16-42).

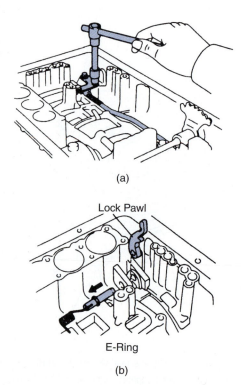

(a)

(b)

FIGURE 16-42 Removal of the bracket allows the park rod to be removed (a). Then the park/lock pawl and shaft can be removed (b).

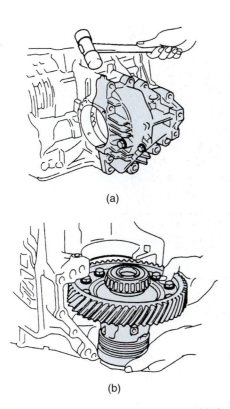

(a)

(b)

FIGURE 16-43   After removing the carrier cover (a), the differential case can be removed from this transaxle (b).

9. On RWD transmissions, remove any remaining parts as required by the manufacturer's instructions. On transaxles, remove the final drive gears and differential plus any other remaining parts (Figure 16-43).

16.6 TRANSMISSION ASSEMBLY

The reassembly procedure for an automatic transmission varies depending on the make and model of the transmission. A service manual should be followed to make sure the parts are assembled in the right order and position and that important checks and adjustments are not skipped (Figures 16-44 and 16-45).

Reassembly begins with a case and subassemblies that are thoroughly clean and reconditioned as necessary. All parts should be thoroughly air dried. Do not dry them with cloth or paper towels, as the lint from the towels can plug filter screens. As the parts are assembled into the case, the bushings and shaft surfaces should be lubricated with transmission assembly lubricant, petroleum jelly, or ATF (Figure 16-46).

Thrust washers are used to separate most of the internal components, and most thrust washers interlock with one of the components next to it (Figure 16-47). It is especially important to hold thrust washers and Torrington bearings in

REAL WORLD FIX

The 1993 Taurus transaxle (AXODE) has been overhauled because of a destroyed planetary gearset. A new gearset, clutches, seals, converter, and solenoids were installed and the valve body was cleaned and inspected. Now there is a flare on the 1–2 shift and, occasionally, a harsh 2–1 shift.

Fix. Reinspection of the valve body did not reveal any problems, but rechecking the low/intermediate band pin length showed that it was slightly bent and 0.004 in. too short. Installation of the correct band pin fixed this problem.

TECH TIP

A transmission should always be assembled with wet bearings and wet clutches. The bearings should be lubricated with assembly lube, petroleum jelly, or ATF. The clutches should be presoaked in ATF for at least 15 minutes.

TECH TIP

The lubrication passages should be checked before transmission reassembly. Blow air into the cooler return port; you should be able to hear or feel air escaping from the bushings connected to this port.

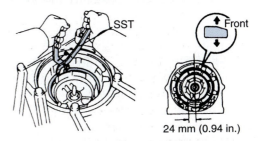

24 mm (0.94 in.)

FIGURE 16-44   This retaining ring locates the overdrive support assembly; note how the tapered side is positioned toward the front of the case.

REAL WORLD FIX

The 4T80-E, 1995 Cadillac was rebuilt because of slippage. On a road test, a definite bump was noticed as soon as the accelerator was depressed, and this occurred in all ranges. Fluid pressures were normal.

Fix. On close inspection, with the transmission partially disassembled and the chain cover removed, it was found that the wrong driven sprocket support seal gasket was installed. Installation of the proper gasket fixed the problem.

FIGURE 16-46   Transmission assembly lubricant or petroleum jelly can be used to lubricate parts and hold them in the proper position.

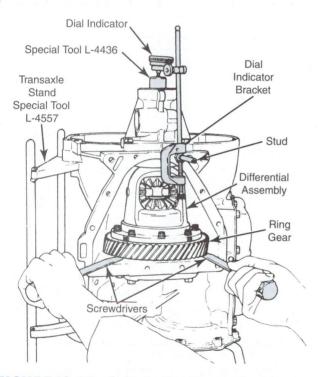

FIGURE 16-45   Checking the differential or gear train end play ensures that the thrust washers have the proper clearance. Note that some transmissions require a special tool to lift the gear train. *(Courtesy of Chrysler Corporation)*

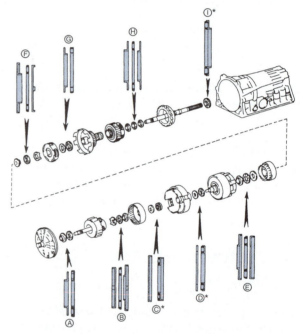

FIGURE 16-47   Thrust bearings and their races must be assembled correctly.

position with either assembly lubricant or petroleum jelly. These parts can easily slip out of position. Ordinary grease should not be used for this because it will not mix with ATF, might stay in a lump, and could possibly clog an orifice. Grease can also change the friction characteristics of the transmission fluid.

Transmission reassembly usually follows a procedure that is essentially a reverse of the disassembly. The last part out is the first part installed. A wise technician takes extra steps to ensure that each part will work properly. The following are some examples:

- The gear train should rotate freely unless there is an intended holding member.
- When a holding one-way clutch is installed, the gear train should turn freely in the direction of output shaft rotation but lock up in the opposite direction.
- When a driving one-way clutch is installed, power should be able to pass through it in the direction of output shaft rotation but the driven part should be able to overrun.

- Each clutch pack or band should have the correct clearance.
- Each clutch and band should operate properly when air checked.
- Every section of the gear train should have the correct end play.
- All tapered roller bearing sets should be adjusted to the proper preload or end play.
- All bolts are tightened to the correct torque.
- The group of bolts securing some parts should be tightened using the proper order.

On some transaxles, an end-play check should be made as the final drive and differential are installed. On other transmissions the differential and transfer shaft bearings must be adjusted to the correct preload. These operations are described in the appropriate service manual. Transaxles using spiral bevel or hypoid ring and pinion gears require adjustment to ensure proper mesh and bearing preload. An additional adjustment is usually required for the input and output bearings for these two gears (Figure 16-48).

16.6.1 Pump Installation and End-Play Adjustment

The final assembly point of many gear trains is the pump. A new pump gasket must be used. Many technicians use two guide pins to hold the gasket in place and align the pump as it

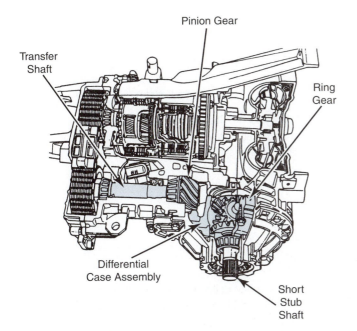

FIGURE 16-48 This transaxle uses a hypoid ring and pinion gearset that requires additional adjustment as it is assembled. *(Courtesy of Chrysler Corporation)*

Transfer Shaft

Pinion Gear

Ring Gear

Differential Case Assembly

Short Stub Shaft

REAL WORLD FIX

The 1994 Chevrolet K2500 pickup (134,000 km) transmission was rebuilt because clutch material was found in the pan while diagnosing a shift problem. The 1–2, 2–3 shift solenoids and pressure control solenoid were also replaced. The vehicle came back with the same shift problem. When the pan was removed, clutch material was found.

Fix. Following advice, the technician checked the rear servo and accumulator and found a hairline crack in the accumulator piston. Replacement of the accumulator piston and new clutch plates fixed this vehicle.

TECH TIP

As a one-way clutch is assembled, it should be checked to make sure it freewheels in one direction and locks in the other. In most transmissions, a holding one-way clutch freewheels in a clockwise direction (same direction as output shaft rotation in forward gears; Figure 16-49). A one-way clutch driven by a friction clutch will normally lock up to drive in a clockwise direction. In some transmissions, the freewheel direction of a one-way clutch is hard to remember, but a service manual often shows how to check it.

TECH TIP

A one-way roller clutch also can be assembled improperly. The accordion spring should preload the rollers in the lock-up direction, and, if possible, place the spring so it will tend to move away from freewheeling race (Figure 16-50).

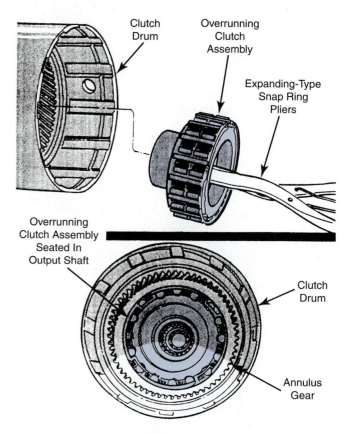

The 1997 Chevrolet Tahoe (78,000 miles) transmission was repaired because of a faulty sun gear shell. It worked well for 2 months/2,000 miles, and problems of delayed 2–3 and 3–4 shifts and erratic speedometer operation began suddenly. A check reveals no DTCs.

Fix. Following advice, the technician removed the VSS and checked the sensor drive gear. It was in the wrong location, and it was discovered that the output shaft could be moved back and forth. The transmission was removed and disassembled, and the snap ring that secures the reaction carrier to the output shaft had fallen out of its groove. Reassembly of this transmission using a new snap ring fixed this problem.

FIGURE 16-49 This overrunning clutch assembly with the inner cam, rollers, and springs should be installed into the clutch drum using a counterclockwise rotating motion. *(Courtesy of Chrysler Corporation)*

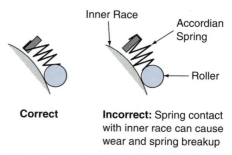

FIGURE 16-50 The accordian spring in some one-way clutches can be installed in a direction so that it will rub against the inner race. This can cause wear and breaking of the spring.

TECH TIP

If one of the ends of a band is noticeably stronger than the other, the strongest end is usually placed at the anchor.

TECH TIP

As a gearset is assembled, each part should turn freely without binding (except for one-way clutches in one direction). It is often possible to make the gearset produce each of its gear ratios by turning the input/turbine shaft and holding the correct reaction member. In many cases, you will need to apply one or more clutches with air pressure.

TECH TIP

Remember to install any required preload device, such as an anticlunk spring, in the proper position, as a center support is installed. Usually a clearance or end-play check is required to ensure that the gear train captured by the center support is free to operate and has the proper clearance.

A center support with a clutch piston must have a fluid passage between it and the case. This passage is often sealed with a special seal that is installed after the center support is installed (Figure 16-51).

As a clutch is assembled, it can be air checked by applying air pressure into the apply passage (Figure 16-53). The clutch should apply without excess leakage and release with clearance at the plates.

A clutch should be stacked with the plates in the proper order and position. There should also be the proper clearance in the clutch stack (Figure 16-52).

Some clutch assemblies are a little difficult to install because of the close fit of the plates over the hub. Swinging the clutch in a kind of spiral direction (as described in Figure 16-54) will work the plates over the hub.

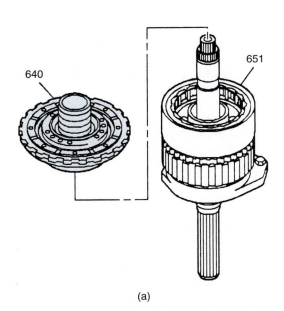

(a)

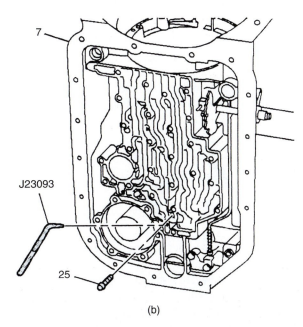

(b)

FIGURE 16-51   After this center support (640) with the rear gear assembly (651) is installed (a), it must be positioned properly using tool J23093 before the retaining bolt (25) is installed (b). On some transmissions, a tube seal should be installed as shown to prevent fluid leaks in the center support and its clutch. *(Reprinted with permission of General Motors)*

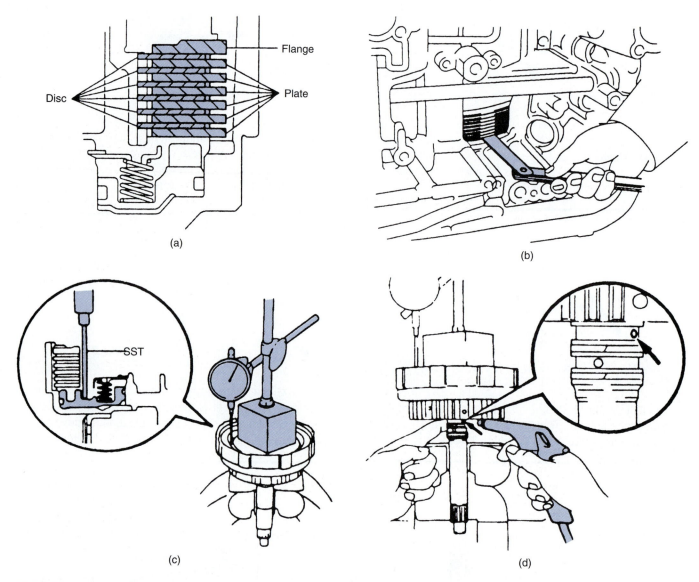

FIGURE 16-52   With the clutch stack correctly installed (a), the pack clearance can be measured using a feeler gauge (b) or a dial indicator (c). Applying the clutch with air allows the piston travel/pack clearance to be measured (d). *(Courtesy of Toyota Motor Sales USA, Inc.)*

TECH TIP

Another problem when installing clutches is weight—one forward clutch assembly weighs about 50 lb (110 kg)—and they are not easy to grasp as you lower them into the case. Special tools are available to provide a way to handle these components.

TECH TIP

You can determine if a clutch is completely installed by measuring its position in the transmission case (Figure 16-55). Another method is to lift the clutch straight up, about 1/4 in. (6 mm), and then drop it. A solid "thunk" indicates the clutch is dropping onto its thrust washer, which is good. If the clutch is dropping onto the edge of a misaligned plate, it makes a quieter, less solid sound.

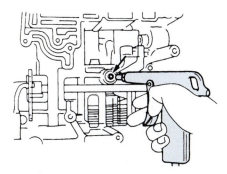

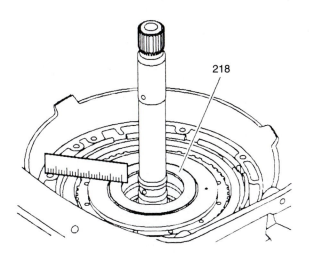

218

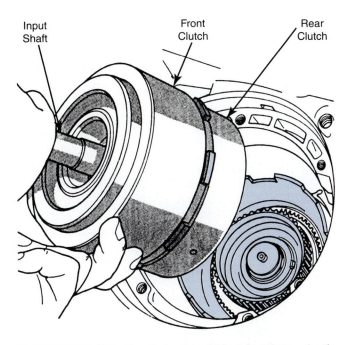

FIGURE 16-53 After the clutch is completely installed, its operation can be checked by applying compressed air to the fluid passage.

Input Shaft   Front Clutch   Rear Clutch

FIGURE 16-54 These front and rear clutches are installed together. The lugs of the front clutch must engage the notches in the sun gear shell, and the rear clutches must engage the splines on the clutch hub. Swinging the input shaft in a spiral motion can help align the plates. *(Courtesy of Chrysler Corporation)*

FIGURE 16-55 The straightedge is used to check the depth of the parts. If the two surfaces are flush, they are assembled correctly. *(Reprinted with permission of General Motors)*

TECH TIP

Most technicians prefer to adjust the end play on the tight side of the specifications. This reduces the thrust movement of the gear train. For example, eight thrust washers between the sizes of 0.076″ (1.92 mm) and 0.122″ (3.11 mm) are available, but one that is 0.15″ (2.94 mm) would provide the least end play that is within specification.

	Inch	Millimeter
Measured End Play:	0.038	0.97
End-Play Specification:	0.005 to 0.036	0.13 to 0.91
Excessive Play:	0.033 to 0.002	0.84 to 0.06
Existing Washer	0.087 to 0.91	2.21 to 2.31
Selected Washer	0.113 to 0.118	2.89 to 2.99
Size Difference:	+0.026	10.68

TECH TIP

If there is no end play after assembly and the transmission is bound, there is a probability that a thrust washer has slipped out of position or a clutch is not completely installed.

is installed (Figure 16-56). The internal end play is always checked and adjusted at this time.

Two common methods are used to check end play: an H-shaped gauge or a dial indicator. The H-shaped gauge is simpler and faster. Place the front gasket in position, adjust the gauge to fit the pump mounting surface, and then adjust the gauge

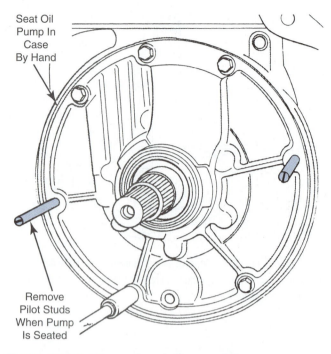

Seat Oil Pump In Case By Hand

Remove Pilot Studs When Pump Is Seated

FIGURE 16-56 The two pilot studs/guide pins properly align the gasket and pump to the transmission case as the pump is installed. *(Courtesy of Chrysler Corporation)*

TECH TIP

After the band servos are installed, many technicians air check the clutch assemblies, servos, and governor as described in Chapter 12. Each of the components should respond with the correct motion or sound and with a minimum of air leakage. If the air checks produce the correct results, the valve body, filter, and pan can be installed.

REAL WORLD FIX

The 700-R4 was overhauled, but when driving in D it will not make a 3–4 shift. The seals and pump were replaced during the overhaul. It was torn down again to replace a torn outer forward clutch seal and forward sprag. It now drags in D-4. Fluid pressures were checked, and they meet specifications.

Fix. A later-model pump with the auxiliary valve body was used during the overhaul; installation of a cup plug to close off the unused lube tube opening solved this problem. When replacing parts, always check the replacement part to make sure that it is exactly the same as the original part. The smallest difference can have a major effect on transmission performance.

TECH TIP

Some technicians check end play using a feeler gauge equal to the largest specified end play. If it enters there is too much end play, and the next larger thrust washer should be installed.

REAL WORLD FIX

The 1988 BMW had a fluid leak at the front of the transmission that was fixed by replacing the gasket between the bell housing and transmission case. It returned with a leak in the same area.

Fix. It was discovered that the retaining bolts pass through the case. Sealing the threads of the bolts with an anerobic sealer stopped this leak.

TECH TIP

When assembling a spring-loaded servo cover, hold the cover inward until each bolt has contact with at least five or six threads.

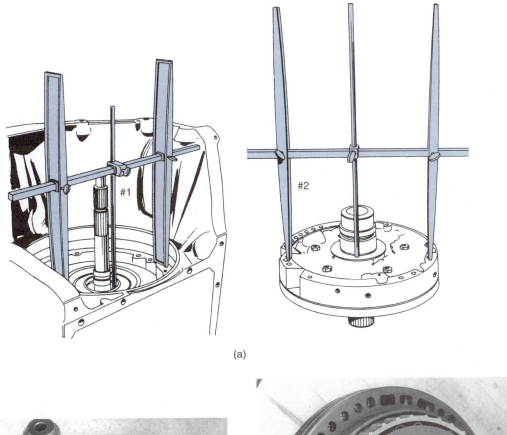

(a)

(b)

(c)

FIGURE 16-57   An H-shaped gauge is being used to check end play (a). It is adjusted to fit the transmission (left) and then moved to check the clearance at the pump (right). A shop-made gauge can be used in the same manner; note the use of an old band to support the gauge at the pump.

rod to touch the thrust surface on the clutch (Figure 16-57). Now turn the gauge over, and place it onto the pump. The clearance between the gauge rod and the thrust surface of the pump is the space you have for the thrust washer plus the clearance for end play.

If the end play is measured using a dial indicator, install the pump using the gasket but without the O-ring. Install and tighten two opposite bolts, and measure the end play as described in Section 16.3.1 (Figure 16-58). Then remove the pump and correct the end play by selecting the correct thrust washers or shims.

The selective thrust washer is normally the No. 1 thrust washer, the one next to the pump (Figure 16-59).

The band servos are installed and the band clearance is checked or adjusted after the pump is installed.

In review, the following general rules are used for transmission assembly:

- New or reconditioned replacement components should always be used.

- New rubber seals and new or very good sealing rings should be used.
- Gaskets and metal-clad seals should be replaced.
- All friction elements should be soaked in ATF.
- All clutches and bands should have the correct clearance.
- All one-way clutches should freewheel in the proper direction.
- All support bushings and thrust washers must be in good condition and assembled correctly.

TECH TIP

When tightening the valve body bolts, use a spiral pattern starting in the center.

TECH TIP

One manufacturer attaches the torque converter housing to the case using aluminum bolts so they have the same coefficient of expansion as the aluminum housing and case. New bolts must be used when the housing is reattached to the case.

REAL WORLD FIX

The 1999 Chrysler 300M (98,000 miles) came in with a second-gear start, no first-gear problem. The fluid is clean and at the proper level. A check reveals no DTCs, and the shift solenoids all have the proper resistance.

Fix. Removal of the transmission revealed earlier transmission service: some of the pan bolts were stripped and cross-threaded, and there was an excess amount of RTV sealant used. RTV chunks were inside the solenoid passages. Replacement of the solenoid pack and filter along with a new pan gasket and ATF fixed this problem.

REAL WORLD FIX

The 1998 Saturn (42,000 miles) transmission had overheated and was overhauled because of a torque converter problem. A new valve body was installed during the overhaul. Now there is no reverse, and reinspection does not reveal the cause.

Fix. An air check shows that the reverse servo was moving properly, but the reverse gear was not. The nut securing the assembly was overtightened. Tightening this nut to the correct torque fixed this problem.

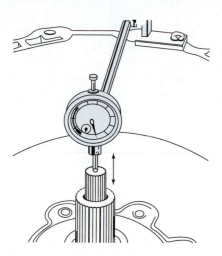

FIGURE 16-58 After the dial indicator is set up, lifting and dropping the input shaft shows the amount of end play. If it is correct, the internal parts have been installed correctly.

TECH TIP

Many technicians pour about 1 quart of ATF into the converter before installation. Remember that the converter must fill before fluid goes to the cooler and back to the transmission lubrication passages.

TECH TIP

If the drive gears do not line up, there is a **stacked converter** on top of the pump gear. If the transmission is installed with a stacked converter and the engine is started, the pump and possibly the converter hub will be ruined.

- All moving parts should be lubricated with ATF or transmission assembly lubricant.
- All end plays should be correctly adjusted.
- All snap rings must be installed completely into their grooves.
- All bolts must be tightened to the correct torque.
- All bolt threads should be lubricated with ATF before installing to reduce thread galling.
- Each hydraulic component should be air checked.
- The gear train should rotate without excessive drag.

16.6.2 Torque Converter Installation

After the transmission is assembled, the torque converter can be installed. The converter should be checked and cleaned as described in Chapter 19 or a rebuilt unit should be used.

The converter must align at three points: turbine spline, stator spline, and pump. Most converters use two flats or notches that engage the pump drive gear, and these notches should be positioned to align with the pump drive gear before installation (Figure 16-60).

Make sure that the converter is completely installed into the transmission before installing the transmission into the vehicle. Some manufacturers provide a dimension for checking converter installation (Figure 16-61).

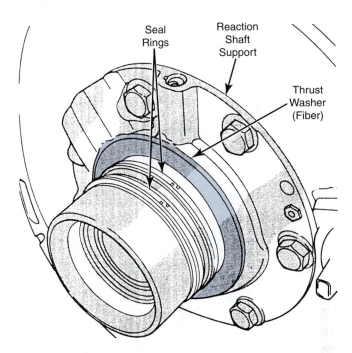

FIGURE 16-59 In most transmissions, the No. 1 (fiber) washer is selective. The technician selects the proper size to adjust the end play. *(Courtesy of Chrysler Corporation)*

TECH TIP

If a torque converter depth dimension is not available, pump tang engagement can be checked by noting how deep the converter is in the housing, rotating the converter a turn or so, lifting the converter back out, and noting if the pump drive tangs are aligned with the location of the converter hub (Figure 16-62). If they are not aligned, the converter was not completely installed and will need to go deeper into the transmission. Most technicians check for proper converter installation as it is being connected to the flexplate. See Section 15.5.

Shops that specialize in rebuilding transmissions to be sold to other shops often use a transmission test machine for quality control checks (Figure 16-63). These machines use an engine or large electric motor to drive the transmission while a power absorber provides a load on the drive shaft(s). They quickly provide a realistic and thorough test of the transmission.

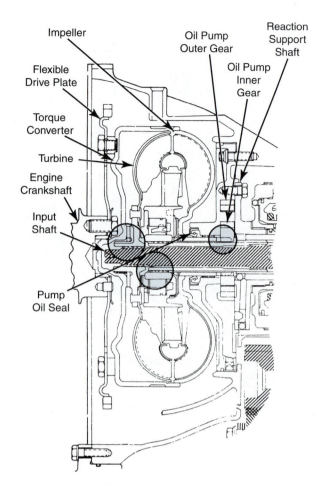

FIGURE 16-60 A torque converter must fully engage the pump, stator support, and turbine shaft (circles).

FIGURE 16-62 The torque converter was rotated and then removed. The pump drive lug (circle) must align with the position of the converter drive tang.

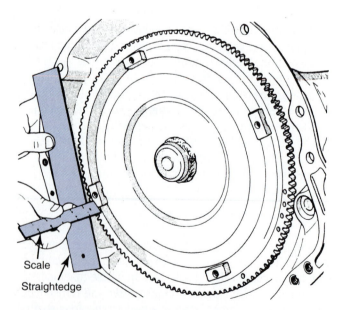

FIGURE 16-61 This check ensures that the torque converter is installed completely into the transmission. *(Courtesy of Chrysler Corporation)*

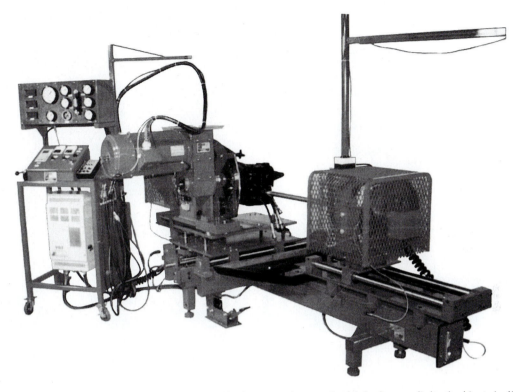

FIGURE 16-63   A transmission is installed in this tester. It will be driven at various speeds while loads are applied to the drive train. *(Courtesy of Axiline)*

SUMMARY

1. Automatic transmissions are removed from a vehicle for overhaul, repair, or replacement.

2. A transmission overhaul includes inspection of all reusable parts, a check of the clearances, and replacement of all gaskets, seals, friction materials, the filter, and worn bushings.

3. Remanufactured transmissions have been overhauled and updated in a factory-like environment.

4. Transmission parts are classified as hard or soft parts. Hard parts are not commonly replaced. Soft parts are commonly replaced during an overhaul.

5. Although the overhaul procedures for various transmissions are similar, there are differences, and service information should always be consulted when overhauling or servicing an automatic transmission.

REVIEW QUESTIONS

The following questions are provided to help you study as you read the chapter.

1. The three repair choices for a badly worn or damaged transmission are:

   a. _____

   b. _____

   c. _____

2. _____ parts are replaced during an automatic transmission overhaul.

3. _____ parts include the pump, clutch drums, and gearsets.

4. To learn about possible health problems and special handling requirements, refer to the _____ _____ _____ _____ (MSDS).

5. Excessive end play is a result of _____ wear.

6. Transmission end play is normally measured with a _____ _____.

7. A technician will change a _____ thrust washer or _____ ring to correct transmission end play.

8. Before reassembly, the parts are washed and _____ dried.

9. As a one-way clutch is assembled into the transmission, it should be checked to ensure that it _____ in the right direction.

10. After a clutch pack is assembled, it should be _____ _____ checked to ensure proper operation.

11. Most technicians set the _____ _____ to the tight side of the specifications.

12. During assembly, all of the friction elements should be _____ in ATF.

13. During assembly, all of the hydraulic units should be _____ checked.

14. The torque converter must align at three points. What are they?

    a. _____

    b. _____

    c. _____

15. Damage could result to the pump or torque converter if the _____ _____ is not properly installed.

CHAPTER QUIZ

The following questions will help you check the facts you have learned. Select the answer that completes each statement correctly.

1. Student A says that some states have rules and regulations that define what an automatic transmission rebuild or overhaul must include. Student B says that an alternative to an overhaul is to replace the transmission with a remanufactured transmission. Who is correct?

   a. Student A

   b. Student B

   c. Both A and B

   d. Neither A nor B

2. Student A says that the torque converter should be left attached to the engine when the transmission is removed from a vehicle. Student B says that the torque converter should be disconnected from the engine and removed with the transmission. Who is correct?

   a. Student A

   b. Student B

   c. Both A and B

   d. Neither A nor B

3. Student A says that the transmission must be thoroughly cleaned right after removal. Student B says that most transmission-holding fixtures allow the student to move the transmission to the best working position. Who is correct?

   a. Student A

   b. Student B

   c. Both A and B

   d. Neither A nor B

4. Student A says that some servos and accumulators require special holding tools or spring compressors to hold the internal spring compressed during disassembly. Student B says that an end-play check should be made before removing the transmission pump. Who is correct?

   a. Student A

   b. Student B

   c. Both A and B

   d. Neither A nor B

5. Student A says that the old gaskets should be discarded as they are removed from the transmission. Student B says that the old gaskets should be saved to match with the new gaskets during assembly. Who is correct?

   a. Student A

   b. Student B

   c. Both A and B

   d. Neither A nor B

6. Student A says that excessive transmission end play is usually caused by a stretched case. Student B says that loose pump bolts are the major cause of excess end play. Who is correct?

   a. Student A

   b. Student B

   c. Both A and B

   d. Neither A nor B

7. During a transmission rebuild, it is good practice to replace

   a. rubber sealing rings.

   b. lined clutch plates.

   c. paper and composition gaskets.

   d. All of these

8. Student A says that special slide hammers are used to pull the pump assembly from the case. Student B says that air pressure in the proper port helps pull the pump. Who is correct?

   a. Student A
   b. Student B
   c. Both A and B
   d. Neither A nor B

9. After the case has been cleaned it should be checked for

   a. damage, warpage, and cross leaks at the worm tracks.
   b. a worn governor bore.
   c. damaged bolt threads.
   d. All of these

10. Student A says that worn or damaged bushings are repaired by driving them out and replacing them with new bushings. Student B says that some bushings are removed by cutting threads in them so a puller bolt can be used. Who is correct?

    a. Student A
    b. Student B
    c. Both A and B
    d. Neither A nor B

11. Student A says that it is good practice to replace all of the friction materials (lined plates, unlined plates, and bands) when rebuilding a transmission. Student B says that lined friction material must be soaked in ATF before it is installed. Who is correct?

    a. Student A
    b. Student B
    c. Both A and B
    d. Neither A nor B

12. Student A says that you should ensure the cleanness of all internal parts by wiping them with a clean shop cloth just before installation. Student B says that petroleum jelly is a good stickum for thrust washers as well as being a good assembly lubricant. Who is correct?

    a. Student A
    b. Student B
    c. Both A and B
    d. Neither A nor B

13. Student A says that all parts should be thoroughly checked for cleanliness and proper working order during reassembly. Student B says that some transmissions have several end-play checks that must be done as the transmission is assembled. Who is correct?

    a. Student A
    b. Student B
    c. Both A and B
    d. Neither A nor B

14. Student A says that transmission end play is normally measured using a dial indicator mounted at the turbine shaft. Student B says that transmission end play is always corrected at the thrust washer No. 1 next to the pump. Who is correct?

    a. Student A
    b. Student B
    c. Both A and B
    d. Neither A nor B

15. Student A says that all the clutches and servos should be air checked right after the valve body has been installed. Student B says that all transmission bolts and especially the valve body bolts should be tightened to the correct torque. Who is correct?

    a. Student A
    b. Student B
    c. Both A and B
    d. Neither A nor B

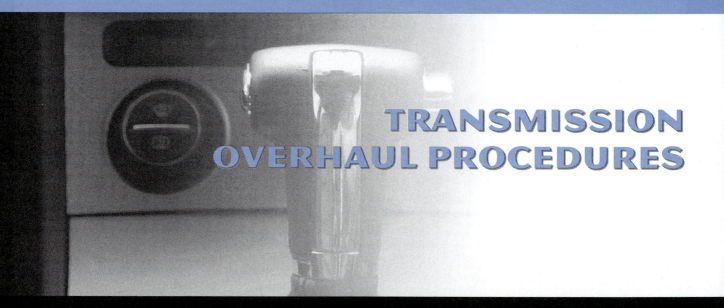

TRANSMISSION OVERHAUL PROCEDURES

OBJECTIVES

After studying Chapter 17, the reader should be able to:

1. Properly perform the standard overhaul procedures.
2. Describe the methods used to clean an automatic transmission and its components.
3. Inspect, remove, and replace bushings and thrust washers.
4. Disassemble, inspect, and assemble a clutch assembly.
5. Remove and replace the various seals used in an automatic transmission.
6. Complete the ASE tasks related to inspection and replacement of bushings, thrust washers, friction material, and seals.

KEY TERMS

17.1 INTRODUCTION

A transmission overhaul is a complete reconditioning that will bring the transmission back to like-new vehicle operation. This requires that worn parts be replaced so the original clearances are restored. An overhaul should include the following:

1. complete disassembly and cleaning
2. careful inspection of each part and component
3. replacement of any worn or damaged hard parts
4. replacement of any worn or damaged bushings or thrust washers
5. replacement of all clutch friction plates
6. replacement of any worn or damaged clutch steel plates
7. replacement of the intermediate band and any other worn or damaged bands
8. replacement of all internal and external seals and gaskets
9. disassembling, cleaning, and reassembling the valve body
10. rebuilding or replacing the torque converter
11. adjusting all clearances to the manufacturer's specifications

Some states have rules and regulations that define the common terms used to describe automatic transmission repair and what must be done to conform to these definitions. Check with your local governing body for any applicable laws that might apply.

17.2 COMPONENT CLEANING

The internal parts, case, and extension housing are cleaned after disassembly. Some technicians set major components aside to be thoroughly cleaned as they are disassembled and serviced. Cleaning methods that are commonly used are hot spray wash, water solution wash, cold dip, and solvent wash. The parts should be dried using compressed air after washing. Each technician or shop has a preferred method of cleaning. Internal transmission wear or overheating is often caused by poor lubrication, which could be the result of a plugged oil cooler in the radiator (Figure 17-1).

A hot spray wash cabinet resembles a large dishwasher (Figure 17-2). The parts are placed inside the cabinet, and the washer sprays the parts with a hot-water-based detergent solution as the parts are rotated. It is an effective and quick cleaner. Newer machines are designed to trap the sludge and dirt to make waste disposal easy and inexpensive. The used cleaning

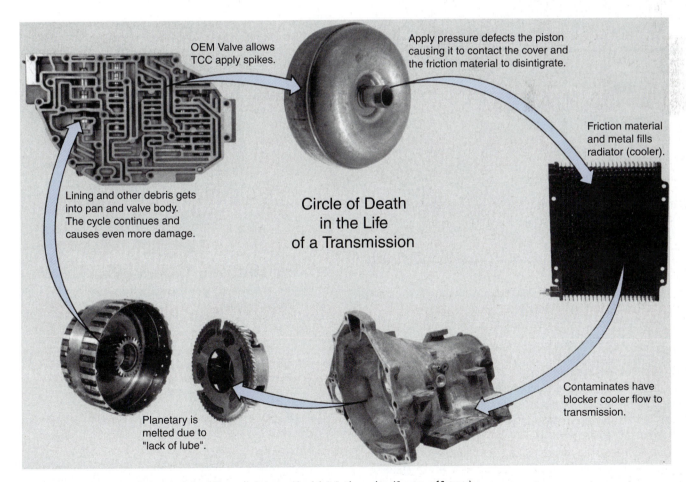

FIGURE 17-1   Expensive transmission failures can be caused by debris in the cooler. *(Courtesy of Sonnax)*

TECH TIP

Transmission parts should never be cleaned or dried by wiping them with a shop cloth. More than one transmission has died from *red rag disease*. Lint left on parts wiped by a shop cloth can clog the filter, blocking the fluid flow into the pump. This can cause an early failure of a perfectly good job.

TECH TIP

You should check the *MSDS (material safety data sheet)* label on the cleaning solution container for concerns during usage and for proper disposal methods.

SAFETY TIP

The petroleum solvent–air mixture from drying the parts is highly flammable. Never use cleaning solvent around an open flame, spark, or source of ignition.

FIGURE 17-2 A spray wash cabinet contains a pump that sprays heated cleaning solution as the parts basket is rotated. (*Courtesy of ATEC Trans-Tool and Cleaning Systems*)

solution, sludge, and dirt waste is an identified hazardous waste that is carefully monitored in many areas.

Cold dipping soaks the parts in a strong cleaning agent. There is no special equipment required. The solution used is relatively expensive, and the used cleaning solution must be disposed of as a hazardous material.

Solvent wash is commonly used for small parts. This method of cleaning parts is labor intensive. The parts are brushed as they are dipped or sprayed with a petroleum- or water-based solvent (Figure 17-3). Petroleum solvents are flammable and can cause redness and soreness of the skin. They are also considered pollutants because of the emissions released into the atmosphere and are treated as a hazardous waste when disposed.

TECH TIP

Rubber seals, Teflon thrust washers, bands, and lined friction plates should not be cleaned in petroleum solvent.

The parts should be rinsed with clear water and blown dry to prevent rusting after cleaning with either the spray washer or cold dip. Solvent wash also requires drying with compressed air to remove any residue.

FIGURE 17-3   This parts washer contains a pump that delivers the heated cleaning solution to a cleaning brush and flexible outlet. *(Courtesy of ATEC Trans-Tool and Cleaning Systems)*

SAFETY TIP

Your hands should be protected by gloves when cleaning parts in solvent.

SAFETY TIP

Be careful as the parts are blown dry. Flying debris can be very dangerous to the eyes or may penetrate the skin.

17.3 BUSHING, BEARING, AND THRUST WASHER SERVICE

Bushings and bearings are used to support rotating shafts. **Thrust washers** are used to separate rotating parts from each other or from stationary parts (Figure 17-4). Bushings are plain metal bearings that require a flow of ATF lubricant to reduce friction. Bearings have much less friction because they have rolling members, either balls or rollers, as well as a lubricant to reduce friction. Bushing, bearing, or thrust washer failure causes wear as the hard parts turning at different speeds rub against each other (Figure 17-5).

Thrust washers are plastic, fiber, or bronze- or tin-lined iron. When end-play positioning is critical or thrust loads are very high, a radial needle bearing commonly called a *Torrington* is used (Figure 17-6). This bearing type uses needle bearings to absorb the loads. These bearings must run against a very smooth, hard surface, either the face of a gear or a race. A bushing or thrust washer must have an operating clearance of about 0.003 to 0.005 in. (0.076 to 0.157 mm) to allow a good oil flow across the bearing surface. Torrington bearings and tapered roller bearings are designed to operate with very little clearance; in fact, excessive clearance or end play can cause a pounding that might damage the bearing.

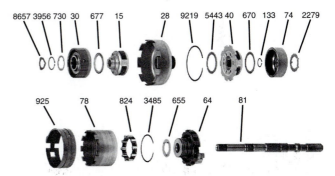

FIGURE 17-4   Parts 8657, 730, 677, 5443, 670, 2279, 6749, and 655 are thrust washers. The nine replaceable bushings for this transmission are not shown. *(Courtesy of Slauson Transmission Parts, www.slauson.com)*

TECH TIP

Thrust washer condition is judged by the appearance of the washer and the surfaces it runs against. The condition of a Torrington is checked by feeling for rough operation under load.

(a)

(b)

FIGURE 17-5   The inner and outer bearing journal of this carrier show severe wear (a). The nylon thrust washer shows that it is deformed and nearly melted (b). Both failed because of poor lubrication and overheating.

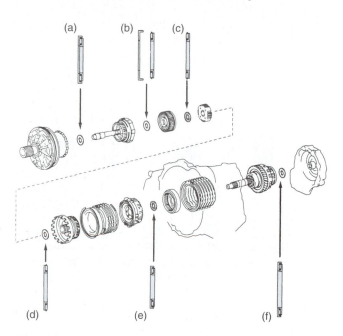

FIGURE 17-6   A thrust bearing can have a specially shaped race at each side or use the transmission component for the race. The race can be part of the bearing or separate. Correct installation is essential.

A bushing is a metal sleeve that is lined with a soft bearing material, usually bronze, tin, or both. An experienced technician judges bushing condition by appearance and feel. Any scoring, galling, flaking, excess wear, or rough operation is cause for replacement (Figure 17-7). A bushing is relatively inexpensive, but the damage caused by a worn bushing is very expensive to repair. Most technicians will not gamble on a

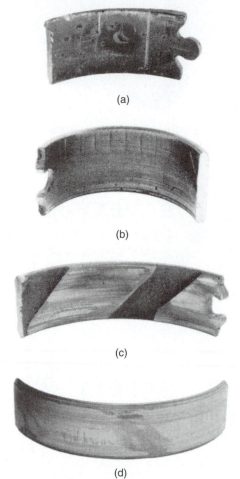

(a)

(b)

(c)

(d)

FIGURE 17-7   These bushings have failed from embedded debris (a), abrasion (b), wiping and overheating (c), and spin out (d). *(Courtesy of Sonnax)*

FIGURE 17-8 A quick and simple check for bushing clearance is to place a strip of paper between the converter hub and bushing. The paper is about 0.003 in. thick, so you should be able to remove it with a slight drag.

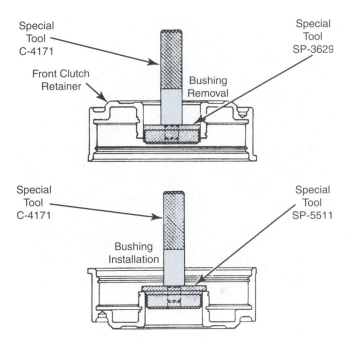

FIGURE 17-9 Special tool SP-3629 is being used to drive the bushing out of the clutch housing (top). Note that special tool SP-5511 for the bushing installation has a lip that prevents installing the bushing too deep (bottom). *(Courtesy of Chrysler Corporation)*

TECH TIP

Most manufacturers do not publish clearance or size specifications for bushings; a few publish thrust washer thickness specifications. If you want to measure bushing clearance to gain experience, use the rule of thumb that anything over 0.006 in. (0.152 mm) is excessive (Figure 17-8).

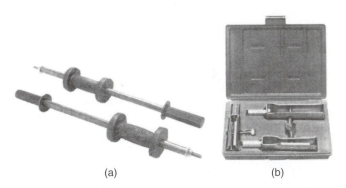

FIGURE 17-10 A slide hammer (a) with a remover adapter (b) can be used to pull a bushing from its bore. *(Courtesy of ATEC Trans-Tool and Cleaning Systems)*

marginal bushing. If in doubt, replace it. Technicians automatically replace every bushing in certain transmissions, and only some in others. The technician's experience with various transmissions helps to decide which bushings will need replacement. The front (pump) and rear (extension housing) bushings are usually replaced during every transmission rebuild.

17.3.1 Bushing Removal

Several methods can be used to remove a bushing. Always check and note the position of any grooves or oil passages. The size and shape of the bore determines the method of bushing removal and installation. If the bore is straight, the bushing is normally pressed or driven straight out the other end of the bore (Figure 17-9). The driving tool is usually a stepped disk that fits into the bushing bore and has a raised shoulder to press against the end of the bushing. The shoulder should be slightly smaller than the bushing outer diameter to keep it from damaging the bushing bore.

If the bore is stepped so the bushing cannot be pressed through, there are removal tools that can pull the bushing out. These tools are often used with a slide hammer. They can enter the bushing and expand to secure a hold onto the bushing or thread into the bushing (Figure 17-10).

A commonly used method to remove a bushing in a stepped bore is to collapse or cut it. A bushing is collapsed by catching the bushing edge with a bushing cutter or sharp chisel and folding it inward (Figure 17-11). This will be easier if you locate the seam in the bushing and work next to it. Another removal method is to cut a groove in the bushing. This is time-consuming, and there is a possibility of damaging the bearing's bore.

FIGURE 17-11 A chisel is being used to cut a groove through the bushing so it can be collapsed. Be careful to not damage the bushing bore.

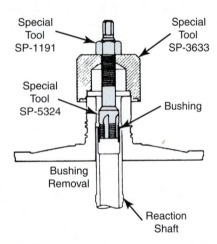

FIGURE 17-12 The special toolset threads into the bushing; turning the nut at the top will pull the bushing out. *(Courtesy of Chrysler Corporation)*

TECH TIP

Very small bushings are usually removed by cutting threads in them so a slide hammer can be threaded into the bushing (Figure 17-12). Some output shaft bushings allow standard bolt threads to be cut into them.

FIGURE 17-13 This band-adjusting screw from a C6 has a cutting groove in the threads, and the nut has been welded into place. With the use of an air wrench, it can cut threads into the bushing at the front of a TH 350 main-shaft; it will bottom in the bore and force the bushing out.

TECH TIP

Technicians are very resourceful; they design special tools that may be better than those designed by the vehicle manufacturer. Some technicians remove the THM 350 output shaft bushing using an impact wrench and a C6 band-adjusting screw modified as described in Figure 17-13.

17.3.2 Bushing Installation

Replacement bushings are available as individual items or part of an overhaul set.

A bushing installer should be used to push the new bushing into its bore to prevent damaging it or the bore. This is

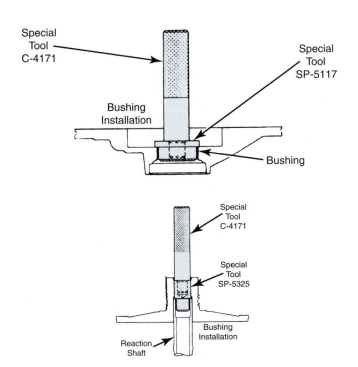

After staking a bushing, you should remove any raised metal with a scraping tool or sharp knife.

Some bushings have a hole that must be aligned with an oil passage to permit lubrication of other parts. It is recommended to use a locking compound such as Loctite® to prevent the bushing from rotating in its bore and shutting off the lube flow.

FIGURE 17-14 Bushing drivers are used to drive bushings into the proper position. *(Courtesy of Chrysler Corporation)*

REAL WORLD FIX

The 1997 Ford Explorer (69,000 miles) has a delay during the 3–4 shift. Under full throttle, there is a definite engine flare. There are no DTCs, and the fluid pressures are normal in all gears. The transmission was sent to a rebuilder, and no problems were found. Testing on a dyno showed good operation.

Fix. Following advice from experienced technicians, the transmission was disassembled. A very close inspection revealed that a bushing inside of a clutch drum had rotated. This blocked most of the fluid passage, leaving about 10% of the opening. Replacement of this bushing fixed this problem.

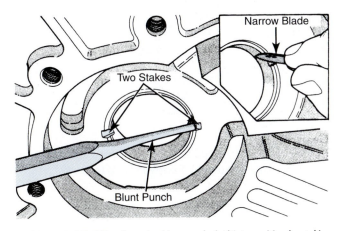

FIGURE 17-15 Some bushings are locked into position by staking them using a blunt punch. Any raised metal is then scraped off. *(Courtesy of Chrysler Corporation)*

often the same tool that was used to remove the bushing. In most cases, the bushing is placed on the tool and pressed or driven into the bore to the correct depth (Figure 17-14). Some bushing drivers have steps so they "bottom out" and stop at the correct depth. A bushing with a groove or oil passage should be aligned in the original position.

In some cases a bushing is **staked** to lock it in place. Staking is usually done using a punch to bend bushing metal into a recess (Figure 17-15).

17.3.3 Tapered Roller Bearing Service

Some transaxles use tapered roller bearings (Figure 17-16). The bearing consists of the *inner race*, *rollers*, **cage**, and **cup**, which is also called a **cone**. These bearings are checked by visual inspection and by rotating the cleaned and lubricated

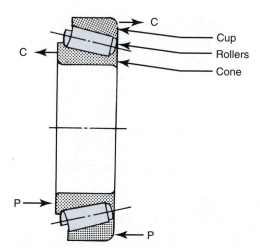

FIGURE 17-16 The cup, rollers, and cone of a tapered roller bearing are machined at an angle as shown. This allows them to resist a thrust in the direction indicated by the P arrows. The bearing is preloaded in this direction; any clearance at the sides of the bearing (C arrows) is called freeplay.

bearing with a pressure between the bearing and cup. Any scoring or flaking of the cup or roller surfaces or a rough feel is cause for replacement. These bearings are often a press fit onto the shaft, and the cup is a press fit into the bore. Special tools are usually required to remove and replace the bearing and its cone (Figure 17-17). If a bearing or its cup are damaged, both should be replaced. If the bearings and cups are to be reused, they should be marked or tagged so a bearing will be installed with the original cup (Figure 17-18).

Tapered roller bearings must be adjusted to get the correct end play or preload. This adjustment is normally accomplished by changing *selective* sized shims that can be positioned under the cup (Figure 17-19). A shim of the proper size is selected to provide the correct end play or preload. The procedure for this adjustment varies between manufacturers (Figure 17-20).

17.4 FRICTION MATERIAL SERVICE

There are three opinions concerning replacement of automatic transmission friction material (lined plates, unlined plates, and bands) during an overhaul:

1. Replace all friction material as a standard practice.
2. Replace all lined plates and the unlined plates and bands as needed.
3. Replace only the worn or damaged items.

The second view is the one held by many technicians. As mentioned earlier, some states (e.g., California) require that lined friction plates be replaced with new parts and the intermediate band be replaced with either a new or relined part if the transmission is being "overhauled" or "rebuilt."

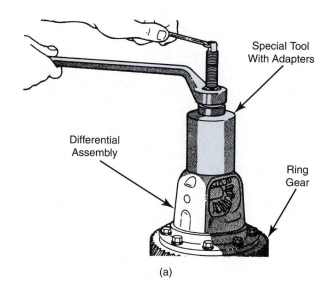

(a)

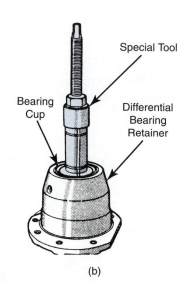

(b)

FIGURE 17-17 Special tools are often required to remove tapered roller bearings (a) and the cups (b). *(Courtesy of Chrysler Corporation)*

FIGURE 17-18 When roller bearings are to be reused, they should be marked or tagged so they can be put back in the same position with the same races/cups.

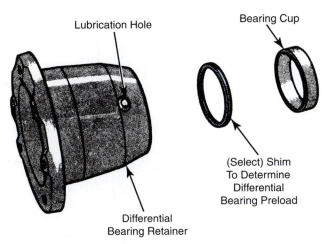

FIGURE 17-19   This bearing set is adjusted with a selective shim placed under the bearing cup; a thicker shim will reduce the clearance or increase the preload on the bearing. *(Courtesy of Chrysler Corporation)*

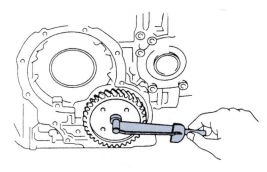

FIGURE 17-20   If this bearing set is adjusted correctly, it will take 2.2 inch-pounds (in-lb) (0.2 N-m) of torque to rotate the differential.

TECH TIP

If the lining appears to be delaminating or coming loose from the core, peel the lining off and look for rust on the steel core (Figure 17-21). Rust is evidence of water damage. Since water also damages nylon parts, it is recommended to replace every nylon washer in the transmission if water damage is present.

17.4.1 Lined Plate Service

If lined plates are to be reused, they should be carefully inspected. The requirements for reuse of a lined plate are as follows:

- The lining wear is minimal.
- There must be no breaking up or pock marks in the lining.

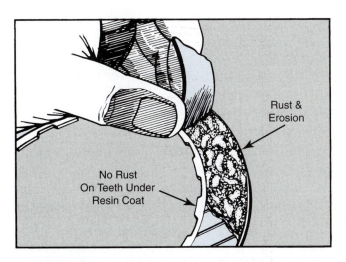

FIGURE 17-21   The lining is lifted off of this friction plate. It shows rust and corrosion that are evidence of water damage. *(Courtesy of Raybestos)*

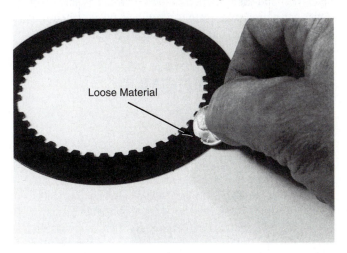

FIGURE 17-22   The lining can be easily scraped from the plate; this disc should not be reused.

TECH TIP

Friction plates that are to be reused should not be washed or soaked in solvent or water-detergent solution. They can be quickly rinsed in solvent and then blown dry if cleaning is needed.

- There must be no metal particles embedded in the lining.
- The lining must not come apart when scraped with a coin, fingernail, or knife blade (Figure 17-22).
- The lining must not have a glazed, shiny appearance.
- The lining material must not be severely discolored.

- The plate must be flat.
- The splined area must be flat and even.

17.4.2 Steel Plate Service

Unlined steel plates are often reused. They must be carefully inspected before reuse:

- The plate must be flat (except for wave or Belleville plates).
- There must be no sign of surface irregularities.
- The splined area must be flat and even.
- Slightly burned plates must be replaced or reconditioned.

A "good" steel plate is reusable. Other than cleaning, no further preparation is needed. The friction surface of the lined plate has to wear slightly until it matches the surface of the unlined plate. Too rough of a steel plate surface produces severe operation and rapid friction material wear. The ideal surface finish for a used steel plate is a tumbled-finish, smooth, very flat surface like that of a new steel plate (Figure 17-23).

TECH TIP

A quick way to check the plates for flatness is to stack the plates and look for any gaps between the plates. Overheated plates tend to warp into either a slightly conical or a "potato chip" shape. Gaps indicate warped, unusable plates. Restack the plates, turning every other one upside down, and recheck for gaps. Any gaps indicate faulty, unusable plates.

TECH TIP

Some shops use a tumbler to recondition used steel plates (Figure 17-24). This machine rotates a basket of plates along with a ceramic medium and soap; the tumbling action creates the small nicks and dents that produce the correct surface finish. Some sources recommend roughing up a steel plate by sanding or blasting with sand, grit, or glass beads, but these processes are considered too time-consuming. Also, blasting may produce a surface finish that is too rough and severe.

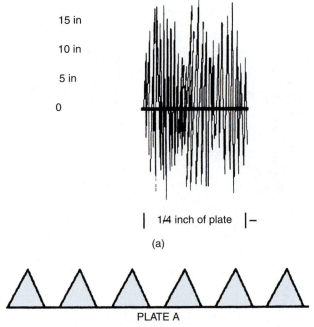

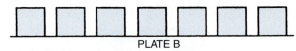

FIGURE 17-23 A profilimeter shows the profile of a steel plate (a); one micro-inch (1μ in) equals 0.000001 in. The actual shape of the surface roughness can vary (b), but both of these plates have the same surface roughness. *(Courtesy of Raybestos)*

REAL WORLD FIX

The 1994 Explorer (82,000 miles) transmission burned up the frictions in the forward clutch after about 4,000 miles. The clutch drum looked good, and the sealing rings were replaced. The case is flat, and the center support has been replaced. The clutch checks out good using a wet air test.

Fix. Using advice from his peers, the technician installed a manual valve index sleeve (an aftermarket repair item). This part keeps the manual valve properly aligned with the bore.

FIGURE 17-24 This tool can rotate a basket of steel plates and special media to cause a tumbling action that cleans and retextures the surface. *(Courtesy of ATEC Trans-Tool and Cleaning Systems)*

17.4.3 Band Service

If a band is to be reused, it should be checked to ensure that:

- the lining material is sound with no breaking up or pock marks
- the lining material does not come apart when scraped with a thumbnail or knife blade
- the lining thickness is almost the same as that of a new band
- the lining material is not badly discolored or does not appear burned
- there are no metal particles embedded in the friction material
- the end lugs appear tight and unworn

If the friction surface on a fabric-lined band has a dark, shiny appearance but is good otherwise, it can be scraped using a knife or bearing scraper to remove the glazed surface. A glazed, paper-lined band should be replaced.

The drum surface for a band must also be in good condition. The drum surface should be very smooth and flat (Figure 17-25). A rough, badly scored drum should be replaced.

17.4.4 New Friction Material Preparation

New friction material must never be used in a dry, unlubricated condition. Dry lining acts like an insulator. It easily overheats and burns from the heat of friction created during

TECH TIP

If the scoring is light and the equipment is available, some technicians true up the drum surface using either an engine lathe or a brake drum lathe. This may require a band with an oversize lining to compensate for the smaller drum diameter.

TECH TIP

Some transmissions use a drum made from a steel stamping rather than from a forging or a casting. These units should be checked for dishing by laying a straightedge along the drum surface (Figure 17-26).

TECH TIP

If the drum surface is smooth but polished, it can be sanded to produce a better finish. If a paper-lined band is used, use 150- to 160-grit sandpaper, and sand in a direction that goes around the drum (Figure 17-27). If a fabric-lined band is used, use coarser sandpaper (40- to 60-grit) and sand in a front-to-back direction.

the first shift. The lined material should be soaked in ATF for at least 20 minutes before installation; some shops soak the plates overnight.

17.5 INTERNAL SEAL SERVICE

An important part of a transmission overhaul is the correct replacement of the internal seals. These are the rubber and metal seals used on accumulator, servo, and clutch pistons

(a)

(b)

(c)

(d)

(e)

(f)

FIGURE 17-25 Two badly worn drums (a and b); both are scored and polished, and (b) shows burn marks. Four faulty bands: (c and d) two broken bands; (e) burned and flaking lining; and f is worn out.

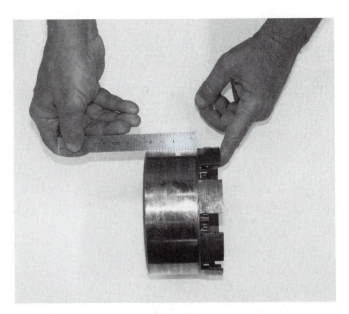

FIGURE 17-26   Stamped steel drums should be checked for dishing. There should be no clearance between the drum and the straightedge.

FIGURE 17-27   If a drum surface is polished, it can be sanded to roughen the surface. If a paper band is used, sand around the drum using 120- or 180-grit emery cloth or sandpaper. If a fabric band is used, sand in a front-to-back direction using 40- to 60-grit sandpaper.

and the rotating metal or Teflon sealing rings used on the pump clutch support, the input shaft, and the governor support (Figure 17-28). Rubber seals should always be replaced during an overhaul. If the metal or Teflon sealing rings are in good shape, it is possible to reuse them, but this is not recommended.

The piston seals of some transmissions are molded directly onto the piston. The piston must be replaced if the seal is damaged or worn excessively.

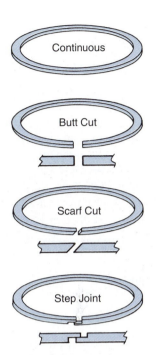

FIGURE 17-28   Four styles of Teflon rings; the uncut, continuous ring requires special tools for installation. The other styles are placed into the groove with overlapping ends positioned properly.

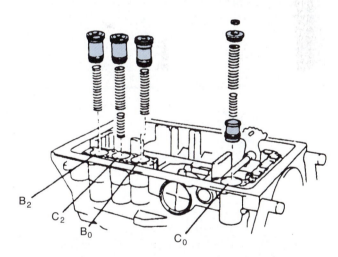

FIGURE 17-29   Each of these accumulator pistons has an O-ring seal that should have a snug fit in the bore. *(Courtesy of Toyota Motor Sales USA, Inc.)*

17.5.1 Fitting Rubber Seals

Always check a seal in the bore where it will operate. In most cases, this takes very little time. An O-ring seal (round or square-cut) is first checked by placing it in the bore by itself (Figure 17-29). If it is slightly larger or smaller than the bore (3% or less), it will work.

TECH TIP

To calculate 3% of the bore, take the diameter, move the decimal point two places to the left, and multiply by 3. For example, a 2 1/4-servo is 2.250 in. Moving the decimal point gives us 0.0225; multiplying by 3 gives us 0.0675 in. The allowable over- or undersize of 3% of 2 1/4 in. is slightly more than 1/16 in.

TECH TIP

The seals can be checked for size by placing them one at a time in their operating position. Start with the seal that is easiest to remove and replace. Place one seal on the piston, lubricate it with ATF, and work it into the bore. Now stroke the piston, and feel for drag (Figure 17-30). A round O-ring should produce some drag; a square-cut seal is okay if it produces a barely noticeable drag. Now remove the piston, remove the seal, install the next seal, and check its drag.

TECH TIP

A lip seal is checked the same way. Just like an O-ring seal, it must produce a drag on the way into the drum, but it is okay if it falls outward when turned over. On a piston that uses three lip seals, you should check them each, one at a time.

17.5.2 Installing Pistons with Lip Seals

The clutch piston should be inspected before seal installation (Figure 17-31). A piston that is manufactured from sheet metal stampings should be checked for broken welds or cracks. Also make sure that the check ball moves freely in its cage and seals properly, as described in Chapter 18.

Inner Seal Installed — Outer Seal Removed

Step #1

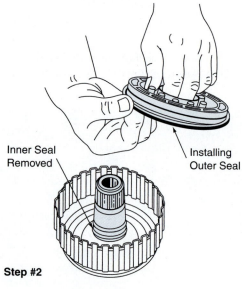

Inner Seal Removed — Installing Outer Seal

Step #2

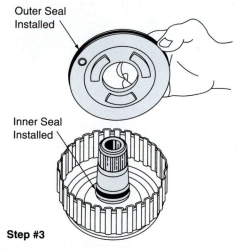

Outer Seal Installed — Inner Seal Installed

Step #3

FIGURE 17-30 The inner piston seal is installed, and the piston is slid into the bore to check its fit (step 1). The piston is removed, and the fit of the outer seal is checked (step 2). Then both seals are installed and lubricated, and the piston is installed for the final time (step 3).

FIGURE 17-31   A piston should be checked for any signs of damage, porosity, nicks at the seal groove, and a missing or stuck check ball.

FIGURE 17-32   Piston and seal installation can be made easier if a film of wax lubricant is smeared around the seals and seal area.

TECH TIP

Wax lubricant, often called **door ease,** is commonly used for vehicle door or hood striker plates. Smearing a film of wax lubricant around the seal and at the edge of the bore is often just enough lubricant to allow the seal to slip into the bore (Figure 17-32).

TECH TIP

Seal installation tools are commercially available or you can make one by rounding the edges of a feeler gauge that is 0.005 to 0.010 in. (0.15 to 0.25 mm) or squeezing a bent, thin piece of piano wire into the end of a small tubing (Figure 17-33). As the piston is being installed, use this tool to coax the seal lip into the bore.

During installation, a lip seal often catches the edge of the bore and will roll outward. This will probably cut the seal lip and cause a fluid leak. Several procedures can be used to

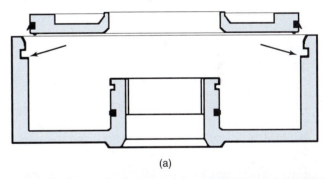

(a)

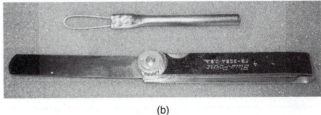

(b)

FIGURE 17-33   When the piston is installed, the seal tends to catch on the upper end of the piston bore (a, arrow). A thin feeler gauge or shop-made seal installing tool can coax the seal past this edge (b).

ease installation and produce a reliable clutch: use a wax lubricant, an installing tool, a seal guide, and precompress the seal lip.

A seal should never be installed dry. Both the bore and the seals should be lubricated with ATF, transmission assembly lubricant, petroleum jelly, or wax lubricant.

TECH TIP

Seal guides are available for some clutch units. These are smooth steel bands with a slight funnel or cone shape (Figure 17-34). They are placed in the drum and lubricated. As the piston is being installed, the guides prevent the seal lips from catching on the edge of the bore.

TECH TIP

Lubegard markets a spray-on product called Seal-E-Zee and a set of application cones that aid lip seal installation.

TECH TIP

Some pistons will not allow a seal guide to be used and precompression is necessary. For example, the front clutch piston of a 46RH/A727 has a ledge that extends outward, well over the edge of the bore. The extension housing sealing O-ring from a Powerglide is slightly smaller than the 46RH/A727 outer seal. If you place the Powerglide seal over the Torqueflite lip seal, it pulls the seal lips tightly inward (Figure 17-35). Leave the O-ring in place for a while (the longer the better); then remove the O-ring and quickly install the piston into the drum. The colder the temperature, the more time you have before the lip seal expands back to its normal size.

TECH TIP

After the clutch is completely assembled, it should be air checked to ensure that the seals are good, the piston strokes properly, and the clutch applies and releases (Figure 17-36).

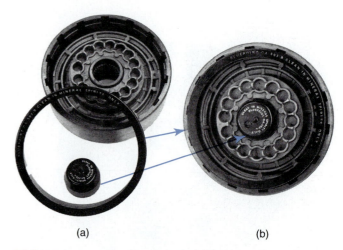

(a)   (b)

FIGURE 17-34 Two seal guides can be placed into the clutch drum. With the new seals lubricated, the piston can be installed without seal lip damage.

FIGURE 17-35 An extension housing O-ring seal has been placed over the piston lip seal of this front clutch. It reshapes the sealing lip to make installation easier.

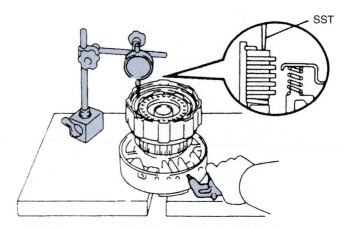

FIGURE 17-36 After the clutch is completely assembled, the condition of the seals can be verified by an air check. The dial indicator will give an accurate measurement of the clutch pack clearance. *(Courtesy of Toyota Motor Sales USA, Inc.)*

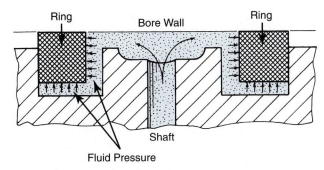

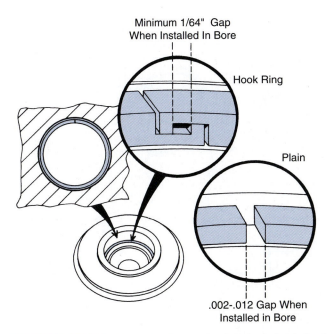

FIGURE 17-37 A sealing ring is forced outward, away from the fluid pressure. It tends to wear into the sides of the seal grooves.

FIGURE 17-38 A metal sealing ring has been hooked and placed into its bore. It should enter with a slight pressure and make full contact with the bore. There should be a slight gap at the ends of the ring as shown.

REAL WORLD FIX

The 1991 Lincoln Continental (105,000 miles) goes into neutral after a stop. Revving the engine will produce a harsh shift back into gear. Shifting into neutral, revving the engine, and shifting back into drive will give normal operation. There are no DTCs, and the fluid pressures are good. A pan inspection shows normal wear.

Fix. The transmission was disassembled. The forward clutch piston was found to be warped and the seal lip was cracked. Replacing the clutch piston and seal fixed this problem.

TECH TIP

If you encounter breakage of metal sealing rings as you install the component over them, check the ring end gap in the component's bore. If the end gap is correct, then fill the ring groove with assembly lube and install the ring so it is centered to the shaft with an equal amount of ring showing all around the shaft. Now, carefully install the component.

17.5.3 Fitting Sealing Rings

A sealing ring has to make a seal on one of its sides and at the outer diameter. Fluid pressure plus the elasticity of the ring pushes the ring outward, where it engages the bore. If the bore is rotating, the sealing ring rotates with the bore (Figure 17-37). Rubbing action should always take place between one side of the sealing ring and the groove. Some sliding action takes place between the ring and the bore. End play allows the bore along with the drum to move forward and backward. Excessive end play causes rapid wear of the sealing ring and possible damage to the ring groove.

A metal sealing ring should be checked by placing it in its bore (Figure 17-38). There should be a tight and close fit between the outer diameter of the ring and the bore. An undersized or odd-shaped ring should not be used. Open-end metal rings should have a slight gap, about 0.002 to 0.015 in. (0.05 to 0.3 mm), between the ends of the ring to allow for

expansion of the ring metal. Slight nicks or imperfections can be smoothed using sandpaper.

Next, check the ring in the groove (Figure 17-39). A hook- or interlock-type ring should be hooked after installation. There should be a maximum of about 0.003 in. (0.07 mm) of groove wear, and the sides of the groove should be smooth and straight. Small imperfections can be smoothed using a small file. Excessive or tapered wear requires shaft or clutch support replacement.

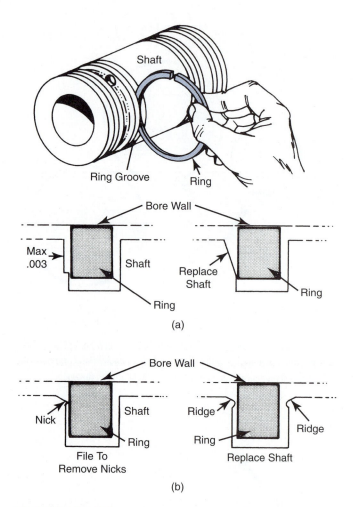

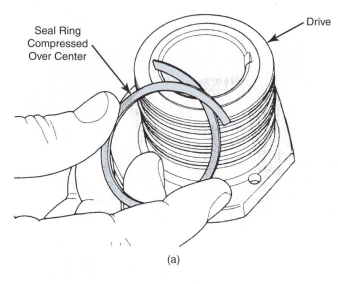

(a)

FIGURE 17-39 Side clearance of a metal sealing ring is checked by placing the ring into the groove and measuring the clearance using a feeler gauge (a). While making this check, look for damage to the seal groove (b).

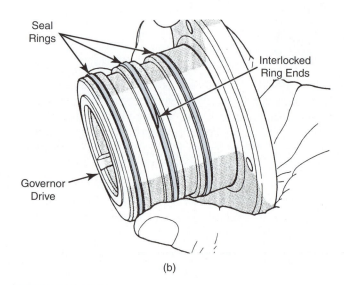

(b)

FIGURE 17-40 Compressing a seal ring helps it fit tight in its groove (a). During installation, make sure the ends interlock properly (b). *(Courtesy of Chrysler Corporation)*

TECH TIP

Be careful when you install the next unit over a sealing ring. The ends tend to stick out, and they can get caught and damaged during installation.

17.5.4 Installing Teflon Sealing Rings

Scarf-cut, Teflon sealing rings are easy to install. Merely place them in the groove with the ends lapped in the correct direction (Figure 17-40).

Uncut Teflon rings require two special tools for installation: an installing tool and a resizing tool. To install a Teflon ring, place the installing tool over the shaft; adjust it to the correct depth if necessary; lubricate the ring and the tool; and slide the ring over the tool and into its groove (Figure 17-41). You can expect the ring to stretch during installation. Next, lubricate the ring and resizing tool, and work the resizing tool over the ring, being sure the ring enters its groove correctly. The resizing tool should compress the ring to the correct diameter. Once the transmission operates and the ring gets hot, it will take the shape of the bore.

FIGURE 17-41 This Teflon seal installation set allows you to stretch a seal ring, position it in the groove, and resize the seal so it has the proper fit. *(Courtesy of ATEC Trans-Tool and Cleaning Systems)*

TECH TIP

Warming the ring in hot water will soften the material and make installation and resizing easier.

TECH TIP

It is helpful to leave the seal resizing tool on the seal until you are ready to install the shaft.

SUMMARY

1. A transmission overhaul includes disassembly, cleaning, replacing worn parts, and reassembling to its original clearances.
2. Transmission parts are cleaned by hand and by automated wash cabinets.
3. Bushings and bearings are carefully checked and replaced as necessary.
4. Clutches are serviced by inspecting and replacing the friction material and seals.
5. Sealing rings must be replaced and the surfaces they seal against must be carefully inspected and serviced as needed.

REVIEW QUESTIONS

The following questions are provided to help you study as you read the chapter.

1. Shop rags should never be used to clean, dry, or wipe parts because they leave _____ on the parts that could _____ the filter.
2. The commonly used methods for cleaning transmission parts are:
   a. _____
   b. _____
   c. _____
3. The condition of a plastic, fiber, or metal thrust washer is judged by the appearance of the _____ and the _____ it runs against.
4. The front _____ bushing and the rear _____ housing bushing are usually replaced during an overhaul.
5. During installation, a bushing must be _____ with any oil grooves of passages.
6. The _____ plates are usually replaced during a transmission overhaul and the _____ plates are often reused.

7. The bands and friction clutch plates should be soaked in ATF for at least _____ minutes before installation in the transmission.

8. A seal ring should be _____ in its bore before installation.

9. After new seals are installed in a clutch and the clutch is completely assembled, it should be _____ checked for proper operation and leakage.

10. A seal ring seals on its _____ and _____ diameter.

CHAPTER QUIZ

The following questions will help you check the facts you have learned. Select the answer that completes each statement correctly.

1. During a transmission rebuild, it is good practice to replace
   a. rubber sealing rings.
   b. lined clutch plates.
   c. paper and composition gaskets.
   d. All of these

2. Student A says that the usual method of cleaning transmission parts is to wash them in solvent and dry them with a shop cloth. Student B says that spray washers are a fast and effective way of cleaning parts. Who is correct?
   a. Student A
   b. Student B
   c. Both A and B
   d. Neither A nor B

3. Student A says that worn or damaged bushings are repaired by driving them out and replacing them with new bushings. Student B says that some bushings are removed by cutting threads in them so a puller bolt can be used. Who is correct?
   a. Student A
   b. Student B
   c. Both A and B
   d. Neither A nor B

4. Student A says that position of the bushing holes or grooves is not important during installation. Student B says that all bushings must be stacked after installation. Who is correct?
   a. Student A
   b. Student B
   c. Both A and B
   d. Neither A nor B

5. Student A says that if a tapered roller bearing cup is worn and needs to be replaced, the rest of the bearing parts also will need to be replaced. Student B says that if a tapered bearing is to be reused it must be installed in its original position. Who is correct?
   a. Student A
   b. Student B
   c. Both A and B
   d. Neither A nor B

6. Student A says that it is good practice to replace all friction materials (lined plates, unlined plates, and bands) when rebuilding a transmission. Student B says that lined friction material must be soaked in ATF before it is installed. Who is correct?
   a. Student A
   b. Student B
   c. Both A and B
   d. Neither A nor B

7. Student A says that an unlined steel clutch plate can be reused if it is smooth and shiny and only has a little bit of "potato chip" warpage. Student B says that a lined plate that shows any darkening should not be reused. Who is correct?
   a. Student A
   b. Student B
   c. Both A and B
   d. Neither A nor B

8. Student A says that seals should always be checked for proper fit before installation. Student B says that seals should never be installed dry. Who is correct?
   a. Student A
   b. Student B
   c. Both A and B
   d. Neither A nor B

9. Student A says that excessive end play causes rapid wear of the sealing rings and possibly the sealing ring groove. Student B says that seal does not rotate in the groove; therefore, the groove could not wear. Who is correct?
   a. Student A
   b. Student B
   c. Both A and B
   d. Neither A nor B

10. Student A says that Teflon sealing rings require special tools for proper installation. Student B says that warming a Teflon seal with hot water will help to size the seal. Who is correct?
   a. Student A
   b. Student B
   c. Both A and B
   d. Neither A nor B

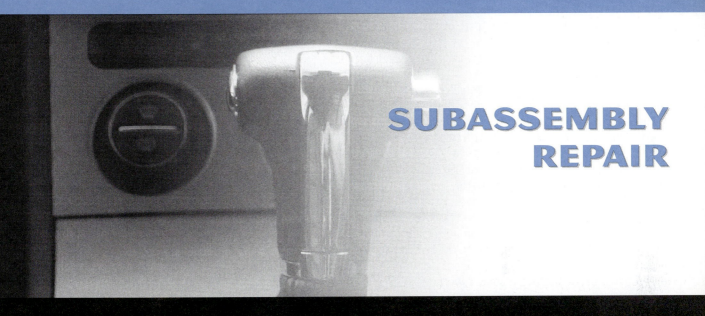

SUBASSEMBLY
REPAIR

OBJECTIVES

After studying Chapter 18, the reader should be able to:

1. Disassemble and reassemble automatic transmission subassemblies.

2. Determine if used subassemblies and their components are usable.
3. Complete the ASE tasks related to off-vehicle transmission/transaxle repair.

KEY TERMS

18.1 SUBASSEMBLY REPAIR

Inspection, service, and repair operations are done to each of the transmission subassemblies as part of the transmission overhaul. These subassemblies include the case, pump, clutch assemblies, gearset, valve body, and governor. Subassembly repair ensures that each component is serviceable and will work properly when the transmission is assembled.

Some technicians disassemble the transmission and all of the subassemblies completely. The components are serviced, repaired, and assembled as the transmission is reassembled. Other technicians choose to disassemble the transmission and service each of the subassemblies separately before starting to reassemble the transmission. The second method is recommended because there will be fewer parts disassembled at one time. This decreases the likelihood of mixing parts, which is easy to do, especially between clutch assemblies, because many parts have a similar appearance. If each subassembly is in good condition and is working properly, the transmission should work properly when completed.

18.2 CASE INSPECTION

Several areas of the case should be checked or serviced after it has been cleaned. These include the bushings, all fluid passages, the valve body *worm tracks* (grooves for the valve body fluid flow), all bolt threads, the clutch plate lugs, and the governor bore.

Some cases have an output shaft bushing, and it should be checked and replaced if it is worn or scored. Bushing replacement is described in Chapter 17. Occasionally a bushing will seize and spin with the shaft, which can ruin the case. The repair procedure is to ream the bore oversize. A bushing with an oversize outside diameter (OD) is then installed to repair the case (Figure 18-1).

Every fluid passage in the case must be clean and open. It is a good practice to blow air into each passage and make sure

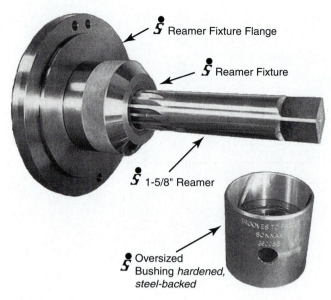

5 Reamer Fixture Flange

5 Reamer Fixture

5 1-5/8" Reamer

5 Oversized Bushing *hardened, steel-backed*

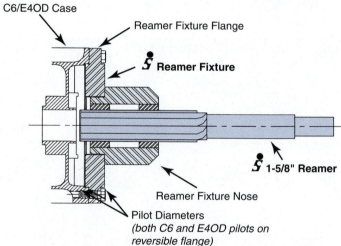

C6/E4OD Case

Reamer Fixture Flange

5 Reamer Fixture

5 1-5/8" Reamer

Reamer Fixture Nose

Pilot Diameters *(both C6 and E4OD pilots on reversible flange)*

FIGURE 18-1 This tool is designed to attach to the rear of an E4OD or C6 case. It guides a reamer that will cut the damaged bore to a larger diameter; an oversized bushing is then used to repair the case and a more durable bushing is installed. *(Courtesy of Sonnax)*

that it comes out the other end. Next, plug off one end of the passage while air pressure is applied; if you hear air escaping, there is a leak.

Check for warpage in the worm track area. Warpage can produce a *cross leak,* which is a leak from one passage to another. A cross leak can cause an unwanted, partial application of a clutch or band that can lead to an early failure. Case warpage is checked by placing a straightedge over the area to be checked and trying to slide a feeler gauge between the case and straightedge.

Most faulty bolt threads are found during disassembly. The telltale sign of failure is when the bolts come out with aluminum on the threads. Damaged threads should be repaired

TECH TIP

The exact location of a leak can be found by a *wet air test* (Chapter 12) or by placing the case under solvent or water as air is applied to each of the passages.

FIGURE 18-2 A flat, smooth file is being drawn (moved in the direction of the arrow) across the valve body area of a case to smooth out any dings or warpage.

TECH TIP

Some technicians **draw file** the valve body area using a 16-in., single-cut file as standard practice. To draw file a case, place the case with the worm tracks upward, lay the file flat, grip each end of the file, and draw the file sideways across the case (Figure 18-2). The file should be drawn in both a lengthwise and crosswise direction. The case is flat when a light cut has been made on all of the raised portions of the worm tracks.

TECH TIP

If a low-mileage transmission has failed because of a burned clutch or band you should check for pressure loss and cross leaks. Check for a cross leak by locating the passages for the two circuits and plug one of the passages with putty and fill it with ATF (Figure 18-3). Fluid leaking from this passage indicates a cross leak, which is probably caused by a crack or porous casting.

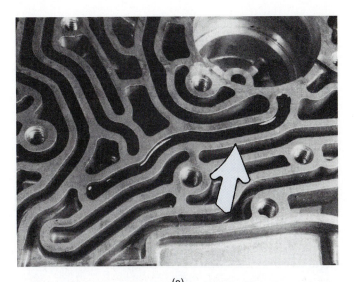

(a)

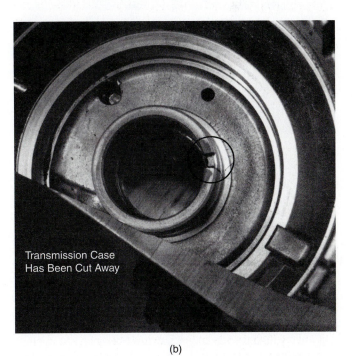

Transmission Case Has Been Cut Away

(b)

FIGURE 18-3 This worm track (arrow) has been closed off and filled with ATF to check for a suspected leak (a). The low-reverse clutch failed because of a pressure loss through a crack (circled) (b). It was found by watching ATF leak out of the crack.

as described in Chapter 14. It is good practice to check all bolt threads visually to make sure they are in good shape. Always replace questionable bolts.

If the transmission has a holding clutch, for example, the low-reverse clutch or intermediate clutch in a THM 350, check the area of the case where the clutch lugs engage the case (Figure 18-4). A badly worn case should be replaced.

FIGURE 18-4 This case shows wear in the area where the low-reverse clutch plates contact the lugs. This case is still usable, but excessive wear might hamper proper clutch apply and release.

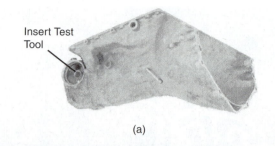

Insert Test Tool

(a)

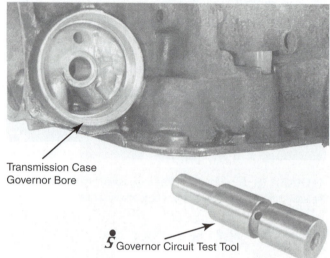

Transmission Case Governor Bore

Governor Circuit Test Tool

(b)

TECH TIP

The governor bore size can be checked by placing the governor into its bore and filling the passages with ATF, as shown in Figure 18-5. The bore should be repaired if the fluid leaks out too quickly (to point A in less than 30 seconds).

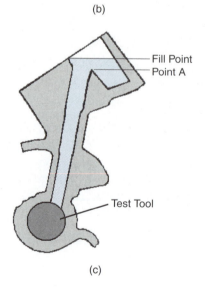

Fill Point
Point A

Test Tool

(c)

FIGURE 18-5 Governor bore wear is checked by placing the case on its back (a); inserting the test tool into the governor bore (b); filling the passage with ATF (c); and seeing how long it takes for the fluid to leak down to point A. *(b is courtesy of Sonnax)*

TECH TIP

Minor scores in a governor bore can be cleaned using a small cylinder hone (Figure 18-6). A worn bore can be repaired by installing a special reaming fixture, reaming the bore oversize, and installing a bushing to return the bore to the original size.

Check the governor bore on cases that have a gear-driven governor. If there is excessive wear in the governor bore, a loss in governor pressure can occur.

The final service step for the case service is to install a new seal for the manual shifter and, in some cases, the throttle

FIGURE 18-6 A small cylinder hone dipped in ATF can be used to smooth out minor scores in a governor bore. It should be turned by hand. Power tools should not be used.

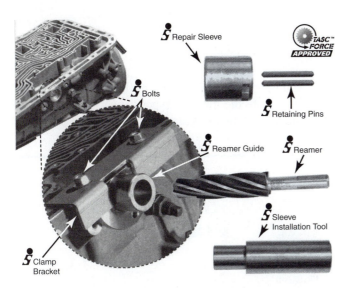

FIGURE 18-7 An A4LD tends to wear the manual shift linkage bore and leak fluid. The case can be repaired by reaming the bore oversize and installing a repair sleeve. *(Courtesy of Sonnax)*

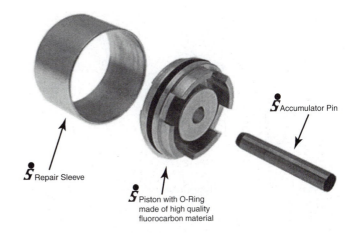

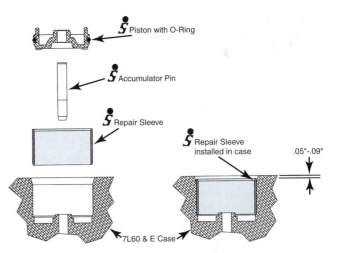

FIGURE 18-8 A damaged or worn accumulator bore can be repaired by installing a sleeve and a matching piston. *(Courtesy of Sonnax)*

TECH TIP

Some transmissions develop a fluid leak around the shift shaft because of a worn bore. A repair kit has been developed that includes a reamer, reamer guide, repair sleeve, and retaining pins (Figure 18-7). The repair sleeve is installed after the bore is reamed oversize.

TECH TIP

Some accumulator bores tend to wear because of repeated accumulator piston oscillation. This produces leakage at the accumulator piston and will ruin the case. A repair sleeve can be installed into the accumulator bore, and this sleeve along with a matching piston will allow the case to be reused (Figure 18-8).

valve linkage or rear bushing seal (Figure 18-9). These operations are described in Chapter 14. After this is done, the case can be set aside until reassembly.

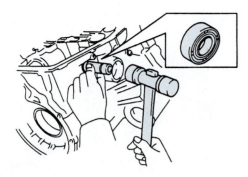

FIGURE 18-9   The manual valve shaft seal is driven into place using a seal driver.

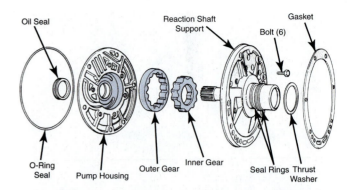

FIGURE 18-10   The pump gears and their cavity are carefully checked for wear and the front seal is normally replaced. *(Courtesy of Chrysler Corporation)*

REAL WORLD FIX

The 1974 Chevrolet Nova (126,000 miles; THM 350) has a late 1–2 shift and no 2–3 shift. Fluid level, TV cable adjustment, and the vacuum modulator are all good. The governor was checked and a bad driven gear was found. The governor gear was replaced, but this did not help.

Fix. Following advice, the technician checked the governor again and the governor bore was found to be bad. A remanufactured transmission fixed this vehicle. The worn governor bore could have been reamed out and repaired.

18.3 PUMP SERVICE

Service of most pumps consists of the following:

- disassembly
- inspection of the pumping members, stator support shaft, front bushing, clutch support surface, and sealing ring grooves
- checking of all valves
- cleaning of all fluid passages, including the *drainback hole*
- replacement of the front seal
- reassembly

Pump disassembly is fairly easy: Simply remove the bolts that secure the cover onto the body (Figure 18-10).

Experienced technicians check a pump by visual inspection. They carefully check the areas where wear normally occurs. Remember that the pump has a high-pressure area, and this high pressure tries to force the gears outward. A technician will inspect these areas:

- sides of the gears or rotors
- the body and cover where the gears run

TECH TIP

As you remove the pump gears or the rotor and slide, carefully note the front–back positioning. Many gears are marked. If the gears are not marked, use a permanent marking pen to identify the front of each gear.

REAL WORLD FIX

The 1982 Buick (2004R; 137,000 miles) transmission came into the shop with no reverse. Disassembly revealed the problem to be caused by worn sun gear splines. The worn parts were replaced, and the unit was rebuilt using a master kit, new pump, and torque converter. On start-up, the unit had excessively high line pressure.

Fix. The high pressure was caused by the wrong regulator valve for the later-model pump. The old valve (no vent) was installed into a bore that required a vented valve. The vent is a passage so line pressure can act on the end of the valve.

NOTE: This is a hard one, but when replacing a pressure regulator valve or its bore, carefully compare the parts to be sure they are the same.

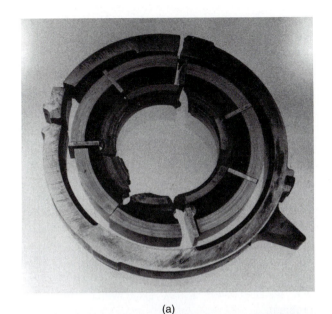

(a)

(b)

FIGURE 18-11 The rotor and slide of this vane pump are broken (a) and the pump body (b) is badly scored. This pump must be replaced.

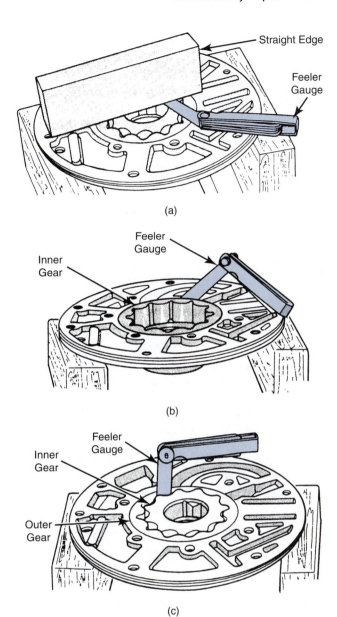

(a)

(b)

(c)

FIGURE 18-12 Clearance checks of the pump gears include end clearance (a), gear-to-housing clearance (b), and gear-tooth clearance (c). *(Courtesy of Chrysler Corporation)*

- flanks of the gear teeth/rotor lobes for score marks
- pump bushing (Figure 18-11)

Manufacturers sometimes publish clearance specifications for the pump wear locations. These clearances can be checked using a feeler gauge (Figure 18-12). A worn pump requires replacement with a new or rebuilt unit.

Vane-type pumps are also checked by visual inspection. Besides the inner slide area, be sure to check the pump guide rings, vanes, rotor, pump guide, slide, slide seals, seal support, slide pivot pin, spring, slide sealing ring, and backup seal (Figure 18-13). If replacement is necessary, the thickness of the rotor and slide should be measured to ensure the correct replacement parts are installed (Figure 18-14).

With the pump disassembled, it is usually easy to remove and replace the front seal and also the bushing if necessary. It should be noted that some manufacturers recommend replacing the pump assembly if the front bushing is damaged. A seal driver should be used when installing the new front seal (Figure 18-15). If a seal driver is not available, a flat piece of 1/8-in. (3-mm) or thicker metal should be placed over the seal to prevent damage while pressing or driving it into place. A damaged stator shaft can usually be pressed out and a new one pressed in while the pump is apart. Upgraded stator support shafts are available for some transmissions (Figure 18-16).

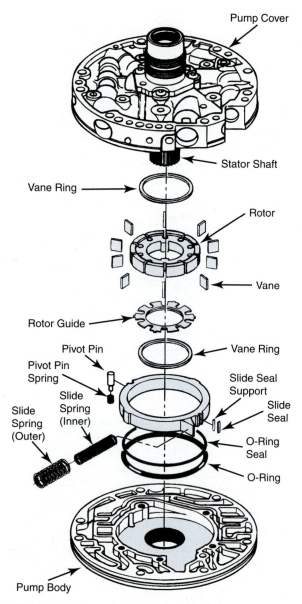

Pump Cover

Stator Shaft

Vane Ring

Rotor

Vane

Rotor Guide

Pivot Pin

Pivot Pin
Spring

Vane Ring

Slide
Spring
(Inner)

Slide Seal
Support

Slide
Seal

Slide
Spring
(Outer)

O-Ring
Seal

O-Ring

Pump Body

FIGURE 18-13 An exploded view of a vane-type pump. Wear checks include the rotor, vanes, slide, pump body, and pump cover.

TECH TIP

Metal caged lip seals are not designed to retain pressure. The fluid that is fed to lubricate the front bushing normally drains back into the transmission case through a drainback hole between the bushing and the seal (Figure 18-17). If this hole plugs up, pressure can build up behind the seal and cause the seal to blow out. Make sure the drain passage is open.

REAL WORLD FIX

The 1993 Chevrolet Blazer (87,000 miles) had a front seal leak that was repaired by installing a new seal, but after one or two weeks, it would begin leaking again. The front pump gasket and O-ring were replaced. The engine crankshaft end play was checked, and it was within specifications. The vehicle returned with the same problem.

Fix. During the next replacement of the seal, the pump bushing was checked and was found to have been spinning in the pump assembly. A new bushing was installed with a new seal, which cured the problem.

REAL WORLD FIX

The 1998 Ford Escort (215,000 miles) was driving at 45 mph when it suddenly neutralled out (no drive or reverse). The technician checked oil pressure and found 0 psi. A check of the pressure regulator valve shows it to be okay. A check of the pump drive shaft shows it was in good condition, and the shaft seems to engage the torque converter splines.

Fix. Following advice, the technician tried the pump drive shaft in the torque converter again, but this time he pulled the shaft about 1/8 in. out from the front of the drive splines. The splines were stripped in this area. A new torque converter fixed this problem.

Some pumps include a clutch piston assembly; the piston seals are serviced as described in Chapter 17.

After the pump has been cleaned, thoroughly checked, and the bushings and seal replaced, it can be reassembled. The gears or rotor and slide assembly should be well lubricated and placed in the pump body.

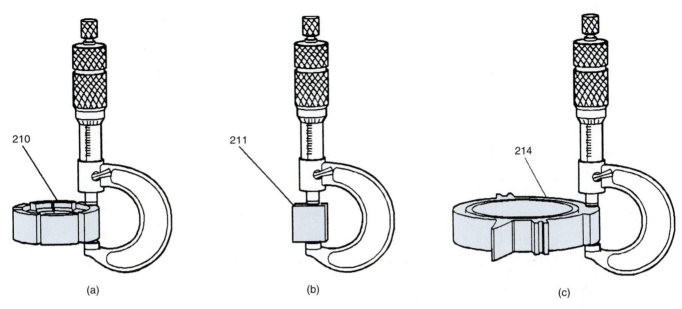

FIGURE 18-14   If replacement is needed for the pump rotor (a), vanes (b), or slide (c), they should be measured to determine the proper size. *(Reprinted with permission of General Motors)*

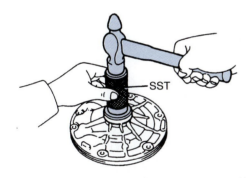

FIGURE 18-15   A new front seal is being installed using a seal driver (SST).

TECH TIP

Technicians normally lubricate all moving parts as they are assembled. Normal automotive grease cannot be used because it is thick and might plug a fluid orifice. Special automatic transmission assembly lubricant, petroleum jelly, or ATF is commonly used. These grease-like compounds will melt and be dissolved before the transmission gets to operating temperature.

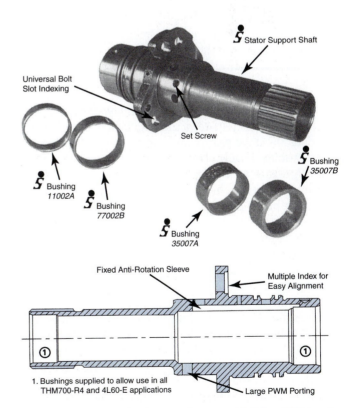

1. Bushings supplied to allow use in all THM700-R4 and 4L60-E applications

FIGURE 18-16   A replacement stator support shaft for a 4L60 transmission that uses a set screw to prevent rotation of the inner sleeve. *(Courtesy of Sonnax)*

Do Not Contact or Damage This Wall When Drilling

Point "A" - Drill a 6.0mm (1/4") Hole 12.9mm (1/2") Deep Max.

Drainback Passage

Point "B" Check For Restriction

Point "C" Drill a 8.0mm (3/8") Hole Do Not Drill Past This Point

FIGURE 18-17   Fluid flowing through the pump bushing must be allowed to flow to the pan through the drainback passage. If this passage is blocked, a drill bit of the proper size should be used to clean it out. *(Reprinted with permission of General Motors)*

TECH TIP

Some technicians lubricate the gears with a heavy coating of transmission assembly lubricant or petroleum jelly to ensure that the pump will prime and start pumping fluid immediately on start-up.

Some pumps require *pump gear alignment* as the gears are installed. This requires a special alignment tool set that positions the drive gear properly to the pump housing and front bushing (Figure 18-18). Improper alignment might cause breakage of the gears or housing or damage to the bushing or front seal. In all cases it is good practice to visually center the pump drive gear to the front bushing as the pump is assembled.

On some pumps, the cover has a much smaller diameter than the body. Here, the cover is merely placed in position and the bolts are installed and tightened to the correct torque. Other pump covers and bodies have the same outer diameter. These diameters are only slightly smaller than the bore in the transmission case. The two outer diameters have to be exactly aligned before tightening the bolts. *Pump cover alignment* is accomplished by using the band shown in Figure 18-19. This band is available commercially, or a very large screw-type hose clamp can be used in its place.

At this point, the pump is ready to be reinstalled.

FIGURE 18-18   These special tools are used to align the pump gears of certain Ford transmissions while the bolts are tightened. *(Courtesy of ATEC Trans-Tool and Cleaning Systems)*

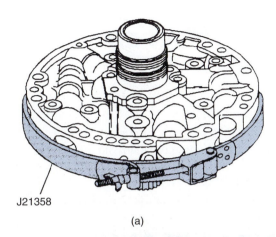

J21358

(a)

(b)

FIGURE 18-19 Special tool J25025-1 is being used to align the pump body and cover before tightening the bolts (a). A long screw clamp can be used for this same purpose (b). *(a is reprinted with permission of General Motors)*

TECH TIP

An alternate aligning method is to place the pump upside down in an empty transmission case before tightening the bolts (Figure 18-20).

FIGURE 18-20 The pump body and cover can be aligned correctly by placing them into the case upside down while the bolts are tightened.

TECH TIP

The torque converter can be used to align the pump gears by placing the pump body on the torque converter hub as the pump is assembled. Torque-tighten the pump cover bolts before removing the pump.

18.4 CLUTCH ASSEMBLY SERVICE

The service procedure for most clutch assemblies is as follows:

- Remove the clutch plates and disassemble the return spring(s) and piston (Figure 18-21).
- Thoroughly clean the parts.
- Inspect the drum, piston, and check ball as well as the bushing and seal ring area.
- Install new seals on the piston.
- Install the piston and return spring(s).
- Install the clutch plates.
- Check the clutch clearance.

Clutch plate removal is usually easy. A screwdriver or seal pick is used to work the snap ring out of its groove. The pressure plate and clutch plates are removed next (Figure 18-22).

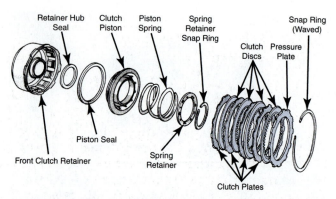

FIGURE 18-21 An exploded view of a clutch assembly; note the clutch stack with four frictions and the strong piston spring. *(Courtesy of Chrysler Corporation)*

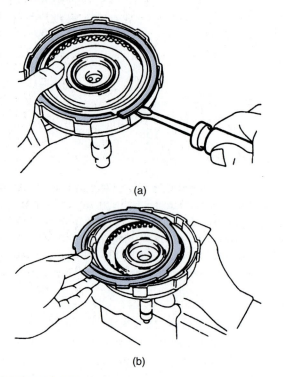

(a)

(b)

FIGURE 18-22 The large snap ring can usually be removed using a screwdriver or seal pick (a) and then the pressure plate and clutch plates can be removed (b).

Always note the position of the pressure plate, the number of lined and unlined plates, and if any cushion plates are used and their position.

A spring compressor is usually required to remove the piston return spring(s) and retainer. There is a large variety of spring compressors, and no one unit will work best for all clutches, because some have a bore in the center, a shaft in the center, or are in the case (Figure 18-23). Many shops use bench- or floor-mounted spring compressors because these are usually faster. Be careful when compressing the spring(s), removing the retainer, and allowing the spring(s) to extend. Some springs store quite a bit of energy (one clutch uses an

TECH TIP

Clutch stacks will vary for a given transmission model depending on the application. Note the order of the plates as they are removed. Check them for wear as described in Chapter 17.

REAL WORLD FIX

The 1995 Impala SS (145,000 miles) transmission was overhauled because of no fourth gear. The 3–4 clutch was badly burned. The case and input drum were replaced because they were badly worn. The transmission now has no low or third gear.

Fix. Disassembling the transmission again revealed that the passage to the forward clutch was plugged with debris. The forward clutch was a used unit, purchased from a dismantler. The input drum had a thorough cleaning. An air check showed proper clutch operation.

A lot of work would have been saved if this used clutch had been disassembled and cleaned during the subassembly repair process.

TECH TIP

While the return springs are being removed, be sure to note the number and location of the springs if all of the pockets are not filled with springs (Figure 18-24).

800-lb [364-kg] release spring). If they fly loose, they can cause injury. Review the safety note following step 7 of Section 16.5.

Some clutch pistons almost fall out of the bore when the springs and retainer are removed. Other pistons have to be

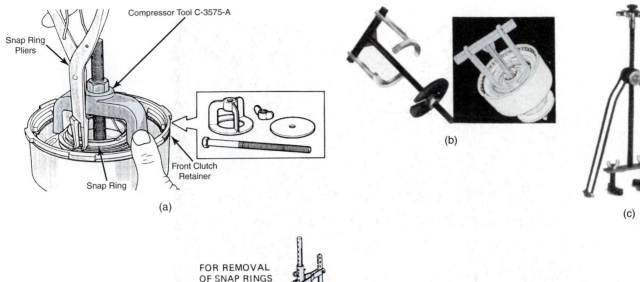

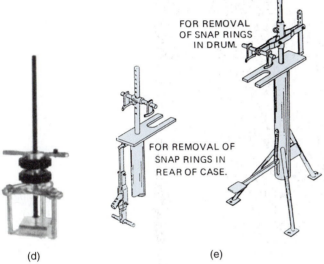

FIGURE 18-23 This variety of clutch spring compressors includes completely portable ones (a, b, and c), a bench-mounted style (d), and a large, foot-operated style (e). *(a, left, is courtesy of Chrysler Corporation; a, right, is courtesy of Kent-Moore; b is courtesy of OTC; d and e are courtesy of KD Tools)*

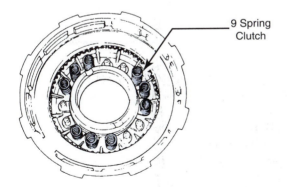

FIGURE 18-24 Some clutch assemblies do not use a spring in each of the pockets. Note how they are arranged in this clutch. *(Courtesy of Chrysler Corporation)*

coaxed with air pressure in the clutch apply oil hole or by slamming the clutch drum piston side down onto a block of wood (Figure 18-25). With the piston out, remove the old seals, wash the parts in solvent, and dry them using compressed air.

REAL WORLD FIX

The 1994 Dodge Caravan (143,000 miles) was working fine when the fluid was replaced a few weeks ago. Since the fluid change, it got stuck in snow, and had to be rocked out. Now it moves forward in all shift lever positions, even neutral. The shift linkage was checked and found to be okay.

Fix. When the transmission was disassembled, the front clutch plates were found to have gotten so hot that they welded together. Rebuilding the transmission fixed this problem.

(a)

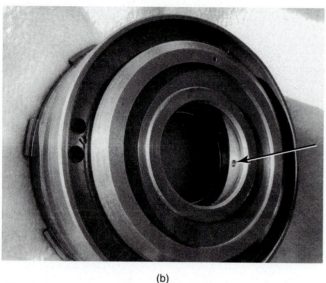

(b)

FIGURE 18-25   A piston can be removed by slamming the clutch downward on a block of wood (a) or applying air pressure in the apply port (b).

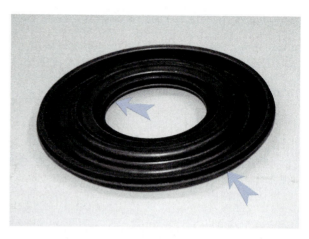

FIGURE 18-26   This piston is made from stamped steel parts that can separate. It is tested by inserting a screwdriver and trying to pry the grooves open with a light pressure.

TECH TIP

Some clutch drums are made from stamped steel parts and these can leak at a weld or a crack next to a weld causing a pressure loss. If you suspect a leaking drum, place the clutch with the bore upward, and fill the piston area with ATF or solvent. If fluid leaks out, you need to replace the drum. Another method is to spray the assembled clutch with a soapy water mix, and air check it using varied low and high pressures.

TECH TIP

Some clutch pistons are made from stamped steel parts that are pressed and welded together. These parts can shift position, which can cause a seal groove that is too wide or too narrow. Check the groove width; it should be slightly wider than the seal. If you suspect a problem, place a screwdriver into the groove, and try prying it wider (Figure 18-26). If the parts move easily, replace the piston.

REAL WORLD FIX

A 1991 Acura has a slip in second gear after it warms up. When cold, the transmission operates normal, and when hot, transmission operation is normal except for second gear.

Fix. A very small crack was found next to a weld in the second drum, and this crack opened up when hot and caused a pressure loss. Replacement of the second drum clutch fixed the transmission.

REAL WORLD FIX

The 1993 Pontiac Grand Am (185,000 km) came in with several problems. Dirty fluid and slippage in all forward gears were found, so the transmission was rebuilt. After the repairs, the test drive showed the slippage was still evident. TV adjustment was good, and fluid pressures were close to normal. The transmission was disassembled again, and a burnt input clutch was found (after only 20 km).

Fix. Following advice, the technician checked the forward input clutch housing, and a crack was found around a weld at the center. Replacing the clutch housing fixed this problem.

TECH TIP

In the heavier cast drums, the ball can be seated by striking the ball using a thin pin punch. This will crush small burrs to make it seat tighter.

The clutch check ball should be captured in its cage but still free to rattle when shaken (Figure 18-27). You should be able to move it with either an air blast or a seal pick. If you suspect that you have a leaky check ball, fill the drum with ATF as just described. It should not leak. The check ball assembly can be removed and replaced in stamped steel drums.

The bushing, seal ring bore, and seal ring grooves should be smooth and free from scores and other damage (Figure 18-28).

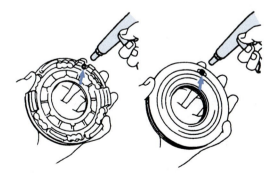

FIGURE 18-27 The check ball should be free to move inside its cage. It should also seal low-pressure air flow in one direction (left) and leak in the other (right).

FIGURE 18-28 This bushing appears usable and the two sealing ring areas (arrows) show normal operation.

REAL WORLD FIX

The 4T60E transaxle in the 1997 Buick LeSabre was overhauled, but it had only first gear. Forcing a 1–2 shift gets neutral. The fluid pressures were okay, and the governor checked out good.

Fix. The transaxle was disassembled, and the second clutch return spring assembly was found to be installed upside down. A more careful check of the parts as they were disassembled would have prevented the problem.

Small imperfections can be removed with a file or by sanding. It should be noted that some turbine shafts have two or more fluid passages. Some passages have a cup plug for fluid flow control. These passages should be clean, open, and not leak into each other.

When the clutch parts check out and are thoroughly clean:

- Install the new seals.
- Thoroughly lubricate the seals and bore.
- Carefully install the piston completely into the bore.
- Replace the return springs and retainer.

If three piston seals are used, be sure they all face in the proper direction.

A clutch is assembled by stacking the parts in the correct order (Figure 18-29). Some units use a thick apply plate next

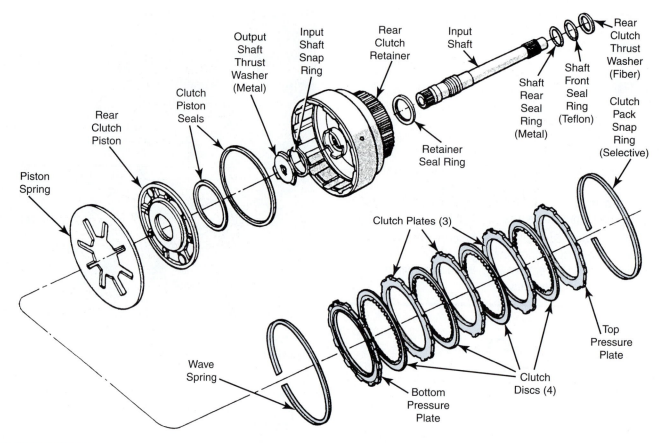

FIGURE 18-29   This rear clutch stack has a selective snap ring, top pressure plate, four friction disks, three steel plates, bottom pressure plate, and wave spring to retain the Belleville piston spring. *(Courtesy of Chrysler Corporation)*

TECH TIP

Always check to be sure the plates turn freely with the clutch released (Figure 18-30). There should never be a drag between the plates with the clutch vertical. If the clutch is laid flat, you should feel a definite drag between the plates.

TECH TIP

If clearance specifications are not available, use the rule of thumb that the clearance should be 0.010 in. (0.5 mm) for each lined plate.

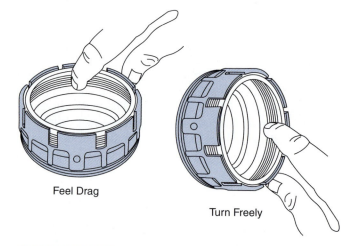

Feel Drag

Turn Freely

FIGURE 18-30   With the clutch assembled and lying flat, you should feel a definite drag if you try to rotate the plates (left). The plates should rotate easily with the clutch vertical (right).

to the piston to distribute the apply force onto the plates. The stack is an alternating series of lined and unlined plates followed by a backing/pressure plate. Some units use a wave, Belleville, or selective plate under the backing plate.

When a clutch pack is assembled, the clearance should always be checked and adjusted if necessary. The clearance check ensures that the clutch is assembled correctly and will

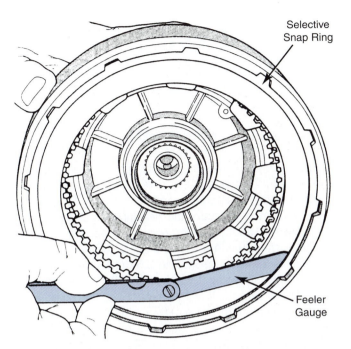

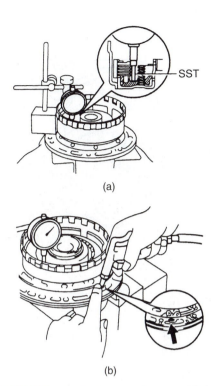

(a)

(b)

FIGURE 18-31 The clutch pack clearance specification for this clutch is 0.025 to 0.045 in. (0.64 to 1.14 mm). A 0.025-in. feeler gauge should enter as shown, but a 0.045-in. feeler gauge should be very tight or not fit in at all. *(Courtesy of Chrysler Corporation)*

FIGURE 18-32 A dial indicator can be set up with the stylus on the piston to measure piston stroke (a). Applying air to the proper passage should cause the piston to stroke so the travel can be measured (b).

produce a smooth shift. Depending on the transmission and the particular clutch, different *selective* parts may be used to adjust clutch clearance. The parts that can be of variable (selective) thickness are the piston, pressure plate, snap ring, apply ring, steel plate, and lined plate. Typically, a selective snap ring is used. Most manufacturers publish clearance specifications for some, if not all, of the clutches used in their transmissions.

Clutch clearance, also called piston travel, is normally measured using a feeler gauge placed between the pressure plate and the snap ring (Figure 18-31). If a waved snap ring is used, position the feeler gauge in the widest area under a wave portion.

TECH TIP

The clearance of a holding clutch can be measured from a point on the transmission case to the clutch pack (Figure 18-33). In others, the clutch has to be assembled temporarily before installation in order to measure the stack height (Figure 18-34).

TECH TIP

Clearance can also be measured using a dial indicator. Position the dial indicator as shown in Figure 18-32, and raise and lower the backing plate to measure its vertical travel, which is the clutch clearance. If a wave or Belleville plate is used, the pressure plate should be pushed downward with a light, even pressure so the cushion plate(s) is not distorted.

TECH TIP

Measuring clutch clearance seems to be a lot of trouble to some, but it is well worth the time if it saves a comeback for a burned-out clutch or poor shift quality.

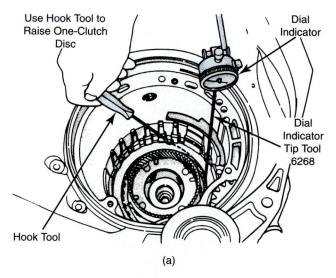

Use Hook Tool to Raise One-Clutch Disc

Dial Indicator

Dial Indicator Tip Tool 6268

Hook Tool

(a)

PART NO.	Thickness
4377150	6.92 mm (.273 in.)
4377149	6.66 mm (.262 in.)
4377148	6.40 mm (.252 in.)
4412268	6.14 mm (.242 in.)
4412267	5.88 mm (.232 in.)
4412266	5.62 mm (.221 in.)
4412265	5.36 mm (.211 in.)

(b)

FIGURE 18-33 This reaction clutch is deep in the case, and the clearance is measured by lifting a clutch plate while watching the dial indicator (a). Clutch clearance is adjusted by selecting the proper reaction/pressure plate (b). *(Courtesy of Chrysler Corporation)*

FIGURE 18-34 This clutch pack is assembled and the height is measured. The height should be within the specified dimensions.

TECH TIP

Many technicians prefer to build a clutch toward the lower end of the clearance to reduce piston travel; this usually produces crisper shift quality. For example, if a 4R70W forward clutch (five plates) has 0.099 in. (2.51 mm) of clearance and a 0.075-in. (1.9-mm) retaining ring, to reduce the clearance to the 0.050- to 0.094-in. (1.27- to 2.38-mm) specification, a snap ring that is either 0.086 to 0.092 in. or 0.102 to 0.106 in. (2.23 to 2.34 mm or 2.59 to 2.69 mm) can be used. The larger snap ring (assume it is 0.104 in.) would be preferred because it would reduce the clearance by about 0.029 in. (0.104 − 0.075 = 0.029 in.) (2.64 − 1.9 = 0.74 mm) to a clearance of about 0.070 in. (0.099 − 0.029 = 0.070 in.) (1.78 mm). The snap ring that is 0.088 to 0.92 in. reduces the clearance by about 0.015 in. (0.38 mm) to about 0.084 in. (2.13 mm)— acceptable but not as good as 0.070 in.

TECH TIP

If the selective parts do not correct the clearance or are not available, clutch clearance can be reduced by using extra-thick steel plates or adding an extra unlined steel or lined friction plate (Figure 18-35). If an additional friction plate is too thick, one or both of the adjacent friction linings can be scraped off using a knife or gasket scraper.

Clutch clearance is adjusted by changing the selective component.

The clutch is ready for installation at this point.

18.4.1 One-Way Clutch Service

One-way clutches are visually inspected during transmission disassembly and reassembly (see Section 16.6). The commonly encountered problems are: severe wear from poor lubrication or metal fragments from a failed part; wear or scoring

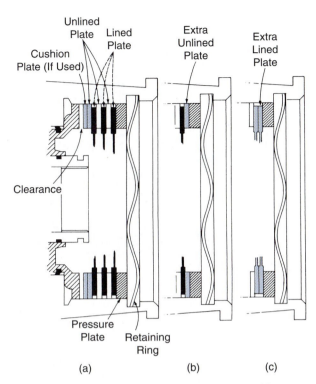

Labels: Cushion Plate (If Used), Unlined Plate, Lined Plate, Extra Unlined Plate, Extra Lined Plate, Clearance, Pressure Plate, Retaining Ring

(a)   (b)   (c)

FIGURE 18-35 Clutch clearance can be reduced by adding an extra unlined plate (a and b) or lined plate (c). If two lined plates are next to each other as in c, clearance can be increased by shaving the lining off one or both adjacent sides of the two lined plates.

REAL WORLD FIX

A 604 transmission from a 1992 Chrysler (72,000 miles) was being rebuilt, and new clutches were being installed. These clutches use five frictions and five steels. The 2–4 clutch pack went together okay, but the low-reverse pack does not have enough clearance, even with the thinnest reaction plate.

Fix. It was discovered that the technician was trying to use 2–4 frictions that are 0.085 in. in place of the thinner low-reverse frictions that are 0.075 in. The low-reverse clutch had the proper clearance when the correct frictions were used.

of the race(s), rollers, or sprags; and a sprag(s) that flips over. One-way clutches should always be lubricated using assembly grease, petroleum jelly, or ATF during assembly. After assembly, they should be tested to ensure that they rotate freely in the proper direction and lock up in the opposite direction.

TECH TIP

Most technicians air check a clutch as soon as it is assembled. This simple operation ensures that the clutch works properly. When air pressure is applied to the clutch, the piston should stroke, squeeze the clutch together, and not leak (Figure 18-36). When air pressure is released, the piston should return to provide clutch clearance. In some cases, a special air nozzle is necessary to reach the apply hole. Placing the clutch over the pump clutch support shaft allows the use of a standard rubber-tipped air gun. Testing through the clutch support shaft also checks the sealing rings.

TECH TIP

Do not air check a clutch before installing the clutch plates. The piston can travel far enough for the piston seal to catch at the end of its bore.

REAL WORLD FIX

The 1996 GMC Vandura G3500 (142,000 miles) came in with a shift problem. A scan tool check showed code 87, solenoid stuck off. Clutch material was found in the pan, so the transmission was overhauled. The vehicle came back after a day with the same problem. The solenoid, fuse, and harness all checked out okay.

Fix. Following advice, the technician disassembled the 4L80E transmission and checked for a leak at the center support. A faulty seal was found, and replacing the center support seal fixed this problem.

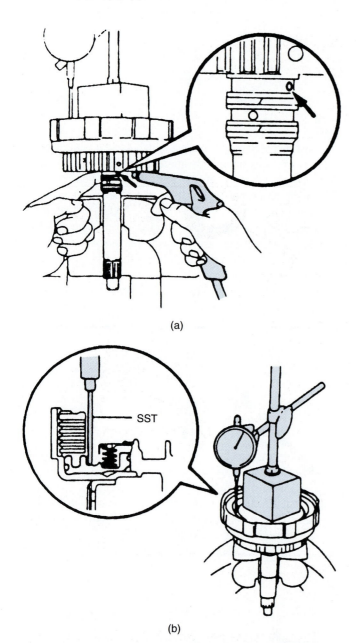

(a)

(b)

FIGURE 18-36   Air pressure is applied to the shaft clutch apply port (a) to apply and air test the clutch piston. The amount of piston stroke and clutch pack clearance are measured using a dial indicator. The special service tool (SST) allows the dial indicator to reach the piston. *(b courtesy of Toyota Motor Sales USA, Inc.)*

If the electronics are disconnected and a CD4E transmission (and most others) will not move forward in drive, there is a large probability that the one-way clutch is at fault.

18.5 GEARSET SERVICE

Servicing gearsets is primarily a visual inspection of the various gears and a side play and rotation check of the planet gears. In some cases there is also an end-play check of the

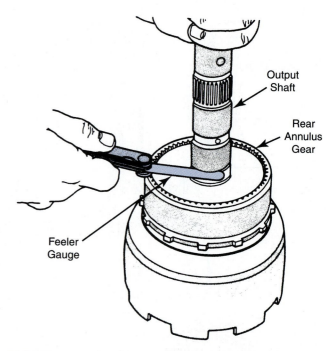

FIGURE 18-37   This gearset should have 0.005 to 0.048 in. (0.12 to 1.22 mm) of end play. A 0.005-in. feeler gauge should enter as shown, but a 0.049-in. gauge should not. *(Courtesy of Chrysler Corporation)*

REAL WORLD FIX

The 1991 Ford Explorer (156,000 miles) transmission was rebuilt. But a road test showed it has a very harsh engagement after the vehicle starts out from a stop. It seems to slam into first gear. The governor was replaced, but this did not help. The valve body was disassembled and rechecked, with no problem found.

Fix. After studying the clutch apply charts, the technician determined that the problem had to be the overrun clutch. An inspection showed that this clutch was bad, and replacing the overrun clutch fixed this problem.

assembled gear train to ensure the thrust washers are not worn excessively (Figure 18-37).

In many transmissions, the gearset comes out one part at a time. A technician always inspects each part as it is removed. After cleanup, the parts are carefully inspected again. Parts to rebuild a planetary are available from aftermarket sources (Figure 18-38).

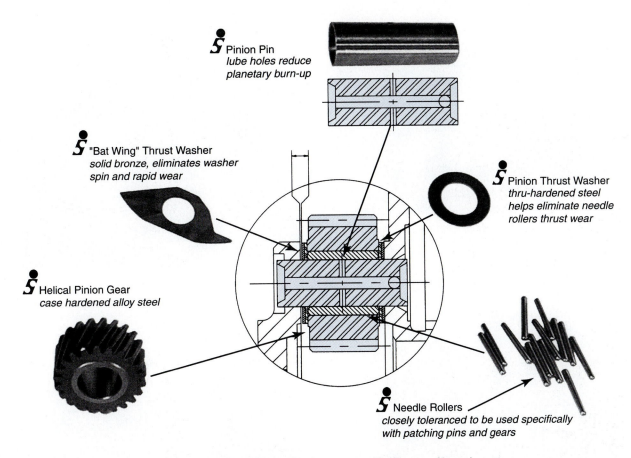

Pinion Pin
*lube holes reduce
planetary burn-up*

"Bat Wing" Thrust Washer
*solid bronze, eliminates washer
spin and rapid wear*

Pinion Thrust Washer
*thru-hardened steel
helps eliminate needle
rollers thrust wear*

Helical Pinion Gear
case hardened alloy steel

Needle Rollers
*closely toleranced to be used specifically
with patching pins and gears*

FIGURE 18-38   This kit includes the parts needed to rebuild a 4L60 planetary assembly. *(Courtesy of Sonnax)*

REAL WORLD FIX

The 2001 Ford Escape (96,000 miles) came in with no drive; it would move forward in manual first or second. There were no DTCs. The transmission was removed, sent to a rebuilder, and reinstalled. A cracked pressure plate and worn friction plates were replaced, but the transmission had the same problem: no drive. The valve body and gaskets were checked and the shift solenoids were replaced, but this did not fix the problem.

Fix. Following advice, the transmission was disassembled, and a bad one-way clutch was found. Replacement of the one-way clutch fixed this transmission.

REAL WORLD FIX

The E4OD in the 1996 Ford F350 (152,000 miles) was rebuilt because of a delayed/no-reverse problem. There were a lot of metal particles throughout the transmission. The transmission was rebuilt, and the torque converter was replaced. After replacing the transmission, there was no drive; it did not move in drive or manual-1. Line pressure was good, and there were no DTCs.

Fix. Following advice, the transmission was disassembled to check the low sprag. It had been installed upside down; reinstalling the low sprag in the proper position solved this problem.

All ring and sun gears should be checked for chipped or broken teeth and worn or stripped drive splines (Figure 18-39). The thrust surfaces at the sides of the gears and any support

(a)

(b)

(c)

(d)

(e)

FIGURE 18-39   Planetary gear train damage shows up as wear (a–d) or cracks and breakage (e).

TECH TIP

Mark the pinion gears before removing the pinion shafts. The gearset can become noisy if you install a pinion gear upside down.

TECH TIP

If gearset replacement is necessary, make sure the new gearset has the same gear ratio. The TCM in electronic transmissions compares input and output speed. If they are not correct, it will illuminate the MIL and set an incorrect gear ratio code.

bushings or bushing surfaces should be checked for scores, wear, or other damage (Figure 18-40). Drive shells should be checked for stripped splines, damaged lugs, or cracks (Figure 18-41).

When checking a carrier, the pinion gears must be undamaged and turn freely. Check for worn or missing pinion

(b)

(a)

(c)

FIGURE 18-40   These three gear train components show severe wear and scoring in the thrust surfaces.

(a)

(b)

FIGURE 18-41   These sun gear drive shells show stripped splines (a) and broken, dislodged splines (b).

REAL WORLD FIX

The 1990 Nissan Maxima (125,000 miles) transmission had no reverse. It was rebuilt, and the clutch plates, band, seals, and solenoid valve assembly were replaced. All the clutches were air checked for proper operation. The transmission was reinstalled, but the original problem is still there. The technician thought that the TCM was the cause of this problem.

Fix. Following advice, the technician checked the fluid pressures, and they were good in drive and reverse. The transmission was then disassembled, and a thorough check found that a sun gear had sheared cleanly from its shaft. Replacing this shaft and reassembly of the transmission fixed this problem.

FIGURE 18-42   This planet pinion gear has too much side clearance; it should be repaired or the carrier should be replaced.

thrust bushings. If they appear sloppy, measure the pinion gear end play and/or side clearance (Figure 18-42). Some manufacturers provide pinion gear side clearance specifications, but if no specifications are available, use the rule of thumb of 0.005 to 0.025 in. (0.167 to 0.635 mm). In some cases, the pinion gear assembly can be removed from the carrier to replace the bearings, gear, or thrust washers. The needle bearings commonly used can make this a tedious task. Shims are available to tighten the side clearance on some carriers.

18.6 VALVE BODY SERVICE

Despite its complexity, the valve body is one of the more reliable parts in a transmission, probably because the valves are so well lubricated. In a way, valves do little, as they move only slightly and only once in a while. Most valve body service operations consist of disassembly, cleaning, checking for free movement, reassembly, and in a few transmissions, adjusting the pressure regulator valve (Figure 18-43). The valve(s) in a governor and pump assembly are serviced in the same manner.

The biggest problem during valve body repair is getting it back together with everything in the right order and location.

Some technicians make a valve organizer by folding a piece of cardboard into an accordion shape (Figure 18-44).

REAL WORLD FIX

The 1995 BMW (110,000 miles) had no reverse, and it would not move backward in neutral with the engine running. The transmission had been repaired a year earlier because of a burned clutch. The internal seals were replaced, but this did not help.

Fix. Following advice from experienced technicians, the valve body was removed and inspected. A small piece (about 3 mm × 5 mm) of foreign material (probably gasket) was found to be blocking movement of one of the valves. Removal of this object fixed this problem.

TECH TIP

Some technicians make a *spring holder,* as shown in Figure 18-45. This unit is shop-made from two electrical box covers and a group of small, 2-in.-long machine screws. Each screw location on the holder is numbered. As a valve and spring are removed, the spring is placed on a screw and the number is written next to the spring in the manual illustration. This does two things: It helps locate a certain spring and helps teach the technician the name of the spring and valve. As each spring comes out, a mental or written note should be made of how it fits the valve, how many coils it has, and its color.

TECH TIP

Most technicians complete a valve body repair as quickly as possible; the longer it takes, the easier it is to forget which spring goes where or how it fits on a particular valve. In many cases, the service manual is only an aid. Each transmission model and version is slightly different. These differences are often in the valve body and are often just a spring change. Remember that when taking a valve body apart, you become the expert in how that particular unit goes back together.

Several methods are used to retain the valve(s) in a bore. Many units use a cover plate that holds one or more valves (Figure 18-46). Removal of the retaining screws allows removal of the plate, valve(s), and spring(s). Many valves use a plug or sleeve at the end of each bore. The plug/sleeve is retained with a keeper, which can be a pin, plate, or key (Figure 18-47). The keeper cannot come out while the valve body is in place on the transmission, and the valve's spring pressure keeps it in place while the valve body is removed. Pushing the plug/sleeve slightly inward allows the keeper to be pulled out easily, and then the plug/sleeve, valve(s), and spring(s) will come out.

An unworn aluminum valve in an unworn valve body might not free fall if it is tested wet; sticking should be tested by feeling the effort required to slide the valve in its bore.

Carefully inspect the valve and valve body for varnish, a light brown or golden brown coating. It can be cleaned off

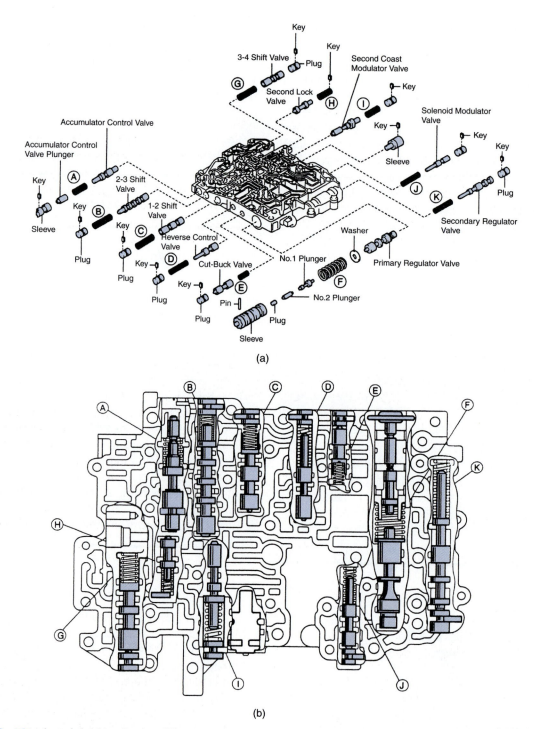

FIGURE 18-43 An exploded (a) and cutaway (b) view of the valve body from a four-speed transaxle. Note the various valve groups and how they are retained in their bore.

TECH TIP

Some valve bodies use a coiled spring pin (roll pin) to hold the valve plug/sleeve in place (Figure 18-48). In some cases, this coiled pin can be pulled out by gripping it with a pair of pliers. In other cases, you will need to make an extractor tool. Grind the flats of a small (about 3/32 in., 3 mm) Allen wrench or the end of a No. 49 drill bit so it tapers to a point, as shown in Figure 18-48. Tap this pointed end into the coiled pin; rotate the pin in a direction that wraps the pin tighter; and as the pin rotates, lift it out of the bore.

TECH TIP

Most technicians place a lint-free shop cloth(s) or a carpet scrap under the valve body while disassembling it. The cloth helps keep the check balls, screws, and pins from rolling away and might prevent a nick or dent in a valve if one happens to drop.

TECH TIP

The reasons for disassembling a valve body are to clean it thoroughly and ensure that all valves are working freely and not sticking. The **free fall** test is a standard check for a sticking valve. Hold the valve body so the bore is vertical. In this position, a steel valve should fall freely from one end of the bore to the other; it should at least fall through the area of normal valve movement (Figure 18-49). Any valve that does not fall freely is sticking, which can be a fault of the valve, the bore, or both.

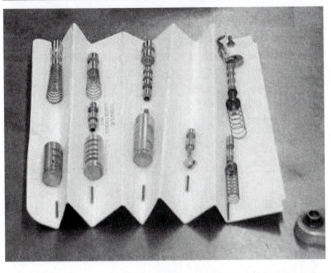

FIGURE 18-44 A sheet of stiff paper has been folded to create this simple valve holder. Note that a valve group can be placed in order and also labeled.

(a)

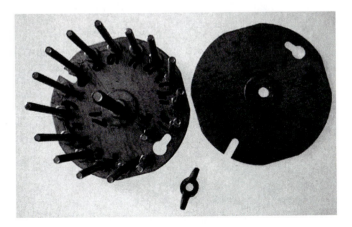

(b)

FIGURE 18-45 This simple shop-made tool is a valve body spring holder. It is made from two electrical box covers, a 1/4 in. × 2-1/2 in. stove bolt and nut, and 16, 8 × 2 in. machine screws and nuts. As a valve is removed, the spring is placed over a numbered peg, and the number is written on a picture of the valve body.

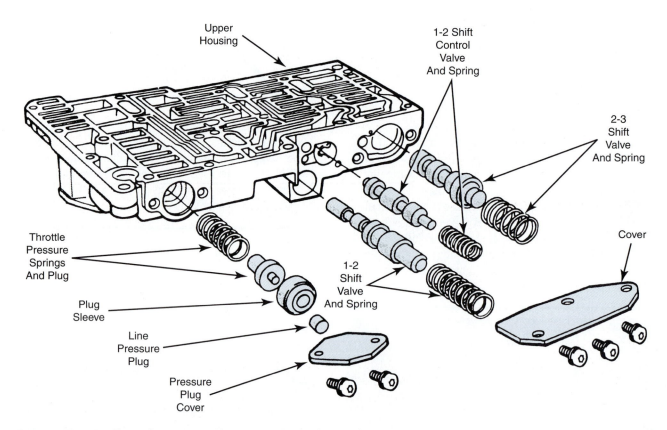

FIGURE 18-46 These valves are retained by two cover plates; with the covers removed, the valves should slide out of their bores. *(Courtesy of Chrysler Corporation)*

Fluid can leak out the end of the bore, past the plug. If a round, aluminum plug is used, it can be enlarged by using a tubing cutter to score a groove around the plug. This displaces and raises metal and should create a tighter fit.

Aluminum valves and valve bodies should be checked for wear. Position the valve so you have something to hold onto, but as deep in the bore as possible. Some valves can be inserted into the bore backward for this check. Next, try to move the valve vertically, and note the amount of movement. Vertical movement should be very small. Compare the amount of movement to a new or known-good valve body.

A wet air test can also be used to check for wear.

Short valves that are located between fluid pressure and a spring tend to tip in the valve bore. This can cause ridges in the bore that can cause the valve to jam (Figure 18-50).

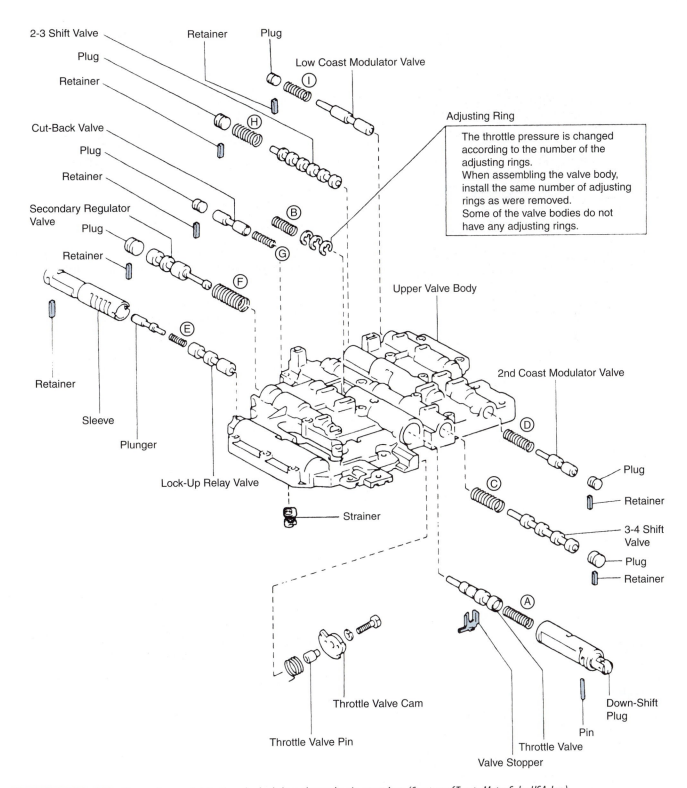

2-3 Shift Valve

Retainer

Plug

Low Coast Modulator Valve

Plug

Retainer

Cut-Back Valve

Plug

Retainer

Secondary Regulator Valve

Plug

Retainer

Retainer

Sleeve

Plunger

Lock-Up Relay Valve

Strainer

Adjusting Ring

The throttle pressure is changed according to the number of the adjusting rings.
When assembling the valve body, install the same number of adjusting rings as were removed.
Some of the valve bodies do not have any adjusting rings.

Upper Valve Body

2nd Coast Modulator Valve

Plug

Retainer

3-4 Shift Valve

Plug

Retainer

Down-Shift Plug

Pin

Throttle Valve

Valve Stopper

Throttle Valve Cam

Throttle Valve Pin

FIGURE 18-47   These valves are held in the valve body by a plug and a pin or retainer. *(Courtesy of Toyota Motor Sales USA, Inc.)*

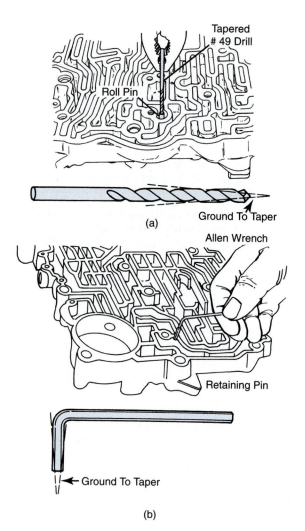

Ground To Taper

(a)

(b)

Ground To Taper

FIGURE 18-48 A drill bit (a) or Allen wrench (b) can be modified so that it enters a roll pin, and then is rotated to lift the pin out. *(Reprinted with permission of General Motors)*

REAL WORLD FIX

The 2000 Ford Mustang (61,000 miles) came in with a complaint of stalling when shifted to drive after the transmission warmed up. A scan tool check showed no unusual activity of the shift or TCC solenoids. The TCC solenoid seemed sticky so it was replaced along with the MLPS, but this did not help.

Fix. The valve body was checked, and several of the aluminum valves were severely scored and worn. Valve body replacement fixed this problem.

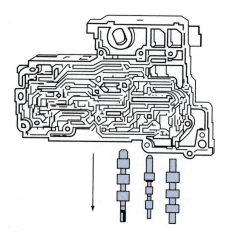

FIGURE 18-49 If the valve body is moved to vertical position, steel valves should slide freely from the bore. Be prepared to catch the valves when making this check.

with carburetor/automatic choke cleaner (Figure 18-51). Soak the valves, springs, and valve body for 5 to 15 minutes, rinse them in hot water, and then dip the valves and springs in ATF and dry the valve body using compressed air.

If a valve is smooth but still sticks in the bore, carefully examine the bore for debris or nicks that might cause raised metal. Small metal particles tend to become embedded in the bores of aluminum valve bodies.

TECH TIP

If a valve is still sticky, inspect it for nicks or dents. The raised metal can be removed using a fine-grit knife-sharpening stone. Lay the valve on the stone and carefully rotate it until all traces of raised metal are gone (Figure 18-52). Be careful not to make a flat or groove on the valve or round off the corners of a land.

TECH TIP

One cure is to drive the metal completely into the aluminum as shown in Figure 18-53. A few sharp taps on the valve is often all that is necessary.

(a)

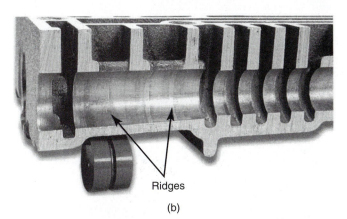

Ridges

(b)

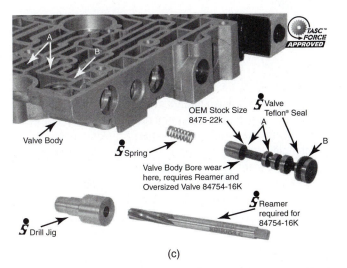

TASC FORCE APPROVED

Valve Body

OEM Stock Size
8475-22k

Valve
Teflon® Seal

Spring

Valve Body Bore wear
here, requires Reamer and
Oversized Valve 84754-16K

Reamer
required for
84754-16K

Drill Jig

(c)

FIGURE 18-50 A valve sag test (a); the valve is inserted backwards into the bore so the inner land is in the area where it normally runs. The valve should not sag off-center. This aluminum valve body has been cut to show the ridges that indicate bore wear (b). Some valve bodies can be saved by reaming the bore oversize and installing an oversize valve (c). *(Courtesy of Sonnax)*

TECH TIP

If tapping does not free up the valve, clean the bore using crocus cloth or a lapping compound. Crocus cloth is a very-fine-grit abrasive cloth. Wrap a section into a tube or roll it with the grit outward, slide this tube into the valve bore, and then rotate it in a direction that tries to unwrap the tube (Figure 18-54). After turning the crocus cloth tube several revolutions, clean the bore and retry the valve fit.

TECH TIP

Some technicians make a lapping compound by mixing household scouring powder and ATF to make a thin paste. This paste is spread onto the valve and in the bore, and then the valve is stroked and rotated in the bore (Figure 18-55). The valve and bore are then cleaned in solvent and dried using compressed air before retrying the valve fit again.

REAL WORLD FIX

The 1996 Ford Taurus (107,000 miles) had an illuminated MIL with no drivability problems. All underhood items checked good. A scan tool check showed code P0761, shift solenoid C circuit stuck in OFF position. Voltage and resistance checks of the solenoid and wiring harness showed no problem. Line pressure was within specifications.

Fix. Following advice, the technician checked the forward clutch control valve and found a broken retainer clip. This caused the spring to bind the control valve, causing it to stick. A new retaining clip fixed this vehicle.

FIGURE 18-51   This valve body is being washed and air dried in a parts washer. It will be cleaned again when the two major parts are separated.

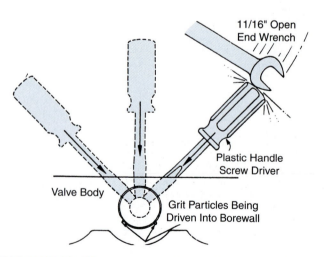

Oil Stone

FIGURE 18-52   Place the valve on the wet sharpening stone and rotate the valve. Slight imperfections and burrs can be removed without rounding off the sharp edges. Do not do this with aluminum valves.

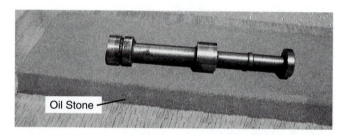

11/16" Open End Wrench

Plastic Handle Screw Driver

Valve Body

Grit Particles Being Driven Into Borewall

FIGURE 18-53   Sometimes a valve in an aluminum valve body will stick in its bore because of grit embedded in the bore wall. This valve can often be freed by gently striking the valve as shown.

FIGURE 18-54   A scored valve body bore can be cleaned by inserting a small roll of crocus cloth into the bore and rotating it in a direction to unroll it. Be very careful to not remove any metal and cause an oversize bore when cleaning the bore of an aluminum valve body.

REAL WORLD FIX

The 1990 Ford Aerostar (130,000 miles) was towed in because the engine died when shifted into drive or reverse. On a test drive, the vehicle operated normally. The fluid level was okay, and there were no DTCs.

Fix. The technician found a TSB that describes this problem and gives a recommended repair. It required removing the valve body, separator plate, overdrive solenoid, retainer, and plug. A stuck shuttle valve was found. Cleaning this valve and bore along with replacing the other parts fixed this problem. New gaskets and O-rings were used during the reassembly.

A valve that has excessive movement, such as a pressure regulator valve, can wear into the bore and cause excess leakage. Leakage can be checked using a wet air test (Figure 18-56). Sometimes the leaking valve can be replaced with an upgraded valve.

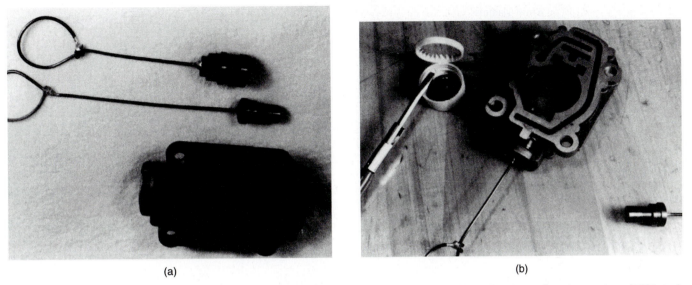

(a)   (b)

FIGURE 18-55   A wire handle has been attached to an old valve so it can be used to lap a governor bore (a). A mixture of scouring powder and ATF is used for the lapping compound (b).

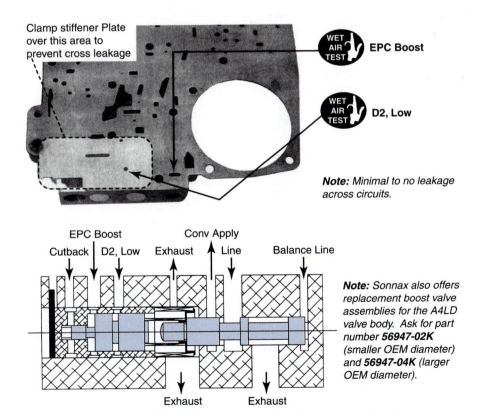

FIGURE 18-56   This boost valve can be checked by putting a small amount of ATF into the EPC boost and D2, low passages and applying low-pressure air to the same passages. More than minimal leakage through the cutback and other passages indicate a worn boost valve or boost sleeve. *(Courtesy of Sonnax)*

Small Diameter
Check Balls (6)

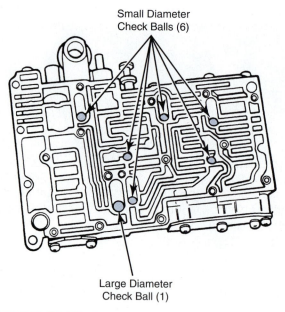

Large Diameter
Check Ball (1)

FIGURE 18-57 This valve body contains one large and six small check balls. *(Courtesy of Chrysler Corporation)*

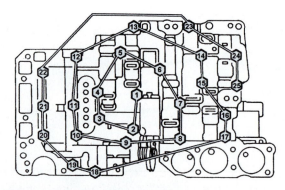

FIGURE 18-58 The valve body bolts should be tightened in order, starting from the center and working in an outward spiral.

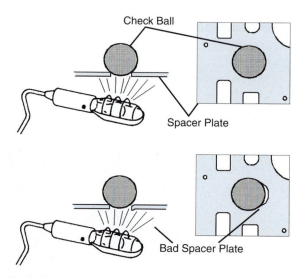

Check Ball

Spacer Plate

Bad Spacer Plate

FIGURE 18-59 A check ball should seal off light from coming through the spacer plate. A problem is indicated if light shines through an opening alongside of the check ball.

TECH TIP

A kit has been developed to repair some valve bores; this kit contains a drill jig (reamer guide), reamer replacement valve, and spring (see Figure 18-50). The reamer is used to restore the bore to be round, straight, and to the correct size for the new valve.

After all the valves, springs, and valve body are cleaned and the valves move freely in their bores, the valve body can be reassembled. The springs should be checked to make sure they are not damaged and do not have distorted coils. Each valve should be dipped in ATF before installation. The reassembly procedure is generally the reverse of the disassembly procedure. As each valve is installed, make sure that it moves freely in its bore. Ensure that all check balls and filter screens are replaced in the proper locations (Figure 18-57). Be sure to tighten each retainer screw to the correct torque (Figure 18-58).

TECH TIP

If a faulty check ball–transfer plate seat is suspected, place the ball on its seat and hold a flashlight behind the transfer plate. Light shining between the ball and transfer plate indicates a problem (Figure 18-59).

The pressure regulator valve spring is adjustable in some Chrysler Corporation transmissions (Figure 18-60). The adjustment can be checked using a small ruler and, if necessary, adjusted using an Allen wrench.

The valve body should now be ready to be installed.

18.7 SOLENOIDS AND SWITCHES

Some sources recommend replacing all switches and solenoids to eliminate a possible cause of future problems. A pulse-width solenoid or pressure control solenoid is in almost constant motion while the transmission is operating; these units wear out. Any external switch that leaks fluid

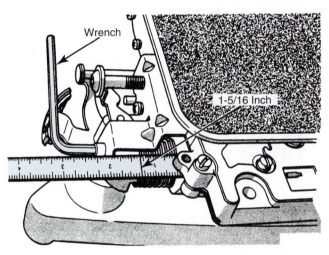

FIGURE 18-60 The pressure regulator spring of this valve body should be adjusted to 1-5/16 in. to get the proper line pressure. *(Courtesy of Chrysler Corporation)*

REAL WORLD FIX

The transmission in the Mercury Grand Marquis taxi (255,000 km) was rebuilt because of a delayed engagement problem. The transmission was replaced, and the vehicle left operating okay. It came back after a few months with a lockup shudder and other symptoms indicating a hydraulic pressure control problem. Scan tool checks did not show any DTCs or electronic control problems.

Fix. Following advice, the technician checked the O-ring on the EPC solenoid, and it was found to be damaged. It was probably damaged during solenoid installation. Replacement of this O-ring fixed the problem.

should be replaced. Switches and solenoids should be cleaned and checked for proper operation as described in Chapter 13.

18.8 DIFFERENTIAL SERVICE

Transaxle differentials should be checked to make sure that the differential gears, thrust washers, and the differential pinion shaft are in good condition (Figure 18-61). A differential can usually be disassembled by removing the lock pin and driving the differential pinion shaft out. This allows removal of the gears and thrust washers (Figure 18-62). The gears should be inspected for chipped or broken teeth and scoring on the bearing surfaces. The thrust washers and differential pinion shaft should be checked for wear and scoring.

Some differentials are combined with a planet carrier that includes a set of planet pinions along with the differential. Like those inside the transmission, these pinion gears must turn freely on their shafts and not have excessive end play. The thrust washers and needle bearings can be replaced. Replacement of the needle bearings can be made easier by applying a thick film of transmission assembly lubricant to stick them in place during assembly.

TECH TIP

If differential clearance is excessive, replace the thrust washers. In many cases, the new thrust washers will correct the clearance.

REAL WORLD FIX

The 1996 Audi A6 (106,000 miles) came in with a no-drive and no-reverse condition. Fluid pressure was good. A scan tool check showed three codes: 0652, range control incorrect signal; 00753, wheel speed sensor or electrical connection; and 00526, brake light switch incorrect signal. The transmission was disassembled and everything looked okay. The input-shaft-to-torque-converter splines were inspected and were found to be good.

Fix. Following advice, the technician disassembled and checked the center differential of this AWD transmission. He found it to be badly burnt and worn. Replacing the center differential fixed this problem.

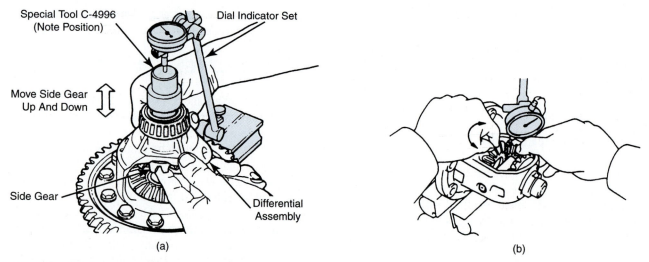

Special Tool C-4996
(Note Position)

Dial Indicator Set

Move Side Gear
Up And Down

Side Gear

Differential
Assembly

(a)

(b)

FIGURE 18-61 Differential side gear end play can be checked using a dial indicator and special tool (a). Another check for the same purpose is to measure the side gear backlash (b). *(a is courtesy of Chrysler Corporation)*

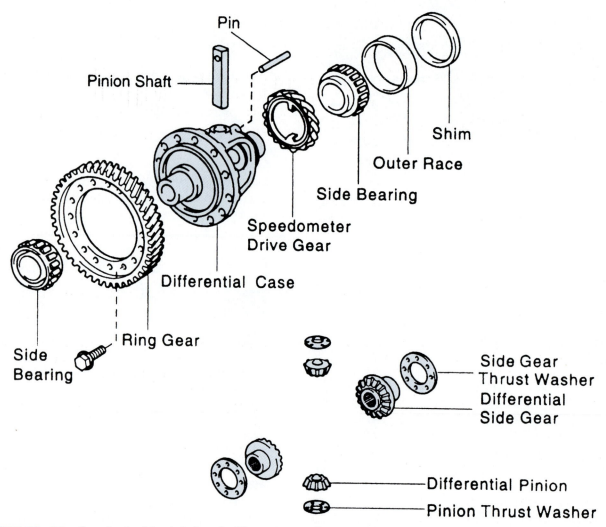

Pin

Pinion Shaft

Shim

Outer Race

Side Bearing

Speedometer
Drive Gear

Differential Case

Side
Bearing

Ring Gear

Side Gear
Thrust Washer
Differential
Side Gear

Differential Pinion

Pinion Thrust Washer

FIGURE 18-62 Removing the pinion shaft allows the differential pinion and side gears with their thrust washers to be removed from the differential case. *(Courtesy of Toyota Motor Sales USA, Inc.)*

SUMMARY

1. Inspection, service, and repair are done to each transmission subassembly during the transmission overhaul.

2. The pump is disassembled and inspected. The bushings and seals are replaced before reassembly.

3. When rebuilding a clutch, the friction plates, piston seals, and bushings are replaced.

4. The valve body is disassembled, cleaned, inspected, and carefully reassembled.

REVIEW QUESTIONS

The following questions are provided to help you study as you read the chapter.

1. The areas of the case that should be inspected are:
   a. _____
   b. _____
   c. _____
   d. _____
   e. _____
   f. _____

2. The pump should be inspected for _____ marks and damage to the gears and housing.

3. When assembling a pump, it might be necessary to _____ the pump halves before torquing the pump body bolts.

4. Like a gear pump, a vane-type pump should be _____ inspected.

5. When disassembling a clutch assembly, note the location of any _____ plates and the _____ and order of the clutch friction and steel plates.

6. Transmission gearsets are inspected for _____ to the gears and pinion gear _____.

7. Valve body repair consists mainly of disassembly, _____, and reassembly.

8. When cleaning a valve body, all of the parts must be kept in _____.

9. Any external switch that is leaking should be _____.

10. If differential clearance is excessive, replace the _____ washers.

CHAPTER QUIZ

The following questions will help you check the facts you have learned. Select the answer that completes each statement correctly.

1. Student A says that a cross leak can cause damage to the clutches or bands. Student B says that damage that would cause a cross leak can be checked using a feeler gauge and a straight-edge. Who is correct?
   a. Student A
   b. Student B
   c. Both A and B
   d. Neither A nor B

2. Student A says that aluminum on the thread of a bolt indicates that the threads in the case are damaged. Student B says that all bolts should be checked for damage before they are reused. Who is correct?
   a. Student A
   b. Student B
   c. Both A and B
   d. Neither A nor B

3. Student A says that a pump can be checked with a visual check or by measuring the clearances. Student B says that worn pump bushing will result in a leaking pump seal. Who is correct?

   a. Student A

   b. Student B

   c. Both A and B

   d. Neither A nor B

4. Student A says that it is good practice to replace all of the friction materials (lined plates, unlined plates, and bands) when rebuilding a transmission. Student B says that lined friction material must be soaked in ATF before it is installed. Who is correct?

   a. Student A

   b. Student B

   c. Both A and B

   d. Neither A nor B

5. Student A says that the location and number of springs in the clutch pack should be noted and that the same number of springs must be placed in the same location during reassembly. Student B says that a clutch piston can be removed with air pressure or by tapping the clutch housing on a piece of wood. Who is correct?

   a. Student A

   b. Student B

   c. Both A and B

   d. Neither A nor B

6. Student A says that the check ball in the clutch piston should rattle when shaken. Student B says that it is okay if the check ball has a small fluid leak. Who is correct?

   a. Student A

   b. Student B

   c. Both A and B

   d. Neither A nor B

7. Clearance in a multiple-disc clutch is adjusted using any of these selective parts, except

   a. clutch pressure plates.

   b. clutch housings.

   c. pressure plate snap rings.

   d. steel plates.

8. Student A says that the gearset is visually inspected for wear or damage to the gear teeth. Student B says that the planet pinion gear end play should be checked using a feeler gauge. Who is correct?

   a. Student A

   b. Student B

   c. Both A and B

   d. Neither A nor B

9. Student A says that the valve and springs must be kept in order during valve body service. Student B says that the valve body springs should be checked for damaged or distorted coils. Who is correct?

   a. Student A

   b. Student B

   c. Both A and B

   d. Neither A nor B

10. Student A says that during an overhaul of a transaxle, the differential should be disassembled and inspected. Student B says that the differential is not a part of the automatic transaxle. Who is correct?

    a. Student A

    b. Student B

    c. Both A and B

    d. Neither A nor B

TORQUE CONVERTER SERVICE

OBJECTIVES

After studying Chapter 19, the reader should be able to:

1. Diagnose torque converter and torque converter clutch problems.
2. Explain the conditions when a torque converter should be reused or rebuilt.
3. Describe the procedure used to rebuild a torque converter.
4. Complete the ASE tasks related to torque converter inspection.

KEY TERMS

Lock-up Clutch Operation (p. 516)
Stator One-Way Clutch Operation (p. 516)

Turbine End Play (p. 516)

19.1 INTRODUCTION

A torque converter is considered to be part of the transmission. It should be serviced or replaced when a transmission is overhauled. A torque converter is always replaced with a new or rebuilt unit if it has an internal failure. Most shops do not rebuild torque converters. There are companies that specialize in torque converter overhaul.

A torque converter does not usually wear out and require replacement. Torque converters tend to collect the metal, dirt, and other debris that enters with the fluid. It is impossible to thoroughly check a torque converter without cutting it open. The internal shape and the centrifugal force inside a torque converter can pack dirt and debris around the outer diameter. Foreign material can also lodge in the clutch lining of a lock-up torque converter (Figure 19-1). It is extremely difficult to remove this material without opening the torque converter. A *reconditioned* or *overhauled* torque converter was cut open, cleaned, inspected, and assembled using new or like-new parts.

Many transmission rebuilders are concerned that removing the torque converter during an overhaul and repositioning it may loosen any internal debris. If the torque converter is not serviced, this debris can leave the torque converter and return to the lubrication passages of the transmission. It may start the wear process in the transmission as soon as the engine is started after the transmission overhaul. The debris might also plug the cooler, causing future problems.

Many shops flush and check the torque converter during every transmission overhaul. Other shops install a rebuilt torque converter as standard practice. High-mileage transmissions, ones that show a lot of metal wear, and units with lock-up torque converters are candidates for replacement. Installing a rebuilt torque converter is more expensive than servicing the existing one. Cleaning and reinstalling a good torque converter is an adequate and safe repair in cases when the transmission is relatively clean.

19.2 TORQUE CONVERTER CHECKS

The torque converter should be checked to make sure it is in usable condition when the transmission is removed. These checks include the *visual condition,* **stator one-way clutch operation, turbine end play,** *internal interference,* **lock-up clutch operation,** and *external leakage.* A torque converter that passes inspection is reusable. One that fails one or more of the checks should be replaced with a new or rebuilt unit. A torque converter that has turned blue from overheating has failed internally and should be replaced.

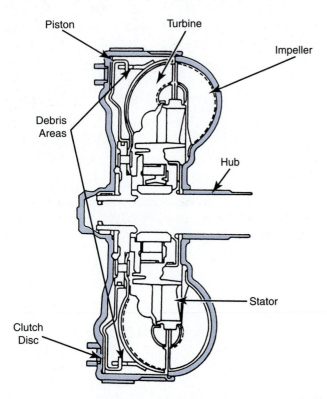

FIGURE 19-1   This cutaway view shows where debris and foreign material will tend to collect inside of the outer rim of a torque converter. *(Courtesy of Chrysler Corporation)*

REAL WORLD FIX

The 1992 Oldsmobile Achieva (162,000 miles) had the transmission rebuilt almost a year ago. Now there is a complaint of a lack of power, and it has been this way since the rebuild. All adjustments are correct, the engine has good vacuum, and a scan tool check shows no trouble codes. A stall check shows a stall speed of 1,560 rpm.

Fix. The stall speed for this vehicle should be 2,760 rpm, so it was determined that the wrong torque converter was installed during the earlier rebuild. Replacement with the correct torque converter solved this problem.

REAL WORLD FIX

The 1991 Acura (85,000 miles) runs good in park and neutral, but the engine dies as soon as it is shifted into gear. Tests reveal no problems outside of the transmission.

Fix. When the transmission was removed, the torque converter was found to be blue from overheating and seized up internally. It had also sent metal particles throughout the transmission. Rebuilding the transmission along with a replacement torque converter was required to fix this problem.

REAL WORLD FIX

The 1991 Nissan Pathfinder (133,000 miles) will not move in any gear. An inspection of the pan revealed some metal particles and dirty fluid. Engine speed does increase when shifted into gear, which is a normal response.

Fix. The transmission was removed, and following advice from experienced technicians, the torque converter splines were checked. They were stripped, and replacement of the torque converter fixed this problem. The shift solenoid pack was also replaced as a precautionary measure.

(a)

(b)

FIGURE 19-2 Converter inspection begins with visual checks to ensure that the pilot, drive lugs, ring gear (if used), hub, and pump drive tangs are in good condition.

19.2.1 Visual Checks

The first checks performed are visual. A technician often performs a visual inspection as the torque converter is removed from the transmission. Visual inspection includes the following:

1. The outside (especially at the welds) for wetness, which might indicate a leak
2. The drive lugs or studs for physical damage (Figure 19-2)
3. The pilot for damage
4. The hub for signs of seal or bushing area wear
5. The pump drive tangs or lugs for wear or damage
6. The starter ring gear, if used, for wear or damage (Figure 19-3)

A torque converter with excessive damage to the hub, pump drive lugs, or converter drive lugs should be repaired or replaced.

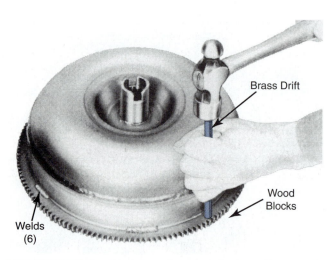

Welds (6)

FIGURE 19-3   A bad starter ring gear can be changed by cutting the welds using a hack saw or grinder and driving the old gear off. The new gear must be secured by welding following the procedure recommended by the manufacturer. *(Courtesy of Chrysler Corporation)*

A small imperfection on the torque converter hub can be cleaned and smoothed using crocus cloth. Roughness or damage that can be felt by running a fingernail or coin across the hub can wear the new front seal.

Stripped or damaged female threads in the drive lugs can often be repaired by installing a thread insert as described in Chapter 14.

19.2.2 Stator One-Way Clutch Check

There are several ways to check a stator one-way clutch. The stator clutch must lock in one direction and slip or freewheel in the other.

To check a one-way clutch, you should:

1. Place the converter flat on a bench top.
2. Reach into the hub so one finger contacts the splines (Figure 19-4).

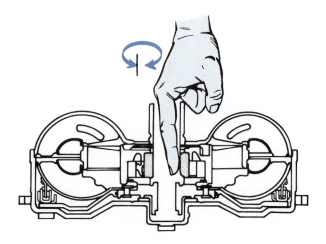

FIGURE 19-4   A stator clutch can be checked by reaching into the hub so your finger contacts the splines. You should be able to rotate the splines in one direction but not the other.

Grip the stator splines using long, thin, flat-jaw snap-ring pliers in order to rotate the stator (Figure 19-5). The added leverage of the pliers allows you to turn the splines in both directions; but in one direction (clockwise), only the inner race revolves. In the other direction, the entire stator and clutch rotate. The difference can be felt, especially if you turn it rapidly.

3. Rotate the splines in a clockwise direction. If you cannot rotate them, the clutch is probably locked.
4. Try to rotate the splines counterclockwise. If you can rotate them, the clutch is slipping. A slipping one-way clutch will cause a vehicle to have a power loss and poor acceleration. A locked one-way clutch will hurt fuel economy because of fluid drag at speeds below TCC lock-up.

A commercial stator-holding tool may be used to check a one-way clutch. This tool can be inserted into a groove in the thrust washer on some stators to keep it and the stator from rotating. Next, a special one-way clutch-tool is inserted into the stator splines, and a torque wrench is used to apply torque to the tool and one-way clutch inner race. The one-way clutch should turn freely in a clockwise direction, and it should lock and hold at least 10 ft-lb (14 N-m) of torque in a counterclockwise direction. Do not apply any more torque than this because the special tool can break.

A torque converter with a faulty one-way clutch must be replaced or rebuilt.

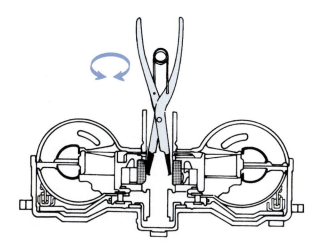

FIGURE 19-5   A stator clutch can be checked by gripping the splines using snap-ring pliers. Rotate the splines quickly; in only one direction, you should feel the weight of the stator.

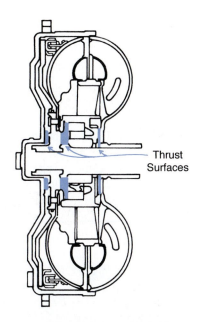

Thrust Surfaces

FIGURE 19-6   The major wear points inside a torque converter are these thrust surfaces. Internal end play increases as these surfaces wear.

REAL WORLD FIX

The 1986 Chevrolet Caprice (2004R transmission; 80,000 miles) makes a grinding/whining noise as soon as the engine is started, and the noise gets louder when shifted into drive or reverse. The noise goes away at speeds above 30 mph. The fluid is clean and at the correct level.

Fix. When the transmission was removed, and the torque converter was removed from the transmission, stripped splines were found on the stator support shaft. A used transmission was installed.

FIGURE 19-7   The special tool is locked into the turbine. Moving the tool handle up and down allows the end play to be read on the dial indicator.

19.2.3 End-Play Check

Thrust washers at the stator and turbine control internal end play (Figure 19-6). End play is normally measured using a dial indicator. Two styles of dial indicator fixtures are commonly used to measure end play. One fixture uses an expandable stem that fits into the turbine splines and is expanded to lock into the splines (Figure 19-7). The dial indicator is positioned and adjusted so the measuring stylus is against the fixture and the dial reads zero. The fixture and turbine are lifted as far as they will go. The travel (end play) is read on the dial indicator.

Another fixture for checking end play is designed so the torque converter sits on top of it (Figure 19-8). The measuring stem is moved upward to contact the turbine splines, and the

dial indicator is adjusted to zero. Then the turbine is lifted as far as possible. The end play is read on the dial indicator.

Some manufacturers publish torque converter end-play specifications. If no specifications are available, use the rule of thumb that 0.030 in. (0.76 mm) is normal and 0.050 in. (1.27 mm) is the maximum end play allowable. A torque converter with excess end play (more than 0.050 in.) should be rebuilt or replaced.

TECH TIP

Turbine or stator clutch end play can be checked by gripping the splines with a pair of snap-ring pliers or your fingers (Figure 19-9). You can feel the end play as the turbine or stator is lifted and then lowered. With experience, you can judge the approximate amount of end play.

FIGURE 19-8 The torque converter is placed onto the end-play fixture. After setting the dial indicator to zero (0), the handle is moved downward to lift the turbine and read the end play. *(Courtesy of TCRS Inc.)*

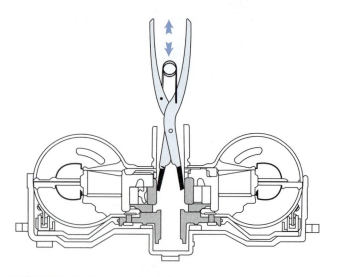

FIGURE 19-9 A quick end-play check can be made by gripping the turbine or stator splines and trying to move the turbine or stator in and out.

19.2.4 Internal Interference Checks

The thrust washers inside a torque converter can wear to the point where the impeller, turbine, or stator can rub against each other. The normal wear pattern caused by the dynamic fluid pressure moves the turbine toward the front of the torque converter and the stator toward the rear. Torque converter interference should be checked twice: Once with the turbine and stator toward the front and again with them toward the rear.

To check a converter for internal interference, you should:

1. Set the torque converter on a bench with the hub up. Gravity will move the turbine and stator toward the front of the torque converter.
2. Insert the transmission pump stator support into the torque converter so the support splines engage the stator clutch splines.
3. Insert the transmission input shaft into the torque converter so its splines enter the turbine splines (Figure 19-10).
4. Rotate the pump and input shaft in both clockwise and counterclockwise directions, one at a time and together. If there is any sign of contact or rubbing, either a rubbing or grating sound or rough feel, the torque converter needs to be replaced.
5. Turn the whole assembly over so the turbine and stator move toward the rear of the torque converter.
6. Repeat step 4. Again, any sign of internal contact indicates a torque converter that should be rebuilt or replaced.

FIGURE 19-10 An internal interference check. The pump body with stator support (a) and clutch with turbine shaft (b) have been installed and are rotated to feel and listen for internal contact. The assembly is then turned upside down and the checks are repeated. Internal contact in either position indicates a faulty converter.

19.2.5 Torque Converter Clutch Checks

The clutch of a lock-up torque converter can fail in several ways: The friction lining can break up or wear out, the pressure plate seals can leak, or the damper assembly can fail. The damper assembly and lining material cannot be checked on the bench. The only way to check them is on a road test or to cut the torque converter open. Lining breakup often shows up as a plugged oil cooler or lining material in the cooler line. Occasionally, a fragment of a broken damper spring can be found in the cooler line. These are definite signs of a faulty lock-up torque converter.

Two styles of testers are available for checking torque converter clutches. One type uses adapters that replace the turbine shaft and allow a vacuum to be exerted on the front side of the clutch plate assembly. If this chamber can hold a vacuum, the center seal and the clutch lining (which forms the outer seal) are good. The second tester style uses adapters that attach to the turbine, which uses air pressure to apply the clutch (Figure 19-11). With the clutch applied, torque is exerted to try to turn the turbine. A good torque converter clutch locks the turbine and prevents it from turning.

Checks of the electronic TCC circuits are described in Chapter 13.

19.2.6 Leak Checks

A torque converter can leak at the welds, fittings, or plugs. Leaking fluid will show up at the bottom of the torque converter housing and can be mistaken for a front seal leak. The difference is the location of wetness on the torque converter.

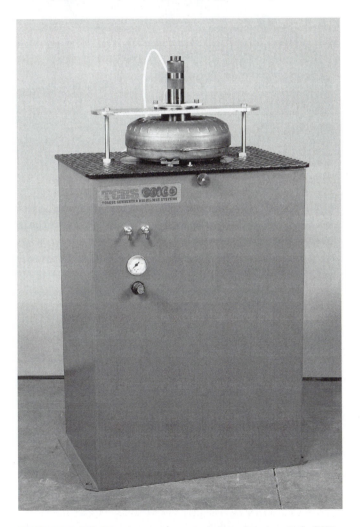

FIGURE 19-11   A torque converter lock-up dyno. It tests the TCC to make sure that it will lock up properly. *(Courtesy of TCRS Inc.)*

REAL WORLD FIX

The 1991 Suburban (126,000 miles) torque converter goes into lock-up in second gear, and then it intermittently releases and reapplies. A scan tool shows the circuit switching. The TCC will release when the brake pedal is tapped as designed. The TCC solenoid, TOT sensor, 3–4 pressure switch, and ECM were replaced, but this did not help.

Fix. Following advice, the technician checked the transmission external wire harness, and he found the insulation had rubbed through, allowing the TCC wire to make an intermittent ground connection. Repairing the wire fixed the problem. This TCC circuit is controlled by an internal governor switch that provides a ground.

TECH TIP

Some vehicles require a TCC with graphite lining. Because this type of lining can conduct electricity, you can check a converter to ensure that it has this lining type. Slide an input shaft into the turbine just far enough to contact the turbine and clutch plate. Now connect an ohmmeter to the turbine shaft and the outside of the torque converter. A continuity reading shows graphite clutch lining. No continuity shows standard lining.

REAL WORLD FIX

The 1993 Toyota Camry (117,000 miles) had the transmission rebuilt because of a worn gearset. All of the soft parts, gearset, and torque converter were replaced. The transmission operation was normal for about 25 miles, and then it stopped working. A scan tool check showed no trouble codes. The filter was found to be plugged with clutch material, but all of the transmission clutches appeared good when inspected. It was noted that the replacement torque converter required different bolts than the original.

Fix. Following advice, the technician checked the front of the torque converter and found six dimples. The installer used six slightly long mounting bolts that dented the front of the converter. Replacement of the torque converter using the proper bolts fixed this problem.

SAFETY TIP

Be sure the assembly is mounted so the adapter cannot be blown out of the hub when it is pressurized.

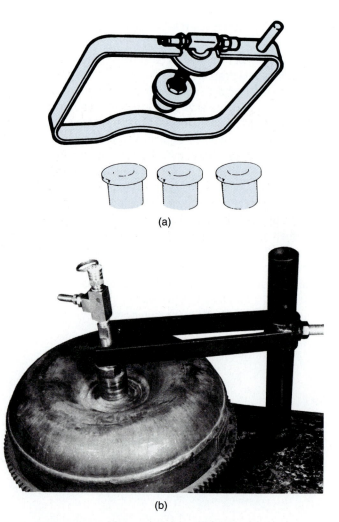

FIGURE 19-12   This torque converter leak-test fixture has adapters to fit hubs of different diameters (a). A different tester is shown with a converter installed (b). *(a courtesy of Kent-Moore)*

The torque converter must be pressurized to test for a leak. A special tool with an expandable plug that fits into the hub and a device to keep the plug in place is used. The plug is equipped with an air chuck to allow pressure to be added (Figure 19-12).

The following description of the procedure to check a torque converter is very general. Always follow the exact procedure for the equipment you are using.

To check a torque converter for leaks, you should:

1. Drain as much fluid out of the torque converter as possible.
2. Select the correct size plug/adapter for the torque converter hub.
3. Place the torque converter and adapter into the holding fixture (Figure 19-13).
4. Tighten the adapter as required, and apply an air pressure of 30 to 40 psi (207 to 275 kPa).
5. Spray a soapy water solution on the areas where you suspect a leak. Foamy bubbles indicate a leak. Some types of test equipment allow the pressurized unit to be

TECH TIP

Very small pinhole leaks can be sealed by peening the hole closed. This is done using a punch and hammer and striking the area immediately around the hole (Figure 19-14). The malleable iron material of the torque converter or weld is forced over into the hole. Larger holes are sealed by welding, which can cause an unbalanced torque converter, or by installing a new or rebuilt torque converter.

immersed in a tank of water. Air bubbles will show the location of any leaks.
6. When finished, completely release the air pressure before removing the test tool.

FIGURE 19-13   A leak test fixture has been placed on the torque converter. It will be inflated with air pressure, and then soapy water will be sprayed on it to identify any leaks.

FIGURE 19-14   Pinhole leaks in a converter can be sealed using a punch and hammer. A series of punch marks around the hole should displace metal to close off the hole.

19.3 TORQUE CONVERTER CLEANING

Torque converters are very difficult to clean because of their internal shape. Most shops use rebuilt torque converters to ensure a completely clean unit without any concerns of internal wear or damage. Trying to clean a torque converter by running solvent or cleaners into it does no good. In fact, it may even be harmful if all the solvent is not removed. A torque converter cleaner is an effective but expensive piece of equipment. It pumps cleaning solvent under pressure through the torque converter in a reverse direction, and at the same time, the device rotates the turbine in order to create a fluid flow that loosens the debris so it can be flushed out. The cleaning operation usually runs until the solvent leaving the torque converter runs clear, about 5 to 15 minutes.

After cleaning, the internal end play should be rechecked. Occasionally, end play increases as varnish or debris is removed.

Exactly how much of the packed dirt and metal debris is removed from a really dirty torque converter can be questioned. Any remaining debris can damage the transmission. Many technicians prefer to rebuild a dirty torque converter. This will ensure complete cleaning and a thorough inspection of the internal components so all worn or faulty parts can be replaced.

19.3.1 Drilling a Torque Converter

It is possible to drill a torque converter to provide a drain opening. This requires installing a plug to seal the opening. Drilling a torque converter is not generally recommended.

TECH TIP

The solvent should be removed completely from inside the torque converter. If the torque converter has a drain plug, this is fairly easy. If there is no drain, drain as much solvent as possible out through the hub. Pour 2 quarts (1.9 L) of clean ATF into the hub, and agitate the torque converter to mix the ATF and the solvent. Then drain as much of the ATF-solvent mixture out through the hub as possible. The small amount of solvent remaining will probably not cause a problem.

TECH TIP

If a pipe plug is used, a recessed-head type should be used because they weigh less and there is a lower possibility of disturbing the balance of the torque converter. If balance is a problem, install two plugs placed exactly opposite each other.

Normally the plug used to fill the hole is a special closed-end pop rivet or a 1/8-in. NPT (National Pipe Thread) plug. The pop rivet is the lightest and quickest to install, but the pipe plug is the most secure.

When drilling a torque converter, it is important not to drill into any of the internal components. Drill only deep enough to penetrate the cover and preferably, into the impeller area (Figure 19-15). With lock-up torque converters, it is important not to drill into the clutch friction area. The hole size is usually 1/8 in. (3.5 mm) if a pop rivet is to be used or 11/32 in. (8.7 mm) if a 1/8-in. pipe plug is to be used. Before drilling, place a depth stop or a piece of tape on the drill bit so you can drill to a maximum depth of 1/4 in. (6.3 mm). This is deep enough to penetrate the outer cover.

After the torque converter has drained, simply remove any burrs from the outside of the hole if you are using a pop rivet. Then apply a small amount of sealant on the rivet; place the rivet into the hole; and use the pop rivet tool to expand the rivet and lock it in place.

After installing a plug, it is good practice to pressure test the converter before installing the torque converter in a transmission.

19.3.2 Cooler Cleaning

Cooler cleaners are designed to clean the radiator oil cooler by forcing cleaning solution or fluid through the cooler lines. This can also be done with a simple fluid pump (Figure 19-16). Cleaning a cooler is normally done by pumping solvent backward through the cooler lines and cooler (called *reverse flushing*).

If you are using a pipe plug, apply grease to the flutes of a 1/8-in. NPT tap to catch the metal chips, and cut threads in the hole. While tapping, make sure not to run the tap into any internal parts. Also periodically back the tap up to break the chips and cut clean threads. Then apply sealing tape or sealant to the threads of the pipe plug and tighten it to 8 ft-lb (10.8 N·m) of torque.

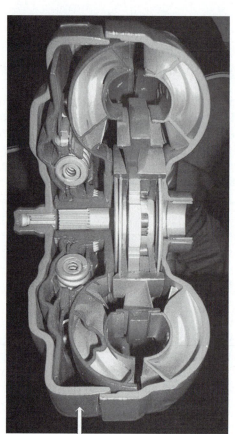

Drain Hole Location

FIGURE 19-15 A hole can be drilled into the torque converter so that it can be drained. This hole should be tapped to accept a small pipe plug.

FIGURE 19-16 This cooler line flusher pumps heated flushing solution through the cooler lines and cooler. A flow meter is used to ensure that the cooler is flowing properly and not plugged. *(Courtesy of G-Tec)*

TECH TIP

Some technicians alternate fluid and compressed air flow to clean the lines and cooler. They may also reverse the flow direction if they feel debris might be caught in the cooler. Be careful if using high-pressure compressed air in addition to fluid flow because excessive pressure can rupture the cooler assembly.

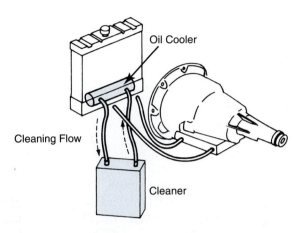

FIGURE 19-17   A cooler flusher is connected to the cooler lines so a cleaning agent can be forced in the reverse direction through the cooler unit until it is clean.

REAL WORLD FIX

The 1995 Dodge D250 truck (120,000 miles) has delayed engagements after sitting for a long time. It works fine after that. A drain-down problem is suspected.

Fix. A Dodge TSB recommended replacement of the cooler line. The replacement line included a check valve to control drainback. Replacing the cooler line fixed the problem.

The cleaner or fluid pump is connected to the transmission end of the lubrication cooler return line. The transmission end of the cooler feed line is opened to return the solvent to the cleaner or to a catch bucket (Figure 19-17). Fluid is then pumped through the circuit until it runs out clear. Some cleaners produce a pulsating solvent flow intended to loosen and remove packed debris. Other units heat the cleaning solution to help remove any wax deposits. After cleaning, the solvent must be blown out of the cooler and lines with compressed air. Any remaining debris in the torque converter and cooler will find its way into the lubrication circuit of the transmission.

19.4 TORQUE CONVERTER REBUILDING

A torque converter is rebuilt by cutting it open, cleaning and inspecting the parts, replacing any worn or damaged parts, and welding it back together. Expensive specialized equipment is required to rebuild a torque converter. The equipment operator should have some machining and metalworking

TECH TIP

If torque converter drainback is suspected, run the vehicle until it is at normal operating temperature, and drive the vehicle through several full-shift cycles. Check and adjust the fluid level if it is low, and shut off the engine. Allow the vehicle to sit for 30 to 60 minutes, then recheck the fluid level and mark it on the dipstick. Allow the vehicle to sit for 24 hours and then recheck the fluid level. If the level has risen by 1 in. (25.4 mm) or more, converter drainback has occurred.

TECH TIP

Flush kits consisting of an aerosol can of flushing solution with adapters to connect to the cooler are available (Figure 19-18). These are popular with many smaller shops that do not have flushing equipment.

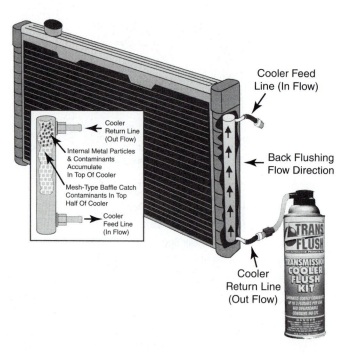

FIGURE 19-18 A cooler can be back-flushed using an aerosol flushing kit. *(Courtesy of Life Automotive Products Inc.)*

The 1993 Camry (75,000 miles) drives okay, but it loses all gears when it gets hot. The transmission was disassembled, and a badly worn gearset was found. The gearset, thrust washers, O-rings, worn frictions, and torque converter were replaced, and the valve body and solenoids were cleaned and inspected. The transmission was reinstalled, but the same problem remained.

Fix. The technician retraced the fluid flow and decided to replace the filter and clean the cooler. These repairs fixed the problem.

REAL WORLD FIX

The 1997 Dodge 1500 Ram pickup (36,000 miles) was repaired after an accident. It had an erratic shift problem, and an inspection of the pan showed a lot of metal, so a remanufactured transmission was installed. After a short test drive, the transmission became noisy with a metallic-type noise.

Fix. The technician learned that this vehicle has a check valve in one of the cooler lines. A thorough cleaning of this clogged valve allowed proper lubrication to the transmission and fixed the noise problem.

skills. These requirements limit torque converter rebuilding to companies that specialize in torque converter rebuilding or the larger transmission shops.

A transmission shop may prefer to rebuild its own torque converters to ensure the correct torque converter for the vehicle. Remember that a transmission model can use torque converters with different stall speeds. Installing the wrong torque converter can cause drastic changes in vehicle performance.

At least eight different torque converters are used with one of the common transaxles. They look about the same and fit any of the flexplates and transaxles. They are easily interchanged, but the result is improper vehicle operation.

A rebuilt torque converter of poor quality can ruin an otherwise perfect transmission overhaul. Some shops have found that it takes about 20 to 30 minutes to rebuild a torque converter—not much more than the time spent to check, clean, and flush or locate an exchange unit.

When a torque converter is rebuilt, all damaged or worn parts are either repaired or replaced as necessary. Rebuilding a torque converter consists of the following operations:

- Inspect the exterior for damage.
- Cut the torque converter open on a specially equipped lathe.
- Inspect the interior components for wear or damage.
- Thoroughly clean the interior parts.
- Disassemble and inspect the stator one-way clutch.
- Replace all worn or damaged parts.
- Prelubricate the internal bearing surfaces.
- Adjust the internal end play.
- Carefully reassemble and weld the two sections together.
- Leak check all welds.
- Balance the assembly.

19.4.1 Disassembling a Torque Converter

Since a torque converter is welded together, the weld must be cut to open the torque converter. The torque converter is mounted in a metal-cutting lathe for the cutting operation. To ensure that it is

REAL WORLD FIX

The transmission in the 1997 Ranger was overhauled because of a broken low and reverse sprag. The overhaul included a master kit, rebuilt torque converter, EPC solenoid, and No. 2 shift solenoid, along with a shift kit. The vehicle came back with a DTC P1743 (TCC solenoid open or shorted) and P1744 (TCC slip/engagement problem). The TCC solenoid and internal harness were replaced. This cured the P1743 DTC. The vehicle still loses TCC operation when it gets hot (about 10 miles), resets DTC P1744, and EPC goes to zero duty cycle.

Fix. Further tests revealed a pressure leak in the TCC apply circuit. The torque converter rebuilder was contacted, and another rebuilt torque converter was installed. The new torque converter fixed this problem.

mounted true, the torque converter is centered to the lathe using an adapter that matches the crankshaft pilot and is bolted to a face plate at the drive lugs. Duplicating the mounting points should give true, wobble-free rotation for accurate machining.

When the lathe is started, runout of the hub can be observed. Excessive hub runout causes wear at the front pump, bushing, and seal and an added strain on the flex plate. It is corrected by careful alignment during reassembly of the torque converter housings. A faulty hub will be removed and replaced at this time (Figure 19-19). The hub weld is cut using a hardened steel alloy cutter bit to remove the weld metal. The new replacement hub is welded in place using an automatic wire welder.

The torque converter housing weld is cut using a hardened carbide cutter bit. A skilled operator will remove just enough of the weld to allow separating the two parts, the front "bowl" from the rear impeller (Figure 19-20). This makes reassembly of the torque converter easier and leaves enough metal for future rebuilding.

19.4.2 Cleaning

A hot spray washer is used to clean the disassembled torque converter parts (Figure 19-21). Some of the parts are cleaned several times as they go through different repair procedures. For example, the front bowl and rear impeller must have the packed-in debris removed, be deburred from the lathe cut, and have the edges beveled slightly to ease reassembly. They are rewashed after these operations to ensure complete cleanliness.

(a)

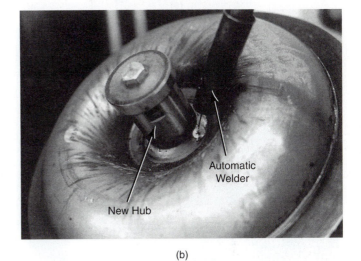

New Hub

Automatic Welder

(b)

FIGURE 19-19 This worn converter hub has been removed to allow replacement (a). A new hub has been installed and welded in place using a special welder (b).

19.4.3 Subassembly Repair

With the torque converter disassembled, the following items are checked and repaired as necessary:

- Torque converter hub: removed and replaced
- Starter ring gear: removed and replaced (Figure 19-22)
- Crankshaft pilot: welded to build up material and machined back to original size
- Drive lugs/studs: removed and replaced
- Turbine drive hub: removed and replaced
- Thrust washers: removed, lubricated, and replaced or upgraded to Torrington bearings
- Support bushings: removed and replaced
- Impeller fins: spot welded to lock in place
- Stator clutch: disassembled, inspected, lubricated, and reassembled

(a)

Cutting Tool

(b)

FIGURE 19-20 To rebuild a converter, first cut it open on a machine lathe (a). A carbide tool is used to cut the weld so the converter can be split apart (b).

- Stator clutch outer race: pinned to lock into the stator
- Clutch lining: relined (Figure 19-23)
- Damper springs or assemblies: removed and replaced

With the exception of the stator one-way clutch, which is always disassembled and inspected, these operations are done on an as-needed basis.

19.4.4 Torque Converter Reassembly

Torque converter reassembly requires several operations:

- Check the height of the stacked components to ensure that the assembled unit is not too long or too short (Figure 19-24).
- Check and adjust the internal clearance to ensure there is correct end play. Adjustment is done by changing or shimming the thrust washers.

FIGURE 19-21 After being cut open, the usable components are placed in a spray washer for thorough cleaning.

Tack Welds

FIGURE 19-22 A new starter ring gear has been installed and tack welded. After ensuring that it is straight, it will be welded securely.

- Make sure the bowl and impeller housings are correctly aligned so there is a minimum of hub runout, and tack weld them securely into position (Figure 19-25).
- Weld the housing in an automatic wire welder to provide a continuous, leak-free weld (Figure 19-26).

FIGURE 19-23   This torque converter piston bonder is used to bond new lining onto a torque converter clutch piston. *(Courtesy of TCRS Inc.)*

(a)

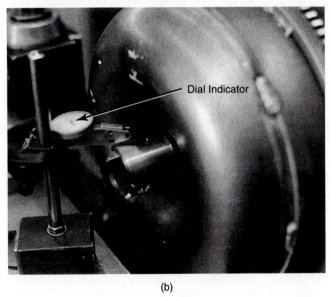

(b)

FIGURE 19-25   This converter is assembled, and the two housings are tack welded together (a). Checks made at this time ensure that the hub is centered and true with the front of the converter (b).

FIGURE 19-24   This fixture is used to ensure that the converter will have the correct overall length after assembly. Shims are added internally to correct end play if necessary.

19.4.5 Postassembly Checks

After the torque converter has been welded back together, it is pressure checked for no leaks (Figure 19-27). This operation is similar to that described in an earlier section. Small leaks can often be repaired by peening the hole closed using a punch and hammer. Larger leaks require rewelding.

The final torque converter rebuilding operation is to balance the assembled unit (Figure 19-28). This compensates for changes in the amount of weld metal and the possible repositioning of the two housing sections. During the balancing operation, the turbine and stator must be locked in a centered position to prevent them from affecting the overall balance. Balancing a torque converter is made more difficult by the three units that can revolve together as one unit or as three separate units.

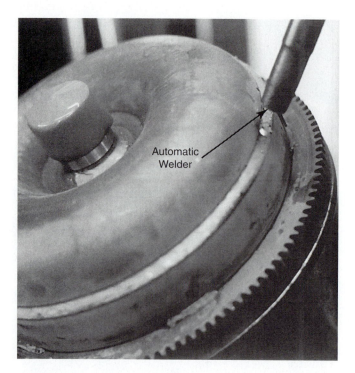

FIGURE 19-26 The assembled converter is welded together on an automatic welder.

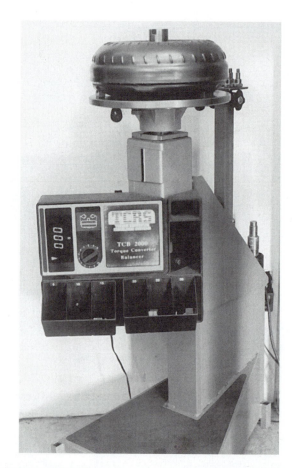

FIGURE 19-28 This converter is balanced using a special balancer. Small weights will be spot welded onto it to correct any unbalance.

FIGURE 19-27 This converter is pressure tested for leaks in this special fixture. Soap will be sprayed on it, and bubbles will show any leaks.

SUMMARY

1. When a transmission is rebuilt, the torque converter is serviced, rebuilt, or replaced.

2. If a torque converter is to be reused, it should be visually inspected for leaks, the one-way clutch operation checked, and internal end play should be measured.

3. Torque converters are rebuilt by disassembling them. They are then inspected, cleaned, parts replaced as necessary, adjusted, and reassembled.

REVIEW QUESTIONS

The following questions are provided to help you study as you read the chapter.

1. Torque converters should be checked for:
   a. _____
   b. _____
   c. _____
   d. _____
   e. _____
   f. _____

2. The six areas of a torque converter that are visually checked are:
   a. Housing for _____
   b. Drive lugs or _____ for damage
   c. Pilot for damage or _____
   d. Hub for signs of seal or _____ wear
   e. _____ drive tangs or lugs for wear or damage
   f. Starter _____ gear for wear or damage

3. If the stator one-way clutch can be easily turned in both directions, it is said to be _____.

4. A customer concern about poor fuel economy or higher-than-normal engine speed could be the result of a _____ stator clutch.

5. As a rule of thumb, the torque converter should have no more than _____ end play.

6. A check for a leaking torque converter is to _____ it and spray it with soapy water.

7. Transmission coolers are flushed out by forcing _____ through the cooler in a reverse direction.

8. Torque converters are welded together and must be _____ to be rebuilt.

CHAPTER QUIZ

The following questions are provided to help you check the facts you have learned. Select the answer that completes each statement correctly.

1. Student A says that a dirty torque converter can ruin a transmission rebuild. Student B says that most used torque converters are worn out. Who is correct?
   a. Student A
   b. Student B
   c. Both A and B
   d. Neither A nor B

2. The visual checks to be made on a torque converter include the condition of the
   a. drive lugs or studs.
   b. hub and pump drive tangs.
   c. pilot.
   d. All of these

3. Student A says that it should not be possible to turn the stator splines in either direction with one's finger. Student B says that normally these splines can be turned both ways by gripping them with a pair of snap-ring pliers. Who is correct?
   a. Student A
   b. Student B
   c. Both A and B
   d. Neither A nor B

4. Student A says that a torque converter with a bad stator one-way clutch should be replaced with a new torque converter. Student B says a torque converter can be rebuilt and the one-way clutch repaired. Who is correct?

   a. Student A

   b. Student B

   c. Both A and B

   d. Neither A nor B

5. Student A says that excessive end play in a torque converter is caused by a worn-out stator. Student B says that torque converter end play can be accurately checked with a pair of snap-ring pliers. Who is correct?

   a. Student A

   b. Student B

   c. Both A and B

   d. Neither A nor B

6. Student A says that a good rule of thumb for the maximum allowable amount of torque converter end play is 0.050 in. Student B says that any torque converter with less than 0.040 in. of end play should be replaced or rebuilt. Who is correct?

   a. Student A

   b. Student B

   c. Both A and B

   d. Neither A nor B

7. Student A says that a stator support and a turbine shaft are needed in order to check a torque converter for internal interference. Student B says that this is a simple check in which one merely rotates parts in the torque converter while listening and feeling for internal rubbing. Who is correct?

   a. Student A

   b. Student B

   c. Both A and B

   d. Neither A nor B

8. Student A says that if the torque converter clutch lining breaks up, it probably plugs the cooler. Student B says that a failed torque converter clutch can cause too little internal end play. Who is correct?

   a. Student A

   b. Student B

   c. Both A and B

   d. Neither A nor B

9. Student A says that during a leak check the torque converter is filled with oil to a pressure of about 80 psi. Student B says that a very small leak at a torque converter weld can be stopped using a hammer and punch. Who is correct?

   a. Student A

   b. Student B

   c. Both A and B

   d. Neither A nor B

10. When a transmission is rebuilt, the torque converter should be

    a. balanced.

    b. painted.

    c. cleaned.

    d. All of these

11. Student A says that a torque converter can be drained adequately by merely turning it so the hub is downward over a container. Student B says that one can clean a torque converter quite well by running a solvent hose into it and turning on the parts washer. Who is correct?

    a. Student A

    b. Student B

    c. Both A and B

    d. Neither A nor B

12. Student A says that after a torque converter is flushed with solvent, it should be filled with ATF and then as much of the ATF/solvent mix as possible should be drained. Student B says that it is possible to completely drain the torque converter by drilling a hole in it. Who is correct?

    a. Student A

    b. Student B

    c. Both A and B

    d. Neither A nor B

13. During a rebuild, a torque converter

    a. is taken apart and cleaned.

    b. has the stator clutch disassembled and checked.

    c. is adjusted to the correct internal end play.

    d. All of these

14. Student A says that special equipment is required to rebuild a torque converter. Student B says that the only sure way to get all of the dirt and debris out of a torque converter is to rebuild it. Who is correct?

    a. Student A

    b. Student B

    c. Both A and B

    d. Neither A nor B

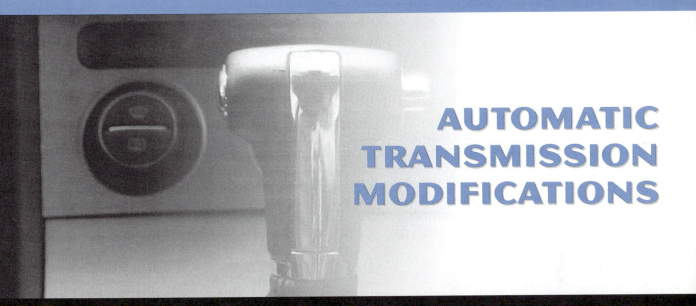

AUTOMATIC TRANSMISSION MODIFICATIONS

OBJECTIVES

After studying Chapter 20, the reader should be able to:

1. Describe the modifications that can be made to improve the reliability or change the operating characteristics of an automatic transmission.

20.1 INTRODUCTION

There are several reasons for modifying an automatic transmission. Most involve matching the transmission to the driver's or vehicle's driving characteristics or operating conditions. Most transmission modifications are intended to improve shift quality and are relatively mild and inexpensive. Other changes, such as those done to produce an all-out race transmission, can be very involved and expensive.

Many transmission repair shops routinely perform minor modifications. When considering transmission modifications, remember that any transmission work that does not follow a manufacturer's recommendations affects the operating characteristics, transmission life, and possibly safety. The manufacturer's warranty may be voided if modifications are made. The technician making the changes is responsible for any adverse results.

When planning transmission modifications, first consider the different stages or levels of modifications:

1. Street usage: changes to improve shift quality
2. Street usage: alter TCC application
3. Street usage: changes to improve fuel economy
4. Street usage: changes to improve strength and longevity
5. Street strip: changes to improve vehicle acceleration rate
6. Racing: numerous changes strictly for racing purposes

Most transmissions are designed and programmed to suit the average new-car buyer. At one time, a major design criteria was to produce a transmission in which the shifts were very smooth, to the point where they could not be felt (Figure 20-1). All shifts have a certain amount of slippage, and the slippage can produce wear and heat. It is possible to change the shift characteristics of many transmissions to the other extreme, a shift that jerks the vehicle and produces tire chirp.

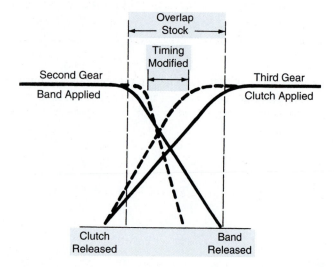

FIGURE 20-1 The overlap period is relatively long with stock shift programming. It is usually reduced to a minimum when transmissions are modified.

We will discuss several types of modifications. Some are inexpensive, such as plug-in electronic modules, a shift kit, increasing the size of a transfer plate orifice, or removing a spring from an accumulator. Other changes are expensive, such as a special-purpose gearset or a highly modified torque converter. Table 20-1 lists various modifications and the ones often used for the modification stages. Each modification will be discussed in more detail.

Most of the stage 5 modifications require specially made, nonproduction parts that are only used on competition units. Although they might provide a benefit for street use, they are usually not worth the cost. Some of the parts for modifying a transmission are available from the new-car dealership or the original equipment manufacturer (OEM). These components are designed for transmissions used with the largest engines or the heaviest or sportiest vehicles. They are designed to handle more torque or provide firmer, tighter operating characteristics. These parts should be used when the transmission requires a warranty. Aftermarket suppliers that service the transmission repair industry are a good source for shift kits, heavy-duty components, and high-performance friction materials. Some suppliers pride themselves in providing parts that cure many transmission weaknesses. All-out racing components are available from companies that specialize in high-performance transmissions and are available through most speed shop catalogs and over the Internet.

Transmission modifications are often developed through a trial-and-error operation. The changes made often depend on the transmission design and are determined after studying its operation, hydraulic circuit, and physical construction. Most technicians use a kit that has already been developed and tested by the supplier.

In order of difficulty, the easiest transmission systems to modify are:

1. Electronic control system
2. Hydraulic control system
3. Torque converter
4. Friction material
5. Gearset

20.1.1 Shift Quality

It is a good idea to determine what a "good shift" is before getting too deep into improving shifts. Most of us realize that too soft of a shift has a lot of slippage that can cause an engine flare and also create wear and heat. Some believe a good shift should be felt by a definite "bump" as the shift occurs, but is this really good? The bump might be a tie-up—being in two gears at one time and thus trying to tear up the transmission.

The two major elements of a good shift are length and firmness. Shift length (duration) is the time period it takes for the shift to occur. Remember that several things *must* occur during a shift. A clutch, band, or one-way clutch must release, another

TABLE 20-1   Modifications to Produce Operating Characteristics

Stage	A	B	C	D	E	F	G	H	I	J	K	L	M	N	O	P
1	X	X		X												
2	X	X		X												
3	X	X	X	X	X	X	?		?							
4	X	X	X	X	X	X	?			X						
5	?	?	X	X	X	X	X	?	X	X	X	X	?	X	?	X

A: shift kit
B: plug-in electronic module
C: increase clutch pack size
D: improve friction material quality
E: added fluid/deep pan
F: added cooling
G: improve lube flow
H: low-ratio gearset

I: lightweight drums
J: high-strength components
K: heavy-duty sprag races
L: low-drag components
M: low-volume oil pump
N: special valve body
O: internal transmission brake
P: converter stall speed change

Symbol: ?—might be made depending on exact usage and other variables.

TECH TIP

As you tear down a transmission that you think shifts too softly, inspect the friction material. Overheated friction material can easily be spotted by the discolored and warped plates. Is it really overheated from shifting too softly?

TECH TIP

Some people equate a good shift with a strong bump, but if you watch the front of the hood during a WOT shift, you can sometimes see it drop sharply and then lift again. If the front of a vehicle drops, the transmission is binding up, trying to stop the vehicle—a very bad thing, indeed.

clutch or band must apply, and the engine speed must change (usually drop) to the rpm required for the next gear. A review of Section 7.7.1 describes this process. Also remember that if one member applies faster, the other member must release faster to prevent a tie-up. The two apply devices must be coordinated or synchronized. A firm shift is felt by the steady pressure at the back of the seat as the vehicle accelerates or a slight lifting of the front of the vehicle during the shift.

20.2 SHIFT IMPROVER KITS

Shift improver kits are the most popular transmission modification. Kits for some transmissions are available from aftermarket transmission part suppliers. Some transmission shops install a shift kit as a standard practice when rebuilding certain transmissions. This is done to increase the life of the rebuild

and to make a noticeable firmness in the shift quality, thus increasing customer satisfaction. The contents of a shift kit vary depending on the transmission and the supplier. It can be a drill bit and direction sheet for increasing an orifice size, a replacement transfer plate, a valve body spring, a spacer block for an accumulator, an orifice plug, or any combination of these (Figure 20-2). Some shift kits are designed to provide changes in stages from the barely noticeable to rather firm shifts.

20.2.1 Orifice Changes

The size of an orifice in the feed passage is used as a major control for the quality of a shift. The speed and/or quality of that shift can be easily altered by changing the size of the orifice. The orifice is normally located in the transfer plate, a part that can be

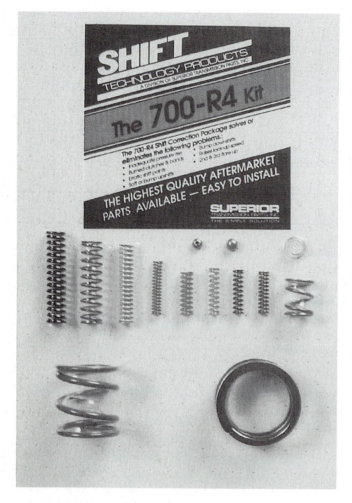

FIGURE 20-2 Shift improver kits vary from minor ones that firm up the shifts to major ones that involve significant internal changes. *(Courtesy of Superior Transmission Parts)*

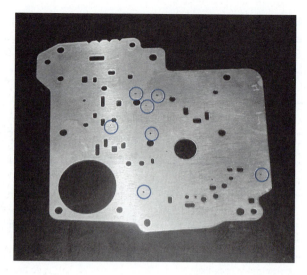

FIGURE 20-3 The small holes in this separator plate are fluid orifices. Checking where the fluid passage goes from an orifice will identify the purpose for that orifice.

TECH TIP

Assume there is an orifice with a diameter of 0.180 in., and we want to increase its size (area) by 10%.

The area of a 0.180-in. hole is $0.180 \div 2 = 0.090$ (radius),

$$0.090 \times 0.090 = 0.008 \text{ (radius squared), and } 0.008 \times 3.1416 = 0.025 \text{ in}^2 \text{ (hole area).}$$

We need to make the area of the hole 0.0025 in^2 larger ($0.025 \times 0.10 = 0.0025$) (area increase) for a total of 0.0275 in^2 ($0.025 + 0.0025$) if we want to increase it by 10%. To determine the diameter of a hole that has an area of 0.0275 in^2, we work through the formula backward:

$$0.0275 \div 3.1416 = 0.00875 \text{ (radius squared), and the square root of this is } 0.0936 \text{ (radius).}$$

Multiplying this by 2 gives us a hole diameter of 0.187 in.

Increasing an orifice diameter from 0.180 to 0.187 in. should increase the flow rate about 10%. Although it appears rather complicated, a simple pocket calculator makes the mathematics rather easy.

easily replaced (Figure 20-3). As described earlier, the speed at which a clutch or band servo strokes to take up a clearance and apply the clutch or band is directly related to the size of the servo piston and the fluid flow rate to the piston. An orifice reduces the flow rate and therefore increases the time for the piston stroke. Simply put, if we were to increase the area of the orifice by 10%, we would increase the flow rate by 10% and reduce the time by 10%. This will speed up the shift and reduce slippage.

Remember that we are referring to the area of the orifice, not the diameter. The area of an orifice is the product of:

$$A = \pi r^2 \text{ or } A = 0.785d^2$$

where

π(pi) $= 3.1416$
$\quad$ r $=$ radius, one-half the hole diameter
$\quad$ d $=$ hole diameter

TECH TIP

When drilling an orifice, finish the hole so there are no burrs or rough edges. These can create fluid turbulence that reduces the flow. Normally the hole is drilled using a sharp drill bit to the desired size, and then a larger drill or a scraper is used to debur or chamfer each end of the hole (Figure 20-4).

TECH TIP

If a hole is too large, the diameter can be reduced by soldering the hole closed or plugging it with a soft rivet and then drilling it to the desired size (Figure 20-5). It is good practice to counterbore each end of the hole before soldering it to give the solder a good mechanical bond. Another method of reducing the diameter of an orifice in a transfer plate is to peen the metal around the hole to displace metal toward the hole. After peening, the orifice should be drilled to the desired diameter.

TECH TIP

The flow through a round passage in the case or a shaft can be closed by driving a cup plug (slightly oversize) into the passage (Figure 20-6). The cup plug is then drilled to provide the desired orifice.

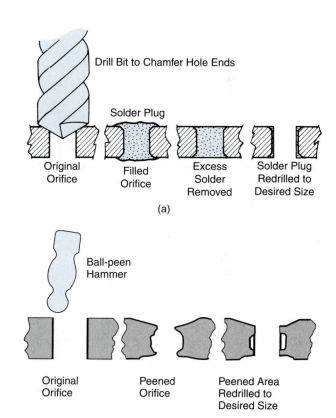

FIGURE 20-5   If an orifice needs to be made smaller, it can be filled with solder and redrilled to the proper size (a); the chamfers ensure that the solder plug does not get pushed out of the hole. Another way of doing this is to peen the hole partially closed before redrilling it to the proper size (b).

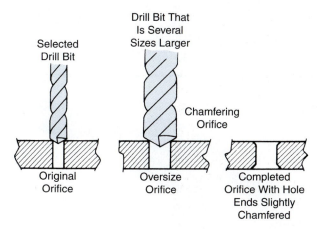

FIGURE 20-4   If a transfer plate orifice has been drilled to a larger diameter, the edges of the hole should be chamfered slightly to remove any possible burrs.

FIGURE 20-6   A small cup plug can be driven into a passage to close it off. It can be drilled to the proper size to provide an orifice.

20.2.2 Accumulator Changes

An accumulator is a relatively easy device to alter. In some cases, it is mounted at the outside of the case to allow quick and easy access. The most common change made with accumulators is to block their motion. If the piston cannot stroke, it will not take fluid away from the clutch or band operation

In a few cases, an accumulator can be blocked by turning the piston upside down relative to the bore and guide rod. Another way to block one is to cut a piece of tubing to a length slightly shorter than the accumulator piston stroke (Figure 20-7). The tubing diameter should be smaller than the piston diameter so it fits against a strong portion of the piston.

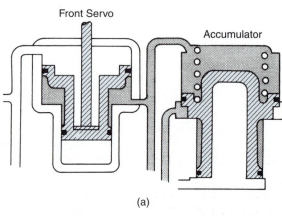

Front Servo

Accumulator

(a)

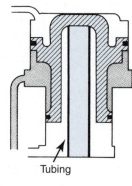

Tubing

(b)

FIGURE 20-7   The action of some accumulators (a) can be eliminated by cutting a piece of thin wall tubing to the right length and installing it to block movement (b). Note that the spring has been removed.

and the application will be faster and firmer. Like modifying orifice size in a transfer plate, blocking an accumulator is fairly easy to change back if it does not produce the desired results.

20.2.3 Programming Changes, Electronic-Controlled Transmissions

Electronic transmission controls can be easily modified by plugging a module between the case connector and the wiring harness (Figure 20-8). In most cases, the electrical harness is disconnected at the transmission end, and the module is connected between the harness and the transmission. Some modules include adjustments so the operation can be tailored to suit the driver's wishes.

20.2.4 Programming Changes, Nonelectronic-Controlled Transmissions

Depending on the intended operation, additional modifications can be made to the hydraulic circuits to reprogram the automatic operation. These include:

- Modulator or modulator rod length to change shift quality and timing
- Shift valve spring to change shift points

If you want to swap an electronic transmission into a vehicle not having electronic controls, an electronic transmission control unit is available (Figure 20-9). This is a system that includes a TPS and wiring harnesses as well as adjustments that allow the tailoring of shift points and shift feel.

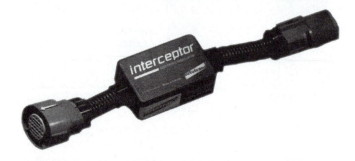

FIGURE 20-8   A plug-in electronic device can be used to change the shift and TCC characteristics of electronically controlled transmissions. *(Courtesy of Autotrans)*

FIGURE 20-9   This E-Place set contains an electronic transmission controller, TPS, VSS, and the wiring harness to connect to the vehicle and transmission. It allows the installation of an electronic-controlled transmission into a nonelectronic-transmission vehicle. *(Courtesy of Autotrans)*

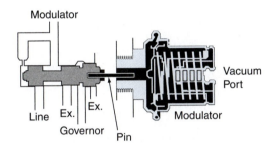

FIGURE 20-10   Line pressure can be increased using a longer modulator pin, turning the modulator adjusting screw inward, or using a modulator with stronger spring pressure.

- Governor weights or springs to change shift points
- Line pressure to apply more pressure on the friction material
- Removal of center seal from clutches using three seals to increase clutch apply force
- Removal of certain check balls to allow increased fluid flow

Shift quality can be changed by modifying the modulator. Many transmission shops install a firmer modulator (one with a high spring pressure or a smaller diaphragm area) or use a longer modulator pin to obtain firmer upshifts (Figure 20-10). A softer modulator or shorter pin is used for softer, smoother shifts. Adjustable modulators can be adjusted to make minor changes in shift quality. In addition to these changes, there are different kits available; one kit is driver adjusted and another technician adjusted. They vary the vacuum signal to the modulator to produce the desired shift quality.

Many shift kits contain one or more replacement shift valve springs. The strength of these springs is altered from

You can see how a modulator change affects the operation if you road test a vehicle after installing a vacuum gauge and fluid pressure gauge as described in Chapter 12. Before making any modifications, make a moderate-to-high-throttle acceleration from a stop to high-gear shift and note the shift quality. This will be the baseline for the next tests. Lower the vacuum available to the modulator, note the effect on the vacuum and line pressure gauges, and repeat the baseline test. Depending on the amount of vacuum, a definite change in shift quality should be noticed. It should be noted that reducing the vacuum signal will not affect full-throttle shifts because the vacuum is zero during wide-open throttle.

Shift timing for all shifts is altered by changing the governor weights or springs. Some manufacturers have a selection of governor weights available. Drilling a hole or cutting away some of the metal in the weights reduces the effect of centrifugal force. This produces lower governor pressure and higher-speed upshifts (Figure 20-11). Adding additional metal onto the governor weights produces earlier and higher governor pressure and lower-speed shifts. Changing the springs has a similar effect. Stronger springs produce later, higher-speed shifts, and weaker springs produce earlier, lower-speed shifts.

stock to produce different shift timing for that particular upshift or downshift.

Many people raise line pressure when reprogramming a transmission by shimming the pressure regulator spring. This produces firmer and stronger shifts, but it also increases the horsepower loss in the transmission and produces more heat in the fluid. A knowledgeable transmission tuner uses other methods that are described in this chapter to produce stronger and firmer shifts. Line pressure increase is used as the last

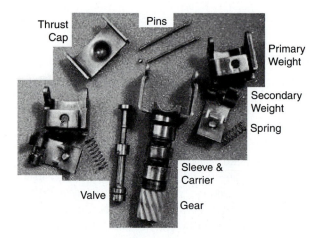

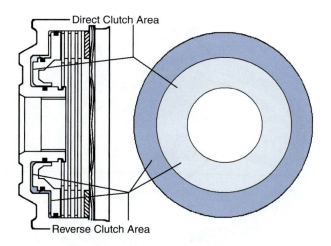

Direct Clutch Area

Reverse Clutch Area

FIGURE 20-12 This direct clutch has two fluid chambers separated by the center piston seal. The inner chamber is used in third gear, and both chambers are used in reverse.

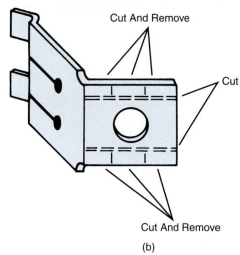

Cut And Remove

Cut

Cut And Remove

(b)

FIGURE 20-11 Cutting material off the secondary weights reduces the centrifugal force of the weights and reduces governor pressure. The result will be later upshifts.

TECH TIP

It is difficult to locate a spring of a particular diameter, length, and strength. A good, complete spring selection is not commonly available. The strength effect of a spring can be increased by stretching it slightly or by placing a shim under one end of it. If tinkering with springs, remember that all straight-wound springs have a constant rate of compression. Even though valve body springs are relatively small, they follow the normal rules for springs. Spring rate refers to the rate of compression relative to the load. This means that if it takes 1 ounce (28.4 g) of pressure to compress the spring 1/4 in. (6.35 mm), it will take 2 ounces (56.8 g) of force to compress it 1/2 in. (12.7 mm), and 3 ounces (85.2 g) of force to compress it 3/4 in. (19 mm). Shimming or stretching a spring causes it to enter further into its rate increase and to do so sooner. If a spring can be shortened by squeezing it, it enters the rate slower and is weaker. The actual strength of a spring is determined by the diameter of the wire, the coil diameter, and number of coils. The thicker the spring's wire, the stronger the spring.

resort. Some tuners can reduce line pressure, and make other changes, to produce the desired result. Reducing line pressure improves transmission efficiency.

Some transmissions use outer, center, and inner seals in the direct clutch pistons and some forward clutch pistons (Figure 20-12). The center seal divides the piston chamber into two separate chambers. These chambers can be filled separately, progressively, or simultaneously. They are normally used to produce smoother neutral–first and neutral–reverse shifts while producing a strong direct clutch in reverse. When building a high-performance transmission, the center seal can be removed to increase the piston area and produce a stronger forward-clutch application. If this modification is done on street-driven vehicles, the 2–3 shift will be considered harsh. Removing the center seal from the direct clutch also produces a severe leak into the reverse passages in third gear. This requires significant altering of the fluid passages.

20.3 CLUTCH PACKS

Clutch pack modifications are used to improve the torque-carrying capacity and the longevity of the transmission. Changes include using the best friction material available, increasing

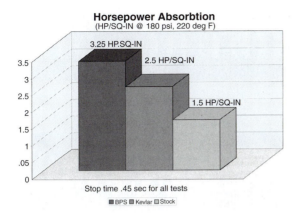

Horsepower Absorbtion
(HP/SQ-IN @ 180 psi, 220 deg F)

Stop time .45 sec for all tests

■ BPS ■ Kevlar ■ Stock

FIGURE 20-13 Special-purpose clutch plates designed for racing have a higher static coefficient of friction that produces firmer shifts that can absorb more torque. *(Courtesy of Raybestos)*

the number of clutch plates, and drilling the hub and drum for improved fluid flow in and out of the clutch plate area.

Friction material quality is important in any transmission. High torque loads or extended transmission life demands using the best material available. This is often a top-quality OEM material with new steel plates. Some shops grit-blast the steel plates. This usually produces a firmer shift, but the rougher plate friction surface causes reduced life expectancy of the clutch lining.

If the transmission is to be used for racing, special-purpose racing clutch plates should be used. These plates use friction material that is designed to absorb the increased torque (Figure 20-13). They also will work better under the higher-heat conditions found in racing transmissions. These friction plates, along with the microfinished steel plates to be used with them, are made to higher standards to ensure proper operation.

20.3.1 Increasing Pack Size

Adding one more friction and a steel plate to a four-plate clutch increases the torque capacity by 25%. The longevity or number of shifts that the clutch can make also increases 25%.

Most manufacturers produce different clutch assemblies with various numbers of plates depending on the engine torque and body weight of the vehicle. The differences that determine the number of plates are usually the piston thickness, pressure plate thickness, drum depth, and hub length (Figure 20-14). In some transmissions, the entire clutch pack assembly must be replaced in order to increase the clutch pack size.

Increasing the pack size can cause other problems. Each pair of plates has a slight drag while released; we can expect a six-plate clutch to have 1/6 more drag than a five-plate clutch. This parasitic drag reduces transmission efficiency and

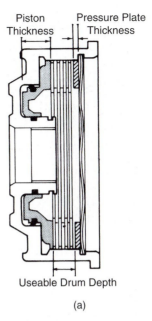

(a)

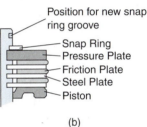

(b)

FIGURE 20-14 In many cases, the number of plates that are used in a clutch is determined by the thickness of the pressure plate or piston (a); in some cases, changing one of these allows another friction and steel plate to be added. In some clutches, the drum can be modified to move the snap-ring groove so another friction and steel plate can be added (b).

TECH TIP

The thickness of the piston from some four-plate clutch assemblies is the thickness of a three-plate clutch piston minus the thickness of one friction plate, one steel plate, and a clearance of about 0.010 in. (0.25 mm) (Figure 20-15). Using the four-plate piston in a three-plate clutch usually allows enough room for an additional friction and steel plate. When doing this, you should always compare the length of the clutch hubs to ensure that the added plate is positioned correctly on the hub. In some transmissions, a clutch with more plates has a longer hub.

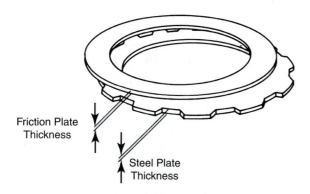

FIGURE 20-15 Measuring the thickness of a lined and unlined clutch plate and adding a clearance of 0.010 in. determines the space required to add an additional plate.

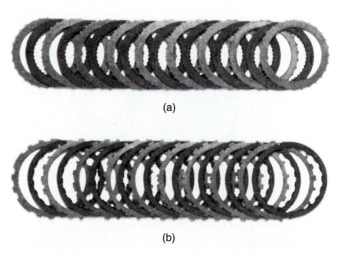

(a)

(b)

FIGURE 20-16 The clutch pack with eight friction plates is designed to replace an AOD six-plate pack (a). The clutch pack with nine frictions replaces the stock six friction, 3–4 clutch pack of a 4L60/TH 700 (b). *(Courtesy of Alto Products Corp.)*

TECH TIP

Some clutches vary the position of the clutch plate retaining snap-ring groove in the drum depending on the number of plates used. The drum can be replaced using one for the desired clutch pack, or a new groove can be machined into the drum to allow more plates to be installed.

Clutch Apply

FIGURE 20-17 When a clutch applies, fluid must leave the area between the plates. Usually it flows out the end of the clutch assembly. It can flow outward if the drum is drilled.

TECH TIP

One aftermarket manufacturer markets thinner clutch plates so more of them will fit into the clutch drum (Figure 20-16). Some sources do not recommend these plates because they have a reduced heat-sink ability. This causes them to run hotter with possible warpage, drag, and overheating problems.

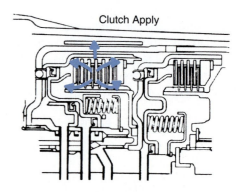

TECH TIP

The clutch for a road or endurance racing transmission needs a little more clearance than a stock unit. About 0.013 to 0.016 in. per plate is recommended.

20.3.2 Drilling a Hub or Drum

Drilling the clutch hub and drum increases the shift speed and clutch longevity. When a clutch is released, fluid must enter between the clutch plates to reduce lining heat, friction, and wear. When a clutch applies, this fluid must leave (Figure 20-17).

increases heat. Another problem is caused by the thinner plates that are often used. A thinner plate does not have as much heat-sink ability; if it absorbs the same amount of heat as a normal thick plate, it will become hotter. If it gets too hot, it can warp and produce still more heat, possibly causing a loss in the static coefficient of friction.

The clutch hubs in many transmissions have holes drilled in them to allow the fluid to escape (Figure 20-18).

Many three-speed Simpson gear train transmissions have a band fitted around the direct clutch drum. This band must

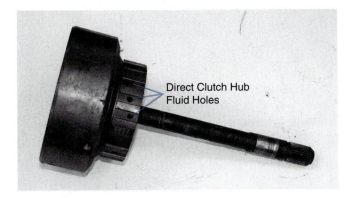

FIGURE 20-18 This THM 700 clutch hub was drilled during manufacture to provide a fluid flow into the clutch area.

TECH TIP

Use 8 to 12 holes of about 1/8-in. (3.17-mm) diameter if drilling a hub. The holes should be spaced equally around the hub so that pairs of holes are directly opposite (Figure 20-19). The hole pattern should be staggered so oil is directed to all of the clutch plates. After the holes have been drilled, remove any burrs from the drilling. Carefully spaced holes of equal size should not disrupt the balance of the hub.

TECH TIP

A series of holes can be drilled through the band friction surface of the drum to reduce band release time. Drill 8 to 12 equally spaced 1/8-in.-diameter holes through the drum. Again, the holes should be staggered across the friction area. The holes should align with grooves for the clutch plate splines (Figure 20-20). The sharp edges of these holes tend to cause band wear. It is good practice to chamfer their outer edge using a 3/16-in. (4.76-mm) or 1/4-in. (6.35-mm) drill bit.

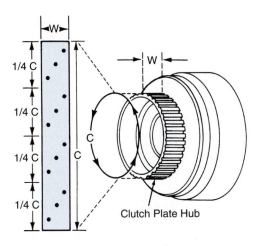

FIGURE 20-19 When drilling a clutch hub, cut a strip of paper to the width and circumference of the hub. Divide the circumference into fourths and then into smaller sections as desired (twelfths are shown). Wrap the paper around the hub, transfer the hole locations, drill 1/8-in.-diameter holes, debur the holes, and clean off any metal chips.

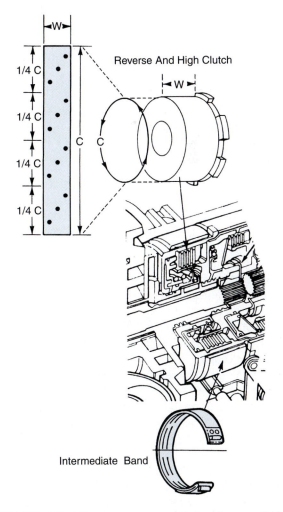

FIGURE 20-20 When drilling a clutch drum, lay out and drill the holes using the same procedure as a hub. After drilling the holes, chamfer the outer edges to remove the sharp edges.

release as the clutch is applied. Clutch apply and band release time can be reduced slightly by routing the fluid from between the clutch plates to the area under the band.

20.3.3 Floater Springs

Floater springs reduce clutch drag. These are thin, wavy springs that fit between the outer edges of the steel plates (Figure 20-21). These springs separate the steels from the friction plates to reduce drag when the clutch is released.

20.3.4 Band Changes

Changes to increase the strength of a band are limited to drilling holes in the drum surface as just described and using the replacement parts available from the OEM manufacturer or specialty aftermarket supplier. Different band levers are available for some transmissions that increase the apply force on the band. Some transmissions use servo pistons of different sizes. Replacing the servo assembly with one of a larger diameter will increase the band apply force and reduce apply speed, but this speed increase can result in timing problems. The band should also be one with the best-quality friction material available.

20.4 IMPROVING LUBRICATION

A transmission's life can be severely reduced if the fluid becomes too hot or too dirty. This applies to all transmissions and especially those used for heavier-than-normal operation, such as RV, trailer towing, off-road, street-strip, or competition operation. Anything that increases fluid temperature will tend to reduce a transmission's life and performance.

Extra-deep oil pans are available from several aftermarket sources. These pans hold 1 to 4 more quarts of fluid than the stock pan (Figure 20-22). The increased fluid provides a larger heat sink, which reduces the rate of heat buildup. The increased surface area, which allows more air contact, provides added cooling. Some deep pans are made from cast aluminum with fins to increase the amount of metal-to-air ratio even more. Some deep pans have air tubes passing through the sump area to provide increased oil-to-air surface area. Most deep pans have an extension to place the filter lower, near the bottom of the pan, to ensure fluid pickup under all operating conditions. A drawback with a deep pan is reduced ground clearance, which might allow the pan to hit road obstructions.

Supplementary transmission coolers are available from many aftermarket sources. These come in kits to make installation easy (Figure 20-23). Coolers are available in different

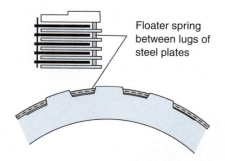

FIGURE 20-21 These thin floater springs (arrow) are placed between the outer edges of the steel plates. When the clutch is released, they will help separate the plates to reduce drag and friction.

FIGURE 20-22 This extra-capacity pan, which holds about two additional quarts of ATF, is finned to provide extra cooling ability. *(Courtesy of A-1 Automatic Transmissions)*

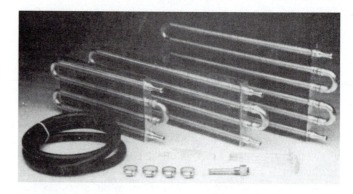

FIGURE 20-23 A supplementary oil cooler can be installed to provide additional cooling capacity. *(Courtesy of A-1 Automatic Transmissions)*

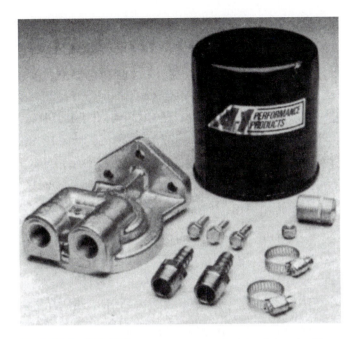

FIGURE 20-24   A filter can be added into the cooler line to remove any contaminants that might clog the cooler. *(Courtesy of A-1 Automatic Transmissions)*

TECH TIP

If installing a remote filter, check to see if it contains a bypass valve. If not, this filter can become plugged as it removes debris from the fluid, and thus restrict the fluid flow through the transmission lubrication passages. Be sure to change filters at the recommended intervals.

TECH TIP

Many racers use synthetic ATF because of the increased ability to withstand high-heat conditions.

TECH TIP

The modification to ensure lube circuit flow is to grind a portion of land 2 (or whichever land separates torque converter feed pressure from line pressure) from the pressure regulator valve or drill a small feed hole (0.060 in., 1.5 mm) in the passage wall between torque converter feed and line or supply pressure. This change might drop line pressure in some gear ranges slightly, but it ensures a converter and lubrication flow at all times.

sizes to suit the cooling needs of different applications. Larger vehicles or heavier loads generate more transmission heat and require more cooling. Cooler setups for street-driven vehicles commonly use rubber hoses with slip-on connections secured by hose clamps. Remember that there is a potential fire hazard should a hose rupture and spray ATF onto a hot exhaust. The coolers for racing/competition vehicles normally use more positive, threaded connections. The coolers using threaded connections also use larger lines to ensure adequate oil flow.

Remote filters can be added to the cooler line if increased longevity is a concern (Figure 20-24). Filters are available in different sizes. Some are rather small, inline devices; others use a standard, spin-on filter cartridge. Filters provide positive cleaning of the fluid returning to the transmission as lubrication oil.

The valve body or pressure regulator can be modified to provide increased fluid flow into the torque converter, cooler, and lubrication circuit. Remember that the pressure regulator valve in some transmissions will shut off flow to this circuit when line pressure falls below the pressure regulator setting.

An abundant quantity of lubrication oil is required for competition transmissions. Some types of competition transmissions require operation in first and second gear at extremely high engine rpm. Under these severe operating conditions, the gearset and the released apply devices must have an adequate fluid flow to reduce friction and remove

heat. Some transmissions have rather complicated and restrictive lubrication passages. They require extensive work to achieve adequate lubrication.

20.5 GEAR TRAIN CHANGES

Replacement planetary gearsets are available from several aftermarket sources—some cater to racing, others to heavy-duty and recreational vehicle (RV) usage. Heavy-duty/RV emphasis

When building a transmission for racing, it is good practice to trace out the cooler-lubrication circuit and study the fluid path. Restrictions can often be reduced by drilling the passages to a larger diameter and removing any sharp corners that might restrict fluid flow. Lubrication flow can be increased significantly in some transmissions. Always use discretion when removing metal from a transmission.

Some all-out racing transmissions, like many race engines, are converted to dry sump lubrication systems. The fluid is pulled from the transmission pan by a scavenger pump and stored in a special reservoir, and the transmission pump intake pulls from this reservoir. This system allows all the air and foam to separate from the fluid in the reservoir and allows additional fluid storage.

A possible disadvantage with the lower gear ratio is that the engine rpm in first gear increases by 10%, and the top speed is reduced by 10%. There is also a greater rpm drop during the shift to the next higher gear. Another disadvantage is the high cost of the gearset.

Remember that electronic-controlled transmissions monitor the input and output shaft speeds to check for slipping. A ratio change can set a DTC and illuminate the MIL.

FIGURE 20-25 Low-ratio gearsets for THM 400, C6, and Torqueflite. They provide a low-gear ratio that is about 11% lower and a 6% lower second-gear ratio than stock. *(Courtesy of A-1 Automatic Transmissions)*

is to increase strength and reduce drag to improve longevity and fuel mileage. Some of these gearsets are made from stronger materials and use improved bearings (Figure 20-25).

The torque capacity of some transmissions can be increased by using upgraded parts from the vehicle manufacturer. For example, a THM 400 can use many of the gear train parts, clutch parts, and other parts from the much stronger 4L80 E.

Lower gear ratios are desirable for certain applications. Several aftermarket sources provide low-ratio gearsets for some popular transmission models. Special-purpose components are relatively expensive. They provide additional torque and pulling power in first and second gears. For example, the replacement gearset for a THM 400 lowers the first-gear ratio from 2.48:1 to 2.75:1. If it is used in a vehicle with a 4:1 rear-axle ratio, the overall ratio is reduced from a stock ratio of 2.48 × 4, or 9.92:1, to the lower ratio of 2.75 × 4, or 11:1. The modified ratio is over 10% lower so it should increase the torque and pulling power by more than 10%.

Low-ratio gearsets are designed primarily for competition vehicles. They are also popular for use in trailer towing, off-road, and RV vehicles that need more pulling power.

Another way to achieve a gear ratio change with RWD vehicles is the addition of an overdrive gearset, which provides one overdrive gear ratio. The most common sets are units placed behind the transmission. These require a shorter drive shaft plus mounting brackets to support the unit and absorb any torque reactions. Overdrive units are available that adapt to the extension housing area of some of the more popular transmissions. This installation, like the addition of a low-ratio gearset, usually requires complete transmission teardown and rebuilding.

20.6 COMPETITION TRANSMISSIONS: STRENGTHENING AND LIGHTENING CHANGES

When the engine's horsepower is increased, the tire size is increased, or the vehicle's load is increased, some stock automatic transmission parts will fail. They are not designed to handle the added torque requirements. Several extra-duty or high-performance parts are available from aftermarket sources to cure the weaknesses in the more popular transmissions. Examples of these parts are:

- The outer sprag race for a THM 350: Special sprag races are over three times as strong as the stock unit.
- The intermediate sprag for a THM 400: Special sprags more than double the strength of the stock unit.
- The Powerglide high clutch hub: The special unit is significantly stronger and more reliable than the stock unit.
- Input shafts for some transmissions are made from stronger steel alloys than the original ones.

Some companies market special parts that allow the use of needle or roller bearings to support the rotating parts and Torrington bearings to replace the plastic or metal thrust washers. These reduce the friction loss and some of the heat that is generated in the transmission. An alternative to the expensive special bearings is to use wider-than-stock replacement bushings or two stock bushings (right next to each other) when possible. Increasing the bushing support area often reduces the amount of wobble and misalignment that a part can produce when spinning at high speed.

Lightweight clutch drums, hubs, and planetary gearset parts are also available for some transmissions. Some clutch drums are rather heavy. The high-reverse clutch of a three-speed Simpson gear train spins about 2 1/2 times faster than the engine in first gear. During a hard acceleration, it takes a significant amount of power to bring this heavy drum up to speed. Bringing the drum to a stop in second gear puts a heavy load on the band. Lightweight components reduce the inertial load, allowing these parts to change speed easier. These lightweight units are made from high-strength aluminum or steel alloys and are rather expensive. They offer the optimum performance in racing situations that demand rapid acceleration. Some lightweight gearset components are drilled with rather large holes to further reduce weight.

20.7 MANUAL SHIFT VALVE BODIES

Manual shift valve bodies eliminate automatic upshifts and downshifts. The shifter has a gear position for each gear, and the driver manually selects the gear range. Most manual shift valve bodies are designed for drag racing and use a reverse shift pattern. The gear positions will be in the order: park, reverse, neutral, first, second, and third. Manual shift valve bodies are also designed for pulling (tractor or truck), off-road, and rally racing vehicles.

Most manual shift valve bodies look like stock valve bodies on the outside. The internal fluid passages and valves have been significantly changed. They are designed so the shifts occur instantly with no lag.

Some drag-racing valve bodies have an internal transmission brake. These units use an electric solenoid that opens passages to shift the transmission into both first and reverse at the same time (Figure 20-26). When the solenoid is deactivated by a driver-controlled switch, the transmission is instantly in first gear only, and the vehicle is free to accelerate. The purpose of this is to produce a rapid response so the vehicle will "launch" instantly, much like a vehicle using a clutch and standard transmission. If used excessively with the converter at full stall, a transmission brake will significantly shorten the life of the converter.

20.8 HIGH-STALL CONVERTERS

Remember that stall speed is the maximum speed that an engine can run against a stalled, stationary transmission input shaft and torque converter turbine. Stall speed is determined by the engine's strength and tightness or looseness of the converter. A high-stall converter is one that allows the engine to reach a higher-than-normal stall speed. When the engine is accelerated against a stationary transmission input shaft, the rpm will flash up to a certain rpm, and this speed will usually drop slightly to the actual stall speed. As described in Chapter 9, the stall speed is primarily controlled by the following factors:

- Converter diameter: The smaller the converter, the higher the stall speed. There is about 30% difference in speed per inch in torque converter diameter.

FIGURE 20-26 A THM 350 valve body with a solenoid valve and tubing added for a transmission brake. *(Courtesy of A-1 Automatic Transmissions)*

- Impeller vane angle: Negative vane angle produces a higher stall speed.
- Stator vane angle: The greater the angle, the higher the stall speed and the greater the torque multiplication ratio.
- Impeller-to-turbine vane clearance: The greater the clearance, the higher the stall speed and the lower the converter efficiency.

High-stall converters are commonly used in drag racing and truck- or tractor-pulling vehicles. On these vehicles, it is important that the engine be allowed to quickly reach the best rpm for producing maximum power. For example, a typical 305 (5-L) engine that is built for racing produces about 90 horsepower at 2,000 rpm and about 350 horsepower at 4,500 rpm. Acceleration from a dead stop with a stock (about 2,000 rpm stall speed) converter begins with an engine turning 2,000 rpm and producing 90 horsepower. A higher-stall-speed converter allows the engine speed at stall to be higher, and the vehicle's acceleration begins with an engine that is producing more power. At coupling speeds, there is very little difference in the performances between the two converters.

Efficiency and torque multiplication ratios are also very important torque converter considerations, as these two factors help determine the amount of power leaving the converter (Figure 20-27).

Most high-performance torque converter manufacturers market a variety of converters. They range from loose, very-high-stall competition converters at one extreme and tight, high-torque, improved-gas-mileage units at the other (Figure 20-28). Tight converters are popular with RV and trailer-towing vehicles as well as vehicles where low-end pulling power and fuel mileage are important. These converters have a lower-than-stock stall speed and often have a greater torque multiplication ratio. If purchasing a special converter, it is recommended to provide the converter manufacturer with the engine torque curve, vehicle weight, final drive gear ratio, tire size, vehicle center of gravity, and the elevation and climate where the vehicle will operate. This information allows the supplier to deliver a unit that will match any special needs.

Heavy-duty torque converters are built to be stronger with reduced internal drag. Some of the internal modifications are brazed fins, a steel turbine hub, a high-strength cover, heavy-duty clutch lining, and improved thrust bearings (Figure 20-29).

All-out competition converters are usually precision remanufactured stock converters. They may have the fins welded or brazed in place for improved strength, stock thrust washers replaced with Torrington bearings, steel turbine splines, and heavy-duty stator clutches installed for improved durability. In some cases the drive lugs are reinforced for added strength (Figure 20-30).

20.8.1 Direct Couplers

Automatic transmissions are used without torque converters for some applications. Direct couplers are used in boats and in some circle-track racing cars. The transmission input shaft and hydraulic pump are driven by a shaft connected directly

TECH TIP

The added horsepower can be a disadvantage if it produces too much wheel spin or breaks drive train parts. Another disadvantage of high-stall speed converters is poor fuel mileage and noise. Imagine driving a car around town that leaves from stops at engine speeds of over 3,000 rpm, and compare this with the average car, which begins accelerating at 1,000 to 2,000 rpm. High-stall converters often prove to be noisy fuel-wasters during normal driving.

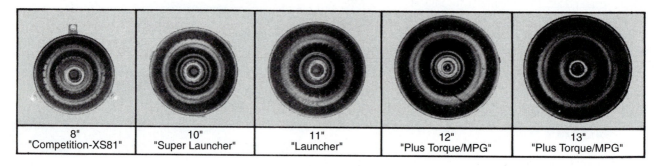

| 8" "Competition-XS81" | 10" "Super Launcher" | 11" "Launcher" | 12" "Plus Torque/MPG" | 13" "Plus Torque/MPG" |

FIGURE 20-27 These five converters are built especially for five different purposes. Note the different diameters that help determine the stall speeds. *(Courtesy of A-1 Automatic Transmissions)*

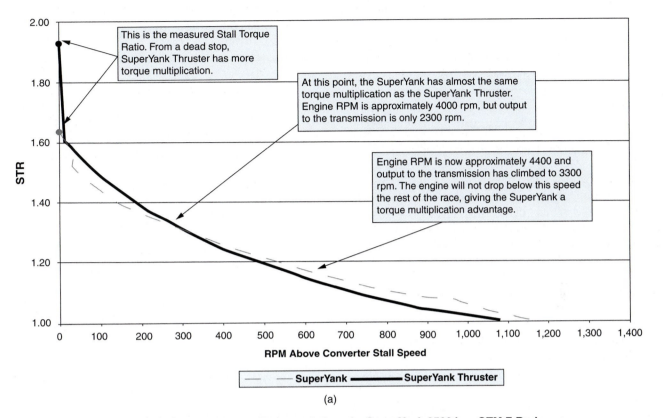

(a)

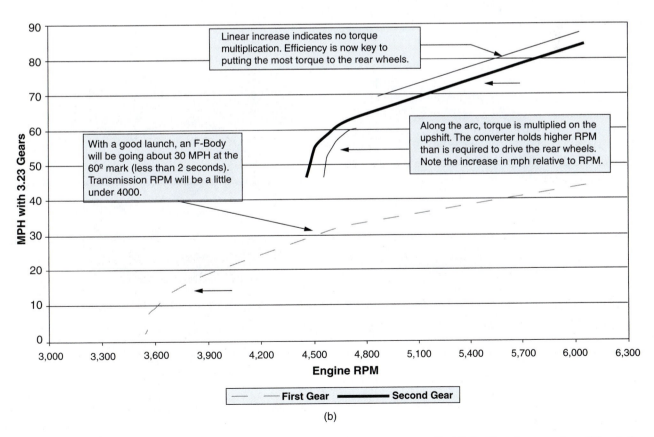

(b)

FIGURE 20-28 Graph a shows the stall torque ratios of two special-purpose torque converters. The full-throttle performance of one of them is shown in Graph b. *(Courtesy of Yank Converters)*

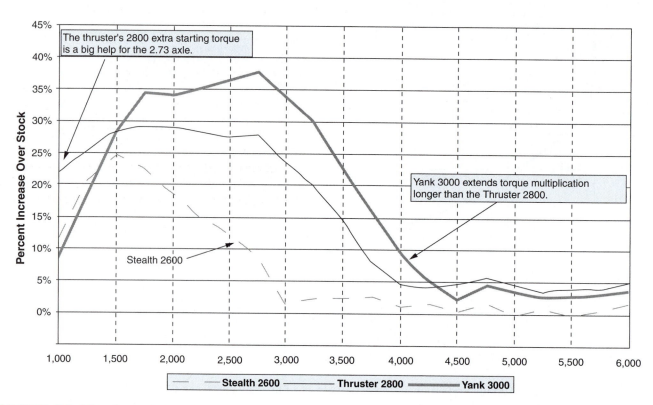

Yank Street Converters
Increase in Torque Compared to the Stock Converter

The thruster's 2800 extra starting torque is a big help for the 2.73 axle.

Yank 3000 extends torque multiplication longer than the Thruster 2800.

Stealth 2600

Stealth 2600 ——— Thruster 2800 ━━━ Yank 3000

FIGURE 20-29   This graph shows the torque increase over a stock torque converter that is available from special-purpose converters. *(Courtesy of Yank Converters)*

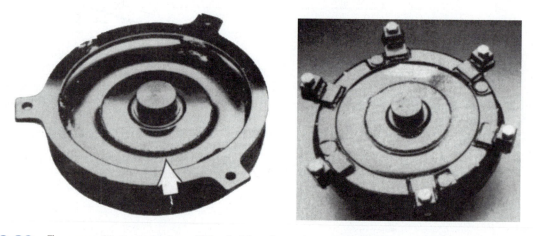

FIGURE 20-30   These competition converters have additional reinforced mounting points. *(Courtesy of A-1 Automatic Transmissions)*

to the crankshaft or flywheel (Figure 20-31). This allows the length, weight of the transmission, and the rotating mass to be reduced significantly. The transmission becomes essentially an in-and-out box with two or three forward-gear ratios plus reverse.

20.9 CONCLUSION

It has been the intent of the authors to introduce you to the aspects, possibilities, and some of the excitement of automatic transmission tuning. It is impossible to cover every aspect

FIGURE 20-31 This coupler attaches directly to the flexplate and is used to drive the transmission pump and input shaft. *(Courtesy of A-1 Automatic Transmissions)*

needed to fully develop a transmission for all of the various vehicles (racing and production) in a book of this type. More than a few knowledgeable manufacturers of specialized transmission components can provide information concerning transmission modifications for those who want to carry this further.

Some transmission tuning, such as shift kit installation and torque converter swapping, is done in the average transmission shop to cure minor transmission problems and improve customer satisfaction. The more specialized work involved in producing a custom racing transmission is done by specialists. It is considered too time-consuming and raises problems of warranty for the average shop if something goes wrong. This type of work is usually left to the highly specialized shop, race car builder, or highly knowledgeable hobbyist.

Performance-oriented automotive magazines occasionally have articles describing automatic transmission performance modifications. Past issues of these magazines can be found in many libraries, and the librarian will help locate the articles. The Internet will also produce useful information on this subject as well as general transmission repairs.

SUMMARY

1. An automatic transmission may be modified for many reasons, such as to improve shift feel, increase road performance, or for all-out racing.

2. The most common transmission modification is installing a shift kit. The kit may by installed by the vehicle owner or a transmission repair shop to improve shift timing and/or quality.

3. More extensive modifications include changing the gear train, increasing the clutch plates, and replacing the valve body.

4. The torque converter can be replaced with a higher-stall unit that will better match the torque output of the engine.

5. Technical articles should be reviewed before making any modifications to ensure the desired the results.

ASE CERTIFICATION

Automotive technicians have the opportunity to voluntarily take the National Institute for Automotive Service Excellence (ASE) certification tests to become ASE-certified automotive technicians. Certification verifies technicians' technical knowledge to themselves, to their employers, and to their customers.

ASE certification requires that you pass one or more certification tests and have at least two years of automotive repair work experience. School training can be used to substitute for part of the work experience requirement, and you may take the certification test(s) before completing the work or school requirement. After taking the certification tests, you will receive the score report, and then when the experience requirement is completed, you will receive the ASE certification.

There are nine automotive service tests, and one is the Automatic Transmission/Transaxle (A2). The A2 test has 50 questions that are taken from the following content areas.

SPECIFICATIONS FOR AUTOMATIC TRANSMISSION/TRANSAXLE TEST (A2)

Content Area		Questions in Test	Percentage of Test
A. General Transmission/Transaxle Diagnosis		24	48%
1. Mechanical/Hydraulic Systems	(12)		
2. Electronic Systems	(12)		
B. Transmission/Transaxle Maintenance and Adjustment		5	10%
C. In-Vehicle Transmission/Transaxle Repair		10	20%
D. Off-Vehicle Transmission/Transaxle Repair		11	22%
1. Removal, Disassembly, and Assembly	(3)		
2. Gear Train, Shafts, Bushings, Oil Pump, and Case	(4)		
3. Friction and Reaction Units	(4)		
	Total	50*	100.0%

*Note: There could be up to 10 additional pretest questions. Your answers to these questions will not affect your score, but since you do not know which they are, you should answer all questions in the test. A recertification test is required every five years. The recertification test will cover the same content areas as those listed here. However, the number of questions in each content area will be reduced by about half.

If you intend to take the A2 test and feel a need to study for it, each of the content areas is divided into groups of tasks. These are the jobs that a drivetrain technician should be able to do. A copy of *The Official ASE Preparation Guide to ASE Automobile Technician Tests* is available from ASE. This guide includes the current Task List and sample test questions with an explanation of how the proper response should be selected. Further help in test-taking skills can be obtained from these sources/websites:

ASE telephone: 1-877-ASE-TECH
ASE website: www.ase.com
ASE Test Preparation: www.asetestprep.com

Prentice Hall ASE Test Preparation Series: http://autotech.prenhall.com or call 1-800-526-0485

AUTOMATIC TRANSMISSION/ TRANSAXLE TEST TASK LIST

A. General Transmission/Transaxle Test Diagnosis

1. *Mechanical/Hydraulic Systems*

Task 1—Listen to driver's concern and road test vehicle to verify mechanical/hydraulic system problems; determine necessary action.

Task 2—Diagnose noise and vibration problems; determine necessary action.

Task 3—Diagnose unusual fluid usage, type, level, and condition problems; determine necessary action.

Task 4—Perform pressure tests; determine necessary action.

Task 5—Perform stall tests; determine necessary action.

Task 6—Perform lock-up converter mechanical/hydraulic system tests; determine necessary action.

Task 7—Diagnose mechanical and vacuum control systems; determine necessary action.

2. *Electronic Systems*

Task 1—Listen to driver's concern and road test vehicle to verify electronic system problems; determine necessary action.

Task 2—Perform pressure tests; determine necessary action.

Task 3—Perform lock-up converter electronic system tests; determine necessary action.

Task 4—Diagnose electronic transmission control systems using appropriate test equipment; determine necessary action.

Task 5—Verify proper operation of starting and charging systems; check battery connections and vehicle grounds.

(The content areas and task list are provided courtesy of the National Institute for Automotive Service Excellence.)

B. Transmission/Transaxle Maintenance and Adjustment

Task 1—Inspect, adjust, and replace manual valve shift linkage and transmission range sensor/switch.

Task 2—Inspect, adjust, and replace cables or linkages for throttle valve (TV), kickdown, and accelerator pedal.

Task 3—Adjust bands, where applicable.

Task 4—Replace fluid and filter(s).

C. In-Vehicle Transmission/Transaxle Repair

Task 1—Inspect, adjust, and replace vacuum modulator, valve, lines, and hoses.

Task 2—Inspect, adjust, repair, and replace governor cover, sleeve/bore, valve, weight, springs, retainers, and gear.

Task 3—Inspect and replace external seals and gaskets.

Task 4—Inspect and repair or replace extension housing; replace bushing.

Task 5—Check condition of engine cooling system; inspect, test, flush, and replace transmission cooler, lines, and fittings.

Task 6—Inspect and replace speedometer/speed sensor drive gear, driven gear, and retainers.

Task 7—Inspect valve body mating surfaces, bores, valves, springs, sleeves, retainers, brackets, check balls, screens, spacers, and gaskets; replace as necessary.

Task 8—Check and adjust valve body bolt torque.

Task 9—Inspect servo bore, piston, seals, pin, spring, and retainers; repair or replace as necessary.

Task 10—Inspect accumulator bore, piston, seals, spring, and retainers; repair or replace as necessary.

Task 11—Inspect and replace parking pawl, shaft, spring, and retainer.

Task 12—Inspect, test, adjust, repair, or replace electrical/ electronic components including computers, solenoids, sensors, relays, fuses, terminals, connector, switches, and harnesses.

Task 13—Inspect, replace, and align power train mounts.

D. Off-Vehicle Transmission/Transaxle Repair

1. *Removal, Disassembly, and Assembly*

Task 1—Remove and replace transmission/transaxle; inspect engine core plugs, transmission dowel pins, and dowel pin holes.

Task 2—Disassemble, clean, and inspect.

Task 3—Assemble after repair.

Task 4—Inspect converter flex (drive) plate, converter attaching bolts, converter pilot, and converter pump drive surfaces.

2. *Gear Train, Shafts, Bushings, Oil Pump, and Case*

Task 1—Inspect, measure, and replace oil pump housings and parts.

Task 2—Check end play and/or preload; determine needed service.

Task 3—Inspect, measure, and replace thrust washers and bearings.

Task 4—Inspect and replace shafts.

Task 5—Inspect oil delivery seal rings, ring grooves, sealing surface areas, feed pipes, orifices, and encapsulated check valves (balls).

Task 6—Inspect and replace bushings.

Task 7—Inspect and measure planetary gear assembly; replace parts as necessary.

Task 8—Inspect, repair, and replace case(s) bores, passages, bushings, vents, mating surfaces, and dowel pins.

Task 9—Inspect, repair, or replace transaxle drive chains, sprockets, gears, bearings, and bushings.

Task 10—Inspect, measure, repair, adjust, or replace transaxle final drive components.

3. *Friction and Reaction Units*

Task 1—Inspect clutch assembly; replace parts as necessary.

Task 2—Measure and adjust clutch pack clearance.

Task 3—Air test the operation of clutch and servo assemblies.

Task 4—Inspect one-way clutch assemblies; replace parts as necessary.

Task 5—Inspect and replace bands and drums.

(The content areas and task list are provided courtesy of the National Institute for Automotive Service Excellence.)

AUTOMATIC TRANSMISSION MODELS

There are many different automatic transmissions models used in modern vehicles. Small booklets/guides are available to help identify them. These guides list the transmissions by vehicle make. The guides shown are available from:

Axiom: www.axiom.com
Transtec:www.TransTec.com
Toledo Trans-kit: www.parker.com
Whatever It Takes: www.wittrans.com

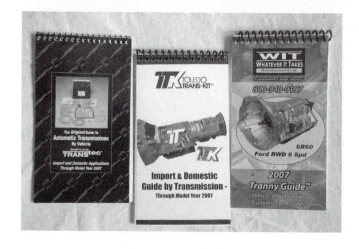

OBD-II TRANSMISSION DIAGNOSTIC TROUBLE CODES

Following is a listing of the transmission diagnostic trouble codes (DTCs) as defined by the SAE. These universal codes can be used to locate the cause of a malfunctioning electronic-controlled transmission. A transmission DTC will appear as **P07XX** or **P08XX.** The P indicates power train. The 0 indicates a generic code; a 1 would indicate a manufacturer-specific code. The 7 or 8 indicates a transmission, and the last two digits indicate the problem area. Remember that other areas such as engine controls can affect transmission operation.

P0700	Transmission Control System Malfunction
P0701	Transmission Control System Range/Performance
P0702	Transmission Control System Electrical
P0703	Brake (Torque Converter) Switch Circuit Malfunction
P0704	Clutch Switch Input Circuit Problem
P0705	Transmission Range Sensor Circuit Malfunction (PRNDL Input)
P0706	Transmission Range Sensor Circuit Range or Performance
P0707	Transmission Range Sensor Circuit Low Input
P0708	Transmission Range Sensor Circuit High Input
P0709	Transmission Range Sensor Circuit Intermittent
P0710	Transmission Fluid Temperature Sensor Circuit Malfunction
P0711	Transmission Fluid Temperature Sensor Circuit Range or Performance
P0712	Transmission Fluid Temperature Sensor Circuit Low Input
P0713	Transmission Fluid Temperature Sensor Circuit High Input
P0714	Transmission Fluid Temperature Sensor Circuit Intermittent
P0715	Input or Turbine Speed Sensor Circuit Malfunction
P0716	Input or Turbine Speed Sensor Circuit Range or Performance
P0717	Input or Turbine Speed Sensor Circuit No Signal
P0718	Input or Turbine Speed Sensor Circuit Intermittent
P0719	Torque Converter or Brake Switch B Circuit Low
P0720	Output Speed Sensor Circuit Malfunction
P0721	Output Speed Sensor Circuit Range or Performance
P0722	Output Speed Sensor Circuit No Signal
P0723	Output Speed Sensor Circuit Intermittent
P0724	Torque Converter or Brake Switch B Circuit High
P0725	Engine Speed Input Circuit Malfunction
P0726	Engine Speed Input Circuit Range or Performance
P0727	Engine Speed Input Circuit No Signal
P0728	Engine Speed Input Circuit Intermittent
P0730	Incorrect Gear Ratio
P0731	Gear 1 Incorrect Ratio
P0732	Gear 2 Incorrect Ratio
P0733	Gear 3 Incorrect Ratio
P0734	Gear 4 Incorrect Ratio
P0735	Gear 5 Incorrect Ratio
P0736	Reverse Incorrect Ratio
P0740	Torque Converter Clutch System Malfunction
P0741	Torque Converter Clutch System Performance or Stuck Off
P0742	Torque Converter Clutch System Performance or Stuck On
P0743	Torque Converter Clutch System Electrical
P0744	Torque Converter Clutch System Intermittent
P0745	Pressure Control Solenoid Malfunction
P0746	Pressure Control Solenoid Performance or Stuck Off
P0747	Pressure Control Solenoid Stuck On
P0748	Pressure Control Solenoid Electrical
P0749	Pressure Control Solenoid Intermittent
P0750	Shift Solenoid A Malfunction
P0751	Shift Solenoid A Performance or Stuck Off
P0752	Shift Solenoid A Stuck On
P0753	Shift Solenoid A Electrical
P0755	Shift Solenoid B Malfunction
P0756	Shift Solenoid B Performance or Stuck Off
P0757	Shift Solenoid B Stuck On
P0758	Shift Solenoid B Electrical

P0759	Shift Solenoid B Intermittent
P0760	Shift Solenoid C Malfunction
P0761	Shift Solenoid C Performance or Stuck Off
P0762	Shift Solenoid C Stuck On
P0763	Shift Solenoid C Electrical
P0764	Shift Solenoid C Intermittent
P0765	Shift Solenoid D Malfunction
P0766	Shift Solenoid D Performance or Stuck Off
P0767	Shift Solenoid D Stuck On
P0768	Shift Solenoid D Electrical
P0769	Shift Solenoid D Intermittent
P0770	Shift Solenoid E Malfunction
P0771	Shift Solenoid E Performance or Stuck Off
P0772	Shift Solenoid E Stuck On
P0773	Shift Solenoid E Electrical
P0774	Shift Solenoid E Intermittent

P0780	Shift Malfunction
P0781	1–2 Shift Malfunction
P0782	2–3 Shift Malfunction
P0783	3–4 Shift Malfunction
P0784	4–5 Shift Malfunction
P0785	Shift/Timing Solenoid Malfunction
P0786	Shift/Timing Solenoid Range or Performance
P0787	Shift/Timing Solenoid Low
P0788	Shift/Timing Solenoid High
P0789	Shift/Timing Solenoid Intermittent
P0790	Normal/Performance Switch Circuit Malfunction
P0801	Reverse Inhibit Control Circuit Malfunction
P0803	1–4 Upshift (Skip Shift) Solenoid Control Circuit Malfunction
P0804	1–4 Upshift (Skip Shift) Lamp Control Circuit Malfunction

J1930 TRANSMISSION TERM ACRONYMS

Automotive terms have been standardized by the Society of Automotive Engineers (SAE) directive J1930. The following is a listing of J1930 automatic-transmission-related terms.

Term	Acronym
Automatic Transaxle/Transmission	A/T
Battery Positive Voltage	B+
Crankshaft Position Sensor	CKP Sensor
Data Link Connector	DLC
Diagnostic Test Mode	DTM
Diagnostic Trouble Code	DTC
Electrically Erasable Programmable Read-Only Memory	EEPROM
Engine Coolant Temperature	ECT
Engine Coolant Temperature Sensor	ECT Sensor
Engine Speed Sensor	RPM
Erasable Programmable Read-Only Memory	EPROM
Flash Electrically Erasable Programmable Read-Only Memory	FEEPROM
Flash Erasable Programmable Read-Only Memory	FEPROM
Fourth Gear	4GR
Keep Alive Random Access Memory	Keep Alive RAM
Malfunction Indicator Lamp	MIL
Mass Air Flow Sensor	MAF Sensor
Park/Neutral Position Switch	PNP Switch
Power Train Control Module	PCM
Programmable Read-Only Memory	PROM
Random Access Memory	RAM
Read-Only Memory	ROM
Scan Tool	ST
Service Reminder Indicator	SRI
Third Gear	3GR

Term	Acronym
Throttle Position Sensor	TP Sensor
Torque Converter Clutch	TCC
Torque Converter Clutch Relay	TCC Relay
Torque Converter Clutch Solenoid	TCC Solenoid
Transmission Control Module	TCM
Transmission Range	TR
Transmission Range Sensor	TR Sensor
Transmission Range Switch	TR Switch
Vehicle Speed Sensor	VSS
Wide-Open Throttle	WOT
Wide-Open Throttle Switch	WOT Switch

Following are other acronyms, not standardized by J1930, that are commonly used.

Acronym	Term
PRNDL	Park/Reverse/Neutral/Drive/Low
PWM	Pulse-Width Modulated
TCIL	Transmission Control Indicator Lamp
TCS	Transmission Control Switch
TFT	Transmission Fluid Temperature
TOT	Transmission Oil Temperature
TRD	Transmission Range Drive
TRL	Transmission Range Low
TROD	Transmission Range Overdrive
TRR	Transmission Range Reverse
TSS	Transmission Speed Sensor

ENGLISH-METRIC-ENGLISH CONVERSION TABLE

Multiply	By	To get/Multiply	By	To get
Length				
inch (″)	25.4	millimeter (mm)	0.3939	inch
mile	1.609	kilometer	0.621	mile
Area				
inch^2	645.2	millimeter^2	0.0015	inch^2
Pressure				
psi	6.895	kilopascals (kPa)	0.145	psi
psi	0.06895	bar	14.5	psi
psi	0.006895	megapascal (MPa)	14.5	psi
Volume				
inch^3	16,387	millimeter^3	0.00006	inch^3
inch^3	6.45	centimeter^3	0.061	inch^3
inch^3	0.016	liter	61.024	inch^3
pint	0.473	liter	0.528	pint
quart	0.946	liter	1.057	quart
gallon	3.785	liter	0.264	gallon
Weight				
ounce	28.35	gram (g)	0.035	ounce
pound	0.453	kilogram (kg)	2.205	pound
Torque				
inch-pound	0.113	Newton-meter (N-m)	8.851	inch-pound
foot-pound	1.356	Newton-meter	0.738	foot-pound
Velocity				
miles/hour	1.609	kilometer/hour	0.6214	miles/hour
Temperature				
(degree Fahrenheit − 32) × 0.556 = degree Celsius				
(degree Celsius × 1.8) + 32 = degree Fahrenheit				

NATEF

CROSS REFERENCE TO NATEF TASKS

Training standards have been developed by the National Automotive Technicians Education Foundation (NATEF) for automatic transmission repair. *Automatic Transmissions/Transaxles* includes information for each of the NATEF tasks. The following identifies each of the NATEF tasks, their priority, and where the related information can be found in the text.

NATEF TASKS: AREA II. AUTOMATIC TRANSMISSION AND TRANSAXLE

The tasks are given a completion priority: 95% of Priority 1 (P-1) tasks must be completed, 80% of P-2 tasks must be completed, and 50% of P-3 tasks must be completed.

II. Automatic Transmission and Transaxle		Section
A. General Transmission and Transaxle Diagnosis		
1. Complete work order to include customer information, vehicle identifying information, customer concern, related service history, cause, and correction.	P-1	12.1–12.3
2. Identify and interpret transmission/transaxle concern; differentiate between engine performance and transmission/transaxle concerns; determine necessary action.	P-1	12.1, 12.4
3. Research applicable vehicle and service information, such as transmission/transaxle system operation, fluid type, vehicle service history, service precautions, and technical service bulletins.	P-1	1.2, 12.2, 12.3
4. Locate and interpret vehicle and major component identification numbers.	P-1	1.1, 10.1, 10.9
5. Diagnose fluid loss and condition concerns; check fluid level in transmissions with and without dipstick; determine necessary action.	P-1	11.2
6. Perform pressure tests (including transmissions/transaxles equipped with electronic pressure control); determine necessary action.	P-1	12.7
7. Perform stall test; determine necessary action.	P-3	12.9
8. Perform lock-up converter system tests; determine necessary action.	P-3	12.6, 19.2.5
9. Diagnose noise and vibration concerns; determine necessary action.	P-2	12.13
10. Diagnose transmission/transaxle gear reduction/multiplication concerns using driving, driven, and held member (power flow) principles.	P-1	12.13.1
11. Diagnose pressure concerns in a transmission using hydraulic principles (Pascal's Law).	P-2	6.2, 12.7
12. Diagnose electronic transmission/transaxle control systems using appropriate test equipment and service information.	P-1	8.3, 13.3, 13.5, 13.6

		Section
B. In-Vehicle Transmission/Transaxle Maintenance and Repair		
1. Inspect, adjust, and replace manual valve shift linkage, transmission range sensor/switch, and park/neutral position switch.	P-2	11.4
2. Inspect and replace external seals, gaskets, and bushings.	P-2	14.3, 14.4, 16.6
3. Inspect, test, adjust, repair, or replace electrical/electronic components and circuits, including computers, solenoids, sensors, relays, terminals, connectors, switches, and harnesses.	P-1	13.3, 13.5, 13.6
4. Diagnose electronic transmission control systems using a scan tool; determine necessary action.	P-1	13.3.5, 13.5.13
5. Inspect, replace, and align power-train mounts.	P-2	14.11, 15.5
6. Service transmission; perform visual inspection; replace fluid and filters.	P-1	11.3
C. Off-Vehicle Transmission and Transaxle Repair		
1. Remove and reinstall transmission/transaxle and torque converter; inspect engine core plugs, rear crankshaft seal, dowel pins, dowel pin holes, and mating surfaces.	P-1	15.2, 15.6
2. Disassemble, clean, and inspect transmission/transaxle.	P-1	16.1–16.5
3. Inspect, measure, clean, and replace valve body (includes surfaces, bores, springs, valves, sleeves, retainers, brackets, check valves/balls, screens, spacers, and gaskets).	P-2	14.9, 18.6
4. Inspect servo and accumulator bores, pistons, seals, pins, springs, and retainers; determine necessary action.	P2	14.10, 17.5
5. Assemble transmission/transaxle.	P-1	16.6
6. Inspect, leak test, and flush or replace transmission/transaxle oil cooler, lines, and fittings.	P-1	14.8, 19.3
7. Inspect converter flex (drive) plate, converter attaching bolts, converter pilot, converter pump drive surfaces, converter end play, and crankshaft pilot bore.	P-2	19.2
8. Install and seat torque converter to engage drive/splines.	P-1	16.6.2
9. Inspect, measure, and reseal oil pump assembly and components.	P-1	18.3
10. Measure transmission/transaxle end play or preload; determine necessary action.	P-1	16.3.1, 16.6.1
11. Inspect, measure, and replace thrust washers and bearings.	P-2	17.3
12. Inspect oil delivery circuits, including seal rings, ring grooves, and sealing surface areas, feed pipes, orifices, and check valves/balls.	P-2	17.5
13. Inspect bushings; determine necessary action.	P-2	17.3
14. Inspect and measure planetary gear assembly components; determine necessary action.	P-2	18.5
15. Inspect case bores, passages, bushings, vents, and mating surfaces; determine necessary action.	P-2	18.2
16. Inspect transaxle drive, link chains, sprockets, gears, bearings, and bushings; perform necessary action.	P-2	16.4.1
17. Inspect, measure, repair, adjust, or replace transaxle final drive components.	P-2	18.8
18. Inspect clutch drum, piston, check balls, springs, retainers, seals, and friction and pressure plates; determine necessary action.	P-2	17.4, 18.4
19. Measure clutch pack clearance; determine necessary action.	P-1	18.4

		Section
19. Measure clutch pack clearance; determine necessary action.	P-1	18.4
20. Air test operation of clutch and servo assemblies.	P-1	12.11
21. Inspect roller and sprag clutch, races, rollers, sprags, springs, cages, and retainers; determine necessary action.	P-1	16.6
22. Inspect bands and drums; determine necessary action.	P-2	16.6, 17.4
23. Describe the operational characteristics of a continuously variable transmission (CVT)	P-3	3.13.3
24. Describe the operational characteristics of a hybrid vehicle drivetrain.	P-3	3.14

ENGLISH GLOSSARY

Accelerate   To increase speed.

Accumulator   A device used to dampen fluid apply pressure so as to cushion or soften a shift.

Actuator   An electronic device that performs a desired function.

Adaptive function relearn   A procedure to reset transmission-operating parameters to base values.

Adaptive learning   Electronic controls that can change operating pressures to compensate for transmission wear.

Additives   Chemicals added to automatic transmission fluid (ATF) to improve the operating characteristics.

Aerated fluid   Fluid of a foamy nature that has been whipped to the point that it contains air bubbles.

Aftermarket   Referring to repair parts produced by companies other than OEM.

Air test   A test using air pressure to ensure proper clutch and band operation.

All wheel drive (AWD)   A drivetrain that automatically drives all four wheels when needed.

Alternating current (ac)   Electrical current flow that reverses direction many times a second.

Ampere   The unit of electric current flow.

Analog meter   A meter that uses needle movement to indicate the values.

Annulus gear   Ring gear, internal gear.

Apply devices   Hydraulically operated clutches and bands and mechanical one-way clutches that drive or hold planetary gearset members.

Asynchronous shift   A shift using a one-way clutch so shift elements do not need to be synchronized, also called a *nonsynchronous* or *freewheeling* shift.

Asynchronous transmission   A transmission using one-way clutches to alleviate shift timing.

Atmospheric pressure   Pressure of the atmosphere around us; generally considered to be 14.7 psi at sea level.

Automatic transmission   A transmission that changes forward-gear ratios automatically.

Automatic transmission fluid (ATF)   The oil used in automatic transmissions.

B+   A connection to battery positive.

Backlash   The clearance between two gears, also called *lash*.

Balanced valve   A valve that is in a balanced position between two opposing forces.

Ballooning   The undesirable expansion of a component, such as a torque converter, because of excessive internal pressure.

Band   A lined metal strap that wraps around a drum; used to stop the drum or hold it stationary.

Band adjustment   An adjustment to set a band to the correct clearance with the drum.

Belleville plate   A clutch plate with a conical shape used to cushion a shift.

Belleville spring   A conical steel ring that gives a spring action because of its resistance to forces that try to flatten it.

Bevel gear   A gear with teeth that are cut at an angle so it can transmit power between shafts that are not parallel.

Bump   A harsh shift condition produced by a sudden and forceful application of a clutch or band.

Case   The rigid housing for a transmission.

Centrifugal force   The force on a revolving object that tries to push it away from the center of revolution.

Check ball   A steel ball that sits on the transfer plate to allow fluid flow in only one direction.

Chuggle   A bucking or jerking condition usually most noticeable during acceleration and when the torque converter clutch is engaged. Chuggle is often engine related.

Circlip   A snap-ring type of ring with a round cross section used to position a shaft in a bore.

Circuit   A path for electrical flow from a power source, through a resistance, and back to the power source.

Circuit breaker   A unit that opens an electrical circuit in the event of excess current flow.

Clutch   A device that controls the power transfer between two points. It can allow or stop the transfer.

Clutch volume index (CVI)   A measurement of the volume of fluid needed to fill a clutch during a shift.

Coastdown   A complete release of the throttle so the moving vehicle slows down; sometimes called *zero-throttle coastdown*.

Coefficient of friction   A reference to the amount of friction between two surfaces.

Conductor   The part of a wire that allows current flow.

Continuity   A circuit or component that has a complete path for current flow.

Continuously variable transmission, CVT A transmission that uses two variable-width pulleys and a belt to change ratios from the lowest to the highest in a continuous, stepless manner instead of fixed ratios.

Control pressure Transmission fluid pressure that is controlled by the pressure regulator valve, also called *line* or *mainline* pressure.

Controller area network (CAN) A method of grouping the various control modules that gives the highest communication priority to vehicle safety.

Converter clutch A clutch in the torque converter that locks the converter during most driving conditions.

Cooler A heat exchanger in the radiator used to cool transmission fluid.

Coupling A clutchlike device that can connect or disconnect the power flow between two components.

Coupling phase A condition where the torque converter turbine speed is almost equal to that of the impeller.

Crescent pump An internal-external gear pump that has a crescent shaped divider.

Cross leak A fluid leak between two separate hydraulic passages.

Cushion plate A wave or Belleville clutch plate that can compress slightly to give a smoother application.

Damper assembly A device that reduces torsional vibrations between the engine and transmissions.

Decelerate Reduce speed.

Delayed When a shift occurs later than expected. Also called *late* or *extended.*

Department of Transportation (DOT) A governmental agency that is concerned with transportation.

Depth filter A fluid filter that can trap foreign particles as they pass through the filter material.

Detent (throttle position) A movement of the throttle to the maximum. *See* Wide-open throttle.

Detent valve A spring-loaded device used to position the manual valve correctly.

Diagnostic connector A terminal built into a vehicle to allow scan tools to read diagnostic trouble codes.

Diagnostic trouble code (DTC) An alpha-numeric code stored in the control module that indicates a malfunction in the transmission or its control system.

Dial indicator A measuring instrument used to measure travel or clearance.

Diaphragm spring A conical-shaped cushion spring, also called a *Belleville* spring.

Differential A gear arrangement that allows the drive wheels to be driven at different speeds.

Digital multimeter (DMM) A meter with multiple functions for measuring electrical activity that uses a digital readout.

Direct clutch The clutch that is applied to provide direct drive.

Direct current (DC) A constant electric current that flows in a single direction.

Direct drive ratio A 1:1 gear ratio.

Directional grooving A pattern of grooves cut into friction plates, and the plates must be positioned with the grooves facing the proper direction.

Double bump Two sudden and forceful clutch or band applications.

Double-wrap band A band design that increases clamping force when applied.

Drain down A problem that occurs when the fluid drains out of the converter.

Drainback hole A passage that allows fluid to drain from an area, example: the front seal cavity.

Drive (1, 2, 3, 4) The gear position that allows the transmission to shift through all of the forward ranges.

Drive axle An axle that supports the vehicle and provides a method of driving the wheels.

Drivetrain The engine, transmission, and other components that drive the wheels.

Driving member The planetary gear member that is the input and is driven.

Drum The drum-shaped enclosure that serves as a housing for a clutch assembly or a friction surface for a band.

DTC Abbreviation for diagnostic trouble code.

Dual-clutch transmission A transmission that uses one clutch to drive the even-numbered gears and a second clutch to drive the odd-numbered gears. It can deliver power in a continuous manner with no lag between gear changes.

Dynamic friction The relative amount of friction between two surfaces that are at different speeds. *See* Static friction.

Dynamic seal A seal in which either the seal or the surface being sealed is in motion.

Early When a shift occurs before the correct speed is reached and causes a lugging or laboring of the engine.

Elastomer Flexible, rubber-like materials commonly used for sealing materials.

Electromagnetic induction (EMI) When electricity is produced by moving a magnetic field over a wire or a wire through a magnetic field.

Electronic control module (ECM) An electronic device that uses various inputs to determine the needed output for a mechanical device to operate properly.

Electronic pressure control (EPC) A transmission fluid pressure control that is varied by a solenoid.

Electrostatic discharge (ESD) A momentary flow of electricity that occurs when an excess of electric charge finds a path to ground.

End bump A condition that produces a firmer feel at the end of a shift. Also called *end feel* or *slip bump.*

End play The amount of movement a gearset or shaft has in a direction that is parallel to the input shaft.

Energy The ability to do work.

Engine braking A condition where engine compression is used to slow the vehicle down.

Engine support A device that supports the engine so a transaxle can be removed.

Environmental Protection Agency (EPA) A governmental agency that is charged with protecting human health and with safeguarding the natural environment: air, water, and land.

Exchange/Used A replacement powertrain component that comes from another vehicle.

Exhaust The release of fluid pressure back to the sump.

External leakage   A fluid leak that escapes to the outside.

Feed-control   A TCM control strategy in which the TCM controls the electrical feed to a solenoid.

Filter   A device that removes foreign particles from fluid.

Final drive   The last set of reduction gears before the power flows to the differential and drive axles.

Firm   A noticeable quick application of a clutch or band that is considered normal.

Flare   A condition that produces an increase in engine rpm with a loss of torque during a shift. Also called *slipping*.

Flex band   A transmission band in which the friction material is backed by a thin, flexible strip of metal.

Flexplate   The thin drive plate that connects the torque converter to the crankshaft of the engine.

Fluid change   To remove and replace the fluid in a transmission.

Fluid check   To check transmission fluid level.

Fluid coupling   A device that transfers power through the fluid.

Fluid diagram   A diagram showing the various fluid paths through a transmission.

Fluid supply   Where the fluid in a transmission is stored, normally the pan.

Fluorescent dye   A dye that glows under fluorescent light that helps us find the source of leaks.

Flywheel   The rotating metal mass attached to the crankshaft that helps even out power surges.

Force   A push or pull measured in units of weights, usually pounds.

Force motor   *See* Pressure control solenoid.

Four wheel drive (FWD)   A drivetrain that can drive all four wheels part of the time.

Freewheel shift   A nonsynchronous shift in which a one-way clutch can freewheel to release a gearmember.

Friction   The resistance to motion between two bodies in contact with each other.

Friction modifier   An additive that changes the lubricity of a fluid.

Friction plate   A clutch plate that has friction material lining.

Front wheel drive (FWD)   A drivetrain that drives the front wheels.

Fulcrum   The pivot/supporting point for a lever.

Fuse   A circuit protection device that will break (open) a circuit if the current flow exceeds the ability of the wire.

Fusible link   A circuit protection device that is made of wire that is smaller than the circuit wire. The link will melt and open the circuit if the current flow exceeds the ability of the wire.

Garage shift   A shift from neutral to drive or reverse.

Gasket   A compressible material used as a seal between two mating surfaces.

Gear ratio   The relationship between two gears determined by dividing the number of teeth on the driving gear by the number of teeth on the driven gear and expressed as a ratio to one.

Gear reduction   A condition in which the driving gear is smaller than the driven gear. This produces a torque increase.

Gearset   Two or more meshed gears.

Gerotor pump   A pump design that uses meshed internal and external rotors.

Governor valve   A hydraulic device that provides hydraulic pressure that is relative to road speed.

Ground   The return path of a circuit. The vehicle's body and chassis normally provides the ground.

Grounded circuit   A circuit that has an unwanted connection to ground causing a short circuit.

Hard codes   Diagnostic trouble codes that are present and stored in ECM memory.

Hard parts   Metal transmission parts that are normally not replaced during transmission repair unless they are worn excessively.

Harsh   A noticeable and unpleasant application of a clutch or band. Also called *rough*.

Hazardous waste materials   Chemicals or components that are no longer needed and pose a danger to the environment or people.

Heavy throttle   An acceleration with the throttle opened more than three-fourths of the pedal travel.

Heli-Coil   A type of bolt thread repair device.

Helical gear   A gear that has the teeth cut at an angle.

Hertz   A unit of measurement of frequency; abbreviated as Hz. One Hz is one cycle per second.

High resistance   Unusual circuit resistance that causes excess voltage drop.

Hunting   A series of repeating upshifts and downshifts that cause noticeable engine rpm changes. Also called *busyness*.

Hybrid drive system   A vehicle powertrain that combines an internal combustion engine with an electric motor(s).

Hydraulic pressure test   A diagnostic test that measures transmission fluid pressures.

Hydraulic schematic   A diagram that shows fluid routing.

Hydraulics   The transfer of power through fluids under pressure.

Hydrodynamics   The action of transferring power through fluids in motion.

Hydrostatic   The action of transferring power through fluids under pressure.

Hypoid gear   A special form of a bevel gear that has the teeth cut in a curvature and that positions the gear on nonintersecting planes; commonly used in rear wheel drive (RWD) final drives.

Idler gear   A gear positioned between two other gears in the gear that is used to reverse the direction of rotation.

Impeller   The input member of the torque converter, also called *converter pump*.

Inertia   The physical property that a body at rest remains at rest and a body in motion remains in motion and travels in a straight line.

Initial feel   A distinct feel that is firmer at the start of a shift than at the end.

Insulator   The plastic, non-conductive material that surrounds an electrical wire.

Internal gear   A gear with the teeth pointing inward toward the center of the gear, also called an annulus or ring gear.

Internal interference   A torque converter check to determine if the internal parts can run into each other.

international Automotive Technicians' Network (iATN)   A web-based organization of technicians in which they help each other solve problems and make repairs.

In-vehicle repair   Transmission repairs that are made with the transmission mounted in the vehicle.

Kickdown   A downshift when the driver pushes the accelerator pedal all the way down.

Kilopascal   A pressure equal to 0.145 psi.

Land   The large-diameter portion of a spool valve.

Late   A shift that occurs above the desired speed that causes over-revving of the engine.

Leak check   A check to determine if there are fluid leaks and where the leak is occurring.

LePelletier gear train   An automatic transmission gear train that combines a simple planetary gearset with a Ravigneaux gearset to produce six or more gear ratios.

Light-emitting diode (LED)   A semiconductor that lights when energized; an LED uses less current than a standard light bulb.

Light throttle   An acceleration with the throttle opened less than half of the pedal travel.

Limp-in mode   A fault condition in which the TCM shuts off the electrical controls to prevent or reduce internal damage. The transmission will operate in a single forward gear.

Line pressure   The fluid operating pressure for most transmission circuits.

Lined plates   The friction plates for a clutch.

Lock-up torque converter   *See* Torque converter clutch.

Loctite   A brand name for a solution that locks bolt threads.

Mainline pressure   *See* Line pressure.

Make (close)   When a switch is closed it will make the circuit, allowing a current flow.

Malfunction indicator lamp (MIL)   An instrument panel amber warning light that flashes to indicate a problem.

Manual (1, 2, 3)   Gear lever positions that will limit forward gear ranges.

Manual linkage   The linkage that connects the shift lever with the manual valve.

Manual valve   The valve operated by the gear selector that directs pressure to the apply devices needed to put a transmission in gear.

Material safety data sheets (MSDSs)   Forms containing data regarding particular substance.

Mechanical diode   A one-way clutch that uses a set of spring-loaded struts for a lighter but stronger clutch action.

Medium throttle   An acceleration with the throttle opened about half of the pedal travel.

Micron   A unit of measurement equal to one millionth of a meter.

Minimum throttle   The smallest throttle opening that can accelerate a vehicle and produce an upshift.

Modulated pressure   The fluid pressure coming from the modulator valve.

Modulator valve   A vacuum device that senses engine load and causes a hydraulic valve to change pressure relative to that load.

MSDS   Abbreviation for material safety data sheets.

Multifunction indicator light (MIL)   The amber warning light that indicates a problem, example: the Check Engine Light.

Multiple-disc clutch   A clutch that uses more than one friction disc.

Needle bearing   A very thin roller bearing.

Nonsynchronous shift   *See* Asynchronous shift

Nonsynchronous transmission   A transmission using one-way clutches that allow an upshift that requires only the application of the next driving or reaction member.

Normally closed (NC)   A switch that is normally in a closed position.

Normally open (NO)   A switch that is normally in an open position.

NVH   Abbreviation for noise, vibration, and harshness.

OBD-II   Onboard diagnostics, regulations that require the vehicle control modules to monitor various functions that can affect vehicle emissions.

OEM   Original equipment manufacturer, the company that produced the vehicle.

Oil cooler   A radiator-like component that reduces the fluid temperature.

Oil filter   The part that removes dirt and debris from oil that is circulated through it.

Oil pan debris check   A check of debris in an oil pan that might indicate possible transmission wear or damage.

One-way clutch   An overrunning clutch that locks in one direction and overruns or freewheels in the other.

Open circuit   A break or interruption in a circuit that will not allow current flow.

Orifice   A restricted opening in a fluid passage designed to reduce fluid pressure while fluid is flowing.

O-ring   A sealing ring made from rubberlike material.

Oscilloscope   A visual display of electrical values displayed on a fluorescent screen or cathode ray tube.

Overdrive   A gear arrangement that causes the output shaft to turn faster than the input shaft.

Overfill   A condition where a transmission has too much fluid.

Overhaul   To completely repair a transmission or other component.

Parallel circuit

Park   A gear range where the output shaft is locked stationary.

Parking gear   A transmission lock that prevents the output shaft from turning.

Passing gear   A forced downshift to the next lower gear.

Pawl   A locking device that fits into a gear tooth to hold the gear stationary.

Pinion gear   A small gear that meshes with a larger gear.

Piston   The moveable portion of a hydraulic cylinder or servo.

Planet carrier   The part of a planetary gearset that contains the planetary pinion gears.

Planet pinions   The gears of a planetary gearset that mesh with both the sun and ring gears.

Planetary gearset   A gearset that contains a sun gear, ring gear, and a carrier with planet pinion gear to produce one or more gear ratios.

Positive displacement   A pump that moves a specified amount of fluid on each revolution.

Pounds per square inch (psi)   A pressure measurement.

Power   The rate at which work is done.

Power shift   A transmission shift that occurs with continuous power flow.

Power train control module (PCM)   The control module that controls engine and transmission operation.

Pressure   A force per unit area; generally measured in pounds per square inch (psi) or units of atmospheric pressure (bars or kilopascals).

Pressure control solenoid   A computer-controlled solenoid that maintains the proper pressure in the hydraulic system of an electronically controlled automatic transmission. Also called a *variable force solenoid* or *force motor.*

Pressure plate   The thick plate that squeezes the clutch pack during clutch apply.

Pressure regulator valve   The valve that maintains the proper pressure in the hydraulic system.

Pressure relief valve   A spring-loaded valve that is designed to release excess pressure.

Pulse-width modulation (PWM)   Operation of a device by an on/off digital signal that is controlled by the time signal so that the device is turned on and off.

Pump   A device that transfers fluid from one point to another.

Pump cover alignment   The process of aligning the two halves of a pump body.

Pump gear alignment   The process of aligning the internal gears to the drive opening.

R&R   Remove and Replace.

Radio frequency interference (RFI)   A high frequency type of EMI that is in the radio frequency band.

Ratio   The relative value between two things.

Ravigneaux gearset   A planetary gearset that uses two sun gears and a planet carrier with two sets of pinion gears.

Reaction devices   A clutch or band that holds a planet gearset member stationary.

Reaction member   The portion of the planetary gearset that is held stationary in order to produce a reduction or overdrive.

Rear wheel drive (RWD)   A drivetrain that drives the rear wheels.

Rebuilt   *See* Remanufactured.

Recalibration   To renew the basic software values of a control module.

Regenerative   The process of braking a vehicle; the energy is used to recharge the batteries.

Regulator valve   The main valve used to control line pressure.

Relay   An electromagnetic switch used to control circuits with relatively high amperage.

Remanufactured   A term used to describe a component that is disassembled, cleaned, inspected, and reassembled using new or reconditioned parts.

Reservoir   A tank or pan where fluid is stored.

Resistance   The opposition to current flow measured in ohms.

Reverse   The transmission gear position that allows the vehicle to back up.

Reverse boost valve   The pressure control valve that increases pressure for reverse gear.

Ring gear   The outer gear of a planetary gearset. Also called an *internal gear.*

Road test   A live test used to confirm proper or faulty vehicle operation.

Roller   The rolling part of a roller bearing.

Roller clutch   A one-way clutch that uses a series of rollers positioned in a special cam for the locking elements.

Rotary flow   The fluid motion inside a torque converter in the same direction as the impeller and turbine.

RPM   Speed expressed in revolutions per minute.

RTV   Abbreviation for room temperature vulcanization.

Schematics   A type of diagram.

Selective   A part that comes in different sizes; the technician selects the proper size.

Separator plate   The unlined clutch plate, also called a *steel* plate.

Series circuit   An electric circuit in which the current flows through more than one load.

Servo   A hydraulic device that changes fluid pressure into mechanical motion or force.

Shift duration   The time period from the start to the end of shift.

Shift feel   A clutch or band application or release that is usually described, for example, as firm or soft.

Shift quality   The subjective feeling of how a shift feels.

Shift timing   When (vehicle speed or engine rpm) a shift occurs.

Shim   A thin metal spacer.

Short circuit   A circuit fault where the current bypasses the major load.

Shrink tube   A plastic tube that shrinks when heated to insulate a wire connection.

Shudder   An easily noticed jerking sensation that is a more severe form of chuggle.

Shuttle valve   A valve used to change a fluid path from one circuit to another.

Signal monitor   A test device used to observe the electric signals being sent to the shift solenoids.

Simpson gear train   A planetary gearset that combines two simple planetaries using a single sun gear.

Single-sided plate   A clutch plate that has friction material on only one side.

Slipping   A loss in torque with a noticeable increase in engine rpm.

Soft   A slow and almost unnoticeable clutch or band apply.

Soft parts   Transmission parts that are normally replaced during an overhaul.

Solenoid   An electromagnet actuator that uses a movable core.

Special service tools (SSTs)   Special tools that have been developed to perform specific repairs.

Spiral bevel gear   A bevel gearset with the gear teeth cut in a curved shape.

Splice   To join two wires.

Spline   A groove(s) or slot(s) cut into a shaft or bore that is used to connect a matching spline.

Spool valve A hydraulic valve that is shaped somewhat like a spool.

Sprag The locking element in a one-way sprag clutch.

Spring holder A special tool used to keep valve body springs in order.

Spur bevel gear A bevel gearset with straight-cut gear teeth.

Spur gear A gear with straight-cut teeth.

Stall A condition where the engine is running but the transmission input shaft is not rotating.

Stall speed The maximum engine rpm that can be achieved with an automatic transmission in gear, with the brakes applied and the accelerator wide open.

Stall test A test that measures engine rpm with a stationary transmission input shaft.

Static friction The relative amount of friction between two stationary surfaces or two surfaces that are turning at the same speed. *See* Dynamic friction.

Static seal A seal between parts that have no relative motion.

Stator A component in the torque converter that is used to change the direction of fluid motion.

Sump The fluid storage point or reservoir; usually the transmission pan.

Sun gear The gear in the center of a planetary gearset.

Supply pressure *See* Line pressure

Surface filter A fluid filter that traps foreign particle on the surface of the filter material.

Surge A barely noticeable engine feel that is similar to chuggle.

Synchronous transmission During an upshift, the timing of the new driving or reaction member must be timed or synchronized with the release of a driving or reaction member.

Technical service bulletins (TSBs) A form that describes a particular vehicle concern and the recommended correction procedure.

Test light A simple tool used to determine if there is voltage at electrical connections.

Throttle position sensor (TPS) An electronic device that signals throttle opening to a control module.

Throttle valve A hydraulic valve that is positioned by throttle linkage.

Thrust washers Bearings that separate rotating parts that turn against each other.

Tie-up A condition where two opposing clutches or bands are attempting to apply at the wrong time. This tends to slow down the engine or vehicle. Also called *fight.*

Torque Turning or twisting effort; usually measured in foot-pounds or Newton-meters.

Torque converter A fluid coupling that transfers power from the engine to the transmission and can produce a torque increase.

Torque converter clutch (TCC) The clutch inside the torque converter that locks the turbine to the impeller to prevent any slippage. Also called a *lock-up torque converter.*

Torque management The process of controlling the amount of torque being transferred to the transmission or drive wheels.

Torque steer A condition where unequal engine torque at the drive wheels causes the vehicle to turn.

Torsional vibrations The natural, uneven power flow from the engine to the transmission.

Transaxle A transmission that is combined with the final drive assembly; normally used in front wheel drive vehicles.

Transmission A device in the power train that provides different forward-gear ratios as well as neutral and reverse.

Transmission control module (TCM) The control module that controls transmission operation.

Transverse Crosswise.

Turbine The output member of a torque converter.

Turbulator An oil cooler design feature that produces turbulence in the fluid flow.

TV linkage The linkage that connects the throttle valve to the throttle.

TV pressure The fluid pressure coming from the throttle valve.

Underfill A condition where a transmission does not have enough fluid.

Unlined plates *See* Separator plate.

Vacuum A negative pressure (below atmospheric); measured in inches of mercury (in. Hg).

Vacuum modulator A vacuum-operated device that replaces TV linkage in some transmissions.

Valley The area of a spool valve between the lands.

Valve A hydraulic device that controls fluid flow.

Vane pump A pump design that uses a rotor with sliding vanes.

Variable displacement A pump that can change the quantity of fluid being pumped at a given speed.

Variable force solenoid *See* Pressure control solenoid.

Variator A vaiable-width pulley used in CVTs.

Vehicle speed sensor (VSS) An electronic device that signals vehicle speed to a control module.

Viscosity The resistance to flow in a fluid.

Viscous converter clutch A torque converter clutch that includes a viscous coupling.

Visual inspection A careful inspection of a component or vehicle using sight and feel.

Voltage drop A voltage loss caused by current flow through a resistance.

Vortex flow A recirculating fluid flow in the converter that is outward in the impeller and inward in the turbine.

Wave plate A clutch cushion plate that is made wavy, not flat.

Weathertight connector An electrical connector that is sealed to prevent water or moisture from entering.

Wet air test An air test used with ATF to show the exact location of a leak.

Wide-open throttle (WOT) Full travel of the pedal to produce maximum power from the engine and full travel of the throttle or detent valve in the transmission.

Work The result of force that changes speed or direction of motion.

Worm tracks The odd shaped passages used to connect the valve body passages to the hydraulic devices.

SPANISH GLOSSARY

Abastecimiento de fluidos   Lugar en donde se almacena un fluido en una transmisión, normalmente es el depósito.

Acelerar   Aumentar la velocidad.

Acoplador   Aparato en forma de embrague que puede conectar o desconectar el flujo de energía entre dos componentes.

Acoplador de fluidos   Dispositivo que transfiere potencia a través del fluido.

Acople manual   Acople que conecta la palanca de cambios con la válvula manual.

Acople TV   Acople que conecta la válvula de la mariposa a la mariposa.

Actuador   Aparato electrónico que realiza una función deseada.

Acumulador   Aparato utilizado para disminuir la presión aplicada del fluido para amortiguar o suavizar el cambio de velocidad.

Aditivos   Químicos añadidos al fluido de transmisión automática (ATF por sus siglas en inglés) para mejorar las características de la operación.

Agencia de Protección Medioambiental (EPA por sus siglas en inglés)   Agencia gubernamental de los Estados Unidos que está a cargo de la protección de la salud humana y del medioambiente natural (aire, agua, y tierra).

Aislante   Material plástico no conductivo que rodea un cable eléctrico.

Ajuste de banda   Ajuste que fija una banda a la distancia correcta con el tambor.

Alineación de la cubierta de la bomba   Proceso de alineamiento de las dos mitades del cuerpo de una bomba.

Alineación de los engranajes de la bomba   Proceso de alineación de los engranajes internos con la abertura de la transmisión.

Alta resistencia   Resistencia inusual de un circuito que causa excesiva caída de voltaje.

Amperio   Unidad de flujo de corriente eléctrica.

Anillo de rodadura   Rodamiento que separa las partes rotantes que giran una contra la otra.

Anillo O   Anillo sellante hecho de material elástico.

Apertura   Condición que produce un incremento en revoluciones por minuto del motor con una pérdida de par durante un cambio. También llamada *Patinaje*.

Atado   Condición en la cual dos embragues o bandas opuestas intentan ser aplicadas en el momento equivocado. Esto tiende a detener el motor o vehiculo. También llamado *vuelo*.

B+   Conexión positiva de una batería.

Banda de doble envoltura   Diseño de banda que incrementa la fuerza de accionamiento cuando es aplicada.

Banda flexible   Banda de transmisión en la cual el material friccionante es respaldado por una banda metálica delgada y flexible.

Banda   Correa metálica alineada que se envuelve alrededor de un tambor; usado para parar el tambor o mantenerlo fijo.

Bloqueo del convertidor de par   *Ver* embrague del convertidor de par.

Bola de retención (Válvula de retención de bola)   Bola de acero que se ubica sobre la placa de transferencia para permitir que los fluidos viajen en una sola dirección.

Boletines de servicio técnico (TSBs por sus siglas en inglés)   Forma que describe un problema de un vehículo particular y el procedimiento de corrección recomendada.

Bomba   Dispositivo que transfiere fluidos de un punto a otro.

Bomba creciente   Bomba de engranaje interno o externo que tiene una separador en forma creciente.

Bomba de paletas   Diseño de bomba que usa un rotor con paletas deslizantes.

Bomba de rotor   Diseño de bomba que usa rotores acoplados interna y externamente.

Caída de voltaje   Pérdida de voltaje causada por un flujo de corriente a través de una resistencia.

Calidad del cambio de velocidades   Sentido subjetivo de cómo se siente el cambio de velocidades.

Calza   Espaciador metálico delgado.

Cambio de fluido   Remover y reemplazar el fluido de una transmisión.

Cambio de potencia   Cambio de transmisión que ocurre con flujo de potencia continuo.

Cambio de velocidad asíncrono   Cambio de velocidad que usa un embrague unidireccional de forma que las partes del cambio no tienen que estar sincronizadas, también llamadas cambio de velocidades *no sincronizado*, o *de rueda libre*.

Cambio de velocidades asíncrono   *Ver* cambio de velocidades asíncrono.

Cambio de velocidades de estacionamiento   Cambio de velocidades de neutro a avance o reversa.

Cambio de velocidades de rueda libre Cambio de velocidades asíncrono en el cual el embrague unidireccional puede tener una rueda libre para liberar un miembro del sistema de engranajes.

Carcasa Cubierta rígida de una transmisión.

Cárter (sumidero) Punto o reserva de almacenaje de fluidos; usualmente es el depósito de la transmisión.

Chaveta Ranura o surco cortado en un eje o rollo que es usado para conectar una chaveta equivalente.

Chequeo de fluido Revisión del nivel de fluido de la transmisión.

Chuggle Condición de resistencia o jaloneo usualmente más notable durante la aceleración y cuando el embrague del convertidor de par está activado. La condición *Chuggle* está a menudo relacionada con el motor.

Circuito Trayecto por el que viaja el corriente eléctrico desde una fuente de poder, a través de una resistencia y de regreso a la fuente de poder.

Circuito abierto Rotura o interrupción en un circuito que no permite el flujo de corriente.

Circuito en paralelo Circuito eléctrico que sigue más de un trayecto desde la fuente de poder hasta la conexión a tierra. Tiene más de una rama o camino.

Circuito en serie Circuito eléctrico en el cual la corriente fluye a través de más de una carga.

Circuito unido a tierra Circuito que tiene una conexión no deseable a tierra causando un corto circuito.

Coastdown Descarga completa del acelerador de forma que el vehículo reduzca su velocidad; algunas veces llamado *Coastdown sin acelerador*.

Código de diagnóstico de fallas (DTC por sus siglas en inglés) Código alfanumérico almacenado en el módulo de control que indica un mal funcionamiento en la transmisión o en su sistema de control.

Códigos duros Código de diagnóstico de fallas que está presente y almacenado en la memoria ECM.

Coeficiente de fricción Cifra que describe la cantidad de la fuerza de fricción que se encuentra entre dos superficies.

Cojinete de agujas Cojinete de rodillos muy delgado.

Conductor Parte de un cable que permite el flujo de corriente.

Conector a prueba de la intemperie Conector eléctrico que está sellado para prevenir la entrada de agua o humedad.

Conector de diagnóstico Terminal situado dentro de un vehículo que permite escanear las herramientas para la lectura de códigos de diagnóstico de fallas.

Continuidad Circuito o componente que tiene una ruta completa para el flujo de corriente.

Control de presión electrónica (EPC por sus siglas en inglés) Control de presión de fluido de transmisión que es modificado por un solenoide.

Control de suministro Estrategia de control en el cual el TCM controla el suministro eléctrico a un solenoide.

Convertidor de par Acople de fluidos que transfiere potencia desde el motor a la transmisión y puede producir un incremento de par.

Corriente Alterna (AC por sus siglas en inglés) Flujo de corriente eléctrica que cambia de dirección muchas veces en un segundo.

Corriente directa (DC por sus siglas en inglés) Corriente eléctrica constante que fluye en una única dirección.

Corto circuito Falla de un circuito en donde la corriente elude la carga mayor.

Cuña Elemento bloqueador en un embrague de cuña unidireccional.

Departamento de transportes (DOT por sus siglas en inglés) Agencia gubernamental de los Estados Unidos que está relacionada con el transporte.

Depósito Tanque o recipiente en donde se almacenan fluidos.

Desaceleración Reducir la velocidad.

Descarga electrostática (ESD por sus siglas en inglés) Flujo momentáneo de electricidad que ocurre cuando una excesiva carga eléctrica encuentra una ruta a tierra.

Descarga Problema que ocurre cuando el fluido sale del convertidor.

Desplazamiento positivo Bomba que mueve una específica cantidad de fluido en cada revolución.

Desplazamiento variable Bomba que puede cambiar la cantidad de fluido que está siendo bombeada a una velocidad dada.

Detenido Condición en la cual el motor está funcionando pero el eje de la entrada de la transmisión no está rotando.

Diagrama de fluidos Diagrama que muestra las diferentes rutas que toman los fluidos a través de una transmisión.

Diferencial Arreglo de engranajes que permite que las ruedas de tracción avancen a diferentes velocidades.

Diodo de emisión de luz (LED por sus siglas en inglés) Semiconductor que se ilumina cuando es energizado; un LED usa menos corriente que un bulbo de luz estándar.

Diodo mecánico Embrague unidireccional que usa un grupo de puntales reforzados con resortes para lograr una menor acción del embrague pero más fuerte.

Dispositivos de ajuste Embragues y bandas hidráulicamente operados, y embragues mecánicos unidireccionales, que impulsan o sostienen los miembros de un engranaje planetario.

Dispositivos de reacción Embrague o banda que sostiene firmemente los miembros de un sistema de engranajes planetario.

Disyuntor Dispositivo mecánico que abre un circuito eléctrico en caso de que ocurra un flujo excesivo de corriente.

DTC Acrónimo en inglés para código de diagnóstico de fallas.

Duración de cambio de velocidades Periodo de tiempo desde el inicio hasta el final de un cambio de velocidades.

Ejes de transmisión Eje que sostiene el vehículo y provee un método de conducción de las ruedas.

Elastómero Materiales flexibles elásticos comúnmente usados como materiales sellantes.

Embrague Aparato que controla la transferencia de potencia entre dos puntos. Puede permitir o bloquear dicha transferencia.

Embrague de convertidor viscoso Embrague de convertidor de par que incluye un acople viscoso.

Embrague de múltiples discos Embrague que usa más de un disco de fricción.

Embrague de rodillo Embrague unidireccional que usa una serie de rodillos posicionados en una leva especial para los elementos fijos.

Embrague del convertidor de par (TCC por sus siglas en inglés) Embrague dentro del convertidor de par que bloquea la turbina del impulsor para prevenir cualquier deslizamiento. También llamado *convertidor de par de bloqueo.*

Embrague del convertidor Embrague en el convertidor de par que bloquea el convertidor durante la mayoría de condiciones de conducción.

Embrague directo Embrague que es aplicado para proveer avance directo.

Embrague unidireccional Embrague de rotación libre que se bloquea en una dirección y rota o rueda libre en la otra.

Empalmar Unir dos cables.

Empaque Material compresible usado como sello entre dos superficies que se unen.

Energía Capacidad para realizar un trabajo.

Enfriador Intercambiador de calor en el radiador usado para enfriar el fluido de la transmisión.

Enfriador de aceite Componente similar a un radiador que reduce la temperatura de un fluido.

Englobado Expansión no deseable de un componente, tal como un convertidor de par, a causa de presión interna excesiva.

Engranaje anular Engranaje de aro, engranaje interno.

Engranaje bisel espiral Juego de engranajes bisel con dientes cortados en forma curva.

Engranaje bisel recto Juego de engranaje bisel con dientes de engranaje de corte recto.

Engranaje biselado Engranaje con dientes que son cortados en un ángulo que permite transmitir fuerza entre ejes que no son paralelos.

Engranaje de anillo Engranaje exterior de un sistema de engranajes planetario. También llamado *engranaje interno.*

Engranaje de dentadura helicoidal Engranaje que tiene los dientes cortados en ángulo.

Engranaje de estacionamiento Bloqueo de la transmisión que evita que el eje de salida gire.

Engranaje de paso Cambio inferior de velocidades al siguiente engranaje menor.

Engranaje hipoide Forma especial de engranaje bisel que tiene los dientes cortados con curvatura y que posiciona el engranaje en planos no intersectantes; comúnmente usados en sistemas de tracción de ruedas traseras (RWD por sus siglas en inglés).

Engranaje intermedio Engranaje posicionado entre dos otros engranajes que es usado para revertir la dirección de rotación.

Engranaje interno Engranaje que tiene los dientes apuntando hacia su centro, también llamado engranaje anular o de anillo.

Engranaje recto Engranaje con dientes de corte recto.

Engranaje sol Engranaje en el centro del juego de engranajes planetario.

Engranajes de piñón Engranaje pequeño que se ajusta con un engranaje grande.

Ensamblaje del amortiguador Aparato que reduce las vibraciones torsionales entre el motor y las transmisiones.

Escape Descarga de presión de fluido de regreso al colector.

Esquema hidráulico Diagrama que muestra la ruta de fluidos.

Esquema Tipo de diagrama.

Estacionar Rango de transmisión en donde el eje de salida es bloqueado estacionariamente.

Estator Componente en el convertidor de par que se usa para cambiar la dirección del movimiento de un fluido.

Fase del acoplador Condición en donde la velocidad de la turbina del convertidor de par es casi igual a la del impulsor.

Filtro de aceite Parte que remueve suciedad y residuos del aceite que circula a través de él.

Filtro de la superficie Filtro de fluidos que atrapa partículas extrañas en la superficie del material filtrante.

Filtro de profundidad Filtro de fluidos que puede atrapar partículas extrañas a medida que pasan a través del material filtrante.

Filtro Dispositivo que remueve partículas extrañas de un fluido.

Firme Aplicación rápida notable de un embrague o banda que es considerada normal.

Flecha de transmisión Transmisión que es combinada con el ensamblaje de conducción final, normalmente usado en vehículos de tracción en ruedas frontales.

Fluido aireado Fluido de naturaleza espumosa que ha sido batido al punto para que contenga burbujas.

Fluido de transmisión automática (ATF por sus siglas en inglés) Aceite usado en transmisiones automáticas.

Flujo rotatorio Movimiento fluido dentro de un convertidor de par en la misma dirección del impulsor y la turbina.

Flujo vórtex Flujo recirculante en el convertidor que está hacia fuera del impulsor y hacia adentro en la turbina.

Frenado con motor Condición en la cual la compresión del motor es usada para reducir la velocidad del vehículo.

Fricción Resistencia al movimiento entre dos cuerpos en contacto mutuo.

Fricción dinámica Cantidad de fricción relativa entre dos superficies que tienen diferentes velocidades. *Ver* Fricción estática.

Fricción estática Cantidad relativa de fricción entre dos superficies en reposo o dos superficies que giran a la misma velocidad. *Ver* Fricción dinámica.

Fuerza Empuje o jalón medido en unidades de peso, usualmente libras.

Fuerza centrífuga Fuerza que actúa sobre un objeto que gira, y trata de alejarlo del centro de revolución.

Fuga cruzada Fuga de un fluido entre dos conductos hidráulicos separados.

Fuga externa Fuga de fluido que escapa al exterior.

Fusible Dispositivo de protección de circuitos que romperá (abrirá) un circuito si el flujo de corriente excede la capacidad del cable.

Fusible tipo alambre Dispositivo de protección de circuitos que está hecho de un alambre que es más delgado que el alambre del circuito. El fusible se derretirá y abrirá el circuito si el flujo de corriente excede la capacidad del alambre.

Golpe Condición de cambio de velocidades ruda producida por el uso repentino y fuerte del embrague o banda.

Golpe bajo Cambio bajo de velocidad cuando el conductor empuja el pedal del acelerador hasta el fondo.

Golpe doble   Dos aplicaciones repentinas y fuertes del embrague o banda.

Golpe final   Condición que produce un sentido más firme al final de un cambio de velocidades. También llamado *sentido final* o *golpe de deslizamiento*.

Grapa circular   Anillo de resorte hendido con un perfil o corte transversal redondo que se utiliza para fijar un eje al interior de un cilindro.

Guía sinfín   Conductos con forma particular usados para unir los conductos del cuerpo de la válvula con los dispositivos hidráulicos.

Hacer (Cerrar)   Cuando un interruptor es cerrado hace un circuito, permitiendo un flujo de corriente.

Helicoidal   Tipo de dispositivo de reparación de rosca de pernos.

Herramienta de servicios especiales (SSTs)   Herramientas especiales que has sido desarrollados para desarrollar reparaciones específicas.

Hertz   Unidad de medida de frecuencia; abreviada como Hz. Un Hz es un ciclo por segundo.

Hidráulica   La transferencia de potencia a través de fluidos a presión.

Hidrodinámica   Acción de transferir potencia a través de fluidos en movimiento.

Hidrostática   Acción de transferir potencia a través de fluidos a presión.

Hojas de datos de seguridad de materiales (MSDSs por sus siglas en inglés)   Formas que contienen datos relacionados con una sustancia particular.

Holgura   Cantidad de movimiento que un juego de engranajes o árbol tienen en una dirección que es paralela al árbol impulsor.

Impulso (1, 2, 3, 4)   Posición de engranajes que permite a la transmisión el cambio a través de todos los rangos de avance.

Impulsor (propulsor)   Miembro de entrada del convertidor de par, también llamado *bomba del convertidor*.

Índice de volumen del embrague (CVI por sus siglas en inglés)   Medida del volumen de un fluido necesario para llenar un embrague durante un cambio de velocidades.

Inducción electromagnética (EMI por sus siglas en inglés)   Ocurre cuando la electricidad es producida por un campo magnético sobre un cable, o por un cable a través de un campo magnético.

Inercia   Propiedad física que hace que un cuerpo en reposo permanezca en reposo, y que un cuerpo en movimiento permanezca en movimiento y viaje en línea recta.

Inspección visual   Inspección cuidadosa de un componente o vehículo usando la visión y el tacto.

Intercambiado/Usado   Componente de reemplazo del tren de fuerza que proviene de otro vehículo.

Interferencia de frecuencia de radio (RFI por sus siglas en inglés)   Tipo de alta frecuencia de EMI que está en la banda de frecuencia de radio.

Interferencia interna   Verificación del convertidor de par para determinar si las partes internas puede funcionar una dentro de la otra.

Juego de engranajes planetario   Juego de engranajes que contiene un engranaje sol, engranajes anillo, y un soporte planetario con un engranaje piñón planetario para producir uno o más relaciones de engranajes.

Juego de engranajes tipo *Ravigneaux*   Juego de engranajes planetario que usa dos engranajes sol y un soportador planetario con dos juegos de engranajes piñón.

Juego de engranajes   Dos o más engranajes acoplados.

Juego mecánico   Espacio entre dos engranajes, también llamado *pestaña*.

Kilopascal   Presión equivalente a 0.145 psi.

Libras por pulgada cuadrada (psi por sus siglas en inglés)   Medida de presión.

Loctite   Marca de una solución que evita que se suelten los pernos.

Luz de prueba   Herramienta simple para determinar si hay voltaje en conexiones eléctricas.

Luz indicadora de fallas (MIL por sus siglas en inglés)   Luz ámbar de emergencia que indica un problema; por ejemplo, la Luz de Revisión de Motor.

Luz indicadora de malfuncionamiento (MIL por sus siglas en inglés)   Luz ámbar del panel de instrumentos que parpadea para indicar un problema.

Manejo del par   Proceso de controlar la cantidad de par que está siendo transferida a la transmisión o las ruedas de tracción.

Manual (1, 2, 3)   Posiciones de la palanca de los engranajes que limitan los rangos de los engranajes de avance.

Mariposa abierta al máximo (WOT por sus siglas en inglés)   Viaje completo del pedal para producir potencia máxima del motor y viaje completo de la mariposa o válvula de detención en la transmisión.

Mariposa ligera   Aceleración con la mariposa abierta menos de la mitad del viaje del pedal.

Mariposa media   Aceleración con la mariposa abierta hasta la mitad del viaje del pedal.

Mariposa mínima   Abertura mínima de la mariposa que puede acelerar un vehículo y producir un cambio superior de velocidades.

Mariposa pesada   Aceleración con la mariposa abierta más de tres cuartas partes del viaje del pedal.

Materiales de desperdicio peligrosos   Químicos o componentes que no son necesitados más y son peligrosos para el medioambiente o las personas.

Medidor análogo   Medidor que usa un movimiento de aguja para indicar los valores.

Medidor   Instrumento de medida que se usa para medir la distancia entre dos objetos.

Mercado alternativo   Referente a partes de repuesto producidas por compañías diferentes a OEM.

Micrón   Unidad de medida igual a una millonésima parte de un metro.

Miembro de dirección   Miembro de engranaje planetario que es la entrada y es conducido.

Miembro de reacción   Porción de un sistema de engranajes planetario que es sostenido firmemente para producir una reducción o sobremarcha.

Modificador de fricción   Aditivo que cambia la lubricidad de un fluido.

Modo cojo   Condición de falla en la cual el TCM apaga los controles eléctricos para prevenir o reducir el daño interno. La transmisión operará en un engranaje de avance simple.

Modulación de pulso ancho (PWM por sus siglas en inglés)   Operación de un dispositivo a través de una señal encendido/apagado que está controlada por una señal de tiempo, de forma que el dispositivo se encienda o apague.

Modulador de vacío   Dispositivo operado al vacío que reemplaza el acople TV en algunas transmisiones.

Módulo de control de transmisión (TCM por sus siglas en inglés)   Módulo de control que controla la operación de la transmisión.

Módulo de control del tren de potencia (PCM)   Módulo de control que controla la operación del motor y la transmisión.

Módulo de control electrónico (ECM por sus siglas en inglés)   Aparato electrónico que usa varios datos de entrada para determinar los datos de salida necesarios para que un aparato mecánico opere adecuadamente.

Monitor de señal   Dispositivo de prueba usado para observar las señales eléctricas que son enviadas a los solenoides de los cambios de velocidades.

Motor de fuerza   *Ver* solenoide de control de presión.

MSDS   Acrónimo en inglés para hojas de datos de seguridad de materiales.

Multímetro digital (DMM por sus siglas en inglés)   Medidor con múltiples funciones, para medir actividad eléctrica, que usa un lector digital.

Normalmente abierto (NO por sus siglas en inglés)   Interruptor que está normalmente en una posición abierta.

Normalmente cerrado (NC por sus siglas en inglés)   Interruptor que está normalmente en una posición cerrada.

NVH   Acrónimo en inglés para ruido, vibración y rudeza.

OBD-II   Diagnósticos y regulaciones a bordo que requieren que el módulo de control de vehículo para monitorear varias funciones que pueden afectar emisiones de vehículos.

OEM   Acrónimo en inglés de Fabricante de Equipo Original, la compañía que produce el vehículo.

Orificio   Abertura restringida en el conducto de un fluido diseñada para reducir la presión de fluido mientras éste fluye.

Orificio de vaciado   Conducto que permite al fluido salir de una zona; por ejemplo: la cavidad de sellado frontal.

Oscilación   Serie repetitiva de subidas y bajadas de los cambios de velocidades que causan notables cambios de revoluciones por minuto del motor. También es llamada

Osciloscopio   Representación visual de valores eléctricos en un monitor fluorescente o un tubo de rayos catódicos.

Par   Esfuerzo de giro o revolución; usualmente medido en pies-libra o Newton-metro.

Par en la dirección   Condición en la cual un par de motor disparejo en las ruedas de tracción causa que el vehículo gire.

Partes duras   Partes metálicas de una transmisión que normalmente no son reemplazadas durante la reparación a menos que estén excesivamente desgastadas.

Partes suaves   Partes de la transmisión que son normalmente reemplazadas durante una puesta a punto.

Patinaje   Pérdida en par con un notable incremento en las revoluciones por minuto del motor.

Piñones planetarios   Engranajes de un sistema de engranajes planetario que se ajusta tanto con los engranajes sol, como los engranajes anillo.

Pistón   Parte móvil de un cilindro hidráulico o servo.

Placa acolchada   Placa de embrague de onda o tipo *Belleville* que se puede comprimir ligeramente para dar un contacto más suave.

Placa de fricción   Placa del embrague que tiene un recubrimiento de material friccionante.

Placa de lado simple   Placa de embrague que tiene material friccionante en un solo lado.

Placa de onda   Placa acolchada de embrague que es ondulada, no plana.

Placa de presión   Placa gruesa que presiona el juego del embrague durante el uso del mismo.

Placa flexible   Placa delgada de manejo que conecta el convertidor de par al cigüeñal del motor.

Placa separadora   Placa del embrague no alineada, también llamada placa de *acero*.

Placa tipo *Belleville*   Placa de un embrague, de forma cónica, usado para amortiguar los cambios de velocidades.

Placas alineadas   Placas de fricción para un embrague.

Placas no alineadas   *Ver* Placa separadora.

Potencia   Ritmo en el cual un trabajo es hecho.

Presión   Fuerza por unidad de área; generalmente medida en libras por pulgada cuadrada (psi) o unidades de presión atmosférica (bares o kilopascales).

Presión atmosférica   Presión de la atmósfera alrededor nuestro; generalmente es considerada igual a 14.7 psi al nivel del mar.

Presión de abastecimiento   *Ver* Presión de línea.

Presión de control   Presión del fluido de transmisión que es controlada con una válvula de regulación de presión, es también llamada *presión de línea o de línea principal.*

Presión de línea principal   *Ver* Presión de línea.

Presión de línea   Presión de operación de fluidos para la mayoría de circuitos de transmisión.

Presión modulada   Presión del fluido proveniente de la válvula moduladora.

Presión TV   Presión de fluido que proviene de la válvula de la mariposa.

Propulsión final   Último grupo de engranajes de reducción antes de que la potencia fluya al diferencial y a los ejes de conducción.

Prueba de aire húmedo   Prueba de aire usada con un ATF para mostrar la ubicación exacta de una fuga.

Prueba de aire   Prueba usando aire a presión para asegurar la apropiada operación del embrague y la banda.

Prueba de carretera   Prueba en vivo usada para confirmar la adecuada o inadecuada operación de un vehículo.

Prueba de detención   Prueba que mide el número de revoluciones por minuto del motor con un eje de entrada de transmisión estacionaria.

Prueba de presión hidráulica   Prueba de diagnóstico que mide la presión del fluido de la transmisión.

Puesta a punto   Reparar completamente una transmisión u otro componente.

Punto de apoyo   Punto de soporte o pivote de una palanca.

R&R   Remover y reemplazar.

Ranurado direccional   Patrón de ranuras cortadas en placas direccionales; las placas deben estar posicionadas con las ranuras en la dirección apropiada.

Reaprendizaje adaptativo   Controles electrónicos que pueden cambiar las presiones de operación para compensar el desgaste de la transmisión.

Reaprendizaje de la función adaptativa   Procedimiento para reiniciar los parámetros de operación de la transmisión a los valores base.

Recalibración   Reiniciación de los valores de software por defecto de un módulo de control.

Reconstruido   *Ver* refabricado.

Red de control de área (CAN por sus siglas en inglés)   Método de agrupar los varios módulos de control que dan la más alta prioridad de comunicación a la seguridad del vehículo.

Red Internacional de Técnicos Automotrices (iATN por sus siglas en inglés)   Organización de técnicos basada en la Internet en la cual ellos ayudan a otros a resolver problemas y a hacer reparaciones.

Reducción de engranaje   Condición en la cual el engranaje impulsor es más pequeño que el engranaje impulsado. Esto produce un incremento de par.

Refabricado   Término empleado para describir un componente que esta desensamblado, limpio, inspeccionado, y reensamblado, usando partes nuevas o reacondicionadas.

Regenerativo   Proceso de frenar un vehículo; la energía es usada para recargar las baterías.

Relación   Valor relativo entre dos cosas.

Relación de avance directo   Relación de engranaje 1:1.

Relación de engranaje   Relación entre dos engranajes determinada al dividir el número de dientes del engranaje impulsor entre el número de dientes del engranaje impulsado, y expresada como la proporción a la unidad.

Relé   Interruptor electromagnético usado para controlar circuitos con relativamente alto amperaje.

Reparaciones en vehículo   Reparaciones de transmisión que son hechas con la transmisión montada en el vehículo.

Resistencia   Oposición al flujo de corriente medido en Ohmios.

Resorte de diafragma   Resorte acolchado de forma cónica, también llamado resorte *Belleville*.

Resorte tipo *Belleville*   Anillo cónico metálico que reacciona como un resorte a causa de su resistencia a ser aplastado.

Retrazo   Cuando un cambio de velocidades ocurre posteriormente a lo esperado. También llamado *tardío* o *extendido*.

Reversa   Posición de los engranajes de la transmisión que permiten al vehículo moverse en reversa.

Rodillo   Parte rodante de un rodillo cónico.

RPM   Velocidad expresada en revoluciones por minuto.

RTV   Acrónimo para vulcanización a temperatura ambiente.

Sacudida   Sensación brusca fácilmente notada que es una forma más severa de *Chuggle*.

Salto   Sensación del motor apenas notable que es similar a un *Chuggle*.

Selectivo   Parte que viene en diferentes tamaños; el técnico selecciona el tamaño apropiado.

Sello dinámico   Sello en el cual el sello o la superficie que está siendo sellada están en movimiento.

Sello estático   Sello entre partes que no tienen movimiento relativo.

Sensación inicial   Sensación distinta que es más firme al inicio de un cambio de velocidades que al final.

Sensor de la velocidad del vehículo (VSS por sus siglas en inglés)   Dispositivo electrónico que envía una señal con la velocidad del vehículo a un módulo de control.

Sensor de posición de la mariposa (TPS por sus siglas en inglés)   Dispositivo electrónico que envía una señal de la apertura de la mariposa al módulo de control.

Sentido de cambio de velocidades   Aplicación o descarga del embrague o banda que es usualmente descrito, por ejemplo, como firme o suave.

Servo   Dispositivo hidráulico que cambia la presión de fluido en movimiento mecánico o fuerza.

Severo   Aplicación notoria y desagradable del embrague o banda. También llamada *brusco*.

Sistema motriz híbrido   Tren de potencia de un vehículo que combina un motor de combustión interna con un motor eléctrico.

Sobrellenado   Condición en la cual la transmisión tiene mucho fluido.

Sobremarcha   Arreglo de engranajes que causa que el eje de salida gire más rápido que el eje de entrada.

Solenoide de control de presión   Solenoide controlado con computador que mantiene la presión apropiada en el sistema hidráulico de una transmisión automática controlada electronicamente. También llamada *solenoide de fuerza variable* o *motor de fuerza*.

Solenoide de fuerza variable   *Ver* Solenoide de control de presión.

Solenoide   Actuador electromagnético que usa un núcleo móvil.

Soporte del motor   Aparato que soporta el motor de forma que el eje transversal sea retirado.

Soporte planetario   Parte del engranaje planetario que contiene los engranajes de piñón planetarios.

Sostenedor de resorte   Herramienta especial usada para mantener los resortes del cuerpo de la válvula en orden.

Suave   Aplicación lenta y casi no notoria del embrague o banda.

Subllenado   Condición en la cual una transmisión no tiene suficiente fluido.

Tambor   Espacio en forma de tambor que sirve como cobertura para un ensamblaje de embragues o una superficie de fricción para una banda.

Tardío   Cambio de velocidades que ocurre arriba de la velocidad deseada y que causa excesivas revoluciones en el motor.

Temprano   Cuando un cambio de velocidades ocurre antes de que la correcta velocidad sea alcanzada y causa un *lugging* o esfuerzo del motor.

Tiempo del cambio de velocidades   Cuando (velocidad del vehículo o revoluciones por minuto del motor) un cambio de velocidades ocurre.

Tierra   La porción de gran diámetro de una válvula de carrete.

Tinte fluorescente   Tinte que brilla bajo luz fluorescente que ayuda a encontrar la fuente de fugas.

Trabajo   Resultado de la fuerza que cambia la velocidad o dirección de movimiento.

Tracción de ruedas traseras (RWD por sus siglas en inglés)   Tren de potencia que impulsa las ruedas traseras.

Tracción en cuatro ruedas (FWD por sus siglas en inglés)   Tren de potencia que puede impulsar las cuatro ruedas parte del tiempo.

Tracción en ruedas delanteras (FDW por sus siglas en inglés)   Tren de potencia que impulsa las ruedas delanteras.

Tracción integral (AWD por sus siglas en inglés)   Tren de dirección que automáticamente mueve las cuatro ruedas de un vehículo cuando es necesario.

Transmisión   Dispositivo en el tren de potencia que provee diferente relaciones de engranajes de avance, así como neutro y reversa.

Transmisión asíncrona   Transmisión que usa un embrague unidireccional que permite un cambio superior de velocidades que requiere solo la aplicación del siguiente miembro de conducción o reacción. Tal transmisión alivia la sincronización de los cambios de velocidad.

Transmisión automática   Transmisión que cambia los diferenciales de los engranajes automáticamente.

Transmisión de doble embrague   Transmisión que usa un embrague para conducir los engranajes pares y un segundo embrague para conducir los engranajes impares. Esta transmisión puede proporcionar energía en forma continua sin lapsos entre cambio de engranaje.

Transmisión síncrona   Durante un cambio superior de velocidades, la duración que el nuevo miembro de impulso o reacción debe tener ajustado o sincronizado, con la descarga de un impulso o miembro de reacción.

Transmisión variable continua (CVT por sus siglas en inglés)   Transmisión que usa dos poleas de ancho variable y una correa para cambiar los diferenciales desde el más bajo hasta el más alto en forma continua y sin pasos, en lugar de diferenciales fijos.

Transverso   Atravesado.

Tren de dirección   Motor, transmisión y otros componentes que dirigen las ruedas.

Tren de engranajes *LePelletier*   Tren de engranajes de transmisión automática que combina un sistema de engranajes planetario simple con un sistema de engranajes tipo *Ravigneaux* para producir seis o más relaciones de engranajes.

Tren de engranajes Simpson   Sistema de engranajes planetario que combina dos sistemas planetarios simples usand un engranaje sol simple.

Trinquete   Dispositivo de bloqueo que se ajusta en los dientes de un engranaje para sostenerlo fijo.

Tubo encogido   Tubo plástico que se encoge cuando se calienta para aislar una conexión cableada.

Turbina   Miembro de salida de un convertidor de par.

Turbulador   Característica del diseño de un enfriador de aceite que produce turbulencia en el flujo de fluido.

Unión a tierra   Camino de retorno de un circuito. El cuerpo del vehículo y el chasis normalmente proveen unión a tierra.

Vacío   Presión negativa (por debajo de la presión atmosférica); medida en pulgadas de mercurio (pulg Hg)

Valle   Área de una válvula de carrete entre las tierras.

Válvula balanceada   Válvula que está en una posición balanceada entre dos fuerzas opuestas.

Válvula de carrete   Válvula hidráulica que tiene forma de carrete.

Válvula de control de detención (posición de la mariposa)   Movimiento de la mariposa al máximo. *Ver* Mariposa abierta al máximo.

Válvula de detención   Tipo de válvula con resortes usado para posicionar la válvula manual correctamente.

Válvula de la mariposa   Válvula hidráulica que está posicionada por un acople de la mariposa.

Válvula de liberación de presión   Válvula apoyada con resortes que está diseñada para liberar el exceso de presión.

Válvula de refuerzo de reversa   Válvula de control de presión que incrementa la presión para el engranaje de reversa.

Válvula gobernadora   Dispositivo hidráulico que proporciona presión hidráulica que es relativa a la velocidad en carretera.

Válvula manual   Válvula operada por el selector de engranajes que aplica presión a los dispositivos necesarios para poner la transmisión continua engranada.

Válvula moduladora   Dispositivo operado al vacío que mide la carga del motor y causa que una válvula hidráulica cambie la presión relativa a esa carga.

Válvula reguladora de presión   Válvula que mantiene la presión adecuada en el sistema hidráulico.

Válvula reguladora   Válvula principal usada para controlar la presión de línea.

Válvula transportadora   Válvula usada para cambiar la ruta de un fluido de un circuito a otro.

Variador   Polea de ancho variable usada en sistemas CVT.

Velocidad de detención   Máximo número de revoluciones por minuto del motor que puede ser alcanzado con una transmisión automática en un engranaje, con los frenos aplicados y el acelerador al máximo.

Verificación de fugas   Verificación que determina si hay fugas de fluidos y en donde están ocurriendo.

Verificación de residuos del contenedor de aceite   Verificación de los residuos en el contenedor de aceite que puede indicar posible desgaste o daño de la transmisión.

Vibraciones torsionales   Flujo natural y no uniforme de potencia desde el motor a la transmisión.

Viscosidad   Resistencia de un fluido a fluir.

Volante   Masa metálica giratoria unida al cigüeñal que ayuda a suavizar los cambios de potencia.

INDEX